WORLD
WRITERS
IN ENGLISH

WORLD
WRITERS
IN ENGLISH

JAY PARINI, EDITOR

VOLUME
II

R. K. Narayan
to
Patrick White

CHARLES SCRIBNER'S SONS®

New York • Detroit • San Diego • San Francisco • Cleveland • New Haven, Conn. • Waterville, Maine • London • Munich

World Writers in English, Volume II

Jay Parini, Editor in Chief

© 2004 by Charles Scribner's Sons. Charles Scribner's Sons is an imprint of The Gale Group, Inc., a division of Thomson Learning, Inc.

Charles Scribner's Sons™ and Thomson Learning™ are trademarks used herein under license.

For more information, contact
Charles Scribner's Sons
An imprint of The Gale Group
300 Park Avenue South, 9th Floor
New York, NY 10010
Or you can visit our Internet site at
http://www.gale.com

Permissions Department
The Gale Group, Inc.
27500 Drake Rd.
Farmington Hills, MI 48331-3535
Permissions Hotline:
248 699-8006 or 800 877-4253, ext. 8006
Fax: 248 699-8074 or 800 762-4058

LIBRARY OF CONGRESS CATALOGING-IN-PUBLICATION DATA

World Writers in English/Jay Parini, editor.
  p. cm
Includes bibliographical references and index.
  ISBN 0-684-31289-1 (set hardcover : alk. paper)-- ISBN 0-684-31290-5 (Volume 1) -- ISBN 0-684-31291-3 (Volume 2)
1. Commonwealth literature (English) -- History and criticism. 2. Commonwealth literature (English)--Bio-bibliography. 3. Authors, English--20th century--Biography. 4. Authors, Commonwealth--Biography. I. Parini, Jay. II. Title. PR9080.5.W67 2003
820.9'9171241--dc22

2003014873

Printed in the United States of America
10 9 8 7 6 5 4 3 2 1

R. K. Narayan

(1906–2001)

JOHN LENNARD

IT IS NOT easy for an Indian novelist to write in English. Though an official language of independent India widely used in law, academia, and journalism, English is more a limited *lingua franca* than a first language. In many rural districts it remains an elite tongue as unknown as Hindi in America; its aesthetic use is restricted to a tiny minority. Even with (at generous estimate) 300 million English-users among India's billion-strong population, demand for new English-language fiction is tiny, and neither utility of use nor a very limited market invite English-language literary effort.

Additionally, for many Indians, English and Urdu (close to Hindi and widely distributed since about 1550, but written in the Mogals' Persian script) remain languages of conquest and colony, alien impositions in which no proper Indian should wish to write. Instead (the nationalist argument goes), writers should work in Hindi, Pashtu, Punjabi, Gujurati, Bengali, Marathi, Telugu, Kannada, Malayalam, or Tamil—or even (according to some purists) classical Sanskrit, slightly more widely understood in India than classical Greek in the United States. Sanskrit aside, the nationalist logic seems clear, but rejects indigenous as well as alien traditions: Urdu for many Indians, and English for some, are first languages, deep-rooted, and have

tremendous Indian literary potential. Urdu, like the Taj Mahal, draws on the rich traditions of Persian (and wider Arabic) culture; English has, besides its own tremendous literary heritage, an enormous vocabulary, an unusual capacity to absorb words from any source-language, and an exceptional global distribution, making it (so the riposte goes) particularly suited to Indian literary needs. The debate is intrinsically political: since the late-nineteenth-century emergence of Indian party-politics one might expect supporters of right-wing, Hindu-supremacist parties such as the Bharatiya Janta Party (B.J.P.) to advocate Hindi literature, and supporters of the centrist, secular Congress Party to be untroubled by the presence of Indo-Anglian novels within the diversity of Indian literature. What neither group can do (though the B.J.P. has certainly tried) is to change the intricate, crazy-quilt history that modern India inherited, primarily but not exclusively from the British.

Under the rule of the East India Company (until 1857) and in formal empire (1877–1947), learning English was an obvious career move, and ensuring the proficiency of (male) children a parental ambition—but only for Indians able to consider such careers or ambitions. Even at its swollen wartime height in 1944–1945, the white population of India never exceeded 300,000 (then about 0.1%), and over three centuries averaged only about 0.05% of the total; such low numbers were possible because the empire, though often military, was substantively mercantile, and relied on Indian troops whose white (and later brown) officers spoke the appropriate vernacular. The adoption of English, therefore, was never imposed, and outside the emergent professional Indian officer-corps its use was largely restricted to five groups: princes and aristocracy (Hindu, Sikh, and Muslim); Brahmins (Hindu priestly caste) who became company and imperial bureaucrats or professional functionaries; Vaisyas (Hindu merchant caste) involved in international trade; upper- and middle-class Muslims (principally in north India) who more or less transferred from Mogal to British administrations; and the Eurasian (mixed-race) population, shunned by both sides but inevitably tending to shadow the dominant power and seek marriage with lower-class whites rather than Indians. There was a considerable spread of English (and creation of Indian English) from military, civil, and domestic service, through cantonment trade, and in cities; rural India was barely ruffled.

Access and attitudes to English also depended on where you were. The political structure of the Raj, little known today, was ludicrously complex but had (and has) substantial consequences. Starting from three primary settlements, Fort St. George (later Madras, now Chennai) in 1640, Bombay (now Mumbai) in 1661, and Fort William (later Calcutta) in 1690, the East India Company expanded steadily but unevenly. In the north, the battles of Plassey (1757) and Buxar (1764) gained it control of Bengal, Oudh (Awadh), Bihar, and Orissa from the faltering Mogal Empire, centered in Delhi. In southern and central India, where Mogal writ never ran or had long failed, there was greater princely resistance: the British twice had to sign expedient treaties with the Mysorean rulers Haider Ali Khan (1728–1782) and Tipú Sultán (1749–1799), and though Cornwallis defeated Tipú at the battle of Mysore (1792), Wellesley (later Wellington) fought him again at Seringapatam (Sriringapatan) in 1799. In 1803, spurred by French interference, Wellesley campaigned in central India, breaking Maratha power at Assaye and Argaum, and taking the strongholds of Ahmednagar and Gawilghur; a further campaign was needed in 1817–1818. The last decades of Company rule saw the aggressive annexation of many princely states, and the consolidation under one rule of more than half the area now comprising India, Pakistan, Bangladesh, and Sri Lanka—but after the Great Mutiny in 1857, control passed to the British Government, who in 1858 declared that Britain had no further territorial ambitions in India. More than six hundred princely states ranging from Hyderabad (as big as Wales) to personal estates of a few acres subsequently signed "Paramountcy" treaties, under which their foreign and defense policies were subsumed by the new Government of India while domestic and civil policies remained sovereign. Most survived within the patchwork-territory of British India until forcibly absorbed into India or Pakistan (in the case of Kashmir, both) after British withdrawal in 1947.

Though a ramshackle polity, the British Government of India created national road, rail, and communications infrastructures, but while English flourished, mass education was never a priority (save in Christian missions). Regional policies were never fully standardized, and in areas isolated by surrounding states, and hinterlands generally, practice was uneven—as it remains today. In princely states language-use and teaching were a matter of autocratic whim, and a function of size and importance: certain larger states, including Mysore (where the Wodeyar dynasty displaced by Haider Ali Khan was re-installed after 1799), became markedly anglophone in palace and (more limitedly) professional culture, and developed state publications in English; in others English was restricted to official correspondence with Britain as Paramount Power and stilted conversation with its resident representative. Generalizations are dangerous, but predictable, interlocking patterns of class and caste, wealth, and urbanization determined access to (higher) education; and across everything runs a North-South gradient.

Explanations of this gradient usually begin with the repeated horse-borne invasions of India from the northwest, through the Hindu Kush from central Asia or along the Gulf Coast from the Near East. Filling the northwestern mountains with hawk-nosed hill tribes, invading the Gangetic plain, pushing through the Vindhya and Satpura ranges into the sub-continental center, waves of invaders over three millennia settled the north with lighter-skinned, sharper-featured, and often Muslim populations. The last great land-invaders, the Mogals, peaking in 1550–1700, ruled a deeply cultured north-central empire, and created in the north the Indo-Islamic architecture (exemplified by the Taj Mahal) now widely considered "typically Indian." The darker-skinned, rounder-featured, Hindu, Buddhist, or animist peoples whose territories were successively invaded were driven south into the tropics, and by about 1750 were concentrated (beyond the Maratha kingdoms of central India, emerging as Mogal power ebbed) in the peninsula between the Malabar and Coromandel Coasts. No land-invaders ever got that far, so gradients of skin-shade (lighter in the north), religion (more Muslims in the north), and imperialization (greater in the north) were created, which with distinct southern languages, climate, diets, and spices made north and south Indian cultures very different.

The British came by sea, and for the first time brought the subcontinent under one regime—but reinforced the gradient of centuries with their own prejudices for lighter skins, bonier features, and Islam as martial, monotheistic, and (like Judaism and Christianity) a religion "of the book." Even after 1857, when the Calcutta army mutinied but the Madras army remained loyal, the British retained an imperial favor for the north. The Mogals were forcibly restricted to north-central India; the British Raj (literally "rule") echoed that restriction to a striking degree in its cultural self-construction, and Re-

alpolitik (politics based on practical rather than theoretical objectives) agrees that if you hold the Ganges, you hold India. Hinduism's sacred river is an unrivaled highway surrounded by immensely fertile land: the government of independent India sits today where the Mogals and British sat, in Delhi, at the head of the Ganges valley in the center of the north. For forty-seven of its first fifty years that government was led by light-skinned, westernized Kashmiri Brahmins (from India's northern frontier), and until the rise of the B.J.P. from Nagpur and the Central Provinces to national government in the 1990s, northern Indians generally dominated the independent Indian polity.

In complicated consequence of these geographies of power, the image of India in English and several major vernacular languages is skewed to the north, especially the cities of the upper Gangetic plain (Delhi, Lucknow, Kanpur), and in Bengali the great delta-metropolis of Calcutta (a British foundation). The south outside Madras/Chennai is neglected, and likely (except, perhaps, for the great central-southern states of Hyderabad and Mysore) to be labeled uncomfortably hot, unpleasantly primitive, and happily unimportant. The southern predominance of Telugu, Tamil, Malayalam, and Kannada, incomprehensible to most north Indians, reinforces this barrier, but helps to insulate the south from the worst of Hindu nationalism, strongest in central and northern India and deeply wedded to Hindi. The south had its own problems with violence in the 1970s–1990s, as the Sri Lankan civil war spilled into Tamil Nadu, but the appalling communal massacres surrounding Partition in 1947 centered on the new borders with West/East Pakistan (now Pakistan/Bangladesh), and neither contemporary lawlessness in Bihar, nor violent communalism in Gujarat and Nagpur, have found any sustained echo in the south.

Relatively speaking, then, the south is quiet, punishingly hot in summer, provincial by Delhi standards, and in English literary terms the merest backwater of the Ganges, or appendage to the Hindu Kush. The only southern Indian from imperial times still widely remembered is Tipú Sultán, for nationalists controversial as a Muslim usurper, and for the British a memorably vanquished foe, whose fabled treasure, cruelty, and barrel-organ shaped as a tiger eating a red-coat have captured imaginations for two centuries (the tiger-organ is still in the Victoria and Albert Museum, London). So it is all the more interesting that the outstanding modern proponent of the Indo-Anglian novel came from a Tamil Brahmin family, lived most of his life in the old princely city of Mysore, and was a master of detachment, writing chronicles of an archetypal southern town, Malgudi, where everything that happened to India in the twentieth century happened too, in its own way.

THE FACTS AND FICTIONS OF A QUIET LIFE

R. K. Narayanaswami (or Narayan Swami), the third of eight children, was born in October 1906 in Purasawalkam, an old neighborhood of Madras notable for its temples. In male south-Indian names of this kind, the first initial indicates the village of paternal origin, the second the father's personal name: Narayan's father was Rasipuram Venkatarama Krishnaswami Iyer (*c.* 1870–1937; "Iyer" denotes a Saivite Brahmin affiliation); Narayan was therefore Rasipuram Krishnaswami, and his brothers include R. K. Srinivasan, R. K. Pattabhi, R. K. Ramachandran, R. K. Balaraman, and R. K. Laxman (a famous political cartoonist who illustrated some of Narayan's books). Krishnaswami Iyer was a schoolteacher and administrator for the Education Service of the Princely State of Mysore; his wife, Gnanambal, a formidable domestic presence, avidly read Tamil literature.

From the age of two, after pneumonia and dysentery left him too weak to travel, and with his mother again nursing, Narayan was raised by his paternal grandmother, Ammani, and uncle Seshachalam in Purasawalkam, while his father worked postings in the Mysorean towns of Chennapatna and Hassan. From 1912 to 1920 (ages 6–14) Narayan attended the anglophone E. L. M. Fabricius Higher Secondary School in Purasawalkam, the only Brahmin in a class of Lutheran converts; conversation at home might be in Tamil or English, Seshachalam being a Tamil scholar-activist and a notable amateur photographer. In leaving their village for Madrassi and Mysorean opportunity, the family had embraced English and begun to distance themselves from caste-consciousness; with the Christian perspectives of his school, Narayan was doubly insulated from the restrictive devotional purism of orthodox southern Hinduism. Early experience of posed photography also helped form an alienated vision; so too did the violent deaths of assorted pets, including a monkey, peacock, parrot, mynah-bird, kitten, and puppy. Moreover, as Narayan grew, Mysorean family reunions were at first distressing meetings with fearsome strangers (especially his besuited father) in hill-towns alien with altitude, cold, and incomprehensible Kannada; if there was later love, another insulating layer developed from natural confusions about this abruptly enveloping family and third language. As he typically understated it, "my grandmother, it seems, had taken me away to Madras when I was only two years old, and I could not think of any other place as my home" (*My Days,* 1974, p. 31).

After outgrowing E. L. M. Fabricius, Narayan briefly attended two other Madrassi schools, C. R. C. High School in Purasawalkam and the prestigious Christian College High School on the Madras Esplanade, but the bullying evangelism and open prejudices of Fabricius Lutherans had already put him off the whole process of formal teaching and examination. His father, deeply anglicized, became in 1921 headmaster of the Maharajah's Collegiate High School in Mysore, and from 1922 to 1924 (ages 16–18) Narayan studied under his father's eagle-eye. He was expected to attend everything, which he did, work diligently, which he did not, and had the permanent run of his father's books and the school library, well stocked with current British, American, and Indian literary magazines. By 1924 he knew all about the postwar London literary scene, and had begun through Walter Scott and Dickens a lifelong concern with the historical and social novel; but both in 1924 and 1925 Narayan failed to graduate, flunking English, then Tamil, more from willful incredulity at the reductiveness of exams than any lack of competence. After each failure he had to wait a year to retake; supported at home, and largely at a loose end, he began in those years a lifelong habit of extended daily walks, crisscrossing his new city with senses wide open. He also read voraciously, and began to write, initially poetic-prose sketches full of romantic description and melodramatic adventure. Both habits became ingrained during four years at the Maharajah's College, University of Mysore (the prose ever maturing and slimming down), and by 1930 the twenty-four-year-old Narayan, B.A., knew he wanted to write novels in English.

For such a career there was no model. Bengali and Hindi literatures had some novelists; Tamil was just being rediscovered as a literary language; Kannada was further behind still; as for English, while there were nineteenth-century examples, the Indo-Anglian novel is now reckoned to begin only with London-based Mulk Raj Anand (b. 1905; *Untouchable*, 1935), Sorbonne-educated Raja Rao (b. 1909; *Kanthapura*, 1938), and Narayan himself. The limpid, realist prose Narayan was evolving was an additional difficulty, offering by the standards of Tamil epic poetry nothing numinously beautiful or metaphorical to hold one's attention. There was also a financial problem: Krishnaswami Iyer had retired in 1928, and money was sufficiently tight that efforts were made to fix Narayan up with a job in the Mysorean Education Service. Twice dispatched to Chennapatna to begin teaching, Narayan twice returned within a few days to Mysore because he found the whole business intolerable and absurd. Thereafter, remarkably by Western standards of bourgeois conformity, his clear assertion of a vocation, however peculiar, was respected; he was left to get on with it, and received continued support in the meanwhile.

Breaking into print from Mysore proved slow work, and Narayan became wearily used to rejection slips. His own habits, of necessity and by choice, were frugal, his only indulgence being two daily cigarettes, but other than from one short story accepted by *Punch,* income was meager. His hopes for his first novel, *Swami and Friends* (1935), completed in 1932, were coming to nothing, and intercontinental postage being expensive, Narayan used a well-placed Mysorean contact, K. R. ("Kittu") Purna (1910–1948), who was studying at Exeter College, Oxford, to relay the manuscript from publisher to publisher. Eventually Narayan told Purna to throw the manuscript in the Thames and forget it, but with unfazed loyalty (and a shrewd sense of how England works) he instead landed it on the desk of Graham Greene (1904–1991), then living in Oxford and since *Stamboul Train* (1932) a rising star among British novelists. Another headmaster's son, Greene fell for *Swami,* and the great literary friendship of Narayan's life began with a warm flurry of letters leading to the publication of *Swami* by Hamish Hamilton in 1935. It was then that Narayan's name was shortened, the publishers disliking the chime of *Swami and Friends* by R. K. Narayanaswami; Narayan himself was too fearfully delighted to object.

The reviews of *Swami and Friends* were good, its sales very low, but from then on Greene (with the remarkable agent David Higham, whom he enlisted) saw successive novels into print with successive publishers: *The Bachelor of Arts* (Nelson, 1937), *The Dark Room* (Macmillan, 1938), and *The English Teacher* (Eyre and Spottiswoode, 1945). Their content is at once a kind of autobiographical *summa* and a detached consideration of the self in others; all are short, many-chaptered novels concerned with experience, not plots. Swami is a little boy, with a boy's thoughts and interests; the adult world impinges as much through misunderstanding as in domestic security, and Swami is hardly the sharpest of his group—but the astonishingly simple narration manages to make readers aware of irony without itself being ironic. The setting is already Malgudi, and at one point the flaring nationalist politics of 1931–1932 intrude as a Gandhian demonstration and *hartal* (strike) leads to a school-boycott-cum-riot and Swami's expulsion for gleefully stoning some school windows—but natural geography, especially the much-loved Sarayu River, the forests leading to the Mempi Hills, and the *maidan* used for cricket, is far more vivid to Swami than the sociopolitics of *satyagraha* (literally "truth-force"; nonviolent protest) or other adult distractions.

In 1934 Narayan married Rajam, fifteen-year-old daughter of Nageswara Iyer, another book-loving Brahmin headmaster. Visiting his sister in Coimbatore (one hundred miles south of Mysore, beyond Ootacamund and the Nilgiri Hills), he saw Rajam at a well and knew immediately that he wanted to marry her. Against all Brahmin tradition he spoke directly to Nageswara Iyer, who was liberal enough to accept this, but a serious traditionalist obstacle arose when Narayan's and Rajam's horoscopes proved incompatible, his having Mars in the Seventh house, indicating early death for Rajam if the marriage took place—for traditionalists a dealbreaker, as it repeatedly is in Narayan's fiction. How he overcame it even his biographers cannot fully explain, but the marriage took place in July; a daughter, Hemavati (Hema), arrived in March 1936, and Narayan again broke tradition by accompanying Rajam back to her mother's for the confinement.

It was the happiest time of Narayan's life—which his fiction both reflects and twists. In *The Bachelor of Arts* a young student, Chandran, at heart an optimist but full of teenage angst, falls in love. Incompatible horoscopes block marriage despite much scheming, and the girl moves away; luxuriating in romantic despair, Chandran lives as a *sannyasi,* a wandering religious mendicant, for nine months, but eventually revolts at himself and returns home. Accepting an arranged marriage, he becomes as adoring of his new schoolgirl-wife as of his lost love, but the novel ends on a open note with Chandran worrying about his wife's failure to write sufficiently often while she completes her schooling.

As imaginary negative parallel to Narayan's married happiness and success in bucking tradition, *The Bachelor of Arts* forms a diptych with *The Dark Room,* a neglected masterpiece considering the life of a traditionally married woman. Savitri endures without complaint the domestic tyranny of self-made insurance broker Ramani, but one day enters the "dark room" of her larder and silently remains there for several days. Scornful of her dumb protest, Ramani goes from bad to worse when he becomes infatuated with a widowed employee; eventually Savitri leaves to attempt suicide in the Sarayu, is rescued, and spends a day in a village temple, before returning to her children and, necessarily, husband. The ending is again exceptionally open with Savitri inert at a window, and though the novel is deeply shaped as a reverse of his personal domestic happiness, Narayan's minimal, noncommittal narration and spare dialogue create a sense, not exactly of fable, but of an exemplary tale needing no embellishment. The best comparison might be with a photo-essay, chapters as small packets of observation individually and collectively implying a world, and in sequence suggesting their particular story is one of many interlocking narratives that might have been told. In Savitri's excursion beyond Sarayu, the richness of Malgudi and environs becomes clearer, and Ramani's employer, Engladia Insurance, with the languorous temptress Shanti Bai, affords alluring glimpses of city-life. Open satire is as suppressed in Narayan's prose as most emotions, but the reflections invited by the ironic substrate of these spare novels are clearly as critically detached from Hindu orthodoxy and its social consequences as from the imperial rhetorics of official 1930s English writing.

Krishnaswami Iyer died in 1937, and the loss of his pension left the family in financial difficulty. They had to move, and Narayan had to begin hack-work while trying more systematically to sell short stories: meeting journalism deadlines for money cut into novel-writing time, but the connections he made in the late 1930s, especially with *The Hindu* (a nationally distributed, Madrassi English-language newspaper) as a vehicle for short stories, were an important lifelong source of income. He also wrote a travel-guide, *Mysore* (1939), commissioned by the state-government. Ends were somehow meeting, and despite gloomy news from Europe things were not too bad in Mysore when in May 1939 Rajam fell ill; the eventual diagnosis was typhoid, and in June she died. As marriage was transformingly happy, so bereavement was a transformation in grief, and there is a simple, potent view that Narayan never truly recovered. Certainly, and very unusually in his culture, he never remarried, and raised his daughter himself.

The need to care for Hema and contribute to household finances meant he had to continue hack-work, and function as a father. It drove him in 1941, as wartime austerity limited his kind of journalism, to publish his own short-lived journal, *Indian Thought,* and from 1943 collections of his stories. His press, Indian Thought Publications (with a wonderful colophon of Ganesh by R. K. Laxman), issued three wartime collections, *Malgudi Days* (1943), *Dodu and Other Stories* (1943), and *Cyclone and Other Stories* (1945), in which snapshots of Malgudi accumulated. It later issued a fourth, *Lawley Road and Other Stories* (1956), and a collection of journalism, *Next Sunday* (1956), full of vivid observations offering a less buffered sense of Narayan than his fiction. Indian Thought still functions in Mysore.

Journalism and the business of printing forced Narayan out and about; inside he remained desolate and fictively barren. Given traditionalist views that must have obtained in Rajam's family (and in all probability been spoken at least once) about the sad consequences of ignoring horoscopes, Narayan might be expected to have turned to the Hindu faith, and he partly did—but his eventual recovery turned on spiritualism and transmuting autobiography into fiction. In November 1939 he was introduced to an amateur medium, Raghunatha Rao, and after a series of séances in Madras in 1939–1940, and extended spiritual training back in Mysore (guided by automatic writing and a resident English occultist, Paul Brunton), he experienced two vital phenomena. In 1941 a powerful, benign divine "Presence" instructed him to recite a variant of an ancient Brahmin prayer, the Gayatri mantra, invoking light (he would recite it all his life); in 1944, in a "willed dream," he had an epiphanic (but casual, untroubled) vision of Rajam and a sense of her companionable benediction, followed on "waking" by joyous consolation. What remained was to create from his terrible and wonderful experiences a novel, *The English Teacher* (1945), which relates bereavement and post-mortal benediction directly, autobiography in the slimmest shell of fiction, gathering to end with a phrase so powerful that in the U.S. it became an alternative title: "grateful to Life and Death."

With it Narayan ended a first phase of fiction, in which autobiography dominates; from *Mr. Sampath—The Printer of Malgudi* (1949) on, successive protagonists have more to do with those Narayan overheard and conversed with on his daily walks and in the course of business than with himself. The memorable Mr. Sampath is of another fictional order than Swami or Chandran, and though certainly concerned with hand-press printing, the novel takes off with an attempt by Sampath and others to establish a film studio. The off-center protagonist, Srinivas, editor and sole author of a progressive journal, *The Banner,* which Sampath prints, comically satirizes Narayan's editorship of *Indian Thought* and brief involvement as a scriptwriter with Gemini Studios, a major Madrassi film company, but the fictional focus has broadened enormously, and for the first time a panoramic sense of Malgudi emerges within a wider frame of Indian life. In the same vein, *The Financial Expert* (1952) chronicles the life of Margayya, a name that means "one who shows the way"—in this case the way to deal with the absurd complexity that happens when shrewd, uneducated farmers confront a state co-operative bank insisting on massed paperwork and incoherent fiscal rules. The situation reflects a Mysore that in 1947 became part of the Indian Republic and lost in a Brahmin diaspora most of the administrative machine that had since 1700 run an efficient, elite state-bureaucracy. *Waiting for the Mahatma* (1955), considered below, relates two young lives and one old one in 1942–1948, covering the coming of independence and establishing the eddying movement of Malgudi through recent history.

Narayan began to move too. All he says in *My Days* about finally breaking "out of the triangular boundary of Madras, Mysore, and Coimbatore" is that, Hema having married and left home, he "felt rather at a loose end. . . . This was the correct moment for the Rockefeller Foundation to think of me for a travel grant. I accepted the proposal" (p. 160). U.S. attention to India increased sharply after 1947, and the Rockefeller, like other foundations, was looking that way, but how the grant came about awaits Narayan's biographers. In any case he made good use of it: stopping in London, he at last met Greene and made their friendship more than epistolary; once in America he met many people and kick-started his reputation; above all, he wrote in only three months *The Guide* (1958), the tragic tale of Raju, mistaken for a holy man, and perhaps his best-known novel. It and successive novels were issued in New York as well as London, Mysore, and New Delhi; film and stage-rights were variously optioned, and from the time he returned to Mysore Narayan was relatively wealthy.

He bought a blue Mercedes, and greatly enjoyed driving to his daughter's and other relatives' houses; he took avidly to wider traveling, returning regularly to London and Manhattan, going in 1961 for the first time to Delhi, and later visiting much of Europe, the Soviet Union, and many of the insular Pacific cultures, including the Philippines, Indonesia, and Australia. But he always returned to Mysore, to his walks, writing-desk, and chronicles of Malgudi. *The Man-Eater of Malgudi* (1961) and *A Tiger for Malgudi* (1983) are considered below; *The Vendor of Sweets* (1967) is a superb comedy of father-son competition, contrasting Gandhian and post-Gandhian generations; *The Painter of Signs* (1976) sees Raman swept from that profession to utter confusion by Daisy, whose mission in life (satirizing Indira Gandhi's forcible-vasectomy programs) is to bring birth-control to the people; the eponymous *Talkative Man* (1986), heard before in Malgudi, tells of Dr. Rann, apparently sponsored by the U.N. but perhaps a fraud; *The World of Nagaraj* (1990) considers the frustrations of that would-be writer while many Malgudians pass through its pages.

Interspersed with novels were memoirs of his first U.S. visit, *My Dateless Diary* (1964), and early life, *My Days* (1974); a new collection of short stories, *A Horse and Two Goats and Other Stories* (1970), and two new-and-selecteds, *Malgudi Days* (1982) and *Under the Banyan Tree and Other Stories* (1985); a second collection of essays, *Reluctant Guru* (1974), and *A Writer's Nightmare: Selected Essays, 1958–1988* (1988); a travel book commissioned by the state government of Karnataka (which includes Mysore), *The Emerald Route* (1977); and three popular prose redactions of Hindu myths and classics decorated by his brother Laxman—*Gods, Demons, and Others* (1964), *The Ramayana* (1972, from the Tamil version by Kamban and dedicated to his uncle Seshachalam), and *The Mahabharata* (1978). His last books were the overlapping *Salt and Sawdust: Stories and Table Talk* (1993) and *The Grandmother's Tale: Three*

Novellas (1993), combining openly autobiographical consideration of his long-dead grandmother Ammani and her grandmother with two last tales of Malgudi.

Driving and international tourism aside, Narayan lived very simply in Mysore, but could not stop distinguished visitors seeking him out (and leaving charmed but bewildered), nor state honors from piling up as anglophone Indians appreciated his achievement. In 1964 he received the Padma Bushan, and in 2000 the Padma Vibhushan, India's second-highest civilian award; from 1985 to 1991 he served by nomination in the Rajya Sabha, India's upper house of parliament, speaking to issues of children's welfare. There were other awards, but despite repeated proposals, never the Nobel; a testy essay, "The Nobel Prize and All That" (in *A Writer's Nightmare*), suggests he became fed up with others' indignation on his behalf. Only when health problems began to impair independence in 1990 did he finally leave Mysore, returning to Madras to live with his daughter and son-in-law.

Narayan's last years were freighted with new grief. Greene died in 1991, ending the longest international literary friendship of the twentieth century, and in 1994, after painful decline, Hema died of cancer. Narayan bore up in appalled numbness, continued to live with his son-in-law and grandchildren, and had the support of many friends, but little can allay the grief of parent for child. Journalism offered some solace, but fiction was again in abeyance, and by the time he could contemplate it once more his own health was failing. He died in May 2001, aged 94.

His biographers Susan and N. Ram, with whom he shared long evenings of talk and reminiscence from 1985, learned more about him than anyone outside his family, including his psychic means of surviving bereavement. Yet even with the help of their admirable biography (of which the first volume, 1906–1945, appeared in 1996), Narayan's life remains deeply private, self-contained, productive yet distant, the greatness of his thought evident only in the refracted vitality of his astonishing fictional creation.

THE NATURE OF MALGUDI

Malgudi, not in any atlas, can be inferentially mapped from the stories that happen there. James Fennelly constructed such a map to illustrate "The City of Malgudi as an Expression of the Ordered Hindu Cosmos" (at an American Academy of Religion Conference, 1978), and had the satisfaction of seeing it published at Narayan's request in *Malgudi Days* (1982). It has three horizontal bands: the Mempi Hills distantly at the top, the Sarayu River one-third of the way down, and Market Road two-thirds of the way down, traversing the town center. Two bridges spanning Sarayu provide vertical bands roughly one-third and two-thirds of the way across: in the west the trunk-road from the Hills crosses into the town as Vinayak Mudali Street and (below Market Road) South Road; in the east the railway (sweeping from the west to a southern station) curves north over the river, towards the hills and distant Trichy. In the center is Fountain Circle, where Ellaman Street crosses Market Road before ending at the Sarayu near the Iswara Temple. Most of Malgudi, including Kabir Street, the Palace Talkies Cinema, and Albert Mission College, is within the area bounded by railway-line and river, but to the west is the Untouchables' village, to the south the New, Lawley, and South Extensions, and to the east the North Extension. There are outlying buildings, Mr. Sampath's house to the southwest and the jail, race track, and Engladia Insurance building to the southeast. North of Sarayu are the cremation grounds, animal hospital, and forest villages scattered across rising, jungled terrain.

Despite a variety of coincident details, Malgudi is not Mysore. It lacks the hilly topography and princely architectural heritage, and in the bustle around Fountain Circle and Kabir Street, among crowds at the temples or by beautiful Sarayu in the cool evenings, the predominant language is Tamil, not Kannada. But Malgudi is certainly south Indian in architecture, climate, and diet, and the attitudes of its Hindus, while capable of being vigorously faithful and doctrinal, are tempered by humility, indecision, good manners, a strong sense of self, and the baking heat. The obvious comparisons are with William Faulkner's Yoknapatawpha County, a setting for many novels and short stories that is and is not Jackson County, Mississippi, where Faulkner lived, and Paul Scott's archetypal province in the *Raj Quartet* (1966–1975). Both help to define Narayan's achievement.

Yoknapatawpha County is a good match for Malgudi, because the Civil War and greater heat of the Confederate states (with all it implies) make for American attitudes stigmatizing Mississippi onto which the Indian North-South gradient can partly be mapped. The parochial good manners, sometimes overreaching shrewdness, and strange, potentially comic ways of Faulkner's human creations, like their excited reactions to newfangled things and mores, would make sense to Malgudians, and detailed comparisons could be attempted. The contrivances and sales-patter of Margayya in *The Financial Expert* (1952) resonate with the dubious ascent of Flem Snopes in *The Hamlet* (1940), *The Town* (1957), and *The Mansion* (1959) toward the bank-presidency he craves. And it is easy to imagine Gavin Stevens, Faulkner's talkative lawyer-narrator, becoming involved with attempts to proceed legally against Vasu in *The Man-Eater of Malgudi* (1961), or Daisy in *The Painter of Signs* (1976). But stylistically the two writers are poles apart: Faulkner's famous syntax, winding orally through histories and genealogies, soil and forest, bone and breath; dragging readers, human action, and the weight of natural millennia together into an extending moment of apprehension; building over paragraphs and pages, novels and years, into a densely tangled crisscrossing mass of partial narrations, is utterly distinct from Narayan's austere prose. Though Malgudi is tremendously present and teeming, Narayan provides in all his tales fewer genealogies than Faulkner provides in one. Nor—at least on the surface—does any history beyond living memory, any knowledge of blood mulched into the soil, trouble the comings and goings of Mr. Sampath, Raman, Nataraj, Nagaraj, the Talkative Man, and other denizens.

It is clear, however, despite profound differences of narrative method, that both novelists reacted as Modernists against late-nineteenth-century clottings of syntax. Faulkner (like Joyce) liquidized it while retaining the volume; Narayan (like Woolf and Beckett) reduced it to a single clear-coating over chosen realities. Scott, a late Modernist, employs both modes (and more) in the shapely web of narrated and ventriloquized histories that constitute his *Raj Quartet*—bulkier than anything of Narayan's, but more compact and structured than Faulkner's sprawling Yoknapatawphan career. Most of the *Quartet* occurs in a town, city, and hill-station in an archetypal province of British India, on the Gangetic plain but stretching north to the foothills of the Himalaya; it has historically accurate systems of administration and transport, and an equally archetypal-realist neighboring princely state, but (as in Narayan) Delhi and other real places are visited at will. In constructing his province Scott sought a form of storytelling that let him bear full witness to his experience, serving in India 1943–1946, of what he called "the British coming to the end of themselves as they were"—a mode of fictional truth occupying the historiographical gulf between all-India histories omitting quotidian life and local studies omitting the larger polity.

Rejecting the semi-*Symboliste* and ahistorical approach of Forster's *A Passage to India* (1924), Scott is far closer to Zola's *Documentation*, weaving a fictional web around absolute fidelity to researched and experienced truth. Although his Mayapore, Ranpur, and Pankot are cousins of Malgudi, they assemble into a particular set of relations which creates a representative British provincial administration, complete with civil, military, and commercial spheres, aware of itself as a subordinate but significant part of a far greater whole: a setting specifically to stage intertwined fictions and histories of 1942–1947, an explanatory backdrop for arrayed people whose good and ill deeds are that fiction and were that history. Like many predecessors, the Japanese Imperial Army attacked India from the north, being held only in the last hills before the Gangetic plain, and it was there Scott did his service, absorbing the spectacle of the Raj from its Delhi seat successfully defending itself at mortal cost. But Malgudi is southern, and its wartime history was quieter. If India's history sometimes arrives, as Gandhi or population-controlling Daisy, and makes for a while a terrific tamasha, or commotion, Malgudi lacks Mayapore's self-consciousness of the metropolis elsewhere, only mildly shares Ranpur's self-consciousness as a seat of administration, and has nothing of Pankot's hill-station militarism and snobbery—all Anglo-Indian phenomena with which Indo-Anglian Malgudi has no truck.

Narayan's account of how it came into being is another deadpan masterpiece:

> On a certain day in September [*Vidayadashami*], selected by my grandmother for its auspiciousness, I bought an exercise book and wrote the first line of a novel ["It was Monday morning."]; as I sat in a room nibbling my pen and wondering what to write, Malgudi with its little railway station swam into view, all ready-made, with a character called Swaminathan running down the platform peering into the faces of passengers, and grimacing at a bearded face; this seemed to take me on the right track of writing. . . .
>
> (*My Days*, p. 76)

One need not believe in this insouciant swimming-into-view to realize that, however fine a microcosm it is, Malgudi lacks Scott's town-planning and topographical sculpture. But he and Narayan are close in namings: "Mayapore" means "City of Illusion" (from Hindi "*maya*," the illusion of the material world, and

"*pur*," equivalent to "-ton" or "–ville"); "Malgudi," according to Narayan

> has no meaning. There is a place called Lalgudi near Trichy and a place called Mangudi near Kumbakonan or somewhere. But Malgudi is nowhere. So that was very helpful. It satisfied my requirement.
>
> (Ram and Ram, *R. K. Narayan*, p. 106)

Suggestive names Narayan knew are one thing, but the euphonious philosophical balance of Mál- (bad) –gúd- (good) –í is apparent. The very opposite of Moore's Utopian nowhere, Malgudi is (despite Narayan's claim) an Indian pan-topia (everywhere), which explains why he responded positively to Fennelly's map of Malgudi as "an expression," not of existing Indian topography or politics, but "of the Ordered Hindu Cosmos."

The stories through which Malgudi is entered are like passes of a camera obscura, whether fleeting scenes, panoramas, or more sustained trackings of individuals, and there are worse ways of approaching Narayan than through Susan Sontag on photography:

> In teaching us a new visual code, photographs alter and enlarge our notions of what is worth looking at and what we have a right to observe. They are a grammar and, even more importantly, an ethics of seeing. Finally, the most grandiose result of the photographic enterprise is to give us the sense that we can hold the whole world in our heads—as an anthology of images.
>
> (*On Photography*, p. 3)

"Malgudi" could be substituted for "photographs" throughout, and each point illuminates the experience of reading Narayan. But as written forms the novel and short story intrinsically lack the transparency, real or supposed, with which photographs are credited, and Narayan had available a range of suggestiveness which visual media lack. Striving for minimalism in prose, he achieved a high degree of universality, and to explore Malgudi demands alertness to both traditional and Modernist modes of meaning.

THE BLESSINGS OF GANDHI-JI

On the surface *Waiting for the Mahatma* (1955) is simple, if by Narayan's standards busy. Sriram, an innocent, self-absorbed twenty-year-old orphan raised by his grandmother, awakens when the Mahatma arrives in Malgudi during his "Quit India!" campaign in 1942; "Mahatma" ("great soul") is the Indian name for M. K. Gandhi (1869–1948), the great reforming nationalist and ascetic, also called "Bapu-ji," ("father"; "-ji" is an honorific). Sriram is properly impressed— but his real concern is a girl in Gandhi's entourage, Bharati, orphan of campaigners for *Swaraj* (self-rule). Drawn by her into the civic comedy caused by Gandhi's decision to stay in the Untouchables' village, Sriram cruelly abandons his grandmother to travel through the Malgudi hinterland with Gandhi. After Gandhi leaves he and Bharati, quietly courting, stay in the hills to continue posting slogans and proselytizing.

The British, understandably in 1942, were less impressed than Sriram with a campaign calling on them leave to India "to God or anarchy"—de facto to the Japanese—and in August 1942 arrested Gandhi and sixty thousand other Congress activists. Knowing how the British would respond when he pushed Congress leaders to vote on "Quit India!" Gandhi instructed supporters to surrender peacefully to police, and Bharati does so, but Sriram (not grasping nonviolence) demurs, pleading a need to see his grandmother. He then becomes involved, through a sinister photographer, Jagadish, with a terrorist campaign waged by the Hindu right in parallel with *Satyagraha*: smallfry, he receives and distributes broadcasts from S. C. Bose (1897–1945) in Tokyo, sets fires, and once plants a bomb. Trying to communicate with Bharati in the women's jail, but frustrated by her Gandhian refusal of subterfuge, Sriram at last goes to see his grandmother, only to find she died the previous night. An unexpected journey to the cremation grounds, amid a great throng of mourners who loved the old lady, provides a perfect Malgudi moment when she revives just as she is about to burn, and the police simultaneously arrive to arrest him.

Hindu belief forbids the grandmother, having left town as a corpse, to return, and with her removal to distant Benares (now Varanasi) on the Ganges, no one remembers Sriram in detention. As a terrorist he is not imprisoned with other Quit-India! detainees, nor released with them in 1944–1945, but placed in the general prison population. Finally freed, he discovers it is January 1948 in an independent India from which East and West Pakistan have been bloodily carved; Jagadish, never caught, tries to console him with albums of Independence Day snapshots, but his only real hope is renewed contact with Bharati, who after her release rejoined Gandhi in Delhi, to campaign with him in areas devastated by the communal massacres of Partition. Finally reunited in Delhi, amid countless orphans Bharati has gathered at sites of massacre, they agree to marry if Bapu-ji gives his blessing. Though very weak, besieged by demands, and fasting in protest at continuing communalism in Bengal, Gandhi receives and blesses them, promising to perform the wedding next morning; as an afterthought he insists they go ahead even if he cannot be there, and steps out to be shot by someone to whom Narayan refers only as "the man." "Two more shots rang out. The Mahatma fell on the dais. He was dead in a few seconds." (*Waiting for the Mahatma*, in *More Tales from Malgudi*, p. 657). There the novel ends, on 30 January 1948.

Early readers knew the name Narayan omits. Nathuram Godse, Gandhi's assassin, was a follower of V. D. Savarkar (1883–1966), author of the ultra-nationalist and -chauvinist *Hindutva* (1924), and a committed Fascist—very much the sort of man whom Sriram, through Jagadish, would ultimately have been serving in 1942–1943. The presence of Godse's name in

Narayan's text of Gandhi's murder would hardly be remarkable; its absence is striking, and draws attention to the names that are given. Allegory, though alive and well in science fiction, is now critically unfashionable and can suggest a heavy-handed one-to-one mapping; Narayan does nothing blunt, but it is striking that Gandhi's death leaves suspended a distracted love-match between Sriram (a name equivalent to "Praise-god," and a favorite warcry of militant Hindus) and Bharati ("Daughter of India"). In itself, of course, "Sriram" is no more remarkable in India than "Jésus" is in the Hispanic world, and "Bha-rati" is a typical name for the daughter of Gandhians—"*Bharat*," "India," is as symbolic as "Britannia" and evokes the nationalist dream—but a final tableau of compromised Hindu activism and India's Daughter uncertainly engaged over Gandhi's corpse is patently more than an unfortunate hiatus in the life of a future Malgudian couple.

However seemingly detached, Narayan's novel is specifically about activism, and it is not only in the ending or the names that symbolic, quasi-allegorical details lurk:

In that huge gathering sitting on the sands of Sarayu, awaiting. . . . Gandhi, Sriram was a tiny speck. There were a lot of volunteers clad in white Khaddar moving around the dais. . . . Police stood about here and there. Busybodies were going round asking people to remain calm and silent. People obeyed them. Sriram . . . wondered if he could do anything to attain the same status. . . .

The river flowed, the leaves of the huge banyan and peepul trees on the bank rustled; the waiting crowd kept up a steady babble, constantly punctuated by the pop of soda-water bottles; longitudinal cucumber slices, crescent-shaped, and brushed up with the peel of a lime dipped in salt, were disappearing from the wooden tray of a vendor who was announcing . . . "Cucumber for thirst, the best for thirst." He had wound a green Turkish towel around his head as a protection from the sun.

Sriram felt parched, and looked at the tray longingly. He wished he could go up and buy a crescent. The thought of biting into its cool suc-

culence was tantalizing. He was at a distance and if he left his seat he'd have no chance of getting back to it. He watched a lot of others giving their cash and working their teeth into the crescent. "Waiting for the Mahatma makes one very thirsty," he thought.

Every ten minutes someone started a *canard* that the great man had arrived . . . to relieve the tedium of waiting. Any person . . . who dared to cross the dais was greeted with laughter and booing from a hundred thousand throats. A lot of familiar characters . . . made themselves unrecognizable by wearing white Khaddar caps. They felt it was the right dress . . . on this occasion. "That Khaddar Store off the Market Fountain must have done a roaring business in white caps today," Sriram thought. Far off, pulled obscurely to one side, was a police van with a number of men peering through the safety grill.

(pp. 458–459)

These paragraphs form a group isolated by blank lines, and are a good example of Narayan's detached simplicity. *Khaddar* is the homespun, homegrown cloth that Gandhi wore and promoted, with the village spinning industry, in tandem with a boycott of imported British cloth, and an economic motif runs alertly throughout the scene, otherwise only the twice-mentioned police and busybodies offer any disturbance to a good-humored pastoral lull. But white is not the only color: the iterated "crescent" of green cucumbers and salt-whitened lime, in conjunction with that "green Turkish towel" serving as a turban, abruptly suggest the national insignia of Pakistan, the green-and-white Islamic crescent. White Khaddar can also disguise familiar characters as members of a potential mob, and those policemen perhaps have good reasons to observe who begins to do what when the Mahatma comes to town.

The political costs of Gandhi's various tactics over the years are rarely counted, and for most people count for nothing beside his spiritual example. There is, however, a strong historical case that he severely underestimated the Hindu Right, unwittingly playing into their hands with the Khaddar campaign, his adoption of the Hindu *dhoti* (compare Nehru's transcultural *sherwani* and *shalwar*), and the simplistic, regressive economics of his village-spinning campaign; another persuasive case can be made that "Quit India!", conceived in panic when it looked as if the Japanese would shortly take over, was a huge mistake, which by putting congressmen behind bars for the duration left a clear field for Jinnah's Muslim League to make Pakistan a political reality, and for the Hindu extremes to claim ordinary loyalties—exactly what happens to Sriram while Bharati is jailed. As the ironizing gap widens between Narayan's narrative detachment and Sriram's faithless desertion of his grandmother, wallowings in imaginary possession of Bharati, and willing violence, mute realities crowd ever more thickly around a prose that remains in itself simple and clear. When only Jagadish can provide Sriram with evidence of the independence he burned and bombed for, over-ironized tragedy trembles toward comedy; but the moment is followed by the disturbing passage through Sriram's train to Delhi of two men examining all passengers, who do not understand Sriram's Tamil but pass on muttering "Hindu" when they see a caste-puncture in his ear. Only then do fellow-passengers explain they were Hindu activists of Savarkar's and Godse's ilk looking for Muslims, whom they would have thrown from the train (p. 640): exactly such people, and their Muslim/Sikh counterparts, were in 1946–1948 responsible for at least 500,000 murders, many in wholesale train-massacres, and the scale of events the two men represent is underlined by the multitude of orphans Bharati cares for in Delhi (pp. 643–644).

Quiet as *Waiting for the Mahatma* might be, and however good-humoredly Malgudian crowds waited for him, in the silence that follows Gandhi's violent death and the novel's abrupt end the questions pressed on its readers are shaped and weighted with a comprehensive neutrality of art that allows a larger contemplation of Gandhi's passion than northern politics

and orthodoxy permit. It is Malgudi in the service of *Bharat*, a report to fellow-Indians of recent experience in a language that bridges communal divisions and, like photographs as construed by Sontag, offers them a new "grammar and, even more importantly, an ethics" of self-representation.

A PAIR OF TIGERS

Tigers are native to India, north and south, but have a particular association with Mysore. Tipú's name probably derives from a word meaning "tiger-like," and his nickname was the "Tiger of Mysore": tiger motifs appear repeatedly on his sword-hilts, insignia, and other personal possessions; in his architecture; in the uniforms of his army and emissaries; and, most famously, in his jeweled tiger-throne and infamous man-tiger-organ, known as "Tipú's Tiger." Made around 1795 by combining French-built musical and automatic mechanisms in a case carved in Chennapatna, it may have been inspired by the death by tiger in 1792, while hunting in the Sundarbans, of a young Scotsman called Munro, son of a general who helped defeat Tipú at Porto Nova in 1781; it was probably made on French commission for presentation to Tipú, which makes it a political image of Mysorean victory over English interlopers, and in its captured career through Wellesley's and various Company offices before winding up in the Victoria and Albert, it remains accurately symbolic. Evidently it cannot now be seen in Mysore—but it is not forgotten, and other tigers can be seen.

Tipú kept two sorts himself: real ones in the palace courtyard, to which executed prisoners were fed (and which Wellesley in one of his first acts as governor of Mysore had shot); and a human equivalent, a palace and personal guard drawn from a Hindu Kshatriya (warrior) caste called *Jettis*—devoted strongmen, traditionally battlefield bone-breakers and civil bone-setters, whom he used in celebrating the great military and expiatory *Dashar* festival every October, and as executioners. Their specialties included neck-breaking, driving nails one-handedly through skulls, and sacred fights against one another using bone knuckledusters and a weapon extending a knuckleduster with hooked blades symbolizing tiger-claws. *Jettis* were in Mysore before Haider Ali and Tipú, and can be seen celebrating the *Dashar* there today, presided over by the surviving Wodeyar claimant to the extinct royal Mysorean title; both there and elsewhere in what were once Tipú's dominions, live tigers can be seen in large, ditch-ringed enclosures that keep them in but not necessarily the public out, and every now and again the news is still enlivened by a tiger's natural reaction to an easy meal. On the other hand, the palaces in Mysore, Sriringapatna, and throughout India are crowded with dead tigers, reduced to rugs or stuffed and mounted—the best of them by successive taxidermists called Van Ingen, members of a Dutch family resident in Mysore since the eighteenth century, and from about 1850 acknowledged masters of taxidermy, patronized by many of the princes who had holiday bungalows at Ootacamund and spent time decimating the wildlife of the surrounding hills.

It is not surprising, then, that Narayan frequently mentions tigers, real or metaphorical, and twice invokes them in titles as a principal organizing motif; nor that those two novels are politically resonant and persistently oblique. *The Man-Eater of Malgudi* (1961), who invades the print-shop and consumes with fearful obloquy the life of shilly-shallying Nataraj, is a massively aggressive taxidermist called Vasu—a man one can never be sure will not stuff one on the spot. Utterly disruptive to all he meets, Vasu wreaks mortal havoc on everything that pads, crawls, swims, or flies within range. Trained by and himself once a *phaelwan* (a traditional fairground strongman, and in modern usage a political bully-boy) before graduating to taxidermy, Vasu is without respect for the natural, majestic, or sacred: the first thing he kills, despite having been refused a license, is a

tiger, its severed head rolling in the back of his jeep; he also kills a tiger cub that in stuffed form becomes his masterpiece of naturalistic taxidermy, and plays a part in the plot, as does compensation for a pet dog he practiced his stuffing on. Surprised to be told an eagle he has shot is sacred, he sees a sales opportunity and proposes to kill more so the faithful can have one each, permanently; he comes his final cropper, mysteriously sudden death from a single blow to the head, in the middle of wild plans to madden Kumar, a beloved village-temple elephant he has already tried to poison, while it is in a Malgudian festival-procession, that it may with suppositious reason be shot for his profit. Throughout all this the narrator, Nataraj, who apparently does nothing to invite Vasu's visitation but merely suffers it, as one might a natural disaster, equally does nothing, and in a harsh view slides from bumbling victimhood to passive conspiracy to the conscious sheltering of a grossly malevolent criminal. The problem is made acute by the shocked, self-risking, and energetic efforts of others to deal with Vasu's menace once his plans for Kumar leak out—Nataraj having kept them to himself until past the eleventh hour.

Though quasi-tragedic in form, and problematic in the gravity of the gulf between Nataraj's inactivity and moral outrage at Vasu's depredations, *The Man-Eater of Malgudi* is zestfully and sometimes achingly funny, a reminder that P. G. Wodehouse (1881–1975), creator of Jeeves and Wooster, is hugely popular in India, and that Narayan was a lifelong fan. But the actions of Vasu and inactions of Nataraj are so extreme that their polarity becomes a dominant narrative concern, and obliges one to consider what reason Nataraj might have for the way in which he simultaneously bemoans and denounces Vasu's behavior yet strives to protect him from the proper consequences of his violence. Noting some curious details in the narrative—Nataraj's inheritance of his proudly owned business premises from "a good Moslem friend who migrated to Pakistan and gave me the first offer" (p. 52); Vasu meeting the *phael-wan* who taught him in Nagpur (p. 17); and the association of his habituation to killing with the Independence struggle and someone called "Hussein who broadened my outlook" (p. 127)—one reading would be of Nataraj, a devout Hindu, as in tortured denial of complicity with an openly violent Hindu sectarianism from which he profits, embodied in Vasu's addiction to killing as pleasure and response. Nataraj's good Moslem friend "migrated" (in 1947) under some kind of pressure, and men like Vasu, *phael-wans* from Nagpur (where the *Rashtriya Swayamsevakh Sangh,* the largest Hindu terrorist organization, is centered), were immediately responsible; of the blind paradoxicality of fascist and National Socialist politics is utterly nailed in Vasu's reply to Nataraj's sentimental protests about the dead tiger cub—"Anyway, it's easier to rear a dead animal." (p. 123).

The sustenance within India of anti-Muslim and anti-Christian violence by the Hindu Right, growing in power and organization throughout the twentieth century and since 1997 in national government, is for many now the great issue of Indian politics. That Narayan represents its personal accommodation in *Man-Eater* is again potently pointed by names: he was beginning his prose redactions of Hindu myth published as *Gods, Demons, and Others* (1964), and uses a subtle reversal—"Vasu," in itself meaningless, suggests (despite his description as a *raksha,* or demon) the name "Vasudev," one title of Lord Vishnu, the protector-aspect of the Hindu Trinity; "Nataraj" (from "*nata,*" dancer, + "*raj*") openly refers to the Cosmic Dance of Lord Shiva, the destroyer-aspect. Shiva's great dance that tramples *rakshas* becomes Nataraj's great shuffle of avoiding responsibility, and as the names speak true it is Nataraj in his silence and guilty inaction who is the destroyer.

Matters are sharpened further by the British resonance of Narayan's title, for *The Man-Eater of Malgudi* summons three oddly distinguished books: *The Man-Eaters of Tsavo, and other East African Adventures* (1907) by Lieut.-Col. J. H. Patterson (1867–1947), who shot among much else the various lions acquiring a taste for coolie during the building of the East African Railroad; and two Narayan would certainly have known, *Man-Eaters of Kumaon* (1944) and *The Man-Eating Leopard of Rudraprayag* (1947) by Jim Corbett (1875–1955), whose remarkable job it was to hunt, throughout India, carnivora officially designated as man-eaters. (Narayan might also have known Kenneth Anderson's *Man-Eaters and Jungle Killers,* 1957, and J. E. Carrington Turner's *Man-Eaters and Memories,* 1959.) There are many more stories about (personally shooting) man-eaters than there are such beasts, but the phenomenon, associated with injury and old age, was while tigers lived wild in large numbers perfectly real, and so were the men who sought to kill them. Corbett was by far the best known (the Rudraprayag leopard in particular, which in 1918–1926 killed and ate at least 125 people and took Corbett several months to stalk, was for a time world-famous) and most remarkable; when he tells you matter-of-factly that, knowing a tiger had been badly injured but allowed to escape, and considering it his duty and mercy to kill the now-dangerous animal, he wound up crawling along a blood-trail, gun-to-shoulder, knowing that when the tiger turned he would have at most a second or two to bring it down head-on and charging, and God willing was able to do so—all with a severe rebuke to the man foolish and cruel enough to have fired a crippling but not fatal shot—he is telling no more than truth. In his lifetime he did exactly that several times, as well as sitting twenty-eight straight nights' fruitless watch over a bridge for the Rudraprayag leopard: the contrast between Corbett's and Nataraj's reactions to the responsibility of a man-eater could not be more different; even in the far more sententious memoirs of inveterate big-game-hunters like Patterson and Anderson, the idea of dithering for months while intolerable predation continues unchecked is simply inconceivable.

Narayan was not (I think) concerned to praise Corbett as British, any more than to condemn

Nataraj as a Hindu, though the possibility of such a reading partly explains the critical silence about his tigers; but he was contrasting via his title efficiency and inefficiency about something self-evidently urgent, as bad for Malgudi as a man-eater and similarly able to run amok. As in *Waiting for the Mahatma*, Narayan the southerner again surveyed from behind his adopted Mysorean ramparts a troubling aspect of the Indian polity primarily rooted in central and northern *Bharat*. John Updike once called him "one of a vanishing breed—the writer as citizen" (*My Days*, p. x), and summoned a comparison with Faulkner as respectful celebrant of the local and parochial. That is fair, but Updike's village-suburb pastoralization of Malgudi is not aware (as he would be with Faulkner) of the modern, all-India critical-political susurrus that sounds whenever the seemingly simple shell of a Narayan novel is held close enough to the ear.

Tigers and Gandhi-ji collide again, quite differently, in *A Tiger for Malgudi* (1983). A faux-naïf foreword says Narayan was inspired by a hermit with a tame tiger who attended a Kumbh Mela festival in the late 1970s, and by the realization that it is smug of humans to "have monopolized the attention of fiction writers" (p. 7); he also reports telling a "smart journalist" who asked, "Why tiger? Why not a mouse?": "So that the chief character may not be trampled upon or lost sight of in a hole" (p. 8). More than half the novel is narrated by Raja, a tiger who moves from wild freedom to circus captivity and performance, putative film-stardom, and an excursion into a greatly discomposed Malgudi, to peaceful life with a self-deprecating *sannyasi* who makes him feel guilty for being a carnivore, old age, and memoirs in a zoo. The novel is slight—Narayan was by then in his mid-70s—but manages to be equally unlike *Animal Farm* and Beatrix Potter, and in its memorable central sweep achieves fabulous high comedy.

The circus-owner who captures and trains Raja, simply called Captain, is all a Malgudian showman should be, and develops an immensely complex act in which after much racing around

the ring and jumping through fiery hoops, Raja and a trained goat share a saucer of milk—or rather, since Raja loathes milk, and the goat has grown insouciant and greedy, Raja tastes the milk and kindly proffers it to the goat, who scarfs the lot. This illustrates not the Christian lion lying down with the lamb, but Gandhian *satyagraha*, India's greatest contribution to the modern world, and brings the Captain admiring fame until, overstepping himself distractedly one night, Raja "chose this moment to shoot forward and nip off the goat's head" (p. 64). The moment is serendipitously captured on film, and Captain recoups via an offer of an epic in which Raja will star until finally dispatched by the hero, played by a cowardly village-*phaelwan* whom the director has more or less kidnapped. The *phaelwan*'s understandable disinclination to try punching Raja to death with Raja's paws on his shoulders means superimposed shots are needed, and Raja spends days being filmed while attempting on hind-legs to reach a goat-carcass repeatedly hoisted away. Before long an electric prod as well as Captain's usual whip are needed, and after a while an irritated Raja knocks the prod from the Captain's hand and in the process accidentally knocks off his head. Proceeding peacefully to Malgudi, rather sorry that everyone runs away, Raja selects a headmaster's office in which to rest; from the ensuing, delightful chaos he is rescued by the *sannyasi*. Thereafter the focus drifts through an odd episode with the *sannyasi*'s wife trying to reclaim him from his forest retreat and Raja's problems with vegetarianism to the zoo and old age.

Though many of the same politically resonant elements occur in *Tiger* as in *Man-Eater* (a *phaelwan*, the inbuilt violence of something intrinsically Indian, and issues of competence in the face of that violence), comedy is far more dominant in *Tiger*, despite the deaths of goat and Captain, and the final onset of natural dotage. In the goat-and-Raja act as a misguided masque of *satyagraha*, Narayan achieves a vividness of political fable that confirms the need to read him with constant alertness to his chronicles—

precisely through their extraordinary southern detachment—as commentaries on issues affecting the Indian polity as a whole. Though the late works are slighter than the novels of his prime, they are still conceived and honed with a master's touch—and his whole art can be found in exquisite miniature in the short stories.

Criticism of Narayan has to date been generally timid (if properly respectful) in the West, and subject in India to earnest insistence on the specifically admirable qualities of Narayan the good Hindu, Brahmin, Gandhian, nationalist, or whatever, as determined by the critic and forcibly attributed to Narayan. His detachment and evident harmlessness, backed by the resistance of his austere prose to short, critically punchy quotation, has so far successfully defeated any appropriation of Malgudi by postcolonial critical-literary thought, whether Marxist, feminist, or subalternist (in striking contrast to the critical receptions of Raj Anand, Raja Rao, and the younger generation of Anglo-Indian and Indo-Anglian novelists including Anita Desai, Salman Rushdie, Vikram Seth, and Amit Chaudhuri). The biography in progress, as of 2003 ending in 1945, does not yet extend beyond the domestic Malgudi of the first four novels, but the second volume should (on the evidence of the first) set a new benchmark for careful close and historically minded reading, of both the fiction and non-fiction—and so open to more sustained, wide-angle investigation the historical-comical-pastoral-tragical (and so political and social) world of R. K. Narayan. My own guess (argued here without detailed biographical information, or space for the evidence of the short stories and the rich problems that form involves) is that for all his evident attractions to literary decency and vegetarianism, Narayan will in time be revealed as a modern tiger of Mysore, his novels as literary bites as absolute in their own graceful, velvet way as Raja's long-pondered and surgically precise nipping-off of a silly goat's head.

Selected Bibliography

WORKS OF R. K. NARAYAN

NOVELS OF MALGUDI

Swami and Friends. London: Hamish Hamilton, 1935.

The Bachelor of Arts. London: Nelson, 1937. (With an introduction by Graham Greene.)

The Dark Room. London: Macmillan, 1938.

The English Teacher. London: Eyre and Spottiswoode, 1945. Published in the U. S. as *Grateful to Life and Death,* Detroit: Wayne State University Press, 1961.

Mr. Sampath. London: Eyre and Spottiswoode, 1949; as *The Printer of Malgudi,* East Lansing: Michigan State College Press, 1957. (The U.K. and U.S. titles are now usually combined, as "*Mr. Sampath—The Printer of Malgudi.*")

The Financial Expert. London: Methuen, 1952; New York: Farrar, Straus and Giroux, 1959; Chicago: University of Chicago Press, 1981. (With an introduction by Graham Greene.)

Waiting for the Mahatma. London: Methuen, and East Lansing: Michigan State College Press, 1955.

The Guide. London: Methuen; New York: Viking, 1958.

The Man-Eater of Malgudi. New York: Viking, 1961; London: Heinemann, 1962.

The Sweet-Vendor. London: The Bodley Head, 1967; as *The Vendor of Sweets,* New York: Viking, 1967. (The U.S. title is now standard.)

The Painter of Signs. New York: Viking, 1976; London: Heinemann, 1977.

A Tiger for Malgudi. London: Heinemann; New York: Viking, 1983.

Talkative Man. London: Heinemann, 1986.

The World of Nagaraj. London: Heinemann, 1990.

A Malgudi Omnibus. London: Minerva, 1994; Vintage, 1999. (Comprises *Swami and Friends, The Bachelor of Arts,* and *The English Teacher.*)

More Tales from Malgudi. London: Minerva, 1997. (Comprises *Mr. Sampath—The Printer of Malgudi, The Financial Expert, Waiting for the Mahatma,* and *The World of Nagaraj;* there is also a helpful glossary of Hindi words.)

Memories of Malgudi. New Delhi: Viking India, 2000. (Comprises *The Dark Room, The English Teacher, Waiting for the Mahatma, The Guide,* and *The World of Nagaraj,* with an introduction by S. Krishnan.)

Magic of Malgudi. New Delhi: Viking India, 2002. (Comprises *Swami and Friends, The Bachelor of Arts,* and *The Vendor of Sweets,* with an introduction by S. Krishnan.)

SHORT STORIES

(Many of Narayan's stories appear in more than one collection; only the contents of those volumes still readily available are given.)

Malgudi Days. Mysore: Indian Thought Publications, 1943.

Dodu and Other Stories. Mysore: Indian Thought Publications, 1943.

Cyclone and Other Stories. Madras: Rock House and Sons, 1945.

An Astrologer's Day and Other Stories. London: Eyre and Spottiswoode, 1947.

Lawley Road and Other Stories. Mysore: Indian Thought Publications, 1956.

A Horse and Two Goats and Other Stories. New York: Viking; London: The Bodley Head, 1970. (Comprises "A Horse and Two Goats," "Uncle," "Annamalai," "A Breath of Lucifer," and "Seventh House"; there is also a brief glossary of Hindi words.)

Malgudi Days. New York: Viking; London: Heinemann, 1982. (A quite different book from the 1943 Mysore collection of the same name; comprises, from *An Astrologer's Day,* "An Astrologer's Day," "The Missing Mail," "The Doctor's Word," "Gateman's Gift," "The Blind Dog," "Fellow-Feeling," "The Tiger's Claw," "Iswaran," "Such Perfection," "Father's Help," "The Snake-Song," "Engine Trouble," "Forty-Five a Month," "Out of Business," "Attila," "The Axe"; from *Lawley Road,* "Lawley Road," "Trail of the Green Blazer," "The Martyr's Corner," "Wife's Holiday," "A Shadow," "A Willing Slave," "Leela's Friend," "Mother and Son"; and eight new stories, "Naga," "Selvi," "Second Opinion," "Cat Within," "The Edge," "God and the Cobbler," "Hungry Child," and "Emden.")

Under the Banyan Tree and Other Stories. London: Heinemann; New York: Viking / Elisabeth Sifton Books, 1985. (A selection from *An Astrologer's Day, Dodu, Lawley Road,* and *A Horse and Two Goats,* with some new stories; comprises "Nitya," "House Opposite," "A Horse and Two Goats," "The Roman Image," "The Watchman," "A Career," "Old Man of the Temple," "A Hero," "Dodu," "Another Community," "Like the Sun," "Chippy," "Uncle's Letters," "All Avoidable Talk," "A Snake in the Grass," "The Evening Gift," "A Breath of Lucifer," "Annamalai," "The Shelter," "The Mute Companions," "At the Portal," "Four Rupees," "Flavour of Coconut," "Fruition at Forty," "Crime and Punishment," "Half a Rupee Worth," "The Antidote," and "Under the Banyan Tree.")

OTHER WORKS BY NARAYAN

Mysore. Mysore: Government of Mysore, 1939.

Next Sunday: Sketches and Essays. Mysore: Indian Thought Publications, 1956.

Gods, Demons, and Others. London: Heinemann, 1964; New York: Viking, 1965; Chicago: University of Chicago Press, 1993; London: Vintage, 2001. (A retelling of stories from the Sanskrit classics the *Mahabharata, Ramayana, Yoga-Vasishta, Devi Bhagavatam,* and *Shiva Purana,* and the Tamil epic *Silapadikharam,* with woodcuts based on temple-decorations, by R. K. Laxman, Narayan's brother.)

The Ramayana: A Shortened Modern Prose Version of the Indian Epic. New York: Viking, 1972; Harmondsworth: Penguin, 1977. (Narayan's version is based on the classic Tamil version by Kamban.)

Reluctant Guru. New Delhi: Orient Paperbacks, 1974.

The Emerald Route. Bangalore: Government of Karnataka, 1977; Columbia, Mo.: South Asia Books, 1999. (With sketches by R. K. Laxman.)

The Mahabharata: A Shortened Modern Prose Version of the Indian Epic. New York: Viking, 1978; Harmondsworth: Penguin, 2001. (With decorations by R. K. Laxman.)

A Writer's Nightmare: Selected Essays, 1958–1988. New Delhi: Penguin Books India, 1988. (Comprises, from *Next Sunday,* "Higher Mathematics," "Fifteen Years," "Allergy," "Horses and Others," "The Vandal," "To a Hindi Enthusiast," "No School Today," "The Non-Musical Man," "On Humour," "Reception at Six," "In the Confessional," "Bride-groom Bargains," "The Scout," "Gardening Without Tears," "Private Faces," "Coffee Worries," "Looking One's Age," "The Great Basket," "Of Trains and Travellers," "A Library Without Books," "A Writer's Nightmare," "Umbrella Devotee," "Next Sunday," "The Sycophant," "The Maha," "Headache," "The Critical Faculty," "Beauty and the Beast," "Memory," "Street Names"; from *Reluctant Guru,* "Reluctant Guru," "My Educational Outlook," "Trigger-Happy," "Better Late," "The Winged Ants," "Taxing Thoughts," "Elephant in the Pit," "The Lost Umbrella," "The Newspaper Habit," "Castes: Old and New," "Curiosity," "The Golden Age," "Rambles in a Library," "At an Auctioneers," "Pride of Place," "Houses, Houses," "A Picture of Years"; and the previously uncollected "Sorry, No Room," "God and the Atheist," "On Funny Encounters," "The Testament of a Walker," "Love and Lovers," "A Matter of Statues," "History is a Delicate Subject," "Junk," "Of Age and Birthdays," "Pickpockets," "Monkeys," "A Literary Alchemy," "The Writerly Life," "The Nobel Prize and All That," "Misguided 'Guide,'" "Indira Ghandhi," "When India was a Colony," "India and America.")

A Storyteller's World. New Delhi: Penguin Books India, 1989.

Malgudi Landscapes: The Best of R. K. Narayan. Edited by S. Krishnan. New Delhi: Penguin Books India, 1992.

Salt and Sawdust: Stories and Table Talk. New Delhi: Penguin Books India, 1993.

The Grandmother's Tale: Three Novellas. London: Heinemann, 1993. (Comprises *The Grandmother's Tale, Guru,* and *Salt and Sawdust.*)

The Indian Epics Retold. New Delhi: Penguin Books India, 1995. (An omnibus edition of *Gods, Demons, and Others, The Ramayana,* and *The Mahabharata,* with woodcuts and decorations by R. K. Laxman.)

The Writerly Life: Selected Non-Fiction. New York: Viking, 2001.

AUTOBIOGRAPHIES

My Dateless Diary: An American Journey. Mysore: Indian Thought Publications, 1964; Harmondsworth: Penguin, 1988.

My Days: A Memoir. New York: Viking, 1974. London: Picador, 2001. (Foreword by John Updike).

BIOGRAPHY

Ram, Susan, and Ram, N. *R. K. Narayan: The Early Years: 1906–1945.* New Delhi: Viking Penguin India, 1996.

CRITICAL STUDIES

(A fuller list of critical articles to 1979 is available in Amritjit Singh, Rajiva Verma, and Irene M. Joshi. *Indian Literature in English, 1827–1979: A Guide to Information Resources.* Detroit: Gale Research, 1981, pp. 347–352.)

Afzal-Khan, Fawzia. *Cultural Imperialism and the Indo-English Novel: Genre and Ideology in R. K. Narayan, Anita Desai, Kamala Markandaya, and Salman Rushdie.* University Park: Pennsylvania State University Press, 1993.

Beatina, Mary. *Narayan: A Study in Transcendence.* New York: Peter Lang, 1994.

Bloom, Harold, ed. *R. K. Narayan.* New York: Chelsea House, 1994.

Goyal, Bhagwat S., ed. *R. K. Narayan's India: Myth and Reality.* Columbia, Mo.: South Asia Books, 1993.

Hariprasanna, A. *The World of Malgudi: A Study of R. K. Narayan's Novels.* Columbia, Mo.: South Asia Books, 1997.

Jha, Ram. *Gandhian Thought and Indo-Anglian Novelists: Mulk Raj Anand, Raja Rao, R. K. Narayan, and Bhabani Bhattacharya.* Delhi: Chanakya, 1983.

Kain, Geoffrey, ed. *R. K. Narayan: Contemporary Critical Perspectives.* East Lansing: Michigan State University Press, 1998.

Mishra, Pankaj. "The Great Narayan." In *New York Review of Books.* February 22, 2001 (http://www.nybooks.com/articles/14016).

Pontes, H. *A Bibliography of Indian Writing in English: R. K. Narayan.* New Delhi: Concept, 1983.

Pousse, Michel. *R. K. Narayan: A Painter of Modern India.* New York: Peter Lang, 1995.

Prasad, V. V. N. Rajendra. *Five Indian Novelists: B. Rajan, Raja Rao, R. K. Narayan, Arun Joshi, Anita Desai.* Columbia, Mo.: South Asia Books, 1997.

Walsh, William, *R. K. Narayan.* London: The British Council / Longman, 1971 (Writers and Their Work).

———. *R. K. Narayan: A Critical Appreciation.* Chicago: University of Chicago Press, 1983.

OTHER WORKS

Anand, Mulk Raj. *Untouchable.* Bombay: Current Book House, 1953; rev. ed., New Delhi: Arnold-Heinemann, 1981.

Anderson, Kenneth. *Man-Eaters and Jungle Killers.* London: George Allen and Unwin Ltd., 1957.

Corbett, Jim. *Man-Eaters of Kumaon.* 1944; Harmondsworth: Penguin, 1955.

———. *The Man-Eating Leopard of Rudraprayag.* 1947; with illustrations, 1954; Delhi: Oxford University Press, 1988.

Faulkner, William. *Novels 1930–1935.* Edited by Joseph Blotner. New York: Vintage, 1981.

Greene, Graham. *Stamboul Train.* London: Heinemann, 1932.

Rao, Raja. *Kanthapura.* 1938; Delhi: Oxford University Press, 1990.

Patterson, Lieut.-Col. J. H., DSO. *The Man-Eaters of Tsavo, and Other East African Adventures.* 1907; London: Fontana, 1973. (With a foreword by Frederick Courtney Selous.)

Scott, Paul. *The Raj Quartet.* London: Grafton, 1978.

Sontag, Susan. *On Photography.* New York: Farrar, Straus and Giroux, 1977; Harmondsworth: Penguin, 1979.

Turner, J. E. Carrington. *Man-Eaters and Memories.* London: Robert Hale Ltd., 1959.

ADDITIONAL REFERENCES

Bhattacharya, Sachchidananda. *A Dictionary of Indian History.* 1967. New Delhi: Cosmo Publications, 1994.

Clark, T. W., ed. *The Novel in India: Its Birth and Development.* London: George Allen and Unwin Ltd, 1970. (Essays on Bengali, Marathi, Urdu, Hindi, Tamil, and Malayalam prose fiction.)

Moienuddin, Mohammad. *Sunset at Srirangapatam: After the Death of Tipu Sultan.* Hyderabad: Longman Orient; London: Sangam Books, 2000. (Contains detailed accounts of the Tiger Throne and of Tipu's Tiger.)

Robinson, Francis, ed. *The Cambridge Encyclopedia of India, Pakistan, Bangladesh, Sri Lanka, Nepal, Bhutan, and the Maldives.* Cambridge, U. K.: Cambridge University Press, 1989.

Ngũgĩ wa Thiong'o
(1938–)

TRACIE CHURCH GUZZIO

IN THE GRIOT tradition found throughout Africa, the storyteller is more than a fabricator of tales; he or she is the keeper of the past and a protector of the culture. Ngũgĩ wa Thiong'o is clearly a griot. His novels, plays, and essays resonate with this ancient and venerable storytelling tradition. Though he has chosen a written form over an oral, and for a time an English tongue over his native Kikuyu, Ngũgĩ practices his art in an effort to treasure the traditions of the past and to ensure their transition into the future. But for a writer in postcolonial Kenya, this is a challenging task. History is a complex construct, a contested space between the colonial era and the past of the indigenous people. The writer must not only preserve the historical memory, he or she must also produce counter histories, ones that revise the stories that other, more powerful forces have told.

Kenya, especially, is a nation faced with deeply entrenched and complex historical issues. Since gaining independence from Britain in 1963, Kenya has been torn between tradition and change. As a politically engaged writer, Ngũgĩ has confronted these conflicts, attempting to echo the voices of the people and their culture. As he asserted in the essay "The Writer and His Past" (in *Homecoming: Essays on African and Caribbean Literature, Culture and Politics,* 1972), the "novelist is haunted by a sense of the past. His work is often an attempt to come to terms with 'the thing that has been,' a struggle, as it were, to sensitively register his encounter with history, his people's history" (p. 39). Ngũgĩ's work struggles to free his people from a cultural colonialism that remained in Kenya after the departure of the colonizers. In this sense alone, his work is inherently political. As the critic Kimani Njogu argues: "Storytelling is for Ngũgĩ a strategy of re-membering what has been dis-membered, building alliances, foreshadowing and keeping hope alive through active engagement. It is for him a way of creating spaces through which alternative voices, long suppressed through the colonial experience, may find expression" (p. 335).

Although Ngũgĩ's work is concerned with history, he sets his novels, plays, and stories in the recent past—in the years of colonial rule in Kenya up to independence and its aftermath. By reading his work, one may trace the move from Kenya's place as a British colony through rebellion to independence to what Ngũgĩ considers neocolonialism—marked by the Kenyan government's reliance on Western interests and capital. Always present in his writing is the inexorable relationship between Kenya and the colonial power. Even after independence, the effects of this historical association are keenly felt. This is true politically and economically as well as culturally. But, according to Simon Gikandi, "Ngũgĩ is unique among African writers of his generation in his refusal to invoke a precolonial world as the site of a stable culture and identity. The reason for this refusal arises, perhaps, from Ngũgĩ's recognition of how difficult it is to discuss a Gikuyu [Kikuyu] culture outside the colonial relationship" (p. 14). Indeed, the dominance of the colonial presence throughout Ngũgĩ's works, even those set after independence, carries his argument that European power did more than steal Kikuyu lands, it stole the culture and history of the people.

In an attempt to recover that loss, Ngũgĩ imbues his fiction and his drama with mythical oral histories, African proverbs, and Kikuyu creation myths. In this way, he reinscribes an oral tradition into his European-influenced prose. But he also reestablishes the Kikuyu story, often regulated and submerged in the colonial text. However, even these moments in his work show the ties to the colonial past. Many of Ngũgĩ's symbols and characters are reminiscent of Christian ideology and biblical motifs and personages. Many of his heroes see themselves as a kind of Moses or Adam, and in some cases Ngũgĩ even draws parallels between a character and Christ. As a child, Ngũgĩ had religious instruction at a missionary school, and his work reflects this biographical fact. But Ngũgĩ's use of Judeo-Christian allusion is more complex. Christianity, brought by the missionaries to Kenya, is part of the oppressive order sprung from colonialism. But it is also responsible for the education that Ngũgĩ received as a child and admired as a young man.

In most of his early work, Ngũgĩ seems to value the hybrid quality of his existent culture, of which Christian doctrine is a part; it is later in his career that he more directly criticizes the European elements, leading to his choice to write in Kikuyu. This shift, occurring in the late 1970s, marks a change not only in his style, but also in his attitudes to neocolonialist influence. At first, in the words of James Ogude, he saw the "possibilities of a syncretic culture, [whereas] in the later novels he displays utter hostility towards anything deemed Western" (p. 13). His work after the play *Ngaahika ndeenda* (1980; English translation *I Will Marry When I Want,* 1982) has increasingly indicated his disillusionment with Kenya's development since independence.

Ngũgĩ's later work has been primarily concerned with the effects of decolonization on the poor and oppressed in the Kenyan nation. His writing became more socialist in tenor, more respondent to the writings of Frantz Fanon and Karl Marx and the call for working-class revolution. He has been critical of the ruling classes of contemporary Kenya and their collusion with Western power, and he has voiced these opinions openly in his work, arguing that lands be restored to the Kenyan lower classes. Ngũgĩ believes that it is through such restoration that the Kikuyu poor will become not only self-sufficient and equal in the eyes of the law, but reconnected to their culture and their history. The land has always symbolized for the Kikuyu their connection to creation and their ancestral past. These ideas, especially in the ways that Ngũgĩ expresses them in his art, has made him a subversive figure in the eyes of the Kenyan authorities, resulting in his imprisonment in 1977. Even after his release a year later Ngũgĩ continued, and has continued, to condemn the policies of the Kenyan government.

Although Ngũgĩ's art reflects his politics and social criticism, his focus has always been on the individual lives of his characters and the people they represent. His narratives and their concentration on the past form what Wole Ogundele has called "a parallel and counterstatement to that of the state" (p. 113), but they also serve as a reminder of the lives lost and buried within the "official" historical record. By incorporating Kikuyu myths and oral style, by including autobiographical events, and by alluding to authentic figures, Ngũgĩ has attempted to reveal the lives of common people overwhelmed by the forces of history.

LIFE

He was born James Ngũgĩ on 5 January 1938 in Kamiriithu, Limuru, near Nairobi in Kenya, and his life is a reflection of the conflicts and changes of his country's recent past. His father, Thiong'o wa Nduucu, was a tenant farmer. Ngũgĩ's mother, Wanjiku, was one of four wives, and Ngũgĩ was one of twenty-eight children in the large, extended family supported by his father's work. As a small child, Ngũgĩ attended a Kikuyu school as part of the independent schools movement. The schools began as a part of the Kikuyu's reaction against the institutions ran by Christian missionaries in the 1920s and 1930s. Most missionary schools forbade traditional Kikuyu practices (such as female circumcisions). Independent schools promoted a balance of Christianity and Kikuyu tradition. While here, Ngũgĩ received a typical African education, but later he left for Alliance High School. Operated by missionaries, the school offered a more colonial British education, something highly valued by both Ngũgĩ and his family. For many native Kenyans, this type of education signaled success and advancement. While at Alliance, Ngũgĩ became strongly influenced by the Christian ideology of the curriculum and the faculty. This exposure is reflected in complex ways in Ngũgĩ's philosophy, writing, and politics throughout the course of his career.

By 1954 Ngũgĩ's perception of his country and the world had been dramatically altered as a result of the Mau Mau rebellion, which had begun in the early 1950s. The Mau Mau was a revolutionary society made up primarily of Kikuyu; members of the society engaged in terrorist activities aimed at driving out European settlers and ending colonial rule in Kenya. Some of Ngũgĩ's family members were imprisoned for collaborating with the rebels, a stepbrother was shot and killed, his mother was tortured, and his brother, Wallace Mwangi, joined the anticolonial forces. These events instilled in Ngũgĩ a strong political and cultural consciousness.

In 1959 Ngũgĩ moved to Kampala, Uganda, to attend Makerere University. It was at Makerere that he became dedicated to studying English literature (including the work of D. H. Lawrence and Joseph Conrad, two writers that he acknowledges as influences). He edited the journal *Penpoint* while at Makerere, and began writing plays, poetry, stories, and criticism. He also met his future wife, Nyambura, whom he married in 1961. In the same year, his first son, Thiong'o, was born. The couple had five more children: another son, Kimunya, in 1963; a third son, Nduucu, born in 1965; and three daughters: Mukoma in 1971, Wanjiku in 1972, and Njooki in 1978.

In 1962 Ngũgĩ's first play was produced. Ngũgĩ wrote *The Black Hermit* in honor of Ugandan freedom from colonial rule, and the play was performed in Kampala at the Ugandan independence celebration. By 1964 Kenya was also celebrating its independence, and that year, Ngũgĩ received a B.A. from Makerere University. The distinction of graduating with honors in English, his second language, was an achievement that convinced Ngũgĩ that he possessed the talent and capability to succeed in a graduate program in English.

In 1964 he accepted a scholarship to attend the University of Leeds in Great Britain. He began studying the literature of the African diaspora, especially the work of Caribbean writers. That year, he published his first novel, *Weep Not, Child*. The following year he published another novel, *The River Between* (1965), which was actually written before *Weep Not, Child*, and he commenced work on his thesis for his graduate degree, a dissertation on Caribbean literature, which was the genesis of his prose collection *Homecoming*, published in 1972. Ngũgĩ would not finish his master's degree at Leeds. Although he submitted his thesis, his academic reviewers requested changes; Ngũgĩ never made those revisions, and he returned to Kenya to accept a position as lecturer in the Department of English at University College in Nairobi. While in this position, he finished and published another novel, *A Grain of Wheat* (1967).

Also while at University College, in 1968, Ngũgĩ constructed a plan with two of his colleagues—Taban lo Liyong and Henry Owuor-Anyumba—for curriculum changes that would result in the abolition of the English Department and its replacement with a department of African literature and languages. In a treatise (reproduced in the appendix of *Homecoming*), Ngũgĩ and his coauthors recommended alterations to English degree programs that would reflect the diversity of languages and literary cultures throughout the world, especially those of Africa and its diaspora. The work equated the reading lists of the curriculum with British colonialism, suggesting that a cultural imperialism still prevailed in the postcolonial universities. The treatise does not affirm that the entire Western offering be abolished; English literature is seen as an important influence on the development of African literature. But to Ngũgĩ and his coauthors, its place in the curriculum should be secondary to literatures and languages of the African people. Ngũgĩ includes courses in oral literature and French and Swahili languages to present a more diverse and more representative curriculum. The treatise advocates that Africa be moved to the "center" of the department's offerings.

In 1969 Ngũgĩ resigned his post at Nairobi University over academic freedom issues and moved back to Uganda, where he had been awarded a fellowship in creative writing at his former school, Makerere University. In 1970 he took an associate professor post at Northwestern University, teaching African literature. His experience in the United States, especially in Chicago, alerted him to the worldwide prejudice against people of color, even in America. Ngũgĩ had read Fanon and Marx while at Leeds, but his time in the United States strengthened his nascent socialism. This is clearly reflected in the novel *Petals of Blood* (1977), which he began early drafts of while at Northwestern. Within a couple of years, Ngũgĩ was back at the University of Nairobi and again a member of the English Department. By 1973 he became chair of the department and implemented the changes to the curriculum that he had argued for in 1968.

Still deeply committed to drama and its importance to the community, Ngũgĩ became involved with the Kamiriithu Community Educational and Cultural Centre in his hometown. He also continued to write plays; his work *The Trial of Dedan Kimathi* was produced by the Kenya National Theatre in 1976. But Ngũgĩ realized that if he really wanted his work to represent and reflect the culture and the lives of the people, as well as spur the community to political action, it had to be written and performed in the language of the people, Kikuyu. This development in Ngũgĩ's aesthetic was echoed in his decision to discard his European name, James, and embrace Ngũgĩ wa Thiong'o, a title that honored his history, culture, and family.

In 1977, the same year that Ngũgĩ legally changed his name, he published *Petals of Blood*, his most Marxist-influenced work to that date, and completed the play *Ngaanika ndeenda* (coauthored with Ngũgĩ a Mirii). The play, written in Gikuyu, marked Ngũgĩ's transition from English-language writing to his native tongue. An immediate success, the play also quickly gained the attention of the government. Within a short time the play's production was halted and its performance license revoked. A month later, on 31 December 1977, Kenyan police arrested Ngũgĩ and confiscated his writing.

Ngũgĩ was never officially charged with a crime, and spent a year in prison without receiving a trial. Although he was chained for some periods of his incarceration, he still managed to write. Composing on scraps of toilet paper that he hid, Ngũgĩ worked on the novel *Caitaani mutharaba-ini* (1980; English translation *Devil on the Cross,* 1987). Despite protests from the international community (including Amnesty International) and famous writers such as James Baldwin, Ngũgĩ remained in jail until 12 December 1978. Following his release, Ngũgĩ fought to regain his university post. There were also constant threats that he would be arrested again. Without a steady position, he toured and wrote. In 1981 he published *Detained: A Writer's Prison Diary,* which described his experience in jail and his resolve to continue his political writing. He continued playwriting with the unpublished, *Maitu njugira (Mother, Sing for Me)* in 1982, but while in England promoting a book, he heard rumors that he would be arrested if he returned to Kenya. The news effectively orphaned Ngũgĩ from his homeland, forcing him into exile.

Since 1982, Ngũgĩ has devoted his energies to voicing his opposition to neocolonialism in Kenya and to cultural genocide, as well as calling attention to the problems of the poor and oppressed in his country. He has lobbied for cultural and literary theorists to reexamine African language and literature from nontraditional Western perspectives. In 1986 he published the novel *Matigari ma njiruungi* (English translation *Matigari,* 1989), for which he received critical acclaim. That same year, a collection of essays, *Decolonising the Mind: The Politics of Language in African Literature,* appeared. Ngũgĩ accepted visiting professor positions at Smith College and the University of Massachusetts at Amherst. In 1989 he became a visiting professor at Yale, where he stayed until 1992, at which time he was appointed to the post of Erich Maria Remarque Professor of Comparative Literature at New York University, where he continued to teach in 2003.

Ngũgĩ has remained a prolific writer and activist. In 1993 he published a collection of his essays under the title *Moving the Centre: The Struggle for Cultural Freedoms.* The following year he was awarded an honorary doctorate in humanities from Albright College. He also began searching for ways to reach even wider audiences with his work. Developing an interest in film, he helped direct the documentary *Sembene: The Making of African Cinema* (1994), and he has written books for children. In 1998 he published *Penpoints, Gunpoints, and Dreams: Toward a Critical Theory of the Arts and the State in Africa,* culled from a series of lectures he delivered at Oxford University in 1996. In 2003 he was at work on a new novel, one that no doubt will continue to examine the problems facing postcolonial Africa. And yet, decades after accepting exile, Ngũgĩ was still considered a controversial and dangerous political force by his government: his work continued to be banned in Kenya.

WEEP NOT, CHILD

The most clearly autobiographical of all of his work to date, *Weep Not, Child,* published in 1964, covers the period of the 1940s to the 1950s, the beginning of the Mau Mau rebellion. Several historical heroes of the rebellion appear in the novel, such as the anticolonial military leader Dedan Kimathi and Jomo Kenyatta (likened to a "black Moses"), who became Kenya's first prime minister after independence. But rather than a documentary of the conflict, Ngũgĩ offers readers a more intimate portrait of a family whose lives are forever altered by the changes occurring around them. In this sense, the novel announces a method typical to Ngũgĩ's work as a whole: embedding personal stories within the national and historical narrative, and balancing authentic events with the fictional lives that are as "true" as the verifiable accounts.

When the novel opens, the historical backdrop is revealed. Since the 1890s, the British colonial government has owned Kikuyu land, selling or leasing it to European settlers, taking it from the Kikuyu people and depriving them of a sound and comfortable living as well as a connection to their ancestral past. This has affected the family at the center of the work. Ngotho, the father, works land that once belonged to his family. He is now a tenant farmer (or *ahoi*), working for subsistence wages. Ngũgĩ's own father lived a similar life. Ngotho's sons have chosen not to live their lives in the same manner. One, Njoroge, chooses the path of education. Njoroge's character and the events that shape his life are reminiscent of Ngũgĩ's own biography. Through this protagonist, we see the struggles of a man caught between the colonial past and the impending postcolonial future. Another son, Boro, fights for the Mau Mau forces. The tension between father and son—Ngotho and Boro—is common in literature as in life, but here it is complicated by the men's differing views of the colonial government and its abuses of Kikuyu land. Ngotho feels the "loss of [his] land even more keenly than Boro; for him it was a spiritual loss. When a man was severed from the land of his ancestors, where would he sacrifice to the Creator?" (p. 110)

Njoroge has altogether different concerns. He has committed himself to a life of schooling and success. Although later he feels guilty for not being a more active participant in the Mau Mau rebellion, he spends most of the novel trying to adapt to the rigors of a colonial education and life. Education is seen as the means to succeed in this society, and Njoroge is hailed as a community hero for being a student: "Somehow the Gikuyu people always saw their deliverance as embodied in education. When the time for Njoroge to leave came near, many people contributed money so that he could go. He was no longer the son of Ngotho but the son of the land" (p. 148). In some ways, this philosophy mirrors that of the white missionaries who run the school, which is especially true of the headmaster: "The best, the really excellent, could only come from the white man. He brought up his boys to copy and cherish the white man's civilization as the only hope of mankind and especially of the black races" (p. 158). Ngũgĩ received a similar education, and both Ngũgĩ

and his character, Njoroge, while young men, believed that education is the best path out of the poverty and oppression that rule their lives.

Njoroge falls in love with a young woman, Mwihaki, whose father, Jacobo, is Ngotho's boss. Mr. Howlands, a European, owns the land that once belonged to Ngotho. Jacobo is associated with Howlands throughout the book; the two work together to keep the land from its rightful owners. Ngũgĩ suggests in his portrait of Jacobo that a culture in which Africans work against one another is even more dangerous than the European presence. Njoroge and Mwihaki's star-crossed love draws these families further into the problems of their society. The reader knows that the young couple's love cannot survive in a context of such violence and conflict.

Boro, more than any other character, perhaps, embodies this context. He returns home from fighting in World War II, a "European fight," only to find his own country in turmoil. His disillusionment over the war embitters him further to the British presence in Kenya. It also isolates him from his father, Ngotho, whom he views as weak. He blames the Europeans for the death of another brother earlier in the novel, and these feelings drive him to join the Mau Mau rebellion. Ngũgĩ here again establishes not only an autobiographical connection to the story, but his intention to highlight individual lives lost in the state's historical record.

When Ngotho dies, Boro at last understands what his father stood for and sees that his allegiance to the uprising has been driven more by hate than by a desire to connect with the land or with the past. Boro kills Mr. Howlands in an act of revenge and seals his fate. By the close of the novel, most of the family is either dead, arrested, or awaiting execution. Njoroge survives, but not because of his luck or his skill; he lives because he has not chosen an active role in the political and social events happening around him. He loses his belief that education will lead him to success or solve the problems of Kenya. And while the novel expresses the importance of a peoples' appreciation for the land and for tradition, it also, somewhat tragically, questions whether or not resistance can affect change in the daily lives of the people. The ending of the novel does offer some hope in the person of Njoroge's mother, who stands as a symbol of love and possible redemption, and by extension suggests that it is the power of love within families which will both unite and heal the wounds of Kenya.

THE RIVER BETWEEN

Ngũgĩ's next published work, *The River Between*, was actually composed before *Weep Not, Child*. Originally titled "The Black Messiah," *The River Between* shares many characteristics with *Weep Not, Child*, though there is less firsthand colonial involvement in the lives of the African characters imagined here. But like *Weep Not, Child*, this work explores men and women devoted to the promise of education and caught between cultures in conflict. The characters of *The River Between* have also lost a connection to the land and to their past, even more prominently than is seen in *Weep Not, Child*.

"The river between" refers to the river that separates two communities and two geographic ridges. The ridges themselves represent the two competing cultures and forces clashing in this country: "The two ridges lay side by side, hidden in the darkness. And Honia river went on flowing between them, down through the valley of life, its beat rising above the dark stillness, reaching into the hearts of the people of Makuyu and Kameno" (p. 152). The land itself is an important character in the novel; its description opens the novel, setting the scene for Ngũgĩ's purpose: to examine the role that the land plays in the tradition and culture of a people. As he indicates in *Weep Not, Child*, if the land is taken from a people, their heritage can be lost as well.

The protagonist of *The River Between*, Waiyaki, shares the same name as a nineteenth-century Kikuyu warrior who resisted British colonial rule. The Waiyaki of this work does not exhibit his namesake's heroism, however. Like other Ngũgĩ characters, he wishes only to pursue his education and one day become a teacher himself. This plan meets with opposition when his father takes him out to a *mugumo* tree (an image that appears elsewhere in Ngũgĩ's work, as a symbol of a community's "roots" and its interdependence on the land) to tell him about his past and his future. Waiyaki discovers that his ancestors were prophets and seers. His father informs him that his fate will be to follow in their footsteps, that in fact he will be a messiah for his community. As in other of Ngũgĩ's novels, there are significant allusions to Judeo-Christian belief, but this work especially uses the image of a Christian savior to explore the effects on the Kikuyu of Christian education and influence.

This announcement about his future comes at a time when Waiyaki is coming to terms with his own identity. He, like the river that lies between the ridges, is caught between two worlds. Both communities are African, but one lives in a more traditional manner, while the other has been highly Christianized and assimilated to Western ways. These competing influences in Waiyaki's life culminate in the prophecy about his future but also in his love for Nyambura, a woman from the "other" side. Like the lovers in *Weep Not, Child*, Waiyaki and Nyambura are destined to be kept apart by social forces. Waiyaki is torn between cultures because of his love and because of his duty. His portrayal here clearly symbolizes the conflict in Kenya during this historical period; but Waiyaki also suffers from a conflict between the needs of the individual and the community. Throughout the novel, images of duality, of things "lying between," reinforce the historical context. The Kenyan nation is not unified as a communal force. Waiyaki may point toward resolution, but he is tempted to embrace the world offered by European culture: "Education was really his mission. . . . Education was the light of the country" (p. 101).

Waiyaki accepts a position as headmaster of a communal independent school (again, similar to an institution that Ngũgĩ attended as a child). The school later decides to expel all females who have been circumcised. Female circumcision, a traditional practice of many African societies, is used in the novel to represent the complex nature of this now hybrid culture. The Christian missionaries and community oppose the practice. The people on one side of the river do not circumcise their female children. However, the other community sees this ritual as part of its heritage. One character in the novel, Muthoni, dies during the circumcision ritual. Waiyaki finds himself at the center of a scandal because he was in attendance at this forbidden practice. Nyambura suffers as well because she is not circumcised. While Ngũgĩ does not take a definitive stance one way or another on the controversial practice, it is clear that he believes such instances to represent complex conflicts between traditional African cultures and Westernized ones. There is no easy solution here, though in other works Ngũgĩ pointedly argues that Kikuyu women have been especially oppressed by the circumstances of their sex and gender roles in the culture. Waiyaki's probable death at the end of the novel implies two possible meanings. Either he has been a typical Christian savior and his death is a sacrifice for the community, or the conflicts within this society are irresolvable. The silence of the people and the land in the concluding paragraph lends support to the latter interpretation.

A GRAIN OF WHEAT

Considered by some critics to be Ngũgĩ's best work, this novel reiterates many of the themes found in his two earlier works. It is certainly a product of Ngũgĩ's growing sophistication as a novelist. The narrative jumps between three different time periods: before the rebellion, after the rebellion, and the day of independence (or *Uhuru*). Several historical figures, including the nationalist politicians Harry Thuku and Ken-yatta, appear in the novel, and Ngũgĩ once again portrays the intimate lives of individuals swept up in the waves of change around them.

Gikonyo and Mumbi are married, but their union has been all but destroyed in the years following the rebellion. Unable to forget his participation in the conflict, and unable to forgive what he sees as Mumbi's betrayal, Gikonyo leads a silent, bitter life. The other main character, Mugo, has also been adversely affected by the rebellion; his family has been similarly torn apart. A misunderstood orphan, Mugo searches for meaning in his life, at times believing that he could be the new Moses, while in desperate situations acknowledging his identification with Judas. We discover later that Mugo has betrayed the hero, Kihika, a man of great faith and conviction—who could have possibly been a true Moses figure. But betrayals permeate the novel, and the lives of the individuals distraught over what has happened to them is magnified by Ngũgĩ to argue that the nation has betrayed the promise of the rebellion and its people as well.

This is a world searching for the promise of new life, for guidance out of the tumultuous past. The desire for change and renewal is embodied in the title image of the grain of wheat. The fecund image of the land and the harvest implies that the land and the people will once again maintain a cooperative relationship that will bring the Kikuyu back to their ancestral past, effecting a renewal. The seeds for this renewal lie in political action: "Then nobody noticed it; but looking back we can see that Waiyaki's blood contained within it a seed, a grain, which gave birth to a political party whose main strength thereafter sprang from a bond with the soil" (p. 12). For many years there have been significant obstacles standing between the Kikuyu people and their land. The description of the colonial officer John Thompson's unfinished work, "Prospero in Africa," reminds the reader of the long tradition of colonial rulers capturing the land, subjugating the conquered, and controlling their lives, forcing the inhabitants to work the very land that once belonged to them. But the novel proposes that that time may be past, if the community unites to solve the problems of their infant nation and the aftermath of colonialism. The repeated images of harvest, seeding, and growth support Ngũgĩ's hope for the future, as does the sacrificial and redemptive death of Mugo and the possibility of a healthy, new start for Gikonyo and Mumbi in their marriage. Even their union is symbolic of mankind and the land being connected in Kikuyu ritual myth. But *A Grain of Wheat* would mark a departure. Later books are characterized by Ngũgĩ's growing disillusionment with Kenya's independent government.

PETALS OF BLOOD

Petals of Blood, published in 1977, would be Ngũgĩ's last novel written in English. Published shortly before his imprisonment, the work is often analyzed by critics in light of Ngũgĩ's political transformation and subsequent arrest. The novel opens with a fire that kills several people. The rest of the novel tries to solve the crime in a series of flashbacks and forwards that uncover the characters' backgrounds and connections to one another and to the victims. The novel exhibits characteristics of the Russian literary theorist Mikhail Bakhtin's description of a dialogic novel. *Petals of Blood* (as well as *Devil on the Cross*) operates not through a single narrative voice but that of a chorus. Multiple discourses, genres, tones, and styles construct the novel, making the work illustrative of a truly communal story.

The title for the work comes from a poem by the West Indian poet Derek Walcott, and the image is an important symbol in the work. The emphasis on the land and the harvest, found earlier in *A Grain of Wheat,* is prominent here as well, though there is a shift in Ngũgĩ's focus. According to Christine Loflin, in *Petals of Blood* "Ngũgĩ moves from the primarily aesthetic and spiritual connection to the land evident in his early novels to an explicitly political and economic relationship between the worker and the land" (p. 269). This is evident in Ngũgĩ's description of a call to arms: "Do not forget your calabash of sour milk. Also your spear and shield. We shall need them in the struggle to come. Gird your loins and always remember everything good and beautiful comes from the soil" (p. 89). The title of the novel ties together the image of the land and of armed struggle, suggesting that the connection between the two is endemic to Kenya and its battle against oppressive forces, whether they be colonial or neocolonial. Ngũgĩ's growing socialism is reflected in scenes like these throughout the book, as well as through the interaction of the characters. At the center of the action is Godfrey Munira, another of Ngũgĩ's schoolteachers educated in the colonial tradition. His goal is to provide the local children of Ilmorog with a solid and stern Western and Christian education. He is portrayed as a passive and ineffectual character throughout the novel. Isolated from his community because of his Western value system, he is also isolated from Kikuyu traditional culture and from nature. He greatly admires his younger and more political colleague, Karega. Karega holds a different position in the classroom than Munira. He sees his duty as an educator in the ways of the people, in the Kikuyu culture. He tries to inspire the children to find value in their past and in their heritage.

Karega, who led a strike when he was a young man, represents Ngũgĩ's new hero. As a man of education *and* action, Karega embodies the best of society. Even Munira sees that Karega is heroic and that he could lead the people to change. But threatening his potential in Munira's eyes is Karega's romantic relationship with Wanja, a woman with an illicit past. Munira takes action against the lovers, ironically spending his energy in a futile and pointless gesture rather than helping the community he has sworn to educate. His misdirected effort has tragic results.

More controversial is the novel's criticism of Kenya's contemporary government and its connection to European power. The bar that burns down at the beginning of the novel is not owned by local people; it is part of a Western corporation. The wealth is not distributed to the people, but to foreigners and to upper-class Kenyans who benefit from their dependence on outside capital. Ngũgĩ argues that this economic relationship fostered by the new, "independent" government is not any better then the colonial powers that once ruled. The neocolonialists are far worse in Ngũgĩ's eyes because they prey on their own people: they are "the drinkers of human sweat, eaters of human flesh" (p. 236). A minor character in the work, Abdulla, is a former Mau Mau resistance fighter, forgotten and exploited by the government that he helped to install. Scenes and characterizations such as these contributed to Ngũgĩ's growing political troubles. Nevertheless, Ngũgĩ is proud of the work and its impact, as he states in the essay "Petals of Love," included in his 1981 collection *Writers in Politics*:

> I am not as a Kenyan ashamed of speaking and writing about the peasants and workers who have built Kenya and who, through their blood and sweat, have written a history of grandeur and dignity and fearless resistance to foreign, economic, political and cultural domination, a history of which we should be proud. If *Petals of Blood* can convey at least that message to us Kenyan readers, I shall be satisfied. Hopefully out of *Petals of Blood,* we might gather petals of revolutionary hope.
>
> (p. 98)

DEVIL ON THE CROSS

Ngũgĩ's first novel written in Kikuyu, *Devil on the Cross,* is one of his most puzzling, yet remarkable, works. Composed on scraps of toilet paper during the year that Ngũgĩ was in prison, the novel highlights the frame of mind and situation of a political prisoner; Ngũgĩ's tone is redolent with satire and sarcasm. Clear heroes are hard to find here. The work's construction and style seems to deliver a message of resistance against Western forms and ideology (in all arenas). Like *Petals of Blood, Devil on the Cross* represents not only a political shift in Ngũgĩ, but a creative one as well. Critic Oliver Lovesey describes the later novels as having a "postcolonial—but also a postmodern—sensibility, self-consciously celebrating their own artificial, constructed nature, mimicking other (especially biblical) plots and phrases, and displaying an unwillingness to accept the 'master narratives' of state-sanctioned historians" (p. 21). Replete with proverbs, oral tales, fabulations, and non-Western linear structures, the novel represents a more indigenous tale than Ngũgĩ had written before.

The novel opens with four characters traveling to a thieves' convention. The participants each formulate their plan to oppress the weak and attain wealth and power. In discovering the plans, the reader becomes acquainted with the histories and intersections of the characters, most especially the four that are central to the story. The frame seems to parody Geoffrey Chaucer's *Canterbury Tales* or Giovanni Boccaccio's *Decameron.* But storytelling in this work is a tool of power, as it has been in the interaction between colonial Europe and Africa for centuries. Whoever writes the history, tells the most "official story," determines the balance of power, the distribution of wealth.

The four main characters operate as allegories more than realized creations: Wariinga, the female revolutionary; Wangari, the worker, a former Mau Mau fighter; Muturi, the activist; and Gatuiria, the intellectual. Each is ineffectual in his or her own way, suggesting perhaps the need for the individual to join forces with others in the community to affect change. This is echoed in the line: "the voice of the people is the voice of God" (p. 8). As in other Ngũgĩ texts, *Devil on the Cross* is notable for its abundance of biblical allusions and images. Besides the obvious reference in the title, there are many resurrection and crucifixion scenes, including

Wariinga's dream of a white devil on a cross that is later removed by black men in suits. The image has several different interpretations, and like a folktale or a biblical story, this scene instructs multiple readers in a multitude of ways.

But the transitory quality of the characters and their inability to accomplish more than revenge or to serve more than their own interests may speak to more than their individual failures. Gatuiria cannot speak his native tongue, a sign of his colonial education, but taken with the other deficiencies of the characters, this inability suggests something more problematic: that this is a country without heroes and with very little compassion or humanity. Very little even happens in the novel. As an allegory of neocolonialism, the narrative offers an indictment of a government that has forsaken the people and whose leadership has failed to address the condition of the land or the suffering of the poor. Only the rich, those plotting to accumulate more wealth and power, succeed.

MATIGARI

The title of Ngũgĩ's 1986 novel, *Matigari,* is a term that means "the patriots who survived the bullets." As a tribute to those who fought in the Mau Mau rebellion, the novel follows the journey of a man named Matigari. We soon discover that this is not his real name, but one he has adopted. His true name is never revealed, and this only adds to the mystery of the character. He is less a realistic than an allegorical figure. As the novel progresses, Matigari becomes less an individual and more an embodiment of the Kikuyu collective. At times he is young, at times old. The character's gender changes as well. And he seems to have the ability to transform himself to suit the situation. A mythic figure to the people he encounters and to those who merely hear about his exploits, his wanderings, his imprisonment with twelve other men, and his ability to work apparent miracles, also likens him to Christ.

Of all of Ngũgĩ's works, this novel is the most symbolic. We know little about this character, only that he is a man who has fought a long time and wishes to go home. On his quest, he is wrongfully imprisoned; he saves the innocent; and he tries to inspire the people to revolt against their oppressors, to fight for the Kenya that the Mau Mau rebellion attempted to create. As people begin to tell stories about him, they also create stories about him. He is less a man and more of the story that he represents to the people that have met him or imagine they have. This characteristic also connects the novel with oral fable, with folktales told over and over again for their instructional value. The stories told about the title character sustain the community and give the people hope for the future. What Matigari represents, what he is searching for, in Ngũgĩ's mind, should be the goal of the people as well.

As Matigari travels, he conducts an almost mystical search: "Where in the country can one find truth and justice?" (p. 82) he wonders. The implication in the novel is that his is a fruitless search. Kenya is a wasteland; its people lost and abandoned. Matigari mourns the condition of the country: "I was trembling with rage, rage of a newly found dignity that comes from having the scales of a thousand years fall from one's eye. I was now human" (p. 22). The only hope for this country is in revolution and in a reconnection to nature.

Although less directly interested in history than some of his other work, the novel still explores the affects of the struggle between the forces of colonial power and the new government. The tone of Ngũgĩ's previous two novels is echoed here as well. Bitterness and disillusionment characterize much of the novel, but there are elements that suggest a possible optimistic future. A scene featuring the *mugumo* tree reiterates what this image symbolizes elsewhere in Ngũgĩ's work; the importance of the past and of the land in building toward the future. The novel's conclusion indicates that the community may yet have reason to hope. Matigari appears at the end of the work as a warrior, and the scene contains symbols of birth, death, and regeneration, of the promise of renewal. Ngũgĩ has stated elsewhere, in *Moving the Centre,* that "Matigari shall one day return" (p. 175). The possibility for a strong, unified, and peaceful Kenya may yet be on the horizon.

Matigari became such a powerful symbol in Kenya that the book drew even more attention than Ngũgĩ's previous works. Within three months of its publication, the novel caught the attention of the Kenyan police who responded to reports that a man named Matigari was roaming the rural districts complaining about the government. Once police discovered that these were fictional accounts, they confiscated copies of the novel and officially banned it from Kenya.

Ngũgĩ's account of the history of the text could read as yet another "story" told about this mythical character, but more importantly it speaks to both the desire of the people to find a hero (fictional or not) and the threat that such hope and inspiration imposes on the neocolonial order. *Matigari* transcends a mere novel here, and becomes an artistic rendering of humanity and faith in the face of years of despair and oppression.

THE PLAYS

Ngũgĩ's plays have not garnered the amount or quality of critical attention that his novels have, despite the fact that they have been a steady source of controversy in his own country. Representative of his work for the theater is *The Trial of Dedan Kimathi,* performed in 1976. This play follows the career of a Mau Mau fighter. Like much of Ngũgĩ's work, it embraces the values embedded in the rebellion, offering a hero for the people to emulate.

It is *Ngaahika ndeenda* (*I Will Marry When I Want*), however, that is Ngũgĩ's most influential dramatic work. His first narrative written in Kikuyu, it marks his move from more conventional writing to a style that clearly reflects his social criticism and politics. His emphasis on the possibilities of workers changing the course of Kenyan history is illustrated in his choice of language. Not all of his audience could read or speak English; Kikuyu is the language of the people. Ngũgĩ's decision to write and perform the play in Kikuyu brought him under the scrutiny of Kenyan officials. Composed of myths, mimes, chants, oral ballads, and stories, the play reenacts Kikuyu traditional ritual—at least symbolically. The emphasis on the folk language and style indicates the work's socialist tenor. The play's performance in 1977 at the Kamiriithu Community Educational and Cultural Centre in Limuru. Kamiriithu, Ngũgĩ's hometown, suited Ngũgĩ's purpose: this was a national theater, devoted to celebrating Kikuyu culture and traditions.

The play was direct in its criticism of the government's dependence on foreign money, its existence as a neocolonial state. In Ngũgĩ's mind, those that benefit from this system are the wealthy Kenyans, while the poor continue to suffer. As in *Weep Not, Child,* the play explores the lives of men and women bound to land that they do not own, working it for barely livable wages or sustenance. Here, however, the owners of the land are not European colonials or their lackeys—the owners are rich Kenyans. Kiguunda works the land belonging to Kioi, owning a half-acre himself. He must decide whether or not he will sell his own plot of land to Kioi in order to finance his daughter's upcoming wedding. It is Kioi's son that Kiguunda's daughter, Gathoni, is engaged to marry. The engagement, however, is the result of her pregnancy, and her father has reluctantly agreed to allow the marriage to take place, even though the prospective groom is his enemy's son.

Kioi convinces Kiguunda that the couple be married in a Christian ceremony, requiring all of the traditional adornments. The planned ceremony becomes more and more expensive, finally forcing Kiguunda to take a loan (from

Kioi's bank), with his precious land as collateral. Gathoni is later abandoned by her fiancée and Kiguunda is unable to pay off his loan. Kioi sells the land to a Western company that intends to build an insecticide plant on the property. With this work, Ngũgĩ criticizes Kenyans who in their greed for Western wealth and prestige forsake their own people. And he points out Christian hypocrisy and its relationship to a culture of oppression. One of the workers sings:

> But they, on this earth, this very earth,
> They are busy carousing on earthly things, our
>   wealth,
> And you the poor are told:
> Hold fast unto the rosary,
> Enter the church,
> Lift up your eyes unto the heavens.
>
> (*Modern African Drama*, p. 317)

If it were not for Kioi's pretensions to Christian living (and Western status), Kiguunda would not have had to sell his land. Kioi places no value on anything except money, ultimately abandoning his family, his people, his faith, and his customs. To Ngũgĩ, Kioi, as a native Kenyan who has sold out to the West, represents the problems facing the contemporary Kenyan nation.

THE CRITICISM

Ngũgĩ has achieved a great deal of success as a novelist and playwright, but he is also, in the words of Oliver Lovesey, an "important theorist of postcolonial and African literature" (p. 21). His collections of criticism have been as influential as his fictional efforts in bringing attention to African language and literature and the issues confronting a postcolonial world. His first effort, *Homecoming,* discusses topics ranging from culture, literature, colonial politics, exploitation, and the significance of the church.

Education and politics are also prominently discussed in *Detained: A Writer's Prison Diary.* Ngũgĩ's description of his imprisonment in 1977 does not just provide autobiographical information from this period, it also reflects on the society that inhibits freedom and artistic expression. It questions the value of Ngũgĩ's own education and the need for the artist to commit to political action (something he was unable to do when he was a young student). He admits that his colonial education does not continue to nourish him as it once did: "What use is your education if it cannot be shared with your own people?" (p. 129). In the text, Ngũgĩ promises to carry on with his work despite the threat of violence or incarceration, and reminds his audience that governments have, throughout history, made a habit of locking away thinkers and artists. His subsequent collections, *Writers in Politics* and *Barrel of a Pen: Resistance to Oppression in Neo-Colonial Kenya* (1986), extend many of these ideas.

Decolonising the Mind: The Politics of Language in African Literature, published in 1986, marked the beginning of his essay writing in Kikuyu. By this time he had already written a play in his native language, and he decided that it was only logical that he argue for the primacy of African literature and language in his own Kikuyu. The initial stages of this decision can be seen even in *Detained,* but *Decolonising the Mind* was written and published after his exile, when his commitment to using his native tongue had deepened. Much of the work is autobiographical, such as his description of meeting the Nigerian writer Chinua Achebe when he was a college student. But the work is also concerned with politics and history. It outlines the Mau Mau rebellion and where it succeeded. It also illuminates the reasons why Kenya (and other African nations) has grown into a neocolonial government.

Ngũgĩ's examination of what happens to a society when its culture and even its language is devalued and lost is most central to this work. Culture and language help a people define and express themselves. If you control this aspect of a community's life, you gain power over the life of the mind—even more lethal than being under the lash. Ngũgĩ equates the history of colonialism in Kenya with the cultural imperialism that continues in its educational systems to this day. Until Kenya can identify with its own voices, Ngũgĩ believes, it will never truly be independent.

The follow-up to *Decolonising the Mind, Moving the Centre: the Struggle for Cultural Freedoms,* published in 1993, explores many of the same issues as Ngũgĩ's earlier work. *Moving the Centre,* however, also shows Ngũgĩ's developing interest in cultural and literary theory, and the essays have broader themes. Influenced by philosophers and critics such as Jacques Derrida, Mikhail Bakhtin, Edward Said, Homi Bhabha, and Michel Foucault, Ngũgĩ reasons that Africa must find its own center, departing from its Eurocentric stance. He traces throughout the collection why this is necessary not for only Africa, but for the rest of the world as well. Too many societies, in Ngũgĩs view, have glued their eyes to the West, ruining their global vision. This has led to fear of the "other," war, terrorism, prejudice, even disease. Ngũgĩ tracks such blindness in history and in literature, citing such examples as the Prospero and Caliban story from Shakespeare's *The Tempest,* and the Robinson Crusoe and Friday tale in Daniel Defoe's famous novel. Authority, knowledge, civilization, humanity all lie in the European characters, but their dark counterparts have represented lust, savagery, laziness, and animalism. This Manichaean binary must be deconstructed by writers and critics to restore a more holistic view of human relationships, and to dethrone the West as the only true cultural power.

Other essays in the collection consider several approaches to this re-centralizing of African culture. Some of Ngũgĩ's essays discuss his growth as a writer and his commitment to Kenya, despite his exile. Others provide his reflections on history and historical figures, such as South Africa's Nelson Mandela. One of the most widely-discussed essays in the collection is "Her Cook, Her Dog: Karen Blixen's Africa." A response to the memoir *Out of Africa* by Isak Dinesen (Blixen's pen name), in it Ngũgĩ condemns the portrait of Africa found in most European literature. He calls *Out of Africa* "one of the most dangerous books ever written about Africa, precisely because this Danish writer was obviously gifted with words and dreams" (p. 133). Presenting Africa as a playground, a dreamland filled with beloved toys, Dinesen, in Ngũgĩ's view, infantilizes the Kikuyu people living on *her* land, land that had been illegitimately occupied only years before. Ngũgĩ accuses the writer of representing racism as love and affection and suggests that Dinesen "embodies the great racist myth at the heart of the Western bourgeois civilization" (p. 135).

Ngũgĩ's essay "From the Corridors of Silence: The Exile Writes Back" describes the events that led up to his exile from Kenya. But the essay really is a call to action, asking writers from all of the world to remember the people they have left behind, the poor, the oppressed—otherwise they will remain voiceless. Ngũgĩ observes that the present condition of the world causes many to feel like exiles in their own land. Such a circumstance is only overcome by individuals united in their humanity.

Ngũgĩ's last collection of essays, organized from lectures given at Oxford University, is *Penpoints, Gunpoints, and Dreams: Toward a Critical Theory of the Arts and the State of Africa.* In many ways, these essays cover old ground. Ngũgĩ states that "the responsibility of Africa's artists and intellectuals to return to the languages of the people has been my theme in books, and in my talks, over the last ten years" (p. 128). But the essays also indicate a return to Ngũgĩ's dramatic roots as well as his growing interest in film. One of the most provocative essays in the work is "Enactments of Power: The Politics of Performance Space." The essay opens with the assertion that the "struggle between the arts and the state can best be seen in performance in general and in the battle of performance space in particular" (p. 37). Ngũgĩ observes that the public space, once a location for learning codes of behavior, governed by poets and philosophers, is now controlled by the state: each group is engaged in a battle now for power. Possibly, this contested space is what led to Ngũgĩ's troubles with the Kenyan government—his use of public space threatened officials' control over public behavior. This essay and others in the collection argue for artists and the common person to fight for their space to speak or write in order to battle the dehumanizing forces of the twentieth and twenty-first centuries.

Whether he is writing children's books, short stories, critical essays, plays, or novels, Ngũgĩ wa Thiong'o remains committed to the struggle of the Kenyan people. Unsatisfied with the unfulfilled promises of governments past and present, Ngũgĩ continues to battle hypocrisy and despair with his stories. Like the griot, he sees his duty as transforming the darkness into a source of hope and enlightenment. While the future of Kenya is uncertain, Ngũgĩ's works are filled with the whispers of prophecy and divination. They forecast troubled times ahead, but like the *mugumo* tree at the center of so many of Ngũgĩ's stories, they also promise a hopeful future lying somewhere beyond present awareness. Ngũgĩ's works forge a new narrative for Kenya—one that is drenched in the bitterness and violence of history, but one that is also resplendent with an imaginative sensibility that is able to re-create the world.

Selected Bibliography

WORKS OF NGŨGĨ WA THIONG'O

NOVELS AND SHORT STORIES

Weep Not, Child. London: Heinemann, 1964; New York: Macmillan, 1969, repr. 1971.

The River Between. London: Heinemann, 1965.

A Grain of Wheat. London: Heinemann, 1967. Rev. ed, 1986.

Secret Lives and Other Stories. New York: L. Hill, 1975; London: Heinemann, 1976.

Petals of Blood. London: Heinemann, 1977; New York: Penguin, 1978, repr. 1991.

Caitaani mutharaba-ini. Nairobi: Heinemann Kenya Ltd., 1980. Translated by Ngũgĩ as *Devil on the Cross.* London: Heinemann, 1982.

Matigari ma njiruungi. Nairobi: Heinemann Kenya Ltd., 1986. Translated by Wangui wa Goro as *Matigari.* London: Heinemann, 1989.

PLAYS

The Black Hermit. Kampala, Uganda: University Press, 1963.

The Trial of Dedan Kimathi. With Micere Mugo. London: Heinemann, 1976.

Ngaahika ndeenda. With Ngũgĩ wa Mirii. Nairobi: Heinemann Kenya Ltd., 1980. Translated by Ngũgĩ as *I Will Marry When I Want.* London: Heinemann, 1982. Reprinted in *Modern African Drama.* Edited by Biodun Jeyifo. New York: W. W. Norton, 2002.

OTHER WORKS

Homecoming: Essays on African and Caribbean Literature, Culture and Politics. London: Heinemann, 1972; New York: L. Hill, 1973.

Detained: A Writer's Prison Diary. London: Heinemann, 1981.

Writers in Politics: Essays. London: Heinemann, 1981.

Barrel of a Pen: Resistance to Oppression in Neo-Colonial Kenya. Trenton, N.J.: Africa World, 1986.

Decolonising the Mind: The Politics of Language in African Literature. London: Heinemann, 1986. Repr. 1997.

Moving the Centre: The Struggle for Cultural Freedoms. London: Heinemann, 1993.

Penpoints, Gunpoints, and Dreams: Toward a Critical Theory of the Arts and the State in Africa. Oxford,U.K.: Clarendon; New York: Oxford University Press, 1998.

BIBLIOGRAPHY

Sicherman, Carol. *Ngũgĩ wa Thiong'o: A Bibliography of Primary and Secondary Sources.* London and New York: Hans Zell, 1989.

CRITICAL STUDIES

Boehmer, Elleke D. "The Master's Dance to the Master's Voice: Revolutionary Nationalism and the Representation of Women in the Writing of Ngũgĩ wa Thiongo." *Journal of Commonwealth Literature* 26, no. 1 (1991): 188–197.

Caminero-Santangelo, Byron. "Neocolonialism and the Betrayal Plot in *A Grain of Wheat*: Ngũgĩ wa Thiongo's Re-Vision of *Under Western Eyes.*" *Research in African Literatures* 29, no. 1 (1998): 139–152.

Cook, David and Michael Okenimkpe. *Ngũgĩ wa Thiong'o: An Exploration of His Writings,* 2d ed. Oxford, U.K.: J. Currey, 1997; Portsmouth, N.H.: Heinemann, 1997.

Gikandi, Simon. *Ngũgĩ wa Thiong'o.* Cambridge U.K. and New York: Cambridge University Press, 2000.

Hale, Frederick. Ngũgĩ Thiong'o's Mau Mau for Children." *Children's Literature Association Quarterly* 20, no. 3 (1995): 129–134.

Hooper, Glen. "History, Historiography and Self in Ngũgĩ's *Petals of Blood.*" *Journal of Commonwealth Literature* 33, no. 1 (1998): 47–62.

Jackson, Thomas. "Orality, Orature, and Ngũgĩ wa Thiong'o." *Research in African Literatures* 22, 1 (spring 1991): 5–15.

Killam, G. D., ed. *Critical Perspectives on Ngũgĩ wa Thiong'o.* Washington, D.C.: Three Continents Press, 1984.

Loflin, Christine. "Ngũgĩ wa Thiong'o's Visions of Africa." In *Critical Essays on Ngũgĩ wa Thiong'o.* Edited by Peter Nazareth. New York: Twayne, 2000. Pp. 261–280.

Lovesey, Oliver. *Ngũgĩ wa Thiong'o.* New York: Twayne, 2000.

Mazrui, Alamin. "Orality and the Literature of Combat: The Legacy of Fanon." *Paintbrush: A Journal of Contemporary Literature* 20 (spring–autumn 1993): 159–183.

Narang, Harish. "Prospero and the Land of Calibans: *A Grain of Wheat.*" In *Critical Essays on Ngũgĩ wa Thiong'o.* Edited by Peter Nazareth. New York: Twayne, 2000. Pp. 123–141.

Njogu, Kimani. "Living Secretly and Spinning Tales: Ngũgĩ's *Secret Lives and Other Stories.*" In *Ngũgĩ wa Thiong'o: Texts and Contexts.* Edited by Charles Cantalupo. Trenton, N.J.: Africa World Press, 1995. Pp. 335–348.

Ogude, James. *Ngũgĩ's Novels and African History: Narrating the Nation.* London and Sterling, Va.: Pluto Press, 1999.

Ogundele, Wole. "Natio, Nation, and Postcoloniality: The Example of Ngũgĩ" In *Ngũgĩ wa Thiong'o: Texts and Contexts.* Edited by Charles Cantalupo. Trenton, N.J.: Africa World Press, 1995. Pp. 111–132.

Osei-Nyame, Kwado. "Ngũgĩ wa Thiong'o's *Matigari* and the Politics of Decolonization." *Ariel: A Review of International English Literature* 30.3 (July 1999): 127–140.

Parker, Michael and Roger Starkey, eds. *Postcolonial Literatures: Achebe, Ngũgĩ, Desai, Walcott.* New York: St. Martin's Press, 1995.

Robson, Clifford B. *Ngũgĩ wa Thiong'o.* London and New York: Macmillan, 1979.

Sicherman, Carol. *Ngũgĩ wa Thiong'o: The Making of a Rebel: A Source Book in Kenyan Literature and Resistance.* London and New York: Hans Zell, 1990.

Williams, Patrick. *Ngũgĩ wa Thiong'o.* Manchester U.K.: Manchester University Press, 1999.

Lewis Nkosi

(1936–)

LUCY VALERIE GRAHAM

A NOTED LITERARY critic and academic in Europe and the United States, South African–born Lewis Nkosi is also known for his incisive journalism and is the author of a number of works of fiction, including two novels. *Mating Birds* (1983), his well-known first novel, has been translated into more than ten languages, and in 2002 he published in English a second novel, *Underground People.* Nkosi, whose literary career has spanned five decades, has been described by the South African critic Andries Oliphant as a "sharp and gifted writer with an irreverent take on life." A world citizen, Nkosi left South Africa in 1961 and has lived and written in contexts as diverse as the United States, the United Kingdom, Zambia, Poland, and Switzerland, where he is currently living. Yet he was definitively marked by his early years as a journalist in South Africa and particularly by his experience working for *Drum* magazine in Johannesburg during the 1950s. Along with other *Drum* journalists and writers of his generation, Nkosi rejected the subservient and dutiful position that was increasingly being forced upon blacks in South Africa by the National Party government of Dr. Daniel François Malan, which came to power in 1948. With cool irony and sardonic wit, the *Drum* writers produced some of the more subversive and critical commentaries on the apartheid system during its founding years. Working for *Drum* in the "hectic decade" of the 1950s, was, according to Nkosi, "the most shaping influence" of his young adulthood. At the time, Johannesburg was "the buzzing centre of all national activity" and the city "seemed to be the only place to be in for any young man trying to write" (*Home and Exile*, p. 9).

Some of Nkosi's critical essays are published in the collections *Home and Exile* (1965), *The Transplanted Heart* (1975), and *Tasks and Masks* (1981). His essays on literature range from critiques of African and African American literature to clear-sighted commentaries on the work of Joseph Conrad and Daniel Defoe. His journalistic essays may be regarded as both autobiographical writing and cultural criticism and have focused on a wide range of subjects. Whether writing about the absurdities of apartheid, the cold glitter of New York, the despair of being an exile in Manhattan, or the pleasures of jazz, Nkosi has produced eloquent and often witty commentaries on society and his position in it. His focus on interracial relations and the unhealed schism between black and white is directed against apartheid ideology and more generally against racist prejudice wherever this may be found in the world.

Nkosi's novels have had complicated publishing histories. This is probably related to his movement across many national borders and his residence in many countries throughout his career. His novel *Underground People* was first published in Dutch in the 1990s and was later published in English by Kwela Books in South Africa (2002). The English version of the novel was revised from a post-apartheid perspective. *Mating Birds* was published in 1986 by St. Martin's Press, New York, and this is generally cited as the first edition. The novel was, however, first published by the East African Publishing House in Nairobi, Kenya, in 1983. Soon after its publication in 1986 it was hailed by critics in the United States, the United Kingdom, and Europe as one of the best works of literature to emerge at that time. Yet the novel had a more ambivalent reception in South Africa, where it was published by Ravan Press, Johannesburg, in 1987. Not only did South African critics appear to take a dim view of a black man writing about an interracial sexual encounter, but the novel's experimental strategies and modernist allusions seemed to be out of place in the territory to which black writing had been relegated in that country.

In apartheid South Africa, the genre of protest writing dominated black literature. Such writing was promoted by what Nkosi has called "solidarity criticism." In an interview with Janice Harris in the early 1990s Nkosi explained that solidarity criticism was based on "paraphrasing the plots of novels showing in what way they were against apartheid and how the heroes of those novels were either good guerrilla fighters or people engaged in resistance against the apartheid state." As Nkosi pointed out, the South African Communist Party, which was closely affiliated with the African National Congress (ANC), was "in favour of socialist-realist type fiction as against texts that were seen as bourgeois, experimentalist or elitist." Black writers who used experimental or playful narrative strategies, or glorified sensibilities that were seen as extraneous to the struggle, were denounced as irrelevant believers in art for art's sake. Nkosi, however, criticized black realist fiction as "journalistic fact parading outrageously as imaginative fiction" (*Home and Exile,* p. 126) and thus tried to open up the debate. He argued against prescriptive views of literature and claimed that it was not necessary for black writers to reflect the conditions in South Africa directly in order to be effective critics of apartheid.

Nkosi saw apartheid as an oppressive system that pervaded every aspect of black experience in South Africa, but he told Janice Harris that he felt that it was not always necessary "to attack it frontally." His novel *Mating Birds* does not articulate an explicit denunciation of apartheid and does not focus on the liberation struggle. Instead it deals with the impossibility of love between a black person and a white person within the language of apartheid. The apartheid state, Nkosi believes, interfered with language and speech. His focus on the concept of desire, and on analyzing the discourse of apartheid rather than its more direct manifestation, indicates his interest in aspects of postmodern and poststructuralist theory. In fact Nkosi has drawn attention to a glaring disparity in South African literature: between white writing, which has been markedly influenced by postmodernism and contemporary literary theory; and black writing, which has for the most part adhered to literary realism. According to Nkosi, this disjunction has not simply been a matter of black writers choosing the mode of realism out of a sense of duty. Nor is it something to be celebrated in the name of "difference." Rather, Nkosi has claimed, this avoidance of "theory" may be traced to the impoverished nature of black education in South Africa and the deprivation and isolation of the black writer under apartheid. Although the political activist Albie Sachs and the writer Njabulo Ndebele have more recently made cases for weaning South African literature away from politics, Nkosi was the first South African writer and critic to have "disputed the pre-eminence of the literature of protest as such" (quoted in Rosenthal, 2002).

Recently Nkosi's work has been given attention for its experimentalism and intertextual allusions and for the philosophical theory it engages with. Spurred on by Nkosi's comments regarding black writing and postmodernism, the South African critic David Attwell has pointed out that, contrary to popular belief, much black writing in South Africa is marked by experimentalism and inventiveness. Attwell (2003) describes *Mating Birds* as a work that "crafts a dispassionate, self-ironizing introspection on the causes and consequences of interracial sexual violence, in a voice that keeps company with Albert Camus's outsider and Richard Wright's Bigger Thomas." Though the plot of *Underground People* moves along quite smoothly in a realist fashion, the novel engages in a dialectical mode with theoretical issues that underpin questions related to freedom, revolution, and democracy. The first full-length—and long overdue—study of Nkosi's work, edited by Lindy Stiebel (University of Durban-Westville, South Africa) and Liz Gunner (University of Natal, South Africa) is scheduled for publication by Oxford University Press in 2004.

EARLY LIFE AND WRITING

Lewis Nkosi was born on 5 December 1936 in Durban, South Africa. He was educated at a missionary boarding school in Zululand. Schools of the type he attended were soon closed by the white Afrikaner Nationalist government which came to power in 1948 and introduced the policy of apartheid. The government's course of action included institutionalizing segregated schooling and the atrocity of "Bantu" education, which was intended to provide an inferior education system for black pupils. Until the collapse of apartheid in the 1990s, Nkosi's was, therefore, the last generation of black pupils to be well educated in South Africa. After completing his

schooling, he became a journalist for *Ilanga lase Natal* (the Natal Sun), *Drum* magazine, and the *Golden City Post*. A letter written to *Drum* in which he emphasized the importance of writing the truth convinced the editors that he had literary talent, and they offered him a job. He was then working for the English-Zulu newspaper *Ilanga lase Natal*, but he accepted the offer of the job at *Drum* when the white proprietor of *Ilanga lase Natal* criticized his lack of deference. When he joined *Drum* in Johannesburg in 1956, Nkosi was twenty years old, and thus early in his writing career he became associated with established *Drum* writers such as Can Themba, Henry Nxumalo, Ezekiel Mphahlele, William "Bloke" Modisane, and Todd Matshikiza. During what was, in Nkosi's words, "the fabulous decade" of the 1950s, *Drum* became the forum for this generation of black writers who had begun to articulate critiques, in reportage and fiction, of the apartheid government.

Embracing a distinctive syncopated and racy style, *Drum* depicted aspects of black urban experience. At that time South Africa was becoming a deeply segregated society. In urban areas black people were forced to live in separate "townships" that were often located on the outskirts of white cities. Notwithstanding the impoverished conditions in the townships, such areas often became active social hubs and developed vibrant underground cultures. The *Drum* writers lived in segregated areas in and around Johannesburg such as Sophiatown—a black enclave in a white area whose destruction was the subject of much campaigning journalism by *Drum* writers—as well as Orlando, Alexandria, and Dube. (Can Themba wrote a famous short story for *Drum* called "The Dube Train.") According to Nkosi, being a *Drum* writer connoted a certain lifestyle: "even in one's personal life one was supposed to exhibit a unique intellectual style; usually urbane, ironic, morally tough and detached" (*Home and Exile*, p. 12). Defying the ban on alcohol, the *Drum* writers frequented *shebeens* (illicit alehouses in the townships), and fraternized with *tsotsis* (criminals), Americanized gangsters, jazz players, and beauty queens. Nkosi claims that the *Drum* writers "brought to South African journalism a new vitality" (p. 10). Although often arrested, once back at work "they wrote up these grim stories of farm labour brutalities, police torture and township riots in a cool sober prose in which they permitted themselves the luxury of a laugh" (pp. 10–11).

Among the *Drum* group was Nat Nakasa, a young journalist from Durban, who became one of Nkosi's friends. It was with Nakasa that Nkosi witnessed the Sharpeville Massacre in 1960. On 21 March a large crowd of black South Africans marched to the Sharpeville police station to protest against the apartheid pass laws, which required black men and women to carry identification with them at all times. This peaceful protest had been organized by the Pan-Africanist Congress (PAC), under the leadership of Robert Sobukwe. The police at Sharpeville fired upon the crowd, many of whom were women and children and were shot in the back. Sixty-nine protesters were killed and 180 wounded. The Sharpeville Massacre was followed by demonstrations, strikes, and riots, and the South African government announced a state of emergency. For Nkosi, Sharpeville marked the end of an era in South Africa. He notes that apartheid became more vicious after 1960: "Sharpeville and the brutal massacre of unarmed Africans marching to a local police station brought us bang into 1960 and a different era altogether. Henceforth the times would be troubled indeed!" (*Home and Exile*, p. 8).

In 1961 Nkosi accepted a Nieman scholarship from Harvard University. The South African government refused to give him a passport, but Nkosi's lawyer, Harold Wolpe, advised him to exploit a legal loophole in the Departure from South Africa Act. Wolpe wrote to the Afrikaner bureaucrats in Pretoria, and Nkosi was eventually issued with a one-way exit permit, which in effect condemned him to a state of exile after leaving South Africa. Nat Nakasa followed him to the United States a few years later. Nakasa,

who was also given one-way exit authorization, was twenty-eight years old when he died tragically on 14 July 1965 after a fall from the seventh story of a New York City skyscraper. Nkosi may have suffered the alienation that characterizes the experience of exile, but his wit and keen sense of irony seem to have been more than a match for the biting cold of the Northern hemisphere. From a condition of banishment he forged a cosmopolitan identity and soon established himself as an acclaimed writer and critic.

During his year at Harvard, Nkosi began writing a three-act play titled *The Rhythm of Violence*, which was published in 1964. Set in Johannesburg in the early 1960s, the play stages the relations between revolutionaries and exponents of the apartheid state. The action centers on a group of black and white students who plan to blow up a gathering of white town officials who are meeting to discuss further apartheid legislation. Nkosi and the other members of *Drum* had developed a penchant for jazz, and the play features discordant jazz music, but Nkosi's eclectic interest in the avant-garde extends to literary form as well. This may be seen in the self-reflexive role-playing within *The Rhythm of Violence*, as two white policemen stage a scenario where one of them "plays" at being a black resistance leader. Much to his own surprise, the policeman finds that he has adopted a position he can identify with. *The Rhythm of Violence* was banned in South Africa, where it was regarded as an incitement to violence.

In an essay on Ezekiel Mphahlele, Nkosi says that toward the end of the 1960s it was revealed that the various foundations that paid for Mphlahlele's studies and for Nkosi's own fees at Harvard were using laundered funds from the Central Intelligence Agency (CIA) with which they supported journals, as well as writers' and artists' clubs, through a "Congress for Cultural Freedom." Nkosi acknowledges that there were no overt attempts to change the collective ideology of African leaders, philosophers, and writers who were provided for by such funds, but he thinks that the CIA wanted to deter African intellectuals and future leaders from turning to the Soviet Union or China for support during the Cold War.

After his year at Harvard, Nkosi left for London. He was able to enter the United Kingdom freely since South Africa was at that time still part of the Commonwealth, though about to withdraw from it. He studied at the University of London and at Sussex University, worked in a multitude of jobs, and became increasingly known as a journalist, literary critic, and radio and television interviewer. His knowledge of African literature enabled him to contribute to publications such as the *Times Literary Supplement, Présence Africaine,* and *New York Review of Books.* His essay on "Farm Jails" was included, with pieces by Nelson Mandela, Albert Luthuli, and Nadine Gordimer, in a series of reports from South Africa titled *I Will Still Be Moved* (1963), which set out to detail "the human consequences" of apartheid. In this essay Nkosi draws attention to the brutality inflicted on African prisoners who were forced into farm labor during the 1950s and 1960s. Chillingly, the beatings, murders, and secret burials on South African farms as documented by Nkosi foreshadowed later violence inflicted by agents of the apartheid state. On farms such as Vlakplaas, suspected black "terrorists" were tortured, murdered, and secretly buried or burned to ashes on open fires. South Africa's Truth and Reconciliation Commission (1996–1998) played a major role in exposing the atrocities that took place on Vlakplaas.

By the time he wrote the essay on "Farm Jails," Nkosi had lived on three continents, and he claims to have had firsthand experience of racism in Johannesburg, London, and New York. Indeed Nkosi's encounters with prejudice and racial discrimination in various parts of the world confirmed W. E. B. Du Bois's prophetic claim, made in *The Souls of Black Folk* (1903), that "the problem of the twentieth century is the problem of the color line." Never losing his wry sense of irony, Nkosi concludes "Farm Jails"

with the following comment regarding Dr. Hendrik Verwoerd, architect of apartheid: "Dr. Verwoerd claims to represent Western civilisation; and I certainly find little ground on which to disagree with him in the present circumstances. Therefore the Western nations had better do something about him soon" (p. 71).

HOME AND EXILE AND *THE TRANSPLANTED HEART*

Home and Exile (1965) is a collection of essays that detail Nkosi's experiences in South Africa, the United States, and Britain from the 1950s up until the early 1960s. The first two sections of the collection are autobiographical, and the third section comprises literary criticism. In the first chapter, "The Fabulous Decade: The Fifties," Nkosi reflects on the time he spent working for *Drum* in Johannesburg and remembers exploits with other *Drum* writers such as Ezekiel ("Zeke") Mphahlele and Can Themba. The essay ends with a discussion of the hypocritical nature of apartheid and the ways in which it has perverted relations between people in South Africa. Nkosi undermines myths of black barbarism and white "restraint" with stories of white men appointed to uphold Christianity or the law who nonetheless sexually exploited black women. This theme was later to be echoed at the end of Nkosi's one-act play "The Black Psychiatrist" (1994), where a white woman is shocked to learn that the black psychiatrist she is trying to threaten and intimidate is her half-brother, born as the result of her father's violation of his black domestic worker.

The Kafkaesque absurdities of the apartheid system are further exposed in the second essay, which criticizes the lack of logic at the heart of apartheid. It includes an anecdote of an African who took a photo of his two black friends only to find himself prosecuted by a white woman who was accidentally snapped while walking past, as well as Nkosi's own account of being arrested by a burly policeman who asks, "What can I charge them with?" To some extent, the essay presages the farcical courtroom scene in Nkosi's novel *Mating Birds,* where the cards are stacked against Ndi Sibiya from the beginning of his trial.

In "A Question of Identity," Nkosi traces the impact of colonialism on African culture and emphasizes the value of an African worldview. He points out that African perspectives may rely on different assumptions than those which give rise to European cultural trends. Whereas European modernism has been fretfully preoccupied with the death of God, for instance, Nkosi points out that in traditional Zulu belief God merely created humans and left them to themselves, an arrangement that was agreeable for both sides. "It is for this reason," Nkosi concludes, "that European anxiety in the Waste Land strikes us as a little self-indulgent, if not an improbable joke" (p. 51).

In two essays on exile, Nkosi relates his experiences in New York. Detailing his arrival, Nkosi describes the city as "an awful kind of grabbing, gold-digging bitch, yet capable of extravagant passions" (p. 59) and Harlem as a segregated, poverty-stricken limbo suffused with the music and culture of jazz. The first essay ends with a memory of the jazz singer Sheila Jordan, whose singing, he claims in the next piece, rescued him from the cold, loneliness, and despair he felt in the wintry city: "She sings ultimately for the disinherited, the outsiders" ("Portrait of Sheila Jordan," p. 76). He records his surprised recognition that a white American woman could convey something to him, a black African.

The essays on literature published in *Home and Exile* range from an analysis of Africa in Negro American poetry to discussions of negritude, African theater, South African censorship, and fiction by black South Africans. There is also a report on a 1962 conference of African writers in Kampala, Uganda, as well as a review (originally published the *Observer* in 1962) of Ezekiel Mphahlele's *The African Image* (1962).

Nkosi's essay against South African censorship titled "Gagged" is an appeal to the British government to rebuke South Africa for its policy of censorship and its gagging of 102 politicians and writers whose words could not be published, distributed, or read publicly in South Africa under apartheid. In an essay on fiction by black South Africans, Nkosi criticizes black realist fiction and states that the strength of African writing in South Africa may instead lie in nonfiction essays. This critique is taken up in his later essays on African literature, particularly in *Tasks and Masks.*

The Transplanted Heart (1975) is a collection of Nkosi's essays written from the late 1960s until 1975. The essays, he claims, were the result of "a watching brief on daily events in South Africa" (p. vii). Although Nkosi was not in South Africa at this time, he continued to follow news stories related to the country and to provide commentaries on the situation there. Most of the essays in *The Transplanted Heart* were written for a news digest bulletin founded by Ezekiel Mphahlele, who was working at that time in Paris as director of the African Section of the Congress for Cultural Freedom.

The Transplanted Heart is divided into three sections. In the first, "Politics," Nkosi responds to current events in South Africa. In the essay from which the collection takes its title, Nkosi focuses on the first heart transplants in South Africa, which were famously conducted by Dr. Christian Barnard. Nkosi takes the concept of a heart transplant both literally and metaphorically. He first makes an analogy between a surgical transplant and white South Africa, which he claims is itself "a 'transplanted heart' beating in an African continent; and here it is the heart and not the body which is rejecting the black tissues around it" (p. 31). He then points to the awful irony that although white South Africans insist on keeping white blood separate from black blood in blood banks, they are happy to accept that a heart, still beating, may be taken for a white man from a "coloured" donor whose wife had not even given permission for her husband's organs to be removed. Nkosi warns that, in a country where black lives are cheap, "doctors in a hurry to possess usable hearts may not do enough to revive black South Africans" (p. 33).

Nkosi also discusses events such as the induction of the new South African prime minister, Balthazar Johannes Vorster, and Vorster's attempts to create a "black ring" of friendly African states around South Africa. Nkosi points out that the South African government saw these potentially friendly states as protection against the more militant African freedom fighters in the north. He predicts, however, that this "ring" will break because the black leaders in these countries have little to gain from alliance with South Africa. Speaking out strongly against South Africa's racist legislation and foreign policy, he claims that although the United Nations Security Council told South Africa to remove its troops from Southwest Africa, the Western powers did not enforce this UN resolution. Commenting on apartheid legislation, Nkosi writes: "As far as the non-white people are concerned the spirit and practice of apartheid, by itself, makes effective rule of law an absurdity" (p. 15). He also criticizes the disastrous "Bantustan" philosophy that forced black people to live in small, segregated "homelands."

Two pieces of travel writing by Nkosi are published in the second section of *The Transplanted Heart*. Here he recounts a trip to Paris, where he spent time with the Afrikaans anti-apartheid writer Breyten Breytenbach, and also writes of the three months he spent at the University of California, Irvine, shortly after the assassination of President Kennedy. In the final section of *The Transplanted Heart*, which focuses on "Music, Writers and Books," Nkosi provides a lively counterpoint to European critics of jazz as he discusses "Jazz in Exile." He praises South African jazz for "carrying the very stench of the bawdy life of the African townships" to Europe: "Even the most obtuse of the

European jazz critics has sensed a quality in SA jazz which is rare outside Negro circles in the US: passion swing, robustness, and an earthiness in the category of Horace Silver's aggressively racial music described sometime ago as 'funk' (p. 98).

In addition to the celebration of African jazz, this section of *The Transplanted Heart* contains tributes to and commentaries on South African writers such as Can Themba, Alex La Guma, Athol Fugard, and Herman Charles Bosman. An essay titled "Robinson Crusoe: Call Me Master" examines the Crusoe story as a colonial myth.

AFRICAN LITERARY CRITICISM

In 1971 Nkosi was appointed visiting regents professor for African literature at the University of California at Irvine, where he spent a year reading African texts and contemplating questions posed by the study of African literature. During the years that followed he began working on an introductory textbook, which was published in 1981 as *Tasks and Masks: Themes and Styles of African Literature.* In this study, which focuses on novels, poetry, and drama produced in sub-Saharan Africa, Nkosi isolates two trends: first, the impulse to express aspects of an essential African culture, and second, a commitment to the task of political and social transformation in Africa. As Nkosi himself acknowledges in the preface to the book, such a dichotomy is mainly useful in broad classificatory terms and should not be applied too uniformly to all African writers.

Nkosi begins his analysis of African literature in *Tasks and Masks* by emphasizing that modern African literature has come into being alongside the struggle for political independence and the establishment of the nation-state in Africa. He also draws attention to a certain anxiety at the heart of African writing, highlighting an "uncomfortable feeling" that, however socially committed a literary text may be, it may be completely irrelevant to the majority of African people, who do not have the benefit of literacy. Like other African literary critics before him, Nkosi asserts that literature in Africa is often accessible only to an educated elite. He also points out that even the best African writers reflect a dependency on colonial language and literary forms.

In *Tasks and Masks,* Nkosi discusses the importance of negritude in shaping and assessing black identity and literature. Whereas colonialism and racism have relied on the denigration of black or African ways of life, negritude seeks to assert the value of black or African tradition and culture. Nkosi quotes M. Leopold Senghor of Senegal, who wrote: "Africa's misfortune has been that our secret enemies, in defending their values, have made us despise ours." Pointing to its roots in European ideologies such as Freudianism, Marxism, surrealism, and romanticism, Nkosi draws attention to an ironic hybridity that characterizes the idea of negritude. He argues nevertheless for the positive role that negritude has played in forming black identity and acknowledges that it is an important area of interest for students of African literature.

In a wide-ranging analysis of writings by Chinua Achebe, Ngũgĩ wa Thiong'o, Ayi Kwei Armah, Ezekiel Mphahlele, Bessie Head, Alex La Guma, Sembène Ousmane, Amos Tutuola, Gabriel Okara, and Wole Soyinka, he then traces the themes and styles of African literature. He commends Achebe's rendering of African society and of the damage done by colonialism, and he pays tribute to the politically transforming visions of Sembène and Ngũgĩ. He examines the engagement between African writing and modernism and critiques black protest writing in South Africa. By tracing themes such as culture conflict in African poetry, he debates the extent to which African poetry can both benefit from tradition and confront the brutalities that have taken root in the wake of colonialism. In a

chapter on African drama, Nkosi challenges the presiding view of traditional African drama as "functional" rather than as "art for art's sake" and asks "for whom" such theater functions. As he points out, even the most traditional drama is often governed by economic and ideological compulsions which have little to do with tradition.

"Constructing the 'Cross-Border' Reader," which was written while Nkosi was a visiting professor at the University of Wyoming, was published in *Altered State? Writing and South Africa* (1994). In this essay he remarks that the term "South African literature" is usually taken to refer to works in English by white writers. Pointing out that a long history of racial segregation has shaped the literature of South Africa, he argues that borders and boundaries between black and white writing must be recognized before they can be overcome. He claims that the detailed descriptions of South Africa in protest writing indicate that such texts aim to inform, and take as their target readership, an international audience. Censorship in South Africa, under which dissent was silenced, produced protest literature that sought readers overseas. He argues that Njabulo Ndebele is one of the few writers to create work that seems to be "almost entirely sealed off or indifferent to the concerns of the white master" (p. 45).

Nkosi pursues his ideas on the engagement between black writing and avant-garde literature in "Postmodernism and Black Writing in South Africa," which was published in *Writing South Africa: Literature, Apartheid, and Democracy, 1970–1995* (1998). In this essay he draws attention to an "unhealed" split between black writing, which has for the most part not incorporated contemporary theory, and white writing, which has been influenced by postmodernist thought. He points out that while many critics cite this disparity as a phenomenon to be celebrated in the name of heterogeneity, it may reveal the damage done to black writers by segregation and "Bantu education." Poststructuralist and feminist criticism, he claims, may have much to contribute to studies of African culture and literature.

MATING BIRDS

Nkosi returned to Africa in 1979 after accepting a senior lectureship at the University of Zambia, where he was appointed professor of literature in 1985. On its first publication by the East African Publishing House in Nairobi, *Mating Birds* created scarcely a ripple in critical circles of the world. This had little to do with the quality of the novel in question, but at the time East African Publishing House was in financial difficulties, had extremely limited distributive power, and was unable to market the book internationally. In 1986 *Mating Birds* was published, with minor changes, by St. Martin's Press in New York to great critical acclaim. Although the novel was sent to the South African censors, the book was found to be "not undesirable" and was released for circulation in the Republic. At that time, the power of censorship in South Africa was declining.

Mating Birds is dedicated to Nkosi's grandmother, Esther Makatini—according to Nkosi, she "washed white people's clothes so that [he] could learn to write." The novel takes the form of a prison memoir, narrated by a black man, Ndi Sibiya, who is on death row in Durban after being accused of raping a white woman, Veronica Slater. Sibiya tells his story in part to the Swiss psychoanalyst Dr. Emile Dufré, whom he describes as "the man from Zurich, my constant visitor, my interrogator, my confessor" (1983, p. 14). Yet Sibiya does not tell Dufré as much as he reveals in his writing. The novel centers on uncertainty, and on close examination it becomes difficult, if not impossible, to be entirely convinced that Sibiya has violated Veronica. In his first-person narration Sibiya admits that his obsession, evoking the intensity of Aschenbach's fixation with a young boy in Thomas Mann's *A Death in Venice*, may

distort his memory of events. Sibiya claims that Veronica was a willing sexual partner. At the same time, he seems unsure whether he raped her or not. He confesses that only she can fill in the gaps in his memory and corroborate his story, but he has hardly spoken to her, and, he asserts, she is lying. Emphasizing his obsessive thought patterns, Sibiya's story circles back to the encounter with Veronica in her seaside bungalow, but he repeatedly breaks off before eventually telling what happened. Allusions to Camus's *L'Étranger* are evident in the beach setting of this incident and in the sunstruck actions of the narrator. Yet when Sibiya's final account of the encounter in the bungalow reaches its conclusion, the reader is confronted with the possibility that Sibiya is innocent and that the bogeyman of racist thinking, the figure of the black rapist, is absent.

In *Mating Birds,* Nkosi clearly plays on, and undermines, a "black peril" theme. In South Africa, "black peril" refers to white fears of black men raping white women. As historians and cultural critics have pointed out, in intercultural contexts such fears are often not related to actual rape statistics but can generally be traced to white sexual jealousy and socioeconomic instability in intercultural contexts. Fear of black male sexuality is also based on racist assumptions and a desire to protect the perceived "purity" of white women. The myth of the black rapist is by no means a uniquely South African phenomenon. It also prevailed in the American South, for instance, where it was used to justify oppressive and racist measures including the lynching of black men. In South Africa fears of "black peril" were used to justify segregation laws, such as the Native Land Act of 1913. Through Sibiya's story in *Mating Birds,* Nkosi seems to circle back on "black peril" narratives in order to subvert them. A black author writing about a sexual encounter with a white woman did not, however, sit easily with many South African critics.

Internationally *Mating Birds* was highly acclaimed. It was chosen as "best of new fiction" by the *New York Times* critic Michiko Kakutani on 22 March 1986 and was in the same year selected as one of that paper's best 100 books. Henry Louis Gates Jr. gave *Mating Birds* a lead review in the *New York Times Book Review* (18 May 1986), where he praised the "lyrical intensity" and "compelling narrative power" of the book. In an article for the London *Guardian* (1 August 1986), Norman Shrapnel summarized the novel and reported: "So stark an outline can give no account of the subtlety and skill that have gone into the structure of this searching—and remarkably, given its dire theme, undepressing—first novel." Paul Pickering, writing for *New Society* (8 August 1986) claimed that "the moral implications of *Mating Birds* are as disturbing as the writing is brilliant." In 1987 *Mating Birds* was awarded a prestigious International Macmillan Silver Pen Prize.

Yet while *Mating Birds* was perceived in the United States and Europe as one of the best pieces of literature to emerge from South Africa, the novel had a more ambivalent reception there. Almost without exception, white literary critics seemed determined to find fault with the novel. Andre Brink (1992) objected to what he referred to as the novel's "predilection for purple prose," its "clichés of soft porn magazines," and "crude erotic fantasies," while Johan Jacobs (1990) abhorred its "sexist drivel" and likened the entire novel to "nothing so much as the elaborate striptease with which the girl seduced the narrator." Although an anonymous reviewer for the *African Communist* in 1987 had lauded "the acuity of [Nkosi's] perceptions of the South African scene," (p. 90), Brink condemned Nkosi for "exaggerating the horrors of the South African situation" (p. 17). Brink insisted:

> There has never been a death-row in Durban; South African court procedure is rather different from the account of it given in the novel; there have never been segregated lectures at any university; quite simply, a trial of this nature could

not have attracted the kind of attention Nkosi claims for his protagonist, whose exploits are alleged to have captured the attention of the entire "civilised world."

(p. 16)

Similarly, Jacobs claimed that "the first fictional veil to go is that of topicality." Evidently South African commentators such as Brink and Jacobs judged *Mating Birds* by the rigid standards of literary realism. In South Africa, black writers were expected to reflect social reality rather than indulge in literary experimentalism. This realist trend, however, had been criticized by Nkosi in *Tasks and Masks,* where he disparagingly referred to the "breadline asceticism," "prim disapproval of irony," and "petty realism" that gave much black writing a "colonial status" (pp. 77–80).

Certain critics also objected to Nkosi's representation of Veronica and to Sibiya's insistence that Veronica "lured" him to her. Sara Maitland, reviewing the novel for the *New Statesman* (29 August 1986), praised Nkosi's "commitment, passion and beautiful writing" but complained that Sibiya's account of Veronica's complicity sounded like "one of the classic defences of all rapists of all races under all regimes" and that Nkosi should have found a better way of exposing injustice than reverting to the "stock image of the pale temptress." In a polemical 1990 critique of J. M. Coetzee's *Foe* and *Mating Birds,* Josephine Dodd protested against the role of Nkosi and Coetzee in introducing South African writing to the rest of the world, claiming that these writers pandered "to the prurient expectations of a First-world audience, supplying details of terrorist rape and interracial sexual excitement" (p. 118). Since it is never proved to the reader that Sibiya has committed a rape, however, such critiques may have been based on shaky assumptions.

As she first presents herself to Sibiya, Veronica is lying on the beach, "heavy, slack and motionless, roasting in the sun and the damp hair clinging to the nape of her neck" (p. 4).

Above her is the sign "Bathing Area—For Whites Only." This "legendary warning" epitomizes apartheid ideology. Public areas such as swimming pools and beaches were segregated in South Africa from the 1940s until the demise of apartheid (p. 4). Sibiya claims that he has not only been accused of raping a woman but that he has also been prosecuted for daring to have sexual relations with a white woman. The Mixed Marriages Act (1949), which prohibited inter-racial marriage, was one of the first laws passed by the white Afrikaner National Party after it came to power; it was followed by the Immorality Act (1950), which made it illegal to have sexual relations "across the colour line." Jacqueline Rose (1995), who has taught Nkosi's novel in a number of seminars, asserts that *Mating Birds* shows the ways in which apartheid is "sexual apartheid as much as, if not before, anything else" (p. 107).

If prohibition is the ultimate law of the apartheid state, then its antithesis, *Mating Birds* suggests, is freedom—the possibility for fulfill-ment, for expression, for liberation from tyranny. Themes of freedom and entrapment are woven together. Though set in prison, Nkosi's novel ends with the "lusty" liberation songs of the political prisoners and with an image of the birds in the air, joyous in their freedom. At the same time as it bonds itself to obsession, sexual desire in Nkosi's novel is also linked to the desire for liberation, to a yearning for a more just time and place where human relationships are not regulated by the discourse of racism. The irony of the relationship between sexual desire and political liberation is most aptly described in a scene where, awaiting death in his prison cell, Sibiya remembers a view from a beach in Dur-ban. Under the blazing sun, he had stared out over the sea, watching the ships on their way to foreign shores:

> I had taken to loitering on this beach, watching the big liners steaming out of the bay for distant shores of Europe, America, and the Far East. In my mood of profound despondency I was thinking, plan-ning, and dreaming of escape from South Africa,

from the life of oppression and wretched exploita-tion. The girl, too, who appeared so unexpectedly on this strand of beach was perhaps part of this dream to escape. Life plays us so many jokes.

(p. 24)

END OF EXILE

In "Constructing the 'Cross-Border' Reader," Nkosi had prophesied the end of apartheid: "For the past decade and a half it has become only too obvious that under the pressure of massive resistance from the oppressed people of South Africa, the apartheid state is at last showing signs of cracking up under the strain" (p. 37). His exile from South Africa ended when he flew back to Johannesburg in December 1991 to at-tend the New Nation Writers Conference. The conference took place after the unbanning of the African National Congress and the release of Nelson Mandela in 1990. From 1989 until 1994, Nkosi contributed a number of essays and reviews to the *Southern African Review of Books,* a literary magazine based there. In 1989 he reported on the "Culture in Another South Africa" conference in Amsterdam, which had been held in 1987. He also reviewed the com-memorative book of keynote addresses, speeches, and analytical papers from the confer-ence, which was published in June 1989. During the symposium more than 300 South African artists "from inside and outside South Africa" met in the Bellevue Theatre in Amsterdam to exchange views. According to Nkosi, the anti-apartheid movement in the Netherlands had become one of the strongest in Europe. For the ten days of the conference Amsterdam was all but taken over by roaming groups of South Africans: "As one wag later put it: 'Amsterdam feels more and more like the alternative capital of another South Africa'" (p. 3). Although the book of the conference, which was filled with glossy photographs and reproductions of artwork, resembled a coffee-table book, Nkosi argued that it had valuable written contributions on art and literature from "the prisonhouse of apartheid" (p. 4).

Nkosi's reflections on the career of his fellow South African writer Ezekiel Mphahlele were published in the *Southern African Review of Books* in 1990. Mphahlele had worked with Nkosi at *Drum* in the 1950s, and in 1990 he had just turned seventy. Like Nkosi, Mphahlele had virtually been forced into exile. As a teacher he had tried to mobilize other educators against "Bantu" education. His attempt to obstruct the system, however, ended when he was banned from teaching in South Africa and left in 1957 to teach at a grammar school in Nigeria. From there he and his family moved to Paris in 1961, where he was offered a post as director of the African Congress for Cultural Freedom. Nkosi notes that "Zeke" was a "literary" writer, but was not cut out, by his own admission, to be a journalist: "It was not only that *Drum*'s diet of 'sex, crime and love stories' alienated him; Mphahlele's temperament was far removed from the outlaw atmosphere which reigned in *Drum*.... Mphahlele resembled a professor in exile" ("Es'kia Mphahlele at 70").

Nkosi praises Mphahlele's autobiography *Down Second Avenue* (1959) as an "enthralling" bildungsroman and lauds his attempts to subvert "the nefarious workings of the South African educational system." However, he claims that Mphahlele's later work, such as *Afrika My Music* (1984), gives intimations of someone who was "probably exhausted by a lifetime of struggle" (p. 34).

In his review of *The Gunny Sack* (1989) by M. G. Vassanji and *Harvest of Thorns* (1989) by the Zimbabwean writer Shimmer Chinodya, Nkosi discusses the role of writers who are from "what is called, hilariously, the 'developing world.'" The case of Salman Rushdie indicates that such writers "are severely punished" for being storytellers, "for the 'crime' of spreading rumours" ("'Commonwealth Literature' Prize Winners," p. 12). At that time Rushdie had been advised not to come to a literary symposium in South Africa—the Ayatolla Khomeini and his followers were baying for Rushdie's blood.

The review was published in 1991, when Nkosi had just taken up a lectureship at the University of Wyoming. He arrived in Wyoming after spending time in Poland, the home of his second wife, whom he met in Zambia. (His first wife, whom he married in the 1960s and with whom he had two daughters, was British.) At Wyoming, Nkosi taught African, South African, and African American literature. According to one of his colleagues, Janice Harris, he brought daily surprises to his hall-mates at the English Department's Hoyt Hall: ". . . the wit and wisdom of the ever-changing collage of international clippings on his office door, the excitement of hearing a cry down the corridor, 'Quick, get Lewis, it's Nadine Gordimer on the phone.' How often does a Nobel Prize winner call a member of the UW English Department?!" Indeed Nkosi and fellow South African writer Nadine Gordimer had been friends since the 1950s. Along with *Drum* friends such as Nat Nakasa, he would visit her home in Johannesburg.

During his time at Wyoming in the early 1990s Nkosi was given a column called "US Diary" in the *Southern African Review of Books*. Here he examined the concept of multiculturalism (July–August 1993) and traced intercontinental networks of acquaintance and influence between African American and South African writers (November–December 1993). He returned to South Africa in time to participate in the country's first democratic election in April 1994. He had been offered a visiting post for a semester at the University of Cape Town (UCT). In one of the "Diaries" (May–June 1994), Nkosi recounts a "post-liberation" celebratory dinner with a group of his peers, including the postcolonial critic Elleke Boehmer, the acclaimed novelist John Coetzee (otherwise known as J. M. Coetzee), Coetzee's Marxist brother, David, and Dorothy Driver, who was at that time an academic in the English department at UCT. Nkosi, who taught many of J. M. Coetzee's novels to American students, describes the man himself as "a mystery, with an interior life which is difficult to fathom." However, Nkosi seemed to get on famously well with Coetzee's brother, who ended the evening by virtually drinking Nkosi under the table.

The year 1994 saw the publication of Nkosi's play "The Black Psychiatrist," which had been written in the 1980s. Janice Harris has described it as "provocative," and the drama certainly ends on an unexpected and powerful note. A black psychiatrist is accosted one morning in his office by a "dazzlingly" attractive white woman who seems to want to charm and intimidate him. She starts narrating to him about her previous acquaintance with the black psychiatrist—she claims to know him from South Africa—but he can't remember anything about her. As Nkosi has pointed out in an interview with Janice Harris: "The question which is always in the mind of the audience is, Who is telling the truth?" The shocking revelation at the end of the play tells as much about their different positions as it does about the hypocrisy of sexual mores under apartheid.

UNDERGROUND PEOPLE

Although *Underground People* was published in 2002, Nkosi began writing the novel in 1978, when he was still a graduate student at Sussex. When he arrived at the University of Zambia in 1979 his work on the novel was already under way, but he decided to put it aside and focus on a short story instead. This short story grew until it became the novel *Mating Birds*. After the publication of *Mating Birds* he returned to work on *Underground People*. Whereas *Mating Birds* focuses on the experience of its narrator, Ndi Sibiya, *Underground People* uses a third-person narrative to incorporate many characters and give a wide-ranging perspective of South African society and of the liberation struggle in the country. The narrative moves from characters and situations to theoretical discussions. Thus far the novel has been well received in South Africa. Jane Rosenthal, who reviewed it for

South Africa's *Mail & Guardian* (1 November 2002), claimed that the novel is "written in a swift and engaging style," and the literary critic Andries Oliphant, writing for South Africa's *Sunday Times* (24 November 2002), concurred: "Lewis Nkosi is in fine satirical form in his new novel."

Underground People was originally intended to be two novels in one, and the early versions of the book bear the traces of William Faulkner's *Wild Palms* (1939). But Nkosi revised the novel many times. The events unfolding in South Africa, particularly the movement toward the end of apartheid in the early 1990s, changed the progression of the plot and required rewriting. The original ending, for instance, depended on the fact that Nelson Mandela was still in jail when the book was published. In the final stages of the original plot, two white lovers, who accidentally stray into the hideout of revolutionary guerrillas, are captured by the guerrillas and used as hostages in exchange for the release of a famous African leader. After Mandela's release in 1990, Nkosi was forced to write a new ending.

The story focuses on Cornelius Molapo, a poet and teacher who lives in one of Johannesburg's segregated black townships. Although set in the late 1980s and early 1990s, the novel seems to weave in cultural attitudes and experiences of the 1950s and 1960s. Indeed, Nkosi has even acknowledged that the character of Molapo is based on the articulate and gutsy Can Themba, Nkosi's colleague at *Drum* magazine during the 1950s. Like Themba, Molapo is an urban dandy, very much the figure of the *Drum* generation. He is a noted jitterbug dancer as well as an eloquent speaker at political rallies, despite being rather cynical about the ability of the National Liberation Movement, of which he is a member, to effect any real changes in South Africa. Molapo's story intersects with that of Anthony Ferguson, the white liberal who works for a London-based human rights organization. Molapo disappears from Johannesburg, and Ferguson is sent to South Africa to find out what happened to him, as it is suspected that Molapo has fallen into the hands of the state security police.

It turns out, however, that Molapo has gone underground and relocated to the rural area of Tambanyane, where he has become involved in a peasant revolution to oust the "Chief" appointed by the apartheid government. Under apartheid, the leaders of black "homelands" were generally puppets of the state. Thus the events described in Nkosi's book are not far removed from actual circumstances in apartheid South Africa. By the end of the novel Molapo has committed his life to the armed struggle of the local Tambanyane people for their land. Although Molapo's whereabouts are being kept secret by the National Liberation Movement, Ferguson tracks Molapo to Tambanyane. The novel ends with a major shootout between the forces of the security police and the National Liberation Movement in the forests of Tambanyane.

In a review of a 1998 biography of Chinua Achebe, Nkosi comments that Achebe considers it his role to "defend African culture" against Western cultural imperialism. Jane Rosenthal claims that this particular authorial mission appears to be quite unlike Nkosi's in *Underground People.* In the novel, Nkosi writes about many aspects of South African culture. His cool irony is balanced by his sympathetic treatment of characters, which even extends to the white Afrikaner policeman Adam de Kock, who is browbeaten by his English bank manager. The most unappealing character, an obdurate and racist white farmer, apparently amused Nkosi so much that he has admitted to becoming quite fond of him.

The novel interrogates dialectical positions through possible points of contact between apparent opposites—in the early pages of the book Molapo mentions "those nodal points where love and revolution intersect." Molapo's life is definitively marked by his love for his beautiful ex-wife, Maureen. Oppositions between the poet and the revolutionary man of action, as well as between the guerrilla fighter and the bureaucratic organizer, are played out, for instance, in the relationship between Molapo and Bulane, a commander in the National Liberation Movement. When Bulane tries to manipulate Molapo into undertaking a dangerous and potentially destructive mission, the latter asks: "How can we be free without love?" Bulane answers: "How can we love without freedom?" Nkosi has claimed that he, as the author, can see the validity of both positions.

Selected Bibliography

WORKS OF LEWIS NKOSI

NOVELS

Mating Birds. Nairobi, Kenya: East African Publishing House, 1983; New York, St. Martin's Press, 1986; Johannesburg, Ravan Press, 1987.
Underground People. Cape Town, South Africa: Kwela, 2002.

PLAYS

The Rhythm of Violence. London: Oxford University Press, 1964.
The Black Psychiatrist: A Play. Weber Studies 11.2 (spring–summer 1994).

NONFICTION

"Farm Jails." In *I Will Still Be Moved: Reports from South Africa.* Edited by Marion Friedmann. London: A. Baker, 1963; Chicago: Quadrangle, 1963.

Home and Exile. London, 1965. Revised and expanded edition, London and New York: Longman, 1983. Pp. 61–71.

The Transplanted Heart. Benin City, Nigeria: Ethiope, 1975.

Tasks and Masks: Themes and Styles of African Literature. Harlow, U.K.: Longman, 1981.

"Constructing the 'Cross-Border' Reader." In *Altered State? Writing and South Africa.* Edited by Elleke Boehmer, Laura Chrisman, and Kenneth Parker. Sydney: Dangaroo, 1994. Pp. 37–50.

"Culture in Another South Africa." *Southern African Review of Books,* August–September 1989.

"Es'kia Mphahlele at 70." *Southern African Review of Books.* February–May 1990. Pp. 12–13.

"'Commonwealth Literature' Prize Winners." *Southern African Review of Books,* March–April 1991.

"US Diary." *Southern African Review of Books,* July–August 1993. P. 24; November–December 1993; May–June 1994. P. 21.

"At the Crossroads Hour." *London Review of Books,* 12 November 1998. P. 24 (Review of *Chinua Achebe: A Biography* by Ezewa-Ohaeto.).

"Postmodernism and Black Writing in South Africa." In *Writing South Africa: Literature, Apartheid, and Democracy, 1970–1995.* Edited by Derek Attridge and Rosemary Jolly. Cambridge and New York: Cambridge University Press, 1998. Pp. 75–88.

CRITICAL STUDIES, REVIEWS, AND INTERVIEWS

Attwell, David. "The Experimental Turn in Black South African Fiction." *Scrutiny* 2 (Pretoria, June 2003).

Brink, Andre. "An Ornithology of Sexual Politics: Lewis Nkosi's *Mating Birds.*" *English in Africa* 19.1 (May 1992). Pp. 1–20.

Dodd, Josephine. "The South African Literary Establishment and the Textual Production of Woman." *Current Writing: Text and Reception in Southern Africa* 2 (October 1990). Pp. 117–129.

Harris, Janice. "On Tradition, Madness, and South Africa: An Interview with Lewis Nkosi." *Weber Studies* 11.2 (spring–summer 1994).

Horn, Anette. "Review Essay: Lewis Nkosi: *Mating Birds.*" *Critical Arts* 5.2 (Durban, South Africa, 1990). Pp. 112–120.

Jacobs, Johan. "Women Represented: Lewis Nkosi: *Mating Birds.*" *Critical Arts* 5.2 (Durban, South Africa, 1990). P. 8.

Oliphant, Andries. "Underground Irony." *Sunday Times* (South Africa, 24 November 2002). P. 4 (Review of *Underground People.*).

Rose, Jacqueline. "Black Hamlet." In her *States of Fantasy.* Oxford: Oxford University Press, 1995.

Rosenthal, Jane. "Notes from Underground." *Mail & Guardian* (South Africa, 1 November 2002). (Review of *Underground People.*)

Siebel, Lindy, and Liz Gunner, eds. *Critical Perspectives on Lewis Nkosi.* Oxford: Oxford University Press, forthcoming 2004.

ZN (anonymous reviewer). "A Sexual Fantasy." *African Communist* 112 (first quarter, 1987). Pp. 89–91 (Review of *Mating Birds.*).

Arthur Nortje
(1942–1970)

PHILIP HOBSBAUM

ARTHUR NORTJE WAS born 16 December 1942 in Oudtshoorn in the Cape Province of South Africa. His mother, Cecilia Nortje, was a colored woman employed as a domestic worker. His father was a young Jewish businessman whose name was withheld, even from Nortje. In his obituary of the South African political leader, Walter Sisulu, David Beresford writes, "It is impossible for anyone who has not shared the experience to fathom the psychological suffering of those born into the no man's land of "Coloured" status in apartheid South Africa."

Cecelia Nortje's family persuaded her to take up residence with her Aunt Piedt in Port Elizabeth. The young Nortje was enrolled in two successive Anglican mission schools, St. James in Sidwell and St. Mark in North End. An influential teacher who remained a mentor well into adult life was James Davidson. Another cultural influence was the Rousseau family, who befriended his mother.

Nortje entered Patterson High School in 1957 where he fell under the influence of Dennis Brutus, a renowned writer and political activist. He recognized Nortje's poetic talent and introduced him to other writers, notably Athol Fugard (1932–).

Nortje sold newspapers and traded in empty bottles in order to supplement the financial support he received from the Department of Education after his school days. He enrolled to study English and psychology at the University College of the Western Cape in Belville, Capetown. This was a segregated institution, intended for Coloureds. A white university would not have been open to him. The medium of instruction was Afrikaans and the facilities minimal. However, he impressed the head of English, a professor Stopforth, and a philosophy lecturer, Adam Small. Nortje was awarded a prize in a literary competition run by the Mbari Writers Club at Ibadan University, and the prizewinning poems were published in *Black Orpheus*.

From the first he seems to have been gifted with remarkable fluency. He had an extraordinary ear for verse. This is attested by his command of pararhyme at an early age, when many a young poet would have been either grammatically trapped by full rhyme or enjoying a suspicious ease in free verse.

"Thumbing a Lift," which was written when Nortje was eighteen, exhibits an unusual maturity both of structure and subject. It begins:

Emaciated sanddunes and grease-black pylons
On afternoons teeming with impurities;

Brittle bitter-brown wire: the sky-blotching
    ravens
Must be September's electrified existence.

I live beside sap-fired willow striplings,
Yet alien to their cause, spring-exultation
Cars pass by the thin thing of my brown thumb
Rhythmically beckoning in painful indication.

Gnats swarm from scumcamps: above the asphalt
Shimmy-shaking witchdoctors gnarled like
    bluegums
Drunkenly perform their corrugated dazzle,
Leering through red heat with futile venom. . . .

(Anatomy of Dark: Collected Poems, p. 18)

Surely this is already accomplished verse. One notes the pattern of assonance: "pylons" / "ravens," "impurities" / "existences," "exultation" / "indication," "bluegums" / "venom." When the pattern is broken, it is for emphasis, as in the nonrhyme of "striplings" / "thumb" at the ends of the fifth and seventh lines of the quotation.

At this point, "the thin thing of my brown thumb," one notices how immediately present to Nortje's mind is the fact of his color. South Africans apply "Coloured" to the children of parents of different races (usually black and white). Such offspring used to be termed "mulattos" or, more insultingly, "half-breeds" or "half-castes." In the early days of Arthur Nortje, under the apartheid government in South Africa of Dr. Verwoerd, such people were treated as second-rate citizens, rating higher than blacks but lower than whites. In a poem called "Apartheid," Nortje wrote, with understandable anger, "the cold and anonymous / men of the world strengthen my enemies."

In this particular poem, "Thumbing a Lift," luxury cars, such as a chromium Chrysler Rambler—"Cream-leather atmosphere, cool man, relaxed"—speed past, his call for a lift unanswered. His hope is, rather, a cattle truck on the horizon.

"What passing bells for those who die as cattle?" Wilfred Owen had written. That pioneer of pararhyme is clearly an influence here. Another probable influence is Gerard Manley Hopkins, who may have inspired such couplings as "sky-blotching" and "sap-fired." In fact, it seems likely that the young Arthur Nortje was to no small extent a product of that influential, *The Faber Book of Modern Verse*, edited by Michael Roberts.

"PREVENTIVE DETENTION"

By 1963, it seemed that Nortje's horizon was already darkening. There is a poem, "Soliloquy: South Africa," that seems to reflect upon a public, just as much as a personal, predicament. Africa is addressed as though she were a recalcitrant woman:

It seems me speaking all the lonely time,
whether of weather or death in winter,
or, as you expected and your eyes asked, love . . .

(Dead Roots, p. 5)

The form suggests, without reproducing, that of a sestina, which repeats the words found at the end of each line and not just their rhyming parts. This particular poem reproduces a line only once, but that specific line carries a special degree of emphasis. It appears not only at the beginning of the poem, in itself a crucial positioning, but at the end—"It seems to me speaking all the lonely time."

Otherwise the effect of repetition is suggested by a patterning of feminine endings (endings on a light syllable) against a minority of masculine endings (endings on a heavily stressed syllable):

All one attempts is talk in the absence
of others who spoke and vanished
without so much as an echo.
I have seen men with haunting voices
turned into ghosts by a piece of white paper
as if their eloquence had been black magic.

The last three lines quoted may be termed the key lines of the poem; those which one might call its dominant. They suggest the ease with which live men can become quite literally ciphers by a bureaucratic measure; indeed, by a mere note upon a page.

In 1963 he spent a further year at college to gain a diploma in education. He took up teaching, and he would not have been unduly subversive to be disgusted by the system that passed for justice in the South Africa of the 1960s.

There is a lyric, "Preventive Detention," also from 1963, that tailors regret and sorrow into physical description. A particular rhyme is sustained throughout, and a refrain is repeated at the end of each four-line stanza, betokening inexorable fate:

> Pale teaboy juggling cups and saucers
> once taught Othello to our class,
> and a spindly scholar's imprisoned because
> winter is in the brilliant grass.
>
> Liberal girl among magnolias born
> was set to clipping dahlias
> in the prison yard, her blonde locks shorn.
> Winter is in the shining grass.
>
> Twine the tattered strands together,
> loves and passions that amass.
> What's discoloured in the blowing clouds
> winters in the luminous grass.
>
> (*Dead Roots*, p. 7)

The refrain is not intact, from one stanza to another. The grass is variously defined as "brilliant," "shining," and "luminous." In the final stanza, the word "winter" alters syntactically from noun to verb.

This poem acts out the confining of these people in "preventive detention"—a euphemism for imprisonment, usually without charge or trial. The scholar is demeaned to being a teaboy, and the "liberal girl" is not only set to menial

gardening tasks but shorn of her locks. One might say that the tone of the poem indicates such punishment was unavoidable. The clouds may be "blowing," but there is in them a discoloration that presages the luminosity of the grass turning to winter. This is certainly the winter of the prisoners' discontent.

LEAVING SOUTH AFRICA

Winter is not the only season. A number of the poems of this period concentrate so much upon fall that they might well be taken to form some kind of sequence. One thinks of "Spell Cold and Ironic" from October 1963, "Go Back" and "Separation," both from 1964, and "Fading Light" and the highly evocative "Windscape," both from 1965. The last begins, turbulently:

> Air-swept slopes of straining weed
> plunge dimly to the dung-dry rocks,
> shore cowers under the bilious sky.
> The oil-scummed green sea heaves and slides
> below my view from concrete heights
> in struggle with the lurching wind.
> Chopping into the curve the white surge
> sprawls among boats in frothing nipples . . .
>
> (*Anatomy of Dark*, p. 136)

What is apparent in these and in several other poems of this period is that the menacing weather is tied up with what seems to be the failure of a love affair—though, of course, these disconsolate poems may refer to different women. The mood, however, is unmistakable: "Dissatisfaction invites me nowhere" ("Hangover"); "Last time I made some love arrangements" ("The Same to You"); "beautiful phantom by failed love fostered" ("Slip of a Girl"); "Wine makes me lose her love" ("Deliberation"); "Is love instinct, life's only hurt?" ("Hamlet Reminiscence"); "I lie in ubiquitous darkness" ("Search"); "barren ground / where roots have struggled and died" ("Absence of Love").

Indeed, the image of dead roots occurs and recurs through the poems of Arthur Nortje. These are not merely the outpourings of adolescent frustration. There is an extra bite in the poems—made, of course all the more poignant by the incidence of an unusually developed verse technique.

Nortje's understandable political disaffection was undoubtedly related quite closely to what seems to have been a series of failed relationships. He is not a tender or accommodating poet. There is a vein of satire very noticeable in his work. Often, it consists in seemingly excessive praise for this or that person or object in a manner that implies a degree of resentment. The mode may owe something to the occasionally grandiloquent style of Ben Jonson, though quite likely it came to Nortje refracted through the sensibility of Hart Crane, another prominent figure in *The Faber Book of Modern Verse*.

"Poem for a Kitchen," on the surface, is tantamount to a hymn of praise for modern fixings. Phrase after phrase suggests appreciation of the amenities: of the Frigidaire: for example, "Metal freezer furred with icicles." The stove, too, receives attention: "a knobbed and dialled monster / with indicators." At the same time there is an element of caricature in all this, that suggests the appreciation is very considerably alloyed with disgust.

The washing machine receives ironic attention:

> What stillness settles round the gleaming
> Hotpoint.
> Having disposed of human jetsam loads
> its thick detergent scum has gurgled seaward:
> filthy tides absorb the black remains.
> And in my cool white shirt of Terylene,
> my healthy socks that hug the feet in nylon,
> and underwear that breathes through pores of
> freedom,
> I smile sweet thanks towards the gleaming
> Hotpoint.
>
> (*Anatomy of Dark*, p. 115)

This is a poetry that thrives on incongruities. In this case, one notices the gap between the elaborate encomium and the mundane nature of its occasion. However magnificent the poet pretends to find the washing machine, that is all it is: a washing machine. To make the point another way: one would expect this atmosphere of panegyric to be bestowed upon an entity partaking of the sublime. Except that examination of the panegyric—"What stillness / . . . / I smile sweet thanks"—implies an overstatement in excess of any occasion that could be readily envisaged. Thus the manner partly is a comedy of humors, where individual traits are stretched and distorted as a mode of commentary.

The commentary here has a moral tendency. What is being satirized is the pretense that one can escape from nature. The normal perceptions of taste and smell seem to be banned from this charivaria. A pseudo-life is celebrated here—not at all, we find out, with the author's approval. He attacks the world of the modern advertisement, that of the opinion-shaping media, the fetishism that impels people to buy and buy and buy, persuaded by brand names.

Further, Nortje satirizes not only the attempt to refine life from raw experience but the false belief that it is desirable or even possible to do so:

> Built-in cupboards are edged with aluminium,
> above which, polished, stands the breakfast
> toaster—
> its plug has copper prongs split down the centre.
> And crystal goblets glitter in the tray
> across from dresser drawers which hold the silver.
> To ban all cooking odours hangs there Kleenaire
> (lavender). It titillates the nostrils.
> The air itself, of course, is sterilized.
>
> (*Anatomy of Dark*, p. 115)

This is a man at odds with the social pressures that shape his environment. So sore and angry a spirit could never feel at home in the world. In "Song for a Passport" he writes forcefully of his frustration: "Who loves me so much not to let me go, / not to let me leave a land of problems?" And in fact he left his land of problems, for London, in 1965.

COMING TO LONDON

He took what seems to have been an increasingly disaffected personality with him. Nevertheless, it appears to have been in his first period in London that some of his finest work was written.

A poem not reproduced in his initially collected works is called "Up Late." It was printed from a manuscript source in an invaluable anthology edited by Gerald Moore and Ulli Beier, *The Penguin Book of Modern African Poetry* (1963, 1968 as *Modern Poetry from Africa*; under its present title, 1984, 1998). This is a key contribution, if one were needed, to the poetry of insomnia. Its setting seems to be a boardinghouse of some kind. The setting is not minimal, as might have been the case in a prison, though the author is able to look back on a period of imprisonment. Here, however, there is a clock, an icebox, a calendar on the wall with a nostalgic scene of home. Yet at the same time there is an absence of human contact. This place, whatever it is, appears to be one where a protagonist can feel very lonely:

> Night here, the owners asleep upstairs:
> the room's eyes shut, its voices dead,
> though I admire it when its mirrors
> oblige me with my presence. Looking ahead
> needs glancing back to what I once
> was, the time that mischance
> borrowed my body to break it by terror.
>
> Now the cameras rest in their elegant
> leather coffins, having caught
> the whirl of streets before the wheels go silent.
> Rain trickles as the red biro writes my heart:
> time demands no attention of the will,
> the clock is yellow with black numerals.

The fact that one is able to notice such minute sounds as the purring of an icebox suggests silence, with not a soul stirring.

Such a quality of attention, coupled with extreme loneliness, is brought out by meter, rhythm, and sound. The verse is formal. A seven-line stanza, akin to the medieval form of rhyme royal, is used. The rhyme scheme consists of a quatrain with alternate rhymes, followed by a couplet, and ending with a line consonant with the first. The poet is not chained to full rhyme: this is variegated with pararhyme. Thus, "upstairs" chimes (rather than rhymes) with "mirrors"; "once" with "mischance"; "will," quite remotely, with "numerals"; while "upstairs" / "terror" is hardly a pararhyme at all.

The meter is a fluid tetrameter, a four-beat movement predominating throughout. Nevertheless, the line varies from three beats to the five beats of "Rain trickles as the red biro writes my heart." The tone is hushed, this quality being enhanced by the diction, with words such as "asleep," "dead," "silent," and "purring" in strategic places.

As the poem develops, the stanzas become less self-contained. There is a tendency for the verse to flow over from the last line of one stanza to the first line of the next, so that the poem ends, musing on loneliness and isolation:

> Give me the whole experience to savour
> who have known waste and also favour:
> time to come may find me eloquent
>
> in other rooms, that reminisce
> of this one so composed in silence. Love,
> the necessary pain, has spurred a search.
> Moving from place to place I always have
> come someway closer to knowing
> the final sequence of song that's going
> to master the solitudes night can teach.

The poem is proleptic of future work. Quite aware as it is of imprisonment, it indicates that any deprivation of human society can give a semblance of jail's unique loneliness. This may be inferred from such phrases as "other rooms that reminisce / of this one so composed in silence."

LOOKING BACK

What may be termed a companion piece is "At Rest from the Grim Place," also found in the Moore and Beier anthology rather than in the collected works. The poem provides a highly atmospheric impression of prison life:

> The sergeant laughs with strong teeth,
> his jackboots nestle under the springbok horns.
> Those bayonets are silent,
> the spear of the nation gone to the ground.
> Warriors prowl in the stars of their dungeons.
> I've seen the nebulae of a man's eyes
> squirm with pain, he sang his life
> through cosmic volleys. They call it
> genital therapy, the blond bosses.

It is easy enough to determine for what "genital therapy" is the euphemism. Though Nortje was not long in prison, one can imagine the effect upon his temperament. Here, the free verse into which he has been excited carries a poignant specificity.

Yet, paradoxically, some of the poem has positive overtones. The anguished query "Why is there no more news?" leads on to an evocation of a more civilized country: "Bluetits scuffle in the eaves of England, / an easy summer shimmers in the water." This indicates that the poem was not written at the time of incarceration but is a recollection, something looked back upon from more tranquil circumstance:

> Curling smoke, a white butt is
> brother to my lips and fingers.
> You watch the ash on grass blades gently crumble.
> Your hands are small as roses,
> they cancel memory.

This evocative free verse is constructed by pitting a line with a strong set of stresses against another with weaker stresses. Thus, in the first line of this quotation, there appears to be a heavy stress on "Curl-," "smoke," and "butt," and weaker stress on "white" and "is," while in the second line, the only stress commensurate with the heavier ones in the first line appears to be on the first syllable of "brother." Although there are stresses on "lips" and on the first syllable of "fingers," they are weaker than that of "bro-." Therefore the first line is composed of more, and stronger, stresses than the second line.

One could pursue the same mode of analysis through the whole quotation, showing how "You watch the ash on grass blades gently crumble," with its prolonged syllable-count and weighty stresses on "ash," "blades" and "crum[ble]," is pitted against the shorter line that follows it, with only one heavy stress, on "ros[es]. Indeed, the whole poem could be anatomized in this way. For, without some such patterning as that, free verse is liable to degenerate into prose.

A different version of free verse is found in another poem of confinement, "Letter from Pretoria Central Prison," also dating from Nortje's London sojourn, August 1966. Here, as in the work of T. S. Eliot, we find what approximates a liberated mode of blank verse; that is to say, the five-stress-per-line, unrhymed form used by the Elizabethan and Jacobean poets. "Letter . . ." more than "At Rest . . ." is anchored to an iambic norm. That is to say, it relies throughout upon alternating heavy and light stresses, though the mode Nortje has chosen accommodates many variegations and departures. Nothing is lost, so far as atmosphere is concerned, in his use of this form:

> The bell wakes me at 6 in the pale spring dawn
> with the familiar rumble of the guts negotiating
> murky corridors that smell of bodies. My eyes
> find salutary the insurgent light of distances.
> Waterdrops rain crystal cold, my wet face in

ascent from an iron basin
greets its rifled shadow in the doorway.

(*Anatomy of Dark*, p. 185)

The poem is written as a retrospect, and there is a developed consciousness of what is going on outside this immediate confinement—a consciousness that leads to some achieved ironies:

Trees are green beyond the wall, leaves through
    the mesh
are cool in sunshine
among the monastic white flowers of spring that
    floats
prematurely across the exercise yard, a square
of the cleanest stone I have ever walked on.
Sentinels smoke in their boxes, the wisps
curling lovely through the barbed wire.

Nortje remarks upon how accustomed one becomes to prison. The person to whom he appears to be writing is also, apparently, confined—in this case, to hospital with a troublesome kidney. Instead of warders, there are "smart nurses" bringing grapefruit. The poem—which, after all, simulates a letter—ends with deliberate abruptness, there being no more space on the paper that, in prison, is stingily provided for correspondence.

LONDON IMPRESSIONS

A related poem, "Autopsy," was written a month later than "Letter from Pretoria Central Prison." It is big (sixty-six lines) and couched in the same mode of free verse as "At Rest from the Grim Place." The subject is the gap between what the author had been taught by his teachers and the realities of the country where they had taught him.

36,000 feet above the Atlantic
I heard an account of how they had shot
a running man in the stomach. But what isn't told

is how a warder kicked the stitches open
on a little-known island prison which used to be
a guano rock in a sea of diamond blue.

(*Anatomy of Dark*, p. 196)

There is here a notable—and dramatic—gap between the quietly descriptive tone, almost that of a didactic exposition in which the gratuitous violence is relayed, and the vicious act itself. The depiction of such brutality would have gained nothing by recourse to melodrama. As in poems previously discussed, the free verse makes for a flexibility of utterance. It even incorporates the odd rhyme, which gives the effect of spontaneity—as though the poem retained certain aspects of a draft. However, it is polished enough when the occasion so requires. Therefore the framework of the poem, describing past teachers, contributes greatly to its central perception.

The poem indeed has its moments of melodrama, chiefly when detailing the aggression that helps to shape the education system Nortje underwent. Here, for example, he seems to be speaking of the political framework:

She who had taught them proudness of tongue
drank an aphrodisiac, then swallowed
a purgative to justify the wrong.
Her iron-fisted ogre of a son
straddled the drug-blurred townships,
breathing hygienic blasts of justice . . .

(*Anatomy of Dark*, p. 195)

However, toward the end of the poem, Nortje is in London and finds himself telephoning one of his teachers. The hiatus between political violence and educational practice seems even more inexplicable:

Over the phone in a London suburb he sounds
grave and patient—the years have stilled him:
the voice in a dawn of ash, moon-steady,
is wary of sunshine which has always been
more diagnostic than remedial.

(*Anatomy of Dark*, pp. 196–197)

The poet professes surprise. What his teachers have imparted seems to him to make no sense of events in the world he has witnessed. That which might send a man into a frenzy appears to have made no essential contact with this particular teacher. He is essentially a creature of the night. The poem ends, as well it might, in an atmosphere of bewilderment:

> The early sharpness passed beyond to noon
> that melted brightly into shards of dusk.
> The luminous tongue in the black world
> has infinite possibilities no longer.
>
> (*Anatomy of Dark*, p. 197)

Along with these bitter utterances, close to political despair, there are some attractive pieces of 1966 describing the early sensations of a newcomer. A degree of reification is experienced in "Spring Feeling"—"In London's hemmed-in slender traceries / fuss the finches." Autumn in the metropolis appears less menacing than that back home: "a wet cane chair drips lonely in the bottom of the garden" ("September Poem"). In "Chelsea Picture" the poet notes, "Dim among mists a starfish floats, the sun / of London autumn, leaves with everything."

Among his "London Impressions," in the poem of that name, are the following:

> Out of the Whitehall shadows I pass
> into a blaze of sun as sudden as fountains.
>
>   . . .Cloudbanks
> lazily roll in the blue heavens beyond . . .
>   . . .
>
> . . . A girl plays games with mirrors
> in Hyde Park . . .
>   . . .
> . . . Sun, you are all I have:
> the grass already welcomes the brown leaves.
>
> (*Anatomy of Dark*, p. 188)

The sense of mild elation is tempered by the feeling of being a stranger without roots in this vast city. There is a degree of freedom, in contrast with the shackles of South Africa, but it is alloyed by a sense of loneliness.

FOLLOWING SYLVIA PLATH

However, a sinister influence began to assert itself. Sylvia Plath's (1932–1963) suicide, followed by the collection *Ariel*, had a galvanic effect on poetry that was by no means all to the good. Along with the young women poets who tried to emulate her passion with only a tithe of her talent stood, somewhat incongruously, Arthur Nortje. He wrote, in an almost ventriloquial assumption of Plath's style, the first of two poems in her honor:

> Hate for the father. A pool of malice in my blood
> dribbles like yellowing water down that cliff-face
>   of ferns.
> His blood confuses mine, I do not forget
> how age corrupts my clarity with snaking pain.
>
> (*Dead Roots*, p. 46)

The savagery of the feeling obscures the verse. That language is inefficient. Placing "corrupts" and "pain" in the same line seems excessive, without the adjective "snaking" to drive the meaning home still further. Further on:

> Night devours the marvellous colours, leans
>   against the window,
> the curtains rustle like stiff silk, the bedroom
>   smells like a ward;
> the scalpel glints of mirrors pierce my dark god
> all I can feel is the burning together of limbs . . .

The force is undeniable, but the reason for all this feverish energy is not immediately apparent. While the poet himself may feel a gross disaffection, his language does not project it with any preciseness. A phrase such as "The scalpel glints of mirrors" conveys nothing with exactitude, while how a mirror "pierces" a god, dark or otherwise, passes the imagination. One necessarily feels that this wonderful pastiche is a product of literature—especially, a sincere admiration for Plath's style—rather than deeply rooted in a specific sensibility responding to specific experience.

"For Sylvia Plath II" is no more focused:

Sensitive as a moon instrument. My
pen bites like a bullet. White and cringing
The paper bleeds black tears, it is inexplicable.

(*Dead Roots*, p. 47)

The likeness to Plath's characteristic rhythm, at least in her later phase, is truly remarkable. However, all this had happened before.

Sixteen years previously, in 1950, young poets read Dylan Thomas, let themselves loose in his mode, and felt themselves to be inspired. Thirty years previously, in 1936, the progenitor of such verse, allowing for stylistic difference, would have been W. H. Auden, and fourteen years before that, most probably T. S. Eliot. Plath was not the best exemplar for a lonely young man exiled from his native land and finding it difficult in his adopted country to form relationships.

OXFORD

By October 1966 Nortje arrived in Oxford to read for a degree in English at Jesus College. At this point began a slow deterioration of personality marked by poems that look like entries in a journal. Nortje seems to have depended increasingly on alcohol and other drugs.

A poem called "Assessment" loses form in a mode of clinical reportage: "I wake clammy from a dream / with eyes that cannot focus on the keyholes, / and the dark is clasping me in soiled sheets." That was autumn, but "Winter: Oxford" proved to bring no comfort:

By the river the raw nerves wince
where wind bends into the trees:
west is a grey afternoon beyond
wet silhouettes of traceries. The grey

current carries the surrendered leaves.
Leaf-blown lanes where tendrils wither
in brittle crevices are paths I take . . .

(*Anatomy of Dark*, p. 204)

Now this is raw material for a poem rather than the poem itself. One notices the opportunities for rhyme that are not taken up. The rhyme would not need to thump home: "trees" and (a favorite word of Nortje) "traceries" would have been one opportunity for pararhyme. Further possibilities of pararhyme have been ignored: "river" / "wither," "nerves" / "leaves," even "silhouettes" and "crevices." The poem seems to need a further recension, to bring the possible rhymes and pararhymes in relation with one another. Alternatively, it could have been written—given Nortje's metrical skill—in a free verse with no need for rhyme.

Around this time Nortje made not altogether successful attempts to incorporate popular elements into the verse. This does not seem to have been necessary. Nortje's own voice was still stronger than anything additional that he took on:

The light I have lamented, poems lost
in half-sleep between the day and the last dark,
my epitaphs for people, elegies, odes
are but the deeper breathing of an age . . .

(*Anatomy of Dark*, p. 209)

Such an elegiac utterance, pertaining almost to the poet William Empson, does not require the acknowledgment that follows—a seemingly quite unnecessary encomium upon the Beatles. "To John, Paul, George, and Ringo":

You, wry John Lennon, the pretty imp
    McCartney,
Harrison the taciturn, gothic-featured Starkey;
the new gospel's four phenomena, they
themselves would laugh at the terminology.

(*Anatomy of Dark*, p. 210)

Quite apart from the fact that the fourth member of the Beatles group was usually called "Ringo

Starr" and not "Starkey," there is a degree of self-consciousness about this name-dropping that sits uneasily with the prevailing tone of the verse. Simply, the effects manifest in the later part of this poem do not accord with those which have appertained earlier.

Sometimes the effect of such popular gestures is not contemporaneousness so much as a kind of intellectual slumming. For example, the stiltedly titled "Discopoem" begins:

> In the middle of my fix I think
> we are all together, a mexican a japanese
> a dolly in a discotheque and mona lisa
> and president johnson and engelbert
>   humperdinck.
>
> The grateful dead at a california weirdo
> brought out their crackle gear, trailed
>   microphones . . .
>
>   (*Anatomy of Dark*, p. 216–216)

Nortje may indeed have had a drug reverie that corresponded to all this. It seems to trade on incongruities, Engelbert Humperdinck being not the nineteenth-century post-Wagnerian composer but a later-twentieth-century popular singer who adopted his name. The Grateful Dead were a post-Beatles rock band. But nothing much is done with his drugged insight. It remains raw material, and is rather strained in its attempt to appear contemporaneous.

Increasingly, the poems appear to be bound up with drugs. At least, this is the inference one must necessarily take from a poem with the title, "Message from an LSD Eater":

> An acute vacuum is imminent
> when grass has withered over the cold fields
> after continuum of anxiety.
> Who has taken a fortunate trip
> beyond the moon, past violet stars, through
>   luminous soundwaves
> invisibly travelling the years' kaleidoscope
> falls back into the sea of capture . . .

As often happens with such poems, there is no verbal equivalent to the power of the hallucinations such a drug as LSD is reputed to inspire. Therefore the would-be verbal equivalent of the experience falls considerably short of the experience itself, and the result is hardly poetry. Oxford seems to have gone stale upon him.

BRITISH COLUMBIA

Fortunately for Nortje, at this point, September 1967, he secured a teaching post in Canada. As with the departure from South Africa, the new scene at first did a good deal to stimulate his writing. The resultant poems are strangely amorphous, but redolent of a delight in language. "Joy Cry" dates from fall 1967, and was written in British Columbia, where Nortje had taken up his new assignment. It begins:

> Apollo's man-breasts smooth and gold-blond
> hold between in the fine-boned cleft
> the kernel of radiant light. Like wind
> youth's madness streams through orifices. The
>   swift
> vivacious morning shoots along the ripples:
> in my loins the swelling pearl moves.
>
>   (*Anatomy of Dark*, p. 125)

This seems to represent the awakening of delight in one's own body; more particularly, the upsurge of sexual desire. It is different in that respect from the autumnal poems of frustration that marked the final years in South Africa, or the gloomy reminiscences of the exile in London. Even so, one notices a series of lost opportunities amid the exuberance. "Blond" and "boned" seem in insufficient correspondence. Even if that suggestion seems officious, the proximity of "gold" and "hold" suggest an incipient rhyme scheme—one that would have done something to shape this outburst of somewhat unfocused exuberance.

Similarly, in the second stanza of this uncharacteristically blithe poem, we find:

> This growing jewel wants to burst
> through coils and meshes the seasons have
>   wrought.

That time can tame the green surge,
that age can quell the riotous blood,
my eyes blind with their glory, shun.
The snow-melt waters roar down the mountain.

(*Anatomy of Dark*, p. 126)

The poem seems to be increasingly burgeoning out of control. Some readers may welcome this. Even so, the final word in the stanza, "mountain," surely calls out for some kind of antecedent. Without it, that word stands oddly isolated; almost incongruously so. Granted the exuberance of the language allows for the rocking rhythm; nevertheless that rhythm itself seems to require some sort of patterning not evident here. On the contrary, there is an allegiance in diction to Dylan Thomas—"the green surge," "the riotous blood"—that makes for obscurity, and even overstatement. There is a putative rhyme at the end of certain lines, in words such as "burst" and "surge." Also the words "quell" and "jewel" could have been brought into some kind of relationship; possibly also "glory" and "waters."

One is glad for Nortje's sake that he was able—after an apparently dreary time—to rejoice, but one cannot help wishing that he had been more able to construct something on which to rejoice. The final stanza of this poem is explicit enough: "The joy cry of virility stirs," "I shall soothe your tender wound." However, it is impossible to feel that the language has caught and held the experience, much less explored it. Having said that, it is only fair to mention that this is one of seven items by Nortje that found their way into *Poems of Black Africa* (1975), edited by Wole Soyinka.

Written at much the same time, so far as one can tell, is another of the Canadian poems, "Night Ferry." This in its size and scale—sixty-four lines—cannot help but be impressive. However, one feels that the author is seeking a new style, having to some extent lost contact with the one he had evolved previously. Walt Whitman is probably behind this big poem of

exploration. The night ferry of the title is used as a symbol for the rite of passage. Its tone is one of questioning. Perhaps the dominant section is the following:

Oily and endless the stream is a truth drug. Pick
up signals from vast space, gather a ghoulish cry
from an astronaut lost for ever, his electronic
panels blipping with danger signs. Below,
crushed like the foil on a Cracker Barrel cheese
    pack
a nuclear submarine no longer muscles
into the thunderous pressure. Is it the infinite
sound I hear that's going where? and to
whom can the intelligence be given? who are you?
Not only this, but also
between us the sensory network registers
potential tones, imaginable patterns
for there are destinies as well as destinations.

(*Anatomy of Dark*, p. 217)

Though Whitmanesque in diction, the rhythm owes little to Whitman's metric. Rather, it echoes the liberated blank verse favored by T. S. Eliot. The language tends to oscillate through various registers. "Panels blipping with danger signs" has the authentic lightness of touch we associate with the better class of science fiction, but it is somewhat debased by the mundane "foil on a Cracker Barrel cheese pack" that follows.

However, though at times crude in detail, the whole poem succeeds in broad effect. It uses a particular crossing in a particular ferry to suggest a new development in a human life:

What purpose
has the traveller now, whose connection is cut
with the whale, the wolf or the albatross . . . ?

(*Anatomy of Dark*, p. 217)

There seems to be the expectancy of encounter with some person, conjectured rather than realized:

O are you daylight, love, to diminish my mist?
Siren, or the breeze's child, forgetful

while reaching through my bones . . . ?

        (*Anatomy of Dark,* p. 218)

The ambition of this poem is something to be admired, but—as with other works previously addressed—a further recension might have brought the vocabulary into more cohesive effect. When the grip slackens, the unwelcome incursion of unhelpful influence tends to supervene. Here, ingeniously but not—given the exalted subject—appositely, there is once more a touch of Dylan Thomas:

    I . . .
    . . . lie
    in half-sleep, knock knock goes
    the who's there night—a to-fro bottle tinkles . . .

        (*Anatomy of Dark,* p. 218)

Through all the images of transit, sea, darkness, and menace, the poem still manages to imply an intermittent hope that some unknown beloved will transpire: "there's you / who must somewhere exist to be regarded / as needy, needed, night-bound: a cherished enigma."

A companion poem, and certainly a poem of exile, is "Waiting," another of the items chosen by Wole Soyinka for his anthology of African poems. Africa definitely is weighing upon Nortje's mind. He can neither live there, apparently, nor forget his country. Images of the sea and of the voyager beset the troubled surface of this poem:

    Origins trouble the voyager much, those roots
    that have sipped the waters of another continent.
    Africa is gigantic, one cannot begin
    to know even the strange behaviour furthest
    south in my swastikaed xenophobic department.
    Come back, come back mayibuye
    cried the breakers of stone and cried the crowds
    cried Mr. Kumalo before the withering fire
    mayibuye Afrika.

        (*Anatomy of Dark,* p. 244)

There is a tempering of hope with despair in this poem. The voyager wonders what can credibly save him. He remembers the verse of the dead poets who sang of lost beauties—"lost" in the sense that he has defaulted by leaving the continent, and also "lost" in the sense that these images are with him only in a ghostly indeterminacy. The continent stands for the forsaken possibility of love: "new magnitude of thought has but betrayed / the lustre of your eyes. . . ." Those eyes have become "the night bulb that reveals ash on my sleeve." That allusion to Eliot's *Four Quartets* is perhaps too evident in this final line. Yet the variegated blank verse that owes such allegiance to Eliot in some of his tenderer moments maybe justifies this degree of reference.

There is a degree of recovery in spirit to be found in "Hope Hotel," a poem of 1968. It is couched in four-line stanzas, and to that extent more disciplined than some of Nortje's other verse of this period. This poem reverts to his earlier acuity of perception. Also, there is a wry neatness and restrained irony redolent of his best efforts. This is expressed in delicately touched pararhymes that seem to deter the less helpful influence. One finds this measure of control right from the very first stanza:

    Dawn light over my hotel notepaper
    with a bird's alert incursion breaks
    in softly potent rhythms to the simple
        provocation
    of rain's splashy dissonance at windows.

        (*Anatomy of Dark,* p. 273)

But perhaps the hope in this poem is illusory after all. The poet appears to have spent the night perusing a book of nudes, presumably as a means of sexual stimulation. He says, mordantly, "the tortoise of the mind / feeds in isolation." He is conscious of the magnificent scenery of his new domicile—"The lush woods luminesce in green explosions." Yet, despite the title of the poem, this does not seem to help: "it is not worth / consideration even now to win back selfhood."

TORONTO

This, however, was almost the last achieved poem that Nortje succeeded in writing. he left British Columbia in June 1969 and moved to Ontario. Here, on 1 September, he took up employment at Alderwood College, a secondary school in Etobicoke, Toronto. This does not seem to have helped. More and more, the poems seem to deteriorate into rough notes. The interest remains, but increasingly it is biographical, rather than literary. If there is a form in these last works, it can best be expressed by describing the poems as having been written in the small hours under the influence of amphetamines:

> My mind hurts with consistent
> intake of chemicals:
> Slim-mint sabbaths, long walks in the dog park,
> librium for angst Mondays . . .
>
> ("Quiet Desperation," *Anatomy of Dark,* p. 337)

March 1970 saw a visit back to London. The verse seems to be moving from diary to a form of therapy. However, no attempt at activity seems to work:

> I walk with an address book
> full of crossed-out numbers, party contacts,
> once-met twice-kissed women who have moved
> to somewhere I will never be. . . .
>
> ("Return to the City of the Heart," *Anatomy of Dark,* p. 337)

There is, even now, a degree of smartness in the verse—indeed, almost wit—but it lacks a context. Such lines do not occur as part of any meaningful construction. There is an arbitrariness in the shape of these later poems. They do not altogether lack structure, but such structure as they have derives from the chance movements of life, not the disciplined consciousness of art.

Back in Toronto by April 1970, Nortje terminated his teaching contract on grounds of ill health. He belabored himself with a sorry awareness of his mixed race. A poem bitterly

named "Dogsbody Half-breed" declares him to have originated in an area that is "bordello for the sea-tossed Dutchman." This work offers few pretensions to verse: the rhythm lurches along like a series of outcries. The most savage of these, whose force gives it a sour quality of its own, comes right at the end:

> and I hybrid, after Mendel,
> growing between the wire and the wall,
> being dogsbody, being me, buffer you still.
>
> (*Anatomy of Dark,* p. 345)

It is not poetry, it is hardly even verse. But no one can doubt its sincerity. No one can ignore such an expression of despair.

This is one of an outburst of nine poems all dating from April 1970 and written in Toronto. "Be At" pictures a man seemingly forever outside a party, hearing young strident voices singing to guitars and drums within. "Asseverations" is a strange, aphoristic piece that harks back to South Africa where, cries the author, he grappled with the hardship of rhyme in shack or hovel. An item called "Shock Therapy" may refer to a metaphorical rather than a literal state of being caught "in the hysteria of silence," tightening the words to pearls of sweat—"shock is the stilling therapy for the poet."

There is the quality of raw emotion in these poems, but little sense of art or technique. A piece simply called "Poem" slaps its emotion on the page before the reader with scant ceremony:

> Become to me a sweet song
> as before said I
>   stone in water mute
> the day burglar of booze
> steals into these defiances of un-
> silent lucubrations . . .
>
> (*Dead Roots,* p. 110)

The line-endings seem to occur arbitrarily.

That is the start of the poem. There follows a series of ejaculations, similar to the kind of writing undertaken by inhabitants of lunatic asylums. These need not be devoid of artistic merit and certainly have a therapeutic value. The poem ends with a cry of despair:

> Become to me as black
> as my hands
>   with the soot of memory
> expunged
>   as in the rose dusk or morninggold
> my love
> my now distant land

A poem from this same month, April 1970, is appositely called "Leftovers." It draws upon popular culture—"buttermilk sky" (Hoagy Carmichael), "tarzaned" (Edgar Rice Burroughs)—to proclaim, rather than enact, what had become in the work of Nortje a pathological mood of disaffection. There is no longer any shape in his poems, but the odd verbal phrase—"the senses whimper," "should the tongue not shrill"—gives this very arbitrariness a surrealistic quality of definition. It is not art, but it is communication, at a basic level.

An ambitious piece of writing, "Nightly," suggests that the poet has peered into dark doorways, seen the ceiling change shape, squeezed out images like pips from a stale orange, felt his loins go numb at the blue burn of alcohol, held back a scream of terror in the ghost-infested midnight. He has sought out anodyne and lived on Benzedrine, only breathing a heavy sigh of relief at dawn when the birds start to wake the universe.

Well, what a night! It is all perfectly credible, but it is not in itself a poem. Rather it is a draft for a poem. One can detect hints toward a metrical shape or a rhyme scheme. But, as it stands, this cento of fifty-one lines would need care and revision to bring it anywhere near the level of articulacy that Nortje had achieved in London some four years previously. Symptomatically, this group of nine poems hastily slapped together and compounded of insomnia and frustration ends with one called, retrospectively,

"South African," displaying the by now familiar range of vocabulary: "nostalgia," "terror," "broken," "stumble," "whip," "beats," "emaciated."

May 1970 brought a further seven poems, superficially more disciplined than the April garnering, but no less redolent of loneliness, insomnia, and amphetamine abuse. Nortje himself terms "Nightfall," though it has a display of metrical form, a set of "unromantic notes." "Poem in Toronto" speaks, literally or not, of "the dormant seed of syphilis / lodger in my skull."

"Native's Letter" refers to past heroes of Afrikaans and of Xhosa culture. One is reminded of T. S. Eliot's "these fragments I have shored against my ruins." The language deteriorates as we look at it: "Darksome, whoever dies / in the malaise of my dear land / remember me at swim, / the moving waters spilling through my eyes. . . ." One misses an objective correlative, to use Eliot's remarkable phrase from his essay on Hamlet. There is more of a shape in this poem than in some others of its group, but one cannot say that rhymes such as "dies" / "eyes" do much by way of shaping this strange emotion. Here, Nortje seems to be wailing for a lost personality—certainly, for lost opportunities.

"A House on Roncesvalles, Toronto 222" is self-reflexive to an extent. It gives us an unfortunately clear idea of what writing poetry by this time meant to Nortje:

> hesitant about whether
> to fetch out pen and paper
> I wonder will thought dribble
> while the radiator weeps into its coils
>   (or will profundities escape
>   before I scan the news and
>   the man who pays for it comes home
>   at 8 o'clock . . .)
>
> (*Anatomy of Dark*, p. 354)

That is near to being automatic writing. Verse cannot be written in this way. It has value only as therapy, and therapy seldom has much to do with literature. Random details crop up as the poem proceeds: "runnels from the nose / find a shallow grave in Kleenex"; "the groin sweats under talc / in the bathroom." There is something juvenile in this kind of writing. Such self-engrossment is unlikely to take the poet anywhere.

The significantly named "Notes from the Middle of the Night" tells an increasingly reluctant reader, "Inside me blooms a sudden wish / to calm fright with a little yellow pill. . . ." The persona displayed seems to be no more than the sum of its sensations: "unlovely the butterfly guts that won't relax / the brain that reeks with guilt feelings. . . ."

RETURN TO LONDON

However, eventually Nortje got back to London. He was there by July 1970. An application to read for a bachelor's of philosophy degree at Jesus College, Oxford, had been successful. But there was not much longer to go. He seems, in "Poem (for?)," to have renewed a love relationship—conducted, so to speak, in parenthesis:

> (I on edge of bathtub watching you
> wash the years
> out of your eyes)
>
> (*Dead Roots,* p. 127)

There is a degree of atmosphere in "The drifting seeds of summer . . . ," London's elusive charm not altogether failing:

> Here I stand in the most
> beautiful of revivals, freshened into
> lovesong tenderness, cool and lyrical
> with no halfway feelings, no
> dryness in the throat, because
> I breathe you.
>
> (*Dead Roots,* p. 128)

But, in a poem he does not trouble to title, love—like so much chronicled in these final works of Nortje—seems to go sour:

> That that is lost and found again
> seldom is as beautiful. Some lustre
> rubbed off in the night amid the neon
> usage. Some sound deadened in a dark chair. . . .
>
> (*Dead Roots,* p. 129)

It is interesting that, probably in an attempt to make sense of his emotions, Nortje at this latest stage reverts to quite strict form. The unnamed poem just quoted is written in fairly tight quatrains. There are pararhymes, as above: "again" / "neon"; "lustre" / "chair." There is a definite, though variegated, five-stress line. The second stanza of the poem runs, not unimaginatively:

> You are saddened looking in a pawnshop:
> in a dusty window, faded, and stained
> see knick-knacks, gilt lamps, second-hand stock.
> Some come to buy, some reluctantly refrain. . . .

Were this the work of a young person, one could certainly see promise in such lines. This is the poet revealing his life as unappealingly used property not many people wish to acquire. In a pawnshop one leaves items of ownership as collateral property against loans of money. Here is the collateral piled up, unredeemable:

> Few come to redeem from the miscellany. These
> items may be wanted but the wherewithal
> is lacking. You sit and read obituaries,
> visit a barbershop, walk around in a fruitstall.

But the plot has slipped slightly. It is the person who leaves the items in exchange for a loan who may be expected to return to redeem them. However, their owner has failed to come up with the money for which they were pawned. They now belong to the owner of the pawnshop and are available for purchase. His customer may or may not wish to buy pieces that have been long in the shop. The final lines, bringing in obituaries, barbershop, and fruitstall, seem

WORLD WRITERS IN ENGLISH

arbitrary. The poem seems to weary of its subject well before it terminates. In any case, there is an absence of focus. The detritus of a life may be tarnished by age and use, but there is a long step from that to such pieces being placed on display in a pawnshop. The absence of focus makes for a degree of self-pity.

A further sonnet of the same period is subtitled, rather than titled, "Love of Perversity." Here the self-pity that tends to disfigure the sonnet previously discussed is let loose, without even appropriate pararhyme or intelligible plot. Instead, there is a kind of wild romantic gesture one associates with the less attractive verbal gestures of Byron. The sestet runs:

> Could I but flay the skins of gentleman
> tough-minded, softspoken, delicate, well-heeled,
> responsible for systems that have bred
> oil tycoons, bankers, men in real estate!
> Businessmen and beggars are equally fraudulent.
> One can see marvels in devil's excrement.
>
> (*Dead Roots,* p. 130)

There follows a set of three sonnets. All may be characterized as outbursts of rancor coupled with both self-aggrandizement and self-contempt. Possibly it is the sonnet form that encourages attitudes of this nature, standing at once aloof and transfixed, blaming the universe for what may very well be the speaker's own fault. One thinks especially of women sonneteers in this connection—Elizabeth Barrett Browning, Edna St. Vincent Millay:

> Supremely individual, flamboyant, proud,
> insane and thirsty for a stable life,
> attacked by love's dementia, and predicaments
>   and loud
> laughter at the skyjackings, world trouble and
>   world strife . . .
>
> ("Sonnet One," *Dead Roots,* p. 133)

Sonnets Two and Three are in a similar vein. The metrical form holds in the anger. Verse of

this last period does not often degenerate into hysteria. But the hysteria is there, manifested by a tendency to look inward. There is a notable absence of regard for external detail. This is solipsism, a world of the poet's own:

> I have drunk up nights and spent the days
> in wild pursuits, life of the libertine:
> do not repent, confess, seek remedies.
> The bourgeois sinners are banned from where I've
>   been. . . .
>
> ("Sonnet Two," *Dead Roots,* p. 134)

One notices the somewhat passé nature of the diction. Expressions such as the Victorian "libertine" and Keatsian "wild pursuits" belong to a register different from that which one might believe available to a poet writing in 1970. "Sonnet Three" is no different in this aspect of matters. "I have tasted potables, edibles, all that flesh / can offer": this is a loose imitation of Byron, in spite of the restrictions of metrical form, and comes across, with all its romantic gesture, as spurious. There are two more sonnets, "Jazz Trio" and "Natural Sinner," of a similar nature.

LAST DAYS

Dispersed among the last sonnets of Nortje are a couple of what can only be called verse epistles, very loose in form, and apparently addressed to himself. They in part concern world events, which, as usual, were distressing in September 1970. These straggling invectives are couched in ill-tuned free verse, full of contemporary allusion, and at times read as though they had been directly transcribed from newspaper reports:

> Hulks of ships clog Suez,
> sandbagged bunkers on either side.
> The Red sea ports are closed.
> Jordan cannot be crossed,
> the Syrians are punished for their impunity.
> Palestine with its ragged refugees
> is won or lost, depending on who speaks the
>   word

through the barrel of whose gun.
They are still fighting in Amman.
At the Wailing Wall they have stopped
knocking their heads against the stone, a
brief respite . . .

("Nasser Is Dead," Dead Roots, p. 131)

This uncouth strain could, charitably, be characterized as cadenced verse, near to lyrical prose. It is something after the manner of Walt Whitman but essentially derives from the Authorized Version of the Bible.

These late documents are of clinical rather than poetic interest. They will tell us little of the Nortje who matters, the poet of the late South African and early London years. Sylvia Plath and, to a lesser extent, Dylan Thomas led him sadly astray. This, as one would expect, appears to be apiece with his personal life. From internal evidence one would surmise that he had difficulty in forming and maintaining relationships. The poems are redolent of insomnia and social unease. Recourse to alcohol and other drugs, mostly amphetamines, proved to be a short-term therapy. Arthur Nortje began a post-graduate program at Oxford, but shortly afterward, on 11 December 1970, took a fatal overdose of barbiturates.

His final poem is dated from Oxford, November 1970. It is called "All Hungers Pass Away." As is the case with so many of these poems, it gives the impression of having been written as an alternative to a night's sleep. In an apparent attempt to contain despair, it is phrased in quatrains. Each line is composed of three heavy stresses, but there are some metrical uncertainties that might have been rectified in further revision. Also, the control over rhyme and pararhyme is, understandably, less certain than in the past:

> All hungers pass away,
> we lose track of their dates:
> desires arise like births,
> reign for a time like potentates.
>
> I lie and listen to the rain

hours before full dawn brings
forward a further day and winter sun
here in a land where rhythm fails. . . .

(Anatomy of Dark, p. 398)

SUMMING UP

Nortje was twice exiled. He was a stranger in his native country where a person of mixed race was a second-rate citizen. He was further exiled in England, where a class system ensures that an individual without personal contacts remains an outsider. The sojourn in Canada does not seem to have helped.

Heinemann brought out a collection of Nortje's poems posthumously. Obviously it contains pieces he would not have wished to be promulgated. Some of the pieces he might have wished to include could have undergone further revision. This collection, however, hangs together with remarkable cohesion. One has a sense of the personality of this sensitive, intelligent, suffering man.

His editors chose to call the collection *Dead Roots*. This is not, perhaps, the most inviting of titles. There are poems of keen satire, of wit, of elegance, that might protest at being gathered under so life-denying an ascription. Yet there is also a certain appositeness. As said previously, this is an image that recurs through the oeuvre. Examples come readily to mind:

> . . . the heart is not a void
> but barren ground
> where roots have struggled and died. . . .

("Absence of Love," Dead Roots, p. 21)

> . . . The rat-toothed sea eats rock, and who escapes
> a lover's quarrel will never rest his roots. . . .

("Cosmos in London," Dead Roots, p. 39)

> . . . You thought she loved you but where is the evidence?

Anchors have snapped and roots are severed.

("The Near-mad," *Dead Roots*, p. 69)

. . . Origins trouble the voyager much, those roots
  that have sipped the waters of another
continent . . .

("Waiting," *Dead Roots*, p. 90)

On reflection, the generic title seems just. However, that is not the whole story. Nortje, this disaffected latest of the last romantics, will survive through those few poems that exemplify the good taste and instinctive form into which his loneliness and grief precipitated themselves. They include "Letter from Pretoria Central Prison," "At Rest from the Grim Place,"

"Autopsy" and, in a quite different vein, "Poem for a Kitchen."

There are also a number of lyrics, modest and unimpressive efforts. However, some of them retain a wayward charm, including "Separation," "September Poem," "Chelsea Picture," "Winter: Oxford," and "Hope Hotel." These are pieces one would like to come across in anthologies. Like the major poems, they have the distinctive stamp of their author's personality. Nobody but Arthur Nortje could have written them.

Note: The author wishes to thank Arthur Nortje's editor and biographer Dr. Dirk Klopper. Without his generous help, this essay would not have taken its present form.

Selected Bibliography

WORKS OF ARTHUR NORTJE

Dead Roots: Poems. London: Heinemann, 1973.

Anatomy of Dark: Collected Poems. Edited by Dirk Klopper, 2000.

"Up Late" and "At Rest from the Grim Place." In *The Penguin Book of Modern African Poetry,* 4th ed., 1998. Pp. 378–380.

SECONDARY TEXTS

Barnett, U. A. *A Vision of Order: A Study of Black South African Literature in English (1914–1980).* London: Sinclair Browne, 1983.

Chapman, M. J. F. "Arthur Nortje: Poet of Exile." *English in Africa,* 6:1 (March 1979): 60.

Berthoud, Jacques. "Poetry and Exile: The Case of Arthur Nortje." *The AUETSA Papers,* 8 July 1983. P. 1.

Dameron, C. "Arthur Nortje: Craftsman for His Muse." *Aspects of South African Literature.* Edited by C. Heywood. London: Heinemann, 1976.

Davis, H. I. "Arthur Nortje: a Forgotten South African poet." *Reality,* 11:4 (July 1979): 5.

———. "The Poetry of Arthur Nortje: Towards a New Appraisal." *UNISA English Studies,* XVIII: 2 (September 1980): 26.

Klopper, Dirk. "Politics of the Self: Exile, Identity, and Difference in the Poetry of Arthur Nortje, *The English Academy Review,* 10 (December 1993).

Leitch, R. G. "Nortje: Poet at Work." *African Literature Today,* 10 (1979). P. 224.

Oyebode, Femi. "Arthur Nortje." *The Oxford Companion to Twentieth Century Poetry.* Edited by I. Hamilton. Oxford University Press, 1994. Pp. 390–391.

Ben Okri

(1959–)

CHRISTOPHER WARNES

ON THE SECOND page of Ben Okri's first novel, *Flowers and Shadows* (1980), a short discussion takes place between the novel's teenage protagonist, Jeffia, and his friend, Ode. The topic is university education and specifically where to go to receive it. Jeffia has decided to stay in Nigeria, to be a "man of home" and "of the land," and perhaps to travel when he is older. Ode, by contrast, has already been accepted to study abroad and argues that "the greatest Africans first had to be men of the world." *Flowers and Shadows* was completed when Ben Okri was only nineteen. Its origins lie in Okri's own experience of waiting to find out if he had been accepted to study at a university in Nigeria. He was not awarded the place and studied in Britain instead, where he decided to remain. Apparent at the outset of Okri's writing career, therefore, is an opposition that will pervade his entire oeuvre. In a variety of different ways, and to different levels of complexity, Okri's poetry, short stories, and novels are preoccupied with a contrast between "home" and "the world," between Nigeria and Britain, between Africa and the West, and between the multitude of shifting concepts, traditions, and modes of expression implied by those terms.

The presence of this opposition should not surprise us. After all, the legacy of colonialism is still so pervasive in the early twenty-first century that any serious work of literature concerning Africa is almost honor-bound to address the relationship with Europe at one point or another. In a general sense, Okri's work has much in common with other African postcolonial fiction, as is clear in its relentless depiction of corruption, poverty, powerlessness, and violence. But although Okri is deeply aware of the extent to which colonialism was an invasion of Africa's social structure, he has asserted in an interview with Jane Wilkinson that colonialism did not really touch the "spiritual and aesthetic and mythic internal structures" of the continent and its people (p. 86). Much of his work, while realistically evoking Nigerian life, is directed at identifying and exploring these internal structures. It is in this respect that Okri stands out among contemporary writers, for he has managed to synthesize an evocation of what he calls the "African world view" with an exploration of form that has taken narrative prose into uncharted territory. He has not limited himself to African themes, however, and draws on a range of religious and mythological traditions, romantic ideas and ideals, social realism, and African folkloric sources in his writing. This cosmopolitan range of influences has allowed him in his later writings to demonstrate that certain "African" qualities of spirit and of perception are in fact wholly available to Westerners, a movement that has culminated in his works in an exploration of the more general condition of humanity, and an assertion of an urgently felt need for spiritual renewal.

LIFE

Okri has been unforthcoming about his personal history in interviews, stating that he prefers to integrate his memories into his fiction. Robert Fraser's 2002 memoir-cum-critical study, *Ben Okri: Towards the Invisible City*, has provided us with some detail about his life. He was born on 15 March 1959 in Minna, Nigeria, to Grace and Silver Oghenegueke Loloje Okri. Silver Okri was a lawyer, trained in England, and Ben spent several years in South London as a child, while his father was studying and supporting his family by working part-time in a launderette. By all accounts, the six-year-old Ben was reluctant to leave London, as well he might have been, for the Nigeria he returned to was on the brink of a civil war, which, through violence and starvation, cost the lives of around a million Nigerians between 1967 and 1970. This conflict is translated into fiction in several short stories, most notably "Laughter under the Bridge," in *Incidents at the Shrine* (1986) which, through the eyes of its child narrator, describes the harrowing human rights abuses carried out by the military in Nigeria during the war.

The Okris lived in one of the less affluent parts of Lagos. Through his father's work as a tenant lawyer Ben learned about the exploitation of the poor by self-serving landlords, and witnessed in the ghetto dwellers around him the resilience, imagination, and dignity that he would later celebrate in much of his fiction. Okri was spared the privations of a ghetto education by attending several boarding schools, initially the Children's Home School in Sapele, then, as

war drew nearer, Christ's High School in Ibadan and Urhobo College in Warri, memorably described in "Stars of the New Curfew," the title story of his 1988 collection. He returned to Lagos in his midteens and studied privately with the intention of taking a degree in science at a local university. During this period he read voraciously from a collection of classics his father had brought back from London. He worked in a variety of low-paid jobs, including as a clerk in a paint company, an experience later coded into fiction in much of his work, especially in his early novels. It was during this period that he began to write. At seventeen his first article was published, an indictment of the abuse of tenants by landlords in the ghetto. He continued to write articles and turned them into short stories which appeared in women's journals and evening newspapers. One of these stories became the novel *Flowers and Shadows*.

Unsuccessful in winning a place at a local university, Okri was drawn, like so many writers before and after him, to London. Arriving in 1978, with the manuscript of his first novel in his luggage, he found the reality of the New Cross section of the city far from the London of his dreams. As he later told Nicholas Shakespeare, "It was as if I hadn't travelled. The houses were boarded up. There were hundreds of rats. I was given a funny room with a broken window through which came the bright yellow light of a street-lamp. It was Nigeria in London, I thought" (quoted in Robert Fraser's *Ben Okri*, p. 37). Traces of his experiences during this period are evident in the short stories "Disparities" and "A Hidden History" in *Incidents at the Shrine* Set in London, both describe the marginal and often desperate lives led by immigrants in the metropolis.

While living in New Cross, Okri took evening classes on Afro-Caribbean literature at Goldsmiths College, and Robert Fraser tells us that it was through the encouragement of his teacher, Jane Grant, that he sent the manuscript of *Flowers and Shadows* to the publishing house of Longman, which published it in 1980. In the same year he was awarded a Nigerian government scholarship and enrolled to study literature at the University of Essex. In 1981 his second novel, *The Landscapes Within,* was published, also by Longman. The following year offered a setback, however, when Okri found that his scholarship had been withdrawn and he was forced into a period of homelessness in London. In 1983 he found work as poetry editor of the weekly magazine *West Africa,* and also freelanced for the BBC Africa service. Throughout this period he was working on his short fictions, and when in 1984 he was awarded a grant by the Arts Council of Great Britain, he began the process of composing the collection of stories *Incidents at the Shrine,* published by Heinemann in 1986. The collection was read and reviewed far more widely under the new publisher than his novels had been, and was awarded the Commonwealth Writers' Prize for Africa and the *Paris Review* Aga Khan Prize for Fiction.

The success of *Incidents at the Shrine* made it possible for Okri to become a full-time writer. In 1988 his second collection of short stories, *Stars of the New Curfew,* appeared, following which Okri began work on the novel for which he is best known, *The Famished Road.* Published in 1991, *The Famished Road* was the first novel to appear by Okri in a decade. In that time he had honed his craft through the writing of short stories, and he had begun to experiment with different modes of storytelling, developing the innovative fusion of African and Western traditions that underlies *The Famished Road.* It was to prove a successful experiment. In October 1991, shortly after accepting a two-year Fellow Commonership in Creative Arts at Trinity College, Cambridge, Okri was awarded the Booker McConnell Prize for Fiction, Britain's most prestigious literary prize. This was undoubtedly the high point of his career thus far.

Okri has found it hard to match the achievement of *The Famished Road* in later works, including the novels that with the 1991 book make up *The Famished Road* cycle. Where the title volume of the cycle held in precarious balance a folkloric, fantastic surrealism on the one hand, and a detailed documentation of life in the ghetto on the other, the novels immediately following it tended to sacrifice realism in pursuit of what can be called a universalist spiritualism. One indication of this shift in emphasis is that it becomes increasingly difficult to show links between Okri's own life experience and his created fictions. In 1992 a volume of poetry, *An African Elegy,* appeared, followed in 1993 by the second novel in *The Famished Road* cycle, *Songs of Enchantment.* Okri's fourth novel, the utopian allegory *Astonishing the Gods,* was issued in 1995. That year, he was presented with a Crystal Award by the World Economic Forum for contributions to the arts and to cross-cultural understanding.

Critical perception that Okri had moved too far away from the realism that had sustained his lyrical and epic flights of imagination in his earlier works was put to rest with the publication in 1996 of the novel *Dangerous Love.* A reworking of *The Landscapes Within, Dangerous Love* is written in a restrained realist-modernist style, and returns to the themes of forbidden love and artistic aspiration that characterized the earlier novel. In 1997 Okri published a collection of essays, *A Way of Being Free.* In the same year he was awarded an honorary doctorate by the University of Westminster and was elected vice president of the English Centre of International PEN, the writers' association. His prodigious output continued with the publication of the third part of *The Famished Road* cycle, *Infinite Riches,* in 1998, and what he called an "anti-spell for the twenty-first century," the book-length poem *Mental Fight* in 1999. In 2002 the novel *In Arcadia* appeared, inspired by the BBC television series *Great Railway Journeys,* with which Okri had been involved six years previously. General recognition has kept pace with his output: in 1998 he was elected a Fellow of the Royal Society of Literature and in 2001 he was named an officer of the Order of the British Empire (OBE). He had come a long way from his days of being homeless and hungry in London.

EARLY NOVELS AND SHORT STORIES

The two novels and two collections of short stories that Okri produced before *The Famished Road* have largely been overshadowed by the triumph of that novel. Usually read for what they tell us about the unfolding project of their author, these works also have much to recommend them on their own terms. *Flowers and Shadows* follows the pattern of the bildungsroman, tracing the evolution of an adult consciousness in its protagonist, Jeffia Okwe. Unlike Okri's later works, *Flowers and Shadows* begins in an affluent part of Lagos, and Jeffia seems to have everything going for him—money, intelligence, looks, a loving family. But by the end of the novel his father and his best friend, Ode, are dead, and Jeffia has been forced to move with his mother to a poorer part of town. The key to this change in fortunes lies with Jeffia's father, Jonan, whose wealth is revealed over the course of the novel to be the result of shady dealings. The novel reads at times like a detective story, with Jeffia learning about his father's corruption through chance meetings with Jonan's victims. Finally, Jeffia's uncle Sowho, who had been wrongfully jailed at Jonan's instigation, returns to claim revenge, and both Sowho and Jonan die in a car chase outside the Okwe home.

The processes by which Jeffia comes to understand himself are at almost every point shown to be bound up with the world of suffering, squalor, dispossession, corruption, manipulation, and exploitation that surrounds him. In this way the novel is as much a commentary on Nigeria as it is on the lives of its individual characters. It is especially through the character of Jonan that Okri makes this link clear. Nigeria, one of the world's largest producers of oil, was experiencing an oil boom in the 1970s. But endemic corruption meant that the revenue generated was squandered and the country became ever poorer. Jonan embodies this corruption, and Jeffia, by virtue of being his son and having benefited from the wealth of his father, is complicit in his father's wrongdoing.

The representation of corruption is common in African literature. Where Okri's portrayal diverges from those of his fellow writers—and where he begins to explore the themes that will dominate his later work—is through his inscription into the novel of cycles of sin and retribution. At the moment in which he is presented with incontrovertible evidence of his father's guilt, Jeffia, shocked almost to the point of madness, thinks to himself, "A son lives out the sins of a father . . . A son lives out the sins of a father" (p. 127). There is a fatalistic dimension here that is apparent elsewhere in the novel, especially in its images of death—the dog with its entrails smeared on the road, the baby beetle being devoured by ants. But equally, Jeffia understands his situation in the terms provided by the Bible, and the novel's ending confirms in almost parabolic form the importance of compassion and forgiveness. Though Okri himself is not religious in any conventional sense, the presence of a fatalistic cyclicality inflected with moral ideas drawn from religious discourse, especially about hope and love, will be a key feature of his unfolding oeuvre.

The upbeat note on which *Flowers and Shadows* ends is missing from Okri's next novel. Like James Joyce's *A Portrait of the Artist as a Young Man*, from which it takes its epigraph, *The Landscapes Within* is a *künstlerroman*, a novel about a young artist coming to terms with the relationships between his art and his surroundings. *The Landscapes Within* is an altogether bleaker novel than its predecessor. Gone are the affluent neighborhood, the wealthy father, and the loving mother of the earlier novel. Instead, our protagonist, Omovo, an aspiring young painter, lives in a ghetto of Lagos with his drunken and depressed father and his father's duplicitous new wife, Blackie. His mother has died some time previously and his two brothers both left home after a dispute with their father.

They have become sailors with little prospect of return, their only contact the occasional note or poem they send home. Omovo has a number of friends, but he does not connect with any of them in the way, for example, that Jeffia did with Ode in the earlier novel. Instead, Omovo is portrayed as solitary, lonely, and alienated by the burden of having to interpret his world through art. The only two people with whom he has any meaningful bonds are Dr. Okacha, an elderly artist who serves as something of a mentor to Omovo, and Ifeyinwa, a young married woman with whom Omovo is in love.

The Landscapes Within reads like a chronicle of Omovo's disgust, punctuated with epiphanies. As was the case with *Flowers and Shadows*, Omovo's perceptions of his surroundings cannot be separated from the wider political context of the nation in which he lives. His painting called *Drift*—an abstract rendering of a pool of filthy water outside his compound, which he calls a "scumscape"—is interpreted by those who view it as a national allegory. The painting is confiscated by the police, who see it as derisive toward the young nation of Nigeria. In the festering, stinking water even the philistine policemen can see reflections of the corruption and decay present in the country.

More than corruption, though, it is violence that is central to the novel's elicitation of disgust. The novel begins with an extract from a notebook, in which Omovo recounts a nightmare about a murdered girl. This turns out to be a premonition, for one night he and a friend find the corpse of a mutilated girl on the beach. We later learn that Ifeyinwa's father had once mistakenly killed a young girl (and then himself, out of remorse) and Ifeyinwa herself is senselessly murdered toward the end of the novel. For Omovo the relations that govern Nigerian society are essentially violent ones. "I've come to realize," Okri told Jane Wilkinson, "you can't write about Nigeria truthfully without a sense of violence. To be serene is to lie" (p. 81). To write "truthfully" is also to experience, as Omovo does, those epiphanic moments "when the landscapes without synchronised with those landscapes within" (p. 206). Through the redemptive qualities of art, hope is able to reenter an otherwise very gloomy world.

Omovo's search for an aesthetic mode appropriate to the realities of Nigeria is also Okri's. The consequences of Okri's interrogation of form are clear in the extent to which *The Landscapes Within* incorporates modernist elements of fragmentation, stream-of-consciousness narration, and surreal juxtapositions. The most chilling of these techniques is the recurrence of an unknown baby's scream that pierces the narration at unexpected moments. There is also an attempt on Okri's part to include specifically African elements in both of these early narratives, the most obvious sign of which can be seen in his characters' use of pidgin. But apart from his incorporation into his text of the language of Lagos's streets, Okri does not get very far in "Africanizing" the mode of his narration. Given that in Nigeria, as in most parts of Africa, ritual, religious, and secular values live side by side, it would seem that, in his quest to find ever more truthful ways of describing the realities of Nigeria, Okri would need to make a place for ritual, myth, and folklore.

The key to understanding the shift between Okri's realistic early novels and the mythic mode he explored in his later fictions can be found in a review he wrote of Amos Tutuola's 1981 novel *The Witch Herbalist of the Remote Town*, for the journal *West Africa*: "Amos Tutuola is a writer who straddles twilights. His fictional world is a haunting terrain; the quests he describes demand from his protagonists the necessities of energy and imagination. . . . *The Witch Herbalist of the Remote Town* is a fascinating and thoroughly enjoyable book. One which I suspect will provide generations of artists with inspiration" (pp. 429–430). Okri is one of those artists inspired by Tutuola, and it is no exaggeration to say that his writing career only took off when he found ways of fusing the lessons he learned from such Western literary masters as Charles Dickens and James Joyce with the influence of his countryman's extraordinary fictions. Writing from the cultural and geographical distance of London, this process initially took the form of a rediscovery of roots, most graphically illustrated in the title story of *Incidents at the Shrine.*

The story begins in the city, with a museum-employee protagonist, Anderson, losing his job to a distant relation of his supervisor. Clearly, Anderson's youthful anxiety, his lowly job, and the presence of nepotism are located in the same narrative terrain as the early novels. After dreaming of his dead parents, and later nearly dying in a fire, Anderson leaves the city to return to his village. Before he gets there he is accosted by three entities identified only as "rough forms," who chase him and cause him to drop the objects he had brought "to show his people that he wasn't entirely a small man in the world" (p. 56). "Incidents at the Shrine," like much of Okri's work, lends itself to study in terms of the work that anthropologists like Victor Turner have done on ritual and liminality, and that which Mary Douglas has done on purification. Thus, the rough forms initiate Anderson into a reality very different from that of the materialistic city. They are both the custodians of the boundary between city and village and symbols of the state of being between boundaries in general. In the village, Anderson will undergo a number of rituals that will purify him and return him to a relationship with his ancestral home.

The crucial moment in Anderson's initiation into the secrets of the shrine comes as his head is forced through a small oiled hole in a door. At first he sees nothing, but gradually, through the pain, he makes out a woman "painted over in native chalk" who is trying to open each of three doors in a gigantic tree. As she opens the third door, Anderson "finally came through" with a crash, though he immediately loses consciousness (pp. 62–63). We are not told what the exact significance of this ritual is—indeed, the story maintains an esoteric silence about its processes of ritual throughout. What can be ascertained,

however, is that Okri derives the symbol of the tree with a magical interior from Amos Tutuola, especially from Tutuola's 1952 novel *The Palm-Wine Drinkard and His Dead Palm-Wine Tapster in the Dead's Town.* "Incidents at the Shrine" begins to develop a Tutuolan sense of spatial and temporal distortion that will be integral to Okri's future fictions.

Okri's next collection of stories, *Stars of the New Curfew,* published two years after *Incidents at the Shrine,* continues to use Tutuolan ideas as a way of exploring issues related to identity, though it is darker in its mood. The pessimism of the later collection, its grotesqueries and its violence, are perhaps the consequence of a visit that Okri made to Nigeria in 1985, when he witnessed the impact of Major General Ibrahim Babangida's recently installed military government. "Worlds That Flourish," for example, has much in common with "Incidents at the Shrine." Both stories tell of a city dweller who journeys back to his rural village after losing his job. But where Anderson's sacking was the consequence of nepotism, the narrator of "Worlds That Flourish" loses his job because he refuses to give his name to a mysterious inquisitor (he remains unnamed to the reader also). This emphasis on naming reminds us of Okri's earlier civil war story, "Laughter under the Bridge," in which speaking the wrong language was grounds for instant execution. Like language, names are indicators of ethnicity, and "Worlds That Flourish" is clearly located in the apocalyptic context of war. The narrator, harassed by thieves, betrayed by his neighbor, and wrongfully arrested for a robbery in which he was the victim, gets into his car and flees an uncannily deserted city. While refueling at a "petrol shack," an old man warns him not to continue. He disregards the warning and shortly thereafter crashes his car into an anthill. He extricates himself from the wreck and continues into the forest, finally arriving at a village.

Unlike Anderson's village, which, apart from its "rough forms" and its sacred shrine house, was nevertheless a real, stable place, the village in "Worlds That Flourish" is thoroughly disorientating and phantasmagoric. Skyscrapers sit alongside huts, some people's feet face backwards, others have wings or three legs and elongated necks. The motif of the magical tree reappears, as the narrator is led by a woman whose skin, like the priestess of "Incidents at the Shrine," is "covered with native chalk" (p. 29) through a door in an *obeche* tree into a spacious and comfortable home. The key to understanding the bizarre nature of this village is provided when the narrator meets his neighbor and learns that the man has been killed by soldiers. Later he comes across his own dead wife, screaming and in great distress. It seems that he is in a town of ghosts, modeled on one of the "Dead's Towns" of Tutuola's *The Palm-Wine Drinkard* and *My Life in the Bush of Ghosts.* In terror, realizing that the "meeting" he keeps being told about will secure his status as "dead," the narrator flees the village and returns to his wrecked car. The story's ending is deliberately ambiguous about whether he will succeed in his attempt to escape death.

In "Worlds That Flourish," the narrator's return to his village constitutes not so much a return to lost origins, but a test of his ability to see beyond the levels of everyday reality. In the city, his neighbor had reprimanded and even betrayed him to the police because—and the point is repeated three times—he doesn't use his eyes. When he reaches the village, he tells us that "slowly my sight returned. At first it was like seeing through milk. When my vision cleared, the voices stopped. Then I saw the village as I had not seen it before" (p. 28). The woman looking after the narrator asks him, "So you can see now?" and he replies, "Yes." The obsession with eyes is found on almost every page—goats, dogs, and chickens stare at the narrator with the eyes of people, a statue of a god has holes for eyes but still "spies" on the narrator, the dead neighbor has three eyes. This emphasis on eyes and seeing is one that will recur throughout *The Famished Road,* and serves to draw attention to

the processes by which our seeing (and not seeing) constructs our sense of reality and of the world.

At the end of "Incidents at the Shrine" Anderson is told by his uncle, the "Image-maker," to return to the city, to collect what he is owed and to find another job. Having reconnected with his roots, with tradition, he is now equipped to live in that locus of modernity, the city. As he crosses the village boundary he is once again approached by the rough forms, but this time they merely paw at him, "as though he had become allied with them in some way" (p. 66). If the rough forms are symbols of a condition of living in between city and village, then their alliance with Anderson suggests that he carries this condition with him as he leaves the village. The narrator of "Worlds That Flourish," like Anderson, does not stay in the village. For him, mangled as he is as a result of the car accident, there will be no hopeful return to life in the city, but it is significant that his experiences in the village have taken place in a zone between life and death. He shares Anderson's quality of not being located in any definite space.

In this "in betweenness" lies the important difference between Okri's use of folklore and that of Tutuola (and others including the Yoruba writer D. O. Fagunwa). Okri's audience is primarily Western. Where the traditional folktale often serves to enforce certain kinds of behavior and to deter others, Okri translates this cautionary element into an illumination of Africanness understood not so much as an essential identity but as a way of perceiving the world. Much of the grotesquerie of his early work is, like that of Tutuola, aimed at instilling a sense of anxiety or confusion. But it does this not in order to reinforce a traditional morality but for the very different purpose of deliberately transgressing the fixed boundaries typical of Western worldviews. Tutuola's world is peopled with folkloric heroes and is marked by clear demarcations between, for example, town and bush. Okri's writing, by contrast, gestures toward a fusion of "Africa" and "Europe," tradition and modernity, the folkloric and the realist. Nowhere is this project more visible or more successfully realized than in Okri's most famous work, the novel that immediately followed the two collections of short stories.

THE FAMISHED ROAD CYCLE

Although most critics would agree with Robert Bennett when he calls *The Famished Road* "a literary tour de force that will soon become a classic of twentieth century fiction" (p. 368), the exact meaning and significance of Okri's Booker Prize–winning novel has proved difficult to pin down. One of the most important concerns facing critics is the question of where to locate the novelistic cycle—which includes *The Famished Road, Songs of Enchantment,* and *Infinite Riches*—in terms of existing narrative traditions. Three options present themselves: the novels have been read as heir to a tradition of Nigerian writing of which Fagunwa, Tutuola, and Wole Soyinka are the most significant exemplars; as part of a trend toward a postcolonial postmodernism visible in the work of other contemporary West African writers such as Kojo Laing, Syl Cheney-Coker, Sony Labou Tansi, and Biyi Bandele-Thomas; and as sharing commonalities with the projects of a global set of writers who engage nonrealist narrative strategies, especially magical realism, in their writings.

The first two of these options point in a general way toward African culture, mythologies, and literature as the most appropriate markers by which to chart one's responses to the novel. The third option emphasizes those places where Okri's narrative has similarities with the literature, ideas, and cultural products of the wider world. These options are not exclusive. From the biblical refrain "In the beginning" that opens *The Famished Road,* it is clear that "Afrocentric" approaches will have to account for the extent to which Okri frequently draws his ideas from non-African sources. On the other hand, approaches that do not acknowledge the literary

and cultural legacy of Nigeria in Okri's narrative impoverish themselves by this silence, and, more importantly, run the risk of reinforcing a potentially offensive cultural bias toward European norms and expectations. *The Famished Road* cycle's great achievement lies precisely in its ability to escape "either/or" logic. It is able to be both "African" and "Western," and a lot more besides.

Although there are important differences between the three novels in the cycle, all are narrated by an *abiku* or spirit child called Azaro, all are set at roughly the same time in his life and concern his relationships with parents, community, and his country, an African state on the brink of independence. *Abiku* are babies that die shortly after birth then return to their mother's womb, only to die again. The *abiku* myth, which is also present in a similar form among West African peoples other than the Yoruba, is clearly related to the high incidence of infant mortality in West Africa. It is common in the literature of the region, appearing in works by writers as different as Chinua Achebe, Soyinka, and Tutuola. Okri takes the concept into new territory, however, for his *abiku,* Azaro, has made the choice to stay in the world. For this choice he is tormented by his spirit companions who continually try to tempt him to leave the world and rejoin them.

The critical interpretations of *The Famished Road* that are most successful in unlocking the novel's secrets are those which, taking the dual nature of the *abiku* as a starting point, develop a distinction between the novel's real, tangible, material dimensions and its surreal, fantastic, esoteric aspects. Of course, such a distinction works only from the vantage point of literary criticism. Within the novel itself, boundaries of all kinds are continually blurred. Nevertheless, it is possible—and perhaps essential—for literary criticism to identify the natures of these two poles before allowing the novel to demolish them altogether. A mythic dimension is apparent in the novel's opening paragraph, which amalgamates Christian ideas about paradise with

Greek myth in order to evoke the "land of beginnings," where "spirits mingled with the unborn" (p. 3), where "tender sibyls" and "benign sprites" float on the "aquamarine air of love" (p. 4). These ideas are then fused to the Yoruba *abiku* myth, which is in turn rewritten through emphasizing its similarities with myths of reincarnation. The most important aspect of the novel's mythic, esoteric side is its use of metamorphosis, understood as a constant, unstable shifting of form and identity that depends on processes of return and recurrence that are never resolved in the novel.

On the other hand, the domain of "the living" is largely represented in a manner similar to that of Okri's early novels. The realistic dimensions of Okri's characters can quite clearly be sketched: Azaro is a boy of around seven years of age who lives with his parents, attends a school that is never described, plays with other children, and has a tendency to wander off on his own. His father, physically powerful and outspoken, earns a tenuous living as a carrier of loads, and occasionally as a night soil, or sewage removal, man. Azaro's mother is a trader of wares. The three share a strong bond of love, although outbreaks of domestic violence are not uncommon. Outside Azaro's family, Madame Koto is the novel's most significant character. She establishes a bar, selling first palm wine, then beer and pepper soup, and the increase in her wealth and status coincides with her courting of powerful politicians. The geography of the realistic dimension of the novel can also be readily mapped: key spaces are the room in which Azaro and his parents live, the compound, the road outside the compound, the bar, the paths and roads that lead into the forest, as well as the forest itself, and the marketplace. Though never specified, it is reasonable to guess that the country is Nigeria and that the city on whose outskirts the novel is set is Lagos. Chronologically, a number of references locate the narrative in the run-up to Nigeria's postindependence elections. The realistic aspect of the novel thus seeks to document the life of the poor in the ghetto of this African city—their struggles against their neighbors, landlords, employers, and politicians, and the encroachments of modernity on their lives.

To a greater or lesser degree, every one of these realistic components carries within it a supernatural charge. Azaro is simultaneously a young child of the ghetto and a spirit child. Dad, a worker, a family man, a resident of the compound, is simultaneously "Black Tyger," a fighting hero of mythical status who defeats ghosts and can make lightning flash from his fist. He becomes a spokesman against spiritual as well as material poverty. Mum, significantly, is the character in the novel who least obviously carries within her a supernatural aspect. In fact, Mum's sorties into the supernatural, whether they take the form of journeys, prayers, or cautionary folktales, are always intended to rescue either Azaro or Dad from dreams or spiritual entrapment—to bring them back to the domain of the living. From the outset it is suggested that Azaro's desire to "make happy the bruised face of the woman who would become my mother" (p. 5) is what causes him to rebel against the cyclicality of birth and death to which he, as an *abiku*, is prone. At the other end of *The Famished Road*, on its last page, Mum can again be seen to be an antidote to the supernatural and to constant transformation: "We have been hungry and full of fear," she tells her husband. "In the morning resume work. Resume your struggles. Be what you are" (p. 500). Madame Koto, like Dad, is also the bearer of a double load of signification. On the one hand, she is a successful entrepreneur; on the other, she is constantly identified with witchcraft. This duality manifests itself in an ambivalence that progressively tilts into stereotype, especially in *Songs of Enchantment*.

Ato Quayson has addressed the difference between the natural and the supernatural dimensions of the novel in terms of a "reality-esoteric axis" (1997, p. 134). It is useful to consider the actions, speech, and presence of a character, or the particular meaning of a place or object in terms of this axis. Many spaces—especially the road, the bar, the forest, and the marketplace—are represented in a realistic fashion and then are "supernaturalized." Although this strategy is not as clear with regard to the representation of the passing of time in the novel, it is still possible to identify the poles on the reality-esoteric axis on which this representation takes place. For example, when Azaro, in a rare moment of standing back from his experience in order to analyze it, notices how the landscape around him is changing, he formulates the change in terms of conventional units of time: "Steadily, over days and months, the paths had been widening" (p. 104). At the other end of the reality-esoteric axis we encounter a very different idea of time: "As I kept watch I perceived, in the crack of a moment, the recurrence of things unresolved—histories, dreams, a vanished world of great old spirits, wild jungles, tigers with eyes of diamonds roaming the dense foliage" (p. 176). As the moment "cracks," it reveals a deeper level of meaning, which has been concealed by concepts like "days" and "months." It appears that Okri is suggesting that behind the apparent reality of linear conventional time lies a mythical time of return, recurrence, and cyclicality.

The problem with Quayson's reality-esoteric axis is that the reader can never be entirely certain of where an object, character, space, or moment registers on it at any given point in the narrative. As he falls asleep one evening, Azaro hears "the air whispering, the walls talking, the chair complaining, the floor pacing, the insects gossiping" (p. 21). Characteristically, any of the following might mean either a literal object or one filled with the supernatural: trees, the forest, stones, lizards, dragonflies, dogs, sunlight, rain, a motorcar, politics, fires, sneezing, illness, rats, chickens. We are warned early on that "one world contains glimpses of others" (p. 10). Within the novel's realistic sides, then, are a variety of narrative shifts and distortions that undermine any attempts to place too fine a definition on what is real and what is not. On the other hand, within the novel's esoteric

dimension, it is also very difficult to separate out dreams, hallucinations, and spiritual reality from one another.

In order to understand better the purpose behind these narrative processes, we need to look to the comments Okri has made about his own writing. In an interview with Jean W. Ross in 1991, Okri rejects labels like surrealism, fantasy, and magical realism, stating that he is not trying to generate any "strange effects" in his writing, but is "simply writing about the place [Nigeria] in the tone and the spirit of the place" (p. 337):

> I'm looking at the world in *The Famished Road* from the inside of the African world view, but without it being codified as such. This is just the way the world is seen: the dead are not really dead, the ancestors are still part of the living community and there are innumerable gradations of reality, and so on. It's quite simple and straightforward. I'm treating it naturally. It's a kind of realism, but a realism with many more dimensions.
>
> (pp. 337–338)

Revealing though this response is, Okri's comments should not be taken at face value. We have already seen how he draws his inspiration from a range of sources, by no means all of which are authentically "African" in any meaningful sense. Even those aspects of *The Famished Road* that do derive from Yoruba myth and folklore come to the novel more through the influence of Tutuola than through any direct connection with "Africanness." Okri's comments presume a certain kind of relationship between art and reality in which a novel—a contrived, complex work of modern art—has the capacity directly and truthfully to embody the "world view" of millions of people living on the continent of Africa. Nevertheless, Okri's comments do help us to understand several aspects of the novels in *The Famished Road* cycle. Most importantly, they alert us to the fact that the realistic and the fantastic dimensions of the novels must be taken as equal in status to one another. Secondly, the concern with interpreting Africa to the West is clearly a project close to Okri's heart. Thirdly, his belief in the role that art can play in understanding culture and the world in general will be a key theme in all of his subsequent writings.

Written during his stay at Trinity College, Cambridge, between 1991 and 1993, *Songs of Enchantment* strives to transfer Okri's insights about the African worldview into more overtly cultural and political terms. One of the ways in which we see this process taking place is through the loose use of the first-person plural in the later novel. No longer does "we" mean just Azaro's family, or the inhabitants of the compound, the road, or even the city. Okri is striving in his use of a plural narrator to evoke a sense of communality. "We" therefore comes to mean all Africans, as it does in the 1973 work *Two Thousand Seasons* by the Ghanaian Ayi Kwei Armah, a novel that clearly influenced *Songs of Enchantment*. On one of his nightly wanderings, Azaro sees his father and his neighbors standing stiff and still in the road. They are transfixed, unable to move, and it occurs to Azaro that this condition is akin to a living death. Suddenly "a great thing heaved in the numbness of [his] mind," and he witnesses a procession of "old souls who had been reborn many times in the magical depths of the continent, and who had lived the undiscovered secrets and mysteries of The African Way" (p. 159). This image of regeneration is based on the version of "the way" that appears in Armah's novel, and gestures toward the lost values that, when rediscovered, will awaken a new age for Africans.

As was the case with Anderson's journey in "Incidents at the Shrine," "The African Way" appears at first glance to point backward to the purity of forgotten African origins. There are differences between Armah's and Okri's "African ways," however. Armah's way means accepting the lessons of reciprocity. Okri's, by contrast, is many things: compassion, fire, serenity, freedom, power, imagination, open-mindedness, the ability to communicate with

humans, animals, and the divine, and openness to transformation. In fact, the African Way in *Songs of Enchantment* encompasses so many romantic notions that it ceases to be nostalgic and becomes a utopian vision of the future. Utopian elements had been present in *The Famished Road*, but there they either appeared in the context of the otherworldly paradise of the spirit children or were confined to Dad's punch-drunk ravings. In *Songs of Enchantment*, such ideals are woven into the very fabric of the novel by means of the communal narration. One important consequence of this process is that Okri's vision rapidly becomes too general to hold only for Africans, and in the works that follow *Songs of Enchantment*, Okri will aspire to take as his audience all of humanity in suggesting ways forward.

By contrast with the rapturous response that greeted *The Famished Road*, critical opinion about *Songs of Enchantment* has been largely negative. Michael Gorra has accused Okri's narrative of lacking "a sense of purposeful form and structure," claiming that "these characters are so permanently on the verge of crisis that the reader stops believing in it" (p. 24). Ato Quayson has pointed out that "unlike the earlier novel, we are from the first never left in doubt that this is a clear-cut war between Good and Evil, represented by the Black Tyger on the one hand and Madame Koto and the Jackal-headed Masquerade on the other. . . . From the start of the novel we know exactly what is going to happen and nothing surprises us" (2000, p. 100). Possibly the most damning critique has come from Brenda Cooper, who argues that "what read as exuberant, busy and kinetic, even to a fault in *The Famished Road* becomes, when repeated in *Songs of Enchantment*, a paradoxical stillness, a fiction trapped in the labyrinth of its own formula, and in a far more reactionary politics" (p. 111). For Cooper, the most obvious symbol of what she sees as Okri's conservatism can be found in his portrayal of women. The ambivalence that characterized Madame Koto in the earlier novel has given way to "male terror of female power" in the sequel. Women's bodies are used as symbols of the nation's illness, and women are cast only as wild "Amazons" or as "priestesses, as the custodians of traditional values and knowledge" (p. 112).

The third novel in the cycle, *Infinite Riches*, published in 1998, largely avoids those aspects of *Songs of Enchantment* denigrated by critics. Madame Koto, absent from the first half of the novel and assassinated shortly after her return, is again presented with the kind of fearful, admiring ambiguity that characterized her portrayal in *The Famished Road*. In fact, we are made aware that it is through the public manufacturing of myth and legend about her that her real self has been distorted out of recognition. Not only does *Infinite Riches* avoid the destructive portrayal of women visible in *Songs of Enchantment*, it could be said to include a feminist perspective. When Dad is wrongfully arrested for the murder of a carpenter, it is Mum and a host of women who storm the police stations to free him. Dad is largely silent in this novel, and he and Mum experiment with gender role reversal throughout. When Azaro is struck by a tree felled by greedy woodcutters, it is Mum who rails against deforestation. There is a strongly felt ecological perspective to *Infinite Riches*, and through the regular meetings Mum has with a group known as "the seven women," Okri comes as close to giving us an image of constructive political mobilization as we will find in his work.

Infinite Riches is, however, so different from its predecessors in the *The Famished Road* cycle as scarcely to merit being considered part of a novelistic cycle. The difference is most visible with regard to the narrative role played by Azaro. In Azaro's suggestive reference to "strange children who are half human, one quarter spirit, and one quarter dream" who are able to see "the indecipherable powers resident on earth in ordinary or invisible forms" (p. 111), we can begin to see the shift that has taken place in Okri's narrative position and focus. Where *The Famished Road* was meticulous about limit-ing itself to Azaro's perspective—a limitation that was counterbalanced by the fact that, as an *abiku*, Azaro's experiences took place on a number of different planes of reality—*Infinite Riches* refuses to limit itself in such a way. The novel is in fact only nominally narrated by Azaro, who is so able to move in dreams into the consciousness of nearly every other character in the novel, from Dad to the British governor-general, that the novel may as well have been written in the third person. Inevitably, this shift between a tightly controlled child's perspective and an omniscient, erudite, knowing gaze is accompanied by technical lapses. It is very hard to take Azaro's astonishment at a telephone or a wristwatch seriously when he is also capable of describing the governor-general's attempts to incorporate the writings of Lord Byron into his memoirs. The central problem confronting Okri in *Infinite Riches* is that his own romantic conception of redemption through art is difficult to reconcile with the technical features that made *The Famished Road* a success.

That extra "one quarter dream" that has been added to Azaro's perspective has given Okri the opportunity to turn *The Famished Road* cycle away from its concern with the African world-view and toward deciphering the hidden powers of the world as a whole. In *Infinite Riches* we can see many of the elements of Okri's earlier work: frustration at corruption and violence, the need for rituals of purification, the emphasis on seeing beyond surface reality, utopianism, elements of religious discourse and romantic notions of art, all translated into a vision that directs itself at understanding and improving the spiritual condition of humanity as a whole. The tendency toward developing universal allegorical symbols of regeneration for humankind becomes far clearer in other writings produced by Okri in the last half of the 1990s and the first years of the twenty-first century.

UTOPIAN WRITINGS

Utopian elements are at their most distilled in Okri's allegorical *Astonishing the Gods*, published in 1995, and in his 1999 book-length poem *Mental Fight*. *Astonishing the Gods* has attracted both high praise and sceptical denunciation. Given Okri's continuing exploration of utopian ideas in his later work, it seems reasonable to speculate that these poles will continue to characterize critical response to his work. The novel features a nameless protagonist who, having discovered that he is invisible, sets out to travel the world in search of visibility. He arrives in a strange, haunting, beautiful island city, complete with Renaissance architecture and the scent of ripening mangoes in the street. With the assistance of three guides, a man, a child, and a woman, the quester undergoes several trials and learning experiences. He learns, for example, that "what you think is what becomes real" (p. 46); that "if you use more than you know that you know, the world will be as paradise" (p. 51); and that "a great law guides the rise and fall of things" (p. 53). Ultimately, he learns the value of silence and of those things that are hidden. Having set out to become visible, he finds "a higher invisibility, the invisibility of the blessed" (p. 159).

To Robert Fraser, *Astonishing the Gods* represents nothing less than "a rethinking of the whole process of interpretation" (p. 85). Fraser links Okri's distrust of names and naming—a distrust that has its roots in the fact that names are markers of ethnicity, and therefore, in the context of the Nigerian civil war, provided a basis for murder—with the "critique of hermeneutics" he finds in this novel. The first voice that the protagonist meets tells him, "We don't believe in names. Names have a way of making things disappear" (p. 6). Later we are told, "When you make sense of something, it tends to disappear. It is only mystery which keeps things alive" (p. 30). Universities are "places where people sat and meditated and absorbed knowledge from the silence" (p. 66). Fraser finds in such assertions evidence for "a heuristic science through which each individual interprets the world uniquely" (p. 86). He goes on to suggest that *Astonishing the Gods* allegorizes the

question of identity. To the extent that "invisibility" is translated from a symbol of oppression into one of enlightenment, this interpretation could be broadened to serve as a metaphor for Okri's work, the way he sees his own life, and his political position.

Other critics have been less generous. Alev Adil, for example, criticizes the style of the novel, claiming that "the journey towards understanding is rather a pompous and obscurantist expedition which continually assures us that hidden behind each elliptical fog of hyperbole there lies the most perfectly constructed vision of harmony" (p. 23). For Adil, the loss of the realism that formed such an important part of *The Famished Road* is to be lamented: "The trouble with Okri's castles in the air is that he writes air well but he doesn't seem moved to write the castles." Finally, Adil sees in *Astonishing the Gods* evidence for a Christian logic that perfection is only achieved through pain, "a message more likely to depress than to astonish" (p. 23). The fact that so few commentators have followed either Fraser's or Adil's lines of criticism is perhaps evidence in itself that Okri's idealistic, apparently antirational approach in *Astonishing the Gods* has proved alienating to most critics. On the other hand, the general popularity of his utopian writings probably derives from their promise of healing and spiritual succor, a promise that depends on the reader moving beyond or outside the language of rationalism.

The connections between *Astonishing the Gods* and Okri's long poem *Mental Fight* are advertised in the last lines of the poem itself:

We can still astonish the gods in humanity . . .
If we but dare to be real,
And have the courage to see
That this is the time to dream
The best dream of them all.

Mental Fight takes its title from William Blake's dream of building a perfect "Jerusalem" in "England's green & pleasant Land." Like

Blake, Okri's grand concern is with the liberation of humanity and the creation of new, humane ways of relating. As mentioned, *Mental Fight* announces itself as "an anti-spell for the twenty-first century." Two sections of the poem were published in the *Times* (London) in January of 1999 and the poem as a whole appeared later that year. At a time of general apprehension and anxiety about the meaning of the millennium, Okri attempts to conjure through his poem a "new world civilisation" (p. 38). The phrase "New Age" recurs throughout the poem, which is dedicated "To Humanity in the Aquarian Age." *Mental Fight* should thus be read both as the culmination of a personal writerly trajectory toward ever more utopian ideals, and as part of the Western cultural phenomenon of New Ageism as it has been studied by, for example, Paul Heelas in his 1996 book *New Age Movement: The Celebration of the Self and the Sacralization of Modernity.*

The New Age brand of utopianism to be found in *Astonishing the Gods* and *Mental Fight* can be contrasted with a subtler, romantic variety to be found in the essays collected in Okri's *A Way of Being Free* and in his 2002 novel, *In Arcadia.* The essays show us another side of Okri's writerly personality and display the workings of a mind engaged with its world, constantly seeking the transformative potential of the everyday. Once again we are in the presence of Okri's dual preoccupation with art and with the conditions that will bring about, as he states in the essay "Redreaming the World," "the first truly universal civilisation in the history of recorded and unrecorded time" (p. 133). In Okri's profoundly romantic view of art, these two preoccupations are, of course, bound up in one another. In "While the World Sleeps," for example, Okri draws on Percy Bysshe Shelley's *Defence of Poetry* to develop a distinction between the "unacknowledged legislators of the world," who "dislike mysteries" (p. 4) and who are "the enemies of poets," and poets themselves, who "remake the world in words" (p. 3). In "Beyond Words," Okri virtually paraphrases

the German Romantic poet and philosopher Novalis when he tells us, "We should keep trying to raise higher the conditions and possibilities of this world" (p. 95).

Okri's essays are at their best when he engages with particular works of art and literature. His comments on race in *Othello* in the essay "Leaping Out of Shakespeare's Terror," for example, represent a significant addition to critical understandings of the play. Similarly, his brief comments on Pablo Picasso's *Minotauromachy* in "Creativity and the Minotaur" contain profound insights into the nature of that etching and of art in general. It is within this context that Okri's novel *In Arcadia* should be read.

In Arcadia, inspired by Okri's experience of making a documentary for the BBC in 1996, traces the journey of a team of six filmmakers from London to Greece in search of the mythical Arcadia. Each of the six is struggling with issues in their personal lives: professional failure, bereavement, financial problems, divorce. Each is therefore presented as in need of the kind of hope that a utopian ideal might present. The journey is fraught with difficulties, not the least of which is that a mysterious personage called Malasso keeps appearing to plague the characters, who seem perpetually on the verge of nervous breakdowns or suicide, with ominous notes. The novel is only superficially concerned with the literal journey of the characters, however, as is clear in the fact that the crew has not even made it out of France by the closing pages. In fact, the journey and the characters are mere pegs on which Okri hangs his speculations about life and death, the nature of modernity, and the role of art in elevating human consciousness.

Arcadia, at least since Virgil, has provided the supreme image of the pastoral idyll. In Okri's view, the dream of Arcadia contains the possibility of healing, wholeness, and happiness. It serves as an antidote to the alienation and disillusionment of modern life. Once again, as in every work by Okri since "Worlds That Flourish," the impetus in *In Arcadia* is toward moving beyond our habitual and limited ways of perceiving the world. The processes by which Arcadia comes to be meaningful depend on a realization that "the world is not all we see . . . the world is an invention of our senses" (p. 68). Arcadia is not so much a geographical place, but an ideal location where thoughts are not separate from reality. The action of the novel culminates, therefore, not in the mountains of Greece, as one might expect, but in a visit to the Louvre in Paris to see Nicolas Poussin's painting *Les bergers d'Arcadie* (Shepherds of Arcadia). And it is not the actual painting that the crew encounters. It is "themselves and their unclear and enigmatic place in the universe, within the shining sphere of life" (p. 202). For Okri, the key to the painting's value and meaning—and hence also the novel's—is the insight that "Death too has been in Arcadia. . . . Death lives concurrent with life; the two streams flow side by side, and sometimes intersect. . . . Immortality and death are conjoined. Beauty and death are linked, happiness and death are coupled" (pp. 205–206). These are familiar themes for Okri, but the artistic frame from which they emerge is entirely new in his novels, if not in his essays.

CONCLUSION

The Famished Road stands out as Okri's masterpiece for good reason. The dazzling array of the novel's rhetorical devices, its uncanny ability to mingle surprise with what seems almost tragically preordained, its hypnotically repetitive, cyclical rhythms, and its evocation of hope and love in the midst of extreme deprivation have all ensured that this novel is likely to be read and reread for a long time to come. In understanding a novel as challenging as this, the more informed the reader is, the more rewarding will be the reading experience. Critics including Quayson have sought to locate Okri's narrative in terms of the Yoruba traditions evident in the work of Tutuola and Soyinka. More recently, Robert Fraser has provided the kind of biographical reading that is useful in understanding Okri's historical and personal contexts. Other critical approaches likely to prove fruitful in the future include ones that take a more comparative outlook and seek to explore the links between Okri's narrative projects and those that have emerged in other parts of the world, especially Latin America.

It is unfortunate that *The Famished Road* has tended to overshadow Okri's other achievements, not only because Okri's early novels are accomplished, significant works or because his short stories compare favorably with the best of the genre, but also because these works illuminate the artistry of *The Famished Road* itself. Okri's works that have followed *The Famished Road* can also contribute to our understandings of, for example, the role that romantic and New Age ideas play in what appears to be an otherwise very African novel. Critics of Okri's later work have objected that there is too much "tell" and not enough "show" in his fictions, and have also lamented the movement away from Africa that has coincided with a movement away from a realistic engagement with the materiality of the world. This process is apparent in *In Arcadia,* which seems to confirm an apparent turn toward thoroughly Western concerns.

Okri's concerns in *In Arcadia* are, however, with the nature of mortality, a universal topic if ever there was one. His contribution can once again be seen to lie in his ability to synthesize Western and African approaches, and in so doing to provide a refreshing perspective on well-worn questions about life and death. *In Arcadia* is implicitly underpinned by Okri's insight in his essay "Amongst the Silent Stones" (in *A Way of Being Free*) that "those who forget death forget how to live. The African world, by opening life into death, by drawing death over the living spaces, gave life more space in which to live, to celebrate, to bear suffering, and to be joyful" (p. 99). Okri's talent has been to show how the perspectives of this "African world" are present—though perhaps forgotten—at the very heart of what is usually thought of as Western.

Selected Bibliography

WORKS OF BEN OKRI

NOVELS

Flowers and Shadows. Harlow, U.K.: Longman, 1980.

The Landscapes Within. Harlow, U.K.: Longman, 1981.

The Famished Road. London: Jonathan Cape, 1991; New York: Nan A. Talese, 1992; New York: Anchor Books, 1993.

Songs of Enchantment. London: Jonathan Cape, 1993; New York: Nan A. Talese, 1993; New York: Anchor Books, 1994.

Astonishing the Gods. London: Phoenix House, 1995.

Dangerous Love. London: Phoenix House, 1996.

Infinite Riches. London: Phoenix House, 1998.

In Arcadia. London: Phoenix House, 2002.

SHORT STORIES

Incidents at the Shrine. London: Heinemann, 1986.

Stars of the New Curfew. London: Secker and Warburg, 1988.

POETRY

An African Elegy. London: Jonathan Cape, 1992.

Mental Fight: An Anti-Spell for the Twenty-first Century. London: Phoenix House, 1999.

ESSAYS

Birds of Heaven. London: Phoenix House, 1996. (Booklet of speeches and essays).

A Way of Being Free. London: Phoenix House, 1997.

OTHER WORKS

Review of Amos Tutuola's *The Witch Herbalist of the Remote Town.* *West Africa* (14 February 1983): 429–30.

"Soyinka: A Personal View." *West Africa* (27 October 1986): 2249–50.

INTERVIEWS

Ross, Jean. "*Contemporary Authors* Interview with Ben Okri." In *Contemporary Authors,* Vol 138. Edited Donna Olendorf. Detroit: Gale Research, 1993. Pp. 337–341.

Shakespeare, Nicholas. "Fantasies Born in the Ghetto." *The Times* (24 July 1986): 23.

Wilkinson, Jane, ed. *Talking with African Writers: Interviews with African Poets, Playwrights, and Novelists.* London: J. Currey ; Portsmouth, N.H.: Heinemann, 1992.

CRITICAL STUDIES

Adil, Alev, "More Narnian than Olympian." *Times Literary Supplement* (10 March 1995). Review of *Astonishing the Gods.*

Appiah, Kwame Anthony. "Spiritual Realism." *Nation* 255.4 (August 1992): 146–148. Review of *The Famished Road.*

Bennett, Robert. "Ben Okri." In *Postcolonial African Writers: A Bio-bibliographical Sourcebook.* Edited by Pushpa Naidu Parekh and Siga Fatima Jagne. Westport, Conn.: Greenwood Press, 1998.

Cezair-Thompson, Margaret. "Beyond the Postcolonial Novel: Ben Okri's *The Famished Road* and Its '*Abiku*' Traveller." *Journal of Commonwealth Literature* 31, no. 2 (1996).

Cooper, Brenda. *Magical Realism in West African Fiction: Seeing with a Third Eye.* London and New York: Routledge, 1998.

Cribb, T.J. "Transformations in the Fiction of Ben Okri," in *From Commonwealth to Postcolonial.* Edited by Anna Rutherford. Sydney: Dangaroo Press, 1992.

Fraser, Robert. *Ben Okri: Towards the Invisible City.* Tavistock, U.K.: Northcote House, 2002.

Gates, Henry Louis Jr. "Between the Living and the Unborn." *New York Times Book Review* (28 June 1992). Review of *The Famished Road.*

Gorra, Michael. "The Spirit Who Came to Stay." *New York Times Book Review* (10 October 1993). Review of *Songs of Enchantment.*

Hawley, John. "Ben Okri's Spirit Child: *Abiku* Migration and Postmodernity." *Research in African Literatures* 26, no. 1 (1995).

Heelas, Paul, *New Age Movement: The Celebration of the Self and the Sacralization of Modernity.* Oxford, U.K. and Cambridge, Mass.: Blackwell, 1996.

Ogunsanwo, Olatubosun. "Intertextuality and Post-Colonial Literature in Ben Okri's *The Famished Road,*" in *Research in African Literatures* 26, no. 1 (1995).

———. Review of *Magical Realism in West Africa: Seeing with a Third Eye,* by Brenda Cooper. *Research in African Literatures* 31, no. 2 (2000).

Quayson, Ato, *Strategic Transformations in Nigerian Writing: Orality and History in the Work of Rev. Samuel Johnson, Amos Tutuola, Wole Soyinka, and Ben Okri.* Oxford: J. Currey; Bloomington, Ind.: Indiana University Press, 1997.

———. *Postcolonialism: Theory, Practice or Process?* Cambridge, U.K.: Polity Press; Malden, Mass.: Blackwell Publishers, 2000.

Wright, Derek. "Interpreting the Interspace: Ben Okri's *The Famished Road.*" *CRNLE Reviews Journal,* 1–2 (1995).

Wright, Derek. "Pre- and Post-Modernity in Recent West African Fiction." *Commonwealth Essays and Studies* 21, no. 2 (1999).

———. "Postmodernism as Realism: Magic History in Recent West African Fiction." In his *Contemporary African Fiction.* Bayreuth, Germany: E. Breitinger, 1997.

Michael Ondaatje
(1943–)

ANYA CLAYWORTH AND CHRIS JONES

PHILIP MICHAEL ONDAATJE, the fourth child of Philip Mervyn Ondaatje and Enid Doris Gratiaen, was born on 12 September 1943 in Kegalle, Sri Lanka (then known as Ceylon), where his family owned a tea plantation. Ondaatje is of Tamil, Sinhalese, and Dutch descent and thus represents the mixed colonial history of his birthplace. His father's alcoholism put great strain on his parents' marriage and in 1945 they divorced. As a result Michael moved to Colombo with his mother. He would see little more of his father, who died in 1965 of a brain hemorrhage. In 1952 Ondaatje left Sri Lanka for England to join his mother, sister, and brother, who had migrated there three years previously. He had attended a school in Colombo that followed British traditions of education, but he had never had to wear a tie to school before entering Dulwich College in London.

Dulwich College has many literary associations. Raymond Chandler and P. G. Wodehouse were pupils at the school, and a friend of Ondaatje's, the novelist and fellow Booker Prize–winner Graham Swift, followed him there. Despite the literary history of his surroundings, Ondaatje was more interested in cricket than literature. A former teacher expressed surprise when Ondaatje won the Booker Prize in 1992, saying that he had always thought Ondaatje was more interested in sports than writing. Ondaatje would not begin to write until 1962, when he went to Canada at aged nineteen, following in the footsteps of his older brother Christopher. He later noted that the impetus to write came from the feeling that Canada was alive with possibilities for him as a young writer. In Britain, he complained of feeling stifled by the great literary tradition.

Ondaatje first became aware of those possibilities and the heady atmosphere of a burgeoning Canadian literary scene when he enrolled at Bishop's University in Lennoxville, Quebec. There he met inspirational teachers of literature and poets such as Ralph Gustafson and Doug Jones, who encouraged him in his own writing. He also met the Canadian artist Kim Jones, whom he married in 1964, subsequently taking out Canadian citizenship. Together they had two children, a daughter, Quintin, in 1964 and a son, Griffin, in 1967. Ondaatje transferred to University College, University of Toronto, and graduated from there with a BA in 1965. His rapid rise to public recognition began the same year, when he won the Ralph Gustafson Award for Poetry. This was followed a year later by the Norma Epstein Award for Poetry and the E. J. Pratt Gold Medal and Award for Poetry. In 1967 Ondaatje completed an MA thesis on the poetry of Edwin Muir under the supervision of George Whalley at Queen's University, Kingston, Ontario, and published his first volume of poetry, *The Dainty Monsters,* with Coach House Press, an independent Canadian publishing house. After his graduate work Ondaatje began teaching at the University of Western Ontario and continued publishing poetry in journals and anthologies, winning the President's Medal from Western. His second book, *The Man with Seven Toes,* appeared in 1969, followed by *The Collected Works of Billy the Kid,* which won the Governor General's Prize for 1970. *The Collected Works of Billy the Kid* was a new departure for Ondaatje in its mix of factual and fictional material to create a kind of narrative collage.

In 1971, despite his growing success as a writer, his contract was not renewed at Western Ontario, largely because he refused to complete a Ph.D. to ensure tenure. Ondaatje's students protested at the loss of such a popular teacher but nonetheless Ondaatje moved to Glendon College, York University. At Glendon, Ondaatje began to teach as a practicing writer rather than as a scholar of literature. His next volume of poetry, *Rat Jelly,* was published in 1973, followed in 1976 by his fictionalized life of the jazz artist Buddy Bolden, *Coming through Slaughter,* which was a cowinner of the *Books in Canada* First Novel Award for that year.

In 1978 Ondaatje returned to Ceylon, but in many ways it was now a foreign state to the Canadian writer, who had left twenty-six years earlier. Even the name of Ondaatje's country of birth had been officially erased in 1972, when Ceylon was renamed Sri Lanka. While he was there he gathered material for his semifictional memoir, *Running in the Family* (1982). He also worked on his next volume of poetry, *There's a Trick with a Knife I'm Learning to Do: Poems 1963–78* (1979), which won the Governor General's Award the year it was published. He spent 1981 as visiting professor at the University

of Hawaii, where he met the television journalist and producer Linda Spalding, who would become his partner following a legal separation from Kim Jones that year. Ondaatje's poems from this period, *Tin Roof* (1982) and *Secular Love* (1984), reflect his personal turmoil at the breakdown of his first marriage and see him beginning to explore the questions of identity that have become the cornerstones of his novels.

Running in the Family marks Ondaatje's first sustained attempt to come directly to terms with his cultural identity. While it is often called a memoir, it is perhaps more accurately termed another exercise in fictionalized biography, as Ondaatje combines his personal history with the fiction of exaggerated family anecdotes. This combination of forms was to be the structural backbone of his first novel, *In the Skin of a Lion,* published in 1987 to international admiration. In addition to developing characters who would reappear in *The English Patient,* Ondaatje sought to outline the history of his adopted country, Canada, and its immigrant population.

Ondaatje's success with *In the Skin of a Lion* led to a volume of his selected poetry, *The Cinnamon Peeler,* being published in Britain in 1989. This was followed in 1992 by Ondaatje's most popular novel, *The English Patient,* which launched him into the mainstream of the international literary scene. The novel won the Booker Prize (the prize was shared with Barry Unsworth's *Sacred Hunger*), making Ondaatje its first Canadian recipient. It also won the Governor General's Award and the Trillium Award. However, the novel's fame was really cemented by the film version, which appeared in 1996. Ondaatje was closely involved in the film's production as a consultant on the set, but the screenplay itself was written by the writer/director Anthony Minghella. The film won nine Academy Awards, including best picture, best director for Minghella, and best supporting actress for Juliette Binoche, who played Hana.

Working on the film of *The English Patient* took Ondaatje back to his early love of film-making, a passion which he explored in 2002 by publishing a book of transcribed conversations with the celebrated film editor Walter Murch (*The Conversations: Walter Murch and the Art of Editing Film*). His experiences on the set also encouraged a change in direction and a return to poetry with his 1998 volume, *Handwriting*. Set entirely in Sri Lanka, *Handwriting* is dedicated to Ondaatje's childhood *ayah,* or nurse. This revival of interest in writing about Sri Lanka was carried into his next novel, *Anil's Ghost* (2000). *Anil's Ghost* took Ondaatje seven years to write and again demonstrates his preoccupation with Sri Lanka, a country to which he feels a sense of belonging, but to which he is reluctant to commit wholly. Ondaatje seems content to define himself as a Sri Lankan Canadian.

LITERARY FORMS

Trying to categorize Ondaatje's writing, according to even basic literary genres, is a surprisingly difficult task. Bibliographies disagree about how many volumes of poetry he has published. This problem is generated partly because Ondaatje often includes earlier sequences within larger collections of new poems. But several of his books simply defy the distinction between poetry and prose. *The Collected Works of Billy the Kid,* for example, does not confine itself to either medium, but alternates between both. A subtitle, *Left Handed Poems,* that appeared in the first edition has been dropped from subsequent reprints, as if to encourage generic ambiguity. Arguably, if one counts *The Collected Works of Billy the Kid,* Ondaatje had published ten volumes of poetry by 2003. There are at least three novels (*In the Skin of a Lion, The English Patient,* and *Anil's Ghost*), and many might also wish to add *Coming through Slaughter* to these. However, the latter is a fictionalized life of Buddy Bolden, a real-life jazz trumpeter who flourished in New Orleans during the early 1900s. It is partly written in the style of documentary reportage and includes excerpts from transcripts of real interviews with people who knew Bolden. *Coming through Slaughter* deliberately blurs the distinction between novel and biography. Ondaatje is careful not to include it among his "formal novels." Similarly, *Running in the Family* is often described as Ondaatje's memoir, but this can give a misleading impression of the book. Ondaatje does reflect on his early boyhood in Ceylon (Sri Lanka) and also incorporates the results of research into his family history, carried out during his return trips to his place of birth in 1978 and 1980. Yet this material is interwoven with poetry and passages of imaginative prose to create a narrative that is neither entirely factual nor entirely fictional. Ondaatje's output as an anthologizer, editor, critic, and filmmaker add further dimensions to his work beyond the normal boundaries of "creative writing." One could argue that part of Ondaatje's literary achievement is this resistance to generic closure, and the opening up of new, hybrid possibilities.

Such a bibliographic exercise can give the impression that Ondaatje's oeuvre is bewilderingly disparate and difficult to characterize. In fact two pervasive thematic concerns give it a coherence which is all the more striking for their presence throughout such a formally various body of work. The first is the proximity of order and chaos; how disciplined patterns may be traced over, or discerned within, seemingly random events and experiences and conversely, how such perceptions of order may easily descend into anarchy. So, in the 1973 poem "King Kong Meets Wallace Stevens" (in *Rat Jelly*), Ondaatje imagines the American poet Stevens thinking of chaos, but also of fences. One could argue that this preoccupation is part of Ondaatje's wider concern with polarities and how opposites collapse into each other, but the slippage between chaos and order is the most common example of this general worldview. The second motif is that of the displaced person or outsider, the antiheroic protagonist of many of Ondaatje's works. A Canadian citizen with a Dutch surname, born to a family of mixed

European and Asian descent in Ceylon, a state whose name would change during the course of his life to Sri Lanka, and educated in England, Ondaatje is himself a migratory or displaced person. It is little wonder, therefore, that this outsider figure should feature so prominently in his work, although its representation occurs in such a variety of guises, some so unlike the author's own circumstances that one must resist the temptation to engage in biographical interpretation, a reading strategy Ondaatje himself disparaged in his critical work on Leonard Cohen (1970). Both these thematic preoccupations are realized in the formal elements of the writing as well as at the semantic or content level. Indeed, the hybridity of genre is a formal expression of the hybridity of identity in the age of globalization. Once the reader becomes accustomed to looking for these patterns within Ondaatje's writing, its multifariousness becomes more approachable, although no less complex.

POETIC ORIGINS

At nineteen Ondaatje began to read poetry widely for the first time at Bishop's University. Early enthusiasms included the symbolist poetry of the modernist writers W. B. Yeats, Wallace Stevens, and W. H. Auden, as well as the dramatic monologues of the Victorian poet Robert Browning. The influence of these writers can be detected in Ondaatje's early work, although ultimately Browning's example proved to be of more enduring use to him. Ondaatje's first book, *The Dainty Monsters,* published in 1967, contains forty-five poems from this period, divided into two sections, "Over the Garden Wall" and "Troy Town." Like all Ondaatje's titles, these three repay close attention. Monstrosity ordinarily precludes any quality of daintiness. The practically oxymoronic title anticipates the yoking of the wild and the tame, the savage and the civilized in many of these poems, an idea which is further developed by the first subtitle. A garden wall is designed to delimit domesticated flora and fauna from the wildlife beyond. To go "over the garden wall" is to transgress this boundary, although ambiguity remains about which side of that boundary the reader now finds him or herself on. This section of the book is populated with animals and birds ranging from the ordinary to the fabulous. We read of sand swallows performing an aerial ballet, weaving patterns in the formless clouds ("Description Is a Bird") and a diminutive dragon being trapped in a badminton net ("Dragon"). The mundane becomes spectacular and the awesome descends into bathos. Parallel antitheses are explored in the second section. "Troy Town" evokes the *Iliad,* the ancient Greek epic by the poet Homer. According to Homer, Troy was the site of a long and bloody siege and is always referred to as a splendid city. Redesignating Troy as a "town" is an act of domestication, and even suburbanization, of a mythical site of conflict. In the two-word phrase one can also clearly hear a pun on the collocation "toy-town," further diminishing the epic grandeur of the allusion. While the first section of the book is largely a kind of modern bestiary, the second part consists more of domestic scenes, families engaged in the everyday conflicts of home life. "A House Divided," for example, depicts a husband and wife fighting nightly battles for control of extra bed-space, and in "The Diverse Causes," the violent primitivist music of the composer Igor Stravinsky rages at the breakfast table as powdered milk is made up. Throughout the poems daily ritual and violence are inscribed within each other. As a whole the collection is often said to be precocious and uneven, despite the lyrical intensity and affective power achieved in some poems (notably "Peter" and "For John, Falling"). Ondaatje has silently acknowledged this by progressively removing *Dainty Monsters* poems from selections of his work. At times the poems are difficult to interpret, and while in later works Ondaatje is often abstruse as a calculated challenge to the reader, it is hard not to conclude that some of the difficulty in *The Dainty Monsters* is due to the young poet not having fully assimilated the symbolist mode he then admired.

Begun in 1966, *The Man with Seven Toes,* published in 1969, sees Ondaatje exploring the possibilities of a longer sequence of interlinked poems to produce a narrative. Based on the documentary sources of a series of paintings by the Australian artist Sidney Nolan, the poems narrate the story of Mrs. Eliza Fraser, who was shipwrecked off Queensland in 1836 and survived in the bush with the aid of an escaped convict. Ondaatje seems to have regarded the work as a partial failure. This judgment may have as much to do with two attempts to perform the work dramatically in 1968 and 1969 in Vancouver, attempts which, by the author's own admission, were not entirely satisfactory. Nevertheless, the poem marks an important stage in Ondaatje's journey from the purely lyric mode to the narrative.

Although *The Collected Works of Billy the Kid,* published in 1970, was Ondaatje's next book chronologically, because it negotiates several genres at once, it will be considered in more detail together with *Coming through Slaughter* (1976), with which it has several affinities. Ondaatje's 1973 collection, *Rat Jelly,* is a more straightforward collection of short lyrics and, together with *Dainty Monsters,* contributed a large number of the poems later included in *There's a Trick with a Knife I'm Learning to Do* (1979), together with a new sequence, "Pig Glass." In several poems in *Rat Jelly,* Ondaatje appears to be writing personally about his present family life in Canada and his memories of family life in Ceylon (some of the latter material he would later cover again in *Running in the Family*). Yet one must be cautious of assuming that the "I" in the poems is the "real" Ondaatje and that his narratives are less personal. Notoriously, Ondaatje often exaggerates and distorts his personal experiences in creating a work of art. Like the protagonist of *Coming through Slaughter,* Ondaatje respects "well-told lies" (p. 24).

EARLY NARRATIVES: *THE COLLECTED WORKS OF BILLY THE KID* AND *COMING THROUGH SLAUGHTER*

It may seem surprising that the first two major works by a Ceylonese-born Canadian should so concern themselves with figures from the foundational mythology of modern America, an outlaw of the Wild West circa 1880 and a pioneer of jazz from the Deep South in the 1900s. It has been suggested that Ondaatje is critiquing the power structures of American society in these two works. This may be true, but it should not be supposed that Ondaatje views America from a disdainful distance. Cowboy movies and jazz records have a global reach and Ondaatje grew up on a diet of westerns, American comic books, and popular music. By the time he was eight he was saturated with the idea of the Wild West. The myths surrounding Billy the Kid and the legendary cornet player Buddy Bolden are simply part of Ondaatje's cultural inheritance and he naturally assumes the right to participate in the retelling of those myths and legends.

In order to relate the story of the notorious Billy the Kid (real name William Bonney), Ondaatje uses a combination of poems, prose poems, extended prose passages, statements by people who knew the outlaw taken from documentary sources, a newspaper interview conducted with Mr. Bonney while in jail, captions from a genuine comic strip, and several photographs, some taken by L. A. Huffman, a nineteenth-century photographer of the frontier. This polyphony of voices and perspectives is not simply part of the narrative, it actually comprises that narrative and effectively displaces the normally central, controlling voice of a narrator. Most of the poems ventriloquize a character (usually Billy), rather than narrate from a third-person perspective. This is a technique Ondaatje learned from Robert Browning's dramatic monologues and it largely replaces the more stable construct of the authorial self which is found in many of Ondaatje's shorter lyrics. The mature novels represent a refinement of these evolving narrative techniques.

Knowing which point of view to trust, learning which voices are reliable and how they relate to one another is, in itself, a process of trust that the reader must learn to establish with the text. Several poems into *The Collected Works of Billy the Kid,* Billy's voice asserts its legitimacy in offering greater reliability than that of previous accounts of his life by virtue of its self-witnessing; "Not a story about me through their eyes, then" (p. 20). However, the authority of this fictionalized persona is of course dubious at best, as it effectively admits in the next sentence, urging us to "Find the beginning, the slight silver key to unlock it, to dig it out. Here then is a maze to begin, be in." Despite providing a personal testimonial, the narrative is incomplete without the reader's participation. We need tools to find a way into the text and, as the disappearing *g* signals (from "being" to "be in"), we need to be alert to blank space and silence as well as what is audible and visible as we move from the beginning of the textual maze to being fully within it. Ondaatje was later to write, in *In the Skin of a Lion,* that "the first sentence of every novel should be: 'Trust me, this will take time but there is order here, very faint, very human'" (p. 146). It is well to bear this in mind when reading *The Collected Works of Billy the Kid;* the sudden juxtaposition of different fragments of narrative through different media, although disorienting at first, is part of the point. Defamiliarized by Ondaatje's textual strategies, we become outsiders to the text, just as Billy is socially excluded from his world. Even the linearity of the narrative is disrupted, for in the very first poem Billy informs the reader that he is killed by a man called Pat Garrett; the beginning of the narrative starts with information about the final climax of the plot, presented from the impossible perspective of the protagonist after his own death. Subsequently the book ranges back and forth over the events of Billy's last months, with little respect for chronology. Disorientation is

encouraged in order to force the responsibility for creating meaning out of disorder onto the reader. We are explicitly made to construct a metanarrative from this wealth of disjuncture and partiality. As consumers of fictional stories, we are always producers of fictional stories, however much we think they are based on objective facts.

This technique of montage, of cutting and splicing, of flashback sequence and juxtaposition, is filmic and reminds us of how images and myths of the Wild West have been promulgated previously. The narrative grammar of *The Collected Works of Billy the Kid* is very like the grammar of cinema and grasping this can give one a way to read the book. Ondaatje, who has made several films, is as much interested in editing and arranging images as he is in creating them. In interviews he has suggested that the book is really a substitute for the film he would have preferred to make, but could not afford to shoot at the time. The inclusion of still photographs and other found materials in the work highlights this editorial (or directorial) aspect of the production of the text's meaning, although it too is problematized. On the page preceding the first poem is a large outline of a box. An italicized paragraph below notes, "I send you a picture of Billy made with the Perry shutter as quick as it can be worked" (p. 5). The reader becomes the recipient of a blank photograph of the book's protagonist, an empty imaginative space which effectively signals the openness of the following text, its resistance to closure. At the very end of the text we are given an actual photographic image of a Billy the Kid, but, rather slyly, it is of the seven-year-old Ondaatje, dressed in a cowboy suit. Ondaatje's final ironic gesture is further admission that it is impossible to engage in the mythology of a figure like Billy the Kid without participating in the mythmaking oneself. Reading the story of the outlaw, Ondaatje has partly written himself into the lead role. However, this is not an act of solipsism, merely an acknowledgment that storytelling can never be a simple, objective act of self-detachment.

In keeping with the multifarious formal and narrative qualities of the text, the portrait of Billy gradually constructed is complex, ambiguous, and open-ended. The title of the book implies that Billy's murders are his works of art, an idea given more prominence by the subtitle of the first edition. Billy's left-handedness, although part of the earlier legendary tradition (testified to by Arthur Penn's 1958 film *The Left-Handed Gun*), also implies his marginality within society, as left-handed people were once commonly thought to be deviant or sinister (the latter word deriving from Latin, in which it means both "left" and "perverse"). The idea that Billy's acts of brutality are his poetry is developed by the first poem, which catalogues these "collected works" in the manner of an epic list under the heading "These are the killed" (p. 6). An uneasy relationship between an artistic temperament and a violent temperament then begins to be sketched out. Acts of creativity and destruction can both spring from a similar impulse. Billy likes to shoot his victims "well and careful" (p. 15), which is how, as the fictional speaker projecting these lyrics (of course he is really projected by them), he likes to compose poetry. Billy often likens scenes of natural beauty to gruesome images generated by watching his victims die:

> In Mexico the flowers
> like brain the blood drained out
> packed with all the liquor perfume
> sweat like lilac urine smell
> getting to me from across a room
>
> (p. 56)

We are not spared from Billy's brutality; he passively observes the vein being pulled from the throat of a dying victim by a chicken, seemingly entranced by the resulting color combination of red and blue. After episodes like this we cannot "buy into" the tradition of Billy as a misguided, rebellious antihero; he is too clearly

psychopathic. Yet neither does Ondaatje allow the reader to demonize Billy easily. Other characters, in whom the text invites us to place more trust, frequently refer to Billy as "boyish and pleasant" and "in good taste" (Paulita Maxwell, p. 19), "charming" (Pat Garrett, p. 43), and "courteous" (Sallie Chisum, p. 87). Billy remains difficult to pin down.

This indeterminacy is aptly illustrated by Billy's own offering of a beginning to his story, his reminiscence of the journey he and Charlie Bowdre had earlier made crisscrossing the Canadian border: "Ten miles north of it ten miles south. Our horses stepped from country to country, across low rivers, through different colours of tree green. The two of us, our crisscross like a whip in slow motion, the ridge of action rising and falling, getting narrower in radius till it ended and we drifted down to Mexico and old heat" (p. 20). Billy and his companion oscillate between two states, being in both but belonging to neither. They constantly transgress a boundary marker which defines the identities of most of the citizens living on either side of it, but which is meaningless to the migratory outlaws.

Critics have often contrasted Billy's unpredictability with the ruthless self-control of Sheriff Pat Garrett, the man who kills Billy, finally enforcing judicial and social order over the excesses of anarchy. Whereas other frontiersmen might be given to spontaneous bouts of binge drinking, Garrett trains himself to drink hard liquor according to a schedule he organizes. He schools himself in French, simply as an exercise in discipline and despite having no one to speak the language with. The text calls Garrett "an academic murderer" (p. 28) and comments that he has equipped himself "to be that rare thing—a sane assassin" (p. 29). Garrett and Billy do come into peaceful contact with each other, staying for a time with mutual friends John and Sallie Chisum on their ranch in the desert. Late-night drinking, conversation, and socializing characterize this period, narrated mostly in the middle sections of the book and providing it with a still, calm center. On the Chisums' ranch a kind of harmonious equilibrium is temporarily achieved between the order and chaos represented by Garrett and Billy. Yet the reader is never totally at ease, having been made aware from the very start that Garrett will kill Billy. Nor does Ondaatje's vision of the world allow for this kind of static opposition between two polarities; one must eventually overcome the other, or the two must bleed into each other. Crisp distinctions between the discipline of the assassin and the spontaneity of the criminal are preserved no more rigidly than those between the Canadian side of the border and the American, between the dainty and the monstrous, between prose and poetry. Ultimately our sympathies are tangled, for Ondaatje wants his readers to find issues of loyalty and identification to be complex and perplexing. His Billy the Kid is a cruel murderer, but has been humanized without being glamorized. As Sallie Chisum spells out, perhaps too crudely:

> There was good mixed in with the bad
> in Billy the Kid
> and bad mixed in with the good
> in Pat Garrett.
>
> No matter what they did in the world
> or what the world thought of them
> they were my friends.
> Both were worth knowing.
>
> (p. 89)

Needless to say, Sallie is not permitted the last words of his text, for even this confession of the double moral nature of humans is too neat a resolution. Instead Ondaatje eats away at the satisfying closure of Sallie's testimony with other poems and increasingly ironic found materials; a photograph of an empty cabin resembling that (or actually that?) in which Billy died; the comic-strip story; the photographic self-portrait of himself, age seven, as a young cowboy placed off-center within a conspicuously large, and mostly (still) blank photograph frame.

Like *The Collected Works of Billy the Kid*, *Coming through Slaughter* consists of a medley of voices and materials, some documentary, some fictional, some fictionalized, all competing to tell and retell episodes from the protagonist's life and downfall from a number of perspectives and points in time. Although *Coming through Slaughter* does include some poetic material, the move toward prose narrative is more complete in this work than in the fully hybrid *Billy the Kid* and is proleptic of Ondaatje's future long narratives, which will more obviously conform to the formal expectations embodied by the novel.

Buddy Bolden was a virtuoso black cornet player who went mad in 1907 while playing at a parade in New Orleans. Bolden spent the rest of his life in an insane asylum in Louisiana, where he died in 1931 having never played another note. Among jazz aficionados Bolden's reputation is legendary and he is often credited with being one of the founders of the modern jazz idiom, a precursor to more famous jazz trumpeters such as King Oliver and Louis Armstrong. However, this preeminence is now impossible to assess, as Bolden, unlike many of his contemporaries, never recorded a single number. His reputation as a pioneering innovator depends entirely on the testimonials of those who claimed to have heard him play. This makes Bolden exactly the kind of figure Ondaatje is drawn to. Indeed, Ondaatje has insisted in interviews that the very attraction of writing *Coming through Slaughter* was that he knew very little about Bolden and therefore had plenty of free rein in filling in the blank spaces of his life.

Like Billy, Ondaatje's Bolden is a self-destructive creative spirit. He is given to bouts of drinking and violent attacks when angered and he loves two women, making it impossible for him to find full emotional fulfilment and ensuring that he remains a divided personality. Bolden can only heal himself into a whole person through his music. A fellow musician overhears Bolden playing privately and is

484

shocked to realize that he is mixing blues tunes with hymns, God's music with the devil's, an innovation of which his contemporary had never dreamed. Temporary resolution of this dichotomy is also suggested at the level of characterization. For just as Billy's unpredictability is countered by Pat Garrett's self-control, so Bolden has a rational foil, his old friend Webb, a policeman who tracks him down when he disappears from his family. Ultimately however, Webb cannot save Bolden from his breakdown.

The interaction of discipline and spontaneity, form and energy are also explored in relation to the medium of jazz itself. Bolden's reluctance to commit his music to wax cylinder is a measure of his idealistic and purist view of jazz, a musical form which values spontaneity and individualism. For an artist like Bolden, recording is at best a mere substitute for performance, at worst a static petrifaction of a fluid, ever-evolving process. The spontaneity of Bolden's own music is emphasized by an incident in which a man is shot in the bar where his band is performing. Bolden immediately changes tempo in order to distract most of the audience with a fast number until the police arrive; his music is a direct response to the ephemeral circumstances of its production; "his whole plot of song covered with scandal and incident and change. The music was coarse and rough, immediate, dated in half an hour, was about bodies in the river, knives, lovepains, cockiness" (p. 43).

Yet Bolden's achievement is his ability to impose patterns on this ephemerality. Listening to Bolden's musical plots is rather like reading Ondaatje's poetic narratives; the experience is challenging, but liberates one from normal artistic conventions. Frank Lewis, who claimed to have heard Bolden's performances, neatly expresses this; "There was a discipline, it was just that we didn't understand. We thought he was formless, but I think now he was tormented by order, what was outside it. He tore apart the plot" (p. 37). Just as Robert Browning and the American poet Ezra Pound (whom Ondaatje also admires) used dramatic monologues and poetic personae as masks to write about personal emotion and experience in a less subjective and self-centered way, so Ondaatje projects his fears and desires through the personae of Billy the Kid and Buddy Bolden, writing about the role of the artist in society without self-indulgence.

Coming through Slaughter has been criticized for not being more political in its depiction of race. Some commentators suggested that a writer born into the legacy of British Imperial rule in the Indian subcontinent should have been more alert to the exploitation of black people in early-twentieth-century New Orleans. Yet it could be argued that the condition of being an "alien" is an experience shared more widely than that of belonging to a distinct ethnic group. In almost all his writings Ondaatje explores the circumstances of those who are in subordinate relationships to the economically or socially privileged. Whether they are black Americans, white American outlaws, or (as in the case of *The English Patient*) those internationally displaced by war, Ondaatje has always given voice to the dispossessed. In any case, explicit racism is present in *Coming through Slaughter*. For example Ondaatje reports black prostitutes being thrown overboard from a riverboat after having been used by whites. It is true that overt racism is depicted primarily in the margins of the book, but Ondaatje wishes to show the richness and diversity, the beauty and the brutality, of relationships within the black community. To depict black American life only in opposition to white America is arguably to diminish its own cultural complexity.

INTERMISSION

When poems from Ondaatje's 1978 collection *Elimination Dance* were included in his 1989 selected poems, *The Cinnamon Peeler*, between poems from *There's a Trick with a Knife I'm Learning to Do* and *Secular Love*, Ondaatje subtitled the section "An Intermission." *Elimination Dance*, along with *Running in the*

Family, published in 1982, can be seen as an intermission in Ondaatje's writing career, coming between the experimentalism of the early work and the maturity of the later novels. Ostensibly both books are also more personal. *Elimination Dance* addresses the breakup of his first marriage and those of several of his friends. Its title alludes to group formal dances in which one couple after another is eliminated from the dance. In *Secular Love* Ondaatje continues to investigate his emotions regarding his separation from Kim Jones and, simultaneously, his new relationship with Linda Spalding. Critics have complained that this collection is solipsistic and indulgent, but while both it and *Elimination Dance* draw more directly on the author's personal experiences than is usual in Ondaatje's work, they treat that material obliquely; an ironical distance is maintained between Ondaatje the poet and Ondaatje the man.

As a fictionalized memoir of Ondaatje's family, *Running in the Family* has an obvious investment in personal history. However, one must always be alert to the dangers of assuming that material Ondaatje presents as factual is actually factual. Christopher Ondaatje, while admiring the way his younger brother Michael captured in the book the atmosphere of the last years of colonial Ceylon, has noted how often *Running in the Family* distorts the facts in its pursuit of a good story. Christopher's own book, *The Man-Eater of Punanai: A Journey of Discovery to the Jungles of Old Ceylon* (1992), provides a more sober account of the same material. However, it would be a mistake to think that Michael Ondaatje is dissembling in *Running in the Family,* trying to deceive the reader into thinking fiction is fact. The text itself lets the reader know exactly what its methods are: "No story is ever told just once. Whether a memory or funny hideous scandal, we will return to it an hour later and retell the story with additions and this time a few judgements thrown in. In this way history is organized" (p. 26). For the alert reader this is not just a statement of how *Running in the Family* operates, but how almost all

Ondaatje's work operates. The construction and organization of history out of retold stories, memories, and scandals is a central concern to the novels that followed Ondaatje's memoir.

IN THE SKIN OF A LION

In the Skin of a Lion represents Ondaatje's first attempt at what he has termed a formal novel. In using this designation, he differentiates the book from his earlier foray into prose, *Coming through Slaughter.* However, *In the Skin of a Lion* does have a certain amount in common with previous works in its mixture of history and fiction. Where *Coming through Slaughter* fictionalizes the life of Buddy Bolden, *In the Skin of a Lion* fictionalizes the history of Ondaatje's adopted nation, Canada, and its immigrant population.

In the Skin of a Lion is by no means a straightforward account, however. While the novel features historical figures such as the millionaire Ambrose Small and historical events including the building of the Bloor Street Viaduct and the Victoria Park filtration plant, the history of the novel is not as it is recorded in history books. Rather, the narrative consists of the previously unrecorded stories of those who actually laid the tarmac on the viaduct and dug the tunnels for the filtration plant. In this way, Ondaatje seeks to challenge notions of the dominant narratives of Canada's past, suggesting that the histories of the marginalized, the forgotten, and the unrecorded have as much right to be told as any other. This is a point which is underlined by one of the epigraphs he chose for the novel, from John Berger's *G*: "Never again will a single story be told as though it were the only one."

The novel questions the very nature of history by combining historical facts with pure fiction. The story of the disappearance of the wealthy theatrical entrepreneur Ambrose Small is a recorded event, but one that Ondaatje takes liberties with. He refers to the Bertillon system of identification, which employed physical measurements, data, and photographs to track criminals and missing persons, when as a matter of historical fact, the police did not have Small's Bertillon record nor were investigators like Patrick Lewis employed to find him. Ondaatje uses such fabrications in order to ask questions about whether and how identity can be established. The combination of fiction and history here calls into question the notion of how "official" history is constructed. History, in this novel, is simply a question of who is writing or telling it.

In the Skin of a Lion sees the debut of three characters who return in *The English Patient*: Patrick Lewis, Hana, and David Caravaggio. The identities of the characters introduced at the very beginning of the novel are not revealed to the reader until the end, when it becomes clear that the anonymous girl portrayed listening to a story in a car is Hana and that the man driving is Patrick. However, this retrospective identification of these characters is made more complex by the fact that the circumstances of the incident as related at the beginning of the novel have changed by the end. In the opening scene, it is Patrick who is driving, with Hana staying awake to keep him company. At the end of the novel, by contrast, it is the inexperienced Hana who is driving, with Patrick lending assistance from the passenger seat:

> — Do you want to drive? he asked.
> — Me? I don't know the gears.
> — Go ahead. I'll talk the gears to you till we are out of town.
> — I'll try it for a bit.
>
> (p. 244)

The inconsistency between beginning and end is deliberate on Ondaatje's part; the discrepancy reflects the narrative's complexity, as each person sees and remembers the story slightly differently.

The anonymity of Hana and Patrick when first introduced to the reader is repeated throughout the novel with respect to several other characters. Alice Gull first appears as a nun who falls from the Bloor Street Viaduct to be caught by Nicholas Temelcoff, a construction worker who is suspended beneath one of the arches at the time. After Nicholas catches Alice, saving her life, he tells her his story in his local bar while she sits silently, having not even uttered a scream as she plummeted toward the ground. The only indication that the experience has had any impact on the silent nun is that she has "found [Temelcoff's] wire shears, and used them to cut away the black lengths of her habit" (p. 48), thus abandoning her identity as a nun. Even as the novel develops, Alice remains reluctant to expose her history. It is up to Patrick to piece the story of his lover together from the photographs and rosary that her daughter Hana shows to him. Patrick can then present his friend Temelcoff with Alice's identity, allowing Temelcoff to see "how he has been sewn into history" (p. 149). Ironically, the clue to Alice's identity has been present in the novel from early on. Alice takes her new name from the mynah bird, Alicia, who lives in Temelcoff's local bar. Her true identity, however, even her name as a nun is left unknown. She is a "Tabula Rasa" (p. 39) that Patrick is left to fill in.

The way in which Alice's identity is revealed reflects Ondaatje's complex use of time in the novel. Although there is a general linear progression from Patrick's childhood to his middle age, time does not move in a straightforward way. Ondaatje hints at things that are then explored in more detail as facts come to light. At the time, Patrick's experience of being woken when a child by mysterious lights seems merely to be an extension of his boyhood interest in insects. He notes that the lights cannot be fireflies because it is winter and he caught the last of the fireflies in his handkerchief at the end of the summer. Time then flashes forward quickly in parenthesis: "(Years later, Clara making love to him in a car, catching his semen in a handkerchief and flinging it out onto the bushes on the side of the road. *Hey lightning bug!* He had said, laughing, offering no explanation)" (p. 20). At this point in the narrative, the reader has not even encountered Clara directly, because she belongs to the sections of the book which concern Patrick as a young man, not as a young boy. The intrusion of this flash-forward allusion to Patrick's lights thus complicates our notion of time in the novel. Patrick cannot possibly know Clara at this point in the narrative, so the reference to her indicates that the story is being told in retrospect. It might even remind the reader that this is a story being told to Hana by Patrick as they drive to collect Clara after the death of Ambrose Small. However, this is not the end of the tale of the lights. Ondaatje returns to it when Alice tells Patrick about the night of Hana's father, Cato's birth: "His father skated three miles for the doctor the night he was born. He skated across the lake holding up cattails on fire" (p. 151). Patrick noted at the time of the incident of the mysterious lights that the skaters seemed to be skating "against the night" (p. 22) and his childhood observation is proven correct when it turns out that the lights were held by Cato's father and his friends, skating for the doctor. Frequently the significance of events and memories is only revealed in their retelling, often after the passage of much time.

THE ENGLISH PATIENT

Like *In the Skin of a Lion*, *The English Patient* addresses questions of history and identity but this time from the setting of Italy in the final months of World War II, an environment and period more remote to Ondaatje, yet at the same time filled with possibilities.

The first thirty pages of the novel signify Ondaatje's intentions to the reader. Two protagonists are introduced, a female who the reader is led to believe is a nurse and a male, her patient, "her despairing saint" (p. 3). Ondaatje does not tell us what the characters' names are, where they come from, or how the male has come to be burned to the bone. Indeed, if David

Caravaggio had not made his long journey to join Hana, it seems likely that the characters would have remained nameless throughout the novel. After all, Hana and the English patient do not use each other's names: she calls him "the English Patient" or simply "the Englishman." The withholding of the characters' identity is a deliberate strategy. Rather than arming the reader with all the information that he or she needs at the beginning of the novel, Ondaatje reveals it slowly and with purpose. He wants the reader to understand the relationship between personal tragedy and the loss of meaningful identity.

This concern with identity is partly predicated on Ondaatje's choice of a wartime setting. War is a time when who you are becomes crucial and when who you are is, in part, determined by where you come from. The English patient recalls that before the war, when he was exploring the desert, his team members came from all over the world and their national identity was unimportant: "We were German, English, Hungarian, African—all of us insignificant to [the Bedouins.] Gradually we became nationless" (p. 138). This is in direct contrast to the situation the characters find themselves in toward the end of the war, when identity has become the central question with which they wrestle. War has left them with a need to know who they are, but also with an understanding that they are not the same people as they were before the war.

The most obvious quest for identity made in the novel concerns that of the burn victim. He had nearly died in a fire when his plane crashed, but he was saved by a Bedouin tribe. His skin has been burned black and his face is unrecognizable, "all identification consumed in a fire" (p. 48). When later questioned by interrogators at a military hospital, indications seem to suggest that the patient is English. As Hana remarks, he knows about English gardens, he speaks English, and he gives signs of having had a traditional English education with his range of reading and classical training. However, as he tells his interrogators, he can also speak German and he knows about the desert: "You should be trying to trick me . . . make me speak German, which I can by the way, ask me about Don Bradman. Ask me about Marmite, the great Gertrude Jekyll" (p. 95). Even after he has been extensively interrogated, his nationality remains uncertain. This episode in the novel raises issues about how identity should be attributed. Is a person to be identified by their language, knowledge, or other cultural indicators? The English patient may indeed know about English country gardens, but only because his English lover Katharine Clifton has told him. He may absorb that knowledge as part of his identity, but it is not a reliable guide to who he is.

To Hana and the sapper Kip, the identity of the patient is of little concern, but Caravaggio is intent on pursuing the matter, convinced that the burn victim is the double agent who betrayed the Allies by leading German agents across the desert into Cairo. He tries to get the patient to admit his identity under the influence of a cocktail of morphine and alcohol. To Caravaggio's amazement, even when heavily sedated, the patient never admits who he is by name. While it is later made clear to the reader that the English patient is actually a Hungarian named Almásy, the point remains that his burned body allows him to erase this identity and to court others. His face is fundamentally altered, his skin burned beyond recognition of ethnic background, and his voice no indicator of nationality. Finally, Caravaggio too allows the patient's identity to remain secret with his pragmatic comment to Hana after he questions the man, "He's fine. We can let him be" (p. 265).

Identity is further complicated by the way in which Ondaatje joins the characters to historical events. This complexity is anticipated by the novel's epigraph, which purports to be from the proceedings of the Royal Geographical Society, in which the speaker regrets the loss of two persons who are characters in the novel. In the same way as the characters from *In the Skin of a Lion* are tied to the history of Canada, so the characters of *The English Patient* are linked to the history of the 1930s and 1940s, the mapping of the deserts and the explosion of the atomic bombs at Nagasaki and Hiroshima. Ondaatje peppers his text with facts from the historical period in which he is working. Kirpal Singh ("Kip"), for example, experiences a sense of racial identity through the explosion of the atomic bombs. Instead of the crystal set providing a comforting musical accompaniment to Kip's work as a bomb-disposal expert, it finally proves formative in putting Kip in touch with "the streets of Asia full of fire" (p. 284). Throughout the novel he has resisted attempts to label his identity according to the color of his skin, his turban, or his eating habits. Kip may have aligned himself with the English patient in his love for condensed milk, but he finally finds that the events of history insist upon his difference from the narrative's Western characters. Kip is not nationless, and the knowledge that it is an atomic bomb that he cannot defuse brings him to the final realization that "His name is Kirpal Singh and he does not know what he is doing here" (p. 287).

The unreliability of history in *The English Patient* is underlined by Ondaatje's use of the Greek historian Herodotus as a touchstone for his text. Herodotus's *Histories* is the text that the English patient uses as his commonplace book, cutting out pages, inserting new leaves, writing diary entries and journal notations in the margins and between sections. He creates a customized text out of an ancient historical authority, a literal illustration of Ondaatje's thesis that history is a palimpsest of stories. The choice of text is also significant. Like *The English Patient*, Herodotus's *Histories* is a combination of ostensibly historically accurate accounts and events which are so far-fetched that they must be fictional. Ondaatje's status as author of *The English Patient* is akin to Herodotus's as author of the *Histories*. Ondaatje implies that, like Herodotus, he too is "the father of history" and "the father of lies."

With the consent and support of Ondaatje, the screenwriter Anthony Minghella made some significant changes in order to represent the novel on the screen. In the 1996 film, the story of Hana (Juliette Binoche) is scaled down to foreground the love story of Katharine (Kristin Scott-Thomas) and Almásy (Ralph Fiennes), and Kip's (Naveen Andrews) role in the film is significantly reduced. The key moment at the end of the novel where Kip hears about the atomic bombs is removed, and his anti-imperial speeches from that section of the novel are cut down to one speech made while reading Rudyard Kipling's *Kim* to the English patient. Caravaggio (Willem Dafoe) is a much more menacing presence in the film and his relationship with Hana is not based on their previous family friendship, as it is in the book, but merely the comradeship of two Canadians abroad. Caravaggio's motives in coming to the Villa San Girolamo, where Hana is caring for her patient, are therefore based on revenge rather than benevolence. Ondaatje recognizes that it was not possible to film the novel as it was but has acknowledged that there was a loss in the translation. He noted in an interview, "It's an irony about the film that a personal death becomes more important than a war crime. But the Hiroshima scene didn't work. In the book I can bring something in in the last chapter that makes it all look ironic; in a film it looks like someone put in the wrong reel." (*The Guardian*, p. 30).

ANIL'S GHOST

Anil's Ghost was published in 2000, having taken Ondaatje seven years to complete. In contrast to either of his previous novels, *Anil's Ghost* focuses exclusively on nonwhite characters. Like *The English Patient, Anil's Ghost* is an antiwar novel of a kind, but this time the war is not on a global scale but a national one. The book takes for its context the civil war waged in Sri Lanka in the mid-1980s and 1990s, when the government was combating both Tamil separatists and

Sinhalese insurgents. Like his 1998 collection of poems, *Handwriting, Anil's Ghost* therefore brings Ondaatje back to the country of his birth and explores the figure of the exile returning to roots.

Anil's Ghost, also like *The English Patient*, concerns a quest for identity. Anil Tissera is a forensic anthropologist who returns to her native Sri Lanka as part of a United Nations human rights investigation. Anil's role is to identify those who died under suspicious circumstances and how they died, with the help of Sarath, a local archaeologist. The driving force of this novel is the identification of a skeleton they name "Sailor," which has been discovered at a government-protected archaeological site. Sailor's bones are immediately identified by Anil as modern. The attempt by those who murdered Sailor to hide his identity among skeletons from the sixth century is thus exposed. In their ability to enter the protected site, the murderers or those who tried to conceal the corpse's identity are revealed to have had government connections. Throughout the novel Anil and Sarath search for the evidence that will reveal the identity of the skeleton. They use science in their attempts toward identification but also Anil's skills of observation. When she sees the head restorer Ananda squatting, she immediately notices his connection to Sailor: "Sailor worked in a mine too. Come here, look at the strictures on the anklebones of the skeleton—this is what Ananda has under his flesh. I *know* this" (p. 179).

Once Ananda reconstructs Sailor's head, identification is made but it is not clear how Anil can use this information. She knows that Sailor is Ruwan Kumara and that he was identified as a rebel sympathizer, ironically by an anonymous hooded man, but it is not clear where this will lead her. There are so many instances of violent death in the novel that Ondaatje seems to suggest that Anil's attempts at identification are perhaps pointless. Ultimately, all that Anil achieves at the end of the narrative is to bring about the murder of Sarath, who appears at his brother Gamini's Colombo hospital as yet another in an endless stream of unidentified corpses. This time, Gamini must cope with the recognition that this is not just another anonymous corpse, but his brother, and in this way, the politics that dominate and terrorize in the novel are brought home to him: "Perhaps they had each assumed they would crash alone in the darkness they had invented around themselves. Their marriages, their careers on this borderland of civil war among governments and terrorists and insurgents" (p. 289).

The identification by Gamini of Sarath's body is paralleled in the text by historical incident. As Gamini is dealing with his brother, President Katagula is assassinated. Although Ondaatje's political leader is fictional, there are obvious similarities between the assassination of Katagula in the novel and the historical assassination of President Ranasinghe Premadasa of Sri Lanka in 1993. Through the interweaving of history and fiction in the novel, the real event of President Premadasa's murder by a suicide bomber is linked to the novel's preoccupation with identification. Premadasa's body was, like Katagula's in so many pieces that it was not possible to pronounce his death for some time, due to lack of evidence that would determine his identity. The novel may fictionalize the episode but asks the same questions as were asked at the time of Premadasa's assassination: "Where was the President?" (p. 294).

Katagula's assassination is just one example of the violence which underpins *Anil's Ghost*. Anil and Sarath, for example, find a stranger, Gunsena, crucified on the road. They think he is merely in a drunken sleep, but their suspicions are aroused by his strange appearance and they return to find him nailed to the tarmac. Ananda's wife disappears after seeing the heads of two of her students on spikes, and Sarath's wife commits suicide by drinking lye. Individuals in the novel are fundamentally changed by their personal experiences of violence; Sarath becomes silent, Gamini a work and drug addict, and Ananda an alcoholic. The ghost of Sarath will, Ananda suggests, always haunt even Anil, who is professionally trained to deal with death. In this way, Ondaatje reflects on the human cost of war. It is all very well for Anil to make her identifications of the dead, but this is of little comfort to those who have lost their loved ones. Anil may make her escape, but others in the novel must remain in Sri Lanka. As Gamini notes, "I could never leave here" (p. 285).

Ondaatje perhaps suggests a cure for the violent world he has depicted through the Buddha statue at the end of the novel. While others concern themselves with the killing fields which surround the statue, Ananda devotes himself again to the art of reconstruction, but this time of a figure of the Buddha, rebuilding it piece by piece. Finally, he paints the eye, in a traditional ceremony described earlier in the novel. As he does so, Ananda recognizes the significance of the natural world around him and of human contact, as represented by his nephew, who holds his tools: "This sweet touch from the world" (p. 307). Although Ondaatje's Sri Lanka is a country torn by the chaos of war, then, it is also one which promises the ordered peace of reconstruction.

Selected Bibliography

WORKS OF MICHAEL ONDAATJE

POETRY

The Dainty Monsters. Toronto: Coach House, 1967.

The Man with Seven Toes. Toronto, Coach House, 1969.

The Collected Works of Billy the Kid: Left Handed Poems. Toronto: House of Anansi, 1970. Repub. without subtitle. New York: Norton, 1974.

Rat Jelly. Toronto: Coach House, 1973.

Elimination Dance. Idlerton, Ontario: Nairn, 1978.

There's a Trick with a Knife I'm Learning to Do: Poems 1963–78. New York: Norton, 1979; Toronto: McClelland and Stewart, 1979.

Tin Roof. Lanntzville, B.C.: Island, 1982.

Secular Love. Toronto: Coach House, 1984.

The Cinnamon Peeler: Selected Poems. London: Pan, 1989. New York: Knopf, 1991; Toronto: McClelland and Stewart, 1992.

Handwriting. New York: Knopf; Toronto, McClelland and Stewart; London: Bloomsbury, 1998.

PROSE

Coming through Slaughter. New York: Norton; Toronto: Anansi, 1976; London: Marion Boyars, 1979.

Running in the Family. New York: Norton; Toronto: McClelland and Stewart, 1982.

In the Skin of a Lion. New York: Knopf; Toronto: McClelland and Stewart, 1987.

The English Patient. New York: Knopf; Toronto: McClelland and Stewart; London: Bloomsbury, 1992.

Anil's Ghost. New York: Knopf; Toronto: McClelland and Stewart; London: Bloomsbury, 2000.

AS EDITOR AND CRITIC

Leonard Cohen. Toronto: McClelland and Stewart, 1970.

The Broken Ark: A Book of Beasts, drawings by Tony Urquhart, with poems compiled by Ondaatje. Ottawa: Oberon, 1971.

Personal Fictions: Stories by Munro, Wiebe, Thomas and Blais. Toronto: Oxford University Press, 1977.

The Long Poem Anthology. Toronto: Coach House, 1979.

Brushes with Greatness: An Anthology of Chance Encounters with Celebrities, with Russell Banks and David Young. Toronto: Coach House, 1989.

From Ink Lake: Canadian Stories. New York: Viking Penguin; Toronto: Lester and Orpen Dennys; London: Faber, 1990.

The Conversations: Walter Murch and the Art of Editing Film. Toronto: Vintage Canada, 2002.

BIBLIOGRAPHY

Brady, Judith. "Michael Ondaatje: An Annotated Bibliography." In *The Annotated Bibliography of Canada's Major Authors.* Edited by Robert Lecker and David Jack. Toronto: ECW, 1985.

FILM

The English Patient. Screenplay by Anthony Minghella. Directed by Anthony Minghella. Miramax, 1996.

CRITICAL AND BIOGRAPHICAL STUDIES

Barbour, Douglas. *Michael Ondaatje.* New York: Twayne, 1993; Toronto: Maxwell Macmillan, 1993.

Bolland, John. *Michael Ondaatje's* The English Patient: *A Reader's Guide.* New York and London: Continuum, 2002.

Hutcheon, Linda. *The Canadian Postmodern: A Study of Contemporary English-Canadian Fiction.* Oxford, U.K., Toronto, and New York: Oxford University Press, 1988.

————. *A Poetics of Postmodernism.* New York and London: Routledge, 1988.

Jaggi, Maya. "The Soul of a Migrant." In *Guardian Weekend* (29 April 2000), pp. 27–31.

Jewinski, Ed. *Michael Ondaatje: Express Yourself Beautifully.* Toronto: ECW, 1994.

Mundwiler, Leslie. *Michael Ondaatje: Word, Image, Imagination.* Vancouver: Talon Books, 1984.

Siemerling, Winfried. *Discoveries of the Other: Alterity in the Work of Leonard Cohen, Hubert Aquin, Michael Ondaatje, and Nicole Brossard.* Toronto and Buffalo: University of Toronto Press, 1994.

Solecki, Sam, ed. *Spider Blues: Essays on Michael Ondaatje.* Montreal: Vehicule Press, 1985.

Spearey, Susan. "Mapping and Masking: The Migrant Experience in Michael Ondaatje's *In the Skin of a Lion." Journal of Commonwealth Literature* 29: 45–60 (spring 1994).

Waldman, Nell. *Michael Ondaatje and His Works.* Toronto: ECW, 1980.

York, Lorraine M. *The Other Side of Dailiness: Photography in the Works of Alice Munro, Timothy Findley, Michael Ondaatje and Margaret Laurence.* Toronto: ECW, 1988.

Alan Paton

(1903–1988)

ANDREW VAN DER VLIES

ALAN PATON'S LITERARY reputation rests almost entirely on his first novel, *Cry, the Beloved Country,* published in 1948. It enjoys a status which the novelist Dan Jacobson calls proverbial, seeming familiar to many South Africans who may never have read it; Nadine Gordimer has described it as the most influential novel ever written about South Africa. It has come to be regarded as both a moving social document—with a profound impact likened by some to Harriet Beecher Stowe's *Uncle Tom's Cabin,* America's most famous abolitionist text—and as an accomplished literary work. In the United States and Britain, Paton is among the very few South African authors of whom many people will have heard or whose work they will have read. His most famous novel continues to be widely taught in many English-speaking countries, and has achieved what might be termed hypercanonical status. It has inspired stage and film adaptations, and by the time of the author's death in 1988 had sold fifteen million copies worldwide.

Paton was a forty-five-year-old civil servant when *Cry, the Beloved Country* was published. He spent the remaining forty years of his life struggling to balance a desire to continue writing—to being the man of letters into which his novel's success transformed him—with a dedication to fighting the injustices which had impelled him to write the novel in the first place. For generations of South Africans, Paton was as much politician as author. He was seen, depending on one's allegiances, as a farsighted champion of nonracialism or as a dangerous liberal in league with those forces which threatened white South Africa's security. In a 1966 piece titled "Interview with Himself" (collected in *Knocking on the Door: Shorter Writings,* 1975), Paton poses as both interviewer and subject, and notes that he had never been able to make writing his life's work; he had got "caught up in politics" (p. 176). He wrote only two further novels, *Too Late the Phalarope* (1953) and *Ah, But Your Land Is Beautiful* (1981), the former attracting a measure of critical appreciation. Both were deeply concerned with the consequences of the racial policies and narrow-minded nationalism of South Africa's National Party government, the party of white Afrikaners (Afrikaans-speakers, descendants of seventeenth- and eighteenth-century Dutch and French Huguenot settlers). Paton published several short stories, two biographies of liberal leaders whom he greatly admired, three memoirs, and a collection of religious meditations. His output as a political commentator and polemicist was enormous, particularly in the 1950s and 1960s.

EARLY LIFE AND CAREER

Alan Stewart Paton was born on 11 January 1903 in Pietermaritzburg, capital of the British colony of Natal, to a Scottish father, James Paton, a court stenographer, and a South African mother of British descent, Eunice James. Natal would join with the Cape Colony and the two former Boer republics defeated in the Anglo-Boer War (1899–1902)—the Transvaal and Orange Free State—to form the Union of South Africa in 1910. Paton's father had been a member of the Christadelphians, a strictly pacifist sect with an authoritarian streak (for example, forbidding marriage to non-Christadelphians). Paton's relationship with his stern, demanding father, and his childhood familiarity with the language of the 1611 King James Authorized Version of the Bible, were lasting influences on his ideas and works. He would reject any group which regarded itself as elite; his writing was imbued with the cadences of biblical language and drew heavily on biblical parable. Paton joined the Anglican (Episcopal) Church in the late 1920s, and his faith came to inform every aspect of his life—his actions as head of a reformatory, his growing involvement in the politics of opposition to racial injustice, and his writing, whether creative or polemical.

The young Paton was a devoted reader, fond of Shakespeare, Milton, the romantics, Alfred, Lord Tennyson, and Robert Browning. His aesthetic imagination was also fired by the natural beauty of rural Natal. After a successful career at school, he went to the university college in Pietermaritzburg, where he was prominent in student politics and the student Christian movement, and was a regular contributor to the college magazine. He graduated with a science degree and in 1925 went as a mathematics teacher to a school in Ixopo, in rural Natal, in the vicinity of which he would set parts of his most famous novel. Here he met Doris ("Dorrie") Olive Lusted Francis, whom he married in 1928, soon after her first husband died; the couple had two sons. Dorrie died in

late 1967, and Paton married Anne Hopkins, née Davis, in 1969; she had become his secretary after Dorrie's death. Paton taught at his former high school in Pietermaritzburg between 1928 and 1935, when he took up an appointment as principal of a reformatory for black male youth at Diepkloof, outside Johannesburg. He effected progressive and far-reaching changes to the reformatory during his term of office (1935–1948), tearing down its barbed-wire fences and introducing greater freedom and responsibility for the boys under his charge.

To understand Paton's contribution to South African literary and public life, one must consider his work in its historical context. He grew up in an English-speaking household, but came, through his parents' example and through early experiences at school and university, to believe in the reconciliation of English and Afrikaans-speaking white South Africans. This was a prevalent concern among politicians during the 1920s, in the face of Afrikaner bitterness after the Anglo-Boer War. Paton claimed that his experiences at Diepkloof ended his unquestioning acceptance of white privilege, and opened his eyes to the suffering, and causes of suffering, of black South Africans. He began to write about the injustices which successive white governments, intent on reconciliation between white South Africans, continued to expect other South Africans to endure. These "other" South Africans, derogatorily categorized as "nonwhites," were classed using the racial terms black, Coloured (a term of self-identification that continues to be in use among the heterogeneous mixed-race community in South Africa), and Indian (descendants of indentured laborers from the subcontinent, forming a large minority, especially in Natal). The right to vote had been determined in the former Cape Colony not by race, but by property; in fact, women as a group were disenfranchised to an extent that black men were not, in the nineteenth-century colony. But attempts to extend this system to the entire country had failed when the Cape Colony became part of the Union of South

Africa in 1910. The Cape Colony became the Cape Province, and was allowed to keep its mixed-race voters' roll, but by the mid-1930s black voters had been removed, and the 1950s would see an extended struggle to remove Coloured voters as well. Soon the political life of the entire country was dominated by white politicians, elected almost entirely by a white electorate, although there were a certain number of white representatives elected by blacks.

One of the few liberal voices in government after 1934 was Jan Hendrik Hofmeyr, an Afrikaner child prodigy who had studied at Oxford, was a professor in South Africa by the age of twenty-two, and administrator of the Transvaal—an appointed position, the highest political administrative post in each of the Union's four provinces—at twenty-nine. Paton met Hofmeyr in 1927 and would be profoundly influenced by him; the British edition of *Cry, the Beloved Country* was dedicated jointly to Dorrie Paton and to Hofmeyr. Through Hofmeyr's reforms, the administration of reformatories was transferred from the Prisons to the Education Department in 1934, and Paton became principal of Diepkloof through Hofmeyr's influence. It was in the hopes of securing the post of director of prisons, again through Hofmeyr's patronage, that he undertook a study tour of reformatories in Britain, Sweden, the United States, and Canada between June 1946 and January 1947. Taking a break from his Swedish tour to visit the seaport of Trondheim in Norway in September, he began in a hotel room there to write about a humble black priest from an area of Natal he knew well. This old man journeys to Johannesburg in search of his son, to find that the boy, induced by poverty and social conditions, has fallen prey to a life of crime. Paton finished the narrative at the home of friends near San Francisco on 29 December 1946. Maxwell Perkins, editor at Charles Scribner's Sons in New York, accepted the manuscript of the novel in February 1947.

Cry, the Beloved Country was published by Scribners in New York in February 1948, and by Jonathan Cape in London the following September. In South Africa, the National Party of Daniel F. Malan won power, unexpectedly, from Field Marshal Jan Smuts's moderate United Party in May of the same year, and set about implementing a more rigorous system of racial separation. Paton wrote in *Journey Continued* (1988), the second volume of his autobiography, that these "were the two decisive events of my life. The first, the modest fame that came from the book, opened many new doors. The second, the coming to power of apartheid, was to close many others" (p. 8).

CRY, THE BELOVED COUNTRY

The opening descriptions of *Cry, the Beloved Country* have come to be almost as widely quoted as Isak Dinesen's description of her Kenyan farm in *Out of Africa* (1937). Paton's novel begins: "There is a lovely road that runs from Ixopo into the hills. These hills are grass-covered and rolling, and they are lovely beyond any singing of it" (p. 3, page references throughout are to U.S. first editions of texts, unless stated otherwise). He presents an image of an earthly paradise, a countryside of fine vistas, of abundant, fertile, and well-managed land. It soon becomes clear, however, that this is countryside occupied by whites; impoverished black farmers and their families, many of which have been fragmented by an exodus of job seekers to the cities, are gathered on poorly managed and overcrowded tribal land barely able to sustain them. The entire novel is structured according to this juxtaposition of unequal social conditions enjoyed or endured by white and black respectively, whether in the rural landscape of Natal and Zululand (the area is now the unified province of KwaZulu-Natal), or in Johannesburg, a city built on the wealth of gold mining and industry reliant on cheap black labor.

The Reverend Stephen Kumalo, the Anglican minister of Ndotsheni, a black settlement in the valley below Ixopo, is summoned by a fellow cleric to Johannesburg to fetch his sick sister, Gertrude. Kumalo makes the journey by train, determined, too, to find his only son, from whom there has been no word for a long time. In the big city, the humble rural priest finds a new and nasty world in which tribal custom and Christian morality have been eroded by dire social conditions. In the words of the young Johannesburg priest Theophilus Msimangu, Virgil to Kumalo's Dante in this urban hell:

> The tragedy is not that things are broken. The tragedy is that they are not mended again. The white man has broken the tribe. And it is my belief . . . that it cannot be mended again. But the house that is broken, and the man that falls apart when the house is broken, these are the tragic things. That is why children break the law, and old white people are robbed and beaten.

(p. 25)

Kumalo finds that his sister has become a prostitute, but that she is willing to take her illegitimate son and go back to Ndotsheni with Kumalo. Stephen Kumalo's brother, John, has become a corrupt political agitator. Kumalo also finds his son with the help of Msimangu, and of kindly white priests and reformatory staff, but it is too late. The boy, Absalom, has shot and killed a white man during a bungled housebreaking, and is to stand trial. The murdered man, Arthur Jarvis, is the son of a white farmer from the hills overlooking the eroded valley of Ndotsheni, and so the novel brings together the lives of the two communities contrasted so effectively in its opening paragraphs. In a cruel ironic twist, Arthur Jarvis was one of the foremost promoters of the cause of black upliftment in Johannesburg, and a prime mover in several charitable concerns to assist young black urban youth, like Absalom.

The novel is rich in Judeo-Christian imagery and patterns. If one of its chief structural devices is pilgrimage, no less important than Kumalo's is the journey to an awareness of social problems made by Arthur Jarvis's father, James. He sits in his son's study reading several of the dead man's essays on his own coming-to-consciousness, and experiences, half-resentfully, a kind of bitter epiphany. The walls of the study are hung with four pictures which serve as ideological icons for Paton and his novel, as much as for his character Arthur. The crucified Christ represents Christian faith, and Abraham Lincoln provides an example of a leader who freed the enslaved and inspired moral courage in his people. Then there is a picture of Vergelegen (literally "situated far away," from the original European settlement on Table Bay at the Cape of Good Hope), the white gabled house of a seventeenth-century Dutch governor of the Cape; as well as a painting of leafless willows by a river in a wintry landscape. Both might be taken to symbolize the relatively early settlement of South Africa by Europeans, and their attachment to the land. This concern invites comparison with a position Paton stated repeatedly in his nonfiction polemical writing on the complexity of race relations in South Africa—that many white South Africans, particularly Afrikaners, unlike recent European settlers elsewhere in Africa, had nowhere else to go, and felt, however paradoxically, African. Arthur represents, for Paton, an ideal of the man of conscience the author himself strove to become. One of the essays which James reads expresses Arthur's wonder that as a child he could read "brochures about lovely South Africa, that land of sun and beauty sheltered from the storms of the world, and feel pride in it and love for it, and yet know nothing about it at all" (p. 170), about the conditions endured by the majority of the population. Paton himself had written something almost identical in a 1946 essay entitled "This Is My Own, My Native Land" (reprinted in *Knocking on the Door*). Stephen Kumalo and James Jarvis meet by accident and learn of their implication in the other's life. Kumalo's son is sentenced to be hanged. Gertrude having run away again, the old priest returns to Ndotsheni with his nephew (Gertrude's son), and with Absalom's pregnant wife. Arthur's grief-stricken parents return to their farm, where his mother, Margaret, dies.

James dedicates himself to helping the people of Ndotsheni: he sponsors the building of a dam, employs an agricultural instructor to teach the people productive and environmentally friendly farming techniques, provides milk for the sick children, and offers to rebuild the dilapidated church. The final relationship between Kumalo and Jarvis offers some hope for interracial understanding. They meet toward the end of the novel as Kumalo makes his way up a nearby mountain to await dawn on the day of his son's execution. Jarvis says, stretching "his hand over the darkening valley": "One thing is about to be finished, but here is something that is only begun" (p. 268). The novel ends with the dawn, and the narrator musing about the coming of a greater metaphorical dawn for the country: "But when that dawn will come, of our emancipation, from the fear of bondage and the bondage of fear, why, that is a secret" (p. 273). In *For You Departed* (1969), Paton would describe *Cry, the Beloved Country* as "a song of love for one's far distant country," as being filled with longing for "that unattainable land where there shall be no more death, neither sorrow, nor crying, for that land that cannot be again, of hills and grass and bracken"; "It is a story of the beauty and terror of the human life" (p. 88–89).

Maxwell Anderson's book for the 1949 Broadway musical based on Paton's novel, entitled *Lost in the Stars* (with music by Kurt Weill), makes much of James Jarvis's conversion to caring liberal by having his character initially more virulently racist. Much of the subtlety of Paton's depiction of a white English-speaker who had previously led an uninterrogated life of privilege, is thus lost in the blurring of old-fashioned English-speaker with nationalist Afrikaner, distinctions which American audiences did not, perhaps, appreciate. The interpretation of Paton's characters as "types," acting out a psychodrama with universal resonance, was widespread in North American and British reviews of the novel. Reviewers were concerned to present the novel as something other than propaganda, due to a reigning critical disdain for

strident political protest at the time. The late 1940s and early 1950s were, furthermore, the early years of the Cold War, when advocacy of extreme political change appeared suspiciously radical to many readers and to the conservative political establishment. Paton's representation of a Christian humanist solution to racial problems served to satisfy a white middle-class American readership concerned with its own racial problems, particularly in the South. The novel became a best-seller in the United States, sold very well in Britain, and was promoted as a school and college text in both countries. The Anderson/Weill adaptation opened on Broadway in 1949, and a film directed by Zoltan Korda was premiered in 1951. Paton won prizes in Britain and America, and soon became a minor celebrity, his text the closest thing to a canonical work of literature by a South African author. It is only with the emergence and critical and public success of works by the dramatist Athol Fugard, and the novelists Nadine Gordimer and J. M.Coetzee, that other (white) South African writers have come to enjoy a similar popular reputation. However, their work has never matched the sales or educational institutionalization of Paton's novel.

Many read *Cry, the Beloved Country* as a parable which sought to awaken South Africa's white population to their complicity in injustice, and to their responsibilities to alleviate the social and political conditions which led to such suffering. The Reverend Stephen Kumalo came to be seen by many of the early reviewers as a representative man, rather than as the specific representative of the oppressed in South Africa. It is thus perhaps unsurprising that many black, Coloured, and liberal white South African intellectuals gave the novel a qualified reception, reading it as a brave complaint against the status quo but viewing with distaste Kumalo's self-abnegation in the face of white largesse. Lewis Nkosi suggested in an essay entitled "The Fabulous Decade" that Kumalo had appeared to young black readers in the late 1940s and the 1950s as an expression of white sentiment, a character whose forbearance and resignation suggested that whites could evade responsibility for racial injustice through acts of charity performed by a few individuals. By the 1980s, in the wake of the 1976 Soweto riots and an upsurge both in violent resistance and brutal state repression, younger white critics also became increasingly vocal in their rejection of Paton's Christian humanist program for reconciliation. Stephen Watson suggested that Paton's presentation of the novel's tragic events as the function of some anonymous Fate obscured their real causes, and neutralized the imperative for political action.

Paton makes use of omniscient, third-person narration, often sounding in cadence like an Old Testament prophet, or the writer of the Psalms. He uses dashes rather than quotation marks to indicate direct speech, a device copied from James Joyce and John Steinbeck. In addition to his chief characters, Paton provides several "choruses" in the form of newspaper reports and passages of the direct speech of numerous anonymous residents of Johannesburg's affluent white suburbs, as well as of its destitute black shantytowns. Many reviewers in South African papers and journals noted that Paton had attempted to convey the essence of a transposed and translated Zulu idiom in the narrated thoughts and direct speech of his black characters, as in the following passage.

Then the chief was silent and alone with his thoughts, and it is not the custom to interpret a chief who is thus occupied with his thoughts. But Kumalo could see that he did not know what to say. He commenced to speak more than once, but whether he checked himself, or whether he could not see to the end of the words that he had in his mind, Kumalo could not say. Indeed a man is always so when another brings heavy matters to him, matters that he himself has many times considered, finding no answers to them.

(pp. 226–227)

Opinion was divided on whether this strengthened the impression of the novel as a

social or ethnographic record, or heightened its parable-like qualities.

The archaic speech of the black characters has been described by critics such as J. M.Coetzee and Tony Morphet as having the effect of portraying the speakers as backward or child-like. There are, certainly, deliberate mistranslations: Coetzee notes in *White Writing* (p. 127) the use of "fire-sticks" for "dynamite," and "chimney" for "mine shaft" in Paton's text (p. 21); Zulu has words for these things which cannot be translated directly as they have been. It is certainly true, too, that Paton's novel gives little idea of any effectively organized black political opposition, instead privileging Stephen Kumalo's reliance on faith and love. Kumalo is quick to chide the new agricultural instructor for suggesting that blacks should aspire to a condition of self-sufficiency in which handouts from conscience-stricken whites might be refused. His brother, John, is portrayed as a selfish, cowardly manipulator, whose confrontational politics are rejected by those characters who act in some measure as spokesmen for Paton's own political stance: "'Perhaps we should thank God he is corrupt,' said Msimangu solemnly. 'For if he were not corrupt, he could plunge this country into bloodshed'" (p. 183). It is true, too, that the legal system is cast as an inscrutable realm, and the legitimacy of laws made exclusively by whites not unduly questioned, although this presentation of the law is that given in the reported speech of the judge who convicts and sentences Absalom. The reader is invited to form his or her own opinion of the matter. The judge declares, self-defensively: "If the law is the law of a society that some feel to be unjust, it is the law and the society that must be changed. In the meantime there is an existing law that must be administered, and it is the sacred duty of a Judge to administer it" (p. 195).

Cry, the Beloved Country is an accurate portrait of social conditions in South Africa in 1946. It does attempt to present, particularly to readers of its time, an argument for the amelioration of social and legal conditions for South Africa's black population. Its reputation endures abroad, while in South Africa, despite an almost universal willingness to regard it as important in its historical awareness-raising effect, it is seen as having been behind the times, even in its time.

TOO LATE THE PHALAROPE

The immediate and extraordinary success of his first novel, and the unlikelihood that he would be able to work with the new National Party administration, prompted Paton to resign his post as principal of Diepkloof in 1948. Hendrik F. Verwoerd, editor of the Afrikaner-nationalist newspaper *Die Transvaler*, had derided Paton's reforms at Diepkloof as pandering to black children. As minister of native affairs from 1952 and prime minister from 1958, Verwoerd would become the chief architect of apartheid, and succeed in reversing Paton's advances at Diepkloof. Between 1948 and 1953 Paton lived on the south coast of Natal, trying to further his writing career. He visited the United States and United Kingdom, wrote short stories and poems, completed a second novel, and began writing a biography. Increasingly, however, he was haunted by racial injustices, and alarmed at the alacrity with which the new government was consolidating its grip on power. When Paton wrote *Cry, the Beloved Country* in 1946, he had retained some hope that the government might act to ameliorate the living and working conditions of black South Africans. The 1948 electoral victory of the National Party put an end to this hope. Furthermore, Hofmeyr died in the same year.

Many of Paton's preoccupations and emotions were channeled into his second novel, *Too Late the Phalarope*, published in 1953. The phalarope is a plover-like bird, the object of a bird-watching expedition which comes too late to effect reconciliation in the strained relationship between the novel's main character, Pieter van Vlaanderen, and his father, Jakob, a strictly

Calvinist and staunchly nationalist Afrikaner patriarch. The novel is highly dramatic, even melodramatic, and needs, in its handling of miscegenation, to be seen in the context both of its setting—a conservative farming area of the eastern Transvaal (currently Mpumalanga Province) sometime after the end of World War II, but before the National Party's electoral victory—and its time of writing.

Pieter van Vlaanderen is a hero in the mold of Greek tragedy: he is a star athlete, an apparently loving husband and father, and a respected policeman. But he is also, the narrator tells the reader, "always two men":

> The one was the soldier of the war, with all the English ribbons that his father hated; the lieutenant in the police, second only to the captain; the great rugby player, hero of thousands of boys and men. The other was the dark and silent man, hiding from all men his secret knowledge of himself, with that hardness and coldness that made men afraid of him, afraid even to speak to him.
>
> (p. 3)

Pieter's tragic flaw is that he succumbs to the temptation of a sexual liaison with a black woman. The Immorality Act of 1927 set out to police extramarital sexual relations; a particular stigma was attached in the (white) public eye to relations between people of different races. The National Party amended the act to reflect this in 1950 (after the novel's is set), and in 1949 it prohibited interracial marriage. Pieter's adultery is shameful enough to the small-town Christian community, but to Afrikaners casting themselves as members of a pure race, his miscegenation is unforgivable. Extremely religious nationalist Afrikaners believed they had fought and died for the right to live on their own land and to rule over conquered native races with whom they believed they had a sacred duty not to mix socially. Revisionist histories and public pageantry such as the centennial reenactment of the Great Trek (the movement of Afrikaner farmers, Boers, out of the Cape Colony and into the interior, to what they would settle as the Transvaal and Orange Free State) in 1938, bolstered their convictions. Paton conveys the sense of their almost literally religious bond with the land in the Afrikaans names of local farms:

> The mist had gone and the stars shone down on the grass country, on the farms of his nation and people, Buitenverwagting and Nooitgedacht, Weltevreden and Dankbaarheid ["Beyond Expectation," "Never Imagined," "Well Pleased," "Thankfulness"], on the whole countryside that they had bought with years of blood and sacrifice; for they had trekked . . . into a continent, dangerous and trackless, where wild beasts and savage men, and grim and waterless plains, had given way before their fierce will to be separate and survive.
>
> (pp. 16–17)

Jakob van Vlaanderen's first name is that of the Old Testament patriarch Jacob, favored son of Isaac, while his surname, literally "of Flanders," evokes Afrikaners' racial and religious roots in the Calvinist Low Countries. He extols the creed of the Afrikaner when declaring that: "the point of living is to serve the Lord your God, and to uphold the honour of your church and language and people" (p. 92).

Pieter's rank in the police is a result of his having served in the army in North Africa during World War II. One of Pieter's subordinates, Sergeant Steyn, a man senior in years but junior in rank (he did not serve in the war), comes to resent Pieter's facility with the English language, his war service, and his apparent haughtiness. Pieter had taken what was known as the red oath, indicating preparedness to serve outside the country's borders (South Africans fought mostly in North Africa and Italy). Many Afrikaners were sympathetic to Germany or at least did not wish to fight for the British Commonwealth, and either refused service altogether or, if enlisted, refused to leave South Africa. Pieter's war record abroad, which includes a Distinguished Service Order, is a point of tension with his conservative father, a man whose bitterness toward the British is undimmed from the Anglo-Boer War. Jakob even refuses to say

the name of the author of the bird guidebook which is Pieter's birthday gift to him, referring to him merely as an "Englishman." As Edward Callan observes, the author, Austin Roberts, bears the same surname as the commander of English forces in the Anglo-Boer War. Pieter commits adultery several times with a black woman named Stephanie, whom he knows as a persistent offender against legislation prohibiting the manufacture or sale of alcohol by black people, the only way she can make money to support her illegitimate child. Steyn observes Pieter talking with Stephanie in a dark street one night and bribes her to deposit, during their next rendezvous, certain items in Pieter's pockets. These serve to corroborate the claim that he has committed an offense under the Immorality Act. Pieter's fall from grace is swift and hard, and brings disgrace to his family in the eyes of the conservative town. Jakob disinherits his son, crosses his name out of the family Bible, destroys all of his gifts, resigns from all public offices, and shuts himself off from the world, vowing never to venture out of the house again. Jakob's sister and Pieter's aunt, Tante Sophie, leaves the household in order to support her nephew. After Jakob's death, apparently from shock, Pieter's mother and his wife support him during his trial. It is suggested that after serving his sentence he and his wife and children will have to start a new life somewhere else.

Critical discussion of *Too Late the Phalarope* has been divided. The novel was generally well received on publication in the United States and Britain, and by elements of the liberal South African press. Sympathetic critics since have regarded it as a powerful and moving story. Later scholars have, in a similar vein to the concerns raised about *Cry, the Beloved Country*'s political vision, critiqued the adequacy and ethical validity particularly of Paton's use of tragedy—the Immorality Act and the community's taboo against miscegenation act as substitutes for Fate or the Gods of Greek tragedy. In Paton's defense, the novel's narrative point of view implies a sense of irony which few commentators have observed. The novel is presented as a narrative, "the story of our destruction" (p. 3), compiled and narrated by Tante Sophie, using her own observations, Pieter's letters from prison, and the diary which he presents to her. Sophie's status as an outsider—she is harelipped and a spinster—allows her to pass as an often unobserved watcher. Yet she shares many of the unquestioned attitudes of her culture and moment: "Then I went off to the kitchen, where old Izak and Lena, who for all their blackness were good Christian souls, were working their heads off for the old master's party" (p. 98). Her attitudes, and an admiration for her nephew which borders on an unhealthy emotional attachment—"when he was a child, I desired to possess him. And now he is a man, I still desire to possess him" (p. 215)—make her a less than entirely reliable narrator. It is in the frequently unremarked ironic distance between author and peripheral but implicated narrator, as John O. Jordan has noted, that the novel's most trenchant critique of Afrikaner and of white society generally, lies. There is nothing in Sophie's narrative, for example, to suggest that Pieter rapes Stephanie, but the unequal power relationship between white policeman and black woman invites speculation about the novel's unwritten violence.

Tante Sophie's act of grieving for Pieter, and of compiling the testimony which is presented as the text of the novel, invites reading as a powerful critique of the misguided and destructive utopian fantasy of racial purity propagated by Calvinist Afrikaner nationalism:

> And I grieve for him, and the house he has made to fall with him, not as with Samson the house of his enemies, but the house of his own flesh and blood. And I grieve for the nation which gave him birth, that left the trodden and the known for the vast and secret continent, and made there songs of *heimwee* [nostalgia and loss] and longing, and the iron laws. And now the Lord has turned our captivity, I pray we shall not walk arrogant,

remembering Herod whom an Angel of the Lord struck down, for that he made himself a god.

> (p. 272)

It was a concern of young liberal Afrikaans intellectuals of the time that Afrikaner purity had itself become an object of unholy worship. In 1957, four years after *Too Late the Phalarope*, Jan Rabie would publish a groundbreaking Afrikaans novel entitled *Ons die afgod* (We the Idol), arguing just this. Although Tante Sophie's narrative may strike a modern reader as anachronistic, even politically incorrect, *Too Late the Phalarope* allowed Paton to explore with great feeling, and prescience, the mind-set of South Africa's ruling caste.

POLITICAL WRITINGS

In May 1953 Paton became one of two vice presidents of the Liberal Party, and in 1956 its national chairman. The party's goal was a society free from the deep-seated racial prejudices which had dominated South Africa for generations; it developed the long-standing liberal tradition in the former English colonies, and appealed to people from all sectors of society. One rallying point was opposition to the National Party government's attempt to remove Coloured voters in the Cape from the electoral roll. After several unconstitutional attempts the government succeeded, by reforming the Senate to give the ruling party the required majority. It was partly these assaults on the merest vestiges of, or foundations for, the extension of the vote to all which prompted liberal associations to unite and reconstitute as a political party. Paton's strongly held views about equality, and his work as a pioneering reformatory head and with numerous other charities, readied him for public life. His political journalism and occasional essays, long directed against racial injustice, were now harnessed to the cause of the party. Selections from a column he contributed sporadically between 1958 and 1966 to the Liberal Party newspaper, *Contact,* are collected in *The Long View* (1968). Some of his political writing is reprinted in *Knocking on the Door.* Peter Alexander's biography gives a comprehensive account of Paton's political life at this time, and a list of his many articles.

Crisis Years for South Africa, a speech given in London in February 1950 to an audience of supporters of missionary work, sketched a short history of South Africa's race "problem," offering a perhaps unexpectedly charitable description of the Afrikaner nationalist government, describing its members as "men influenced by the great ideals of Christianity—ideals of justice and love" (p. 4), but as men whose fear of losing their self-declared right to govern themselves overwhelmed their humanity. The speech gives an insight into Paton's desire to demystify South African affairs and render them less simplistic than usually depicted for foreign audiences. It also makes clear Paton's belief that Christians had a "responsibility to speak out against any action or attitude which is inspired by fear" (p. 7). This was a guiding principle of his political life. Several short histories of South Africa followed, all attempting to explain apartheid's injustices in historical context, and expressing the hope that South Africans would find the moral courage to confront their fears and move together toward a common society. *South Africa Today* (1953) ends with the declaration that the "logical opposition to White Nationalism and its 'no equality in church and state,' is a Liberal policy of 'equal rights for all civilized men'" (p. 30). *The Land and People of South Africa* (1955), published in Britain as *South Africa and Her People* (1957), was aimed at high school students and cast as a guided tour around the country and its problems. *South Africa in Transition* (1956) presented a similar tour, this time with photographs by the American photographer Dan Weiner.

In the very personal *Salute to My Great Grandchildren* (1954), part of a series of pamphlets published by a small liberal church press, Paton poses questions about the future political situation to his imagined descendants, seeking in the process to cast contemporary actions and opinions into context:

> Tell me, children, why did we do all this? Why did we propound policies that the mind so completely rejects? Do you see it all clearly? Were we so afraid that we no longer knew sense from nonsense? Were our great policies not children of reason at all, but of fear? Do you see that the water-diviner was deceived by the sewer?
>
> (p. 5)

The People Wept (1958) deals with the Group Areas Act, legislation which declared areas reserved for specified racial groups and had the effect of shifting a large number of black, Coloured, and Indian South Africans out of areas they had long occupied. They were often shifted from what were to be made largely white towns and cities into inconveniently located and poorly serviced townships. Paton's intentions were clear: "It is only when white South Africans realise what these inhumanities are, that they will understand clearly the nature of the laws to which they have consented; and as for people abroad, this booklet will provide them with a true picture of what is happening" (p. 2). *The Charlestown Story* (1959) presented the case history of one such "clearance."

Hope for South Africa (1958), a short work sketching South Africa's history and outlining the Liberal agenda, contains a tongue-in-cheek explanation of the meaning of the designation "liberal" in the view of conservative white South Africans: "It is liberal in South Africa to want educated Africans to have a parliamentary vote; it is more liberal to want them to be able to stand for parliament; it is even more liberal to want all Africans to participate fully in the processes of government" (p. 6). His novel about politics and the Liberal Party in the 1950s, *Ah, But Your Land Is Beautiful* (1981), enlarges on the term's associations: "It is hard to describe the detestation in which the words *liberal, liberalism,* and *liberalist* are held in white Pretoria. Liberalism denotes moral looseness and

504

degeneracy. White liberals are people who will hop into bed with blacks at the drop of a hat" (p. 79). The Suppression of Communism Act of 1950 was broad enough in its definitions of undesirable opposition to be used against any opponent of apartheid, and was invoked repeatedly to restrict Liberal Party members. Paton himself feared arrest at times, even penning a declaration in the early 1960s, "Under Threat of Arrest," published later in *Knocking on the Door,* for his wife to release in the event of his detention. He traveled to the United States to receive the 1960 Freedom Award from the New York organization Freedom House, a prize awarded since 1943 to defenders of civil liberties including Winston Churchill, Franklin D. Roosevelt, Dwight D. Eisenhower, George Marshall, and Dag Hammarskjold. Paton's passport was withdrawn by the authorities on his return to South Africa; it was only restored in 1970. The Liberal Party was finally made illegal under the Prohibition of Interference Act in 1968, and disbanded rather than restrict its membership to one racial group as demanded by legislation. Paton continued writing and speaking against apartheid and its injustices until his death on 12 April 1988, just two years before the release of the black South African political leader Nelson Mandela and the legalization of formerly proscribed political parties.

SHORT FICTION AND POETRY

Paton's short fiction and verse written in the period 1948 to 1960 suggest an ambivalence, a tension between the claims of the personal and the public. This was true particularly after 1953, but poems from 1948–1949, collected in *Knocking on the Door,* pose keenly the dilemma of the conscience-stricken writer. In "To Walt Whitman," he ponders his own late development as a published writer:

> And why did he not sing before? Why, duties,
> Duties and resolutions, programmes and crusades,
> Solemn undertakings, religious obligations,

> And plans to revolutionise the world,
> All crowded in upon him, till night came,
> And pen stared at paper, waiting for a voice
> That never spoke.
>
> (p. 62)

At the same time, however, words are the means by which he might, he wrote in the poem "I Have Approached," "waken the sleeping consciences" and "call back to duty the absenting obligations / To assault again, night and day, month and year / The fortresses and bastions of our fears" (p. 74). In a speech given in the United States in 1949, "Why I Write," Paton quoted another of his poems in answer to imagined questions: "Why does he write at all? . . . Or why if he writes, does he not follow the conventions?" (p. 82). His poem, "Could You Not Write Otherwise?" answers in its penultimate stanza:

> Simple I was, I wished to write but words,
> And melodies that had no meanings but their
>   music
> And songs that had no meaning but their song.
> But the deep notes and the undertones
> Kept sounding themselves, kept insistently
> Intruding themselves, like a prisoned tide
> That under the shining and the sunlit sea
> In caverns and corridors goes underground
>   thundering.
>
> (p. 83)

The much-anthologized "To a Small Boy Who Died at Diepkloof Reformatory" juxtaposes the pathos of the death of a child with the activity engendered in numerous departments of state by the minor transgression which landed him in detention, and with the documents and words which remain the only evidence of his short and troubled life. Paton makes a play on the idea of committal—the commission of his body to the earth following the child's commission to the reformatory, for an offense "in whose commission / Millions of men are in complicity" (p. 69).

Several of Paton's short stories from the 1950s were published as *Tales from a Troubled Land* in

New York, and, arranged differently, as *Debbie Go Home* in the United Kingdom in 1961. Most deal with experiences at Diepkloof. Of these, some are mere vignettes ("The Worst Thing of His Life" and "The Elephant Shooter," sketches of members of his staff). All show the narrator, the principal, in an ambivalent light—as having failed in some way, or as learning unexpectedly from his charges. In "Ha'penny," a small boy at the reformatory spins an elaborate tale about his supposed family, based on his having observed a real family in his hometown. The principal investigates and discovers that the child is an orphan; the woman claimed for his mother will have nothing to do with the child, as she is Coloured and he is black. The child, nicknamed Ha'penny, sickens when he discovers that the principal has uncovered his invention. The woman has a change of heart and arrives, pretending for the child that she is his mother, but it is too late, and he dies. "The Divided House" features a boy called Jacky who claims to want to become a priest, but constantly breaks the law. In "Death of a Tsotsi," a young gangster wants earnestly to reform, but is threatened by his old cronies and murdered by them on his release. "The Waste Land" is a taut, atmospheric description of a man escaping a mugging.

"Sponono" is perhaps the most interesting of the "Diepkloof" stories in the collection, describing the attachment to the principal of a young delinquent who repeatedly reprimands him for failing to act compassionately. The story plays deftly with ideas of the distinction between forgiveness and the need to bear the consequences of wrongdoing. Paton and Krishna Shah worked the story into a play which was performed in South Africa in 1962 and 1963 before transferring in 1964 to Broadway, where it was well received critically but not popularly, and had only a short run. Including the characters from "Ha'penny" and "The Death of a Tsotsi," it added a chorus and culminated in a dream sequence in which Sponono acts as judge of the principal's Christian trusteeship, exploring in a fascinating manner some of Paton's own

anxieties about his politics. Clyde Broster edited a useful anthology of the stories, poems, and other writings from and about the Diepkloof period in 1986 as *Diepkloof: Reflections of Diepkloof Reformatory*.

Three stories in *Tales from a Troubled Land* and *Debbie Go Home* are not set at Diepkloof. "A Drink in the Passage" describes, from the perspective of a successful black sculptor, a friendly advance from a well-meaning young white man. The story illustrates the extent to which fear of the "other," and legislation which all but criminalizes interracial contact, has alienated people of all races from carefree interaction and understanding. "Life for a Life" is a scathing portrayal of the lack of due legal process in the country. An elderly shepherd dies in mysterious circumstances in custody for questioning over the murder of his vicious farmer master. The story exposes the absurdity of the official answers given to the man's distressed but determined wife, Sara. In "Debbie Go Home," the title story in the British edition, Paton explores the manner in which politics divides members of a family. Jim de Villiers is a Coloured worker who may be laid off because of the introduction of job reservation for white workers. He arrives home to find his wife fitting an expensive ball gown on their daughter, whom she wants to attend the debutante ball, at which the (white) provincial administrator will be the guest of honor. Jim explodes: "'You've got some high white folks to receive our girls,' he said. 'They'll smile at them and shake their hands, and the Administrator will talk a lot of shit about the brotherhood of man and the sisterhood of women. But if one of our girls went to his house next week, it would be to the back door'" (pp. 12–13, British ed.). The son, Johnny, is active in the radical Unity Movement, and plans to picket the ball. The story's depiction of issues affecting the Coloured community was particularly pointed, and timely.

Other short stories and fictionalized reminiscences are collected in *Knocking on the Door*. The narrator of "Bulstrode's Daughter" recounts how, on a ship's journey, Bulstrode and half of the passengers on board are gravely offended that the narrator allows his children to play with the children of another passenger, a distinguished Indian man. "The General" is a strange tale of affection between two childhood friends, both generals in the South African army. "The Hero of Currie Road" features an elderly man who feels a sense of desperation at the racial divisions in the country, but strives to maintain his liberal principles in the face of criticism from the left and the right. "Sunlight in Trebizond Street" is an impressionistic tale of the psychological torture used on white radicals in police custody.

BIOGRAPHY AND AUTOBIOGRAPHY

Paton produced two biographies, both of leading public men who served, in qualified ways, as models for his life as a liberal and as a Christian. Both works are important in their own right, as well-researched records of influential lives. They are important, too, as examples of considered prose, revealing a certain artistry in their construction. Paton had begun to research a biography of J. H. Hofmeyr soon after his onetime mentor's death in 1948, but set it aside in 1952 on realizing that Mrs. Hofmeyr, who had lived with and dominated her son throughout his life, had particular ideas about the kind of book it should be. Paton took up the project again at the time of her death, in 1959, and it was published in 1964 in Britain, and issued in the United States the following year, in slightly abridged form. Hofmeyr is revealed in Paton's judicious and thorough picture as a flawed hero, a superb manager and efficient minister but without the courage to put into practice those comparatively radical ideas about equality for which Paton had come to admire him. He was the champion of the principle of equality, but could not effect changes which Paton felt would have ameliorated much suffering. Paton called it a biographical symphony, and it is an important piece of writing for any student of his oeuvre.

The second biography is of Geoffrey Clayton, *Apartheid and the Archbishop* (1973). Clayton, an Englishman, came to South Africa in 1933 as bishop of Johannesburg. In 1948 he became Archbishop of Cape Town, and so the head of the Anglican Church in South Africa, which was and is known as the Church of the Province of South Africa. In Paton's words, after Hofmeyr's death in 1948, Clayton was, for the next eight years until his own death in 1957, the "foremost upholder and defender of Christian liberal principle and practice" in South Africa (p. 170). Clayton realized that he had no choice but to make his church a voice of opposition to apartheid. He tried to hold the line between pietism—the view that the church should have nothing to do with politics, but only with the practice of faith, strictly defined—and activism—which rejects a Christianity that does not pay attention to politics and society. He came into conflict with priests including Michael Scott and Trevor Huddlestone for, as he saw it, using the church carelessly for their own political ends. Paton wrote about both figures in his political essays, and Father Vincent in *Cry, the Beloved Country* is based on Father Huddlestone, who is also a "character" in *Ah, But Your Land Is Beautiful.*

Clayton was often derided by the government for interfering with its affairs. His final conflict with it came when he decided to lead his church in defying new legislation which would ban mixed-race church services and disallow the use of a church by different races. Clayton died on the afternoon on which he was to sign a letter to the government indicating his opposition. *Apartheid and the Archbishop* is a meticulously researched work, containing much detail which will strike the modern general reader as perhaps of interest only to scholars of church history. It is significant, however, as Paton's record of a man he deemed to have led the examined, Christian life, in a country which he believed would be healed were everyone to follow such a model.

In 1967 Paton's wife, Dorrie, died. His tribute to her, published as *Kontakion for You Departed* in Britain and as *For You Departed* in the United States in 1969, mixes memories of their courtship and life together with accounts of his grief at her death and record of the political situation at the time. Paton drew the structure of his elegiac memoir from the Kontakion, an Orthodox service of remembrance and grief for the departed, but also an affirmation of faith. Sixty-nine passages are arranged as antiphon: odd-numbered passages are set in the immediate present, the aftermath of Dorrie's death, and even-numbered passages relate chronologically the couple's courtship and life together. Callan, in his monograph guide to Paton's work, finds in this deliberate counterpoint the book's "homiletic theme: while yesterdays may be recalled, they cannot be relived. This is a clear warning against the temptation to seek some Edenic or Arcadian past, a desire that can become a morbid growth in nations that deify the past" (p. 112). The memoir recalls Dorrie's strength in their joint struggle in the Liberal Party. As such, it is forcibly and uncompromisingly political. It was even necessary to amend South African copies of the British edition of the text so as not to fall afoul of restrictive legislation, it not being permitted to quote a banned person in South Africa, something Paton's memoir did. His description of a police raid may also have been deemed to have contravened legislation forbidding the revelation of any details about the operations of the security police.

Paton wrote autobiographical sketches, such as the "Case History of a Pinky," published by the South African Institute of Race Relations in 1971 and reprinted in *Knocking on the Door*. But in 1980 he published the first volume of his autobiography as *Towards the Mountain*, its title taken from Isaiah's vision of peace to come: the lion lying with the lamb on a holy mountain. The metaphor of life as a journey to a goal of spiritual satisfaction structures the entire work, as it structured *Cry, the Beloved Country* (which

itself had ended on a mountain). In 1988 the second and last volume of his autobiography appeared as *Journey Continued.* Both are highly readable recollections of an extraordinarily full life, and provide invaluable context for reading Paton's fiction and for considering his public achievements. They are also, however, as most autobiographies tend to be, occasionally vague and disingenuous. Peter Alexander's biography, *Alan Paton* (1994), fills many of the gaps.

STILL CRYING FOR THE BELOVED COUNTRY

Paton's final novel, *Ah, But Your Land Is Beautiful* (1981), was the first of a projected trilogy which would have presented a fictionalized account of the Liberal Party and other opposition organizations from the early 1950s to the late 1970s. The novel preceded the second volume of Paton's autobiography, suggesting that a fictionalized account of the politics which largely dominated his life was an important precursor to presenting these events in a first-person, nonfiction narrative. The title is both ironic and wistful, echoing the unknowing, often unseeing tourists who exclaim: "Ah, but your land is beautiful. That's what they say, the visitors, the Scandinavians and the Germans and the British and the Americans" (p. 35). Some do see the pain and injustice, and look toward Paton's longed-for ideal community: "There is talk of another land too, where the tears have been wiped from every eye, and there is no more death, neither sorrow, nor crying, nor any more pain, because all those things have passed away. But here in the land that is so beautiful, they have not passed away" (p. 36). The novel has six parts—"The Defiance Campaign," "The Cleft Stick," "Come Back, Africa," "Death of a Traitor," "The Holy Church of Zion," and "Into the Golden Age." Each presents a series of episodes of omniscient third-person narration in addition to a series of vignettes, letters, fictional newspaper reports, and reported or direct speech of numerous anonymous voices not unlike those in *Cry, the Beloved Country*. There are numerous characters, several plotlines, and independent incidents. All conspire to create a mosaic-like picture of opposition to the government.

The Defiance Campaign involved several high-profile acts of civil disobedience, carried out by such figures as Patrick Duncan, son of a former governor general of South Africa, and the Mahatma Gandhi's son Manilal (who grew up and lived in South Africa). Among the novel's cast of characters are the Bodasinghs, a wealthy Indian family whose eighteen-year-old daughter, Prem, in her final year of high school, repeatedly defies the ban on nonwhite readers in the city of Durban's Municipal Reference Library. She eventually falls in love with Hugh Mainwaring, president of the activist National Union of South African Students, and himself the son of a government official, the chairman of the Natal Executive. Prem is wounded in a drive-by shooting, almost certainly carried out by the security police. Mr. Wilberforce Sibusiso Nhlapo, the headmaster of J. H. Hofmeyr High School at Ingogo, in Zululand, attempts to negotiate student activism and the threatened revolt of some of his more radical colleagues as he tries to attend to the education of his pupils. Another character, Robert Mansfield, is the headmaster of Newcastle High School in Natal. He attempts to organize racially mixed sports events, but resigns his position when these events are prevented by parents' opposition and government threats. He is harassed by means of obscene and threatening letters, his car is tampered with, his house is bombed, and he eventually emigrates to Australia. Mansfield is based, very loosely at least, on Paton and his experiences in the Liberal Party. Paton is arguably also represented by another character, Philip Drummond, elected national chairman of the party (as was Paton), and described as a Pietermaritzburg man (as was Paton), "respected by both conservatives and evangelicals, with private means, a proficiency in

Zulu, and an ironic way of speaking that concealed qualities of quite another order" (p. 107).

Numerous unrelated incidents are narrated in an attempt to convey a wide range of actual and metaphorical events. Black mourners at a white man's funeral are turned away. A white judge goes to a black church to wash the feet of a black woman as a symbolic apology, kisses them too, and is observed by a journalist who sees that it is reported widely, leading to divergent opinions—even among whites. A Coloured man who has lived his life as a white is discovered by the police, loses his job, is made to leave the white residential area, and is left by his disgusted white wife. White lawyers assist without charge blacks harassed or arrested on spurious or petty charges. Three brothers, sons of a prominent Afrikaner, join the Liberal Party in the face of charges of having deserted their people. There are descriptions of Trevor Huddleston assisting black inhabitants of Sophiatown as they leave their homes (which are soon to be destroyed) for a new township miles away. Paton describes Archbishop Clayton's resistance to the government, and his death before he can sign his letter of protest against the Native Laws Amendment Act's clauses restricting multiracial worship.

Interspersed throughout the novel are letters from a fictional Afrikaner civil servant in Pretoria, Gabriel van Onselen—initially an apparently staunch supporter of his nationalist bosses—to his liberal, spinster aunt, Trina, in Natal. These letters, often apparently responding to his aunt's expressions of disquiet at the excesses of apartheid, betray van Onselen's own increasing unease, although he does not allow himself to question the course on which the country is set. The zeal with which he supports the aims and ideals of policies of racial segregation, particularly as espoused by "Dr Hendrik," the barely (and unnecessarily) disguised Hendrik Verwoerd, comes to appear a desperately held defense against fear: "The whole magnificent plan of Separate Coexistence is taking shape under our very eyes" (p. 57). van Onselen's letters provide a vehicle for Paton to damn Afrikaner nationalist politicians and their supporting officials—sometimes perhaps too theatrically—in their own (imagined) words. It also allows him to provide a survey of government policy as a backdrop to the rest of the novel: the reader learns about the attempts to amend the voters' roll, for example, and about the farcical mass treason trial of 1956 to 1960, through these letters.

The novel ends with the death of Prime Minister Strijdom and the imminent accession of Verwoerd as the Afrikaner hero who will lead the country into a supposedly golden age of racial segregation. van Onselen finds it difficult to accept that this grand design might cause unforeseen suffering, but comes to believe that the country will be ostracized in the international community if the National Party continues on its course: "I have no time for these fanatics. The history of the Afrikaner is one of courage but also of resourcefulness and intelligence. The word *kragdadig* used to be a noble word, meaning powerful and resolute in deed. But it is gradually acquiring a second meaning, that the doer of the deed has more power than sense" (p. 220). The van Onselen sections of the novel are among the most intriguing and daring. In the end, they become absurdist, although whether Paton intended this effect as a critique of the distorted utopia of Afrikaner ideology, or whether he simply overreaches, is unclear. van Onselen's immediate superior, a much-vaunted ideologue, is trapped soliciting a black woman and, improbably, in a dreamlike sequence, sentenced to death for committing treason against the Afrikaner race in the process. van Onselen treats the man's mother with grace and respect, and eventually moves into the dead man's room in her home.

Ah, But Your Land Is Beautiful is not, by critical consensus, a great novel. Alexander quotes a review from the *Washington Quarterly* which described it as more fact than fiction, and

thus, "alas, a corresponding diminution of the artistry and technical skill needed to carry off so ambitious an enterprise" (p. 407). It was the mixed reception it received which encouraged Paton to get on with writing *Journey Continued* rather than the final novels of the trilogy. It is, however, an intriguing mixture of fact and fictionalized fact—the author's note states that many characters are "real," often thinly disguised—and provides a moving if melodramatic account of the opposition to apartheid between 1952 and 1958.

CONCLUSION

Paton declared himself impatient with those who denied an artist the right to promote a cause, or the politician the right to be literary, for fear of criticism for producing propaganda. He believed that one could be both artist and activist. His status as well known author of a still widely read novel was generated by the phenomenal early reception of *Cry, the Beloved Country*. Paton's legacy as a political thinker is highly contested, and his reputation as a literary artist has been debated. *Cry, the Beloved Country* remains a point of contact for almost all South African writers; it is the proverbial work which, for good or ill, captured the attention of a readership abroad, of that heterogeneous group all too often still constructed, for cultural and economic reasons, as the ideal imagined audience for (white) South African writing.

In *South Africa and Her People* (1957), Paton expressed the hope that the ideal of racial separation, the ideological impetus of apartheid, would lose its "lodgement in the white mind":

In 1960 the massive wall may show a crack.

In 1970 the crack may have become a breach.

In 1980 the waters may be pouring through.

In 2000 the river may be flowing quietly to the sea, with only a few ruins left of its former impediment, to be preserved as historical monuments of the folly of mankind.

(p. 138)

His prognosis was prescient—the early-twenty-first-century reader is separated by a decade from the unbanning of opposition parties in South Africa, from the release of Nelson Mandela and the victory of the African National Congress in the country's first all-race elections. It is a moot point whether the ruin of apartheid has also consigned to the status of an historical monument Paton's corpus of writing. His work (and not just *Cry, the Beloved Country*) rewards continued and renewed consideration by readers interested in the highly fraught relationship between political protest and creative writing, and in the processes of literary canonization.

Selected Bibliography

WORKS OF ALAN PATON

NOVELS

Cry, the Beloved Country: A Story of Comfort in Desolation. New York and London: Scribners, 1948, repr. Harmondsworth, U.K.: Penguin, 1958; New York: Collier Macmillan, 1987.

Too Late the Phalarope. New York: Scribners, 1953; London: Jonathan Cape, 1953; Cape Town: Frederick Cannon, 1953; London: Panther, 1958; Harmondsworth, U.K.: Penguin, 1971.

Ah, But Your Land Is Beautiful. Cape Town: David Philip, 1981; New York: Scribners, 1981; London: Jonathan Cape, 1981; Harmondsworth, U.K.: Penguin, 1983.

MEMOIRS/AUTOBIOGRAPHIES

Kontakion for You Departed. London: Jonathan Cape, 1969. Repub. as *For You Departed.* New York: Scribners, 1969.

Towards the Mountain: An Autobiography. New York: Scribners, 1980; London: Jonathan Cape, 1980; Cape Town: David Philip, 1980.

Journey Continued: An Autobiography. London: Oxford University Press, 1988; New York: Scribners, 1988; Cape Town: David Philip, 1988.

POLITICAL WRITING

Crisis Years for South Africa: Report of a Speech by Alan Paton. London: South Africa Church Office, 1950.

South Africa Today. London: Lutterworth, 1953.

Salute to My Great Grandchildren. Johannesburg: St Benedict's Booklets, 1954.

The Land and People of South Africa. Philadelphia: Lippincott, 1955, rev. 1964; Toronto: Longman, 1955. Repub. as *South Africa and Her People.* London: Lutterworth, 1957, rev. 1970.

South Africa in Transition. Photographs by Dan Weiner. New York: Scribners, 1956.

The People Wept: Being a Brief Account of the Origin, Contents, and Application of that Unjust Law of the Union of South Africa known as the Group Areas Act of 1950 (Since Consolidated as Act No. 77 of 1957). Kloof: Alan Paton, 1958.

The Charlestown Story. Pietermaritzburg, South Africa: Liberal Party of South Africa, 1959.

The Long View. Ed. by Edward Callan. New York: Praeger, 1968; London: Pall Mall, 1969. (Contains a selection of Paton's column "The Long View," published in the Liberal Party journal *Contact,* the speech given on his acceptance of the Freedom Award in 1960, and some other uncollected pieces.)

Hope for South Africa. London: Pall Mall, 1958; New York: Praeger, 1979.

Save the Beloved Country. Melville, South Africa: Hans Strydom, 1987; New York: Scribners, 1987.

OTHER WORKS

Debbie Go Home: Stories. London: Jonathan Cape, 1961. Revised and republished as *Tales from a Troubled Land.* New York: Scribners, 1961.

Sponono. With Krishna Shah. New York: Scribners, 1965; Cape Town: David Philip, 1983.

Instrument of Thy Peace: Meditations Prompted by the Prayer of St. Francis. New York: Seabury, 1968; London: Collins, 1970.

Knocking on the Door: Shorter Writings. Edited by Colin Gardiner. Cape Town: David Philip, 1975; New York: Scribners, 1975; London: Rex Collins, 1975. (Contains poems, short stories, political essays, and pamphlets, many not previously published.)

Diepkloof: Reflections of Diepkloof Reformatory. Edited by Clyde Broster. Cape Town: David Philip, 1986.

MANUSCRIPTS

An extensive collection of Paton's manuscripts and letters is held by the Alan Paton Centre at the University of Natal, Pietermaritzburg, KwaZulu-Natal, South Africa, which also preserves his library.

BIOGRAPHIES

Hofmeyr. London: Oxford University Press, 1964. Republished in abridged form as *South African Tragedy: The Life and Times of Jan Hofmeyr.* Edited by Dudley C. Lunt. New York: Scribners, 1965. Repubished as *Hofmeyr.* Cape Town: Oxford University Press, 1971.

Apartheid and the Archbishop: The Life and Times of Geoffrey Clayton, Archbishop of Cape Town. Cape Town: David Philip, 1973; New York: Scribners, 1973. London: Jonathan Cape, 1973.

STAGE AND FILM ADAPTATIONS

Lost in the Stars: A Musical Tragedy. Adaptation of *Cry, the Beloved Country,* libretto by Maxwell Anderson, music by Kurt Weill. New York: Sloane Associates, 1950; London: Jonathan Cape and Bodley Head, 1951.

Cry, the Beloved Country. Screenplay by Alan Paton and John Howard Lawson. Directed by Zoltan Korda, starring Canada Lee and Sidney Poitier. London Film Productions, 1951.

Cry, the Beloved Country: A Verse Drama Adapted from Alan Paton's Novel. By Felicia Komai with Josephine Douglas. London: Edinburgh House, 1954.

Too Late the Phalarope. By Robert Yale Libott from Paton's novel. Presented by Mark K. Frank at Belasco Theater, New York (11 October 1965.) Script unpublished.

Lost in the Stars. Screenplay by Maxwell Anderson (play) and Alfred Hayes (screenplay). Directed by Daniel Mann. American Express / Cinévision Limitée, 1974.

Cry, the Beloved Country. Screenplay by Ronald Harwood and Joshua Sinclair. Directed by Darrell Roodt, starring James Earl Jones and Richard Harris. Distant Horizon, Alpine Films Ltd., Videovision Entertainment, 1995.

CRITICAL STUDIES AND HISTORICAL BACKGROUND

Alexander, Peter F. *Alan Paton: A Biography.* New York: Oxford University Press, 1994. (Contains the most comprehensive bibliography of Paton's work.)

Baker, Sheridan, ed., *Paton's* Cry, the Beloved Country: *The Novel, The Critics, The Setting.* New York: Scribners, 1968.

Callan, Edward. *Alan Paton.* Rev. ed. Boston: Twayne, 1982.

Chapman, Michael. *Southern African Literatures.* London: Longman, 1996.

Coetzee, J. M. *White Writing: On the Culture of Letters in South Africa.* New Haven, Conn.: Yale University Press, 1988.

Davenport, Rodney, and Christopher Saunders. *South Africa: A Modern History,* 5th ed., New York: St. Martin's Press, 2000; London: Macmillan, 2000.

Foster, Malcolm. *Cry, the Beloved Country: Notes.* Toronto: Coles, 1970.

Gardner, Colin. "Alan Paton: Often Admired, Sometimes Criticized, Usually Misunderstood," in *Natalia* 18 (December 1988).

Gordimer, Nadine, and David Goldblatt. *Lifetimes under Apartheid.* London: Cape, 1986. (A record of conditions under apartheid with photographs by Goldblatt and text by Gordimer.)

Hartnett, C. P. *Paton's* Cry, the Beloved Country *and* Too Late the Phalarope *and* Tales from a Troubled Land: *A Critical Commentary.* New York: Monarch, 1965.

Hooper, M. J. "Paton and the Silence of Stephanie." *English Studies in Africa* 32, no.1 (1989).

Iannone, C. "Alan Paton's Tragic Liberalism." *American Scholar* 66, no. 3 (1997).

Jacobson, D. "Nostalgia for the Future." *Times Literary Supplement* (29 July 1988).

Jordan, John O. "Alan Paton and the Novel of South African Liberalism: *Too Late the Phalarope.*" *Modern Fiction Studies* 42, no. 4 (1996).

Luthuli, Albert. *Let My People Go.* London, Collins, 1962.

Matlaw, Myron. "Alan Paton's *Cry, the Beloved Country* and Maxwell Anderson's/Kurt Weill's *Lost in the Stars*: A Consideration of Genres," in *Arcadia: Zeitschrift fur Vergleichende Literaturwissenschaft* 10, no. 3 (1975).

Medalie, David. "'A Corridor Shut at Both Ends': Admonition and Impasse in Van der Post's *In a Province* and Paton's *Cry, the Beloved Country.*" *English in Africa* 25 (October 1998).

Morphet, Tony. "Stranger Fictions: Trajectories in the Liberal Novel." *World Literature Today* 70, no. 1 (winter 1996).

Nash, Andrew. "The Way to the Beloved Country: History and the Individual in Alan Paton's *Towards the Mountain.*" *English in Africa* 10, no. 2 (October 1983).

Nixon, Rob. *Homelands, Harlem and Hollywood: South African Culture and the World Beyond.* New York and London: Routledge, 1994.

Nkosi, Lewis. "The Fabulous Decade: The Fifties," in *Home and Exile.* London: Longmans, Green, 1965.

Parker, Kenneth, ed. *The South African Novel in English: Essays in Criticism and Society.* London: Macmillan, 1978.

Paton, Anne. *Some Sort of a Job: My Life with Alan Paton.* New York: Viking, 1992; London: Penguin, 1992.

Ridden, G. M. *Alan Paton: Cry, the Beloved Country: Notes.* Harlow, U.K.: Longman, 1983. (A volume in the York Notes series popular among British high school students and university undergraduates).

Rive, Richard, "The Liberal Tradition in South African Literature." *Contrast: South African Literary Journal* 14, no. 3 (July 1983).

Smith, Malvern Van Wyk. *Grounds of Contest: A Survey of South African English Literature.* Kenwyn, South Africa: Juta, 1990.

Sparks, Allister. *The Mind of South Africa.* London: Heinemann, 1990; New York: Knopf, 1990.

Stevens, I. N. "Paton's Narrator Sophie: Justice and Mercy in *Too Late the Phalarope.*" *International Fiction Review* 8, no. 3 (winter 1981).

Thompson, J. B. "Poetic Truth in *Too Late the Phalarope.*" *English Studies in Africa* 24, no. 1 (March 1981).

Vigne, Randolph. *Liberals against Apartheid: A History of the Liberal Party of South Africa, 1953–1968.* New York: St. Martin's Press, 1997.

Watson, Stephen. "*Cry, the Beloved Country* and the Failure of Liberal Vision." *English in Africa* 9, no. 1 (May 1982).

Caryl Phillips

(1958–)

GAIL LOW

CARYL PHILLIPS IS one of the most talented and prolific contemporary British writers of Caribbean descent. A critic, playwright, broadcaster, essayist, and screenwriter, he is also a novelist of repute. His fictions explore the history and legacy of slavery, colonialism, racism, and postwar migration with complexity and great sensitivity. If his works exhibit a keen historical sense, they are modulated by their focus on individuals caught in the maelstrom of larger historical forces outside their control. In Phillips's oeuvre one sees a fascination with voice and the way a combination of diverse voices forms a choral unity within the structured whole of a novel. This musical rendering of individual voices is perfectly suited to Phillips's imaginative invocation of diverse and dispersed stories across the New World. Many of Phillips's novels are narrated by separate personas or told in such a way that readers gain an intimacy with the workings of individual minds and hearts. Despite his ethical concerns, he is a writer not afraid to take chances. His character studies range from victims of oppression to the oppressors themselves and are seldom tempered by authorial interjections. Phillips's travel writing is also accomplished, and his chronicles of journeys through Europe, Africa, the Americas, and Israel return again and again to the question of belonging and not belonging. His overriding concern with exile, displacement, longing, memory, and ancestry place him at the very center of a twentieth-century literary poetics of identity.

BIOGRAPHY

Caryl Phillips was born on 13 March 1958 in the small Caribbean island of St. Kitts. He was only four months old when his parents immigrated to Britain; theirs was one family among hundreds encouraged to journey from the British colonies and dominions to help with labor shortages during postwar reconstruction. Phillips grew up in a white working-class district of Leeds, England, and went to what he describes as "mainly white-dominated middle-class schools. Despite doing well academically, in interviews and essays Phillips has spoken often about the confusion and pain of racist encounters in his formative years, when he was constantly challenged over his right to live in Britain. Migration, the end of empire, and the crisis of British identity at a time of decolonization yoked immigration and race together in the national imagination as the "coloured problem." Such anxieties over race provoked spectacular backlashes, notably the Nottingham and Notting Hill race riots in

London of 1958 and the "Keep Britain White" campaigns led by right-wing political parties. A senior Conservative politician, Enoch Powell, made an infamous address in 1968 cultivating paranoia about a Britain filled with dark strangers; he sought actively to incite racial hatred by predicting violent reactions against immigration that would produce "rivers of blood." The legacy of Powell's depiction of black Britons as foreigners was far-reaching. Unsurprisingly, such a climate of insecurity and racialized tension made for an unsettled childhood. Phillips has written that when he was a young boy, "Britain's ambivalence" toward him and his family "could cause a stranger, a friend, or even a teacher to turn" suddenly against him. Questions of home, tribal ties, national allegiances, and their rhetorical landscape would become abiding themes in all of Phillips's work, and diaspora, exile, and not belonging are key preoccupations.

Phillips went to Oxford University in 1976 to study experimental psychology and neurophysiology, but he soon switched to English literature and language. He maintained a lively interest in the dramatic arts, directing plays by Henrik Ibsen, Harold Pinter, Shakespeare, and Tennessee Williams, among others. His first forays into creative writing manifested themselves in plays for theatrical production. At Oxford his encounters with a fellow student who was a black American encouraged him to explore what it meant to be "black" British. The mid- to late 1970s were landmark years in the history of black Britain, for they bear witness to the growing anger and politicization of black people in London. These political movements also drew strength from the civil rights campaigns in the United States, and Phillips speaks wryly of being a "truculent afro-sporting rebel" who, like many other black youths, turned deliberately away from the tolerance of his parents' generation. The street violence that erupted in Notting Hill in 1976 and in Lewisham in 1977 became a platform on which a generation of black youths protested their exclusion from society.

A visit to the United States undertaken in his second year at Oxford also impacted on his awareness of a wider black community. In memoirs and interviews Phillips has described reading Richard Wright's *Native Son* on a Los Angeles beach as an epiphanic moment. Wright's "deeply felt sense of social indignation" and imaginative exploration of the effects of racism on individuals struck a chord, and the novel's narrative power sparked Phillips's literary ambitions. Furthermore, the discovery of other African-American writers such as Amiri Baraka, Ralph Ellison, James Baldwin, Nikki Giovanni, and Sonia Sanchez opened his eyes to a rich tradition of black writing that was lacking in Britain. He felt not only that he could aspire to the status of a writer but that what he had to say was important and should be heard: "the fundamental problem was, if I was going to continue to live in Britain, how was I to reconcile the contradiction of feeling British, while being constantly told in many subtle and unsubtle ways that I did not belong." After graduating from Oxford, Phillips worked in Edinburgh and immersed himself in the theater and writing for radio broadcast. *Strange Fruit* (1981), *Where There Is Darkness* (1982), and *The Shelter* (1984) were written and produced in quick succession.

Phillips's return to the Caribbean island of his birth in 1980 and prolonged spells living between St. Kitts and England engendered what would later develop into a heightened preoccupation with belonging to two cultures, in particular the ambivalent and hybrid nature of allegiances. It also let him see displacement—being "of and not of" an identifiable national and cultural polity—as a "gift" rather than a curse. If his encounter with African-American writers offered him a literature that gave voice to his experiences as a black person, Phillips's discovery of Caribbean writers like George Lamming and Sam Selvon gave those experiences specificity. For Lamming and Selvon had themselves migrated to London in the 1950s; their novels of emigration were imbued with "the uncomfortable anxieties of belonging and not belonging" in a way that matched Phillips's own life experiences and those of many of his generation. The formal inventiveness of these writers also taught Phillips to think about the form of the novel and to see its technical problems and possibilities as "structural gamesmanship." Later Phillips was to praise the distinctiveness of Caribbean aesthetics and assert that its formal inventiveness was in part based on its historical and cultural hybridity. In *The Atlantic Sound* (2000), he writes, "Its restlessness of form, its polyphonic structures, its yoking together of man and nature, of past and present, its linguistic dualities and unwillingness to collapse into easy narrative closure . . . enables Caribbean writers and thinkers to easily slip the restrictive noose of race to which those of the African-American tradition seem so firmly wedded."

In 1990 Phillips was offered a creative writing residency at Amherst College in Massachusetts and in 1997 a full professorship. As of 2003, he was living and teaching in the United States. Phillips's interest in slavery, like that of other contemporary British writers such as the novelist Fred D'Aguiar and critic Paul Gilroy, in some ways reflects his transatlantic intellectual and academic connections. These writers' preoccupations with slavery can be traced to the influential work of African-American intellectuals like Henry Louis Gates Jr. and novelists like Toni Morrison. Yet it would equally be true to say that transatlantic connections have been part and parcel of a black diasporan cultural aesthetics that began with slavery. Phillips's ethical agenda has not waned with time, and his 2003 novel *A Distant Shore* seeks to highlight the human story behind the anonymous statistic of the refugee. In adjacent stories of an aging Englishwoman and an asylum seeker from Africa, the novel seeks to forge kinship and connections across the borders that separate various dispossessed and marginalized peoples.

Phillips's restless energy and diverse range of interests from music to tennis to weighty social causes are reflected in the subject matter of his prolific nonfiction output, including two volumes of travel writing (*The European Tribe*, 1987, and *The Atlantic Sound*), as well as a richly textured collection of essays (*A New World Order*, 2001) and an edited anthology on the game of tennis (*The Right Set: A Tennis Anthology*, 1999). In his relatively short career as a writer, he has received many prizes and awards. *The Final Passage* (1985) won the Malcolm X Prize for fiction and *The European Tribe* took the Martin Luther King Memorial Prize; *Crossing the River* (1993) was short-listed for the prestigious Booker Prize and awarded the James Tait Black Memorial Prize. Phillips has been awarded a British Council fellowship, a Rockefeller Foundation Bellagio residency, and a Guggenheim fellowship and was made a fellow of the Royal Society of Literature in 2000.

NOVELS OF MIGRATION: CARIBBEAN AND BRITAIN

Phillips's early works all have for their subject the experience of migration or reflection on the changes that such experiences have brought to bear on individuals. Many of the celebrated novels of Caribbean migration, such as George Lamming's *The Emigrants* (1954), Samuel Selvon's *The Lonely Londoners* (1956), and V. S. Naipaul's *The Mimic Men* (1967) focus on men. In *The Final Passage* (1985), Phillips rewrites the story of the postwar Caribbean from a woman's point of view. Leila's desire to migrate stems from her wish to escape a Caribbean that she associates with secrets and lies, cycles of poverty, macho attitudes, sexism, and the legacy of slavery—a place, she asserts, "overburdened with vegetation and complacency." London, in contrast, is imagined as a place of escape, a dream of new beginnings and achievements. Yet London turns out to be vastly different from her dreams; seen through Leila's eyes it is a place of decay, poverty, pollution, litter, emotional gloom, and the downright hostility evident in the signs "No vacancies for coloured, No blacks,

No coloureds." Leila's predicament is exacerbated by the fact that she is a young pregnant woman who has to take care of an infant. The novel charts Leila's gradual seclusion and the contraction of her world to the sitting room of her derelict house in the company of her very young children. Her isolation is physical as well as mental; she retreats into herself and becomes so dissociated from her surroundings that finally, in an ambiguous ending, the narrator describes her as "leaving England behind."

Both *Strange Fruit* (1981) and *Where There Is Darkness* (1982) are bleak plays that explore what it is to be a West Indian in Britain. Phillips explains in an interview with C. Rosalind Bell that *Strange Fruit* is about generational difference, the conflict that results in part from the sacrifices his parents' generation had to make and "the contradictions that this created in them," and also from the "second generation not knowing how to relate to the Caribbean," to Britain, or to their parents. *Strange Fruit* focuses on a single mother and her two sons. The mother is a schoolteacher whose journey to Britain was made in order to escape her drunken husband and to seek a better future for her young sons. She has had to struggle hard in order to provide them with a sound education, and it is clear from her speeches that the sacrifices she made and the hostility she endured were so that her sons might succeed in life. Yet both sons rebel against what they see as their mother's complacency and acceptance of racism. The sons are angry and disenchanted; one proclaims to his white girlfriend, "You try and kick out those of us who are already here and stop anyone else from coming in. Well, it ain't fucking working, is it? We're a beautiful people, a talented, resourceful, strong, dark people, a people just waking up. We're growing and you're scared shitless." But if these young men protest their treatment as foreigners and second-class citizens in a land that should be home, the older son's recent trip back to the Caribbean to meet his relations also makes him realize that he does not belong in the Caribbean. Alvin remarks in hurt and confu-

sion, "when I tried to talk to them, our own relatives, not just any black people, you know how they treated me? Like a stranger in a very strange land, and that's how I felt." Alvin's return makes him question his assumptions that home must be in the Caribbean or Africa and that all black people are brothers. He realizes that he has to find his own answers to the question of belonging and that no one can do it for him. Like his brother, Errol, he chooses to leave home. Their anger and estrangement renders their mother's sacrifices meaningless and her situation unbearable, and she commits suicide.

Whereas *Strange Fruit* examines the mother-son relationship, *Where There Is Darkness* focuses on the father. The play opens with Albert Williams'ss goodbye party on the eve of his departure for the Caribbean after twenty-five years in Britain. Like the mother and sons in *Strange Fruit*, there is very little communication between Albert and his father because they have different expectations and outlooks on life. The father's macho treatment of women causes further friction between his son and his black girlfriend and between him and his wife. By the end of the play Albert is quite clearly a broken man who has little understanding of his family, his relationships, or his environment, and his desire to return to the Caribbean seems to be motivated by escape. Elsewhere, in Phillips's 1986 novel *A State of Independence*, a central character like Albert returns to the West Indies after twenty years in Britain. Yet he finds that there is no return; his country has moved on, his relations and friends have drifted away, and his relatively comfortable experiences in Britain encourage him to find fault with the poverty of the environment to which he has returned and to object to its future development and inevitable corruption funded by "State-side" capitalism.

From this cluster of early texts one can see some of Phillips's developing preoccupations. *Strange Fruit, Where There Is Darkness,* and *The Final Passage* offer a critique of black masculinity and irresponsibility. The central male figures in all three texts are characterized by their unthinking cruelty to women and their selfish focus on their own interests. Errol in *Strange Fruit* uses his girlfriend for his own sexual pleasure and is oblivious to her emotional needs; that she is white renders her a convenient figure to blame for all the unpleasantness in his life. Similarly, Albert in *Where There Is Darkness* is not only verbally abusive to his white wife but also physically violent; his actions provoke his son's girlfriend to remark in exasperation, "I've never heard of anyone as selfish as you. You're like all black men, think the world owes them a favour so they can behave how they like, whether it's throwing bottles and bricks at the police or smashing women's faces." The gendering of migration in *The Final Passage* highlights the specific difficulties faced by migrant woman, who may have children and family to care for in contrast to their husband's relative freedom to roam the city for work or leisure. But Phillips is concerned with more than simply recounting the experiences of women: *The Final Passage* is written from the point of view of a woman, and it is particularly convincing in its portrayal of feminine vulnerability. This interest in what women think and experience marks all of Phillips's subsequent fictional writing. Also, *Where There Is Darkness* and *The Final Passage* show an early interest in experimenting with narrative form. In the former, flashback scenes are embodied within the present time of Albert's goodbye party and motivated by his memory of past events, but the frequency of these scenes also works to disrupt the logic of the play's narrative time. *The Final Passage* uses different focalizers in the first half of the novel to present different views of the same sequence of events or set of circumstances. The novel eschews narrative linearity through a very deliberate delayed disclosure of information regarding characters' pasts or motivation, thereby suggesting the fragmentation of individual life and historical understanding in the Caribbean.

NOVELS OF SLAVERY

Since the later years of the twentieth century, critiques of modernity have sought to question the ethnocentric basis of some of our fundamental beliefs about culture, civilization, rationality, and aesthetics, pointing out the link between the growth of European civilization and the history of slavery and imperialism and arguing that the consolidation of a modern European identity was based on its relationship with "others" and "outsiders." Phillips's work in the 1980s and 1990s can be located within this wider debate. For a time he was writing concertedly about slavery. He defends this obsession in his fictional work by arguing that "the root of our problem—of all those people, white and non-white, who live in Europe or the Americas—is to do with the forces that were engendered by the 'peculiar institution.'" Coming to terms with the past, he believes, is integral to "understanding where we are or where we might be going." Two novels from this period, *Cambridge* (1991) and *Crossing the River* (1993), expose how the beauty and wealth of the European world at home and abroad is founded on the savage exploitation and labor of the slaves, and crucially, explore the impact and legacy of slavery on both black and white, masters/mistresses and slaves, and their descendants.

Cambridge allows the larger debate linking modernity with slavery to be played out as a personal tragedy for its two central characters, Emily Cartwright, the mistress of a plantation, and Cambridge, a slave. Emily, daughter of an absentee English planter, is sent by her father to his Caribbean estate prior to an arranged marriage with an elderly man. She complains that such a commercial transaction is undertaken simply to benefit her father's future, and she starts her journey as one sympathetic to the abolitionist cause. She writes that she means to act as her father's conscience, keeping a record of the "pains and pleasures" "endured by those whose labor" enables her father "to continue to indulge himself in the heavy-pocketed manner to which he has become accustomed." Her relative innocence and position as a woman and visitor contributes to her estrangement from planter society, and in the early days she embraces this marginality, seeing herself as different and "set apart" from the white planter class. Yet with time, her stay on the Caribbean island reveals the extent of her complicity with the slave-owning community and how much she subscribes to their racialized prejudices. Emily switches sides; her affair with Mr. Brown, the overseer and manager of her father's plantation, is expressive of a willingness on her part to be identified as a slave owner. When Mr. Brown's brutality and injustices are revealed for what they are, Emily has to come to terms with what exactly her position entails. Her early idealism and abstract support for the abolitionist cause is shown to be a form of disavowal and willful blindness to the fact that slave labor has contributed as much to her position as lady as to her father's position as a wealthy gentleman in English society.

In the epilogue to her story, Emily's realization of her complicity in the plantation economy and her reactions to the stillbirth of her illegitimate child forces a confrontation with herself about who she really is and precipitates a mental breakdown. Her identification with the island and her friendship with her black maid, Stella, suggests that she does come to terms with how and what the island has made her. Yet Emily's own mental instability makes it very difficult to judge whether her openness and intimacy with Stella at the end is simply the product of a deranged mind or whether it signals the possibility of personal growth. What comes to the fore in Phillips's representation of the character is the pathos of her vulnerability and her marginality in the wake of slave emancipation—in this she is not unlike her literary predecessor Antoinette Cosway in Jean Rhys's *Wide Sargasso Sea* (1966).

The story of Cambridge's enslavement serves as a necessary counterpoint to the blatant prejudices voiced by those in the planter class. By offering us the tale of his capture and enslavement, Phillips shows the inhumanity that indicts all that freely partook of the trade in human lives. Cambridge's education, literacy, and fortitude are testament to his will to survive. Formerly an African named Olumide, his transformation into "an Englishman, albeit a little smudgy of complexion" represents his naive acceptance of European ideals. That he chooses to treat his master "as one man to another" contributes to his own demise. But if his assimilationist beliefs can be criticized, the savage treatment meted out on him is nothing less than a bitter condemnation of the civilization he aspires to.

Cambridge consists of three main narratives that are bookended by a prologue and epilogue. The first two of the three narratives are written in first-person voices of the slave mistress and the slave. The third appears to be a fragment from a proslavery newspaper giving details of Cambridge's death. These three narratives can also be characterized by their generic affiliations—that of the Englishwoman's diary or journal of travel, the slave narrative, and the colonial anti-abolitionist newspaper concerned with the rights of settlers and slave masters. In reproducing the genre, conventions of speech, syntax, and phrasing that mimic previous accounts of either planter or slave, Phillips creates a real feel for period and locality. Laying these three different narratives alongside each other without authorial comment forces readers to mediate between the self-contained realities of these vastly different social worlds and provides rich opportunities for ironic self-exposure. But Phillips never forces the situation through authorial commentary or mediation. What readers are left with at the end of the novel is a fractured and at times incommensurable account of plantation life and the principal characters involved in the tragedy.

The importance of creating and establishing character in a historical reconstruction seems crucial to Phillips's aesthetics, and his prominent use of the first-person voice and attempt to reproduce a textual and linguistic mimicry of a different age makes his writing distinctive. In his interview with Bell, Phillips speaks of undertaking an immense amount of historical research in order to "hear" his characters tell their stories and of his own role as that of a "conduit" for voices from the past. His fascination with first-person voice stems from his sense that it conveys a "flexible intimacy" that is not possible with "the straightjacket of the third person." According to Phillips, it also offers a powerful way to engage with complex historical questions and to rewrite the received wisdom of official history by encouraging readers to understand and "digest what they're saying, and somehow rework them." The combination of voices in Phillips's mature work lends them a choral quality in which one hears each distinctive sound but whose juxtapositions and layering forms the musical unity of the novel as a whole.

Nowhere is this more evident than in *Crossing the River.* Designed to make a "connection between the African world" and the "diasporan world" of African descendants, the novel comprises the first-person voices of an African father who laments his selling of his three children to the owner of a slave vessel; a slave woman remembering her family and reliving her past; an Englishwoman recounting her affair with a black soldier; and letters between a captain of a slave ship and his wife and between a slave repatriated to Liberia and his former patron, framed within a third-person account of their relationship. Three of the four sections of the novel are substantive, and these belong to the life stories of Nash, Martha, and Travis. These are not the original children sold by the African father but are figuratively associated with these children through their names and their common history of slavery; each of their

accounts is a permutation of the base matrix of loss and belonging that is invoked in the African father's lament in the prologue and epilogue. Their stories are individualized, but they are also emblematic and symbolic stories of survival of the black slave diaspora, exploring the poetics of kinship, social memory, and the renewal of identity. The continuity across time and place established in the novel is at once imaginative and fictive, but it also encourages readers to perceive that such continuity must be restaged through memory and that such remembering establishes an enduring link with the trauma of dispersal that constitutes the middle passage. *Crossing the River*'s inclusive understanding of diasporan poetics—for the novel embraces both black and white stories—is one that offers an alternative conception of freedom and belonging across and within racial lines.

The insistence that black and white histories are inextricably linked carries across from *Cambridge* to *Crossing the River.* The first section of the novel details the story of the freed slave Nash and his former master, Edward Williams. Edward's story is written in the third person but Nash's letters from Liberia to his mentor father and slave master are reproduced with the narrative. Again, Phillips provides very little narrative mediation between these different characters; as a result readers are forced to arbitrate between different perspectives and positions. Edward is presented at times as a benevolent patron and disinterested philanthropist, but, like Emily Cartwright in Phillips's earlier novel, it is also evident that his "well-liveried" domestic slaves contribute to his elegant lifestyle; his underlying racism surfaces very quickly when he lands in Africa. Nash Williams, made in the image of his master, inherits much of his master's mind-set, viewing Africa as a place of darkness and in dire need of education and religious instruction. The relationship between freed slave and master is likened ironically to that of son and father; it contains many of the emotional expectations of familial relationships, but it is imbued with little of their responsibilities. Nash's repatriation to Liberia is literally an abandonment, for his requests for financial help, supplies, and emotional support are not met. When Edward finally travels to Liberia, ostensibly to look for Nash, who goes missing, it is a journey to exorcise his personal ghosts, his homosexuality, and the discovery of his pedophilia. The revelation of Edward's abuse of Nash and other young slaves indicates a betrayal of trust that parallels the betrayal of the African father who sells his offspring into slavery.

If Nash's and Edward's stories in "The Pagan Coast" reflect a desire for kinship and love despite their abrogation in the actual treatment of each other, Martha's narrative, "West," explores the bond that endures among kinfolk in spite of separation and loss. Martha is depicted as a black pioneer whose journey westward across America is undertaken not in search of gold but of freedom and family. She dies tragically before she arrives in California, but her remembrance of her lost relations on her deathbed offers an imaginative transcendence. In Martha's narrative, the past is as real and vital as the present. This is signaled by a shift from past tense to present tense and from third-person to first-person voice, corresponding with the shifts between a narrator who details Martha's dying moments to Martha's own narration of her past. Ironically the past tense of the main narrative is actually the present time of Martha's impending death, while past events of Martha's life are narrated in the present tense. In "West" the past is coterminous with the present; the novel seems to suggest a fundamental relationship between time, space, memory, and a posited connection between various peoples. If memory is the space where linear narrative time is interrupted and dislocated, then diaspora is a spatialized unity of kinship between slaves and their descendants as a "many-tongued chorus of common memory." For all Martha's journey are travels in search of family and journeys that re-create her original family, and in this she echoes the original father of the prologue who hears his

children's voices; like him, she presides over stories of love and abandonment. Yet in contrast to the story of the original African father, and unlike Edward's, hers is a story of survival and a re-creation of kinship, not a story of parental guilt resulting from betrayal.

The third narrative, "Crossing the River," is very brief and belongs to James Hamilton, the captain of the slave ship *Duke of York*. Hamilton's letters and logbook draw on John Newton's eighteenth-century *Journal of a Slave Trader*. Hamilton's repetitive commercial record of the buying and selling of people as commodities and his bargaining strategies are in stark contrast to the pathos of Martha's tragedy. Hamilton's letters to his wife speak of the toll that his slave-trading career has taken on his temperament and suggest that the disavowal of his occupation and all it entails is increasingly difficult to maintain. He writes that "a continued indulgence in this trade and a keen faith cannot reside in one breast" and that "the warring passions of both love and hatred" cannot be contained in the same heart. The reader learns that Hamilton is an orphan who has not come to terms with his father's death and that his current separation from his wife adds to his desire for love and security. Yet the irony of his enforced breakup of slaves' families and kin is lost on him.

The last section, "Somewhere in England," belongs to Travis, the third of the "three children" sold into slavery but reimagined in this section as a black soldier in World War II Britain. His story is narrated by his English wife and lover, Joyce. Their romance ends with Travis's death in Italy and with Joyce giving up their baby son, Greer, for adoption. Greer returns to meet his birth mother for the first time at the close of their story. The section is written in the form of diary entries, but the journal is not assembled chronologically, nor are its individual entries of equal length. The entries work associatively, and the journal as a whole reads like an irregular patchwork of the significant moments of Joyce's life, such as her observation of the arrival of the American soldiers, the villagers' responses, her courtship with her first husband, Len, and their subsequent stormy relationship, in addition to her interracial romance. Joyce's nonconformity and her flouting of convention mark her as an outsider to the village community she lives in, but it is her marginality and loneliness that enable her to sympathize with the American soldiers' unease as "objects of curiosity." Throughout Joyce's diary, no mention is made of the fact that some of the GIs are black, even though she mentions a visit by an officer whose remarks gesture toward the racial divide between the "us" of the villagers and officers and the "them" of some of the regiment. For Joyce color has little significance, and it is not until her divorce and remarriage to Travis that one has a sense of the taboos they break by their love and the barriers that are erected to separate them. Yet despite Travis's early death, he survives in memory and through his son. Greer's decision to seek his birth mother points to the primacy of kinship, but crucially, it is a kinship that must be reconstituted rather than simply inherited. Greer's return symbolizes the survival of the child in the face of separation and closes the cycles of pain, separation, and betrayal that occur as motifs throughout the novel.

Within *Crossing the River* one encounters fathers, sons, daughters, and lovers searching relentlessly for kinship. The African father of the prologue and epilogue waits by the estuary of the river to listen for the voices of his "children," Nash, Martha, and Travis. Nash Williams in Liberia writes of wanting to return to his "father," mentor, and former owner, while Edward's guilt at betraying Nash propels him on a journey to the African interior to find his protégé. Martha's journey westward to California is framed as a search for her daughter. James Hamilton writes of his homesickness and loneliness; he dreams of being united with his wife and of learning more of his recently deceased father. Joyce's relationship with her mother is characterized by rejections, by her first lover through betrayal and by her first husband through conflict and abandonment. Joyce finds a brief respite in Travis but gives up her baby for adoption when he is killed. These sons and daughters of slave descendants, fractured by history, sink "hopeful roots into difficult soil" to survive the crossing and arrive on "the far bank . . . loved." In this diasporan chorus, Phillips also includes others in his poetic epilogue to the novel, like the drug addict in Brooklyn, the barefoot boy in Sao Paulo, the child prostitute and her mother in Santo Domingo. As the voices of the characters combine with that of the original father and other characters that people the novel, what emerges is a choral invocation of all those who have been marked by the history of slavery.

RACISM AND ANTI-SEMITISM

Diaspora is also a concept that is associated with the dispersal of Jews from their homeland, and Phillips, whose grandfather was Jewish, makes explicit links between racism and anti-Semitism. In memoirs, Phillips writes of an early sympathetic identification with the Jewish experience of anti-Semitism because it struck a chord with his own experiences of racism as a child. Because the Holocaust and Jewish persecution were topics in books, television documentaries, and the educational curriculum in a way that other forms of racism were not, Phillips remembers, in *The European Tribe,* "vicariously channell[ing] a part of my hurt and frustration through the Jewish experience." His interest in Jewish history is reflected in his fictional work and nonfiction writing on the creation of Europe's first ghetto in fifteenth-century Venice, and in his powerful characterization of the effects of the Holocaust and its memory on individual survivors. Phillips's third and sixth novels, *Higher Ground* (1989) and *The Nature of Blood* (1997) respectively, draw parallels between racial rituals of exclusion against black and Jewish people, the breakdown and traumatic dispersal of families, and their subsequent sense of loss, exile, and dispossession.

Higher Ground is made up of three individual but interlinked stories: "Heartland," the story of an unknown African who works for European slave traders; "Cargo Rap," the story of Rudi William, an African American imprisoned for armed robbery; and "Higher Ground," the tale of Irina, a Polish Jew who migrates to England on the children's transport during World War II, "shipwrecked" and without family, spending the rest of her life locked within herself, "staunching memories like blood from a punched nose." All three characters in *Higher Ground* are solitary and alienated figures who attempt, with varying degrees of success, to connect with others.

Written in the first person, the unknown African collaborationist in "Heartland" justifies his actions as a strategy for survival. He does not cultivate any emotional attachment to the Europeans living in the fort or to the Africans that arrive, for he has the task of separating family, village, and linguistic groups in order to break their spirits and forestall slave rebellions. The collaborationist's carefully cultivated isolation is broken when he forms a relationship with a girl he helps recruit and who later is raped by officers and soldiers. His feelings for her enable him to remember past social and emotional bonds and reawaken an empathetic capacity that allows him to connect with those he has helped enslave. The narrative ends with an imaginative and aesthetic invocation of such affiliation in a "choral chant" that sings of a promise to return to the "heart" land despite separation and exile.

Exile is the emotional terrain of the next two narratives. "Cargo Rap" comprises letters to family members written by Rudi William from his prison cell. His letters tell of his anger with, and alienation from, an American society that has committed acts of horrendous violence and violation against black Americans. Rudi reminds

his readers that 55 percent of prisoners are "Africans" that live on the "bottom level" of an American "social swill bucket." His rhetoric is inspired by the Black Power, decolonizing, and revolutionary movements of the 1960s, and he believes victims of oppression should rise up against their capitalist oppressors. Yet if his anger is understandable, his rage is sometimes indiscriminate; he is dogmatic rather than penetrating in his responses and seems to view history, as Phillips later remarks in *The Atlantic Sound*, "through the narrow prism of [his] . . . own pigmentation." For example, he blames his father for failing to be revolutionary. Rudi exhorts him to read Frantz Fanon, Marx, and Lenin "in order to discipline his mind," chastises him for not being "the strong natural African man" and warns him against being "some knock-kneed, shoe shuffling clown right out of a minstrel troupe." He wants his family to learn Chinese in order to read Mao. He calls his mother a "quisling" and castigates her for not seeing the "chains" of enslavement she wears because she works for a white woman. His attitude toward women is often misogynistic; he suggests at one point that they are the black man's "greatest enemy," needlessly emasculating their menfolk and rendering them infantile by looking after them. Rudi is prickly and defensive and suspicious of anyone who offers to help. Yet it is also equally obvious that he is constantly provoked and physically assaulted in prison, and his letters indicate increasing signs of physical and mental deterioration. In his last letter, addressed to his recently deceased mother, he compares his incarceration with enslavement on a plantation. But as the letter proceeds, it becomes ambiguous whether the associations are simply metaphorical or whether Rudi really thinks he is living on a slave plantation. "Higher Ground," the last of the three narratives, is written from the point of view of Irina, a Polish Jew who finds refuge in England through *kinder* transport but whose survival is the worst kind of punishment. Irina is haunted by the memories of her family who perished in World War II.

Without family, friends, or relations, she feels she has no identity; she is a woman emotionally marooned in a strange land, dreaming always of the past. Her vulnerability renders her an easy target for others' abuse. She finds herself institutionalized after a suicide attempt. Irina meets a young West Indian, Louis, near the end of the section, and for a fleeting moment they seem to strike up a sympathetic friendship. But Louis, who is himself homesick and adrift in a London that is hostile to new immigrants, has already decided to return home rather than face what he describes as "a life of spiritual poverty." Irina, at a breaking point, suffers another mental breakdown and awaits her return to the hospital.

All the stories in *Higher Ground* are united thematically in their exploration of exile, displacement, and alienation; all their central characters are emotionally adrift and lost, lacking the social, familial, or communal ties that would anchor them to a place called home. Characters find themselves caught up in situations that echo one another, for example in their various forms of incarceration, whether they be slave forts, American prisons, mental institutions, or even the prison house of the self. All three main characters aspire toward emotional fulfillment and connection with others, but all are "shipwrecked." Only the African collaborator finds peace, ironically, at the moment of his enslavement. Phillips develops slavery as a powerful trope by addressing it squarely at the start of the novel in order to explore its legacy on the fragmentation of self and culture. Irina's and the unknown African's stories are not only linked metaphorically—Phillips seems to be arguing for the commonality of these traumatic histories of separation and dispersal.

Higher Ground can be read as a forerunner to *The Nature of Blood* (1997), for both are concerned with the parallels between slavery and Jewish persecution in their history and effects. But whereas *Higher Ground* offers a more coterminous reading of racism, dispossession, disruption, and a severance of kinship ties, Phil-

lips in his later novel explores the meaning and concept of diaspora, exile, and belonging primarily through the history of anti-Semitism. *The Nature of Blood* is a stylistically sophisticated and ambitious attempt to offer multiple characters with different histories and locations, all of whom are given their own voices. The novel features Eva Stern, a young Jewish concentration-camp survivor, and chronicles the gradual disintegration of her life and family in Hitler's Germany. It also details her internment in Bergen-Belsen, the deaths of her friends and relations, and her attempts to come to terms with being a Holocaust survivor. Alongside Eva's narrative, and inextricably tied to it, are stories of Jewish persecution in fifteenth-century Europe and a fleshing out of Othello's story. Minor characters are also given their own voices, including Stephan, an uncle who presides over the formation of Israel as a Jewish state, and Malka, a black Ethiopian Jew who, despite the promise of being returned to her motherland, Israel, is treated like an outsider. While the novel is narrated predominantly in the first-person voices of the major characters, third-person is used in discursive historical sections detailing the creation of a Jewish ghetto, the setting up of the gas chambers, and in the novel's conclusion. Yet despite the use of the third-person voice, there is little attempt to use the convention to frame and situate the book's many voices and strands. The novel moves abruptly from voice to voice and from one location to another across history. Each new story adds a different layer and encourages a rethinking of the preceding story; the similarity of situations and differences of responses force a reconsideration of character. At times the novel's disjointed stops and starts and its complex layering actually frustrate the progressive unfolding of the story.

The temporal linearity of narration is interrupted strikingly through flashbacks, where the "violence of memory," memory not only of the living but also of the dead, characterizes a traumatic reliving of the painful past associated particularly with Holocaust survivors. Other characters show an inability to relinquish the memory of things past. Like the itch of a phantom limb that will not go away, one of the characters remarks that despite the freedom promised by the creation of a Jewish homeland, the "old world" can never be put to rest or surrendered. Linearity is also undercut through dramatic irony. Eva's and Othello's narrations of their own lives possess a curious prophetic quality that they are unaware of. This is in part because their stories are narrated in the present tense: the general outcomes of their stories are common knowledge, so their speeches gain a kind of dramatic irony through readers' knowledge of what is to come. For example, Othello's thoughts on his wife and the difficult life ahead of him read like a premonition of their tragedy—an outcome that is logically outside the story of Phillips's novel, which ends with their blissful union. Repetition also disrupts linear chronological time. Phillips highlights the structural similarity between the persecution of Jews in fifteenth-century Venice and Hitler's final solution, pointing to parallels between the herding of Jews into ghettos in the fifteenth century and the concentration camps of the twentieth. The effect is to render history as a traumatic and temporal repetition. This repetition is furthered by the careful use in different stories of certain visual motifs such as ashes and the flight of birds, which has the effect of echoing what previously occurred. Such motifs also create connections and patterns across time and enable the novel to achieve a poetic and structuring synchronicity in the face of the fissiparous energies of its different tales.

Metaphors of kinship, genealogy, ancestry, and origin function to transform peoples across temporal zones into a "people." Phillips's novel can be read as an extended meditation on the nature of diaspora—of blood and belonging across generations and consequently also of histories of not belonging. When asked in an interview to comment on the influence of William Styron's novel *Sophie's Choice* on his novel

Higher Ground, Phillips pointed to a racism that both black people and Jews struggle against and reflected on how both communities have been forced to experience a collective severance of family ties. The loss of kinfolk and the trauma associated with that experience is one of the central pillars of *The Nature of Blood*. The very first character we meet in the novel is a doctor in the newly formed nation of Israel, haunted by the loss of his wife and child, both of whom chose America over Israel. A boy he talks to at a refugee camp in Cyprus speaks of the loss of his parents in the war and of the emotional wrench of returning to his family home only to find it has been taken over. The refugee camp is full of what its American director calls "orphaned and unattached" young people. Eva's liberation from internment at Belsen is greeted with the question, "Do you have family?" Her survival in spite of the horrors of the camp and the deaths of her father, mother, sister, and friends forms the kernel of her traumatic rehearsal of the past. She relives moments in the camp that spelled the separation and destruction of families, a camp "with no regard for affiliation." Having survived with no family is tantamount to enduring a living death, and Eva spends all her time recreating her family through memory and hallucinations; her waking and dreaming lives are blurred in an absolute yearning for human connection. In the novel the killing of Jews in the camps echoes the earlier horror and loss of the sanctioned murder of three Venetian Jews falsely accused of killing a Christian boy for ritual sacrifice in fifteenth-century Europe. History repeats itself. Violent persecution and racism structures Jewish identity as outsiders; they are dispossessed and deterritorialized across history.

Family is crucial to the forging of connections and the replication of those connections through the ages. Yet in the novel there is a gap between family understood as one's immediate relations and family understood more metaphorically as collective ancestry, ethnicity, and as a "people." The novel ponders "the nature of blood" by looking at what these ties exclude as well as include. The creation of the state of Israel is meant to substitute ties of affiliation for filiative relations. In the novel, one of Stephan's main tasks is to prepare refugees from postwar Europe for settlement by fostering in them an emotional, mental, and psychic investment in their new country that goes beyond political identity to become essentially familial identity. This is not the country of Israel, Stephan asserts, but "our country." This new "familialized" identity promises to make good the loss of family and kinfolk, but Stephan by his own admission is still haunted by memories of his past. Malka, who is black but Jewish, is fed on the same dreams, but her return to Israel is one of racist encounters, cultural shock, and an aggressive marginalizing of her family, all of which contribute to its breakup. Malka objects to the myth of the "return": "you say you rescued me. Gently plucked me from this century, helped me to cross two more, and then placed me in this time. Here. Now. But why? What are you trying to prove?" In demanding that Malka typify an ideal Jewishness, the state repeats the tragedy of familial destruction and loss. It stands in real danger of making her a genuine outsider in a way she has never before encountered. Similarly, Othello's story and his travels in the Jewish ghetto of the city also lay bare the deep-seated antagonisms that underlie racial tensions. Othello knows that he can never belong by virtue of his skin color and his cultural difference. He remains an outsider who is at best tolerated as a "prized acquisition," a necessary evil, or an entertaining spectacle. In daring to marry Desdemona he contravenes racial taboos and risks the little he has. Other stories serve to remind one of the exclusions of these assertions of blood but equally of the necessity to reach across borders. Rosa's marriage to a Jew puts her own life at risk, but her steadfast commitment to her ideals is heroic. Her choice of pronouns in her conversations with Eva, "if we do not fight, then we are lost," is both inclusive and transgressive. It resists the history of Jewish persecution by Christians in modern Europe and the policing of racial and ethnic borders that would find its ultimate expression in the logic of Hitler's death camps.

TRAVEL WRITING AND ESSAYS

Phillips's travel writing is anchored to his wider social and cultural preoccupations. *The European Tribe* (1987) was the result of a yearlong trip through Europe that recasts the "grand tour" as an exploration of tribalism, nationalistic fervor, and the racism of Europeans' postcolonial castigation of others within their national borders. Its seemingly contentious premise that European cultures are tribal in nature is borne out most startlingly by the eastern European wars of ethnic cleansing and to a lesser degree by the sometimes intractable difficulties that have obstructed the path to establishing the wider polity of the European Union. *The European Tribe* is part autobiography and memoir, part anecdote, part travelogue, part history, part sociology, and part literary criticism. It records Phillips's experiences in Morocco, Spain, and Britain's colonial outposts Gibraltar and Northern Ireland, as well as Poland, France, Italy, the Netherlands, Germany, Norway, and Russia. In fortress Europe, Phillips contends, "you must create a class of people who are not you. Who are different. Who are outsiders. Who can never be you. Who are less than you." In Gibraltar, Phillips finds a Britain more anachronistically British than at home, where food, architecture, music, and television all bear traces of "British sociocultural aggression." Cultural borderlines are insistently invoked between the island and the mainland in a land where the tourist board welcomes visitors with the slogan: "You'll also receive a warm welcome from the people of Gibraltar, because just like you, we're British." In the other surviving outpost of empire, Belfast seems to be a city still under siege, with military patrols, barbed wire barricades, and entrenched religious and ethnic factional divisions even after years of Anglo-Irish strife. Such an environment breeds insularity: a land on the one hand caught between a youthful army "defending a cause they do not understand, full of antagonism towards a people they do not want to understand," and on the other, Irish youths whose lives revolve around the twin principles of prejudice and bigotry toward anyone existing "outside their own religious and political sphere." A visit to the Jewish district of Venice provokes a meditation on Europe's history of anti-Semitism and Shakespeare's plays *The Merchant of Venice* and *Othello,* both of which detail the tragic fate that is meted out to outsiders in sixteenth-century Venice. It also shows the candidly autobiographic nature of Phillips's musings: he explores Othello's characteristic traits (neurosis, impetuosity, and jealousy) as a direct product of his ambiguous position as a "black European success" story, allowing Phillips to muse on his own sense of being "of and not of Europe." Phillips's vicarious identification with Jewish persecution stemming from his own troubled history sensitizes him to the manner in which Shylock is tolerated and patronized because he fulfills a financial need; when he is no longer deemed useful, he is "shamefully castigated" as an "outcast." From France's colonial migrants to Germany's guest workers to the rise of the political right in Europe, it is difficult to avoid the conclusion that Europe's "haves" have ruthlessly exploited the "have nots." The mixture of populations and cultures within its borders cannot simply be put down to the continued arrival of outsiders; instead, Europe must face up to its colonial past and recognize that these alleged foreigners are now an inextricable part of the continent.

If *The European Tribe* was written in part as Phillips's attempt to come to terms with his sense of himself as belonging to Europe and his desire to be acknowledged as European, *The Atlantic Sound* (2000) is a highly crafted and self-reflexive travelogue that presents identity as something that transcends the borders of nation states. Phillips's travels from the Caribbean to Britain, from the West Coast of Africa to the American South, are journeys undertaken in the shadow of and in relation to earlier transatlantic passages of slavery or postwar migrations. To the contemporary discourse on diaspora Phillips here contributes self-reflexive and critical reflections on the nature of home and belonging, but he also puts forward a case for a new language of historical and global connectedness. The "Atlantic sound" invoked in his title relates to the ocean where migrations and sea-journeys were undertaken by sailors, traders, slaves, officials, and ordinary people from Africa, the Caribbean, Europe, and America, all shaped by the legacy of slavery and the traffic in slaves. But in many ways the stories that Phillips unearths—both historical and contemporary—are "soundings" of the peoples whose destinies have been affected by these forces. *The Atlantic Sound* is made up of separate journeys collected into three sections, "Leaving Home," "Homeward Bound," and "Home." In a preface Phillips tells of reenacting his parents' arrival in England by boat, and the book is drawn to a close by his examination of the claims by African Americans residing in Israel that they have returned home.

Phillips's opening journey on a "banana" boat between the Caribbean and Britain repeats the postwar exodus of people from the Caribbean to seek a new life in the "mother country." But if this journey is not a "crossing into the unknown," as it was for his parents, neither does it represent "closure" for him. Phillips's account of the nineteenth-century Ghanaian John Ocansey's journey to Liverpool to seek reparation for a business fraud makes the timely point that travel has not always been from Europe to the far-flung uncivilized corners of the globe. Written from Ocansey's point of view, the travelogue offers a glimpse of the strangeness of English life and customs in the nineteenth century, the religious and filial piety of this Christian West African, and the intertwined histories of Liverpool and West Africa. Phillips's own account of his visit to Liverpool is written as a postscript to Ocansey's earlier narrative and is intended to be read in relation to it. In the company of a black Liverpudlian, Phillips looks at how much the modern city has sought to erase traces of its inglorious past; a walk through the civic and commercial center unearths Liverpool's hidden history, and the absence of black people calls attention to Phillips's own visible presence. The drive through the predominantly black district of Toxteth yields a tale of disenfranchisement and inner-city decline untouched by the urban regeneration found elsewhere in Liverpool. Yet he also notes somewhat ironically that the Liverpool-born black community (LBBs) also jealously guards its own territory, longevity, and authenticity against what it sees as new arrivals, whether they be war refugees from Somalia or postwar Caribbean migrants.

The middle section of *The Atlantic Sound* examines the motivations of individuals and groups that seek to return to what they see as their African motherland. An encounter with a fellow passenger on the flight outward elicits the knowing remark that he is returning home. Such complacency is countered by Phillips's repeated aside to the reader, *"no I am not going home"*—he offers an understanding yet skeptical view of the overwhelming romance of home. There is a touch of Naipaul's testiness as Phillips describes the predictable scenes of soliciting and begging that greet the metropolitan traveler in lesser-developed lands. His interviews with a Ghanaian pan-Africanist and an African American returnee expose a tale of two lives: the former takes advantage of the sentimentality of back-to-Africa movements while the latter seems content with his own status as exile in a land to which he can contribute. Phillips's West African trip is undertaken for the purpose of attending a pan-African festival celebrating "a time when the diasporan family returns to Mother Africa to celebrate the arts, creativity and intellectual achievements of the Pan African world." In contrast to an assumed familial homogeneity of the festival's rhetoric, Phillips sees cultural differences assert themselves. The great "return" cannot deliver, precisely because Africa is not

being treated as a real historical locale but rather the stuff of fantasy and wish-fulfillment: "Africa cannot cure. Africa cannot make anybody feel whole. Africa is not a psychiatrist." In a fit of "diasporan fatigue," Phillips finds dignity in the historical figure of Phillip Quaque, who "returns" to Africa after being educated in England by missionaries, an exile in his own homeland. In the story of Quaque, Phillips finds a complexity of identity and multiplicity of allegiances that are unacknowledged in the rush to see Africa as a panacea for contemporary ills.

The story of Judge J. Waties Waring's interventions in South Carolina's segregationist laws is the subject of the third section of the book. His presence in the story is prefigured in the historical connections alluded to earlier between Liverpool and Charleston, both being towns whose prosperity was based on slavery. This Charleston judge was formerly a pillar of his somewhat conservative community. But his remarriage to a northerner and his growing objections to segregationist practices in the South resulted in his estrangement from his own town. His dissenting judgment on the legitimacy of "separate-but-equal" educational practice predates the landmark civil rights case that put an end to legalized segregation by two years. For his efforts, the judge was ostracized and treated like a "pariah in the land he loved;" Waring had little choice but to exile himself from Charleston after his retirement. Yet his legacy of dissent and justice was part of the wider movement towards equal rights for all American citizens.

The epilogue that closes *The Atlantic Sound* looks at the African American settlement in Israel. This self-contained settlement is doggedly American and stands out from its environment in a somewhat surreal fashion. Despite living over thirty years in a "world that does not recognize them" in a land they "cannot tame," and despite flying the Israeli flag, the members of the community still assert that they have indeed "come home." From these differing stories Phillips concludes that there can be no closure, despite a longing for the secure simplicity of home or of "race." In *A New World Order* (2001), Phillips asserts more explicitly that no one feels fully at home: "These days we are all unmoored. Our identities fluid. Belonging is a contested state. Home is a place riddled with vexing questions." Even the Englishwoman who begins *A Distant Shore* remarks, "England has changed. These days it's difficult to tell who's from around here and who's not. Who belongs and who's a stranger." But this ambivalence, uncertainty, and lack of closure is seen as a positive state; if Phillips has a "home," it is that of an Atlantic imaginary.

Selected Bibliography

WORKS OF CARYL PHILLIPS

NOVELS

The Final Passage. London and Boston: Faber and Faber, 1985.

A State of Independence. London: Faber and Faber, 1986; New York: Farrar, Straus, and Giroux, 1986.

Higher Ground. London and New York: Viking, 1989.

Cambridge. London: Bloomsbury, 1991; New York: Knopf, 1992.

Crossing the River. London: Bloomsbury, 1993; New York: Knopf, 1993.

The Nature of Blood. London: Faber and Faber, 1997; New York: Knopf, 1997.

A Distant Shore. London: Secker and Warburg, 2003.

PLAYS

Strange Fruit. Oxford: Amber Lane Press, 1981.

Where There Is Darkness. Oxford: Amber Lane Press, 1982.

The Wasted Years. London: Methuen, 1985.

The Shelter. Oxford: Amber Lane Press, 1984.

TRAVEL WRITING

The European Tribe. London: Faber and Faber, 1987; New York: Farrar, Straus, and Giroux, 1987. (A 1992 reissued London Picador edition contains a new forward by the author.)

The Atlantic Sound. London: Faber and Faber, 2000; New York: Knopf, 2000.

COLLECTED ESSAYS

A New World Order. London: Secker and Warburg, 2001; New York: Vintage, 2002.

EDITED ANTHOLOGIES

Extravagant Strangers: A Literature of Belonging. London and Boston: Faber and Faber, 1997.

The Right Set: A Tennis Anthology. London: Faber and Faber, 1999; New York: Vintage, 1999.

FILM SCRIPTS

Playing Away. London and Boston: Faber and Faber, 1987.

The Mystic Masseur. Merchant Ivory Productions, 2001.

MANUSCRIPTS

Caryl Phillips's manuscripts and papers are held at Beinecke Library, Yale University, New Haven, Conn.

BIBLIOGRAPHY

A comprehensive bibliography compiled by Bénédicte Ledent is available at http://www.ulg.ac.be/facphl/uer/d-german/L3/cppres.html.

INTERVIEWS

Bell, C. Rosalind. "Worlds Within." *Callaloo*, 14.3: 578–606 (1991).

Birbalsingh, Frank. "Caryl Phillips: The Legacy of Othello, Parts 1 and 2." In *Frontiers of Caribbean Literature in English*. Edited by Frank Birbalsingh. London: Macmillan, 1996. Pp. 191–197.

Davison, Carol Margaret. "Criss-Crossing the River." *Ariel*, 25.4: 91–99 (October 1994).

Eckstein, Lars. "The Insistence of Voices." *Ariel* 32.2: 33–44 (April 2001).

Jaggi, Maya. "Crossing the River." *Wasafiri*, 20: 25–29 (autumn 1994).

———. "The Final Passage." In *Black British Culture and Society: A Text Reader*. Edited by Kwesi Owusu. London and New York: Routledge, 2000. Pp. 157–168.

"The Other Voice: A Dialogue between Anita Desai, Caryl Phillips, and Ilan Stavans." *Transition*, 64: 77–89 (1994).

Saunders, Kay. Interview. *Kunapipi*, 9.1: 44–52 (1987).

Sharpe, Jenny. "Of This Time, of That Place." *Transition*, 68: 154–161 (winter 1995).

Swift, Graham. "Caryl Phillips." *Kunapipi*, 13.3: 96–103 (1991).

CRITICAL AND BIOGRAPHICAL STUDIES

Benítez-Rojo, Antonio. "Three Words toward Creolization." In *Caribbean Creolization: Reflections on the Cultural Dynamics of Language, Literature, and Identity*. Edited by Kathleen M. Balutansky and Marie-Agnès Sourieau. Barbados: University Press of the West Indies, 1998. Pp. 53–61.

Birat, Kathie. "Delegated Dominion: Language and Displacement in *Cambridge* by Caryl Phillips." *Revue française d'études américaines*, 72: 26–36 (March 1997).

Cheyette, Bryan. "Venetian Spaces: Old-New Literatures and the Ambivalent Uses of Jewish History." In *Reading the "New" Literatures in a Postcolonial Era*. Edited by Susheila Nasta. Cambridge and New York: D. S. Brewer, 2000. Pp. 53–72.

Di Maio, Alessandra. "Diasporan Voices in Caryl Phillips's *Crossing the River*." In *Multiculturalism and Hybridity in African Literatures*. Edited by Hal Wylie and Bernth Lindfors. Trenton, N.J.: Africa World Press, 2000. Pp. 367–376.

Flint, Kate. "Looking Backward? The Relevance of Britishness." In *Unity in Diversity Revisited: British Literature and Culture in the 1990s*. Edited by Barbara Korte and Klaus Peter Müller. Tübingen: Gunter Narr Verlag, 1998. Pp. 35–50.

Ilona, Anthony. "Crossing the River: A Chronicle of the Black Diaspora." *Wasafiri*, 22: 3–9 (autumn 1995).

Innes, C. L. "Wintering: Making a Home in Britain." In *Other Britain, Other British*. Edited by A. Robert Lee. London: Pluto, 1995. Pp. 21–34.

Julien, Claude. "Surviving through a Pattern of Timeless Moments: A Reading of Caryl

Phillips's *Crossing the River.*" In *Black Imagination and the Middle Passage.* Edited by Maria Diedrich, Henry Louis Gates Jr., and Carl Pedersen. Oxford and New York: Oxford University Press, 1999. Pp. 86–95.

Ledent, Bénédicte. "Voyages into Otherness: *Cambridge* and *Lucy.*" *Kunapipi,* 14.2: 53–63 (1992).

————. " 'Overlapping Territories, Intertwined Histories': Cross-Culturality in Caryl Phillips's *Crossing the River.*" *Journal of Commonwealth Literature,* 30.1: 55–62 (1995).

————. "Remembering Slavery: History as Roots in the Fiction of Caryl Phillips and Fred D'Aguiar." In *The Contact and the Culmination: Essays in Honour of Hena Maes-Jelinek.* Edited by Marc Delrez and Bénédicte Ledent. Liège, Belgium: L3, 1997. Pp. 271–280.

————. *Caryl Phillips.* Manchester, U.K.: Manchester University Press, Contemporary World Writers Series, 2002.

Low, Gail. " 'A Chorus of Common Memory': Slavery and Redemption in Caryl Phillips's *Cambridge* and *Crossing the River.*" *Research in African Literatures,* 29.4: 122–140 (winter 1998).

————. "Separate Spheres?: Representing London through Women in Some Recent Black British Fiction." *Kunapipi,* 21.22:23–31 (1999).

O'Callaghan, Evelyn. "Historical Fiction and Fictional History: Caryl Phillips's *Cambridge.*" *Journal of Commonwealth Literature,* 29.2: 34–47 (1993).

Okazaki, Hank. "On Dislocation and Connectedness in Caryl Phillips's Writing." *Literary Criterion,* 26.3:38–47 (1991).

Rahbek, Ulla. " 'I Am 200 Years Old Now, and Getting Older': Blackness in Caryl Phillips's Plays from *Strange Fruit* to *The Shelter.*" In *Dialoguing on Genres.* Edited by Ulf Lie and Anne Holden Rønning. Oslo: Novus Press, 2001. Pp. 113–125.

————. "Confusion Hits Us Every Time: Contemporary Black British Literature." In *Identities and Masks: Colonial and Postcolonial Studies.* Edited by Jakob Lothe, Anne Holden Rønning, and Peter Young. Kristiansand, Norway: Høyskoleforlaget, 2001. Pp. 65–80.

Sarvan, Charles P., and Hasan Marhama. "The Fictional Works of Caryl Phillips: An Introduction." *World Literature Today,* 65.1: 35–40 (1991).

Schäffner, Raimund. " 'Identity Is Not in the Past to Be Found, But in the Future to Be Constructed': History and Identity in Caryl Phillips's Novels." *Unity in Diversity Revisited? British Literature and Culture in the 1990s.* Edited by Barbara Korte and Klaus Peter Müller. Tübingen: Narr, 1998. Pp. 107–126.

————. "Assimilation, Separatism, and Multiculturalism in Mustapha Matura's *Welcome Home Jacko* and Caryl Phillips's *Strange Fruit.*" *Wasafiri,* 29: 65–70 (spring 1999).

Sharrad, Paul. "Speaking the Unspeakable: London, Cambridge, and the Caribbean." In *De-scribing Empire: Post-Colonialism and Textuality.* Edited by Chris Tiffin and Alan Lawson. London and New York: Routledge, 1994. Pp. 201–217.

Smethurst, Paul. "Post-Colonial Island Chronotope." In his *The Postmodern Chronotope.* Amsterdam and Atlanta: Rodopi, 2000. Pp. 219–266.

Thieme, John. "Removing the Black-Face: A Different 'Othello Music'" In his *Postcolonial Con-texts: Writing Back to the Canon.* London and New York: Continuum, 2001. Pp. 155–169.

Varela Zapata, Jesus. "Translating One's Own Culture: Coming Back from the Metropolis in Caryl Phillips's *A State of Independence.*" In *Translating Cultures.* Edited by Isabel Carrera Suárez, Aurora Garcia Fernandez, and M. S. Suárez Lafuente. Oviedo-Hebden Bridge: KRK/Dangaroo Press, 1999. Pp. 397–406.

Peter Porter

(1929–)

SEAN O'BRIEN

PETER NEVILLE FREDERICK Porter was born at Kangaroo Point, Brisbane, Australia, on 16 February 1929, to Marion Main and William Porter. His parents were thirty-nine and forty-four years old respectively. The child of older parents may well have early intimations of mortality, but in Porter's case the education was brutal: his mother died suddenly of a burst gall bladder when he was nine years old. From then on, he wrote, he was "locked out of paradise." Much of his poetry negotiates between the brute facts of death and loss and the impulses of art, which are to celebrate, to give form, and to preserve.

Having lost his mother, Porter, already sensing himself exiled, spent nine years at private boarding schools run by the Anglican Church. After this he worked for a time as a trainee reporter and a warehouseman until, on 2 January 1951, he boarded the steamer *Otranto* from Brisbane, joining the great postwar migration of young Australians to Europe and in particular to London, capital and symbol of the British Empire.

In the title poem to his 1970 collection *The Last of England,* Porter wrote: "You cannot leave England, it turns / A planet majestically in

the mind" (*Collected Poems,* vol. 1, p. 145). This startling statement of affection, by a son of a notably resentful colony, shows Porter's ability to live imaginatively with contradiction and in two places at once, knowing himself to be both an outsider and an inheritor, viewing exile as homecoming. Porter is also more European in his attitudes than many British writers. He accepts a role of stewardship, preserving and commending European culture (literature, music, Renaissance and baroque art) for a British audience. The position is not comfortable, but it is productive. He has certainly seemed easier with his role than some of his Australian critics, such as Les Murray, who at one time viewed him as a deserter.

When Porter arrived in London on 19 February 1951, three days after his twenty-second birthday, he was a young man of wide and ambitious reading (for which he could thank the unapologetic seriousness of Australian literary education), with strong but undeveloped literary ambitions. He did not have, and has never acquired, a university degree. The term "autodidact" has pejorative overtones in middle-class English life. It suggests the disordered learning of the untrained, as well as the insecurity of those driven to overcompensate for a lack of "proper" grounding. Such assumptions have as much to do with social class as with educational attainment. Porter has prospered in part because while he has come to understand the class system he has never given in to it, and in part because his appetite for literature and all other forms of artistic experience far outweighs the discouragement exercised by snobbery.

Porter was also fortunate to come to London in the years following World War II, when the social mobility promised by the Labour governments elected in 1945 and 1950 was, albeit untidily and patchily, in evidence. Economic conditions were austere, and food rationing, introduced in wartime, was still partly in force. But there was work, though not necessarily of a congenial kind, and there was sympathetic company, like that of Porter's lifelong friend, the Australian novelist Jill Neville (1932–1997). Porter nonetheless spent much of the decade sunk in depression, trying both to write and to find a way to make a life as a writer.

An important part of Porter's development as a poet and as a literary professional was his membership in a poetry workshop called the Group, whose members included well-known or emergent poets including Alan Brownjohn, George MacBeth, and Peter Redgrove. A forerunner of the informal workshops now common in Britain, the Group sought to apply the rigorous close reading methods known as "Practical Criticism" developed by I. A. Richards and the very influential Cambridge critic F. R. Leavis (and in the United States, as the "New Criticism," by Cleanth Brooks and W. K. Wimsatt) as an antidote to belletristic critical impressionism. As the 1950s drew to a close Porter combined an increasingly busy literary life with a job at Notley's advertising agency, where the poet Gavin Ewart and the novelist William Trevor also worked.

In 1961 Porter's first collection, *Once Bitten, Twice Bitten,* was published, quickly followed by *Poems, Ancient and Modern* (1964) and *A*

Porter Folio (1969), by which time Porter, who had not published a poem until he was thirty, was among the best-known younger poets working in Britain. He had, it seemed, sprung from nowhere. The poet and critic Stephen Spender, an influential and extremely well-connected literary commentator, was driven to ask: "Who is Peter Porter?"

Porter's work combined contemporary satire with broad allusion to European and Australian culture and history, as well as showing awareness of contemporary American poets including Robert Lowell and John Berryman. He offered a striking alternative to the dominant modes in English poetry at the time. These were the avowedly anti-cosmopolitan Movement (whose leading representatives were Philip Larkin and Kingsley Amis), which rejected modernism and the cultural allusiveness that is central to Porter's poems; and the new nature poetry written by Ted Hughes, which concentrated on landscapes, wild animals, and the elements. Porter's early reputation was sealed with the publication of *The Last of England* in 1970, which marked the beginning of his long-term relationship with Oxford University Press and of his life as a full-time writer.

In 1961 Porter married Jannice Henry, a nurse, with whom he had two daughters, Katherine (b. 1962) and Jane (b. 1965). While Porter's poetic reputation grew steadily in the 1960s and 1970s, Jannice herself, especially after an attack of meningitis in 1967, grew increasingly unhappy and became an alcoholic. When she died in 1974 the coroner gave an open verdict, but Porter himself remains certain that she committed suicide. *The Cost of Seriousness* (1978), whose subject is Porter's relationship with Jannice, is a work of guilt and elegiac love, widely regarded as Porter's most important book, in the title poem of which he delivers the loaded, ambiguous phrase "The cost of seriousness is death" (*CP*, vol. 1, p. 338).

In 1974 Porter began the first of many visits to Australia. Poems such as "An Australian

Garden" from the 1975 collection *Living in a Calm Country* (*CP*, vol. 1, p. 282) begin a re-examination of his complex Australian inheritance as exile and returnee. This study of his origins and attitudes to them has been a major feature of his work ever since, running in tandem with a continuing concern with the ways in which poetry is meaningful in the present day.

In 1983 the first edition of Porter's *Collected Poems* was published to great acclaim. The range of Porter's work was vast, his interests omnivorous. History, music, painting, literature, language, politics, religion, ideas, love, sex, gossip, domestic life, place, time, cats—there was little in the humanistic sphere that did not in some way attract his attention. The modes of his work were similarly varied—aphorism, dramatic monologue, pastoral, and satire were among the most prominent. He displayed a wide-ranging curiosity about technique, moving between strict traditional forms and the freer experimental shapes and measures of modernism and postmodernism. The gods of his literary universe were Shakespeare, George Herbert, Robert Browning, and W. H. Auden, but he was also extremely interested in Wallace Stevens and John Ashbery. The catholicity of his taste also figured in his work as a critic and reviewer of poetry, music, and art.

In 1983 Porter met Christine Berg, who was to train as a child psychotherapist. They married in 1991 and at the time of writing in 2003 have eight grandchildren between them. Porter maintains a prolific rate of publication. A two-volume expanded edition of the *Collected Poems*, including work from a further seven books, appeared in 1999, followed by a new collection, *Max Is Missing*, in 2001.

The body of Porter's work is huge. There are seventeen full collections of poetry and a number of collaborative works with the painter Arthur Boyd. Porter has edited a number of selections from other poets' work as well as anthologies. He has been a prolific critic, essayist, and reviewer. His work is enormously vari-

ous as well as prolific, and all this essay can attempt is to offer a cross-section of its riches.

EARLY WORK

The most powerful emotion when Porter writes of childhood in Australia is fear. "A Christmas Recalled" (*CP*, vol. 1, p. 7) looks back at a family party held "in our huge summer" (a characteristically striking and Audenesque phrase that describes time in terms of size). He remembers lying in bed "drinking up my fear" in Schweppes lemonade while next door the adults make cocktails. When talk turns to the threat of war with Japan, the thought of death comes, not for the first time, to the child's mind. Death "was a word like 'when,' / and not a thing like cat."

"Ghosts," from the "1962–63" section of *Collected Poems*, gives a picture of Marion Porter, but we also see that she died too soon for her son to grasp his mother as a personality: "The inheritance I had, her only child, / Was her party melancholy and a body / Thickening like hers, the wide-pored flesh / Death broke into twenty years ago" (*CP*, vol. 1, p. 50). Porter describes himself as the "late child of a late marriage," and the pun is deliberate and excruciating. The sole surviving child among five miscarriages, Porter feels himself to be more than averagely acquainted with death. Without engaging in psychoanalysis, there is a sterile quality in the child's relationship with his inhibited father, which also contributes to the creation of Porter's imaginative world. "Forefathers' View of Failure" depicts a Calvinist tribe of nineteenth-century Scots emigrants, hardworking, hard-drinking men who "stencilled failure's index on their brains" (*CP*, vol. 1, p. 3) and saw no purpose in the possession of an imagination. It was a world inimical to an imaginative and (as Porter puts it in "Ghosts") "feminine" small boy.

Unsurprisingly, Porter's voyage to London seems to have been undertaken with literary ambitions but few expectations of happiness. The past is not to be shed: its contents are summed up in "Ghosts" as "The nightmares that I have, the memories of love."

In *Poetry Today: A Critical Guide to British Poetry 1960–1995*, the poet and critic Anthony Thwaite said of some of Porter's early London poems: "Soon this work will require footnotes" (p. 71). The young Porter, getting to grips with London, is certainly fascinated by names, details, the temporary excitement of fashionable places. It is not a world he belongs to, but "John Marston Advises Anger," named for the Jacobean playwright, satirist, controversialist, and author of *The Malcontent* (1604), shows that the poet is at the same time complicit with that world's desires, a malcontent drawn to the bonfire of the vanities.

> Those jeans and bums and sweaters of the King's
>   Road
> Would fit Marston's stage. What's in a name,
> If Cheapside and the Marshalsea mean Eng. Lit.
> And the Fantasie, Sa Tortuga, Grisbi, Bongi-Bo
> Mean life? A cliché? What hurts dies on paper,
> Fades to classic pain. Love goes as the MG goes.
> The Colonel's daughter in black stockings, hair
> Like sash-cords, face iced white, studies art,
> Goes home once a month. She won't marry the
>   men
> She sleeps with, she'll revert to type—it's part
> Of the side-show; Mummy and Daddy in the
>   wings,
> The bongos fading on the road to Haslemere
> Where the inheritors are inheriting still.
>
> (*CP*, vol. 1, p. 20)

In this dense, angry, energetic passage, Porter begins by contrasting the enduring imaginative reality of London locations such as Cheapside (found in Jacobean theater) and the Marshalsea (the debtors' prison described at length in Charles Dickens's *Little Dorrit*) with the fleeting glamour of London clubs and coffeehouses at the beginning of the 1960s. We know that Porter's loyalties lie with literature, but there's a

sense in which it can't compete with the sexy here and now, where "Love goes as the MG goes." This seemingly meaningless slogan, of a kind often found in advertising, becomes richly suggestive in this context. Love "goes" in several senses: it goes as a car goes, that is, it works; it goes as a car departs, that is, it fades; and it "goes" in the vernacular English sense of the phrase for a sexually promiscuous woman, "She's a goer." In Porter's hands the simile pulls in an unexpected direction—rather than producing an atmosphere of glamour and romance, the sense is of something mechanical rather than naturally occurring. The mechanical is also predictable—and Porter knows exactly what the Colonel's daughter will do when her flirtation with bohemian artistic life is over.

The sense that sex and class are somehow organized to the outsider's disadvantage is something Porter returns to more than once. "Beast and the Beauty" tells of being taken up and then dropped by an upper-middle-class girl: "wine-wise young barristers and gentlemen- / farmers fought for her hand. In the loft there waited trunks / Of heirlooms to be taken seriously" (*CP*, vol. 1, p. 15). Abandonment is bad enough, but the poem entertains the sobering thought that despite the snobbery and superficiality of the girl in question, she still has something the young man wants, as he waits "for a lustful kiss to bring / Back his human smell, the taste of woman on his tongue." Fulfilment it seems, would have nothing to do with morals or the marriage of true minds. Porter was later to write, in "Half-Mast Poems," of the way the world is really organized: "Two Nations! / The Rich and the Poor, the South and the North? / No, the attractive and the unattractive" (*CP*, vol. 1, p. 132).

Porter's early years in London coincided with the development of the Cold War and the arms race between the United States and the Soviet Union. It was a time of mass political activism in Britain, notably by the Campaign for Nuclear Disarmament. The possibility of nuclear war generated a widespread atmosphere of alarm, and the Cuban Missile Crisis of 1962 brought the world to the brink of destruction. It was in this atmosphere Porter published what is perhaps his most famous poem, "Your Attention Please." In this dramatic monologue an anonymous government spokesman explains that attack is imminent and gives advice on what to do. The speaker's tone is of chilling reasonableness:

> Some of us may die.
> Remember, statistically
> It is unlikely to be you.
> All flags are flying fully dressed
> On Government buildings—the sun is shining.
> Death is the least we have to fear.
> We are all in the hands of God,
> Whatever happens happens by His Will.
> Now go quickly to your shelters.
>
> (*CP*, vol. 1, p. 46)

The poem is both hilarious and horrific. As well as offering bland allegations of divine support, the speaker somehow converts the wreck of ordinary life into science fiction, as though the listeners have never really inhabited the ordinary world of their previous lives but have just woken into a parallel sphere. Dream and nightmare are very significant powers in Porter's imagination. He has spoken of dreams as a kind of private epic, and in his imaginative world the walls of ordinary reality are not the less permeable for their adamantine character. As the speaker in "The Last of the Dinosaurs" remarks, "life is a dream or very nearly" (*CP*, vol. 1, p. 96).

Supposing the world stands at risk of destruction, what is there in it that Porter would defend? In the first place, art. Porter is extremely knowledgeable in music and visual art as well as literature. The art for which he cares most is clearly music, which, he reminds us in the third of the "Three Poems for Music," "was stolen from a God" (*CP*, vol. 1, p. 123). Had he been able to choose, Porter might well have been a composer instead of a poet. Music is free of the problems of content and meaning: it represents itself alone, whereas writing and poetry must gesture at a purity of utterance they can never reach. Music's very freedom from meaning seems to us to speak of paradise, and yet, according to the early poem "Walking Home on St. Cecilia's Day" (St. Cecilia is the patron saint of music), it is "useless, impartial as rain in a desert" (*CP*, vol. 1, p. 16). Its perfection both uplifts us and reminds us of the realm of earthly sorrows to which we must return after the song's enchantment. When the music ends, we weep, like Caliban in *The Tempest*, to dream again.

"All art," wrote the critic Walter Pater (1839–1894), "constantly aspires to the condition of music." It is in part Porter's awareness of the inaccessibility of that condition that draws him to such an intensely detailed rendering of the world of places, people, and objects. Few poets are as novelistic in this regard as Porter. He has absorbed Auden's description of the novelist as one "who can become the whole of boredom" and "be among the Filthy filthy too" (*Collected Poems*, ed. by Edward Mendelson, 1991, p. 180). The sequence "The Porter Songbook" from *A Porter Folio* (*CP*, vol. 1, pp. 133–138) addresses this paradox. The contents of this songbook are for the most part clearly *un*musical, full of the kind of circumstantial detail that lyrics tend to exclude, though their themes of erotic passion and disenchantment would certainly seem suited to the work of the great nineteenth-century German composers of lieder (songs), such as Franz Schubert, Robert Schumann, and Hugo Wolf. The way in which even music can help to enforce disenchantment is touched on in "The Sadness of the Creatures," one of Porter's most powerful and harrowing poems, in which history is scaled down to the situation of "two people not disposed / to argue" [who] "have met so / oblique a slant of the dark / they can find no words for / their appalled hurt but only / ride the rearing greyness" (*CP*, vol. 1, p. 166). Among the furnishings of this despairing scene are "one hundred and seven Bach / cantatas at the last count."

Porter's constant references to the arts are not simply a matter of allusion for its own sake. His imagination tends to re-create the world of certain works or their creators inside his poems, according them a status equal to reality. Early examples are "Madame de Merteuil on the Loss of an Eye" (*CP*, vol. 1, p. 62), "The Word of Simon Raven" (p. 64), "The Great Poet Comes Here in Winter" (p. 74), and "Fantasia on a Line by Stefan George" (p. 99). The first is spoken by a leading character in Pierre Choderlos de Laclos's novel of erotic corruption, *Les Liaisons Dangereuses* (1782). (Dramatic monologue is a favorite form for Porter, and two of its masters—Shakespeare and Robert Browning—are among Porter's masters too.) Simon Raven (1927–2001) was an English novelist whose ten-book sequence *Alms for Oblivion* (1964–1976) followed the fate of a large cast of mad, bad, dangerously lustful, and avaricious upper-middle-class English people from 1945 until the 1970s. The poem is a comic and melancholic synopsis of actual and potential events in the Raven world, exactly noting Raven's fascination with sexual grotesquerie and sadism (aspects of which recur in *After Martial*, Porter's 1972 translations from the Roman satirist): "Israeli agents / Put pubic lice in Prince Mohammad's beard, / Doctor Boyce cuts off his cousin Kate's / Clitoris." Porter's use here and elsewhere of narrative cross-sections and fragments anticipates by nearly twenty years the New Narrative phase of English poetry exemplified by the work of James Fenton and Andrew Motion.

The third example, "The Great Poet Comes Here in Winter," is a semicomic and half-mad interior monologue by the German poet Rainer Maria Rilke (1875–1926) at Schloss Duino near Treste in Italy, where he wrote parts of his great visionary work *Duino Elegies* (1912–1922). In it Porter reveals his sense of the frequent absurdity of the lives and personalities of great artists—though this in no way undermines his devotion to their work:

> Whether there will be
> Any mail from Paris or even broccoli

> For dinner is in doubt. My hat blew off the
>   planet.
> I knelt by the infinite sand of the stars
> And prayed for all men. Being German, I have a
>   lot of soul.

> (*CP*, vol. 1, p. 75)

The mingling of the profound and the trivial, the grave and the absurd, are characteristic, as is the inventive energy that creates a kind of aria for Rilke's voice.

The complexity of Porter's imaginative relations with art can be illustrated by "Fantasia On a Line By Stefan George" (*CP*, vol. 1, p. 99). The poem begins with the opening line of the eighth part of George's *Das Buch der hängenden Garten,* "Wenn ich heut nicht deinen leib beruhre" (If today I do not touch your body), which Porter freely renders as "I shall die if I do not touch your body." George (1868–1933), a leading German poet of his time, is perhaps now best remembered for the fact that Arnold Schoenberg set his poems to music—which is where Porter originally encountered his work. Thus a poem is "translated" into a musical setting and then translated back into another (very different) poem. Porter's work is, we see, conspicuously intertextual. It draws on, alludes to, and at times expands on existing literary works, and it expects readers to follow its lines of reference. He also assumes a familiarity with European musical and visual arts traditions, and his imagination includes an ever-expanding museum of artistic and historical references. This is an attitude strongly associated with poetic modernism, as in the poems of T. S. Eliot and Ezra Pound, where allusion is a means of preserving and perhaps renewing a threatened cultural heritage. It is also, in a rather different sense, an important component of postmodernism, where it is sometimes assumed that writing supplants writers, so that all texts are at some level made of quotations. Porter would dispute the latter interpretation, since he values the individual sensibility that informs a text. With characteristic energy and confidence he has made use of the technique without assenting to the allegations that theory has attached to it. Indeed, in "The Sanitized Sonnets" (*CP*, vol. 1, pp. 171–176) he reduces allusion to a kind of macaronic shorthand, a storm of obliquely related aphorisms and resonant phrases, as if parodying the air of catastrophe found in Eliotic modernism while showing parody to be an authoritative contemporary response to the artist's situation.

The famous statement by the German philosopher and critic Walter Benjamin that "there is no monument to civilization which is not also a monument to barbarism" might have been made specially for Porter. His work is full of a sense of the presence, and of the interpenetration, of good and evil. In "Annotations of Auschwitz," the man in the street, told of the murder of six million people in the Nazi death camps during World War II, blandly remarks, "It's nothing to do with me" (*CP*, vol. 1, p. 38): thus, by doing nothing, the complacent civilian makes thinkable the very crime from which he tries to separate himself. As well as artists and passersby, Porter is particularly interested in the moral life of the powerful or exceptional. One of his finest early poems, "Soliloquy at Potsdam," is spoken by Frederick II, the Great, king of Prussia (1712–1786), architect of the militaristic state which was in turn to lead to the unification of Germany in the nineteenth century. Frederick combined wide learning, intellectual curiosity, accomplishment as a musician and composer, brilliance as a military commander, and enlightened yet despotic rule—all of which fascinates Porter. Frederick is the only assessor of his vision for his people: "Who else in Europe /Could take these verminous, clutching creatures / And break them into men?" He allows liberty of thought but not of deed:

The reformers sit at my table,
They talk well but they've never seen a battle
Or watched the formed brain in the flogged body

Marching to death on a bellyful of soup and
    orders.
There has to be misery so there can be discipline.

                        (p. 49)

Whereas in Browning's classic dramatic monologue "My Last Duchess" (first published in *Dramatic Lyrics,* 1842), the reader is invited to overhear the nature of power and to criticize and even condemn its possessor, in Porter's poem the relationship between reader and subject is imagined rather differently: we are to be the awed recipients of the king's table talk; there is no question of our being asked to comment. The privilege of witness is sufficient—more, indeed, than we deserve. By this means Porter memorably dramatizes the arrogance of power.

Porter's early work, then, takes in a vast range of material, but rather than seeming merely eclectic in its interests, it offers us access to an immensely civilized and endlessly curious mind in the process of mapping itself—a task so large as to resemble painting the Golden Gate Bridge, by definition never to be finished. Porter's is often a frightening world, but it is also continuously exciting. Porter states in "The Old Enemy" (from *Preaching to the Converted,* 1972) that "God is a Super-Director / Who's terribly good at crowd scenes, / But He has only one tense, the Present" (*CP*, vol. 1, p. 189). Keeping pace with this is a life's work.

ART AND DEATH: *THE COST OF SERIOUSNESS* AND AFTER

Porter is not a systematic thinker and certainly not a philosopher. As he states in his essay "A Place Dependent on Ourselves: Poetry and Materialism": "I find all philosophy difficult, from the Greeks through to today's practitioners. . . . I don't feel guilty at not understanding philosophers, since I don't enjoy them either, except for the more gamey aphorists . . . Pascal, Lichtenberg and Nietzsche. . . . Except for [Wallace] Stevens there are no great poets who are too difficult to understand" (*Saving from the Wreck: Essays on Poetry*, p. 186). Porter is by no means immune to ideas, however; rather it is the case that in his poems they are more likely to figure dramatically, as part of the texture of experience, than as ideas in themselves. Much of his interest naturally concentrates on art, its status in the world, its capacity for truth, the nature of the artist, and art's connections with morality.

The central experience of Porter's middle years was the death of his first wife, Jannice. It would be vulgar and unhelpful to read the resulting book, *The Cost of Seriousness* (1978), as direct autobiography—poetry's seriousness must sometimes lie in making something *out* of experience—and so, while it seems clear that the poems in this pivotal collection arise from personal grief, guilt, and suffering, they are works existing in their own right. For Porter, only in this way, by upholding the autonomy of poetry in the face of an accompanying critique of the capacities of what the title poem calls "those forgettable objects, words" (*CP*, vol. 1, p. 338) can grief be fully and respectfully observed.

"An Exequy," the major elegiac poem in the book, deliberately takes a famous model, "An Exequy to His Matchless Never to Be Forgotten Friend" by Bishop Henry King (1592–1669), a masterpiece of grief and tenderness addressed to his wife, Anne (d. 1624), in which personal loss and Christian consolation are persuasively balanced. Porter lacks King's theological certainties, but he employs the frame of King's poem. This is partly to show that in an atheistic or agnostic society, salvation is sought in love of others, with an emphasis on the erotic, rather than the love of God, and partly because artistic models outlive the beliefs that may originally have animated them (for example, one of Porter's great loves is the church music of J. S. Bach). In "An Exequy," the poet has vivid dreams of his wife in various guises, which prompt him finally to address her and to imagine her return at the time of his own death:

> I owe a death to you—one day
> The time will come for me to pay
> When your slim shape from photographs
> Stands at my door and gently asks
> If I have any work to do
> Or will I come to bed with you?

(p. 328)

The poignant plainness of the language contains a powerful and troubling ambiguity. Death is both a desired state of reunion and a necessary punishment for unspecified personal failures (his dead wife knows the poet's "heart, / in every cramped and devious part"). The couple will meet again in death (going "to bed"), which here has an erotic charge (sex was formerly known as "the little death"). Notwithstanding these grimmer overtones, the poem speaks with great tenderness, which of course only emphasizes the absoluteness of the couple's separation. In a later poem, "The Future," Porter speaks of a certain type of poetry as "lyrical erotica I have no talent for" (*CP*, vol. 1, p. 381), but the combination of directness with complexity here proves otherwise. "An Exequy" also indicates a degree of confidence in relation to literary history that is the preserve of the major poet.

"An Exequy" is immediately followed by "The Delegate," spoken, we infer, by the poet's dead wife and an altogether darker piece of work—not so much a riposte to or denial of the first poem as a firm adjustment of its terms, marking a refusal by the poet to let himself off the hook. Like "An Exequy," it is rich in the paradoxes of disbelief. For example, though we may be atheists, habit, inclination, and the precedents of language itself make it necessary for us to imagine an "afterwards" we do not believe exists, and this "afterwards" becomes part of our understanding and of our creation of reality. Porter's work makes frequent and vivid dramatic use of such fictive states, but the effect here is harrowing, for the dead woman speaks with a tender familiarity that is nonetheless unsparing:

I am always receding,
my ambition is to accomplish
non-existence, to go out and close the door
on ever having been.

(*CP,* vol. 1, p. 332)

Furthermore, the ghost knows herself to be a creation of the poet and delivers back to him convictions he may hold but may find it painful to admit outside the confines of the writing room:

I have an immense truth to give you—
In the end, we are condemned
only for our lack of talent.
          There is no morality,
no metered selfishness, no cowardly fear.
What we do on earth is its own parade
and cannot be redeemed in death.

So the imagined source of consolation becomes an agent of despair (as a demon might impersonate an angel, except that this demon is truthful). The only source of immortality (in the artist's view) is the fame conferred on talent, supposing he possesses it—a thought that imprisons him with the "licensed selfishness" of art, whose primary task is to serve its own creation. Its enlistment in moral causes, it is implied, is a secondary matter. The resulting art may indeed be morally serious and engaged, but this says little about the artist—or the audience, for as Porter states in "The Cost of Seriousness," "A public worthy of its / artists would consist of whores and monsters" (*CP,* vol. 1, p. 338). The ruthless unmasking of the self also involves the abandonment of any illusions about the nature of society. Its pains and appetites are not a partial or special case but part of its texture, along with all the other possible kinds of behavior, including admiration for art. Humanism is forbidden to escape into sentimentality; grief and death are real; they are among our defining experiences.

The poet's wife is not his only accuser. "A Lecture by My Books" is another brilliantly paradoxical piece, in which the author's library diagnosis the exact nature of his failure:

You cannot write tonight. We own all
the words you will ever need to make a shape
of permanence. But they were used by
men who felt along the lines
to life. We are dead
who kept the watch for you while your
     landscapes burned.
We stand like stelae
on the road to Hell. Fear us.

(*CP,* vol. 1, p. 334)

Artistic impotence here becomes a source of critical condemnation by the language itself, and artistic obligations are no more escapable than the prison of language itself. Those "forgettable things, words" turn out to be jailers. We should remember at this point that Porter's work has never been less than wholehearted; he has staked his imaginative life on it, and here, in a brilliant fictive contrivance, he finds himself wanting. If the scope of language is limitless, punishment by failure is similarly without limit. The cost of seriousness is death because in the poet's world, seriousness is life itself, which proves unequal to the struggle with death. In Porter's hands the ancient trope of the poet's inadequacy takes on a fresh power.

The Cost of Seriousness can be described as a postmodernist work. For example it recognizes the existence of its linguistic medium at every turn, showing the inseparability of the poetic "self" from the text and history of texts. Secondly it exploits this awareness to substantiate experiences—dreams of visitation, imagined colloquy with the dead—normally felt to be impossible in a post-religious age. It shows a strong sense of "play," but, more interestingly, the "play" is always in the service of a basic moral seriousness: the sins and guilt of the poet are, we are given to understand and to feel, *real* and consequential beyond the borders of the text.

The slightly eerie combination of excitement and sorrow felt by the reader of these poems shows an altogether deeper effect than the self-regarding aestheticism to which some postmodernist writing is prone. Porter's impatience of theory, and his own strong literary practicality, serve as reminders that these alarming poems, with their glimpses of death and hell, with their dreadful sense of deserved punishment, with their permanent stoicism, are, after all, products of human and human*ist* endeavor rather than of an authorial attempt to shed the humanistic tradition on the grounds of its outmoded essentialism. More plainly, they are the works of a bitterly gained artistic maturity. "A Philosopher of Captions," from Porter's subsequent collection, *English Subtitles* (1981), closes with a sense of "embarrassment" that "pain is the one immortal gift of our stewardship" (*CP*, vol. 1, p. 368). The "pain" may be loss (the death of Jannice, and of Marion Porter), or it may be less easily ascribed, like "the little stone of unhappiness" in "What I Have Written I Have Written" from the same volume, which is restored to its owner with relentless regularity. It is inextricably linked with this life—the poet's—and his unhappiness; it may be the corollary of his art, but it can no more serve as an excuse than the unhappiness may hope for relief. "Duty is better than love, / it can suffer no betrayal" (CP, vol. 1, p. 377) is accordingly both a statement of great moral exactitude and a cry of desperation.

"IN THE NEW WORLD HAPPINESS IS ALLOWED": PORTER'S RETURNS TO AUSTRALIA

"The Delegate" closes: "everything must be remade." An earlier poem, "Anger," from *Living in a Calm Country* (1975), insisted on the need "To give no part / of oneself to death / before the time" (*CP,* vol. 1, p. 271). Another piece from *The Cost of Seriousness,* "Non Piangere, Liu," which deals with the continuing arrival of mail for Porter's late wife, concludes:

> Do not cry, I tell myself,
> the whole thing is a comedy
> and comedies end happily.

> The fire will come out of the sun
> and I will look into the heart of it.

> (*CP,* vol. 1, p. 352)

Juxtaposed like this, the poems hardly offer an affirmation, but they show a kind of persistence and even a capacity for wonder. As Porter began to return to Australia more frequently during the 1970s, the country of his birth took on the role of the New World, the site where everything must be remade.

While for Porter the idea of Australia is inextricably linked to his mother's premature death, in *Living in a Calm Country* it becomes a place of mingled surprise and recognition as well. As might be expected, Porter uses existing literary ideas to mediate his renewed experience of his birthplace. "On First Looking into Chapman's Hesiod" is both an important poem of the period and a key work in his career as a whole. The title alludes to Keats's sonnet "On First Looking into Chapman's Homer," where the work of the prolific Elizabethan translator George Chapman (1559?–1634) gave Keats imaginative access to a "new" world—the heroic world of Homer's Greek heroes and gods. Porter, readily adopting the urbane manners of a Roman city-poet, examines the rural life from which some of his ancestors came: this too is both a new world (Australia was "discovered" by eighteenth-century explorers) and an old one, in that its rituals and customs have ancient Greek precedents. The Greek poet Hesiod (fl. 700? B.C.), in "The Works and Days of Hands," gives a firsthand account of farming life on the Aegean island of Euboea. Virgil was to draw on this poem in the *Georgics*. As a Roman poet might read Greek legends as the prehistory of his civilization and see himself as an Athenian of his own day, Porter brings an anthropological interest to his origins. What he discovers is comprehensible and recognizable, but it is also foreign to a dweller in cities "where one escapes from who one is and who / One was, where home is just a postmark / And country wisdom clings to calendars" (*CP*, vol. 1, p. 286).

Porter offers a critique of Australian society through the lens of Chapman's translation. He finds "the same blunt patriotism, / A long-winded, emphatic, kelpie yapping / About our land, our time, our fate." His unease at an agrarian-populist destiny projected out of a culture that is both narrow and self-admiring is apparent. The ruralism of some Australian writers makes him uncomfortable too:

> One day they're on the campus,
> The next in wide hats at a branding or
> Sheep drenching, not actually performing
> But looking the part and getting instances
> For odes that bruise the blood. And history,
> So interior a science it almost seems
> Like true religion—who would have thought
> Australia was the point of all that craft
> Of politics in Europe? The apogee, it seems,
> Is where your audience and your aspirations are.

These lines are double-edged. One the one hand they seem surprised, even fascinated, by Australia; on the other there is an undertone of mockery, skepticism, and anxiety. To a Europeanized mind, this looks like a provincial country with intolerant nationalism in the making, in the name of authenticity. Thirty years on, Porter has been proved right.

Curiously, "On First Looking into Chapman's Hesiod" produced a rapprochement between Porter and Les Murray (1938–), the eminent Australian ruralist poet who had previously felt that Porter had "betrayed" his birthplace: "I used," Murray wrote, "to make snide remarks about [Porter] selling out one's country to curry favour with the metropolitan enemy" ("My New Country Enjoys Good Relations with Death," *Sydney Morning Herald*, 14 February 1976, p. 15). Now Murray saw such comments as "silly." As a "Roman" poet, Porter, it seems, had learned from an English ironist too, the metaphysical poet Andrew Marvell, whose "Horatian Ode upon Cromwell's Return from Ireland" is a masterpiece of Janus-faced political commentary. In the New World, it

seems as if irony might be contraband. A much sterner elaboration of Porter's themes occurs in "In the New World Happiness Is Allowed," when Australia is described as "the end of the world with deep-freezes" (*CP*, vol. 1, p. 337) and a place poisoned by racism. He concludes: "Forgive me, friends and relatives, / for this unhappiness. I was away from home."

Despite his doubts about Australia in general, and the pain of his own childhood memories, Porter did not abandon Australia. Instead he made imaginative incursions there on his own terms. In "An Australian Garden" he uses some elements of pastoral. In the English poetic tradition this has come to mean the contemplation of nature through models of the natural, in which the wildness of the natural world is brought to order, for example in a garden which may recall the Garden of Eden before the Fall. Again, Marvell's work stands at Porter's shoulder: Marvell's "The Garden" is perhaps the greatest English pastoral poem. Porter's garden is not Eden; it is full of the evidence of death, and of the inescapability of the past, but in contemplating the utterly unclassical Australian garden, Porter proposes a new kind of liberty, a readiness to see the world and its people as they are and live with that knowledge:

> Where is the water, where the terraces, the Tritons
> And the cataracts of moss? This is Australia
> And the villas are laid out inside their eyes:
> It would be easy to unimagine everything,
> Only the pressure made by love and death
> Holds up the bodies which this Eden grows.
> (*CP*, vol. 1, p. 284)

A comparable note of restrained affirmation is sounded in "Under New Management," where, in a pastoral landscape, the poet declares himself "god of this place, my own savannas" (*CP*, vol. 1, p. 358). The affirmation of a kind of imaginative autonomy will prove important in Porter's later work.

Though life may not obediently supply the symmetries desired by art, and though Porter is a poet for whom a state of rest is unthinkable, subsequent poems on Australian themes indicate a gradual establishment of perspective on his own history as well as an accommodation to Australia's sheer otherness. Two poems from his 1987 collection *The Automatic Oracle* exemplify this adjustment, as Porter explores Australian landscapes to find his place in them. "The Melbourne General Cemetery" finds Porter describing a kinship with this city of the dead, not from some morbid appetite but through a recognition that the world possesses an equalizing order. This, or somewhere like it, is where we shall all end up, but equally this is a fact susceptible to contemplation and to art:

> Almost able now to live
> In life or death, this stalker looks
> At those he loves, appreciative,
> And knows them pictures and the books
> Of Thanatation his to give.
>
> (*CP,* vol. 2, p. 87)

The obscure word "Thanatation," derived from the Greek *thanatos,* meaning death, seems to be a coinage referring to the poet's power to remember and then lay to rest the dead. The slightly eerie blend of affirmation and melancholy of the mood is typical of Porter and is mirrored in "Southsea Bubbles," where he visits his grandparents' house and remembers "a family tree / sited in hell" before a complex modulation of tone refers us back to the title. The English South Sea Bubble of 1720 was a state-sponsored financial fraud built on investors' credulity:

> Play history for melody
> and not for truth,
> possums and sparrows
> waltz the roof.
>
> And I must hear before I die
> this oracled South
> speak true love
> from a lying mouth
>
> (*CP,* vol. 2, p. 88)

What *might* have been, what was perhaps wished for and intended, deserves to be remembered (or imagined, an act originating with memory) even though it never happened, and even if the poet's affirmation is a bitter one. This uncomfortable complexity of mood is something Porter has commented on with black humor elsewhere: "I am fond of the overdone. Of Luca Signorelli / and Castagno. I'll never learn simplicity. / I don't feel things strongly. I was never young" ("The Story of My Conversion," *CP,* vol. 1, p. 279). Gradually, though, this very complexity of response allows Porter to consider the imagination itself in relation to Australian weather and landscape in another pair of poems, "The Wind at Bundanon" and "The Ecstasy of Estuaries."

All landscapes are allegorical to Porter; doubly so since he often reads them through prior experience of art. In "The Wind at Bundanon," "This merciless blowing has to be / a metaphor of something." Alert to his own habits, Porter, for whom landscapes are most frequently found framed in art galleries, reads the weather. He makes it supply on a large scale the portents absent from the landscape itself, despite the wind and sky's resistance to the habits of pathetic fallacy:

> . . .The wind has helped us
> draw the face of death. Suppose we had to find
> a passage of the Styx—a goat, a pile of coins,
> a strangled chook beside—better this wind
> than gods about their business. With fingers
> in its eyes, it paints itself a holocaust,
> back to our dreams, The Wonder Book of
>   Sunsets,
> The Raft of the Medusa, a world on fire.
>
> (*CP,* vol. 2, p. 119)

Still more surprising is "The Ecstasy of Estuaries," where, for a time, place is valued for itself: "Rest here, that have no absolute" (*CP,* vol. 2, p. 116). Porter, though, cannot resist ironizing as he affirms, as the anachronistically elevated tone of this line indicates. Neither can he prevent invasion by memory and comparison.

But at the conclusion he does concede the autonomy of place, a state for which the imagination is seeking its own equivalent: "This ecstasy of estuaries prepares / a tableland for time to wander in." Porter's restlessness, though, is immediately at work again, finding that the far-off and supposedly unspoiled place is also susceptible to irony. "Woop Woop" (the name Australians use to evoke an archetypally remote settlement in the Outback) is a lovingly detailed account of a small town, the seeming quintessence of provincialism, which is in fact changing even as the poet imagines it. With all such places, the visitor has come just too late to see the real thing—"despite remoteness and the different sorts of fly, / it has suburban aspects" (*CP*, vol. 2, p. 113). And yet, in the teeth of the evidence, Woop Woop will go on fueling dreams of simple authenticity. The very untidiness of daily reality offers a form of half-imagined reassurance that looks rather like belonging. "National Service" returns to Brisbane, the city of Porter's birth, for a wry, deliberately artless, and bathetic excursion, conducted as though in the manner of an untutored Outback poet with far more matter than style, through a personal history of Australian-ness. The excursion also reads as an exorcism. Is it so terrible to be Australian? Apart from anything else, it's inescapable. It may as well be accepted with democratic grace:

> I moved on: I live in London: I'm grown quite
>   mannerly
> But death will put me on the tram to Annerley
>
> And I'll look out for the familiar sign on the shop
> *Bushells Blue Label:* I'll have got to my stop.
>
> (*CP*, vol. 2, p. 289)

"EXHALATIONS OF THE ABSTRACT": IMAGINATION AND FORM

In his lecture "Poetry and Materialism," Porter writes: "Artists are celebrant sceptics, engaged doubters, defiant cowards. They wish to surmount the prose of transcendence with the poetry of reality" (*Saving from the Wreck*, p. 197). The phrasemaking is striking, the meaning hard to determine, until we grasp that "transcendence" is devalued by its association with, for example, religious doctrine—a matter of the letter rather than the spirit. But there is a sense that meaning shifts and wavers in Porter's work, like objects seen underwater. This is a state of affairs with which Porter professes himself happy in another lecture, "The Poet's Quarrel with Poetry," where he makes a distinction between the demands of philosophy and those of poetry. Intending to vanquish the philosophers, he argues:

> Logic is only glue after all: it sticks thought together. Poetical glue is association, language affinities sometimes beyond meaning, and metrical and sound patterning insist on being heard. So whatever the subject matter of a poem, its development may diverge from what it would be in another form of expression. Poetry is also tied to specific vocal techniques, and resembles a lawyer's plea in court more than a philosopher's logical and linear expression.
>
> (*Saving from the Wreck*, p. 175)

This is not an appeal to the irrational for validation, nor is it an embrace of randomness. Porter is attempting to take account of the fact that composition may be fruitfully affected by contingency. He is also making a further important point: that a poem is rarely an attempt to illustrate a truth that the poet already possesses fully, although the completed poem may well prove to contain a proverbial element. He directs us back to the medium of which poems are made—that is, language itself—and he illustrates the poet's special preoccupations by offering a further useful distinction:

> I have come up with a proposal as to why poetry seems difficult for readers of literature in general. In prose you can say that your main purpose is *telling*. In poetry it is *making*. A poem is analogous to a painting, a piece of sculpture or a musical composition. Its material is language, and often

that language will be almost mosaically fitted together, with words as the pieces of the mosaic.... Poetry is charged with feeling and meaning. . . . But first it has to satisfy the shapeliness of its hope.

(*Saving from the Wreck*, pp. 171–172)

Here Porter awards poetry the literary primacy it is often felt to have lost to the novel. He does this by showing the poet's attachment to language as an a priori condition rather than a role deliberately assumed. The direct relation between the maker and the language is the source both of poetry's authority and its difficulty in an age which continually insists that, even in art, language should serve utility.

The poet Porter most often shadows in his discussions of poetry is Wallace Stevens, whom he greatly admires. His relationship with Stevens needs some examination. Porter is extremely worldly; he has much greater interest than Stevens in everyday life, in sex and the passing show of cultural fashion. Where Stevens expects the world to come to him, Porter goes out and immerses himself. Porter's work is in this sense poetically *impure*. Where Stevens subjects the world to a unifying style of the imagination, Porter's poetry, while it has a quickly recognizable signature, contains a good deal more evident improvisation. His intention is not to emulate, still less to imitate Stevens, but to seek means by which the authority Stevens confers on the poetic imagination can be demonstrated in subject matter and diction that are frequently remote from those of the great American poet. Part of what Porter admires in Stevens is "a love of abstraction mixed with materialism . . . it has a lean and hard resonance" (p. 176). What Porter appears to mean by "abstraction" is the ability to render abstract ideas as experiences rather than flatly denotative tokens. It appears, then, that Porter sees in Stevens a poet free of the dissociation of sensibility T. S. Eliot saw as the affliction of post-Renaissance literature.

To state the obvious, Porter's poems are frequently far from simple. His pursuit of imaginative accuracy yields little to the recently fashionable claims of accessibility. One reason for the difficulty is that his poems are crammed with highly specific, often aphoristic but equally often un-anchored detail; the reader may infer the overall theme but struggle to follow the intricacy of the melodies that serve to dramatize it, because of the speed of transition between registers and kinds of diction. Claude Rawson has commented illuminatingly on this state of affairs. Reviewing *English Subtitles*, he notes the attraction for the modern writer of "the stab of sudden comprehension, incomplete and fleeting, but capable of piercing deeper than discursive talk" (*London Review of Books*, 16 July–5 August 1981, pp. 14–15). He goes on to note that Porter's aphorisms "readily merge . . . into a surrounding context in a way that denies undue status, even of a momentary sort, to self-enclosed crystallizations of experience. But there is no doubting their importance in the poems, and in his ideas of how poems work." What Porter seems to have undertaken in some of his finest later poems is to write a language that can accommodate abstraction in the sense described above and include it in a discourse whose dramatic character expands to include abstraction among other contributing factors rather than being disabled by it. "Stratagems of the Spirit" (a title taken from Stevens's "Credences of Summer"), from the 1989 volume *Possible Worlds*, is an extraordinarily brisk but surefooted dream-lecture on the history of symbolism, its exhaustion by interpretation, and the continuing necessity of it in a secular age:

> we
> Must think ourselves alive and newly-landed,
> Star-faced Linnaeans hearing musical
> Communiqués no erudition robs
> Of freshness—we must pace our footfall on
> The temple steps and listen for the sun.
>
> (*CP,* vol. 2, p. 154)

Necessity here does not mean desirability: it means the inextinguishable habit of the imagination. The temple at the close may be that of the god of light, Apollo, but what we do there is seek for an illumination that breaks down the barriers between the senses.

In "The Poet's Quarrel with Poetry," Porter quotes a remark attributed to the Australian poet John Forbes that "Eloquence is the only truth" (*Saving from the Wreck*, p. 173)—a slippery comment open to misuse but one whose meaning becomes clear in the context of Porter's poem, which serves the truth by dramatizing those imperatives that the imagination both serves and enforces. Yet while Porter rises to an eloquence comparable, though not akin, to Stevens'ss, "Stratagems of the Spirit" does not mark an artistic point of arrival. "Exhalations of the Abstract" (another Stevensian title, though in fact it is invented) tests the same imperative against the grimmer setting of a friend's hospital bed, noting his "fright" and, in the teeth of the evidence, proposing an alternative truth to the one we know:

All language is of objects and the rose
Surprising you above the window sill
Is one strayed word returning to the fold,
A dividend extracted from abstraction.
Among the dead the aunts have not relaxed
Their stark vocabulary and prune for hope.

(*CP*, vol. 2, p. 210)

Porter's artistic enthusiasms include the baroque. At some points his work crosses into the rococo. A love of elaboration for its own sake may be viewed with suspicion, but in Porter's poems there come points, as in this quotation, of near-equality between the demands of meaning and those of form—as if he views the world as a vast music-making machine, one whose task is not to preserve individual moments but to go on extending the music. It is a prospect in equal measures chilling and awe-inspiring.

In "The Cost of Seriousness," Porter writes of his failing to achieve his "goal / of doing without words, that / pain may be notated some real way" (*CP*, vol. 1, p. 338). At a distance of more than a quarter century, we can see that,

while the crisis of conscience and artistic conviction underlying the poems of that period was agonizing for Porter, his work survived it with a renewed sense of poetry's powers, and that this renewal was strongly linked to a grasp of poetry's limitations. Poetry may be only words, able to do no more than gesture at the crises that seem to require them; but the Ariel-like capacity of language to be everywhere and nowhere is a major freedom, while the impulse toward poetic form does honor to experience, mourns it, re-creates it as best it may, and lends it permanence. The understanding that poetry is a part of the world like anything else is the positive element in Porter's sometimes horrifying sense, summarized in "The Delegate," that "There is no morality, / no metered selfishness, no cowardly fear" (*CP*, vol. 1, p. 333). If it is true that there is no underlying moral order to guarantee the meaning of experience, the existence of art is all the more remarkable, while "music's huge light irresponsibility" ("Walking Home on St. Cecilia's Day," *CP*, vol. 1, p. 16) seems wholly justified, as does poetry's aspiration to share it.

Porter's position in relation to twentieth-century poetry is complex. Part of his poetry's necessary impurity has arisen from his embrace of both modernism (exemplified by the complex and nonlinear work of Eliot and Pound) and the antimodernist reaffirmation of poetic tradition made by W. H. Auden, with its developing faith in traditional form and in rationality. In the hands of their inheritors these two lines of development have sometimes appeared mutually exclusive and even antagonistic. Much influential postwar poetry in Britain, exemplified by Philip Larkin (1922–1985), eschewed the irrationalism and cultural showing off it saw in modernism, preferring to trace the well-made poem back through Auden and into the work of Thomas Hardy (and in doing so accept limitations of scale). Successors to the modernists, including Charles Tomlinson (1927–), have read the work of Larkin and other Movement poets as timid, suburban, and artistically reactionary. Porter, to a unique degree, has seen that while poetic modernism involves a sense of catastrophe, and antimodernism a sense of continuance, the poet experiences and needs to encompass both versions of the world—indeed to see them as inseparable. He has described this position with typical wit and eloquence in a profile in an Australian literary journal:

> Most people seem to think about writing literature that one uses experience and that experience should be as fresh as it can be. . . . It ought to be about taking a car down to the beach, or about looking at a flock of galahs, or even about Sydney cocktail parties, but it should not be about other works of art, nor even about ancient Italian cities. This seems to me to be a pre-empting of human imagination. It suggests to me that if reading books is not one of the major experiences of your life, why do people bother writing them? For many people what they read, or look at, or listen to, is primary experience.
>
> (*Westerly*, 27.1, March 1982, p. 47)

Art, he insists, is "primary experience," not in order to exclude the other experiences referred to (there are plenty of beaches, birds, and parties in Porter's work) but to accompany and enrich them and to refuse to allow art to be subordinate to an alleged "real world" whose proponents are frequently one-eyed at best. Porter is offering a defense of seriousness and a refusal to abandon tradition simply because someone has set off the fire alarm again; but he is a wit, not a sermonizer, and he delights in the absurdities language

presents as well as in its attempts to invoke the truth. Several of his poems are based on misreadings—"Civilization and Its Disney Contents," "A Bag of Pressmints," "Brides Come to the Poet's Window." One of the most recent, "The Western Canoe," jumbles the title of Harold Bloom's *The Western Canon* (1994) and plays with the possibilities of installing the Imaginary Museum of Culture in a water-based theme park. In satirizing those who would overstate the claims of art, Porter offers a sane balance. The comedy concludes with the possibility that "Hot in headphones, brushing off the monkeys," Mr. Kurtz, the immensely civilized trader-turned-cannibal from *Heart of Darkness*, one of the great bogeymen of modern literature, will "reappear upriver" (*CP*, vol. 2, p. 294). It is this sane, experienced, unillusioned but perpetually curious view of the world that allows Porter the kind of extended, richly imagined eloquence for which he is likely to be remembered, for example in imagining afresh a cosmos founded on and consisting of music:

> Behind us is the deep note of the universe,
> The E-flat pedal on which time is built,
> Spreading and changing, both a subtle
> Growth of difference and a minimalist
> Phrase, with bridges crossing it and staves
> Of traffic on its tide, a broad bloodstream
> To carry to the delta full mythologies.
>
> (*CP*, vol. 2, p. 152)

Selected Bibliography

WORKS OF PETER PORTER

POETRY

Once Bitten, Twice Bitten. Lowestoft, U.K.: Scorpion Press, 1961.

Poems, Ancient and Modern. Lowestoft, U.K.: Scorpion Press, 1964.

A Porter Folio: New Poems. Lowestoft, U.K.: Scorpion Press, 1969.

The Last of England. Oxford: Oxford University Press, 1970.

Preaching to the Converted. Oxford: Oxford University Press, 1972.

After Martial. Oxford: Oxford University Press, 1972.

Living in a Calm Country. Oxford and New York: Oxford University Press, 1975.

The Cost of Seriousness. Oxford and New York: Oxford University Press, 1978.

English Subtitles. Oxford and New York: Oxford University Press, 1981.

Collected Poems. Oxford and New York: Oxford University Press, 1983.

Fast Forward. Oxford and New York: Oxford University Press, 1984.

The Automatic Oracle. Oxford and New York: Oxford University Press, 1987.

Mars. London: Andre Deutsch, 1988.

A Porter Selected. Oxford: Oxford University Press, 1989.

Possible Worlds. Oxford and New York: Oxford University Press, 1989.

The Chair of Babel. Oxford and New York: Oxford University Press, 1992.

Millennial Fables. Oxford and New York: Oxford University Press, 1994.

Dragons in Their Pleasant Palaces. Oxford and New York: Oxford University Press, 1997.

Collected Poems. 2 vols. Oxford and Melbourne: Oxford University Press, 1999.

Max Is Missing. London: Picador, 2001.

ESSAYS

Saving from the Wreck: Essays on Poetry. Nottingham: Trent, 2001.

AS EDITOR

The English Poets. With Anthony Thwaite. London: Secker and Warburg, 1974.

The Faber Book of Modern Verse. With Michael Roberts. London: Faber and Faber, 1982.

Complete Poems by Martin Bell. Newcastle: Bloodaxe, 1988.

Oxford Book of Modern Australian Verse. Oxford: Oxford University Press, 1988.

New Writing 6. With A. S. Byatt. London: Vintage, 1997.

CRITICAL STUDIES

Bennett, Bruce. *Spirit in Exile: Peter Porter and His Poetry.* Melbourne and New York: Oxford University Press, 1991.

Grubb, Frederick. "Exile, Vigour, and Affluence: Peter Porter." In his *A Vision of Reality: A Study of Liberalism in Twentieth Century Verse.* London: Chattto and Windus, 1965.

O'Brien, Sean. "Peter Porter: A Planet in the Mind." In his *The Deregulated Muse.* Newcastle, U.K.: Bloodaxe, 1998.

Steele, Peter. *Peter Porter.* Melbourne and New York, 1992.

Thwaite, Anthony. *Poetry Today: A Critical Guide to British Poetry 1960–1995.* Harlow, U.K.: Longman, 1995.

A. K. Ramanujan
(1929–1993)

RAJEEV S. PATKE

OVER THIRTY YEARS of life and work in the United States, Attipat Krishnaswami Ramanujan made several distinguished reputations for himself: as poet, translator, folklorist, and scholar. In India he is widely admired for his poems in English; in the United States he is better known for his many sensitive and scholarly translations of Tamil and Kannada classics into English. The poems and translations share several features with the scholarship: meticulous care about detail, incisive phrasing, omnivorous curiosity, a dry sense of irony, a wide-ranging adaptability to ideas and their affective power, and a startling capacity for original collocations and insights that act as a two-way mirror between Indian cultures and Western modes of thought.

LIFE

Ramanujan was born in 1929 in Mysore, an ancient and beautiful city in the central southern Indian state of Karnataka. He came from a Brahmin family of Tamil descent and grew up in a trilingual environment. Edward C. Dimmock Jr. and Krishna Ramanujan report in their introduction to his *Collected Essays* that "When he spoke to his father on the second floor study of the family's three-storey house . . . he used

English. Downstairs, with his mother in the kitchen, Tamil was spoken. And on the streets outside, he communicated in Kannada" (p. xiv).

Ramanujan's father was a professor of mathematics at the University of Mysore. He also studied astronomy and astrology and had a large collection of books in English, Kannada, and Sanskrit. In 1980 Ramanujan wrote about the trouble he had making sense as a teenager of his father's multiple and apparently contradictory commitments to astronomy and astrology: "I had just been converted by Russell to the 'scientific attitude.' I (and my generation) was troubled by his holding together in one brain both astronomy and astrology; I looked for consistency in him, a consistency he didn't seem to care about, or even think about" (*Collected Essays* 1999, p. 36).

An early poem, "Self-Portrait" (*Collected Poems* 1995, p. 23), speaks of his reflected image in a windowpane as the portrait of a stranger signed in a corner by his father. The influence of the father on the son was as decisive as it was troubling to the son. Ramanujan's mother, though a typical orthodox housewife of the times, was well read in Tamil and Kannada. The literate and layered dimensions of a multilingual culture were thus a part of his early environment. As noted by several commentators, the symbiotic tension between upstairs and downstairs was to expand from its narrowly familial aspect in Ramanujan's life and become symbolic of the polarization of linguistic inheritances that characterize his discourses on the task of the translator of Indian languages, in which Sanskrit acquires a paternalistic authority variously complemented, supplemented, or supplanted by the maternal resources of regional languages.

In what his editors describe as "a subtly serendipitous event," at age seventeen he overslept and failed an examination. The extra year he had to spend before graduating also saw him begin to write. First he tried his hand at radio plays, then he moved on to stories and poems. His daughter Krittika reports, in her prefatory essay to the *Collected Poems* (1995), that "his favourite poets were Shelley and Yeats," and adds that while he always loved Yeats, in later life he came to prefer Wallace Stevens and William Carlos Williams (p. xv). The latter's influence is clearly discernible in the kind of terraced look to the printed free verse that became Ramanujan's staple. One of his interviews, and several poems, also acknowledge the influence of Ezra Pound. In college he first studied science but was persuaded by his father to sustain his interest in language and literature. Ramanujan secured a B.A. degree with honors in English from Maharaja's College, Mysore, in 1949 and then took up a job teaching English in the Malayalam-speaking state of Kerala. The following year his father died of a heart attack. In the 1950s, Ramanujan taught in several colleges, ranging from Quilon to Belgaum and Baroda. In 1957 he became a fellow at Deccan College. This institution, situated outside Pune, in the Indian state of Maharashtra, had a well-established reputation in the fields of linguistics and archaeology. The following year he secured a graduate diploma in theoretical linguistics from Deccan College. In 1959, at what can be seen in retrospect as the midpoint of his life, he left for the United States on a Fulbright grant to study linguistics at Indiana University.

Ramanujan was to spend the rest of his life—thirty-three years—in the United States. He obtained a Ph.D. in linguistics from Indiana University in 1963 and started his American teaching career as an assistant professor at the University of Chicago, where he worked in the department of South Asian Languages and Civilizations and in the Linguistics department as well as with the Committee on Social Thought. At his sudden death on 13 July 1993 he was William E. Colvin Professor of South Asian Languages and Civilizations at Chicago. He also taught for short periods at several other U.S. universities, including Harvard University, University of Wisconsin, University of Michigan, University of California at Berkeley, and Carleton College. Widely respected as a scholar of South Indian languages, translator, Indologist, and folklorist, he received several honors, including the Padma Sri (1976), the fourth-highest award conferred by the government of India for distinguished service in any field of human endeavor, and a MacArthur Foundation fellowship (1983), popularly known as a "genius grant" and given for "exceptional creativity, promise for important future advances based on a track record of significant accomplishment and potential for the fellowship to facilitate subsequent creative work."

Since his death, his widow, Molly Daniels-Ramanujan, who holds a Ph.D. from the University of Chicago's Committee on Social Thought, has supervised the publication of his collected poems, essays, and uncollected works with the help of several of Ramanujan's equally distinguished colleagues. After his death, and in recognition of the excellence of his translations, the South Asia Council of the Association for Asian Studies based in Ann Arbor, Michigan, established the A. K. Ramanujan Book Prize for Translation. The award of $1,000 is given every other year and is intended to recognize the first publication in English of original translations from a South Asian language from any historical period. The first award, given in 1996, was won by Rajagopal Parthasarathy's *Cilappatikaram of*

Ilanko Atikal (The Tale of an Aklet): An Epic of South India (1993). Subsequent winners are: for 1998, Patrick Olivelle's *Upanisads* (1996); for 2000, Stuart Blackburn's *The Fatal Rumour: A Nineteenth Century Indian Novel* (1998); and for 2002, George L. Hart and Hank Heifetz's *The Four Hundred Songs of War and Wisdom* (1999). The legacy of Ramanujan's commitment to translation thus flourishes past his death in works that he would have admired and encouraged.

RAMANUJAN'S INDIA

An India of the mind—compounded from the influences of his formative years and his reading in several languages, and combining the interests of the scholar with those of the translator—underlies the achievement of Ramanujan's poems in English. The orientation evidenced or implied by his poetry grows out of his concerns and preoccupations as an Indologist and translator. Therefore, even if the poetry was written mostly in the United States, its significance is best appreciated in the context of Ramanujan's notion of an Indian legacy, a notion that developed as an interaction between his formative years in India and his later, more self-reflexive scholarship, which made India his exclusive object of academic study. For Ramanujan, India is a complex set of cultural systems, "stratified yet interconnected" (*Collected Essays*, p. 9). They shape his sense of self and his work, as they do that of other Indians, especially those born in families where the practices of Hinduism prevail.

The specific systems of culture that interested him are Brahmanical in orientation. That is, they reflect the beliefs, attitudes, and practices of a specific part of the caste system which has divided Indian society for more than two thousand years into the profession-based, male-descended, and noninterchangeable categories of Brahman (priest), Kshatriya (warrior), Vaisya (merchant or trader), and Sudra (servant or

untouchable). The interaction between, and the combined effects of Jainism, Buddhism, and Brahmanism shaped a set of mainstream religious beliefs, and cultural traditions that became known in ancient India as the *marga* (literally "path," metaphorically "way of life"), which Ramanujan refers to as the "so-called Great Traditions (*Collected Essays*, p. 26). But the *marga* traditions do not exist, or coexist, except in further interactions with other systems. Ramanujan identifies three such parallel systems of practice which "invert, oppose and otherwise reflect on" the *marga* traditions. They become directly pertinent to his interests as scholar and translator, and indirectly they influence all his poems in English: folklore, bhakti ("the personal/devotional revolutionary form of Hinduism that comes into vigorous being first in the sixth-century Tamil area," *CE*, p. 26), and Tantra ("an esoteric system of spiritual exercises"). As Ramanujan puts it, "*Tantra* inverts, and extreme forms of *bhakti* subvert; folk forms rework and domesticate the orthodox brahmanical traditions" (*CE*, p. 27).

The relation of the paternalistic influence of Sanskrit to the maternal resource of the bhakti tradition that found its expression in the regional languages of central and south India is described by Ramanujan in the form of a tension or resistance: "The imperial presence of Sanskrit, with its brahmanical (*smrti*) texts of the Vedas and the Upanishads, was a presence against which bhakti in Tamil defines itself, though not always defiantly (*Hymns for the Drowning* 1981, p. 109).

Ramanujan's poems are thoroughly immersed in the influences of both traditions: the Sanskritic Brahmanism is acknowledged grudgingly or involuntarily, while the poet makes many overt statements that are subversive of the paternal and express a more natural affinity for the maternal. In his translations, bhakti becomes the source of inspiration that draws his creative energies into a form of celebration that mixes several impulses: the invocatory, the commemorative, and the elegiac.

The same is true of the form of the Indian folktale, which Ramanujan collected, edited, and translated assiduously. It feeds the anecdotal side of many of his poems in English. The folktale is to epic what the bhakti poem is to the Sanskrit lyric. It arises from common stock; it speaks from and for the people, even when it handles supernatural or legendary material; it is oral in transmission and generally emanates from women. In that sense it represents the feminine and maternal perspective on experience and folk wisdom. It supplements, and sometimes subverts, the male-dominated perspective of the Sanskrit tradition of narrative.

Some, like Tejaswini Niranjana (1992), have accused Ramanujan's attachment to Indic regional cultures as an essentializing and post-romantic tendency symptomatic of a colonial or postcolonial mind-set, while others, such as Vinay Dharwadker (1999), have offered a vigorous defense of Ramanujan's practice and theory of translation. The specific nuances Ramanujan discovers in the bhakti traditions give some purchase to either persuasion, and the debate retains a capacity to polarize opinion in the informed reader:

> The poem evokes the primal, the essential experience of *bhakti:* not ecstasy, not enstasy [shamanic trance], but an embodiment; neither a shamanic flight to the heavens or soul loss, nor a yogic autonomy, a withdrawal of the senses—but a partaking of the god. . . . A *bhakta* [worshipper] is not content to worship a god . . . he needs to possess him and be possessed by him . . . to embody him in every possible way.
>
> (*Hymns for the Drowning,* pp. 115–116)

The work that draws Ramanujan's creative energies as translator is of the kind in which resistance is most manifest. Invoking Shakespeare's line "How with this rage shall beauty hold a plea," he remarks of over three hundred years (sixth to ninth centuries A.D.) of Tamil history that "Not only did poetry, sainthood, and art 'hold a plea,' they helped renew, unify, and reconstruct the culture" (*Hymns for*

the Drowning, p. 106). His introduction to *Speaking of Siva* (1973) insists that in such poetry "Alienation is not discontinuity" (p. 33). In his discussion of the strength of the regional traditions in Tamil, Kannada (and, by implication, Marathi, Bengali, etc.), he writes: "The simplicity and vigor of a colloquial dialect represents a revolt against Sanskrit, a defiance of the 'language of the gods' and of the ritual and brahmanical learning it represented" (*CE,* p. 330). This corresponds in a curiously literal way to how Ramanujan represents his father and his friends in the poem "Astronomer," in which their "Sanskrit zodiacs" are "forever troubled" by "the kidneys / in his Tamil flesh" and "the woman smell . . . down there" (*CE,* pp. 36–37; *CP,* p. 134).

This complex and bi-gendered cultural inheritance shapes a set of shared values and attitudes whose influence can be felt in the critical traditions of the Indian regional languages. Ramanujan is articulate and explicit about what is entailed in either. In "Is There an Indian Way of Thinking?," a paper prepared for a 1980 workshop in Chicago, he first clears the air of several misconceptions about what it means to be an Indian, then he goes on to delineate what he regards as traits characteristic of a mode of thinking and feeling that creates the rich poetic traditions he was to spend his life translating into English.

In popular conceptions, the typical or archetypal Indian is portrayed as irrational and inconsistent, prey to superstition, prone to emotionalism, and victimized by a submissive belief in karmic destiny and a fatalistic determinism that paralyzes free will and choice by attributing everything bad or good in any one life to the deeds or misdeeds of a past incarnation. This Indian also suffers from the "apparent inability to distinguish self from non-self" and is characterized by the absence of any clear notion "of a universal human nature" (*CE,* p. 39). Ramanujan counters these clichés with the qualification that the modes of thought and feeling that may be characterized as Indian are largely context sensitive, whereas the ability to universalize and idealize is based on cultures that are drawn to context-free rules and modalities. His defense of an Indian sensibility is complemented by a negative attitude toward India's introduction to modernity: "One might see 'modernisation' in India as a movement from the context-sensitive to the context-free in all realms: an erosion of contexts" (*CE*, p. 49). In contrast, the genre of traditional lyric poetry, as exemplified in Indian civilization predating modernity, serves Ramanujan as an illustration of how a culture can be context specific:

> Texts in the Indian traditions may be historically dateless and anonymous, but their contexts, uses, efficacies, are explicit. . . . Tamil (and Sanskrit) lyrics are all dramatic monologues; they imply the whole "communication diagram": who said what to whom, when, why, and often with who else overhearing it.
>
> (*CE*, p. 42)

This tradition draws upon an entire taxonomy of landscapes, flora, fauna, and corresponding emotional states that create a comprehensive ecosystem of human predicaments, feelings, ideas, and their natural correlates from which any individual poem or poet creates meaningful utterance. In this ecosystem, the poet or poem is never alone. The individual situation, poem, and poet are all part of a larger system that is always implicit in its entirety whenever any part of it is explicitly evoked. Since all and any utterance takes place only within this context-sensitive system, the whole is always implied in the part that is uttered. All poetry is thus part of a single nature-culture continuum: "in the Tamil poems, culture is enclosed in nature, nature is reworked in culture, so that we cannot tell the difference" (*CE*, p. 44). The implication for the act of writing is immediate and overwhelming. The poet writing within the older Indian systems is never solitary. Poetic utterance is never an isolated act. The poet always writes within the continuum of nature and culture: "He posits a familial self, a 'self-we regard,' sees no phase of separation/

individuation from the parental family as in modern America" (*CE*, p. 46). The "Hindu concern with *jati*—the logic of classes, of genera and species, of which human *jatis* are only an instance" (*CE*, p.47)—thus provides the Indian poet with a grammar of poetry and a poetics of culture. This grammar and poetics enriches, and in its turn is enriched by, Ramanujan's long series of translations from Kannada and Tamil and his work with Indian folktales. Beyond the challenge of the specific word, sentence, meter, rhyme, image, or figuration, his translations seek to evoke a densely peopled and context-sensitive culture. The poems in English are unable to come up with anything to correspond to what the translations attribute to the imagined Tamil past. While the poet's interactions with ancient and medieval Indian culture, as mediated by Tamil poetry, represent the poeticized past as a source of positive values, his poems in English fail to discover the same richness of experience in his personal memories of India, or in his personal life in the United States.

RAMANUJAN THE TRANSLATOR

The entire body of Ramanujan's translations may be described, in his own terms, as a sustained act of personal repossession, as crucial to his sense of self as his own poems. The introduction to *Poems of Love and War* (1985) acknowledges that "Even one's own tradition is not one's birthright; it has to be earned, repossessed. . . . One chooses and translates a part of one's past to make it present to oneself" (p. xvii). The afterword to *The Interior Landscape* (1967) notes that the tradition of poetry to which he is attracted "is an impersonal tradition" (p. 99). His introduction to *Speaking of Siva* (1973) adds: "Both the classical [in Sanskrit and in the regional languages] and folk literature of India work with well-established languages of convention, given personae, and elaborate metrical patterns that mediate and depersonalize literary expression (p. 53).

As a specific instance of this general tendency, the ecosystem of early classical Tamil literature, as enshrined in a work of grammar and poetics called the *Tolkāppiyam* (c. 100–300 A.D.), divides poetry into two classes: *akam* (interior) and *puram* (exterior). In his many discussions of translations, Ramanujan repeatedly invokes this division as a shaping force on poetic convention in the regional Indian literatures. *Akam* deals with "the 'inner' poetry of emotion, especially the varied emotions of love in its changing aspects" (*When God Is a Customer* 1995, p. 9). It is "directly about experience, not action" (*The Interior Landscape*, p. 103). *Puram* deals with the exterior world of heroic action, community, war, kingship, and other zones of public experience. The *akam* tradition recognizes several types of love (such as well-matched, mismatched, unrequited), and each of the principal types from that repertoire develops a recognizable set of symbolic conventions. Thus each of five types of symbolic region or landscape is considered as appropriate for a corresponding *uri* or phase of love (such as elopement, union, separation, patient or anxious fidelity, and infidelity), and "each phase of love gets its characteristic type of imagery from a particular landscape" (*CE*, pp. 203–204). The "five real landscapes of the Tamil country (hills, seashores, agricultural areas, wastelands, and pastoral fields) become, through this system, the interior landscapes of Tamil poetry" (*CE*, p. 224). The personae who voice the utterance of a poem are limited to a range of characters typified through their relation to others and to the theme: hero, heroine, friend, mother, concubine, passerby, and so on.

Likewise, *puram* poems develop a corresponding vocabulary of interrelated persona, landscape, mood, and imagery. Furthermore, "the two themes, love and war—*akam* and *puram*—become metaphors for one another: contrasted in theme and structure but unified by imagery" (*CE*, p. 214). The difference is that "*akam* poems tend to focus attention on a spare single image; in *puram* poems, the images rush and tumble over one another" (*The Interior Landscape*, p. 101). In either tradition, for the

individual poet "the design is given but the details are his to use" (*The Literature of India*, p. 172), and "the external world is continuous with, and expressive of, inner experience" (*When God Is a Customer*, p. 13). The afterword to *The Interior Landscape* (1967) notes that for five or six generations the classical Tamil poets were able to sustain a formalized language of symbols and conventions that created a miraculously wonderful tradition: "The spurious name *Cankam* [fraternity, community] for this poetry is justified not by history but by the poetic practice" (p. 115).

The difference between this fraternity, as cherished in Ramanujan's translations, and its absence, as reflected in his English poems, is between a poet firmly rooted within the nourishing network of associations and conventions that constitute a communal culture, and a poet writing without the benefit of a sense of communal belonging. In one case, "The Literary ideal is impersonality" (*Speaking of Siva*, p. 53), which evokes communal unity as an abstraction of roles and relations from the specificity of interpersonal selfhood; in the other, the ideal remains confined within a romantic commitment to subjective self-expression and an involuntary drive toward the modern diminution of solitary selfhood.

Ramanujan grew up in Mysore, which is part of the Kannada-speaking state of Karnataka. He thus came to the language as part of his social environment. His translations in *Speaking of Siva* (1973) focus on a medieval religious tradition (at its most intense between the tenth and twelfth century A.D.) whose followers worship the incarnation of the Hindu god Siva, in a tradition that Ramanujan claims has analogues to European Protestant movements. The correspondences Ramanujan avers (though these have been challenged by Niranjana, 1992) include protest against mediators like priests, support of the underdog, preference for regionalism through language, belief in arbitrary grace, and belief in the doctrine of the mystically chosen elect. Ramanujan's strategy as translator works on the following principles: "Not to match the Kannada with the English, but to map the medieval Kannada onto the soundlook of modern English; in rhythm and punctuation, in phrase-breaks, paragraph and lineation to suggest the inner form of the originals as I see them (*Speaking of Siva*, p. 13). He quotes with approval a dictum from St. John of the Cross, in which to *translate* "is to reconstitute as nearly as possible the *effect* of a certain cause" (p. 13). The Kannada form of the *vacana* ("what is said") belongs to an oral tradition, "not only a spontaneous cry but a cry for spontaneity" (p. 38). Yet, for poet and translator, "Without a repertoire of structures to rely on, there can be no spontaneity" (p. 38).

As for Tamil, his mother tongue, Ramanujan's essay "On Translating a Tamil Poem" points out that "The poems I translate from Tamil were written two thousand years ago in a corner of South India, in a Dravidian language relatively untouched by the other classical language of India, Sanskrit. . . . Over two thousand Tamil poems of different lengths, by over four hundred poets, arranged in nine anthologies, have survived" (*CE*, p. 219).

Translation, as the task of attempting the impossible, is enabled for Ramanujan by four articles of faith: (1) a belief in what Ramanujan regards as the explanatory fiction of universals that subsidize linguistics and literary study ("If such universals did not exist . . . we would have had to invent them," [*CE*, p. 229]); (2) the presence of interiorized contexts within a poem, such that the properties and conventions of an entire culture are assimilated and exemplified by any given poem; (3) the systematicness of bodies of poetry, "the way figures, genres, personae, etc. inter-mesh in a master-code" (*CE*, p. 230); and (4) structural mimicry, that is, the treatment of relations, not items; phrases, not words; rhythms, not meters; and syntactic pattern, not morphology as the elements to "carry across" in translation.

The introduction to *Hymns for the Drowning* (1981) treats translation as a form of transposition and recognizes several levels of difficulty to the task: "Items are more difficult to translate than relations, textures more difficult than structure, words more difficult that phrasing, linear order more difficult than syntax, lines more difficult than pattern. Yet poetry is made at all these levels—and so is translation" (*Hymns for the Drowning*, p. xvi).

In terms of the specific problems presented by Tamil, Ramanajun notes that "the 'left-branching' syntax of Tamil is most often a reverse mirror image of the possible English" (p. xvii). His strategy chooses to translate "unit by syntactic unit and to try and recreate the way the parts articulate the poem in the original" (p. xvii).

The special technical resource that Ramanujan discovers in the Indian regional poetic traditions is that of a Hopkinslike "inscape": "The *Tolkappiyam* calls this technique of using the scene to describe act or agent *ullurai* ('the inner substance')" (*The Interior Landscape*, p. 109). In the afterword to *Poems of Love and War* (1985), Ramanujan describes them as "insets," the key element in the conduct and progress of a classical Tamil poem: "this progression [from the basic cosmic elements to the specific component of a landscape] is also the method of the entire intellectual framework behind the poetry: moving from first elements to native elements to human feelings" (pp. 244–245). Likewise, the features that attract Ramanujan to his Indian linguistic materials are a complex manifold: their assimilation of spontaneous utterance into the illusion of spontaneous form; their assimilation of individual expression into communal modalities; their resourceful resistance to the homogenizing and colonizing power of Sanskritic culture; and finally, their capacity to combine the devotional with the sensuous.

When such poetry succeeds in producing the effect it intends, "grammar becomes poetry, and poetry becomes theology" (*Hymns for the*

Drowning, p. 126). To a poet in the bhakti tradition, god is like a mother tongue, and to lose the mother tongue is "to be exiled into aphasia" (p. 138). From a different but related metaphorical perspective, bhakti partakes of the sense of touch in two contrary senses, it is contact as in merging, and it is contact as in "contagion" (p. 147). In its obsessive and all-consuming aspects, love of god is both dissolution and disease. The Telugu songs translated in *When God Is a Customer* (1994), make the courtesan the major figure in this poetry of love, as "an expressive vehicle for the manifold relations between devotee and deity." It is not a mere matter of expressing the sacred through the profane, because "for these devotees love of god is not *like* a sexual experience. . . . it is erotic in its own right" (p. 19). The afterword to *Hymns for the Drowning* remarks that "the entire erotic tradition has become a new signifier, with *bhakti* as the signified" (p. 160). The interpenetration of the sacred and the profane might be said to be the peculiar power of Ramanujan's materials in Kannada, Tamil, Malayalam, and Telugu. In his own poems, a fund of personal experience and memory undergoes a modern poetic treatment that can be said to be like a reverse image or a photographic plate as a negative to the positive of his classical and medieval Indian models.

RAMANUJAN THE POET IN ENGLISH

Ramanujan's collected poems in English are much slimmer in size than the body of his translations into English or his collected essays. During his lifetime he published only three volumes (1966, 1971, and 1986), and a selection (1976). A sizable body of later, uncollected poems has been published posthumously in *Collected Poems* (1995) and *Uncollected Poems and Prose* (2001). The relative meagerness of his poetic output is partly accounted for by his daughter Krittika: "Ramanujan worked on these poems off and on for many years, as was his habit. He often joked that poems were like babies, they dirtied themselves and he had to

clean them up. He said it took him ten years to really finish a set of poems" (*CP,* p. xv). The first three volumes are the principal focus of the large body of critical analysis and commentary that has followed them from India since the 1970s and 1980s. Although he has been represented in a number of anthologies from Britain and the United States, he figures there less as a major poetic voice from India, or from the United States, than for the representative position he can be made to occupy in the context of the diasporic and hyphenated condition of the Indo-American. In *The Hybrid Muse* (2001), Jahan Ramazani can still speak, from the United States, of Ramanujan as needing an introduction and "poised on the brink of worldwide recognition" (p. 75). In India, meanwhile, he has for a long time occupied a position of eminence among Indian poets writing in English in the twentieth century.

Ramanujan's poetry is all of a kind: dry, spare, and unsparing. Its wry scrutiny surveys the personal self, family relations, and more general human situations and predicaments with an impersonality that can appear sharp and cold. His range of tones, moods, and content is narrow and distinguished by an odd mix of the distant and the impersonally intimate. Critics have sometimes expressed unease or disquiet about its limitations. S. Nagarajan, for example, writing in 1972, notes Ramanujan's reliance on unmediated images in his poems and complains of "the relative failure to offer an intellectually satisfying comment upon his experience" (p. 20). The later verse is slightly more expansive, but the feature highlighted by Nagarajan continues to mark all of Ramanujan's poetry. When the effect works, a poem comes across as densely allusive and elliptically complex. When the effect fails to impress, the poem appears unresolved or evasive in its response to the issue or experience that has triggered it into being. This is partly due to the fact that in Ramanujan's poems in English—unlike the world of his translations—fraternity and community are evoked only as an implied absence. Correspondingly, a sense of the sacred as interwoven in the profane is almost completely effaced from the poems in English, as if the will to grace had been turned inside out by a corrosive spirit of modernity that did not spare the poet or his subject matter.

The work of the widely admired Indian graphic artist S. G. Vasudev offers an oblique but telling insight into the typical quality of Ramanujan's work in English: its starkness. Vasudev was introduced to Ramanujan in the 1960s by Girish Karnad (playwright and filmmaker, also noted for his powerful film version of Anantha Murthy's Kannada novel *Samskara*, which was translated into English by Ramanujan in 1989). In "Tribute to A. K. Ramanujan," Vasudev collected for exhibition over forty drawings inspired by Ramanujan's poems and translations. In the essay accompanying an exhibition of these drawings at the Nehru Centre in London during December 2002, Vasudev recounts that when he showed Ramanujan the cover designs that he had prepared at the poet's request for his first Kannada book of poems, *Hokkulalli Hoovilla* (No flower in the navel), the poet asked:

"Don't you want to use any more colour?"
I said, "No. I can only conceive of your poems in black and white."

The starkness of Ramanujan's poetry may be described as an affect of absence and separation. One way of glossing it is to point to the world that is both lost, and kept from loss, in his translations. In the afterword to *Hymns for the Drowning* (1981), Ramanujan writes of the love poetry inspired by "what is called *viraha* in Sanskrit, *mullai* and *neytal* in Tamil poetics" (p. 156). Such poems speak of absence rather than presence, and the pain of separation rather than the joy of union.

The distinction parallels the central theological one between the Lord's otherness (*paratva*) and his easy access (*saulabhya*)—a distinction that characterizes the *ālvārs*' [bhakti poets'] experience of being: its nearness coupled with its mysterious otherness, its unavailability. The latter makes the former precious, precarious, a thing of grace. . . . The otherness is a condition of grace. So is separation a condition for *bhakti*.

(pp. 156–157)

It can be argued that his poems in English are a host of recursive variations on the theme of *viraha*.

THE STRIDERS (1966)

Ramanujan's style, poetic strategies, and mannerisms reveal themselves as fully formed in his earliest poems. The volume was a Poetry Society recommendation when first published. The poems are all written as reflections in free verse, terse, laconic, and gnomic. A poem like "Two Styles of Love" (*CP*, p. 11) stands out for being neatly turned out in staidly rhyming quatrains. Ramanujan rarely uses traditional forms, rhymes, or meters. In this respect, his poetry aligns itself with the formal tradition of modern poets such as Ezra Pound and William Carlos Williams, and the exceptions merely highlight the norm. His preferred line length is short, and groups of lines are usually arranged on the page in irregular stanzas that follow the tone of the speaking voice. Line breaks are used to accentuate images and the surprising impact of transitions carefully prepared for and sprung across a syntax stretched across line breaks. The verse line is rarely end-stopped. This preserves a sense of quirky energy in the poem's momentum, never allowing the reader to rest content until an entire poem has been read, if even then.

Ramanujan's images can surprise, first with their oddity and then with their aptness. Collocations can be unexpected, as in his very first poem, "The Striders" (*CP*, p. 3). The initial stanza gives the image of water bugs perched on water in such a way as not to break the water's skin. The second stanza remarks that it is not just prophets that walk on water. The effect is disconcerting, since the perspective does not explicitly diminish prophets or elevate bugs. It simply holds the two apparently discordant images in insouciant balance. The poem ends by reversing the associations of sky and water, as the bug "drowns eye- / deep / into its tiny strip / of sky" (*CP,* p. 3). Such poetry is knowing in manner and surefooted in its zigzag down the serrated line breaks. The reader is likely to be impressed but also likely to be left uncertain about how to take the impression.

Ramanujan has a natural propensity for unusual associations. A book that has gold on its spine reminds him of "Snakes" (*CP,* pp. 4–5). The marks on their hoods look like the lorgnettes of some terrible aunt. The bodies are like tongues that lick the floors they cross. The tassel his sister uses to braid her hair reminds him of scales. Stepped on, a snake's belly is like a lotus stalk. The spasms that strike poet and snake drain both of their fear, leaving the poet free to walk in the woods. Meanwhile, the reader's walk through the poem is likely to leave behind a sense of disquiet at the mastery with which queasiness has been conjured up, and disquiet that the poem has no apparent intention exorcising it. The same is true of the recollection of a half-naked female corpse grained by the sand that is brought to memory when the poet is offered "Breaded Fish" (*CP,* p. 7) to eat. The imagery of snakes and dead fish recurs throughout the poetry. An extra digit to the hand marks three stanzas of "The Opposable Thumb" (*CP,* p. 6). Water dripping from the "slightly incontinent mouth" (*CP,* p. 9) of a tap sounds like a silversmith's mallet next door and then like a woodpecker. The poem ends with the wish that a tree might shriek and writhe like the dead snake in a crow's mouth. In "Still Life" (*CP,* p. 12) a woman leaving the poet after lunch is evoked through the shape of her bite on a sandwich. In another poem dominated by a surreal yellow, the heat of the day is like sulfur mines, the father sits in the yellow of a sunflower, and the poet's voice wonders if an unborn daughter shall show jaundice in her eyes.

In "Sometimes" (*CP,* p. 26), "the day has weals / on her back, as if / she had slept on a rafter." Such odd collocations of details throng poem after poem, sharp like crow's feet.

Ramanujan's predilection for certain types of images is supplemented at the level of figurative language by a characteristic habit of metaphors in metamorphosis. In "Looking for a Cousin on a Swing" (*CP,* p. 19), the metaphor of "the lunging pits / of her feeling" shades off first into a suggestion of "innocent" sexual groping and then into "the crotch of a tree." Similarly, "Lac into Seal" returns to the image of "the armpits of trees" (*CP,* p. 50). The interchange between inner and outer worlds, as between the human and the natural, presents a darker version of what is also encountered in the systematic symbology of his translations from Tamil and Kannada. Likewise, the folklorist's love of tales figures in a number of poems where the poet uses the yarn as an oblique or allegorical way of getting to an ugly and uncomforting truth. Such poems are equally deft at evoking contemporary incidents, childhood memories, and old wives' yarns about wandering princes and enchanted animals.

The effect of allusions to Indic materials is sometimes disconcerting, as in "Anxiety" (*CP,* p. 29), where the poet can find no relief in metaphor, though "Flames have only lungs. Water is all eyes." The poem "Conventions of Despair" is explicit about giving up on the modishness of being modern because

I must seek and will find

my particular hell only in my hindu mind:
must translate and turn
till I blister and roast

(*CP,* p. 34)

And "Still Another View of Grace" returns to the obsession with purging, or failing to purge, the Brahmin within:

Bred Brahmin among singers of shivering hymns
I shudder to the bone at hungers that roam the
   street

                                          (*CP*, p. 45)

The edginess of tone characteristic of Ramanujan's first volume feeds on its own uncertainties, on its fear that for a man falling, the only floating is "the amniotic floating without hands," without "the sudden catch / of grace" (*CP*, p. 51). Glass in fist, the "Case History" of such a self-alienated individual faces

   . . . several rows
of futures that could not reach any past.
                                          (*CP*, p. 47)

RELATIONS (1971)

The title and epigraph of Ramanujan's second volume indicate a fundamental ambivalence about the self in its relations to family:

   But living
among relations
binds the feet.

                                          (*CP*, p. 56)

A poem like "Of Mothers, among other things" bears this out in its focus on the mother as an old woman. Her hands are like claws, her clothes hang loose on her body. Present age and former youth—the one seen, the other smelt—are held in stereoscopy with such immense strain that the poet's tongue "licks bark / in the mouth" (*CP*, p. 61). What is stared at unblinkingly is the aging; what the mother was, or might have been, in youth is evoked indirectly, as the smell of a petal upon a twisted "blackbone tree" (reminiscent, as commentators love to point out, of Pound's haiku-like poem about "petals on a wet black bough"). The evocation of tree and petal enacts the co-presence of contrary states: the tree is gnarled and endures, like the poet's old mother; the petal is soft, and fragile, like her youth. The

poet never knew his mother as young. In that sense, her youth is like an absence that the image of the petal vivifies for the present, not as memory, but as an imagining. Present age and imagined youth are both realized in the present tense of the poem as metonymies from nature. The ugliness of age and the pathos of youth are both evoked in terms of tree and petal. The human, in being associated and merged with the natural, becomes less personal, more distanced, enabling the poet to regard the compound emblem of tree-mother and age-youth with a gaze ambivalently split between fascinated horror and wonder.

Sexuality is latent in much of Ramanujan's poetry, and his sexual images tend to evoke taboo or transgressive aspects of sexuality. As Anjali Kadekodi and others have noted, the physicality of the mother is a recurrent motif for metaphors that engage indirectly with the Oedipal and incest motifs in myth and literature. Ramanujan's essay "The Indian Oedipus" notes that in his Indian materials "the son never wins, almost never kills the father-figure" (*CE*, p. 387). Many of his own poems skirt this territory in their treatment of the figures of father and mother. The poet is fond of discovering himself implicated—through complicitous affinity or direct genetic inheritance—in the sexual life of parents and grandparents. Spiders remind him of a grandfather in the role of fisherman-lover imprinting his nets on the "great swinging grandmother" who bites him, below (*CP*, p. 62).

Loving, eating, and hating go closely together, as if ancestors were Borneo spiders. "Love Poem for a Wife 1" speaks of husband and wife as being distanced by unshared childhoods. Nostalgia becomes a peculiar emotion when felt about experiences that are not part of personal memory. The images in photograph albums become "family rumours" (*CP*, p. 65). The metaphor of the poem was made literal in the image of Ramanujan and his parents that was used for the cover of *Relations* (1971). Wendy Doniger remarks: "that amazing photograph . . .

he sitting, she standing, towering above him, both of them firmly embedded in the head of Ramanujan" (*CE*, p. 5). The double image symbolizes the odd aptness with which Freudian determinism superimposes itself on Hindu karmic destiny to imply that we carry—like a third eye planted in the middle of our foreheads—the ghost of our ancestors in our selves, as Aeneas had carried his father, Anchises, on his back in his diasporic voyage from falling Troy to the Rome of his future. Ramanujan is reported to have been "both embarrassed and amused" (*CE*, p. xv) by the cover.

Ramanujan's poetry may be read as symptomatic of how the solitariness of his poetic self mapped real, imagined, and desired networks of relationships in a reverse (and hence desolating) analogy to the positive embedding that had sustained the Tamil poets and personae of his translations. As an antidote to unshared pasts, the poet talking to his wife invokes, in what can be recognized as only a half-facetious remedy, the Egyptian custom of marriages between siblings and the Hindu custom of child marriage predicated on the conjunctions of astrology.

Trying to remember what is not a memory becomes a compulsive obsession in Ramanujan's poetry, like "an amnesiac / use of memory" (*CP*, p. 76). In such a predicament, "Nothing / at all is family to that estrangement," and like a branch separated from its trunk, the poet's persona would like to trace a path back to "the inverse / branching under the earth" (*CP*, p. 76). The senses roam loose in such poems. Touch and smell verify what is close and near, but in bewildering isolation, with no sense of coherence or continuity to perception. The poetry becomes a welter of smells, "skin listening," and "a seeing ear," but without a face or body to hold the synesthesia together, "eyes groping for the hidden hooks" (*CP*, p. 93). Women carrying baskets on their heads, buffaloes swatting flies, gulls' eggs on grass, human buttocks parted in outdoor defecation are all noted in sharp col-

location. The effect produced by such sequences avoids whimsicality while giving a blank shrug to the oddness of the reality seen, as if in passing from the distance of a train window. Iridescence and horse piss, lovers or houseflies rubbing legs, all become equal grist to an unrelenting mill of observation, whose even-paced neutrality is belied by the choking sense that "ancient hands are at my throat" (*CP*, p. 79).

A poem like "Entries for a Catalogue of Fears" is sardonic in confessional self-deprecation. The fears the poet is eager to acknowledge are endless. One stanza alone begins with depths, heights, father, insects, iodine in the eyes, sudden knives, urchin laughter, and ends with "add now / men in line / behind my daughter" (*CP*, p. 86). The aptest metaphor the poet can find for his predilection is of vultures

and their unerring arts

of picking

on soft parts

like testicles and coconut brains.

(*CP*, p. 88)

Somewhat anticlimactically, through all such gristle, the poet's self-dramatization reassures him that for "THE HINDOO: the only risk" is "heartlessness" (*CP*, p. 90). His regret is that "poems / cannot flay like eyes or hurt / like a fall on a sidewalk" (*CP*, p. 94), although he works hard at bridging the distance through his scavenging for unsettling images and unnerving associations. The list of what he can come up with is characteristic: male priests with "whiskered nipples," fingers that grow lizard faces, an unborn granddaughter face floating like praying mantis. Yet the poet affirms that he does not shudder. The kind of reading such poems requires is not very different from what Ramanujan recommended, after Jerome McGann, for the apparently very different poetic worlds of the Tamil and Kannada classics: "We respond to a system of presences and absences; our reading then is not linear but what has been called 'radial'" (*CE*, p. 15).

"Prayers to Lord Murugan," the longest and most ambitious poem in *Relations,* illustrates the affinity between Ramanujan's poetic world and the classical Tamil past of his translations. The poet reports that the sequence of poems was triggered in 1967 by a dissertation submitted at Chicago on the iconography of the Tamil deity by Fred Clothey. The poem alludes to this field of scholarship and to a sixth century poem called *Tirumurukarruppatai:*

> My poem, too, talks about some Indian attitudes to the Indian past, with which I was somewhat despondently preoccupied at that time. I had felt that Sanskrit itself and all that it represented had become an absence, at best a crippling and not an enabling presence, that the future needed a new past.
>
> (*CE*, p. 192)

"A future in need of a new past," and despondency about ever realizing a future that could shed or replace his personal memories might well describe all of Ramanujan's poems in English. His sequences function as a series of "anti-prayers": "The past works through the present as the present reworks the past" (*CP*, p. 192). That might well serve as the most apt description of his entire project of translation, treated both literally and as metaphor.

How the past is meant to revive the present is evident, for example, in section 3, which asks in prayer if, in the fight against the fruit fly, the red flower will ever come to the branches of the "blueprint" city. Lord Murugan, as the deity of the greenness in nature, can cause flowers to bloom red, and he also allows the fruitfly to prosper. How can the blueprints of our utopias ever get realized, the poet fears, when the principle of growth is also the principle of decay in nature.

Section 4 asks for replacements: grey pottery replaced by copper and iron; nightmare virgins by white-haired witches. Section 5 says, "We eat legends and leavings." This refers to the manner in which contemporary India is content to make capital out of past legends, which are the detritus with which India fuels its contemporary aspirations. The Indian rural practice of using dried dung as fuel is linked sardonically to the modern aspiration to send human beings into space.

How the present changes the past is revealed when wishes disguised as prayers highlight and underline the woes of the modern world. Our collars are white, our blood brown. We have lost our face and our five senses. We are the nonliving unable to be born. We need relief from our own prayers. Thus, sardonically, Ramanujan draws the curtain over a second volume as unremittingly bleak as his first, leavened primarily by his stark honesty and his avidity for what we might hide "in the reeking / crotches of rotten timbers" (*CP*, p. 92), like the "pins and needles / at amputees' fingertips" (*CP*, p. 116)

SECOND SIGHT (1986)

Ramanujan's third collection follows the first two after a relatively longer gap in time. It is slightly different in tone. The first two volumes come across as tense, concentrated, elliptical. Each word, line, and group of lines has a sharp precision, as of stones set intricately by an expert working with a miniature. The Indian poet and translator R. Parthasarthy remarked in the 1970s on how the early poems have something hard and brilliant about them. In contrast, *Second Sight* is almost relaxed. Poems tend to develop in a more leisurely fashion. This can be misleading, since these poems are as complex in their evocations and allusions as the early ones, just as deeply thought and felt. The eye for disquieting detail remains as alert as ever. "In the Zoo" (*CP,* pp. 128–29) combines scavenger birds with Madras lawyers with grandmother's maggoty curds. The habit of drawing upon the less likely members of the mineral, vegetable, and animal kingdoms for analogies and figures in metamorphosis remains alive and well.

But the overall effect is more personal and more ruminative. What felt like intrusiveness in some of the early poems now feels like an intimacy in which the poet includes the reader in a casual intentness. Here the poet tries out experiments in prose poems, and these are more successful than his occasional forays into irregular "sonnets." Otherwise, the preference for a William Carlos Williams type of free verse remains constant, though the movement of syntax over line breaks is now managed less self-consciously. The train of allusions and associations is more willing to wander, no longer as determined as previously to ambush the reader with sudden turns of thought and phrasing.

This volume stands out for several habits of feeling that recur through the first two volumes and here acquire greater prominence. The poetic persona in Ramanujan had always sustained a tenuous sense of self. Individuation had amounted to isolation. Poems had been wont to convey experiences that were virtually out-of-body. The face in the mirror was often either blank or imprinted with familial memories and nostalgia for what was not even personal memory. Images from nature impinged on poetic consciousness in a manner that evacuated personality. The poet had cultivated a sensibility attuned to dissociated images, sights, sounds, and smells. These tendencies come to the fore in *Second Sight*. Here the mind becomes acutely self-conscious of its contingent physicality; the self becomes detached from the body; present experience merges with memory, and memory merges with nostalgia for other times, other places, and other bodies. Death is always just round the corner. The myths of karma and rebirth, and the parallel myth of destiny as predicted or predicated in the stars, become a

continuous motif, like a half-forgotten but subliminally ubiquitous refrain or drone. In "Drafts" the self is recognized as "a copy of lost events," a DNA sequence endlessly repeatable, without an original (*CP*, p. 157). A long anecdotal poem about a "Highway Stripper" becomes a pretext in which the stripping away of blouse, shoes, panties, bra, and "even the woman / he was wearing" (*CP*, p. 166) becomes the occasion for the poet to acknowledge himself a perpetual transvestite, "moulting, shedding" vestiges like vestments until finally he couples with nothing.

Lists, in Ramanujan, serve as an antidote to the fixity of the self. The fascination with lists is put to serious use in the very first poem of the volume, "Elements of Composition," (*CP*, pp. 121–123), which assimilates the decomposition of selves into the process of continual rebirth. "Questions" takes up the same theme from the point of view of "Eating, being eaten," of "being born over and over," of "sucking at the nipple." Birth is imaged as if it were a true memory:

> my head's soft crown bathed in mother's blood,
>> wearing tatters of attachments, bursting
>
> into the cruelties
> of earthly light, infected air?
>
>> (*CP*, p. 131)

Death, birth's alter ego, is made into a familiar presence in *Second Sight*. The body after death holds a Donne-like fascination for Ramanujan. Burial, cremation, dismemberment, dissection—various cultures' methods for disposing of bodies are examined and rejected in fear mixed with morbid fascination. Decay and dying are not readily turned away. But the poet still has the recourse of not being born yet:

> I am not yet
> May never be
>
>> (*CP*, p. 170)

The mode of storytelling so cherished by Ramanujan the folklorist makes several appearances in the volume. Each time, a story from the remembered or legendary past is turned to a contemporary application. To that extent not everything is cast in a purely negative light. The early volumes had been deft in their assimilation of historical reference into the poetic matrix. *Second Sight* expands the poet's scope by making room for, and taking note of, some of the more widely publicized horrors of the contemporary world: Hiroshima, Vietnam, My Lai, Biafra. Thus, at least in part, and in passing, Ramanujan is able to imply that his "intricate / diagrams of Dravidian kinship" (*CP*, p. 180) map a topography that expands its field of reference beyond the Tamil and the Indo-American diasporic to the all-encompassing realm of the contemporary.

THE BLACK HEN (1995)

The final section of Ramanujan's posthumously published *Collected Poems* (1995) represents a selection made by friends from a larger body of material, of which other portions are published in the *Uncollected Poems and Prose* (2001). The latter brings together thirty-one additional poems, two interviews, and two prose pieces. The editors argue the case for a poet struck by death in his prime, with much of his best work yet to come. But it is also possible to recognize a certain dilution in the last poems, despite, or perhaps because of, their relative profusion. The best of the poems, such as "Salamanders," return to the familiar and forlorn motif of how "We, denizens of this nowhere nothing" (*CP*, p. 202) might, like newborn salamanders, hope to sustain and renew a sense of being "forever unborn." "Traces" inscribes, or discovers, this desire embedded in fossils "waiting for people to decipher / and give themselves a past / and a family tree" (*CP*, p. 204). "Birthdays" wonders if "death / throes are birth pangs" (*CP*, p. 206), such that our dispersal in death might begin a new "reworking" of our "mother-matter." Rebirth becomes an enticing option when death

feels close. But karmic destiny is also part of a system that has been denied and resisted by the doubts of a modern rationalist. In "Mythologies 2" the poet prays to the midnight sun: "slay now my faith in doubt" (*CP*, p. 226).

Jahan Ramazani underlines the link between Ramanujan's propensity for metaphor and the tendency of postcolonial writing to present itself in terms of perpetual displacement and fragmentation: "Split vision is characteristic of postcolonial literatures, a seeing of cultures in terms of one another" (p. 74). Ramanujan as translator and poet provides double confirmation for this reading. One of his last poems ends with the rhetorical concession that despite work as a form of resistance to dreaming, the urge to dream keeps returning to "a blue Mysore house in Chicago" (*CP*, p. 249). "Waterfalls in a Bank" offers punning recognition of a related predicament:

> as I transact with the past as with another
>
>> country with its own customs, currency,
>
> stock exchange, always
>
> at a loss when I count my change . . .
>
>> (*CP*, p. 189)

This "Hindoo" is glad, beyond any superstitious claim for "second sight," if he can sometimes regain even his "first, and only / sight" (*CP*, p. 191). Modernity itself, like the postcolonial or the diasporic condition, becomes a form of hyphenation from which, as Tejaswini Niranjana observes in *Siting Translation* (1992), there is no escaping into some unfissured origin. Ramanujan's achievement is to have written from within such a fissure, not in order to close the gap but, in trying continually to bridge it, to have shown how wide it really was. The effect of his sharpest poems and translations is like a recognition that

> Sight may strike you
> Blind in unexpected places.
>
>> (*CP*, p. 186)

Selected Bibliography

WORKS OF A. K. RAMANUJAN

POETRY IN ENGLISH

The Striders. New Delhi and London: Oxford University Press, 1966.

Relations. New Delhi, London, and New York: Oxford University Press, 1971.

Selected Poems. New Delhi, London, and New York: Oxford University Press, 1976.

Second Sight. New Delhi, London, and New York: Oxford University Press, 1986.

TRANSLATIONS

Fifteen Poems from a Classical Tamil Anthology: A Translation. Calcutta: Writers Workshop, 1965.

Some Kannada Poems: A Selection. With M. G. Krishamurthi. Calcutta: Writers Workshop, 1967.

The Interior Landscape: Love Poems from a Classical Tamil Anthology. Bloomington and London: Indiana University Press, 1967, 1975.

The Song of the Earth and Other Poems. With M. G. Krishnamurthi, Michael Garman, and Rajeev Taranath. Calcutta: Writers Workshop, 1968.

Selected Poems of G. Sankara Kurup. Translated from the original Malayalam by A. K. Ramanujan and others. Calcutta: Dialogue Publishers (distributors: Stechert-Hafner, New York), 1969.

Speaking of Siva. Harmondsworth, U.K., and Baltimore: Penguin, 1973.

Hymns for the Drowning: Poems for Visnu by Nammalvar. Princeton, N.J.: Princeton University Press, 1981.

Poems of Love and War: From the Eight Anthologies and Ten Long Poems of Classical Tamil. New Delhi: Oxford University Press, 1985; New York: Columbia University Press, 1985.

Samskara: A Rite for a Dead Man. New York: Oxford University Press, 1989. (A translation of U. R. Anantha Murthy's Kannada novel.)

When God Is a Customer: Telugu Courtesan Songs. With Velcheru Narayana Rao and David Shulman. Berkeley and Los Angeles: University of California Press, 1994. Reprint, New Delhi: Oxford University Press, 1995.

COEDITED OR COAUTHORED WORKS

The Literature of India: An Introduction. Edward C. Dimock Jr., A. K. Ramanujan, and others. Chicago and London: University of Chicago Press, 1974.

Another Harmony: New Essays on the Folklore of India. Edited by Stuart H. Blackburn and A. K. Ramanujan. Berkeley: University of California Press, 1986.

Folktales from India: A Selection of Oral Tales from Twenty-two Languages. Selected and edited by A. K. Ramanujan. New York: Pantheon, 1992.

The Oxford Anthology of Modern Indian Poetry. Edited by A. K. Ramanujan and Vinay Dharwadkar. New Delhi: Oxford University Press, 1994.

A Flowering Tree and Other Oral Tales from India. By A. K. Ramanujan. Edited with a preface by Stuart Blackburn and Alan Dundes. Berkeley: University of California

Press, 1997. Also available at http://ark.cdlib.org/ark:/13030/ft067n99wt/.

SELECTIVE LIST OF CONTRIBUTIONS TO JOURNALS AND BOOKS

"Parables and Commonplaces." In *Writers in East-West Encounter: New Cultural Bearings*. Edited by Guy Amirthanayagam. London: Macmillan, 1982. Pp. 138–149.

"Foreword." In *Folktales of India*. Edited by Brenda E. F. Beck et al. Chicago: University of Chicago Press, 1987.

"Annayya's Anthropology." (Short story.) Translated from the Kannada by Narayan Hegde. *IndiaStar Review of Books*. Also available at http://www.indiastar.com/hegde1.html.

BOOKS IN KANNADA

Proverbs. 1955.

Haladi Meenu. 1966. (Translation of an English novel.)

Gadegalu. 1967.

Modern Kannada Fiction: A Critical Anthology. Edited by M. G. Krishnamurthi. Grammatical notes by A. K. Ramanujan. Madison: Department of Indian Studies, University of Wisconsin, 1967.

Hokkulalli Huvilla. 1969. (Poems.)

Innastu Hosa Kathegalu. Dharwad: Manohara Granthamala, 1972.

Mattu Itara Padyagalu. Dharwad: Manohara Granthamala, 1977. (Poems.)

Mattobbana Atmakate. Dharwad: Manohara Granthamala, 1978. (Novella.)

Kuntobille. 1990. (Poems.)

COLLECTED WORKS

The Collected Poems of A. K. Ramanujan. New Delhi: Oxford University Press, 1995.

The Collected Essays of A K. Ramanujan. Edited by Vinay Dharwadkar and others. New Delhi: Oxford University Press, 1999.

Uncollected Poems and Prose by A. K. Ramanujan. Edited by Molly Daniels-Ramanujan and Keith Harrison. New Delhi and New York: Oxford University Press, 2001.

The Oxford India Ramanujan. New York, Oxford, New Delhi: Oxford University Press, 2003.

AUDIO

Indian poet A. K. Ramanujan reading from his poems (sound recording). 1985. Library of Congress, Washington, D.C., control number: 89741361.

BIBLIOGRAPHY

Sharrad, Paul, Shyamala Narayan, Marvin Gilman, Kerry Lyon, and Richard Lever. "Bibliography of Criticism of Indian Literature in English (1970–1990)." (Arranged by writers' names, then alphabetically by critics' names.) Available at http://www.uow.edu.au/arts/icd/publications/india_%20a-nan.pdf.

CRITICAL AND BIOGRAPHICAL STUDIES

Barche, G. D. "A. K. Ramanujan's 'Two Days': A Stylistic Study." In *Indian Poetry in*

English. Edited by Birendra Pandey. New Delhi: Atlantic, 2001.

Bhabha, Homi. "Indo-Anglian Attitudes." *Times Literary Supplement,* 3 February 1978, p. 136; 21 April 1978, p. 445.

Bhashyam, Kanaka, and Chellappan, K. "Encounter and Synthesis in the Poetry of A. K. Ramanujan." *Journal of Indian Writing in English* 12.2: 96–104 (1984).

Bhatnagar, M. K., ed. *The Poetry of A. K. Ramanujan.* New Delhi: Atlantic, 2002.

Char, M. Sreerama. *Prayer Motif in Indian Poetry in English.* Calcutta: Writers Workshop, 1988.

Chindhade, Shirish. *Five Indian English Poets: Nissim Ezekiel, A. K. Ramanujan, Arun Kolatkar, Dilip Chitre, R. Parthasarathy.* New Delhi: Atlantic, 2001.

Clothey, Fred W. *The Many Faces of Murukan: The History and Meaning of a South Indian God.* The Hague and New York: Mouton, 1978. (Includes Ramanujan's poem "Prayers to Lord Murukan.")

Das, Bijay Kumar. "Ramanujan's 'A River': An Explication." *Journal of Indian Writing in English* 13.2:24–26 (1985).

Devy, G. N. "Alienation as Means of Self-Exploration: A Study of A. K. Ramanujan's Poetry." *Chandrabhaga* 6:5–19 (1981).

Dharwadker, Vinay. "A. K. Ramanujan's Theory and Practice of Translation." In *Post-Colonial Translation: Theory and Practice.* Edited by Susan Basnett and Harish Trivedi. London: Routledge, 1999. Pp. 114–140.

Dwivedi, A. N. *A. K. Ramanujan and His Poetry.* Delhi: Doaba House, 1983.

———. *The Poetic Art of A. K. Ramanujan.* Delhi: B. R. Publishing Corporation, 1995.

Ezekiel, Nissim. "Two Poets: A. K. Ramanujan and Keki N. Daruwalla." *Illustrated Weekly of India* (18 June 1972). Pp. 43–45.

Gowda, H. H. Anniah. "Indian Plays and Poems in English: Karnad's *Tughlaq* and Ramanujan's *Relations.*" *Literary Half-Yearly* 14.1:3–10 (1973).

Guptara, Prabhu. "The Individual and the Community in the Poetry of A. K. Ramanujan." In *Individual and Community in Commonwealth Literature.* Edited by Daniel Massa. Malta: Old University Press, 1979. Pp. 177–187.

Jha, Rama. "A Conversation with A. K. Ramanujan." *Humanities Review* 3.1 (1981).

King, Bruce. "The Poet's India I: Ezekiel, Ramanujan, Patel, Daruwalla, Shiv Kumar." In his *Modern Indian Poetry in English.* New Delhi: Oxford University Press, 1987. Pp. 110–128; 2d ed., 2001.

———. *Three Indian Poets: Nissim Ezekiel, A. K. Ramanujan, Dom Moraes.* New Delhi: Oxford University Press, 1991.

Koelnserger. Ernst W. "Minimal Lines, Animated Surfaces." *The Hindu* (1 December 2002). (Article on, and interview with, S. G. Vasudev.) Also available at http://www.hinduonnet.com/mag/2002/12/01/stories/2002120100160200.htm.

Kulshrestha, Chirantan. "The Self in A. K. Ramanujan's Poetry." In *Contemporary Indian English Verse: An Evaluation.* Edited by Chirantan Kulshrestha. New Delhi: Arnold/Heinemann, 1980. Pp. 175–186.

Lall, Emmanuel Narendra. *Poetry of Encounter: Three Indo-Anglian Poets: Dom Moraes, A. K. Ramanujan, and Nissim Ezekiel.* New Delhi: Sterling, 1983.

Marudanayagam, P. "Relations as Shackles: A. K. Ramanujan's Tamil Moorings." In *Modern Indian Poetry in English: Critical Studies.* Edited by Nila Shah and Pramod

Nayar. New Delhi: Creative Books, New Delhi, 2000.

Mehrotra, A. K. "A. K. Ramanujan." In *An Illustrated History of Indian Literature in English*. Edited by Arvind Krishna Mehrotra. New Delhi: Permanent Black; New York: Columbia University Press; London: Colin Hurst, 2002. Pp. 295–307.

Mirza, Taqi Ali. "A. K. Ramanujan's 'Particular Hell.'" In *Indian Poetry in English: A Critical Assessment*. Edited by Vasant A. Shahane and M. Sivaramkrishna. Madras: Macmillan, 1980. Pp. 152–162. Reprint, Atlantic Highlands, N.J.: Humanities, 1981.

Mishra, R. S. "A. K. Ramanujan: A Point of View." *Chandrabhaga* 1:60–66 (1979).

S. Nagarajan. "A. K. Ramanujan." In *Contemporary Indian Poetry in English*. Edited by Saleen Peeradina. Bombay: Macmillan, 1972. Pp. 18–21.

Naik, M. K. "A. K. Ramanujan and the Search for Roots." *The Humanities Review* 3.1:14–19 (1981). Reprinted in *Contemporary Indo-English Poetry*. Edited by Bijay Kumar Das. Bareilly: Prakash Book Depot, 1986. Pp. 8–18. Also reprinted in *Living Indian English Poets: An Anthology of Critical Essays*. Edited by Madhusudan Prasad. New Delhi: Sterling, 1989. Pp. 13–23.

———. "Landscapes and Inscapes." *Kavya Bharati* 1:65–71 (1988).

Nair, Rama. *"Of Variegated Hues:" The Poetry and Translations of A. K. Ramanujan*. New Delhi: Prestige, 2002.

Nerlekar, Anjali. "Of Mothers, among Other Things: The Sources of A. K. Ramanujan's Poetry." *Wasafiri* 38 (spring 2003). (Special issue: "Poetry." Laura Chrisman and Steve Yao, guest editors.)

Niranjana, Tejaswini. *Siting Translation: History, Post-Structuralism, and the Colonial Context*. Berkeley: University of California Press, 1992.

Parthasarathy, R. "How It Strikes a Contemporary: The Poetry of A. K. Ramanujan." *Literary Criterion* 12.2–3 (1976). Reprinted in *Osmania Journal of English Studies* 13.1:187–199 (1977), "Special Number on Contemporary Indian Poetry in English," edited by V. A. Shahane and M. Sivaramakrishna.

Patel, Geeta. "King, Three Indian Poets: Nissim Ezekiel, A. K. Ramanujan, Dom Moraes." *Journal of Asian Studies* 51.4 (1992). (Review.)

Patke, Rajeev S. "Ithacan Voyages: The Poetry of R. Parthasarthy and A. K. Ramanujan." In *New Perspectives in Indian Literature in English: Essays in Honour of M. K. Naik*. Edited by C. R. Yaravintelimath, G. S. Balarama Gupta, C. V. Venugopal, and Amritjit Singh. New Delhi: Sterling, 1995. Pp. 112–120.

Patke, Rajeev S. "The Ambivalence of Poetic Self-Exile: The Case of A. K. Ramanujan." *Jouvert: A Journal of Postcolonial Studies* 5:2 (winter 2001). Also available at http://social.chass.ncsu.edu/jouvert/v5i2/rspatk.htm.

Raghunandan, Lakshmi. *Contemporary Indian Poetry: With Special Emphasis on Nissim Ezekiel, Kamala Das, R. Parthasarathy and A. K. Ramanujan*. New Delhi: Creative Books, 1990.

Ramazani, Jahan. "Metaphor and Postcoloniality: A. K. Ramanujan's Poetry." *Contemporary Literature* (spring 1998). Reprinted in his *The Hybrid Muse: Postcolonial Poetry in English*. Chicago and London: University of Chicago Press, 2001. Pp. 72–102.

"Remembering A. K. Ramanujan: On the Art of Translation." *Indian Literature* 168 (July–August 1994). (Special Issue.)

Reuben, Elizabeth. "The Presence of the Past: The Sense of Time in the Poetry of A. K. Ramanujan." *Journal of Indian Writing in English* 17.1:13–20 (1989).

Singh, Satyanarain. "Ramanujan and Ezekiel." In *Contemporary Indian English Verse: An Evaluation.* Edited by Chirantan Kulshrestha. New Delhi: Arnold/Heinemann, 1980. Pp. 165–174.

Shulman, David. "Attipat Krishnaswami Ramanujan (1929–1993)." *Journal of Asian Studies* 53.3:1048 (1994).

Sreermacher, M. "The River's Argot in Three Indo-English Poets: A. K. Ramanujan, K. N. Daruwalla, and Nissim Ezekiel." *Poetry* 10:11–13 (1986).

Srivastava, R. K. "Reflection of Growing Dehumanization in Ramanujan's Poetry." In *Contemporary Indian-English Poetry.* Edited by Atma Ram. Calcutta: Writers Workshop, 1989. Pp. 51–63.

Swain, Rabindra K. "A Home Away from Home." (Review of *Uncollected Poems and Prose.*) *Contemporary Poetry Review.* Available at http://www.cprw.com/Swain/Ramanujan.htm.

Venkatachalapathy, A. R. "Obituary: A. K. Ramanujan." *Economic and Political Weekly* 28.31:1571 (1993).

Jean Rhys
(1890–1979)

CLARE CONNORS

JEAN RHYS'S ELLIPTICAL and yet engaging novels and stories seem purposefully to resist definition. Are they feminist attacks on the power of the patriarchy, or hopeless tales of female dependency and inadequacy? Are they comic or tragic? Should they be read as "West Indian" or "European" fiction? Do they suggest the futility of existence, or demonstrate a triumphant mocking of the worst fate can produce? Are they modernist or postmodern? In her tales of women who work in not-quite respectable professions, are always in need of money, and are frequently ostracized by the society that has made them what they are, Rhys at once teases us to make pronouncements upon her fiction, and suggests that to do so would be to fall into the very categorizing methods it is her business to question. Elusive as it is, the work of this Dominican-born novelist has mesmerized literary critics since it returned to critical attention in 1966 with the publication of *Wide Sargasso Sea*. Describing displaced and socially disadvantaged women, many of them non-British, Rhys's texts have proven fertile ground for analysis by feminist and postcolonial critics, yet their enduring literary value is not simply a product of the critical schools which have seized upon them. Mimicking her spectral heroines, Rhys's precisely crafted texts have a power to haunt beyond their specific ideological commitments, or the details of authorial autobiography on which they draw. Like the snatches of jazz songs they often quote, Rhys's novels and short stories linger, at once ripe for analysis and yet productively recalcitrant to definitive interpretation.

BIOGRAPHY

Rhys's fiction draws heavily on incidents from her life, yet it is important to know about those incidents not so much in order to recognize them as they recur in the work, as to understand the creative uses to which they are put. Ella Gwendoline Rees Williams was born on 24 August 1890, to a Creole mother of Scottish and Irish descent and a Welsh father. These hybrid and non-English origins partially explain the unhappy time she first had when she came to cold, gray England in 1907, initially to study at the Perse school in Cambridge. In 1909 she trained briefly at the Academy of Dramatic Art, before leaving to become a chorus girl (like Anna in *Voyage in the Dark*) under a variety of aliases including "Vivien," "Emma," and "Ella Gray." Her first affair, with Launcelot Hugh Smith, an older man, began in 1910 and lasted for two years until Smith broke off the affair. He "pensioned her off," paying her regular sums of money, until in 1919, partly to escape from this dependence, Rhys contracted her first marriage, to Jean Lenglet, a Dutch-French poet and journalist. Initially living in Holland, they soon moved to Paris, where in 1920 her son William died at the age of three weeks. The death of a child haunts many of her literary heroines. Her daughter Maryvonne was born in 1922, and the following year Rhys met Ford Madox Ford, who encouraged her writing. Lenglet was imprisoned for currency irregularities, and Rhys went to live with Ford and his partner Stella Bowen, in a ménage-à-trois transmuted into fiction in her first novel, *Quartet* (1928). Under Ford's patronage *The Left Bank and Other Stories* was published in 1927. Leslie Tilden Smith became her literary agent in the same year, and would soon, following her estrangement from Lenglet and a move to London, become her lover. When her divorce came through in 1933 she was free to marry him, which she did in 1934. Maryvonne chose to live with her father. Even the early days of their relationship were far from idyllic. Smith was thriftless, and the couple were frequently impecunious and had to appeal to relatives for money. During this time Rhys's three first novels were published: *Quartet* in 1928 (under the title *Postures* in its British imprint), followed by *After Leaving Mr. Mackenzie* in 1930 and *Voyage in the Dark* in 1934. They were quietly received, and Rhys earned almost nothing from the royalties.

The Dominica which Rhys lovingly memorializes in her prose was an abiding personal love, although she was able to revisit it only once in 1936, when she spent an extended holiday there with her husband, paid for out of the substantial inheritance which he had received after his father's death, and which he ran through in less than two years. While the visit did not completely live up to her nostalgic expectations—she found the heat difficult, and the slow life somewhat boring—it provided valuable resources for her subsequent depiction of the island in *Wide Sargasso Sea*. Rhys's penultimate

novel, *Good Morning, Midnight,* was published in 1939, coinciding with the outbreak of war. Leslie Tilden Smith died suddenly on 2 October 1945. The shocked Jean was helped to sort out his affairs by Smith's cousin Max Hamer, whom she married in 1947. There ensued difficult times for Jean. She remained in obscurity throughout the 1940s and 1950s, her work unremembered and out of print and her health in decline. In addition Max was arrested, and subsequently imprisoned, for stealing check forms from his firm, intensifying the emotional and financial problems Jean was facing. The year 1949 brought a partial resurrection of her fortunes—she was "rediscovered" by the actor Selma Vaz Dias, who wanted to perform an adaptation of her *Good Morning, Midnight.* On the other hand this was also the year in which Rhys was herself imprisoned (albeit only five days) for a breach of the peace, involving an incident with a neighbor who had been harassing her. Vaz Dias's initial performance of the dramatic monologue, in 1949 to an audience in the Anglo-French Arts Centre, did not much increase the neglected author's audience. A similar script was used for a broadcast on the BBC's Third Programme in 1957. This performance was excellently received by the listening public, and Diana Athill of Andre Deutsch publishers was introduced to Rhys's work by Francis Wyndham, who himself had been a longtime admirer of her novels. Athill and Wyndham were to be important forces in bringing Rhys back to public attention, and it was their initial warmth and encouragement that nudged her back into the writing she had for some time been unable to countenance. She signed a contract for the novel that was to become *Wide Sargasso Sea* in 1957, although it was not to appear until 1966, the same year in which her husband, Hamer, died. Rapturously received by the critics, this novel precipitated a revival of her other work, much of which was reissued in the ensuing years. Two more collections of short stories, *Tigers Are Better-Looking* and *Sleep It Off Lady*, were published in 1968 and 1976 respectively, and Rhys died in 1979, leaving a fragment of an autobiography, *Smile Please,* which was published posthumously.

LEFT BANK AND *QUARTET*

Rhys's first publication, *The Left Bank,* a book of twenty-two short stories published with an introduction by Ford Madox Ford in 1927, marked hers out as a mature literary talent from the start. Her vignettes of moments in the lives of inhabitants of Paris's *Rive Gauche* are not primarily interested in characters or, despite the book's title, purely in physical environment. While never becoming falsely abstract, they instead convey states of mind, emotions, and physical conditions through a series of briefly observed episodes. The Left Bank in these stories is as much a psychic as a physical landscape, and this blending of place with feeling will be a recurrent feature of Rhys's later urban topographies. The collection's first story, "Illusion," sets the stage for the way in which a brief event will provide illumination into a character's psyche. The narrator describes how, calling one day on her plain, proper, and very British friend Miss Bruce, she learns that the latter has been admitted to a hospital. Opening the doughty Miss Bruce's wardrobe to find a nightgown for her, she is surprised by "a glow of colour, a riot of soft silks" (pp. 32–33). It becomes clear from this fleeting glimpse into her domestic interior that Miss Bruce suffers from "that thirst to be loved which is the real curse of Eve" (p. 34). A similarly illuminating cameo is seen in the page-and-a-half-long "In the Luxemborg Gardens," "where a "depressed young man" who has been meditating on "the faithlessness of women" (p. 71) quickly moves off in pursuit of a young nurse, with an alacrity that proves his own hypocrisy and fickleness. Physical conditions too are exposed to scrutiny—"Hunger," for example, describes both the physical and mental stages passed through by someone undergoing a five-day period without food. Showing that the order of the stories in this first book has been as meticulously planned

as their internal elements have been crafted, this is followed by "Discourse of a Lady Standing Dinner to a Down-and-Out Friend," a complacent monologue by a wealthy woman interspersed with her parenthetical personal reflections. The three consecutive "West Indian" stories in the book—Rhys's first treatment of a locale that continued to haunt her literary imagination to the end—are also interrelated. The first one, "Trio," which describes three West Indian people at dinner, concludes, "it was because these were my compatriots that in that Montparnasse restaurant I remembered the Antilles" (p. 85), thus paving the way for the recollections of the "savage and lost" (p. 88) Dominica in "Mixing Cocktails" and "Again the Antilles."

The ending of "Trio" is also significant stylistically, in its strange shift from a purely descriptive prose style to the self-referential allusion to the novelist's own memories. Similar fractures in the "realist" illusion can be seen in "Mixing Cocktails," where the reminiscences of the Dominican house in the hills are interrupted with an address that can only be meant for the reader: "I am speaking to you; do you not hear?" (p. 89). Other features of what will become Rhys's distinctive style are also to be discerned in this early collection. Her penchant for ellipsis—the trailing off of the narrative due to despair, inconsequence, whimsy or some other reason—is already apparent here, as for example in the reflection "Horrible World . . ." (p. 129) in "Learning to Be a Mother." Here the ellipses seem to mark a fading out of consciousness: "So I must have slept" is the next sentence. At the end of "The Grey Day" ("The poet paid for his drinks . . .") they suggest the continuance of a futile existence: it is as though nothing more need be said. Economy is a further feature of Rhys's style that is remarkable from the outset. The opening of "Vienne" displays well her deployment of the brief sentence, and equally short paragraph: "Funny how it's slipped away, Vienna. Nothing left but a few snapshots" (p. 193). There are signs, however, that Rhys is still learning her craft. "Mannequin," for example, the tale of a young woman beginning her first job in an expensive clothes shop, describes an episode which will later form the basis of one of Sasha Jansen's recollections in *Good Morning, Midnight.* In the former the narrator describes with heavy-handed irony how Mme Veron, the proprietress of the shop, "smiled imperiously and engaged her [Anna] at an exceedingly small salary" (p. 60). In the later novel, on the other hand, we are left to notice the smallness of Sasha's salary ourselves, through the fact that the sum she receives when she is dismissed from work is exactly the same as the price of one of the dresses she covets. These symptoms of immature writing aside, however, it is clear that Ford's encomium to her stories at the end of his introduction ("Miss Rhys' work seems to me to be so very good, so vivid, so extraordinarily distinguished by the rendering of passion, and so true, that I wish to be connected with it" pp. 26–27) is amply merited.

Given the warmth and generosity of Ford's patronage, Rhys's first novel could be said to have bitten the hand that fed. In *Quartet* Ford provides the model for the odious and uncomprehending Heidler, and Rhys's affair with him, while living in his house with him and his partner Stella Bowen, is remarkably similar in outline to her heroine Marya's ménage-à-trois with the Heidlers. Autobiographical details also feed into the reasons for Marya's neediness. Just as Rhys had been left stranded by her husband Jean Lenglet's imprisonment for currency irregularities in 1924, so Marya is left alone, engulfed by "a vague and shadowy fear" (p. 28), upon her husband Stephan's sudden arrest and conviction for theft. One should be wary, however, of reading the story as a simple roman-à-clef. Rhys, for example, was in 1924 already an aspiring writer, to be published later the same year, and through her relationship with Ford she met many influential modernists including Joyce, Stein, and Hemingway. Marya, on the other hand, while she reads "quantities of books. All sorts of books" (p. 10), is not in any

sense an author. Indeed, the only time we see her writing, it is a desperate letter to Heidler once he has jilted her: "Words. To make somebody understand" (121). Rhys's own words have been more successful in making generations of readers understand—and the understanding she seeks is not primarily comprehension of her own personal predicament. Her concerns are with the relationship between the personal and the social and cultural. She anatomizes the multiple conditions of alienation of her marginalized heroines, exploring the structures of power that both produce and punish them. *Quartet* is just the first full-length example of this critical and analytical process.

Marya Zelli is an alien for a variety of reasons; her class, her nationality, her gender, and her sexuality all conspire to ensure that she does not "belong." An impoverished English woman abroad in Paris and married to a Pole, she does not after four years "know any of the English people in Paris" (p. 8), yet seems not to know any Parisians either. And when she does meet her compatriots, the desolate Miss De Solla and the Heidlers, there is no sense of homecoming, but rather a mutual incomprehension. She is spoken of in her presence "in the third person as if she were a strange animal or at any rate a strayed animal—one not quite of the fold" (p. 12).

The title under which the novel originally appeared in Britain, *Postures,* captures the way in which Rhys seeks to interrogate the artificiality of the tacit rules that decide who is inside and who is outside the fold. The behavior that sustains such rules must be carefully choreographed, or composed, like a musical quartet. The "quartet" of the later title also refers, of course, to the complicated patterns of relationship the novel charts. For most of its duration it focuses on a trio, detailing Marya's entry into the Heidlers' home and the complicated series of dynamics between the three. Initially, Marya shies away from the invitation to seek sanctuary with them on the grounds that she's "got used to the idea of facing cruelty" and that it will make her "soft and timid" so that she will "have to start getting hard all over again afterwards" (p. 42). These scruples themselves turn out to be cruelly ironic. Far from finding comfort and kindness under her benefactors' roof, she is quickly ensnared by a series of unwritten codes to do with gender, sexuality, and the cultural institution of marriage. Propositioned by the "majestic and paternal" (p. 47) Heidler, her first impulse is to resist. Despite having a "longing for joy" (p. 59), she asks Lois Heidler to lend her some money to enable her to leave the home and escape temptation. Lois's interests do not lie in this direction, however. She knows that if Marya leaves, Heidler will follow, leaving her a deserted wife—beyond the pale of the social norms to which she herself, with her fondness for select and carefully chosen gatherings, subscribes. Instead, she effectively prostitutes the already socially marginal Marya to her marriage, mocking her scruples ("The matter with Mado is that she's too virtuous," p. 61) and refusing to allow her to escape, on the grounds that Heidler will "get tired of her as soon as she gives in" (p. 64). Eschewing the depiction of romantic or feminist ideals of female solidarity, Rhys suggests that in fact socially successful women secure their position through complicity with the social systems that oppress their less fortunate sisters. Surrendering to circumstances and becoming part of this exploitative threesome, Marya falls prey to society's double standards. She is condemned as a prostitute ("the *grue*," p. 66) by those who divine the true nature of her relationship, and criticized by the Heidlers for being too emotionally honest to "play the game" (p. 89) and socialize with them, in order to uphold the fiction of a happy household. She is already culturally and socially beyond the pale, with her foreign surname and criminal husband; her poverty and the coercive force of Lois's desire to retain her own social centrality thus propel Marya also into a sexual wasteland.

Despite this novel's fascination with trios and foursomes, then, two-sidedness and duplicity form the main focus of its criticism and satire. Heidler incarnates the sexual double standard by which male promiscuity is tolerated while women who have more than one partner are condemned. Upon Stephan's release from prison, the trio becomes a quartet. They meet and dine—the only time they are ever together as a foursome—and then Marya returns to her husband's hotel room with him. This action triggers Heidler's revulsion from Marya ("I have a horror of you. When I think of you I feel sick." P. 115), and his separation from her. Hypocritically, he asserts, "I've never shared a woman in my life, not knowingly anyhow, and I'm not going to start now" (p. 115). When Marya points out his duplicity, and the fact that she has had to share him with his wife for many months, he replies, "I don't know what you mean" (p. 115). It is as though the sexual double standard is so culturally engrained as to be invisible and unintelligible. Marya's own name points to the long history of bifurcated images of women as either pure and virginal or corrupt prostitutes, invoking both the Virgin Mary and Mary Magdalene. In that she is presented as both sexually experienced and yet more innocent of social deceit than her respectable corruptors, her character undoes the oppositional logic which seeks to categorize women as either "virgin" or "whore." Indeed, when she sees a statue of the Virgin Mary in church, she rereads it in her own terms, thinking that "she suggested not holiness but rather a large and peaceful tolerance of sin" (p. 74).

While Marya strives to resist society's violent, hierarchical encodings and stereotypical straitjackets, however, she is frequently ensnared by them. Towards the end of her relationship with Heidler, he has installed her in a hotel as his mistress, his "*petite femme*" as he calls it. Of this title she thinks: "It was, of course, part of his mania for classification. But he did it with such conviction that she, miserable weakling that she was, found herself trying to live up to his idea of her" (p. 92). Ideals of femininity are internalized perforce, the novel suggests, since only by living up to social ideals are women rewarded, either emotionally or materially. Early on in the novel, in Miss De Solla's rooms, Marya scrutinizes drawings of "groups of women. Masses of flesh arranged to form intricate and absorbing patterns" (p. 8). *Quartet* is preoccupied with how women are socially "arranged," usually solely in terms of their "flesh." It also shows how these arrangements happen through society's images of women in the first place. Mado (as Marya is nicknamed) is "made over" by the world's pigeon-holing categories of femininity. Discussed as though she were a doll by the Heidlers (p. 67), unable to fit comfortably into society's definitions of her as either a wife, a mistress, or a prostitute, she feels "like a marionette, as though something outside her were jerking strings that forced her to scream and strike" (p. 82). This image of the disempowered heroine, like a puppet on a string, will recur throughout Rhys's fiction, conveying the coercive and manipulative effects of duplicitous expectations upon behavior and indeed identity.

Marya seems ultimately to be completely vanquished by the forces that control and constrain her. Alone in her hotel bedroom with Stephan, she confesses to him that she has had an affair with Heidler, whom she loves. He attacks her, and as she falls she knocks her head, "crumple[s] up and [lies] still" (p. 143). Her last words are "I didn't mean . . ." (p. 143). Unable ever to signify in her own terms, she can only express her failure to express herself, to "mean." More positively, we might argue that she remains a resistant textual enigma to the last. The narrative voice seems to silence her, adopting Stephan's point of view as he heads off to the Gare de Lyon with another woman ("*Encore une grue*" he thinks, p. 144: another tart), but we are left pondering the image of the fallen Marya. Is she dead or alive? Rhys's heroine leaves us unable to classify her right to the end.

AFTER LEAVING MR. MACKENZIE

The very title of Rhys's second novel suggests the extent to which women might be defined according to male standards: its heroine seems to be positioned unpromisingly in terms of the aftermath of a relationship, and thus identified solely through "Mr. Mackenzie." At the novel's opening, the jilted Julia Martin is living in "a cheap hotel on the Quai des Grands Augustins" (p. 7) in Paris, surviving on a weekly allowance received from Mr. Mackenzie's lawyers. Her life is monotonous, anxious, melancholic, and alcoholic: her landlady disapproves of her habit of coming home "accompanied by a bottle. A man, yes; a bottle, no. That was the landlady's point of view" (p. 9). Throughout the novel we will receive a variety of "points of view" of Julia Martin. Our introduction to the multiplicity of perspectives on her comes in the scene that precipitates all the subsequent action of the novel. Instead of the weekly check for three hundred francs she has become accustomed to receiving, Julia is sent a final sum of fifteen hundred francs, along with a letter instructing her that her weekly allowance will henceforth cease. She follows Mr. Mackenzie into a restaurant, and returns the check to him, slapping him in the face with her glove, in a gesture melodramatic and yet ineffectual, before leaving. The scene is narrated from Mr. Mackenzie's point of view. Before Julia arrives, we are privy to his complacent self-reflections, and his slightly less smug recollections of the affair. We learn that he has "adopted a certain mental attitude, a certain code of morals and manners" (p. 18) from which he rarely departs. This code, moreover, is "perfectly adapted to the social system" (p. 18). His concern, it is made clear, is with social appearances. Thus Julia's arrival initially frightens him, discomposing his self-possession. She is "pale as a ghost" (p. 22), and this allusion to her spectrality (the first of several in the novel) points both to the fragile insubstantiality of her embattled identity and to the fact that "she haunted him, as an ungenerous action does haunt one" (p. 21). Again, the marginality of Rhys's heroine's identity seems at once to remove her agency and yet, paradoxically, to give her a certain, albeit attenuated, power. She haunts and unsettles, even while she cannot definitively act.

The scene in the restaurant is not only viewed from Mr. Mackenzie's perspective, however. After Julia leaves, he looks around the room and initially thinks that "nobody had noticed anything" (p. 27). However, he subsequently realizes that in fact a "dark young man" (p. 27) has seen the whole incident. The narrative then adopts this dark horse's point of view: George Horsfield, it transpires, has witnessed Julia's "scene" in a bad looking-glass in which "the actors had been slightly distorted, as in an unstill pool of water" (p. 28). Significantly, he has seen only the back of Mr. Mackenzie's head ("round and pugnacious—somehow in decided contrast with his deliberately picturesque appearance from the front." P. 28): perspective, Rhys suggests, is everything. Horsfield is to some extent outside ("hors" in French) the ordinary fields of vision, and perhaps better able to identify with the marginalized Julia or at least to "see" her better.

In terms of plot, Horsfield's intervention is crucial. He replaces the fifteen hundred francs Julia has impetuously returned to Mr. Mackenzie, and he also makes the suggestion that Julia return to London. Her visit to her native country forms the main middle section of the novel; we follow Julia as she encounters her sister and her dying mother, indifferently begins an affair with Horsfield, and tries to acquire money from her uncle and her former lover, before returning, at the book's close, to Paris. If *Quartet* showed a woman who was outside the fold, *After Leaving Mr. Mackenzie* charts a failed return to the place where its heroine ought to be at home. Repeatedly, we see her framed, judged, and usually condemned by those from whom she seeks understanding. Her uncle Griffiths sums her up as a bad lot; her sister Norah,

herself an impoverished woman, though "respectable" in a way Julia is not, is hostile and jealous towards her; and her former lover Neil James sees her as one of those tactless "resurrections of the past" (p. 79). Significantly, it is only her dying and incapable mother who seems to recognize Julia in an authentic and meaningful way. Although Norah has warned her that "she doesn't know anybody" (p. 52), there is a moment when the sick woman looks "steadily at her daughter" and whispers the words "orange blossom" (pp. 71–72). We learn that Julia's mother, who had once been "the warm centre of the world" (p. 77) for her daughter, had spent her childhood in South America, and said of England that it was not "a country to be really happy in" (p. 76). Rhys's first novelistic depiction of postcolonial exile, then, is fleeting, but nonetheless important. Julia's exchange of glances with the mother who was once so central to her life suggests that true recognition might only come between fellow outcasts. However, within the context of the novel this moment does not seem able to provide any grounding or meaning to Julia's liminal life. Her mother dies, and she is cast out of the family home for arguing with her sister after the funeral.

Julia's failures to achieve recognition form part of a more general meditation in the novel about the notion of identity. What makes us who we are? Are our characters produced by internal qualities, or are we produced by our environment and other extrinsic factors? To Horsfield she recounts how she tried to tell her life-story to a painter for whom she was sitting (another person, then, who makes images of her) and how the painter, Ruth, refused to believe her account. The failure of recognition Julia experiences through this lack of comprehension on the part of the ruthless Ruth is annihilating, "like looking over the edge of the world" (p. 41). In the light of this shock to Julia's sense of self, even material documents of identity— photographs, letters, marriage certificates, passports, the papers about her dead baby— seem inadequate. She tells Horsfield:

It had all gone, as if it had never been. And I was there, like a ghost. And then I was frightened, and yet I knew that if I could get to the end of what I was feeling it would be the truth about myself and about the world and about everything that one puzzles and pains about all the time.

(p. 41)

What is questioned, then, is whether one has an identity apart from the social forms that encode and ratify it. Julia is represented, in the face of the failure of such documentation to shore up her sense of self, as a revenant. Her identity is insubstantial and precarious, and yet she lives on, outlasting all official descriptions of her.

These debates about identity could be seen to participate in age-old philosophical discussions about free will and determinism, or the twentieth-century existentialist interrogation of the relationship between existence and essence. There are certain problems with simply reading the novel as presenting a philosophical dialectic, however. Julia says of her encounter with Ruth, "It was as if I were before a judge, and I were explaining that everything I had done had always been the only possible thing to do. And of course I forgot that it's always so with everybody, isn't it?" (p. 40). Mr. Horsfield's reply—"Well, I think there's a good deal of tosh talked about free will myself" (p. 40)—endorses Julia's musings by translating them into a more philosophical (and therefore traditionally masculine) discourse. His position is a far cry from Uncle Griffith's complacent individualistic motto, "everybody has to sit on their own bottoms" (p. 61), and yet its overtly philosophical character seems in some way to miss the specificity of Julia's position. Rhys implies, perhaps, that the abstract terms of philosophy do not take sufficient account of gender. Later in the novel the debate about free will and determinism again founders over the issue of sexual difference. When Julia asks her former lover Neil James, "Do you think I could have done differently?" (p. 82), he replies that while before the war he had no time for people "who didn't get

on," now he is far more sympathetic to those whom he calls his "mad friends" (p. 83). But he proceeds, "mind you, women are a different thing altogether. Because it's all nonsense; the life of a man and the life of a woman can't be compared. They're up against entirely different things the whole time" (p. 83). Even if one acknowledges that one's identity is determined by forces outside one's control, one still cannot generalize a philosophical model that would account for both male and female positions, since the determining forces (the "things" they are up against) are always "different." Thus what seems to be a debate in the novel between free will and determinism, or between "essential" and "existential" views of the self, is inflected also by debates about the differences between men and women.

The emphasis both on the difference of perspective and on the fact that one might be determined by other people's views, is not only discussed thematically in the novel but also conveyed through its style. For its frequent use of ellipses, its shifting point of view and free indirect discourse, Rhys's mature literary technique (fully visible in this novel for the first time) has often been linked to the stylistic innovations of the modernists. In some ways, perhaps, it would be better to call it postmodern. For example, whereas Virginia Woolf, one of Rhys's modernist literary forebears, seems to some extent to validate the mobile and shifting qualities of her characters' interior, subjective lives against the harsh impositions of the "objective" world, Rhys is less certain about the possibility of demarcating any sort of secure inner-world for her creations. The opening paragraph of *After Leaving Mr. Mackenzie*, describing Julia's arrival in her Parisian hotel, displays many of the uncertainties that will ensue.

After she had parted from Mr Mackenzie, Julia Martin went to live in a cheap hotel on the Quai des Grands Augustins. It looked a lowdown sort of place and the staircase smelt of the landlady's cats, but the rooms were cleaner than you would have expected. There were three cats—white

Angoras—and they seemed usually to be sleeping in the hotel bureau.

(p. 7)

Initially we seem to be presented with an omniscient narrative voice, discussing the affairs of the heroine in a dispassionate and objective manner. Soon, however, the language takes on the coloring of Julia's own vocabulary and point of view in the disjunction between how the place looks and smells and how it actually is. In what is apparently a classically modernist technique, the pretensions to objectivity are undercut by an emphasis on the importance of the subjective position. However, things become more complicated in the use of the second-person pronoun "you." Addressing and implicating the reader, this colloquial usage ("one" might be the more standard form, and would certainly be the pronoun Woolf would deploy) suggests in fact that the point of view of the "I" is always necessarily routed through what "you" might expect. There is no private realm of the self here, untainted by the world of the "you," and yet on the other hand the dispassionate objective language of the world is necessarily hijacked by the individual and subjective perspective and tone of the heroine. Once again, then, this time at the level of style, the novel seems poised between two alternatives—between essence and existence, free will and determinism, the claims of the self and the impositions of the world.

This undecidability, both of style and of theme, remains to the novel's end. Having shown a last—and typical—encounter between Julia and Mr. Mackenzie, in which her request for the loan of a hundred francs shocks his "romantic" (p. 137) posturings, the narrative concludes: "The street was cool and full of grey shadows. Lights were beginning to come out in the cafés. It was the hour between dog and wolf, as they say" (p. 138).

Just as *Quartet* ends with Marya's failure to signify and a narrative enigma as to her fate, so *After Leaving Mr. Mackenzie* terminates in an "in-between" state appropriate to the borderline

status of its heroine, and to the novel's either/or ambivalence about key philosophical oppositions. The last three words "as they say" are equally ambivalent. On the one hand, the tyranny of the "they" seems to have won out, as the localized points of view the novel has adopted give way to a clichéd French expression for the dusk ("entre chien et loup": between dog and wolf, as Rhys translates). On the other hand, the acknowledgment that these are "their" words seems to ironize and frame them, asserting once again a more colorful and subjective point of view. "As they say" at once endorses the "they" and the "I": the novel is shifty and ambiguous to the last.

VOYAGE IN THE DARK

Rhys's third novel is narrated in the first person, but from its opening onwards it is clear that we are not going to be able to rest easily in a realm of subjective certainties: "It was as if a curtain had fallen, hiding everything I had ever known. It was almost like being born again" (p. 7).

Anna Morgan's rebirth will not be a matter for celebration. Transplanted from the warm and happy world of her West Indian island (about which we only learn through her memories) to chilly England, Rhys's first fully realized postcolonial heroine will receive a cold baptism, inducted into duplicitous social mores and exploitative sexual relationships. Hers is not a voyage of discovery in this alien country, but a journey into the heart of various darknesses.

More obliquely than Rhys's later novel, *Wide Sargasso Sea, Voyage in the Dark* is also a rewriting of another text. At the start of the novel, Anna is reading Emile Zola's *Nana*, the story of a Parisian prostitute set just before the Franco-Prussian War of 1870. Zola's eponymous character is beautiful but selfish, vulgar, greedy, and vain. Rhys suggests straight away the partiality of this perspective, through the words of Anna's friend Maudie: "I bet you a man writing a book about a tart tells a lot of lies one way and another" (p. 9). Anna, whose very name seems to suggest a purer version of Zola's Nana (which is a colloquial French word meaning "chick"), will to some extent be able to put the record straight, revealing the ways in which society produces the prostitution it then hypocritically condemns.

Her story begins with her life as an impoverished chorus girl, on tour in the bleak English provinces. The least worldly-wise of her colleagues—ironically many of them mock her for her virginity—she is alienated and miserable and suffers from "the cold nights, the damned cold nights" (p. 15). When she is wooed by the attentive Walter, romance and warmth initially seem to enter her life. He takes her out to dinner, graciously escorts her home when she refuses to sleep with him, and sends her money and flowers. Having caught a cold, Anna prevails upon him to help her, but this bid for comfort seems to entail an unwritten bargain in which her body will be exchanged for his protection. They sleep together, and he slips money into her purse. Thus begins Anna's slow decline. As Walter's lover she is relatively protected, but once he jilts her, cruelly and by proxy through his friend Vincent, she is completely lost. Depressed and abject, she strays into a series of relationships, which become more and more overtly financial in motivation.

It is the stark anatomizing of the material basis of sexual relationships that makes this aptly named novel so dark. While Anna might seem profligate or at least naïve for her comment that "money ought to be everybody's. . . . You can tell that because you get accustomed to it so quickly" (p. 24), her view is placed in stark counterpoint with that of Maud's acquaintance, who asserts that "a girl's clothes cost more than the girl inside them" (p. 40). Rhys is depicting a world in which the female body is viewed as a commodity, and courtship rituals and romance have become a matter of economic exchange. Women necessarily become complicit with this process. Maudie's advice to Anna ("The thing with men is to get everything you can out of

them and not care a damn." pp. 38–39) initially shocks her, but the novel suggests that there is little room for a more romantic position to hold sway. Women without a steady income face an intolerable impasse. Unable to achieve the status of respectable married women unless they have the money already to look respectable, they can only acquire such money through selling themselves. "Isn't it rotten when a thing like that falls through just because you haven't got a little cash?" (p. 136) bemoans Maudie of this double-bind. In this world where money and presents stand in for male responsibility and affection, the boundaries between romantic relationships and prostitution become blurred. Defending her friend Laurie, Anna asks: "why shouldn't she be a tart? It's just as good as anything else, as far as I can see" (p. 109).

Whereas in her earlier novels, the worst consequences of Rhys's heroines' banishment from the "fold" of polite society seems to be poverty and condemnation, here—in keeping with the greater emphasis on a materialist analysis—Anna suffers profound physical consequences too. She becomes pregnant and has to have a back-street abortion, paid for by the absent Walter. The birth motif with which the novel begins is thus given a blackly ironic twist at its close: new life is terminated, and the pronouncement of the emergency doctor, called to stop Anna hemorrhaging, that she'll soon be "ready to start all over again" (p. 159) is nightmarishly repeated as the novel concludes: "starting all over again, all over again . . ." (p. 159). Trailing off into ellipses, the idea of a new start is represented simply as a repetition of the same bleak story, with no possibility for return, recovery, or renewal.

If *Voyage in the Dark* sounds like Rhys's most vicious attack on the values and economics of patriarchal sexual ideology, it nevertheless also represents a damning critique of the women who connive in this system. Anna's decline is hastened by her treatment at the hands of a series of women who exploit her before abandoning her. Indeed, it is only when she is turned out of her lodgings by her landlady for coming home late ("I don't want no tarts in my house," p. 26) that she turns to Walter for help and is first seduced by him. Ironically, the landlady's desire to avoid the appearance of immorality produces precisely the situation she holds in such horror. Hypocritical distinctions between the appearance and the fact of immorality also lie behind the treatment she later receives from Ethel. Reeling from her rejection by Walter, Anna is befriended by Ethel, who persuades her to rent a room in her flat and invest in her beautician's business. Insisting that she is "the best masseuse in London" and that her business is "straight and above board" (p. 115), Ethel is nevertheless marked out from the first by her profession as trading in human flesh. Her moral double standards are made explicit when she implies that she will turn a blind eye to Anna's sexual liaisons, provided she receives more rent. "All done by kindness" (p. 134), Anna bitterly remarks, of Ethel's silent complicity. It is only when Anna manifests in her depressed behavior the sense of degradation she feels that Ethel asks her to leave, remarking that "there are ways and ways of doing everything" (p. 142). Anna's mistake, like Marya Zelli's in *Quartet,* is to retain an essential honesty about the sexual economy in which she participates.

Anna's anomie arises not simply because of her gender and class, but also because of her cultural difference from those around her. Memories of the unnamed West Indian island of which she was a fifth-generation inhabitant punctuate the drab narrative of London life like traumatic fragments that cannot be either assimilated or abolished. Anna suggests the incommensurability of her past home and her present location when she says "if England is beautiful, it's not beautiful. It's some other world. It all depends, doesn't it?" (p. 45) The name of her former home, Constance Estate, suggests its function for her as a constant touchstone in the face of her current baffling existence. Yet while we feel all the pathos of Anna's exile, Rhys does not romanticize the West Indies, or Anna's

relationship to it. One of her key memories is of seeing "an old slave-list" (p. 45) and of worrying that the "sins of the fathers" (p. 46) are visited on their children. The symbolism here is complicated. To the extent that Anna's Creole family were historically complicit with, and derived their wealth from, the violent history of slavery, it is difficult to continue to read her simply as an innocent victim. On the other hand, this recollection draws attention to the stark fact of Anna's own sexual enslavement, preventing us from simply relegating to the past, or to a distant country, the horrific notion of a trade in bodies.

GOOD MORNING, MIDNIGHT

If *Voyage in the Dark* was savage and unremitting in its exploration of sexual slavery and social exclusion, Rhys's penultimate novel seems at once funnier and yet more sinister. The fey tone of its title, taken from the Emily Dickinson poem that also forms the book's epigraph, captures well the witty but disturbingly uncanny style of *Good Morning, Midnight.* Comedy—the chirpy and incongruous salutation of midnight—tugs against the tragedy of the fact that the blackness of the night is being sought and embraced. Its plot is the slightest of all Rhys's novels. Sasha (or Sophia) Jansen has been lent some money to have a short break in Paris. While there she dyes her hair and buys a hat. There are several human encounters, all of them difficult to gauge in terms of their value for our heroine. She is disturbed by the presence of a salacious white-dressing-gowned man in the next-door hotel room, but is befriended by some Russians, from one of whom she buys a painting, and a gigolo, who initially mistakes her for a wealthy woman and then tries to seduce her. At the close of this almost plotless narrative, we see Sasha willing the return of the gigolo, René, who has left without taking the money she has contemptuously offered him. As her hotel room door opens, however, she sees not the figure of René but the white dressing-gown of her despised neighbor, who has come to take advantage of her distress. The story concludes with her pulling him towards her, ambiguously affirming the value of human contact with a strange echo of the climactic ending of Molly Bloom's monologue in Joyce's *Ulysses*: "Yes-yes-yes. . . ." (p. 159).

In some ways *Good Morning, Midnight* is a crystallization of the essential traits of Rhys's earlier novels. Sexual exploitation, poverty, definition through the male gaze, and the function of make-up and clothing are all anatomized. One might be forgiven for thinking that there is little new in this fourth narrative of a down-and-out heroine inhabiting a series of seedy Parisian rooms. To read the book in this light, however, and to posit, as some critics have done, a generic "Rhys woman," is to ignore the subtle ways in which Rhys's penultimate novel is about repetition, sameness, and identity, and also about the interweaving of past and present narratives about the self. Returning to her hotel room, Sasha says: "This damned room—it's saturated with the past. . . . It's all the rooms I've ever slept in, all the streets I've ever walked in. Now the whole thing moves in an ordered, undulating procession past my eyes. Rooms, streets, streets, rooms. . . ." (p. 91). The past presses on the present, domestic and urban spaces mimicking and recalling one another in a ghostly fashion. In an odd way *Good Morning, Midnight* itself seems haunted by the ghosts of the rooms and streets of Rhys's other novels, both alluding to and ironizing them. Whereas Julia Martin's penchant for powdering her face in *After Leaving Mr. Mackenzie* is simply presented as a defensive tic, for example, here Sasha's first-person narrative voice ironizes her own fetish for disappearing into bathrooms to compose herself and reapply her makeup: "Lavabos . . . What about that monograph on lavabos—toilets—ladies? . . ." (p. 10) Rhys's own preoccupation with the small urban spaces her liminal heroines make their own seems also to be satirized here. More significantly, the repetitions and echoes of this familiar yet strange narrative

question the extent to which rectilinear stories of progression and development can ever be existentially true. "I don't believe things change much really; you only think they do. It seems to me that things repeat themselves over and over again" (p. 56) says Sasha. While this statement most obviously casts in doubt the possibility for amelioration or improvement in her life (the most significant change she experiences in the novel is of her hair color), it also serves to question whether there was ever any definable point that precipitated the decline in the first place. Rhys eschews the "traumatic" model in which depression, despair, and failure can be tracked back to, and blamed upon, a single cataclysmic event. When René says to Sasha, "Something bad must have happened to make you like this," she replies "One thing? It wasn't one thing. It took years. It was a slow process" (p. 146). Just as there is no one thing which has brought Sasha to her present condition, so no definitive act will change it.

Elements of the "slow process" which brought Sasha to her present condition of stasis and despairing repetition are conveyed to us through flashbacks. More than any of Rhys's other novels, *Good Morning, Midnight* shuttles between past and present, as Sasha wanders the streets with the "gramophone record" repeating in her head "here this happened, here that happened . . ." (p. 15). In particular she recalls a range of jobs she has had—as a mannequin, a tour-guide, a teacher of English, and a transcriber of fairy-tales. Her memory of the first forms a nightmarish, but also comic, reprise of the incidents of Rhys's earlier short story "Mannequin." There the heroine, Anna, on her first day of work in a clothes shop, becomes lost in a labyrinth of corridors and is momentarily unable to find her way to the dining room for lunch. Symbolic of the fact that she is cast adrift in an alien world, this anecdote nevertheless has a happy ending. Anna arrives at the right room, and gradually becomes accepted by her new colleagues. The story finishes with her happiness at being part of Paris. Even such compromised moments of felicity are refused to Sasha in the later reworking of the episode. Sent by her boss, whom she has already signally failed to impress, to take a letter to the "kise" (his ignorant mispronunciation of "caisse," the counting house) she wanders panic-stricken about the building. The anecdote is comically rendered ("I try another passage. It ends in a lavatory. The number of lavatories in this place, c'est inoui," p. 23) but also manages to convey the horror and panic that arise in such situations of embarrassment and impotence: "I walk up stairs, past doors, along passages—all different, all exactly alike. There is something very urgent that I must do. But I don't meet a soul and the doors are shut" (p. 23). Clearly, we can read the episode as emblematic of Sasha's existential condition, shut out and alone and impelled onwards without any clear sense of what she is doing. The garbled goal (kise/caisse) of her mission is significant too—suggesting that she is unable to reach the financial hub of things.

In a larger sense still, all the narratives of past professions interwoven into *Good Morning, Midnight* raise questions to do with identity, and the extent to which people can ever happily fill the roles society decrees for them. "Please, please, monsieur et madame, mister, missis and miss, I am trying so hard to be like you" (p. 88), entreats Sasha in what appears to be an address to the "hypocrite lecteur" of the novel. Interestingly she relates her existential predicament to language: "Every word I say has chains round its ankles" (p. 88). Society's use of language is thoughtless, clichéd, and naïve. Like the fairy tales Sasha is paid to take down, it dupes its speakers into false and sometimes sentimental beliefs. "Everything is born out of a cliché, rests on a cliché, survives by a cliché. And they believe in the clichés—there's no hope" (p. 36). The most awful instance both of the power of cliché, and of social straitjacketing, comes in the memory of Sasha's dead child. Two of Rhys's other heroines—Marya and Julia—share this kind of memory with her, and of course with their author Rhys, but it is in this novel that the

death of the child is treated most fully. Sasha recalls lying in the maternity ward, unable to sleep and worrying about money, "money, money for my son, my beautiful son. . . ." (p. 50). The matron's solution to her patent anxiety is to bind her body in bandages, so that she can return to her pre-maternity figure. She is swaddled like a mummy in her painful constraints, and her literal bondage is both a product of her social bondage—since underlying the practice is the assumption that she will be more materially successful or valuable if she is physically unscarred—and a metaphor for it. "And five weeks afterwards there I am, with not one line, not one wrinkle, not one crease. And there he is, lying with a ticket tied round his wrist because he died in a hospital" (p. 52). The dead son himself is symbolic of the violent molding and categorizing tendencies of social institutions, labelled and docketed even in death.

In the world Rhys describes here, motored by the tabulating power of language and gendered and class-based assumptions, it becomes difficult to tell what is human and what is not. Looking at the "damned dolls" in the clothes shop, Sasha thinks "what a success they would have made of their lives if they had been women" (p. 16). The most successful women are those who are the most doll-like and inhuman, as befits her later drunken and surreal image of the world as "an enormous machine, made of white steel" with "innumerable flexible arms, made of steel" (p. 156). Conversely, and in an uncanny reversal, the inanimate comes to seem animate. Rooms are humanized ("'Quite like old times,' the room says," p. 9), sympathizing with the women who inhabit them, even as they are rejected by the outside world.

If Sasha's alienation is not, most immediately, attributed to her race (though her nationality is never made clear to us, any more than it is to the patron of the hotel who demands her papers: "Nationality—that's what has puzzled him," p. 13), a significant anecdote related by one of her Russian friends foregrounds this as a key cause of social alienation. Employing another uncanny image which confuses the human and the inanimate, he describes a poor "mulatto" woman who lived near him in Notting Hill, and who was "like something that has turned into stone" (p. 80). Ostracized and mocked by those around her and living with an "Angliche" husband who tells her that she "imagines" the hostility she meets, this Martiniquaise who is "no longer quite human, no longer quite alive" (p. 80) seems to point onwards, across the twenty-five year gap before Rhys's last novel was published, to the tragic figure of Antoinette in *Wide Sargasso Sea*.

WIDE SARGASSO SEA

The Creole in Charlotte Brontë's [*Jane Eyre*] is a lay figure—repulsive which does not matter, and not once alive which does. She's necessary to the plot, but always she shrieks, howls, laughs horribly, attacks all and sundry—*off stage*. For me (and for you I hope) she must be right *on stage*. She must be at least plausible with a past, the *reason* why Mr Rochester treats her so abominably and feels justified, the *reason* why he thinks she is mad and why of course she goes mad, even the *reason* why she tries to set everything on fire and eventually succeeds. (Personally, I think *that* one is simple. She is cold—and fire is the only warmth she knows in England.)

(*Letters 1931–1966*, pp. 156–157)

Rhys's *Wide Sargasso Sea* is possibly the most artistically successful prequel ever written, and these comments, from a letter she wrote to Selma Vaz Dias in 1958 some eight years before its publication, suggest why. In writing her own account of the events which precede the narrative of *Jane Eyre*, Rhys is concerned both to place on stage what Brontë viewed as beyond representation and to make it come alive. Here she suggests that while "madness" might be a real enough phenomenon, it is socially produced, and therefore, as she repeatedly insists, has "*reasons*," even if it is not rational. That which is silenced and incarcerated in Brontë's novel is here given a voice, and a narrative. Bertha

Mason, renamed "Antoinette" by Rhys, recounts from her own point of view the story of her marriage to Rochester (who is never explicitly named) and her move to England.

In keeping with Rhys's insight into the complexity of questions of identity, inflected as they are by issues of race, gender, and class, she does not simply present one "reason" for Antoinette's descent into madness. As with *Good Morning, Midnight*, the "traumatic" narrative is inadequate to account for her experiences. In some ways, indeed, they represent an uncanny repetition of her mother's life. The similarly named Annette, left alone and abandoned by her neighbors, sees a way out through her marriage to the recently arrived Englishman, Mr. Mason. It is Mason's failure to understand his environment, and the black Jamaicans who work for him, that causes the latter to set fire to the family home, bringing about the death of Annette's ailing son Pierre. These events, which—we are left to infer—drive Annette mad and lead to her premature death, parallel in outline Antoinette's story. She too marries an Englishman, Rochester, and it is his failure to understand her, or the environment of their honeymoon island (modeled on Dominica), which causes him to punish and constrain her, renaming her with the ugly forename "Bertha," and making his Antoinette a "Marionette" (p. 99). From Antoinette's point of view, his renaming of her (like his use of the power of the English law to appropriate her inheritance, which passes to him upon their wedding) is no better or less powerful than the magical practices of "obeah" known to her nurse Christophine. Her use of a love potion to attempt to restore his love for her is from this stance vindicated. For Rochester, on the other hand, it is the last instance of the dangerous, intoxicating, but hostile properties of the oppressive honeymoon residence where "everything is too much. . . . Too much blue, too much purple, too much green. The flowers too red, the mountains too high, the hills too near" (p. 42). Tellingly it is the quiddity of the West

Indian environment which Rochester rails against here. Wanting to appropriate everything to his own schemes of reference, he cannot cope with things being as they are—with the flowers being red, and the mountains high. The main source of his revulsion from Antoinette also derives from his desire to categorize the world according to his own neat schemes of reference. He is already suspicious of Antoinette's cultural and racial identity ("Long, sad, dark alien eyes. Creole of pure English descent she may be, but they are not English or European either." p. 40), and his growing abhorrence of his wife is fanned by a letter from Daniel Cosway, who describes himself as a "half-way house" (p. 59) relation of Antoinette's, and suggests that the latter is both congenitally mad and having an affair with her mixed-race cousin Sandi. Fears of miscegenation and of madness intermingle in his appalled reaction to his wife. Rejecting Christophine's proposal that he return half Antoinette's dowry and leave (a suggestion that he suspiciously, again reading the world according to his own lights, accords to a financial motive—"She Christophine, would take good care of Antoinette (and the money of course)" (p. 102), he takes her back to England with him, "a mad girl" with a "doll's voice" (p. 110). Here, in the third part of the novel, the overt events of the narrative join up with the plot of *Jane Eyre*. Imprisoned in a room, and guarded by Grace Poole, Antoinette is haunted by memories of the past and unable to recall her own more recent acts of "mad" violence. Significantly, the other inhabitants of the house think of her as a ghost. Displaced from her home, deprived of her personal and racial identity as well as her property, Antoinette is a revenant in the home of which she ought to be the mistress. The "reasons" for her madness are multiple, but they have been sensitively staged for us by Rhys's narrative.

Whilst Rhys's fascination with *Jane Eyre* is most obviously motivated by its exclusion of one particular West Indian figure, her engagement with the novel has larger social and cultural

ramifications. For a long time, Charlotte Brontë's first published book was viewed as a proto-feminist manifesto, describing the travails of the underdog Jane as she battles against the patriarchal establishment, finally winning through with an inheritance and a happy marriage to a humbled and symbolically castrated Rochester. Rhys's earlier novels have already suggested her suspicions of this sort of teleological success story, and of women who end up triumphantly winning the social game. As recent "postcolonial" readings of *Jane Eyre* (many of them undertaken in the wake of Rhys's novel) have shown, Jane's happiness is only in fact achieved through the exploitation of colonized peoples—the inheritance which brings her independence, for example, arises from colonial trade, with its historical involvement in slavery. The mid-Victorian success story is thus dependent upon the occluded narratives of other races, and of other people. It is important, therefore, that in putting on stage what Brontë had kept in the wings, Rhys does not simply replace one person's narrative with another's, inverting *Jane Eyre*'s power hierarchies and making the marginal central. "There is always the other side, always" (p. 82) says Antoinette, and Rhys bears this in mind in *Wide Sargasso Sea*. Antoinette is accorded a large proportion of the narrative, but in the key middle section of this three-part novel, Rochester takes over the narration. Other voices speak up too. The distinctive Creole patois of Antoinette's nurse Christophine is cited in the opening paragraph, for example: "They say when trouble comes close ranks, and so the white people did. But we were not in their ranks. The Jamaican ladies had never approved of my mother, 'because she pretty like pretty self' Christophine said." (p. 5)

Opening with the "they say" which ended *After Leaving Mr. Mackenzie*, this striking beginning represents a confused web of identities. The apparently impersonal wisdom of "they say" is shown to be racially specific ("we were not in their ranks"), performing in miniature the move Jean Rhys carries out in the novel as a whole, where *Jane Eyre*'s claims to tell universal truths about freedom and the power of individual endeavor are shown to be predicated upon colonialist and racist assumptions. Christophine's distinctive accents present a counter-voice, but this too is alien, intervening into the standard English of the narrative from outside. Antoinette and her mother, Annette, are multiply displaced. Coming from the French colony of Martinique, Annette is an alien in Jamaica, fitting in neither with the indigenous black population, nor with the Jamaican "white people," whether Creoles or recent settlers. Simple black/white oppositions no longer provide adequate models of identity and difference. Whereas Brontë establishes a stark binary between the mad and passionate Bertha and the quiet and constrained Jane, the similar juxtaposition of Antoinette with the black Tia is less simple. That they are presented as a pairing is clear on several occasions—Tia steals Antoinette's dress, for example, leaving behind her own. And as they are leaving their burning home, Coulibri, and Tia throws a stone at Antoinette and then begins to cry, Antoinette describes a process of apparently oppositional mirroring: "We stared at each other, blood on my face, tears on hers. It was as if I saw myself. Like in a looking-glass" (p. 24). Here we see a mutual interaction, both violent and painful: a far cry from the hygienic symbolic practices of *Jane Eyre,* where Bertha is presented as an alter ego, but never looked at on her own terms. *Wide Sargasso Sea* is thus remarkable both for the success with which it gives eloquent speech to a muted voice, and for the way in which it rethinks the whole business of telling one's own story, and bears in mind that there is "always the other side."

TIGERS ARE BETTER-LOOKING AND *SLEEP IT OFF LADY*

Rhys did not write another novel after this late-coming success, but she did produce two further volumes of short stories, *Tigers Are Better-Looking* (1968), which also contained selected stories from *The Left Bank,* and *Sleep It Off Lady* (1976), her last published work. The title story of the first volume aptly invokes the civilized savagery which is the theme of so much of Rhys's work, and which continues to be exposed in these collections. The violence implicit in social relations and mediated by cultural forms is powerfully treated in *Tigers* in the "The Day They Burned the Books," in which the white Mr. Sawyer beats and abuses his wife as a "damned, long-eyed, gloomy half-caste" (p. 41). After his death, Mrs. Sawyer gets her revenge by destroying his precious books, in a conflagration which shocks the child narrator. We might read this act as a destruction of the cultural forms that mediate colonial aggression, but Rhys seems to suggest that while Mrs. Sawyer's hatred is understandable, it, too, is nevertheless violent and destructive.

In *Sleep It Off Lady,* the anomie and alienation that had become Rhys's themes are given a new treatment in her consideration of age and aging. The title story describes the treatment Miss Verney receives at the hands of a society that treats her either indifferently or cruelly. Her fear of aging is symbolized through her desire to get rid of the garden shed which "would survive" long after her death, and her terror of the sinister rat that inhabits it. Her concerns are ignored by her neighbors, and when she collapses in her back garden, she is deliberately left there by a local child, who parrots at her the words of her mother, before adding her own cruel admonition: "'She ought to take more water with it,' my mum says. Sleep it off lady" (p. 171). Miss Verney dies, and the doctor's verdict, "very widespread now—a heart condition" (p. 172), provides an ironic commentary on a more serious lack of heart in society. Themes of aging and death are also picked up in "Rapunzel Rapunzel," in which the narrator describes an elderly woman who retains her beautiful hair as though to "reassure her that she was still herself" (pp. 140–141). When her hair is cut off, in a thoughtless act by a hospital hairdresser that seems symbolic of many other violences against women in Rhys's work, the woman collapses and her death is seen to be imminent.

Perhaps the most literally and metaphorically haunting story in this final volume, however, is its last one, "I Used to Live Here Once." Returning to an old home in the West Indies, the female character from whose point of view the story is recounted approaches and greets two children, saying to them "I used to live here once" (p. 177). They fail to hear or acknowledge her, but suddenly feel cold and enter the house. "That was the first time she knew" (p. 177), the story chillingly concludes. Having spent her literary career describing women who have only a spectral existence in their social milieux, and having herself been reported dead before she "returned" with her masterpiece *Wide Sargasso Sea,* Rhys at the last ventriloquizes an "actual" ghost. This haunting voice, speaking beyond the grave to announce its alienation and sense of displacement from home, seems a fitting one with which to have concluded her oeuvre. Like Rhys's own texts, it lives on and returns to haunt, powerful and compelling despite its dispossession.

Selected Bibliography

WORKS OF JEAN RHYS

NOVELS

Quartet. London: Chatto and Windus, 1928. (First published as *Postures.* The Penguin edition, reprinted with a new introduction by Katie Owen in 2000, has been used in this essay.)

After Leaving Mr. Mackenzie. London: Jonathan Cape, 1930. (The Penguin edition, reprinted with a new introduction by Lorna Sage in 2000, has been used in this essay.)

Voyage in the Dark. London: Constable, 1934. (The Penguin edition, reprinted with a new introduction by Carole Angier in 2000, has been used in this essay.)

Good Morning, Midnight. London: Constable, 1939. (The Penguin edition, reprinted with a new introduction by A. L. Kennedy in 2000, has been used in this essay.)

Wide Sargasso Sea. London: Andre Deutsch, 1966. (The Penguin edition, reprinted with new editorial matter by Angela Smith, has been used in this essay.)

SHORT STORIES

The Left Bank and Other Stories. London: Jonathon Cape, 1927.

Tigers Are Better-Looking. London: Andre Deutsch, 1968. (This also reprints a selection of stories from *The Left Bank.*)

"Temps Perdi" and "I Spy a Stranger" in *Penguin Modern Stories.* London: Penguin, 1969.

Sleep It Off Lady. London: Andre Deutsch, 1976.

The Collected Short Stories. New York: Norton, 1987.

Tales of the Wide Caribbean. Ed. Kenneth Ramchand. London and Kingston, Jamaica: Heinemann, 1985.

OTHER WORKS

My Day. New York: Frank Hallman, 1975. (Three autobiographical pieces.)

Smile Please. London: Andre Deutsch, 1979. (A partial autobiography, published posthumously.)

Letters, 1931–1966. Edited by Francis Wyndham and Diana Melly. London: Andre Deutsche, 1984.

SECONDARY WORKS AND BIOGRAPHICAL STUDIES

Alvarez, A. "The Best Living Novelist." *New York Times Review of Books,* 17 March 1974, 6–7. (An important document in establishing Rhys's literary reputation.)

Angier, Carole. *Jean Rhys.* London: Andre Deutsch, 1990. (Has a tendency to use the fiction as evidence for the biography.)

Bowlby, Rachel. "The Impasse." In her *Still Crazy After All These Years.* London: Routledge, 1993. (An important discussion of Rhys's relationship to modernism.)

Carr, Helen. *Jean Rhys.* Plymouth: Northcote House, 1996.

Emery, Mary-Lou. *Jean Rhys at "World's End": Novels of Colonial and Sexual Exile.* Austin: University of Texas Press, 1990.

Frickey, Pierrette, ed. *Critical Perspectives on Jean Rhys.* Washington, D.C.: Three Continents Press, 1990.

Harrison, Nancy. *Jean Rhys and the Novel as Women's Text.* Chapel Hill and London: University of North Carolina Press, 1988.

Howells, Coral Ann. *Jean Rhys.* London: Harvester Wheatsheaf, 1991. (A useful introduction that explores feminist, Caribbean and modernist approaches to Rhys.)

Kloepfler, Deborah Kelly. *The Unspeakable Mother: Forbidden Discourse in Jean Rhys and H.D.* Ithaca, N.Y., and London: Cornell University Press, 1989.

Le Gallez, Paula. *The Rhys Woman.* Basingstoke: Macmillan, 1990.

Look Lai, Wally. "The Road to Thornfield Hall: An Analysis of *Wide Sargasso Sea.*" In *New Beacon Reviews: Collection One.* Edited by John La Rose. London: New Beacon Books, 1968. (This was the first article to consider the *Wide Sargasso Sea* as a Carribean text.)

Malcolm, Cheryl. *Jean Rhys: A Study of the Short Fiction.* London: Prentice Hall, 1996.

Raiskin, Judith. "Jean Rhys: Creole Writing and Strategies of Reading." *Ariel,* 22: 4 (1991) 51–67.

Elaine Savory. *Jean Rhys.* Cambridge: Cambridge University Press, 1998.

Spivak, Gayatri. "Three Women's Texts and a Critique of Colonialism." In *The Feminist Reader: Essays in Gender and the Politics of Literary Criticism.* Edited by Catherine Belsey and Jane Moore. London: Macmillan, 1989. (This important essay reads *Wide Sargasso Sea* alongside *Jane Eyre.*)

Staley, Thomas. *Jean Rhys: A Critical Study.* London: Macmillan, 1979.

Tiffin, Helen. "Mirror and Mask: Colonial Motifs in the Novels of Jean Rhys." *World Literature Written in English,* 17, April 1978, 328–341. (This article was the first to bring together feminist and colonial readings of Rhys's work.)

Thomas, Sue. *The Worlding of Jean Rhys.* London: Greenwood Press, 1999.

Arundhati Roy

(1961–)

JEFFREY F. L. PARTRIDGE

ARUNDHATI ROY IS one of the most remarkable and controversial figures of contemporary Indian life. She shot to international fame when her 1997 novel *The God of Small Things* (for which she received advances of $2.2 million) received Britain's most prestigious literary award, the Booker Prize—a first for a female Indian writer. Since 1997 she has devoted herself to activist causes in India and to writing about such political issues as the 1998 entry of India and Pakistan into the nuclear arms club and the ill effects of globalization and U.S. foreign policy. Roy explains the central concern of her writing in her 2003 book *War Talk:* "the theme of much of what I write, fiction as well as nonfiction, is the relation between power and powerlessness and the endless, circular conflict they're engaged in" (p. 46).

Roy is controversial for both literary and extraliterary reasons. *The God of Small Things* created a sensation worldwide. According to Julie Mullaney, the novel "was completed in May 1996, launched in April 1997 in Delhi, and won the Booker Prize in London in October 1997. Published in over forty different languages, it has sold over six million copies worldwide" (p. 13). Since its publication, at least six scholarly books and numerous scholarly journal articles have been written about the

novel. However, not a few Indian readers found it distasteful and disrespectful. Communist Party members in India objected to the novel's depiction of one of their leaders, Syrian Christians of Kerala objected to the depiction of their community, and some Indian readers objected to Roy's depiction of India. Some literary critics disliked its plot structure and others disliked the way Roy experimented with language. A lawyer in Kerala even registered a lawsuit against Roy on grounds of public immorality.

Extraliterary controversies emanate from Roy's political writing and activism. Roy has made headlines for her active involvement in demonstrations against the Indian Supreme Court's decision to allow the construction of the Sardar Sarovar dam in central India. Her actions landed her a jail sentence and a fine for contempt of court. Moreover, Roy's three books of political essays, gathered from her articles in prominent Indian magazines and often reprinted by international publications such as *Der Spiegel, Christian Science Monitor, Le Monde, The Guardian,* and *El País* openly criticize the Indian government, the Indian Supreme Court, global corporations, and the U.S. government. In India she is seen by some as a passionate upholder of truth and by others as a self-indulgent megalomaniac.

In *Power Politics* (2001), Roy explains her shift from novelist to political writer as a moral compulsion: "In the midst of putative peace, you could, like me, be unfortunate enough to stumble on a silent war. The trouble is that once you see it, you can't unsee it. And once you've seen it, keeping quiet, saying nothing, becomes as political an act as speaking out. There's no innocence. Either way, you're accountable" (p. 7). Like George Orwell, who said in his famous essay "Why I Write" that he was driven to write politically because of the great upheavals of his age (most notably the rise of fascism), Arundhati Roy sees the political issues of her age as too serious for a serious writer to ignore. Unlike Orwell, however, Roy has yet to find an appropriate authorial identity between the impartiality that literary aesthetics seems to demand and the partisanship of the political activist.

Suzanna Arundhati Roy was born on 24 November 1961 in the southeastern state of Kerala, India, home to a fairly large Syrian Christian community and the world's first democratically elected communist government. Her hometown of Ayemenem, with its virulent mix of religious and political ideologies (Christian, Hindu, Muslim, socialist), provides the backdrop for the novel that would make her famous. There are also many parallels between *The God of Small Things* and her family. Although not twins like her characters Estha and Rahel, Arundhati and her brother were the only children of Rahib and Mary Roy, who, like their fictional counterparts, divorced when the children were still young. Rahib Roy was a tea plantation manager (like Ammu's husband in the novel) and a Bengali Hindu; Mary Roy was a Syrian Christian schoolteacher who later became an activist for the rights of women in India. As Ian Buruma puts it in "The Anti-American," "Arundhati imbibed dissent with her mother's milk."

Arundhati attended architecture school in New Delhi after leaving home at the age of sixteen and living in a Delhi slum to save money. She made little use of her honors degree in architecture professionally, but the principles of architecture have profoundly influenced her work as a writer. In an interview with Taisha Abraham for *ARIEL*, she describes writing *The God of Small Things* as analogous to "designing a building" (p. 90). Writing the novel "was really a search for coherence—design coherence—in the way that every last detail of a building—its doors and windows, its structural components—have, or at least ought to have, an aesthetic, stylistic integrity, a clear indication that they belong to each other, as must a book" (p. 91).

Another impact on Roy's novel was her experience with the film industry. She acted in a film called *Massey Saab* (1985), directed by Pradeep Krishen, whom she later married. She went on to write for a documentary film (*How the Rhinoceros Returned*), a television series (*The Banyan Tree*), and two screenplays (*In Which Annie Gives It Those Ones* and *Electric Moon*, 1992). Roy describes her experience with film and television as a kind of apprenticeship for her novel, saying in the interview with Abraham that "Writing screenplays was a tremendous discipline that helped me to hone my writing muscles before I began *The God of Small Things*, which was artistically by far the most ambitious thing that I have ever done" (p. 90). Roy found a kind of freedom in writing her novel that she had not experienced with screenwriting: "That brooding, introspective, circular quality of the narrative would have been hard to achieve in cinema" (p. 90).

THE GOD OF SMALL THINGS

The God of Small Things is a finely textured, intricate novel set at the intersection of the "big" history of postcolonial India and the "small" histories of individual lives. The "Small God" of the novel's title refers to the persistence of the individual will (what Roy calls "a sort of enforced optimism," p. 20) to maintain sanity and order in the face of national and historical chaos, "that vast, violent, circling, driving, ridiculous, insane, unfeasible, public turmoil of a nation" (p. 20). In the novel, this national strife is represented by the continued stratification of society by a caste consciousness that renders some privileged and others "untouchable" and which relegates women to a position of subservience to men. The rise of Marxism in Kerala, the state in southeast India in which the novel is set, promised an equality that would transcend class, caste, and gender differences, but, as seen from the example of Marxists such as Comrade Pillai and the communist sympathizer Chacko, the new ideology becomes another way of exploiting the underprivileged for the benefit of what the novel calls "Men's Needs" (pp. 292, 160). Added to the inequality endemic to India's social history is the impact of British colonialism on the national psyche, creating the fawning deference to the colonial "masters" and the self-hatred found in characters such as Pappachi, Baba, Chacko, and Baby Kochamma. The "Small God" is found in the victims of those forces, characters such as Rahel, Estha, Velutha, and Ammu. These characters dare to stand against the strictures of society by violating society's codes, acts that define them as strong and heroic but also as doomed to ostracism and figurative and literal death. Roy describes the two forces this way: "That Big God howled like a hot wind, and demanded obeisance. Then Small God (cozy and contained, private and limited) came away cauterized, laughing numbly at his own temerity" (p. 20).

The story, when finally pieced together, is not complicated, but Roy's way of weaving memory and imagistic events together complicates the action in order to reveal the complex web of memories and feelings experienced by the characters. Rahel returns to Ayemenem, Kerala, in 1993, upon learning that her twin brother, Estha, has returned to live there after their separation over twenty years earlier. On a fateful December night in 1969, Mammachi (Estha and Rahel's grandmother) learns that her twenty-seven-year-old divorcée daughter, Ammu (Estha and Rahel's mother) has been sneaking off to have sex with a Paravan "untouchable" named Velutha. Mammachi locks Ammu in her room. The frightened children decide to row across the river to hide out in an abandoned colonial house, and their cousin, Sophie Mol, begs to go with them. Sophie has just arrived from England with her mother, Margaret, who married and divorced Chacko (Estha and Rahel's uncle) while he was attending Oxford. The boat capsizes and Sophie drowns. Estha and Rahel hide in the colonial house and find that their mother's lover, Velutha, is also hiding there after learning that his father, Vellya Paapen, has informed Ammu's mother that Ammu and Velutha are lovers. In an attempt to salvage the family's reputation, Baby Kochamma, Estha and Rahel's grand aunt files a fabricated statement at the police depot that claims Velutha raped Ammu and kidnapped Estha and Rahel. The police, incensed by the effrontery of the "untouchable," beat Velutha mercilessly, and he dies later in a police cell, but only after Estha is coerced into accusing Velutha of kidnapping him and Rahel. After the funeral for Sophie Mol, Estha is sent to Madras to live with his father, and Ammu is forced to leave home. Rahel eventually marries an American man and moves to the United States.

This story line, however, is broken into shards and scattered across the novel so that the pieces are not entirely put back together until the end. This postmodern technique of fracturing, dismantling, and recycling fragments and juxtaposing events and images in an otherwise straightforward story is integral to the content of the novel. As with any good work of fiction, the novel's form is inseparable from its content. In one of two metafictional references in the novel to her storytelling approach, Roy describes the memory of 1969 as being

like the salvaged remains of a burned house—the charred clock, the singed photograph, the scorched furniture—[that] must be resurrected from the ruins and examined. Preserved. Accounted for. Little events, ordinary things, smashed and reconstituted. Imbued with new meaning. Suddenly they become the bleached bones of a story.

(p. 32)

We begin just as the recently returned Rahel begins, with "the bleached bones": Ammu's divorce and return to Ayemenem with the twins; the mysterious connection between the twins; the Orangedrink Lemondrink Man; Sophie Mol's funeral; Ammu's ostracism; Estha's betrayal of Velutha; Baby Kochamma's love for Father Mulligan; a polluted river. But each of these "bleached bones" reveals one piece of the puzzle that begins to make sense only as more information is weaved into the tale.

Inspector Thomas Mathew's treatment of Ammu is a good example of Roy's method. On page 9 we learn that the inspector taps Ammu on her breasts with his baton and tells her to go home. We imagine that Ammu is mistreated because the inspector is simply an uncouth chauvinist who abuses his power to make advances on women. Over 200 pages later, however, we have learned that Ammu came to the police station to set the record straight, and this new information is the impetus for the inspector's behavior:

Later, when the real story reached Inspector Thomas Mathew, the fact that what the Paravan had taken from the Touchable Kingdom had not been snatched, but *given*, concerned him deeply. So after Sophie Mol's funeral, when Ammu went to him with the twins to tell him that a mistake had been made and he tapped her breasts with his baton, it was not a policeman's spontaneous brutishness on his part. He knew exactly what he was doing. It was a premeditated gesture, calculated to humiliate and terrorize her. An attempt to instill order into a world gone wrong.

(p. 246)

Even this is not the full story. Fifty pages later we learn that the inspector is angry with Baby Kochamma for filing what he now realizes is a false statement. He knows that his department's brutal treatment of Velutha may cost him his job or worse if Ammu is allowed to enter a statement saying that she was a willing sexual partner rather than a rape victim. The inspector thinks, "True he was a Paravan. True, he had misbehaved. But these were troubled times and technically, as per the law, he was an innocent man. There was no *case*" (p. 298). The actions of the police inspector are repeated several times, but each time the reader perceives those actions in light of new evidence. Our experience of the events becomes like that of the children: like Rahel, and, one presumes, like the now-silent Estha, we confront the events of that night in December 1969 as bits and pieces of memory in a charred-out home, "the bleached bones of a story."

The second metafictional passage suggestive of Roy's technique is a reference to the classical art of Kathakali. Kathakali is a combination of dance and drama based on Hindu mythology that dates to seventeenth-century Kerala. In the 1990s of *The God of Small Things,* Kathakali dancers perform truncated versions of their epic dances for tourists who are busy applying suntan lotion to their bodies while lounging poolside. On their way home, these dancers visit a temple to "ask pardon of their gods" for "corrupting their stories" (p. 218). Like the river, now a polluted cesspool smelling of "shit and pesticides bought with World Bank loans" (p. 14), the traditional folklore of Kerala is sacrificed on the altar of progress for the nation—what Roy calls, in one of her political essays discussed below, "the greater common good." However, in Roy's description of true Kathakali performances we learn that *The God of Small Things* may not owe its structural design to postmodern trends in fiction but to the traditional Kerala art of Kathakali. The novel's structure is perhaps an attempt to recover the aesthetics of Kathakali.

Kathakali discovered long ago that the secret of the Great Stories is that they *have* no secrets. The

Great Stories are the ones you have heard and want to hear again. The ones you can enter anywhere and inhabit comfortably. They don't need to deceive you with thrills and trick endings. They don't surprise you with the unforeseen. They are as familiar as the house you live in. Or the smell of your lover's skin. You know how they end, yet you listen as though you don't. In the way that although you know that one day you will die, you live as though you won't. In the Great Stories you know who lives, who dies, who finds love, who doesn't. And yet you want to know again.

(p. 218)

This is also an appropriate description of *The God of Small Things*. We know what happens in the novel from the outset. We know Sophie Mol comes to Kerala and dies. We know that Estha and Rahel are blamed for her death. We know that Estha betrays someone he loved. We know that Estha is separated from Rahel and that Ammu goes away. There are few surprises left after the first chapter; the only question that remains is how everything fits together. Moreover, the recursive nature of the novel, its repeated phrases (the "God of Loss," the "God of Small Things," "viable die-able age," the "Heart of Darkness," the "History House"), and its revisited events give the novel a Kathakali-like familiarity, which Roy describes as a story that is "as familiar as the house you live in."

The tourist resort in which the Kathakali perform is built on the grounds of what Roy calls the "Heart of Darkness" or the "History House," the colonial home Estha and Rahel hide in after Sophie Mol's drowning and the site of Velutha's beating at the hands of the Kottayam police. The abandoned home is also the site of Velutha and Rahel's nightly rendezvous. Roy refers to it as the "Heart of Darkness" because its now-deceased owner, Kari Saipu, was an "Englishman who had 'gone native,'" and was therefore "Ayemenem's own Kurtz. Ayemenem his private "Heart of Darkness" (p. 51). The reference to Joseph Conrad's famous novel that

paints colonial Africa as the bowels of savagery reverberates through the novel—as for instance when Ammu bristles at a comment by Margaret and says, "Must we behave like some damn godforsaken tribe that's just been discovered" (p. 171) or when Margaret's friends in England warn her that "when you travel to the Heart of Darkness . . . *Anything can happen to anyone*" (p. 311). The attitude toward Africa symbolized by *Heart of Darkness* therefore acts as a colonial pretext to the India of *The God of Small Things*. The wife beater Pappachi, the ineffectual Rhodes scholar Chacko, and the self-important Baby Kochamma are all marked by their deference to British culture, Chacko only less so because he is aware of the irony of his Anglophilia (p. 52).

Pappachi (Estha and Rahel's grandfather) represents the epitome of the colonial Indian's attitude toward the British Empire. He is one of the novel's most pathetic and most dangerous characters (although Baby Kochamma rivals Pappachi as a female version of the same dangerous attitude). Once the imperial entomologist under British rule, Pappachi slid in rank and importance after independence until he returned to Ayemenem to jealously watch his wife's business thrive and his own stature diminish even further. When his daughter, Ammu, returns home after divorcing her alcoholic husband because he wanted to make her a concubine to his English boss (at the boss's suggestion), Pappachi refuses to believe her because "he didn't believe that an Englishman, *any* Englishman, would covet another man's wife" (p. 42). Pappachi spends his waning years walking the streets of Ayemenem in his British suit and returning home to beat his wife with a brass vase, an evocative image of the postcolonial mind-set: he exalts English culture and denigrates his own. According to Ammu, "Pappachi was an incurable British CCP, which was short for *chhi-chhi poach* and in Hindi meant shit-wiper. Chacko said that the correct word for people like Pappachi was Anglophile" (p. 50).

Of all the characters in the novel, Chacko is most keenly aware of the family's postcolonial situation. Chacko teaches his niece and nephew that their family's Anglophilia is a kind of curse. In Chacko's opinion, "they were a family of Anglophiles. Pointed in the wrong direction, trapped outside their own history and unable to retrace their steps because their footprints had been swept away" (p. 51). The reference to footprints is possibly a reference to "untouchability." Velutha "left no footprints on the sand, no ripples in the water, no image in mirrors" (p. 250) because as a Paravan "untouchable" he was nonexistent in the eyes of Kerala society. A lack of footprints particularly signals untouchability because in Pappachi's day, "Paravans were expected to crawl backwards with a broom, sweeping away their footprints so the Brahmins or Syrian Christians would not defile themselves by accidentally stepping into a Paravan's footprint" (p. 71). Thus the novel seems to suggest that to be a family of Anglophiles in postcolonial India is to experience a kind of ostracism analogous to untouchability. In drawing this comparison, we should note that the Paravan still suffers the worst fate in the novel, so Roy is not attempting to say that Anglophiles and untouchables suffer equally.

What the novel does clearly state is that Rahel and Estha's family have fallen out of step with postindependence India. Chacko explains that being "trapped outside their own history" is like being locked outside "an old house" with its lights on and voices whispering inside:

> "But we can't go in," Chacko explained, "because we've been locked out. And when we look through the windows, all we see are shadows. And when we try and listen, all we hear is a whispering. And we cannot understand the whispering, because our minds have been invaded by a war. A war that we have won and lost. The very worst sort of war. A war that captures dreams and re-dreams them. A war that has made us adore our conquerors and despise ourselves."
>
> (p. 52)

Chacko expresses here a disconnection with India caused by the colonial legacy he has inherited. The war they had won was independence from the British crown; the war they had lost was the war of the mind: although a man like Chacko is no longer physically a subject of the British Empire, he will always be so mentally. He and his family are doomed to "adore our conquerors and despise ourselves." In this sense, and again in Chacko's words, they are "prisoners of war" who "belong nowhere" and "sail unanchored on troubled seas" (p. 52).

The novel's postcolonial critique of Indian Anglophile behavior may explain why betrayal occurs in various forms throughout the book. The Anglophile deference to the British described by Chacko, and instantiated by Pappachi's habit of beating Mammachi, is a form of betrayal. Self-denial, as Chacko calls it, is betrayal of self. This postcolonial betrayal is compounded by a series of smaller betrayals. Vellya Paapen's betrayal of his son, Velutha, is occasioned by his deep feelings of deference to Mammachi: "as a Paravan and a man with mortgaged body parts [Mammachi paid for his glass eye], he considered it his duty" (p. 242). The Kathakali dancers betray their gods to serve the tourist market. The people of Kerala, with the help of the World Bank and the globalism it represents, have betrayed the environment, turning their once sparkling river to filth. Julius Caesar is betrayed by Brutus again and again in Estha's childhood games (p. 79), an act that prefigures his own betrayal of Velutha. In what is called "the last betrayal" (p. 267), Comrade Pillai refuses to help Velutha in his time of need. Pillai even denies that Velutha is a member of his party in order to disassociate himself from the cursed Paravan.

The fact that Velutha is a carpenter, betrayed by those closest to him, denied by the one man who could help him, and finally executed brutally brings to mind the sufferings of Christ at the hands of Pontius Pilate and the Sanhedrin. Jesus, a carpenter from Nazareth, was betrayed by one of his twelve disciples and denied by another, and he was beaten and executed. Yet if Roy intends an analogy between Velutha and

Christ, the analogy ends here. For Velutha, and for the untouchables he represents, there is no resurrection in the story. No one receives new life through his death. No tiny band of followers explodes into a major movement.

Another kind of betrayal in the novel is the act of transgressing the "love laws." Transgressing laws is a betrayal of those laws and the body that lends them authority. However, since the love laws are presented in the novel as an unfair restriction on the individual will, this kind of betrayal is a positive one, although in the case of Ammu and Velutha it comes with dire consequences. The novel uses this forbidden love between a "touchable" and an "untouchable" to explore the depths of society's self-righteous, racist, and pharisaical attitudes but also to suggest that these attitudes are ingrained deep in human nature. When the police attack Velutha we are told that they are only "history's henchmen" who were "sent to square the books and collect the dues from those who broke its laws" (p. 292). The police, in other words, are acting out a part. They represent "civilization's fear of nature, men's fear of women, power's fear of powerlessness" (p. 292). Loving an untouchable, divorce, and incest are all types of transgression in the novel. What Rahel realizes upon her return to Ayemenem is that "Ammu, Estha and she were not the worst transgressors. . . . They all broke the rules. They all crossed into forbidden territory. They all tampered with the laws that lay down who should be loved and how."

As the above discussion of structure suggests, "return" is a central motif in *The God of Small Things*. Like the Ithaca of the *Odyssey*, about which Estha writes in his primary school notebook and the adult Rahel reads upon her return home (p. 150), Ayemenem is the place to which the twins finally return. The impetus for telling the story is Rahel's return to Ayemenem after learning that Estha was, as Roy puts it, "re-returned" to Ayemenem after the twins' father purportedly immigrated to Australia. Through Rahel's return we begin to piece together the

family history and the events of 1969. The return to Ayemenem is metaphorically a return to memory, a chance to mend the brokenness of the past, which is most likely the reason for Rahel's return from the United States after divorcing her American husband. Pappachi, Chacko, Baby Kochamma, Ammu, Rahel, and Estha all return to Ayemenem at various points of time, further reinforcing the centrality of Ayemenem in their lives and in the family's narrative.

The one moment in time to which no one can return is the time before the rise of Marxism, before the British, before the Dutch, before the arrival of Syrian bishops, "when the Love Laws were made" (p. 33). The love laws, the novel argues, are as much to blame for the events of the story as the arrival of Sophie Mol (pp. 33–34). These are the laws that decree "who should be loved, and how. And how much" (p. 33). Without these laws, there is no transgression in the story. Velutha has not committed a crime by sleeping with Ammu. Ammu is not locked in her room. The children do not run away. Sophie Mol does not drown. Thus the explanation for Rahel and Estha's incest toward the end of the novel is found in this final attempt to return. The image of Estha and Rahel "fitted together like stacked spoons" is an image of fetal return. The fact that "what they shared that night was not happiness, but hideous grief" (p. 311) is not to say that they feel shame at their act of incest. Rather, the "hideous grief" comes with the realization that they can never return to the time before the love laws, the time when they were together in their mother's womb.

Given its themes of incest and forbidden love and its unbecoming vision of postcolonial India, it is not surprising that *The God of Small Things* has been the subject of controversy in India. Communists and other left-wing groups objected to Roy's politics. Aijaz Ahmad in "Reading Arundhati Roy Politically" charged Roy with pandering to "the prevailing anti-Communist sentiment" in India and claimed she has "neither a feel for Communist politics nor perhaps rudimentary knowledge of it" (quoted in Sharma and Talwar, p. 10). Some Marxists took exception to Roy's portrayal of the communist leader E. M. S. Namboodiripad, whom she repeatedly refers to as "Soviet stooge, running dog" (for example, p. 285). Namboodiripad, the only blatantly historical figure in the novel, wrote a critical rebuttal of Roy's novel in the Communist Party magazine, *Ganashakti.* The novel also stirred debate among communist factions. According to R. S. Sharma and Shashi Bala Talwar in *Arundhati Roy's* The God of Small Things: *Critique and Commentary,* some Communists accused Roy of slandering the party leadership while others argued that "Roy has truthfully exposed the hypocrisy and dishonesty" of party leadership in Kerala and that "she has staunchly upheld the cause of the downtrodden" (p. 10).

The explicit treatment of sex, masturbation, and incest in the novel incited much debate as well. While critics such as Ahmad argued that Roy was simply aping Euro-American bourgeois literature, others were outraged. Shabu Thomas, a lawyer from Kerala, filed a lawsuit against Roy for outraging public decency. Some Syrian Christians and other citizens of Kerala were unhappy with what they saw as Roy's negative portrayal of their community, questioning whether a cross-caste love affair would have prompted such violent responses by the community. In Roy's view, the criticisms of her novel highlight the ways that images of India are manipulated and controlled by the Indian elite and politicians. Roy commented, "India is a country that lives in several centuries, and some of the centuries have not been at all pleased with my book. But I say replace ethnic purity and 'authenticity' with honesty" (quoted in Mullaney, p. 70).

Finally, the language and style of *The God of Small Things* has drawn much attention and adds fuel to an ongoing debate on the role of the Anglophone writer in India. Some critics worry that the world's view of India is in the hands of a small elite of Indian writers who write in a language that is not even indigenous to India. However, the language of Roy's novel has been praised by critics within and without India for evoking a realistic image of life in Kerala without exoticizing its people and culture. As James Wood wrote in *The New Republic,* "the great pleasure of *The God of Small Things* flows from its language, and its delight in verbal comedy. . . . Language is the playground of its politics." Roy's writing has been compared to that of James Joyce for its inventiveness and that of William Faulkner for its strong sense of regionalism. Roy's style is often compared to that of the father of modern Indian writers in English, Salman Rushdie. But Roy's mastery of the novel's language and style should leave no readers in doubt that they are in the hands of a skillful and original individual talent. Her greatest achievement in this extraordinary first novel is her narrative voice, a voice that weaves in and out of time periods and various characters' consciousnesses while maintaining steady control of her subject. Her narrative voice offers a sensitive portrayal of the powerless in the hands of the powerful, the "small" in the hands of the "big," and does so without sentimentalizing or underestimating those characters.

POLITICAL WRITINGS

Roy's three books of political essays to date extend one major theme from *The God of Small Things:* they argue on behalf of "the small," a stance that prompted Member of Parliament Balbir K. Punj to satirically call Roy "the Goddess of small things" (*Outlook,* 27 May 2002). The "small things" at the heart of Roy's passion are the people whose homes and fields are submerged by mega-dam projects in rural India, the destitute who suffer in poverty and illiteracy while the Indian government pours billions into its nuclear arms program, the Muslims of Gujarat who were persecuted in what she calls Hindu nationalist "pogroms" in 2002, and the innocent and helpless individuals of the "ancient" civilizations of the world adversely affected by U.S. foreign policy and corporate globalization. Like Velutha and Ammu condemned to death and ruin by a pharisaical society, the small people of Roy's political essays suffer similar fates under uncaring powers (the Indian government, the United States government) and inhuman forces (globalization, capitalism). As she writes in *The Cost of Living* (1999).

> We have to support our small heroes. (Of these we have many. Many.) We have to fight specific wars in specific ways. Who knows, perhaps that's what the twenty-first century has in store for us. The dismantling of the Big. Big bombs, big dams, big ideologies, big contradictions, big countries, big wars, big heroes, big mistakes. Perhaps it will be the Century of the Small. Perhaps right now, this very minute, there's a small god up in heaven readying herself for us.
>
> (p. 12)

Roy claims in *Power Politics* that *The God of Small Things* is "no less political than any of my essays" (p. 11). Her specific reference to the "small god" thesis in her political writings invites readers to explore the political implications of the novel. There are no mega-dam projects and nuclear bombs in *The God of Small Things,* but the novel's examination of upper-caste attitudes toward the lower castes and of those who would transgress the boundaries is analogous.

The reader is also encouraged to link the novel with her political writings by the title of her first collection of essays, *The Cost of Living* (1999), which is taken directly from the novel; indeed one might even assume from its title that *The Cost of Living* is a kind of sequel to *The God of Small Things,* and in a way it is. At the moment when Velutha enters Ammu in their first sexual encounter on the riverbank, Roy writes, "the cost of living climbed to unaffordable heights; though later Baby Kochamma would say it was a Small Price to Pay" (p. 318). "Living," then, is following one's passions. The "cost" is the price one pays for transgressing society's moral code in following one's passions.

For Baby Kochamma, the moments of Ammu's and Velutha's passion were not worth the price: Velutha's violent death and Ammu's ostracism and—Baby Kochamma's true concern—the shame brought upon the family. The novel suggests, however, that Ammu's life was already a kind of death—a woman divorced and in love with an "untouchable" has no hope of living the life that she wants. She is incarcerated by her society's love laws and caste prejudices. But in that act of transgression with Velutha, Roy writes, "She lived" (p. 319).

There are at least two ways in which Roy carries over the notion of "the cost of living" to her political writing. One is the personal cost for the writer who stands up against her government to cry foul. In *The Cost of Living*, Roy writes,

> When I told my friends that I was writing this piece, they cautioned me. "Go ahead," they said, "but first make sure you're not vulnerable. Make sure your papers are in order. Make sure your taxes are paid." My papers are in order. My taxes are paid. But how can one *not* be vulnerable in a climate like this? Everyone is vulnerable. Accidents happen. There's safety only in acquiescence. As I write, I am filled with foreboding.
>
> (p. 108)

The only safety available to Ammu and Velutha is to forget about each other, to stifle their passions and desires, to live "in acquiescence" to the moral code of their society. Roy sees her own position as a writer in disagreement with her government in similar terms. By stepping out of her role as a novelist and openly attacking the policies of her government, she refuses the safety of "acquiescence" and chooses instead to transgress social norms by exposing what she sees as her government's hypocrisy no matter what the cost.

Roy has, in fact, paid a price for her opposition. Her lengthy essay on the government's disregard for the people displaced by the impending construction of the Sardar Sarovar, a massive dam being built in central India on the

Narmada River, was published in *Outlook* and *Frontline,* two major Indian periodicals, in June 1999. This article, her active involvement in demonstrations, and of course her fame as India's Booker Prize winner, made Roy the most prominent opponent of the dam project. The article also drew a censure from the Indian Supreme Court, accusing Roy of attempting to "undermine the dignity of the Court" (*Power Politics,* p. 97). On 13 December 2000, Roy took part in a demonstration outside the Supreme Court in opposition to the court's decision to allow the Sardar Sarovar project to continue. The rally was peaceful, but Jagdish Parashar, R. K. Virmani, and three other lawyers submitted a petition against her and two other demonstrators for allegedly shouting slogans against the court and physically threatening the opposing lawyers. The Supreme Court entertained the charge and issued a summons to the three demonstrators even though the local police station had seen the original charge as unworthy of attention.

Roy wrote an affidavit, which is published in its entirety in *Power Politics,* in which she criticizes the actions of the court. In her words, the court's willingness to entertain the lawsuit against the three defendants who "publicly . . . questioned the policies of the government and severely criticized a recent judgment of the Supreme Court . . . indicates a disquieting inclination on the part of the court to silence criticism and muzzle dissent, to harass and intimidate those who disagree with it" (p. 102). The Supreme Court threw out the case against Roy and the other defendants on 28 August 2001, but on 5 September 2001, issued a new contempt of court charge against Roy for what it judged to be her unfair criticism of the Supreme Court in her affidavit. The Court found Roy guilty of contempt of court in its proceedings on 6 March 2002, sentencing her to three months in jail or a 2,000 rupee fine. Roy elected to spend one symbolic night in jail and then to pay the fine.

The other sense in which the "the cost of living" idea carries over from *The God of Small Things* is in Roy's championing of "small" people in her essays. Roy argues that in India it is possible to get statistics on everything from cricket scores to stock market performance to the number of "vasectomies in a given year,"

> But the government of India does not have a figure for the number of people who have been displaced by dams or sacrificed in other ways at the altars of "national progress." *Isn't this astounding?* How can you measure progress if you don't know what it costs and who has paid for it?
>
> (p. 17)

The cost of living in India, Roy claims, is borne by the poorest people, mostly made up of "untouchables" like the Dalits and the aboriginal Adivasis. "It's like having an expense account," she argues. "Someone else pays the bills. People from another country. Another world. India's poorest people are subsidizing the lifestyles of her richest" (p. 19). While this argument is not congruent with the case of Ammu and Velutha transgressing the moral code, it does extend Roy's metaphor of living costs which first appears in *The God of Small Things.*

In making these connections between her novel and her political essays, Roy is clearly leveraging her notoriety as the author of *The God of Small Things.* Roy sees herself as caught between her political activism and her novel's success. On the one hand she intentionally uses her fame to bring greater publicity and broader awareness to the causes she believes in; on the other she does not want to appear as a "hero" in battles where others are suffering in more heroic ways than she. In her acceptance speech for the fourth annual Prize for Cultural Freedom by the Lannon Foundation, based in Santa Fe, New Mexico, Roy said, "I accept this prize knowing that there are many people around the world who deserve it more than I do. Unknown, invisible people who are raising their voices and fighting the fight at much greater cost to themselves than I could ever claim" (*Outlook,*

23 January 2003). Similarly, in her statement upon release from jail Roy explained that she decided to spend a symbolic one night in jail and pay the fine because serving the entire three-month sentence might make Roy "a martyr for a cause that is not mine alone" (*Outlook,* 7 March 2002).

Nevertheless, one of the most consistent criticisms Roy faces is the charge that her political writings are self-serving and egotistical. Ian Buruma, in an article entitled "The Anti-American," talks of Roy's snobbish tone and her "tendency to sound preposterous." Buruma paraphrases Ramachandra Guha from his November 2000 article in the *Hindu* as saying that Roy's "vanity and her self-indulgence devalues the work of serious activists" (*Outlookindia.com,* 4 May 2002, first published in *The New Republic*). Reeta Sinha, in "What Makes Me an Expert on Arundhati Roy," talks of the "me-myself-and-I attitude which permeate[s] her essays" (*Outlookindia.com,* 16 January 2002). The *Publishers Weekly* reviewers of *The Cost of Living* point out the irrelevance of digressions that call attention to herself and detract from the issues at hand: "fully a fifth of the article ["The End of Imagination"] is devoted to a friend telling Roy that she has become so famous that the rest of her life would be 'vaguely satisfying,' which is a fair description of this book" (20 September 1999). Despite these criticisms, and as even Buruma concedes, issues such as the Sardar Sarovar dam have come to the attention of more people—more of the average population who do not normally read political essays—because Roy has utilized her fame as the author of the Booker Prize–winning *The God of Small Things.*

THE COST OF LIVING

The two essays that make up this slim volume were published previously in *Outlook* and *Frontline.* "The End of Imagination" came out as a cover story in both publications in July 1998, a year after *The God of Small Things* and in the wake of the media frenzy over the Booker Prize. "The Greater Common Good" was published in *Outlook* and *Frontline* in June 1999. Out of all her political writing, these two essays most clearly bridge the distance between Roy's artistic aims in her novel and her passion as an activist.

"The Greater Common Good," which appears first in the volume, protests the building of the Sardar Sarovar dam in the Narmada River valley, running from central Madhya Pradesh state through Gujarat state to the Arabian Sea. The ninety-page, heavily footnoted article documents the "heroic" efforts of the Narmada Bachao Andolan (NBA), an organization of anti-dam activists and victims of the Sardar Sarovar project, to convince the Indian government to halt construction of the Narmada Valley development projects. Roy argues that the "war" is not between "modern rational, progressive forces of 'Development'" and "a sort of neo-Luddite impulse—an irrational, emotional 'Anti-development' resistance, fueled by an arcadian, pre-industrial dream" (p. 10). This "crude" dichotomy suggests that those opposed to the dam projects are selfishly putting their own needs above "the greater common good" of the nation. Roy argues, however, that the government's position, far from seeking the benefit of the greatest numbers in the population, actually seeks to serve itself, the Indian elite, and the city dwellers at the expense of millions of rural people, archaeological sites, sacred temples, farms, villages, and the environment. She even equates the actions of the Indian government to Nazi Germany's extermination of the Jews, saying, "shall we just put the Star of David on their doors and get it over with?" (p. 55).

"The End of Imagination" is a shorter but similarly impassioned essay on India's May 1998 test detonation of a nuclear bomb. The essay argues that India's entry into the nuclear race ushers in a new age of horror for the Indian people and continues a nightmare for the rest of the world. Roy is aware that the case against nuclear weapons, even as deterrents, has been made before: "There can be nothing more humiliating for a writer of fiction to have to do than restate a case that has, over the years, already been made by other people in other parts of the world, and made passionately, eloquently, and knowledgeably" (p. 94). Since the Indian government raised the issue again by testing a nuclear weapon, Roy feels obligated to revisit the case against nuclear arms. "Silence," she claims, "would be indefensible" (p. 94). While she may make the case as "passionately" as other writers have, Roy unfortunately does not make it as "eloquently" or "knowledgeably." Her rhetoric often slips into adolescent satire, as in the following:

> But let us pause to give credit where it's due. Whom must we thank for all this? The Men who made it happen. The Masters of the Universe. Ladies and gentlemen, the United States of America! Come on up here, folks, stand up and take a bow. Thank you for doing this to the world. Thank you for making a difference. Thank you for showing us the way. Thank you for altering the very meaning of life.
>
> (p. 101)

She also resorts to melodrama: "From now on it is not dying we must fear, but living" (p. 101) and "The air is thick with ugliness and there's the unmistakable stench of fascism on the breeze" (p. 105) as well as racialized critique, claiming nuclear weapons are "the ultimate colonizer. Whiter than any white man that ever lived. The very heart of whiteness" (p. 101).

The two articles in *The Cost of Living* are linked by Roy's argument that dams and nuclear bombs both wreak havoc on ordinary citizens. She writes, "Big Dams are to a nation's 'development' what nuclear bombs are to its military arsenal. They're both weapons of mass destruction. They're both weapons governments use to control their own people. Both twentieth-century emblems that mark a point in time when

human intelligence has outstripped its own instinct for survival" (p. 80).

POWER POLITICS

Power Politics (2001) brings together five previously published essays on subjects ranging from the role of writers in society and the right of citizens to protest the Supreme Court to the damaging effects of corporatization, the September 11 World Trade Center terrorist attacks, and the United States' 2001 military campaign in Afghanistan. The book marks two developments in Roy's writing career: the extension of her critical lens from national to international issues and her attempt to frame a writing identity between novelist and activist.

Her argument in "The Algebra of Infinite Injustice" has earned Roy such titles as anti-American, America-basher, and demonizer of the United States. Her basic argument is that the terrorist attacks of 11 September 2001, were not incited by jealousy of America's freedom, as George W. Bush asserted, but by "the U.S. government's record of commitment to and support for exactly the opposite things—to military and economic terrorism, insurgency, military dictatorship, religious bigotry, and unimaginable genocide (outside America)" (p. 108). She states that she, as a writer, has been put in the uncomfortable position of having to speak the cold truth at a time when sympathy for the United States is at an all-time high. "But then it falls to the rest of us to ask the hard questions and say the harsh things. And for our pains, for our bad timing, we will be disliked, ignored, and perhaps even silenced" (p. 109). Roy's assessment of the situation is not particularly "harsh"—such commentaries emanate from political commentators such as Noam Chomsky, novelists such as Norman Mailer, and countless television commentators both inside and outside the United States—yet some critics have taken exception to the way in which Roy states her views. She claims that Americans may be confused as to why they are so hated, but the rest of the world is not. The rest of the world shares "the tired wisdom of knowing that what goes around eventually comes around" (p. 108). Margaret Wente, columnist for the *Globe and Mail,* claims in her article "Soft on Fascism" that Roy's argument is a kind of "gotcha" criticism, an almost gleeful claim that "it's their own fault after all" (*Outlook,* 18 October 2001; *Globe and Mail,* 16 October 2001).

The first essay in the collection, "The Ladies Have Feelings, So . . . Shall We Leave It to the Experts," is Roy's most extended discussion on the relationship between her political activism and her role as a writer. The essay, based on a talk she gave at Hampshire College in Massachusetts on 15 February 2001, responds to the general perception in the Indian media that Roy is inappropriately stepping out of her role as a novelist by writing political articles, an opinion stated plainly by the Indian Supreme Court a year later. Roy, the court claimed, has wandered "from the path on which she was traversing by contributing to the [sic] Art and Literature" (*Outlook,* 7 March 2002). Roy contests the notion that a fiction writer has no business commenting upon political issues and claims instead that it is the "best and greatest" writers who recognize that "there is an intricate web of morality, rigor, and responsibility that art, that writing itself, imposes on a writer" (p. 5). In other words, a writer may turn her back on society—she has that right—but she who takes her position as a writer seriously will be unable to ignore the important issues of her day.

Roy complains about the term used to describe her four years after her only novel was published. She claims that she is no longer called a "writer." Now, because of her political essays, people refer to her as a "writer-activist," a label she dislikes because it suggests that she is less than a true writer. The "activist" tag to the title suggests, according to Roy, that "I take sides. I take a position. I have a point of view. What's worse, I make it clear that I think it's right and moral to take that position, and what's even

worse, I use everything in my power to flagrantly solicit support for that position" (p. 11). As Reeta Sinha points out, taking sides and having a point of view does not give other writers the title of activist, so why should it Roy? Still, since "everything in my power" includes marching in demonstrations, challenging the Supreme Court, speaking at political rallies throughout the world, and spending a night in jail for contempt of court, it is surprising that Roy does not see her political activism as the logical explanation for the title. She acts the part of an activist and should not see anything demeaning in being called one.

WAR TALK

The title piece in Roy's third book of political essays revisits the nuclear weapons issue four years after India and Pakistan conducted nuclear bomb tests in 1998 (the article "War Talk: Summer Games with Nuclear Bombs" first appeared in *Frontline* in June 2002). "War Talk" is a short but impassioned rumination on the apocalyptic implications of India's and Pakistan's commitment to nuclear weapons. In it Roy also briefly revisits the issue of fiction writing, suggesting that writing fiction under the shadow of a potential nuclear holocaust is more than a low priority for her. She suggests that the public's desire for more fiction from her is morally reprehensible while we are living under the shadow of impending disaster.

As seen above, Roy's definition of herself as a writer has undergone various transformations. First, her success as a novelist gave her the opportunity to bring political issues to the attention of a wide audience—an audience that very likely would not have read her writing if she were not the author of *The God of Small Things.* She was then an acclaimed novelist interested in political issues. Next, the prominence and frequency of her political writing revealed to the public that political activism was not simply a sideline for Roy but that she was defining herself as more than a fiction writer. The appellation "writer-activist" may not have sat well with her, but it seemed to have stuck. Now, in her third book of political essays, Roy's public image is beginning to shift from "novelist" to "activist." Five years after the publication of *The God of Small Things,* Reeta Sinha posed the tongue-in-cheek question, "one novel makes her a fiction writer?" (*Outlook*, 16 January 2002). As the novelist title fades, Roy seems rankled by the public's eagerness for her to put down her political pen and get back to fiction.

In the article "War Talk," Roy seems unopposed to leaving the fiction writer image behind at this point in her career. Here she makes these comments on the way the nuclear threat dwarfs the issue of fiction writing for her:

> The last question every visiting journalist always asks me is: Are you writing another book? That question mocks me. Another book? Right *now*? This talk of nuclear war displays such contempt for music, art, literature, and everything else that defines civilization. So what kind of book should I write?
>
> (p. 7)

Although in this statement Roy still holds literature and the arts up as the bastion of civilized society, her outrage at being asked continually whether she is writing another novel suggests that literature is for her almost frivolous in the face of serious social issues. More to the point, Roy, who elsewhere extols the virtues of the artists of the world as the speakers of truth in a world of deceit, seems weary of the public's insistent reference to her fiction writing. The journalists' question "mocks" her because it suggests that the public listens to her because of her one novel, not because of her knowledge, skill, and opinions as a political writer. Her influence remains anchored in a literary success in 1997, and, despite her attempts to move on, the public is still waiting for her to get back to her real calling.

In another essay in *War Talk,* however, Roy continues to frame herself publicly as a writer of fiction and nonfiction. In "Come September," an essay that claims rather crudely that America's September 11 is not the only September 11 in history and that many other nations have suffered worse disasters, many thanks to American foreign policy, Roy suggests that fiction and nonfiction are tools she uses to expose the "excesses" of the powerful (p. 46). Revealing the truth behind these powers, moreover, is something she feels compelled to do as a writer:

> Stories reveal themselves to us [writers]. The public narrative, the private narrative—they colonize us. They commission us. They insist on being told. Fiction and nonfiction are only different techniques of storytelling. For reasons I do not fully understand, fiction dances out of me. Nonfiction is wrenched out by the aching, broken world I wake up to every morning.
>
> (p. 45)

While Roy attempts to equate fiction and nonfiction as "only different techniques of storytelling," the fact that one "dances out" of her and the other is "wrenched out" suggests again that in her view fiction writing is the softer of the two modes of expression. Fiction "dances"—it is easy, ornate, sublime; but political essays are "wrenched out"—they come from the gut, and they tell painful truths. *War Talk,* her fourth book, reveals more than Roy's views on nuclear arms, American "imperialism," and the heroic efforts of Noam Chomsky (an article written as the foreword to a 2003 edition of his *For Reasons of State*); the book reveals a writer still struggling with her identity and her relationship to her craft.

Roy's political books have been touted by some as powerfully written and courageous. (Salman Rushdie in a blurb for *The Cost of Living* called it "brilliant reportage" and "passionate, no-holds-barred commentary," and Howard Zinn and Noam Chomsky in advance praise for *Power Politics* described her writing as "penetrating" and "impressive," respectively.) Others decry her political writing as histrionic, self-indulgent, and sensational. The criticisms of her writing are worth looking into because they get to the root of her unevenness as a political writer. On the one hand, her notoriety brings attention to social and political issues in India that many Indian voters and the international community might otherwise not recognize. Her political essays are not detached and emotionless but rather reveal a human passion to right the wrongs of the world and come to the aid of the poor and needy. Moreover, her articles are thoroughly footnoted with references to other articles and documents, which suggests that she has done her homework. On the other hand, Roy's political writing is far less accomplished than her fiction. Her passion often comes through in what Buruma calls a "shrill" voice. The shrillness is due mainly to the abundance of hyperbolic statements, melodrama, and an almost adolescent sarcasm (as noted previously) in her essays. A *Publishers Weekly* review of *Power Politics* sums up these weaknesses: "Although her passion and agitation on these issues is commendable, her writing lacks analysis, and her generalized outrage and hyperbole make much of her criticism wooden. She tends to switch between issues of trade and her fame, losing the reader" (30 July 30 2001, p. 72).

Buruma points to more flaws in her writing that tend to diminish their impact. One is the hyperbolic argument of "moral equivalence," as when Roy claims that global enterprises such as Coke or Nike operate on the same principles as terrorism and when she says George W. Bush and Saddam Hussein and Osama bin Laden are all interchangeable (Buruma, *Outlook,* 4 May 2002). The other is "the misleading quotation": Buruma clarifies that when, in 1996, Lesley Stahl of CBS asked then Secretary of State Madeleine Albright what she thought of U.S. economic sanctions killing children in Iraq, Albright first

explained that she did not believe children had died because of the sanctions before saying the difficulties caused by sanctions were a price worth paying to contain Saddam Hussein. By leaving Albright's explanation out of the quote, Roy has Albright saying that killing a half a million children in Iraq is a price worth paying.

Buruma argues that certain people in the West, namely academics and the "global intelligentsia," champion Roy because "she has positioned herself, successfully, as an authentic Third World voice." But the danger, in Buruma's view, is that Roy's polemics against the West (most notably the United States) "gives criticism a bad name" and resorts to a kind of "Occidentalism, or Said in reverse." While Edward Said, in his famous book *Orientalism,* argues that historical views of Asia were invented by the West as the "Other" to European morality and culture, Buruma charges Roy with similarly demonizing the West.

Political writers by definition express opinions on contentious issues and are thus expected to face opposition. That Roy is criticized by those who do not share her views (for example, Brooke Unger, the South Asian bureau chief of the *Economist,* and Margaret Wente of the *Globe and Mail*) is no indictment against her. However, what writers such as Ian Buruma, Ramachandra Guha, and Reeta Sinha deplore about Roy's political writing is its lack of sophistication. After three books of political essays, Roy's writing has come nowhere near the elegance and sophistication of the fiction writing displayed in her novel. What remains to be seen is whether the writer will continue as a novelist and whether the activist will develop into a more powerful and effective political writer.

Selected Bibliography

WORKS OF ARUNDHATI ROY

FICTION

The God of Small Things. New York: Random House, 1997; New York: HarperPerennial, 1998.

NONFICTION

The Cost of Living. New York: Modern Library, 1999.

Power Politics. Cambridge, Mass.: South End Press, 2001.

War Talk. Cambridge, Mass.: South End Press, 2003.

CRITICAL AND BIOGRAPHICAL STUDIES

Abraham, Taisha. "An Interview with Arundhati Roy." *Ariel: A Review of International English Literature*, 29.1: 89–92 (January 1998). (Brief but informative discussion of the language debate in Indo-Anglian literature.)

Ahmad, Aijaz. "Reading Arundhati Roy Politically." *Frontline*, 8 August 1977, p. 101. (An oft-cited article on politics in Roy's novel.)

Bhatt, Indira, and Indira Nityanandam, eds. *Explorations: Arundhati Roy's* The God of Small Things. New Delhi: Creative, 1999. (Contains several lucid and informative essays among two dozen.)

Bing, Jonathan, et al. Review of *The Cost of Living. Publishers Weekly,* 20 September 1999. Pp. 61–62.

Boehmer, Elleke. "East Is East and South Is South: The Cases of Sarojini Naidu and Arundhati Roy." *Women: A Cultural Review,* 11.1–2: 61–70 (spring–summer 2000).

Bose, Brinda. "In Desire and in Death: Eroticism as Politics in Arundhati Roy's *The God of Small Things.*" *Ariel: A Review of International English Literature,* 29.2: 59–72 (April 1998). (Argues that "Roy's politics . . . exist in an erogenous zone; the erotics, however, are not totally divorced from the world of 'actual' politik.")

Buruma, Ian. "The Anti-American." *Outlookindia.com,* May 4, 2002. First appeared in the *New Republic,* 29 April 2002, p. 25. (Incisive review of *Power Politics* and Roy's political writing.)

Chew, Shirley. Review of *The God of Small Things. Times Literary Supplement,* 30 May 1997.

Dhawan, R. K., ed. *Arundhati Roy: The Novelist Extraordinary.* London: Sngam, 1999.

Dodiya, Jaydipsinh, and Joya Chakravarty, eds. *The Critical Studies of Arundhati Roy's* The God of Small Things. New Delhi: Atlantic, 1999. (Poorly edited volume with "Postcolonial Feminism" and "Fictions of Caste" being the only bright spots.)

Durix, Carole, and Jean-Pierre Durix, eds. *Reading Arundhati Roy's* The God of Small Things. Dijon, France: Editions Universitaires de Dijon, 2002.

Kakutani, Michiko. Review of *The God of Small Things. New York Times,* 3 June 1997, p. 20.

Mullaney, Julie. *Arundhati Roy's* The God of Small Things: *A Reader's Guide.* New York: Continuum, 2002. (Excellent discussion of Roy's place among postcolonial Indo-Anglian authors.)

Oumhani, Cécile. "Hybridity and Transgression in Arundhati Roy's *The God of Small Things.*" *Commonwealth Essays and Studies,* 22.2: 85–91 (spring 2000).

Pathak, R. S., ed. *The Fictional World of Arundhati Roy.* New Delhi: Creative, 2001. (Contains a number of highly critical articles.)

Pietiläinen, Petri, and Jopi Nyman, eds. "The American Dream as the Authentic Experience: The Reception and Marketing of Arundhati Roy as a Post-Colonial Indian Writer." *Text and Nation: Essays on Post-Colonial Cultural Politics.* Edited by Andrew

Blake. Joensuu, Finland: University of Joensuu, 2001. Pp. 103–125.

Sharma, R. S., and Shashi Bala Talwar. *Arundhati Roy's* The God of Small Things: *Critique and Commentary.* New Delhi: Creative, 1998. (The best book from an Indian press on the novel. Includes an informative overview of controversies.)

Sinha, Reeta. "What Makes Me an Expert on Arundhati Roy?" *Outlookindia.com,* 16 January 2002. (Critical and sometimes cheeky article on Roy's political writing.)

Tirhankar, Chandra. "Sexual/Textual Strategies in *The God of Small Things.*" *Commonwealth Essays and Studies,* 20.1: 38–44 (autumn 1997).

Updike, John. "Mother Tongues." *New Yorker,* 3 June 1997, pp. 156–159. (Calls Roy's novel a "Tiger-Woodsian debut.")

Salman Rushdie
(1947–)

PETER FILKINS

FOR ALMOST A quarter of a century Salman Rushdie has been a lightning rod for political controversy while also writing some of the most important and inventive novels published in English. Though his first novel, *Grimus* (1975), met with critical disdain and disappeared from the scene in a blaze of befuddlement, his second novel, *Midnight's Children,* published in 1981, is a postmodern classic. It was his fourth novel, however, that set Rushdie on the world stage, though ironically enough, the condemnation that greeted *The Satanic Verses* (1988) forced Rushdie to retreat into hiding for nearly a decade. The poster child for free speech, the articulate defender of the secular imagination in the face of fundamentalist edict, and the weary target of hatred and disdain from both East and West, Rushdie at times seems to have been swallowed whole by the "Rushdie Affair." Only through the effervescence of his fictive imagination and the clarity of his moral thought has he managed to survive as a writer, though the shadow of the controversy continues to haunt him.

Born in Bombay and educated in private English schools in both India and England, Rushdie has always straddled two worlds. Raised in a Muslim family devoid of a strict religious atmosphere, in numerous interviews he cites the cosmopolitan, multi-ethnic, Hindu, and secular world of Bombay as his most important influence, while the "idea of India" also granted Rushdie a deep love of "multiplicity" as a philosophical approach to life. "We have understood that each of us is many different people," he says in writing on "India's Fiftieth Anniversary," and adds, "The nineteenth-century concept of the integrated self has been replaced by this jostling crowd of 'I's. And yet, unless we are damaged, or deranged, we usually have a relatively clear sense of *who we are.* I agree with my many selves to call all of them 'me.' This is the best way to grasp the idea of India" (*Step Across This Line,* 2002, p. 163). As Saleem Sinai says in *Midnight's Children,* "I have been a swallower of lives; and to know me, just the one me, you'll have to swallow the lot as well" (p. 4). The same could be said of Rushdie.

Rushdie's embrasure of multiplicity, however, was radically challenged when his family moved to Karachi, Pakistan, in 1964. There he experienced firsthand the repressive atmosphere of Pakistan's theocracy and military government during his summers at home, causing him to later describe the partitioned country as a "peeling, fragmenting palimpsest, increasingly at war with itself. . . . a failure of the dreaming mind" (*Shame,* 1983, p. 92). After losing his own faith at age fifteen, Rushdie would increasingly see fundamentalist religion as the sworn enemy of free thought, a standoff later brought home to him through the Rushdie Affair. Though many of his characters long for spiritual grounding, and while Rushdie himself continues to value the role of belief and prayer in individual lives, dogma and orthodoxy represent, to his eyes, the death of public life. His entire output as a writer, in fact, can be seen as an effort to return to the multifarious and diverse roots of Bombay. For it is there in the Bombay of the fictive mind that he sees humanity's best hope in "hybridity, impurity, intermingling, the transformation that comes of new and unexpected combinations of human beings, cultures, ideas, politics, movies, songs" (*Imaginary Homelands,* 1992, p. 394).

"Home," however, became for Rushdie not only a place that he could not return to, but something which he no longer believes even exists. Writing about the movie of *The Wizard of Oz,* which Rushdie considers his first literary influence after seeing it as a ten-year-old in Bombay, he argues that "the real secret of the ruby slippers is not that 'there's no place like home' but rather that there is no longer any such place *as* home: except of course, for the home we make, or the homes that are made for us, in Oz, which is anywhere, and everywhere, except the place from which we began" (*Step Across This Line,* pp 29–30). Yet Rushdie does not see the loss of home as a disadvantage, but rather as a boon to the creative imagination. For twin to his passionate celebration of multiplicity has been his consistent advocacy of the state of migrancy as the quintessential mode of modern experience. He acknowledges that "when the writer who writes from outside India tries to reflect that world, he is obliged to deal in broken mirrors, some of whose fragments have been irretrievably lost," yet he is also quick to add, "But there is a paradox here. The broken mirror may actually be as valuable as the one which is supposedly unflawed" (*Imaginary Homelands,* pp. 10–11). Furthermore, Rushdie sees this experience as not only inherent to Indian

emigrant writers, but also to the human condition. Because "there is no longer any such place *as* home," our humanity is made common through the fact that "the past is a country from which we have all emigrated," whereas "the writer who is out-of-country and even out-of-language may experience this loss in an intensified form" (*Imaginary Homelands,* p. 12). Such loss, however, becomes our collective gain, for "the migrant is not simply transformed by his act; he also transforms his new world. Migrants may well become mutants, but it is out of such hybridization that newness can emerge" (*Imaginary Homelands,* p. 210).

Rushdie eventually reconfigured his thoughts on the migrant condition to include "the dream of leaving" as an archetype as powerful and valuable as "the dream of staying," even going so far as to say that "The most precious book I possess is my passport" (*Step Across This Line,* p. 367). Mary Karr reports that in a talk Rushdie gave at Syracuse University in March 2002, he declared, "The dream of staying has been incredibly privileged, because it relates to the idea of belonging, of roots, of nation, of tribe, of clan. All kinds of very important cultural constructs require us to think that staying put is a very good idea. . . . [But] the itch to leave home—the dream of away—is actually as important as the countervailing dream of home, though it gets much less cultural airtime" (*The Chronicle of Higher Education,* 13 September 2002). Similarly, Rushdie has praised "Over the Rainbow" as the "anthem of the world's migrants. . . . a grand paean to the uprooted self, a hymn—*the* hymn—to Elsewhere" (*Step Across This Line,* p. 13). This transforms migrancy from a condition into a cultural imperative, one that Rushdie's own life has both mirrored and fulfilled. But whether "the dream of leaving" is in the end a viable construct of reality is a question that runs through Rushdie's writing and much of his life. "This unbelonging—I think of it as *disorientation,* loss of the East—is my artistic country now," Rushdie observed in 1999 (*Step Across This Line,* p. 266), and one has to wonder what ultimate effect such a condition has on his creative psyche. Even Rushdie would agree that the literary value of his novels must in the end be the final arbiter of his contribution as a writer, no matter his profile as a defender of humanism and free speech.

ABRACADABRA

The newness that Rushdie brought into the world was made plain with the publication of *Midnight's Children* in 1981. Through the life of Saleem Sinai, born at the exact hour of India's independence in 1947, Rushdie launched a new era in postcolonial writing by creating a new type of language. At its heart was the hybrid, hotchpotch multiplicity of India's true nature, but in shaping a language to describe that nature Rushdie also seized hold of the colonizer's tongue and refashioned it as his own. Inspired by G. V. Desani's 1948 novel *All About H. Hatterr,* Rushdie sought to mimic the rhythms peculiar to Indian English in a way that gave the language credibility as a comic and creative tool. Whether it be Reverend Mother's repeated use of "whatsitsname" as a verbal tic, or Padma's complaint about Saleem's incessant need for "all this writing-shiting" (p. 21), or Saleem's compressed response of "ouchmynose" to his geography teacher's crazed tug on Saleem's nose while exclaiming "*thees* is human geography!" (p. 277), Rushdie's idiom revitalized English and was triumphant in handing back to the colonized the dignity and power of speech in a tongue that was recognizably their own.

This urge to reconstruct and refashion also spills over into Rushdie's narrative technique. In many interviews he has openly acknowledged his debt to writers such as Laurence Sterne, Günter Grass, Jorge Luis Borges, Italo Calvino, Franz Kafka, and Gabriel García Márquez, particularly for how they helped him to formulate a magic realism that would enable him to render the complexity of India's spiritual and historical reality. The breaking up of Saleem's

poor body, singular, unlovely, buffeted by too much history. . . . [crumbling] into (approximately) six hundred and thirty million particles of anonymous, and necessarily oblivious dust" (p. 37), corresponds to the partition of India at its founding, just as the ability of midnight's children to communicate telepathically depicts the unity and hope of the first generation born into independence. Allegory, however, can be a closed system of symbols. Rushdie is careful to question the automatic linkage fostered by allegory, for his anarchic narrative style is bent on fighting against such closed systems. As Saleem points out:

> Midnight's children can be made to represent many things, according to your point of view; they can be seen as the last throw of everything antiquated and retrogressive in our myth-ridden nation, whose defeat was entirely desirable in the context of a modernizing, twentieth-century economy; or as the true hope of freedom, which is now forever extinguished; but what they must not become is the bizarre creation of a rambling, diseased mind. No: illness is neither here nor there.
>
> (p. 240)

This last admonition springs from Saleem's worry that Padma thinks he is "cracking up" in more ways than one, particularly when he gets lost in what, to her, seem like numerous implausible tangents while telling his story. Saleem's insistence on intentionality, however, is itself another allegory. Behind it lies his own claim that, through communication with midnight's children, "I had entered into the illusion of the artist, and thought of the multitudinous realities of the land as the raw unshaped material of my gift" (p. 207). Hence, both Saleem and Rushdie make clear that the rambling, multidimensional nature of their storytelling is its own point while at the same time refusing to be pinned down to any single interpretation of it.

"Unreality is the only weapon with which reality can be smashed, so that it may subsequently be reconstructed," writes Rushdie in *Imaginary Homelands* (p. 122). In an early interview he explains that "*Midnight's Children* was partly conceived as an opportunity to break away from the manner in which India had been written about in English, not just by Indian writers but by Western writers as well" (quoted in James Harrison's *Salman Rushdie*, p. 4). In this manner, Rushdie's aim is as much political as it is aesthetic. By reshaping the novel about India, he seeks to reshape India's reality as well, for throughout his career Rushdie has maintained that "reality is an artefact, that it does not exist until it is made, and that, like any other artefact, it can be made well or badly, and that it can also, of course, be unmade" (*Imaginary Homelands*, p. 280).

Nor is this a mere philosophical trope when it comes to Rushdie's fiction. Saleem's warning that "to understand me, you'll have to swallow a world" (p. 458) also carries with it the assumption of his own ability to interpret, and thus shape the world we are meant to swallow. "Who what am I?" asks Saleem in his unique breathless rhythm. "My answer: I am the sum total of everything that went before me, of all I have been seen done, of everything done-to-me. I am everyone everything whose being-in-the-world affected was affected by mine. I am anything that happens after I've gone which would not have happened if I had not come" (p. 457). Thus Saleem is India and India is Saleem, an equation posited by Rushdie in order to undermine the hegemony of an Indian government that during the 1975 Emergency declares that "*Indira is India and India is Indira*" (p. 509). By extension, then, so too is Rushdie, or at a minimum, *Midnight's Children* seeks to not only represent, but also embody and make real the India found within its pages. "Abracadabra" is the name of the "special blend" of chutney Saleem makes in Mary Pereira's pickle factory (p. 548), and through the "chutnification" of language, history, and myth, both Saleem and Rushdie strive to give India "shape and form—that is to say, meaning" (p. 550).

The same cannot be said for Pakistan, for there Rushdie finds that the multifarious and shape-changing nature of reality is the first victim "in a country where truth is what it is instructed to be" (*Midnight's Children*, p. 389). Rushdie explores this bleak condition further in his 1983 novel, *Shame*, a book that stands in stark contrast to *Midnight's Children*. As James Harrison points out in *Salman Rushdie*, "The whole atmosphere in *Shame* is . . . the antithesis of the inclusiveness that characterizes most of *Midnight's Children*. From the multiple, muddled, all-embracing world of a thousand and one stories about a thousand and one children . . . —that is, from an inclusive Hindu world—we have moved to the embittered, rejecting world of Islam" (pp. 87–88). Rushdie's satire of the Pakistani regime is scathing to say the least, so much so that throughout the book he can hardly restrain himself from entering directly into the narrative. This occurs in only a couple of places in *Midnight's Children*, most subtly when one hears Rushdie's own voice delivering Saleem's conclusion, "We must live, I'm afraid, with the shadows of imperfection" (p. 548). By contrast, in *Shame* the author steps front and center when he informs us:

> The country in this story is not Pakistan, or not quite. There are two countries, real and fictional, occupying the same space, or almost the same space. My story, my fictional country exist, like myself, at a slight angle to reality. I have found this off-centering to be necessary; but its value is, of course, open to debate. My view is that I am not writing only about Pakistan.
>
> (pp. 23–24)

Though this sounds like a passage from an introduction to the novel, it is woven into the novel itself. In his effort to reveal "what-must-on-no-account-be-known, namely the impossible verity that barbarism could grow in cultured soil, that savagery could lie concealed beneath decency's well-pressed shirt" (p. 219), the depth of Rushdie's outrage is measured by the distance he keeps from his characters while at the same time injecting himself more directly into the narrative. The thug dictator, Raza Hyder, and the corrupt politician, Iskander Harappa, seem more like stick figures than like live human beings, but the narrator's meditations give vent to a deeper consciousness. "I, too, like all migrants, am a fantasist," writes Rushdie as the revealed narrator. "I build imaginary countries and try to impose them on the ones that exist" (p. 92). To the degree that this happens out of his moral ire, the novel works as a powerful indictment of Pakistan while also functioning as a protest against rigidity and oppression everywhere. Yet, as James Harrison observes,

> No longer are we playing games with a narrator of great charm but dubious reality. It is all too clear who and what is being satirized, who and what we are to disapprove of. . . . When Saleem indulges in such pontifications in *Midnight's Children*, the reader is usually invited to take them with a pinch of irony. By choosing to speak so clearly and confidently in his own voice in *Shame*, however, Rushdie exposes himself to the danger of taking himself more seriously than he would a surrogate
>
> (*Salman Rushdie*, p. 81)

The result illustrates Rushdie's own imposing will when it comes to matters of tyranny, a conviction that would not only cause *Shame* to be banned in Pakistan, but set the stage for Rushdie's own life-and-death drama.

SNAKES AND LADDERS

Rushdie's achievement has always carried with it a kind of double edge. Because of his English schooling and his move to Britain in the 1960s, many critics have been sensitive to his status as a cosmopolitan writer, even going so far as to accuse him of depicting the East through the same stereotypes created by the West. Writing about Rushdie's affinity for cartoon-like characters, Timothy Brennan notes in *Salman Rushdie and the Third World*, "Characterisation in any conventional sense barely exists—only a collection of brilliantly sketched cartoons woven together by an intellectual argument. . . . His novels, in short, are metafictions, and their range of interest neo-colonial. That is, they are novels about Third-World novels" (pp. 84–85). While Brennan sees this as an interesting aspect to Rushdie's fiction that complicates his role and place in postcolonial literature, other critics sometimes bristle at Rushdie's razor-sharp satire. D. C. R. A. Goonetilleke sums up an aspect that troubles many a reader, particularly in the East, when he admits, "Rushdie does seem too ready to present his compatriots of yesterday as mindless, illogical, brutal, bloody and boorish. There is hardly any attempt to communicate *understanding* to the reader" (*Salman Rushdie*, p. 149).

This side of Rushdie has generally been credited to his supposed "arrogance." Some see the source of his brand of satire as a postcolonial writer attempting to subvert, if not reinvent, the fictional modes handed to him through the distortions and simplifications imposed on India by the colonial mind. Others see Rushdie as merely a postmodern novelist more attached to the West than to the East, his novels representing attempts to establish his cleverness or escape from the world he has left behind. Since *The Satanic Verses*, Rushdie has become the clarion voice for secular pluralism and free speech opposed to what he has posited as the backwardness and fundamentalism gripping much of the East through Islam. His insistence on the importance of his cause, however, as well as his refusal to cease criticizing the West for its racist attitudes toward the Third World, has also led to accusations of arrogance from the very societies whose underlying principles of freedom and multiplicity he passionately defends. At times Rushdie has found himself between a rock and a hard place, a man without a country, reviled by many from the world he has tried to give voice to while clinging to the life raft of his own cause.

One could argue that, sadly enough, Rushdie seems to be a writer born for such trouble.

Beneath his advocacy for more open societies, and behind his love of the multiplicity and "hotchpotch" of Bombay, is a vision that holds "duality" at the center of life's real grounding. This view is captured in a passage of *Midnight's Children* in which Saleem muses about his love of the board game Snakes and Ladders:

> All games have morals; and the game of Snakes and Ladders captures, as no other activity can hope to do, the eternal truth that for every ladder you climb, a snake is waiting just around the corner; and for every snake, a ladder will compensate. But it's more than that; no mere carrot-and-stick affair; because implicit in the game is the unchanging twoness of things, the duality of up against down, good against evil; the solid rationality of ladders balances the occult sinuosities of the serpent; in the opposition of staircase and cobra we can see, metaphorically, all conceivable oppositions. . . .

> (p. 167)

All of this would seem well and fine as a model of spiritual life or even fiction, but Saleem points out the hitch in Snakes and Ladders as a metaphor for daily life when he admits later in the same passage, "I found, very early in my life, that the game lacked one crucial dimension, that of ambiguity."

Rushdie discovered this for himself with the issue of the *fatwa* by Iran's Ayatollah Khomeini in February of 1989 calling for his death as a blasphemer against Islam because of his depiction of the prophet Muhammad in the *Satanic Verses*. Though the situation soon turned into the high-profile contest of ideas characteristic of his own fiction, in reality it also became a deadly serious matter for both Rushdie and East-West relations. For Rushdie, the situation was clear. "Those who oppose the novel most vociferously today," he wrote in 1990, "are of the opinion that intermingling with a different culture will inevitably weaken and ruin their own. I am of the opposite opinion. . . . *The Satanic Verses* is for change-by-fusion, change-by-joining. It is a love-song to our mongrel selves" (*Imaginary Homelands,* p. 394). Ironically, Rushdie's target

in his "love-song to our mongrel selves" was no longer the colonial mentality, but a powerful force from within his own culture. This also made his satire of Muhammad and Khomeini seem much more volatile to those who were insulted by it, for rather than coming from the historical racism of the West, it was generated by what they saw as an act of betrayal by one of their own. Though Rushdie felt he had simply climbed another rung on the ladder of his own artistic development, he awoke one morning to find himself riding the back of a snake.

Srinivas Aravamudan points out the potential harm posed by Rushdie's satire when in "Being God's Postman Is No Fun, Yaar" he writes:

> Many of those who have risen to Rushdie's defence . . . have done so in the name of essentialized versions of Literature, Free Speech, Criticism, Democracy, the West, or Islam; and often these appeals are deemed to have a universally critical and metasocial function. I will argue, however, that a careful reading of Rushdie's book precludes the defence of satire within such terms; a secular defence-initiative, like the Strategic Defense Initiative, could be used as a tactical offensive weapon. Defending satire of a longstanding historical and cultural "other" of the West, such as Islam, can very easily . . . serve the function of insulting and frightening the adversary, ultimately doing the ideological work of cultural imperialism.

> (*Reading Rushdie,* M. D. Fletcher, ed., p. 189)

In response to this charge, Rushdie insisted on the "fictionality of fiction" (*Imaginary Homelands,* p. 393), but the trouble is that from the very start of his career Rushdie has insisted on the ability of fictions to shape *reality.* Even in *The Satanic Verses* he sees the potential hubris that he risks when, as narrator, he muses, "A man who sets out to make himself up is taking on the Creator's role, according to one way of seeing things; he's unnatural, a blasphemer, an abomination of abominations. From another angle, you could see pathos in him, heroism in his struggle, in his willingness to risk: not all mutants survive" (p. 49). What was lost amid the hullabaloo of the Affair is that this is said of

Saladin Chamcha, a character who has tried to remake himself as an Englishman but failed, mostly at the hands of England's racism. By the end of *The Satanic Verses* he returns to India and his dying father, regaining along the way a sense of continuity he no longer thought he had, but which has become his own as a result of "*selected* discontinuities, a *willing* re-invention" (p. 427).

Politics, indeed, often lacks "one crucial dimension, that of ambiguity." One of the ironies of Rushdie's career is that his situation has also demanded that he enter the realm of politics in order both to keep his cause visible and to seek a positive resolution to it. This, too, has caused him to sacrifice ambiguity at times, for whereas his novels may be characterized as fictions interspersed with ideas, the latter of which are then subject to modification and irony through plot twists, characterization, and unreliable narrators, his essays and editorials are by definition much more direct espousals of ideas. While this has helped Rushdie articulate the importance of free speech and secular inquiry like few others have had to do before, it has also at times revealed a surprising, dare one say "fundamentalist" side to a writer opposed to the same. Writing in 1997 about the growing predominance of religion worldwide, Rushdie states, "To choose unbelief is to choose mind over dogma, to trust in our humanity instead of all these dangerous divinities." Later in the same essay he adds, "To my mind religion, even at its most sophisticated, essentially infantilizes our ethical selves by setting infallible moral Arbiters and irredeemably immoral Tempters above us. . . . (*Step Across This Line*, pp. 143–144). One could imagine the same spoken by Jean-Paul Sartre, but from Rushdie's mouth such words take on a special tone, one heightened in his response to the terrorist attacks of 2001, when he writes, "If terrorism is to be defeated, the world of Islam must take on board the secularist-humanist principles on which the modern is based, and without which their countries' freedom will remain a distant dream" (ibid., p. 341).

One would be hard pressed to quibble with Rushdie's passionate defense of humanist values, but when he continues to insist that the real game at stake is Art vs. Islam, some amount of air is sucked out of his argument. In his Tanner Lectures on Human Values, delivered at Yale University in 2002, Rushdie asks, "And now, in the aftermath of horror, of the iconoclastically transgressive image-making of the terrorists, do artists and writers still have the right to insist on the supreme, unfettered freedoms of art?" (*Step Across This Line*, p. 379). Unsurprisingly, his response is that artists have not only the right, but also the responsibility. Yet there is something too insistent about the question. "*WHAT KIND OF IDEA ARE YOU?*" asks the satirical poet Baal in one of Gibreel Farishta's dreams (*The Satanic Verses*, p. 335), and at times Rushdie himself has risked seeming more an idea than a writer. "I admit the dilemma," he writes on the tenth anniversary of the *fatwa*:

> Ignore the politics (which I'd love to do), and my silence must look enforced or fearful. Speak, and I risk deafening the world to those utterances, my books, written in my true language, the language of literature. I risk helping to conceal the real Salman behind the smoky, sulfurous Rushdie of the Affair. I have led two lives: one blighted by hatred and caught up in this dire business, which I'm trying to leave behind, and the life of a free man, freely doing his work. Two lives, but none I can afford to lose, for one loss would end both.
>
> (*Step Across This Line*, p. 265)

ALL YOU NEED IS LOVE

Another reason that Rushdie has been criticized in the East is that, despite creating a language that seeks to give expression to those who were denied it under colonialism, his fiction has failed to offer a vision that replaces the colonized one he undermines. In *Cultural Imperialism and the Indo-English Novel*, Fawzia Afzal-Khan writes, "Rushdie, by refusing to mythologize history in his first three novels, successfully avoided historical petrification. However, this debunking of myth, and of the other genres used by him, could finally be construed as a failure on his part to construct a viable alternative ideology. . . . [P]erhaps because of the surreal nature of his own predicament, he is unable to quite fully rehabilitate the genre of myth in a fashion that could provide a viable solution to the historicity of the postcolonial impasse" (p. 175). Rushdie would certainly counter that any such ideology runs the risk of the reductive categorization inherent to racist attitudes, whereas "from the very experience of uprooting, disjuncture and metamorphosis (slow or rapid, painful or pleasurable) that is the migrant condition . . . can be derived a metaphor for all humanity" (*Imaginary Homelands,* p. 394). This expansiveness is further supported by what Rushdie sees as the culminating end to secular pluralism, namely the acceptance and dignity of love versus the denigration and violence imbued through hate. Rushdie implies this as an end for writing itself when he draws an analogy between Saleem's thirty pickle jars and the same number of chapters "chutnified" in *Midnight's Children* as Saleem hopes, "One day, perhaps, the world may taste the pickles of history. They may be too strong for some palates, their smell may be overpowering, tears may rise to eyes; I hope nevertheless that it will be possible to say of them that they possess the authentic taste of truth . . . that they are, despite everything, acts of love" (p. 550).

Yet nowhere in Rushdie are we given a portrait of mature, sustained love. In the reconciliation between Saladin Chamcha and his father at the end of *The Satanic Verses* there is great tenderness, but with the death of the father the relationship comes to an end. Moraes Zogoiby, the narrator of *The Moor's Last Sigh* (1995), falls hopelessly in love with Uma Sarasvati, and even goes so far as to link Rushdie's belief in the migrant condition with the beauty of love when he says, "I wanted to cling to the image of love as the blending of spirits, as mélange, as the triumph of the impure, mongrel, conjoining best of us over what there is in us of

the solitary, the isolated, the austere, the dogmatic, the pure; of love as democracy, as the victory of the no-man-is-an-island, two's-company Many over the clean, mean, apartheiding Ones" (p. 289). However, Uma tries to murder "the Moor," and it is betrayal that remains the modus operandi of all the relationships in the novel. In fact, given that *The Moor's Last Sigh* is in many ways a rewrite of *Midnight's Children*, it is interesting that Moraes is betrayed by his parents as well, whereas in the earlier novel parents tended to play inept, even slightly corrupt, but nonetheless loving roles.

Saleem and Padma in *Midnight's Children* represent the most sustained relationship of romantic love in Rushdie's novels, but theirs is a highly allegorical union. Padma, the "lotus goddess" whose name means "The One Who Possesses Dung" (p. 21), sits at Saleem's elbow, "bullying [him] back into the world of linear narrative, the universe of what-happened-next" (p. 38). Mothering him, feeding him, calling for the doctor when worried about him "cracking up," she eventually proposes marriage, her love perhaps being the "cabbalistic formula, some awesome abracadabra" capable of releasing Saleem from his fate, though even he concedes that "Love does not conquer all, except in the Bombay talkies" (p. 530). The novel ends with an image of Saleem's dissolution among India's vast numbers, though paradoxically there is also the hope and expectation that he and Padma will soon marry. That hope, however, is a philosophical one, for as a symbol of pedestrian reality, versus Saleem's mythic undertaking in the telling of his story, Padma represents "what is" while Saleem strives for "what might be." Their union, if successful or even possible, would be the culmination of Rushdie's project, namely the wedding of the diurnal and the mytho-poetic, of the real and the ideal, of the mundane and the magical in a symbiotic relationship that would allow each to flourish in the other's eyes.

Such a "state" is the providence of love at its most nourishing and supportive best, but hardly can such a model serve a "state" or nation, though Rushdie would seem to argue otherwise. Even the "state of love" attained by Saleem and Padma would seem a false one, for rather than a genuine love interest, Padma serves most of all as a stand-in for the reader. Her urge to know "what-happened-next" is our own as readers. We may possess more sophistication than she does in our ability to analyze and even second-guess the tale itself, but we are no less the targets of Rushdie's urge to seduce and transform through his hybrid vision.

Aurora's use of the Moor as a subject for her painting in *The Moor's Last Sigh* corresponds to the potential sway Rushdie holds over us as readers and reveals his own awareness of this problem:

> There was no stopping her. Around and about the figure of the Moor in his hybrid fortress she wove her vision, which in fact was a vision of *weaving*, or more accurately interweaving. In a way these were polemical pictures, in a way they were an attempt to create a romantic myth of the plural, hybrid nation . . . of the present, and the future, that she hoped would evolve. So, yes, there was a didacticism here, but what with the vivid surrealism of her images and the kingfisher brilliance of her colouring and the dynamic acceleration of her brush, it was easy not to feel preached at, to revel in the carnival without listening to the barker, to dance to the music without caring for the message in the song.
>
> (p. 227)

As Catherine Cundy observes in *Salman Rushdie*, "The arrogance of the creative artist, which is arguably necessary, and the sincere political beliefs of the individual man often appear in conflict and at best reside in uneasy compromise with each other" (p. 11). Given the messianic and willful control that the above passage confesses to in the pursuit of "a romantic myth of the plural, hybrid nation," it is clear that Rushdie is aware of such uneasy compromise being the more likely, if not more complex, relation formulated by reader and nation alike rather than the fuzzier notion of

universal love which he sometimes latches onto when all else fails.

Rushdie's most tender book, *Haroun and the Sea of Stories* (1990), contains another sustained relationship of love, though again it is filial in nature. The noble effort of the boy Haroun to save his father, Rashid, and cleanse the Sea of Stories of the pollution dumped into it by the evil Prince of Silence, Khattam-Shud, is a delightful tale that reads as a transparent allegory of Rushdie's own struggle against the Ayatollah Khomeini and the "silence" imposed through the *fatwa*. The idealism inherent in the Guppees' cause links to Rushdie's notion about love as an end in itself when Mali the Floating Gardener makes clear King Bolo's motivation in rescuing Princess Batcheat from the Citadel of Chup: "It is Love. . . . It is all for Love. Which is a wonderful and dashing matter. But which can also be a very foolish thing" (p. 121). Indeed, what Haroun wins in saving the Sea of Stories is not only the restoration of his father's talent for telling stories, but also the return of his mother, Soraya, after she reconsiders her affair with the clerk Sengupta. By restoring the flow of stories Haroun also restores reality, since, as the Water Genie observes, "To give a thing a name, a label, a handle; to rescue it from anonymity, to pluck it out of the Place of Namelessness, in short to identify it—well, that's a way of bringing the said thing into being" (p. 63). The novel also infers, however, that by restoring "reality" Haroun also restores his "home." At the end of the book the world of the Guppees is left behind as Rashid and Haroun return to the dreary world of Kahani. His mother having returned, Haroun realizes, "I honestly don't need to go anywhere at all" (p. 211). But this is a fairytale, thus implying that this is not how things usually work out in reality. It is also a sentiment that flies in the face of Rushdie's more recent support of "the dream of leaving," as well as his contention that Kansas is a boring, washed-out place Dorothy rightly wishes to flee. Haroun may charm us with his courageous effort to save the Sea of Stories and secure familial love, but in

Rushdie's extended oeuvre such longing for stability is an aberration rather than the norm.

In fact, flight has become the central theme of Rushdie's most recent fiction, for both *The Ground Beneath Her Feet* (1999) and *Fury* (2001) present characters possessed of an inescapable urge to flee family, home, and mature, adult love. In both of these books Rushdie links his earlier celebration of hybridity and fragmentation with what he sees as the inevitable trials and disappointments of love. In *The Ground Beneath Her Feet,* for instance, the narrator Rai reflects on the tumultuous relationship between the singer Vina Apsara and her high school sweetheart and fellow musician, Ormus Cama:

> No, this is a story of a deep but unstable love, one of breakages and reunions; a love of endless overcoming, defined by the obstacles it must surmount, beyond which greater travails lie. A hurdler's love. The forking, fissured paths of uncertainty, the twisted mazes of suspicion and betrayal, the plunging low road of death itself: along these ways it goes. This is human love.
>
> (p. 322)

Indeed, the novel supports this view through the sprawling tale of Vina and Ormus's inability to escape the imprisonment of fame and live together as husband and wife. "Freedom to Reject is the only freedom. Freedom to uphold is dangerous. Life is elsewhere. Cross frontiers. Fly away" (p. 146), muses Rai, and it is clear that Vina and Ormus share his vision, however helplessly. "Home," with its corresponding stability, is not only something that never existed; in a perverse manner it becomes the enemy in Rushdie's later fiction. It is as if after having suffered a decade of enforced homelessness at the hands of the *fatwa,* as well as forty years of migrancy since leaving Bombay for England and school in the early 1960s, Rushdie has chosen not only to embrace his condition, but also to turn it into a supreme ideal whose counterpart of stability and staying is anathema if only because it is an option no longer available to him.

The underlying bitterness of this vision is confirmed by Malik Solanka in *Fury.* A historian of ideas born in Bombay who, like Rushdie, leaves England after many years to move to New York, Malik comes "to America as so many before him to receive the benison of being Ellis Islanded, of starting over," though in his case this also involves an urge to have his past erased. "Give me a name, America," he asks, "make of me a Buzz or Chip or Spike. Bathe me in amnesia and clothe me in your powerful unknowing. Enlist me in your J. Crew and hand me my mouse ears! No longer a historian but a man without histories let me be" (p. 51). What possesses Malik in the Land of the Free, however, is the latent, if not manifest fury of a country guilty of greed and overconsumption inhabited by a society powerless to change it, a place where "people were stressed-out, cracking up, and talking about it all day long in superstrings of moron cliché" (p. 115). It would be one thing if the narrator were to comment on such desperation with irony or nostalgia, but instead both Rushdie and Malik turn their disorientated condition into a full-blown vision of life:

> Life is fury, he'd thought. Fury—sexual, Oedipal, political, magical, brutal—drives us to our finest heights and coarsest depths. Out of the *furia* comes creation, inspiration, originality, passion, but also violence, pain, pure unafraid destruction, the giving and receiving of blows from which we never recover. The Furies pursue us; Shiva dances his furious dance to create and also destroy. But never mind about gods! . . . This is what we are, what we civilize ourselves to disguise—the terrifying human animal in us, the exalted, transcendent, self-destructive, untrammeled lord of creation. We raise each other to the heights of joy. We tear each other limb from fucking limb.
>
> (p. 31)

The duality of creation and destruction has always been at the heart of Rushdie's fiction.

But part of the darkness involved here is that such a vision, rather than seeing the world as potentially magical, posits it as a sham. One wonders to what degree Rushdie's own homelessness has come to seem to him the only lens through which to view the world. At the end of *Fury,* the disillusioned Malik returns to England to spy on his son and former wife together with her new man in a park. The fury that erupts in Malik is understandably "awful and immense, a roar from the Inferno, the cry of the tormented and the lost" (p. 259), but the problem comes when Rushdie wishes to turn it into a universal condition based solely on his own personal experience of displacement and loss. This seems especially indulgent when, at the very same time, he continues to advocate the major catalyst for such loss, namely the human urge for flight. Malik calls out to his son Asmaan while bouncing in a children's bouncy castle in the park, the book closing on the picture of the son's "only true father taking flight like a bird, to live in the great blue vault of the only heaven in which he had ever been able to believe" (p. 259), a statement and a condition which remains true for Rushdie as well.

IMPORTANCE AND INFLUENCE

One wonders what kind of novelist Rushdie would have become had the affair over *The Satanic Verses* never occurred. While the opaque system of allusions that made up his first novel *Grimus* could hardly have predicted the inventive brilliance of *Midnight's Children,* the latter also remains unmatched in its achievement. *Shame* is a fine and biting satire, perhaps the best political allegory of its generation, and *The Satanic Verses* is also formally ambitious in its mixing of realism and fantasy by alternating narrative chapters with those that record Gibreel's dreams. *Haroun and the Sea of Stories* showed that it is possible to write a children's story that also speaks to adults, as did George Orwell's *Animal Farm.* But after these, all of which were written or at least begun before Rushdie was

forced into hiding, there is a real dropping off. It is as if, quite understandably, if not sadly, Rushdie has had to write in a vacuum, such that the subject of his novels has become Salman Rushdie trying to figure out how to write a novel rather than the story and characters themselves.

Malik Solanka gives voice to this very problem at the end of *Fury.* A maker of philosophical dolls whose invention becomes a worldwide hit and marketing nightmare, Solanka is horrified when a coup takes place in a province of India, led by rebels who seem to have modeled themselves on Solanka's dolls and his personal relations, such that:

The masks of his life circled him sternly, judging him. He closed his eyes and the masks were still there, whirling. He bowed his head before their verdict. He had wished to be a good man, to lead a good man's life, but the truth was that he hadn't been able to hack it. As Eleanor [Malik's wife] had said, he had betrayed those whose only crime was to have loved him. When he had attempted to retreat from his darker self, the self of his dangerous fury, hoping to overcome his faults by a process of renunciation, of *giving up,* he had merely fallen into new, more grievous error. Seeking his redemption in creation, offering up an imagined world, he had seen its denizens move out into the world and grow monstrous; and the greatest monster of them all wore his own guilty face.

(p. 246)

While there is immense pathos in this passage if it is read as a transparent statement about Rushdie's own beleaguered state after a long road of sacrifice and affliction, Malik also ends up only a puppet or doll standing in for Rushdie himself. Many a character has such a relation to his or her creator, but the problem in *Fury* is that Malik is never fully realized as a character in his own right. Rushdie's talent as a magic realist has never allowed him to develop characters who live and breathe in a realistic manner. Even though the realism of his later novels captures the artificial reality of a postmodern world of shallow fame and mass consumerism, his characters are more like ideas than people, while his narrators and protagonists seem only to have experienced the world on terms specific to Rushdie himself. Again, the same can be said of many a novel, but in the case of Rushdie, his life has been so unique and so much a myth unto itself, that it becomes difficult to read the novels as anything other than a window into Rushdie's own circumstances rather than a metaphorical reflection of the world at large.

Now that he has gradually been able to come out of hiding, we can only hope that Rushdie finds a way to engage more immediately with the societies and characters he writes about. His newfound love of New York and America would seem to provide him with fresh material for his fiction, though neither *The Ground Beneath Her Feet* nor *Fury* has paid off in this way. One of the reasons why, perhaps, is that America is not a land that holds a set of myths shared by all. There are many political myths, such as the idea of the melting pot, manifest destiny, self-reliance, or the self-made man, that have been rich resources of fictional critique and satire from Melville to Fitzgerald, Hemingway to Bellow. But what does not exist is a set of tales similar to the rich tradition of Hinduism and Islam, and which Rushdie spent the better part of his early career tapping into and reconfiguring in order to create a new order of myth for the East. While he has never created a completely viable vision or ideology that could replace the remnant colonialism he revealed or the fundamentalism he condemned, he nonetheless had material to work with that his Eastern audience shared and that the West wished to learn more about. America, while a kind of myth in itself, offers no Shiva or Kali or Muhammad as backdrop for the stories that Rushdie wishes to reinvent in order to demonstrate their relevance for today.

There is no question, however, that Rushdie remains one of the major novelists of his generation and is well-deserving of the attention and praise granted his work after winning the Booker Prize (1981), the Whitbread Prize (1988), and France's prestigious Commandeur dans l'Ordre des Artes et des Lettres (1999), among others. Given the troubled rift between East and West and the calamitous events that have erupted from such division, Rushdie would seem poised to write the great novel of these troubled times. Even a return to the magic realism of *Midnight's Children* could well serve the unique position he holds as a writer who understands the East, is unafraid to criticize the flaws of the West, and can parody and debunk misconceptions forwarded by each. Such a work could also continue the breakthrough that Rushdie has brought to fiction, namely a use of language that captures the way in which English has been used by colonized peoples and migrants in order to shape their reality rather than be victimized by it. In addition, Rushdie's mythic imagination has the ability to draw upon the past in order to help us understand the present in much the same way that novels such as Günter Grass's *The Tin Drum* or Gabriel García Márquez's *One Hundred Years of Solitude* did for their own cultures. *Midnight's Children* already accomplished this feat for India, and in a more troubled manner *Shame* did the same for Pakistan. But though Rushdie continues to articulate the ideas of migrancy as the principle metaphor of the early twenty-first century, only *The Satanic Verses* has spoken to this condition extensively, and only then within a British-Indian colonial context. Now that Rushdie's own migrancy has extended further to New York, and now that much of the world seems poised to continue its own transformation through displacement or upheaval, the time would seem ripe for Rushdie to attempt a kind of global fiction that could capture both his moment and our own.

In an interview conducted in 1994 at the time of the publication of *East, West*, a collection of his short fiction, Rushdie claimed that "the most important part of the title was the comma. Because it seems to me that I am that comma—or at least that I live in the comma" (quoted in D. C. R. A. Goonetilleke's *Salman Rushdie*, p. 131). Indeed, as Goonetilleke goes on to point out, the collection itself reflects Rushdie's "understanding of separate but connected worlds" (p. 131). Because some of the stories are set in the East, and some derive from his later migration to the West, such a fusion makes sense when looking at the shape of the entire book. However, Rushdie has yet to accomplish such a fusion in a novel, though he remains the best candidate to do so. In works such as *Midnight's Children* and *Haroun and the Sea of Stories,* he has already fused Western magic realism with Eastern storytelling, while also creating an English that fuses the tongues of colonizer and colonized alike. But if the globalization of reality, myth, and storytelling has evolved through the media, movies, and modern life, Rushdie possesses the talent to render it.

Or simply inspire it. Though there are not many novelists who have been directly influenced by Rushdie, his prominence has certainly allowed many writers to gain visibility, as well as to feel a certain legitimacy in speaking from a world stage rather than just to their own cultures. Indian writers such as Vikram Seth, Rohinton Mistry, Amitav Ghosh, and Arundhati Roy have gained wide attention largely because Rushdie put postcolonial literature on the map. As an essayist and reviewer, Rushdie also continues as a passionate and eloquent spokesman for free speech and the values of pluralism and humanism. In this role he has also written on writers of many different cultures, thus providing readers with a way to see connections between major writers of our time. Finally, as a commentator and columnist sensitive to the best and worst of both sides of the cultural divide, he shares a valuable (if at times flawed) perspective, one able to raise impertinent and uncomfortable questions that might otherwise be ignored, but which Rushdie remains attuned to as the perpetual outsider.

"I am the bomb in Bombay, watch me explode," says Saleem Sinai on the last page of *Midnight's Children* before he goes on to conclude that "it is the privilege and the curse of midnight's children to be both masters and victims of their times, to forsake privacy and be sucked into the annihilating whirlpool of the multitudes, and to be unable to live or die in peace" (p. 552). As a young novelist working part-time in an ad agency while trying to write a second novel after the failure of his first, Salman Rushdie could have hardly known how portentous these words would prove to be. Perhaps more than any other living writer, he has been an artist who both has been shaped by our time and continues to shape how we read our time through him. This duality alone makes him unique among his peers, while the invention and nuance of his best work has helped to open and expand our appreciation of the East and West alike. That he has paid a great price for his efforts is unfortunate, even tragic. That he has done so with such conviction and authority is a benefit and privilege granted to us all.

Selected Bibliography

WORKS OF SALMAN RUSHDIE

FICTION

Grimus. London: Gollancz, 1975; New York: The Overlook Press, 1979; Penguin, 1991.

Midnight's Children. London: Jonathan Cape, 1981; New York: Knopf, 1981. (The 1991 Penguin edition is cited in this essay.)

Shame. London: Jonathan Cape, 1983; New York: Knopf, 1983. (The 1989 Vintage International edition is cited in this essay.)

The Satanic Verses. London: Viking, 1988; New York: Viking, 1989.

Haroun and the Sea of Stories. London and New York: Granta Books/Penguin, 1990.

The Moor's Last Sigh. London: Jonathan Cape, 1995; New York: Pantheon, 1995.

The Ground Beneath Her Feet. New York: Henry Holt, 1999.

Fury. New York: Random House, 2001.

East, West. London: Jonathan Cape, 1994; New York: Pantheon, 1994.

NONFICTION

The Jaguar Smile: A Nicaraguan Journey. London and New York: Viking, 1987.

Imaginary Homelands: Essays and Criticism 1981–1991. London and New York: Granta Books/Penguin, 1992.

Step Across This Line: Collected Non-fiction, 1992–2002. New York: Random House, 2002.

The Wizard of Oz. London: British Film Institute, 1992.

SECONDARY WORKS

Afzal-Khan, Fawzia. *Cultural Imperialism and the Indo-English Novel.* University Park, Pa.: Pennsylvania State University Press, 1993. (Important study of the novels of R. K. Narayan, Anita Desai, Kamala Markandaya, and Rushdie and the ideologies found within their work.)

Appignanesi, Lisa and Sara Maitland, eds. *The Rushdie File.* New York: Syracuse University Press, 1990. (Collects articles on and responses to the Rushdie Affair from around the world.)

Ashcroft, Bill, Gareth Griffiths, and Helen Tiffin, eds. *The Empire Writes Back: Theory and Practice in Post-Colonial Literatures.* London and New York: Routledge, 1989. (An important study of the way that postcolonial writers such as Rushdie have shaped English narratives on their own terms.)

Bhabha, Homi K., ed. *Nation and Narration.* London and New York: Routledge, 1990. (Contains essays on the concept of the nation and who speaks for it, including Bhabha's analysis of *The Satanic Verses* in "DissemiNation: Time, Narrative, and the Margins of the Modern Nation.")

Booker, M. Keith, ed. *Critical Essays on Salman Rushdie.* New York, G. K. Hall, 1999. (Collects essays on Rushdie's writing up through *The Moor's Last Sigh.*)

Braziller, George, ed. *For Rushdie.* New York: Braziller, 1993. (Essays by Arab and Muslim writers in support of Rushdie during the Affair.)

Brennan, Timothy. *Salman Rushdie and the Third World: Myths of the Nation.* New York: St. Martin's, 1989. (Examines the tension between cosmopolitan writers and de-colonization movements with Rushdie as a prime focus of discussion.)

Chauhan, Pradyumna S., ed. *Salman Rushdie Interviews: A Sourcebook of His Ideas.* Westport, Conn.: Greenwood Press, 2001. (Collects important interviews with Rushdie from 1981 to 1999.)

Clark, Roger Y. *Stranger Gods: Salman Rushdie's Other Worlds.* Montreal and Kingston, Canada: McGill-Queen's University Press, 2001. (Examines the role of myths and mysticism in Rushdie's fiction.)

Cohn-Sherbok, Dan, ed. *The Salman Rushdie Controversy in Interreligious Perspective.* Lewiston, NY: Mellen Press, 1990.

Cronin, Richard. *Imagining India.* New York: St. Martin's, 1989. (Looks at the struggle of postcolonial writers to capture the complexity of Indian society and history.)

Cundy, Catherine. *Salman Rushdie.* Manchester, U.K.: Manchester University Press, 1997. (Concise discussion of Rushdie's work up through *The Moor's Last Sigh* with a useful chapter on the critical overview of his work.)

Durix, Jean-Pierre. *The Writer Written: The Artist and Creation in the New Literatures in English.* New York and Westport, Conn.: Greenwood Press, 1987. (The chapter on *Midnight's Children* looks at it as a metafiction.)

Fletcher, M. D., ed. *Reading Rushdie: Perspectives on the Fiction of Salman Rushdie.* Amsterdam: Rodpoi, 1994. (Excellent collection of essays that includes important articles by Uma Parameswaran, Keith Wilson, Fletcher, Brennan, Booker, Sara Suleri, and Srinivas Aravamudan.)

Goonetilleke, D. C. R. A. *Salman Rushdie.* New York: St. Martin's Press, 1998. (A concise survey that looks at the connection between Rushdie's life and work.)

Grant, Damian. *Salman Rushdie.* Northcote House, 1999. (Balanced discussion of Rushdie's novels as historical documents and imaginative creations.)

Hamilton, Ian. "The First Life of Salman Rushdie." *New Yorker,* 25 December 1995: 90–113. (A biographical profile of Rushdie's life up until the *fatwa.*)

Harrison, James. *Salman Rushdie.* New York: Twayne, 1992. (Well-balanced discussion of the major themes in Rushdie's work. Contains a useful chapter on the history, religion, and politics of India.)

Karr, Mary. "The Domestic Verses of Salman Rushdie." *Chronicle of Higher Education,* 13 September 2002: B: 7–10. (Brief consideration of Rushdie's new life in America.)

Kundera, Milan. "The Day Panurge No Longer Makes People Laugh." In his *Testaments Betrayed.* New York: HarperCollins, 1993. (A meditation on Rushdie's plight and the future of the novel.)

MacDonogh, Steve. *The Rushdie Letters: Freedom to Speak, Freedom to Write.* Lincoln: University of Nebraska Press, 1993.

Parameswaran, Uma. *The Perforated Sheet.* New Delhi: Affiliated East-West Press, 1988. (Collects her essays on Rushdie's first three novels.)

Petersson, Margareta. *Unending Metamorphoses: Myth, Satire and Religion in Salman Rushdie's Novels.* Lund, Sweden: Lund University Press, 1996.

Rao, Madhusudhana M. *Salman Rushdie's Fiction: A Study: The Satanic Verses Excluded.* New Delhi: Sterling, 1992. (A structuralist study of Rushdie's work.)

Rodgers, Bernard F. Jr. "Imaginary Homelands." In his *Voices and Visions.* Lanham, Md.: University Press of America, 2001. (Survey of Rushdie's work and career up through *Imaginary Homelands.*)

Sanga, Jaina C. *Salman Rushdie's Postcolonial Metaphors.* Westport, Conn.: Greenwood Press, 2001. (Examines the themes of migration, translation, hybridity, blasphemy, and globalization in Rushdie's work.)

Suleri, Sara. *The Rhetoric of English India.* Chicago and London: University of Chicago Press, 1992. (Her chapter on Rushdie examines the nature and sources of blasphemy in his work.)

Taneja, G. R., and R. K. Dhawan, eds. *The Novels of Salman Rushdie.* New Delhi: Indian Society for Commonwealth Studies, 1992. (A collection of hard-to-find essays mainly by Indian critics.)

Olive Schreiner

(1855–1920)

ANDREW VAN DER VLIES

FOR MANY OBSERVERS and critics, and for many readers throughout the British Empire and in the United States until at least the middle of the twentieth century, the name of one South African writer was almost synonymous with the land of her birth: Olive Schreiner. She became inextricably linked to the South African landscape to which her most famous novel, *The Story of an African Farm* (1883), had given convincing fictional embodiment for the first time. The novel has often been claimed as the first South African novel in English, even though it was written when "South Africa" was a geographical, rather than a political, designation. It is also frequently described as among the first and most important of the novels of the "New Woman" in Britain, the forerunner of work in the later 1880s and 1890s by Sarah Grand, Mona Caird, and George Egerton. Its success was remarkable, and its author's reputation enduring. Schreiner spent much of the rest of her life trying to complete a narrative that she expected would eclipse *The Story of an African Farm* in expressing her ideas about gender and colonialism, but she left what was published posthumously as *From Man to Man* (1926) unfinished at her death. She published a collection of allegorical works, *Dreams* (1890), which became immensely suc-

cessful, and produced much writing on South African politics and society. For many, her *Woman and Labour* (1911) was a guiding text of early-twentieth-century feminism, and many proto-feminist writers and thinkers—from Charlotte Perkins Gilman to Vera Brittain—claimed her as a mentor.

Schreiner was a colonial, a writer resident for long periods in Britain, a dreamer resident in the Cape Colony, the Transvaal Republic, and finally in the Union of South Africa (formed in 1910 from the union of British colonies and former Dutch or Boer republics). Like so many writers from South Africa who sought to make their reputations abroad over the ensuing century, she felt keenly the difficulties of creative life on the margins, removed from the perceived center of intellectual and cultural life in Britain. Like many English-speaking colonials of her time, she had grown up referring to Britain as "home." But the manner in which she sought, throughout her life, to balance an intellectual engagement with this distant "motherland" with a passionate commitment to the land of her birth, the source of much of her inspiration, illustrates the fluidity of identities forged in and between the colonial periphery and the metropolitan center. Hers was a transnational career, and her work resists definition as exclusively South African or British.

THE COLONIAL EXPERIENCE

Schreiner's father, Gottlob, was a German-born missionary who met and married Rebecca Lyndall, the daughter of an English nonconformist minister, while studying in London. Olive Emilie Albertina Schreiner was born on 24 March 1855, at Wittebergen, a mission station in the mountains of the northeastern Cape Colony, near Basutoland (now Lesotho). She was the ninth of twelve children, and was named after three dead brothers. Her father was dismissed for breaching missionary regulations about trading, and the family dispersed when Schreiner was twelve. She spent several years living with various of her older siblings, and with family friends, in the interior of the Cape Colony, in Cradock, Dordrecht (where she had a failed relationship with an older, Swiss man), and in 1872 and 1873, at the diamond diggings at Kimberley. Here she started writing a novel, *Undine,* which was published posthumously in 1928. While acting as a governess on remote farms in the semiarid interior of the Eastern Cape known as the Karoo between 1874 and 1881, Schreiner worked on what became *The Story of an African Farm,* and on a manuscript entitled "Saints and Sinners" (which she regarded as her favorite), published as *From Man to Man.*

In March 1881 she left for Britain, where she hoped to train for a medical career—there was nowhere for women to study medicine in the Cape Colony. Schreiner's health was fragile and, forced to abandon her plans, she stayed with an elder brother, a schoolmaster, and then settled in London. Schreiner had developed an asthmatic condition in late adolescence, and suffered chronic ill health for the rest of her life, although the exact nature and extent of her illness has been a source of great contention among her biographers. By the mid-1880s, she was using quinine and bromide regularly; it is difficult to

separate symptoms from side effects and real physical distress from psychosomatic frailty. The Britain Schreiner encountered was one in which an indigenous socialist tradition was taking shape as the economic depression of the 1870s and 1880s revealed a failure of Victorian capitalism to ameliorate domestic social inequalities. Schreiner became closely involved in intellectual circles exploring the implications of this failure, forming close attachments with many radical thinkers of the time, including Havelock Ellis, Karl Pearson, Eleanor Marx, and Edward Carpenter. She engaged in extensive correspondence with Ellis, in particular, and prepared papers on what was known as the "woman question"—women's rights—and its relation to social Darwinism. At the end of 1886, suffering from mental and physical strain after the collapse of a relationship with Pearson, Schreiner left Britain for extended periods of recuperation in France and Italy, at Alassio on the Italian Riviera. Here she wrote many of the "dream allegories" which would become so popular with British readers in the 1890s. She made two trips to Britain before returning to the Cape Colony in October 1889, after an absence of more than eight years.

Schreiner delighted in once again being in the land whose landscapes and climate she had missed, but she was also critical of the parochialism she found there. To alleviate her asthma, she moved from Cape Town to the drier climate of Matjesfontein, a railway stop in the Karoo between Cape Town and Kimberley, in March 1890. She became acquainted with Cecil Rhodes during this period, but her initial admiration for this British-born mining magnate, Cape politician, and arch imperialist, was soon revised, and she became one of his most implacable opponents. She spent six months in Britain in 1893, and on her return in February 1894 married Samuel Cron Cronwright, an Eastern Cape farmer with political aspirations. In sympathy with her feminist ideas and reputation as an author, he changed his name to Cronwright-Schreiner while she kept hers. They lived on his farm near Cradock, but moved to Kimberley later in 1894 on account of her health, and to Johannesburg in 1898, where they remained until the outbreak of the Anglo-Boer War the following year.

FINDING A VOICE

Between 1881 and 1883 Schreiner published several of her dream allegories in a magazine produced by her brother's school in Eastbourne, England. "Dream Life and Real Life: A Little African Story," "The Adventures of Master Towser," and "The Lost Joy," were all republished in *Dreams* and in *Dream Life and Real Life* (1893). Her first attempt at a novel, probably substantially complete by 1876 although only published seven years after her death, most directly foreshadows many of the concerns of her later novels. In the eponymous heroine of *Undine*, Schreiner attempts to draw an independent-minded character who apprehends and seeks to negotiate the gendered limitations of opportunities and expectations experienced by women at the time. Undine Bock, the "queer little child" of Schreiner's narrative, grows up on a Karoo farm, a strange, free-spirited, freethinking child who startles her mother and her governess by exclaiming that she wants nothing to do with the cruel, judgmental God of strict evangelical and Calvinist Christianity: "I don't want to go to heaven, and, if God wants to, he can send me to hell and I will never ask him not to, *never*. I know I'm very wicked, but I'm not half so wicked or so cruel as he is. Nothing is, not even the devil" (p. 18). This is daring material for a novel written in the early 1870s.

In England, Undine is bullied into attending chapel by her grandparents, her cousin, and by the man to whom she is attracted, the cold and domineering Albert Blair. Albert, his brother Harry, and their father George all fall in love with her; she is heartbroken when Albert casts her off, but decides that she must, nonetheless,

serve him. She does this by agreeing to marry George—symbolically crushing a rose as she does so, a drop of blood from her finger staining her white dress—on the condition that he give her fifty thousand pounds. She gives birth to a daughter, but the baby does not survive. George dies shortly after, and Undine confounds her gossiping, jealous relatives by disappearing, leaving the estate to his sons, both of whom had been disinherited by their father. She returns to the Cape, and travels with an improbably caricatured colonial family (the Snappercaps) to Kimberley, where she discovers that Albert Blair has died of fever. She sits with his body on the night before his burial, before going out to lie beneath stars. They seem to speak to her, soothing her anxieties about death: "Without death there is no change, without change no life; without the shedding of blood no good thing" (p. 372). The Undine of German myth is a water nymph who obtains a human soul. In *Undine*, the character's hope of salvation lies in a connection with an organic universe rather than in salvation predestined or sanctioned by a cruel judgmental God. The novel ends with the kind of suggestive, open-ended conclusion which Schreiner would develop in *The Story of an African Farm*: Undine is described apparently asleep, or perhaps dead, with "nothing else to be seen in the little yard" (p. 374).

Samuel Cronwright-Schreiner, in his introduction to *Undine*, explained that during their married life Schreiner had never mentioned the manuscript to him, but had apparently given an incomplete version to Havelock Ellis in 1884 insisting that it never be published. After her death, Cronwright-Schreiner discovered the missing final pages of the manuscript among his wife's papers, and published a reconstructed text. It is intriguing to speculate, however, on the extent to which Schreiner meant the text to be merely a working out of ideas which she would develop more successfully in *The Story of an African Farm* and *From Man to Man*. Undine's rejection of orthodox Christianity foreshadows Waldo's in *The Story of an African Farm* in its nature and method of exposition. In fact, several episodes in *The Story of an African Farm* are modeled directly on *Undine.* Like the character Waldo in the former novel, Undine is troubled at night by a ticking clock which reminds her of the numberless souls which she is led to believe are damned: "Thousands, O Lord, are going to destruction every moment" (p. 5). And just as Waldo will do, Undine tries to "sacrifice" a mutton chop on a makeshift altar in the sun, calling on God to prove his existence, or at least disprove his indifference. Undine's declaration to George that she does not love him, but will be a good wife to him, rehearses Rebekah's renegotiation of the terms of her marriage in *From Man to Man,* but not as successfully. Undine's apparently irrational attraction to Albert foreshadows Lyndall's attraction to her anonymous lover in *The Story of an African Farm*; Lyndall knows he will only love her for her ability to perform a female role, rather than as an equal. Albert tells Undine that it is "a matter of supreme indifference" to him what she believes, so long as she does nothing "peculiar," as there is "nothing so hateful in a woman as eccentricity of any description" (p. 147). Undine's actions are less clearly psychologized than Lyndall's, however, and seem to reinforce, rather than challenge, what the critic Carolyn Burdett has called a "sacrificial femininity." Burdett argues that the "repulsiveness of the men in *Undine* simply serves to fuel the process by which the woman is held responsible for male desire and punished for it" (p. 35).

The opening chapters of both *Undine* and *The Story of an African Farm* are strikingly similar in their descriptions of a farm in the Karoo by night, bathed in a mystical moonlight, and by day, baking in the harsh rays of the African sun. But in *Undine,* within a couple of chapters and with little explanation, the scene has moved to an imagined England of visiting clergymen, rose-covered country cottage gardens, and endless white snow. The few critics who have commented on the novel in the late twentieth and early twenty-first centuries have

regarded the later chapters, set in New Rush, the diamond fields which later became Kimberley, as the most convincing. Schreiner clearly learned from writing this often unconvincingly melodramatic first novel that, as expressed in her preface to the second edition of *The Story of an African Farm,* the writer must "sit down to paint the scenes among which he has grown"; "He must paint what lies before him."

THE STORY OF AN AFRICAN FARM

Schreiner sent the manuscript of her most famous novel to five publishers between 1880 and 1882. Before arriving in Britain, she sent a copy to family friends in Lancashire. They sent it to an Edinburgh publisher, David Douglas, who advised changes. The large firms Macmillan, Bentley, and Smith, Elder all rejected the manuscript in 1881 and 1882, and Schreiner rejected the terms she would have received from Remington, a firm specializing in collaborative half-profits publishing, often of colonial material. The novel was finally accepted in 1882 on the recommendation of George Meredith, the reader for Chapman and Hall, and published in January 1883 under the pseudonym Ralph Iron (her name first appeared, in parentheses, on the title page in 1887, and editions of the book began appearing under her own name beginning in the early 1890s). Schreiner rejected and resented inferences that she had made substantial alterations to the manuscript in line with Meredith's suggestions. There had been some concern that circulating libraries and railway booksellers would be reluctant to stock a novel with a freethinking, unwed mother as heroine. It was reviewed widely in the critical press, and widely acclaimed. Different interest groups found different elements to praise: the novel gave voice to women's aspirations, it explored the dilemmas of spiritual individuals in an age suffering a crisis of faith, it was an example of a new kind of romance which would revivify English writing, it was a moving portrayal of colonial conditions. Despite the critical readers' reports from some of the publishers which rejected the manuscript, and in spite of some critical reviews in the religious press, the novel became a small publishing wonder, selling many tens of thousands of copies in its first decade, many more than anticipated. It had at least fifteen editions during Schreiner's lifetime, and there have been many more since her death.

Em and Lyndall, the daughter and niece of an Englishman, grow up on a farm in the Karoo looked after by the man's Dutch widow, Tant Sannie. A kindly old German man, Otto Farber, is overseer of the farm's sheep and ostriches. His son, Waldo, is a friend of the girls. Bonaparte Blenkins, an impoverished Irish immigrant whose first name suggests both Ralph Waldo Emerson's critique of Napoleon as the power of intellect without conscience, and whose surname has its roots in an archaic word for deception, arrives on the farm, eager to trick his way to a living. He turns Sannie against Otto (who dies after being dismissed), becomes overseer, tutor to Em and Lyndall, and presides over a reign of terror. Several critics have read him as Schreiner's caricature of the rapacious colonizer. He is finally driven off by Sannie when he makes advances to a visiting relative of hers. A young man called Gregory Rose rents part of the farm and falls in love with Em, but switches his affections to Lyndall on her return from four years away at boarding school. She accepts his proposal of marriage, but, on the evening of the wedding, runs away with a former lover to the Transvaal. Gregory Rose traces Lyndall, and finds her dangerously ill; she has given birth to a child which died soon after birth. He dresses as a female nurse and, unrecognized, takes care of her until she dies. In the meantime, Waldo has left the farm to travel around the colony. He returns to the farm to discover that Lyndall is dead. Em and Gregory are to be married, and Waldo, going out to sit in the sun one day, dies while musing about the unity of nature and the human soul.

The narrative is set in the arid interior of the Cape Colony in the late 1850s and the 1860s, concluding in 1867, when the Cape was on the verge of the industrialization and social and political upheaval which would follow from the discovery of diamonds later that year. For the most part an omniscient third-person narrative, it veers between parody, satire, and bildungsroman, with frequent digressions drawing on multiple narrative forms: dream, sermon, romance, allegory, hunting tale, confession, letter, song. Later critics, unsure of how to account for the many different registers and modes of storytelling employed in the novel, have frequently regarded it as earnest, but aesthetically unsuccessful. Yet it was warmly received by many late-Victorian critics as a bold novel of ideas, an intelligent exploration of the anxieties and tensions of an age in which religious certainties had been destabilized, and accepted notions about gender were under sustained review. It is this, as much as its foreshadowing of modernist aesthetic techniques, which makes *The Story of an African Farm* worthy of continued consideration. Its multivocality marks it as a narrative whose very form enacts the emotional and spiritual dilemmas of its protagonists. In the words of Joseph Bristow in his introduction to a 1992 edition of the novel, "Schreiner's demonstrably high level of consciousness about what may and may not be achieved by various narrative conventions" alerts the reader to the kind of formal intervention she envisages her work performing (p. xi). Carolyn Burdett comments that Schreiner's exploration of chance, which seemed to her (and seems to her chief characters) to structure existence, is mirrored by contingency in its mode of narration. Malvern van Wyk Smith, Joyce Avrech Berkman, and Irene Gorak are among many later critics who have contributed to a reevaluation of the novel's technique. In her preface to the second edition of the novel, Schreiner wrote, in a formulation which some regard as a forerunner of a distinctly modernist aesthetic, that the human life could be "painted according to two methods": the "stage method," in which "we know with an immutable certainty that at the right crises each one will reappear and act his part"; or "the method of the life we all lead. Here nothing can be prophesied. There is a strange coming and going of feet. Men appear, act and re-act upon each other, and pass away." The novel opens with a description of the farm's stunted bushes and rocky outcrops bathed in moonlight, and describes the spiritual torment endured by the fourteen-year-old Waldo, who, like Undine, lies awake listening to a clock which makes him think of the many millions of souls who are, according to the strict Calvinist theology which dominated the religious life of Dutch or proto-Afrikaner communities, condemned to perdition. During the day, in the baking heat, he calls on God to show himself as he did to the Israelites in the Old Testament. The universe, it seems increasingly to Waldo, is governed by chance and cruelty, not by a divine, beneficent God. Blenkins destroys his prized sheepshearing machine, a senseless act of cruelty which is compared with Waldo's dog playing with and eating a defenseless beetle. Both acts reflect the vulnerability of the human and natural worlds alike to inscrutable forces: "It was all play, and no one could tell what it had lived and worked for. A striving, and a striving, and an ending in nothing" (1992, p. 74). Part 2, which has this last statement as its epigraph, opens with a parable-like exposition of the development of a child's apprehension of the spiritual life. Entitled "Times and Seasons," this is an allegory of the growth and loss of faith. It is an allegory of Waldo's progress toward a radical scepticism:

> Now we have no God. We have had two: the old God that our fathers handed down to us, that we hated, and never liked; the new one that we made for ourselves, that we loved; but now he has flitted away from us, and we see what he was made of—the shadow of our highest ideal, crowned and throned. Now we have no God.
>
> (p. 113)

In a world where "all things are driven about by a blind chance" (p. 114), the mind turns to nature. Waldo's apprehension of a great unifying force in nature is clearly influenced by Emersonian transcendentalism; Schreiner knew Emerson's essays well, and her pseudonym, Ralph Iron, as well as the names Waldo and Em, echo the American philosopher's name. Existence is seen not as "a chance jumble," but as "a living thing, a *One*" (p. 118). At the end of the novel, stripped of the need to find comfort in an expectation of Christian salvation, Waldo becomes part of this apprehended whole: "It is but the individual that perishes, the whole remains" (p. 259).

In the first narrated action of part 2, Waldo is seen carving a wooden post for his father's grave. A stranger, apparently a passing colonial sophisticate, stops to rest on his journey and offers an allegory by way of interpreting Waldo's carving. His narrative, of a hunter's quest for a white bird (representing "Truth"), seems to suggest the triumph of a supremely rational, scientific view of the universe, one which offers Waldo a means of conceiving a new way of operating despite the contingency he has glimpsed. The hunter pursues the bird for many years, and eventually climbs the mountains of "Dry-facts and Realities" (p. 130), after which he dies. Waldo ecstatically embraces the allegory. The stranger gives him a copy of the English philosopher Herbert Spencer's *First Principles* (which a man had given to Schreiner as a child under similar circumstances) but warns, as he leaves, that Waldo should not become detached from his relationship to the land on which he works. Much later, while on his travels, Waldo comes across the stranger, but feels that the man looks down on him for being uneducated and unsophisticated. Waldo's search for a truth beyond that of his own existence in the natural world of the farm is finally as futile as the hunter's. It leads him back home, to realize that what the stranger had implied was that the positivist scientism offered in his allegory, and in Spencer, must be mediated by a species of knowledge related to Waldo's own experience in the natural world he knows and understands.

If Waldo is the embodiment of Schreiner's struggle with spirituality and situatedness, it is in Lyndall's story that the young author embodied her arguments about the nature of women's dependency, and the hypocrisy of Victorian attitudes to women's status and to sexual activity. Lyndall's discussions with Waldo, Gregory Rose, and her anonymous lover about the position of women, reveals a fierce critique of the social conditioning of gender roles. She is scathing about the indoctrination practiced in girls' schools; women are conditioned to be inferior to men, she explains to Waldo. "We all enter the world little plastic beings," but "the world tells us what we are to be, and shapes us by the ends it sets before us. To you it says—*Work*; and to us it says—*Seem!*" While boys are taught that they can "gain all that human heart desires," girls are taught that "Strength shall not help you, nor knowledge, nor labour" (pp. 154–155). Women may be allowed, Lyndall declares, "a little longing when we are young, a little futile searching for work, a little passionate striving for room for the exercise of our powers," but a "woman must march with her regiment. In the end she must be trodden down or go with it; and if she is wise she goes" (pp. 155–156).

Tant Sannie asks: "If the beloved Redeemer didn't mean men to have wives what did He make women for?" (p. 262), but Lyndall rejects the conception of marriage as a woman's lot. For her, marriage without love "is the uncleanest traffic that defiles the world" (p. 156), and while Em's idea of love is of service, Lyndall strives for a new kind of relationship. She accepts Gregory's proposal, she tells him, not because she loves him, but for the mere expedient of having a married name. Gregory Rose's "womanhood"—his donning of Em's mother's clothes in the farmhouse loft, and of the nurse's outfit in chapter 12 of part 2—marks him as a New Man, the equivalent of Lyndall's New Woman, one who is not interested in possessing women for their stereotyped femininity. His name, Gregory Nazianzen Rose, emphasizes his dual nature, his masculinity and femininity: Saint

Gregory of Nazianzus was a fourth-century Christian bishop in Asia Minor, credited with an important defense of Christ's twofold nature, human and divine. And yet Gregory is often harshly treated by Lyndall. And she does not, after all, marry him. Furthermore, Schreiner's three principal female protagonists—Undine, Lyndall, and Rebekah (in *From Man to Man*)—all share apparently irrational attractions for strong, cruel, domineering men, despite their vaunted desire for independence. Lyndall knows that she will never be free if she marries her lover. She accuses him of having resolved to love her only because she seemed unattainable. She is prepared to go away and live with him as long as they love each other, but will not enter into a marriage which she knows will not be one of equals. Rather than portray an ideal relationship between the sexes, Schreiner's novel portrays, and enacts, the practical impossibility of its achievement under the prevailing circumstances in late-Victorian (colonial) society.

Joyce Avrech Berkman and Anne McClintock both consider the extent to which Schreiner repeats colonial platitudes about race in apparent contradiction of her supposed championing of native rights. In *From Man to Man*, Rebekah is guilty of uncomfortable Jewish stereotyping, about which all that can be ventured in Schreiner's defense is the evidence of Rebekah's explicit condemnation of racial discrimination to her sons; Schreiner also published a pamphlet against anti-Semitism, denouncing Russian pogroms, in 1906. Much of her stereotyping of black Africans—underlining the imperial myth of native laziness, for example—might be said, at least in *Undine* and *The Story of an African Farm*, in which it is most pronounced, to reflect a young author's naive repetition of the kind of language which was commonplace in the Cape Colony. Schreiner's biographers Ruth First and Ann Scott suggest that her depiction of the relationships between adults and children in *The Story of an African Farm* makes a statement about the violence of colonialism. Lyndall, Waldo, and Em are victims of a narrow-minded religion, and a parochial anti-intellectualism, which seeks to maintain hierarchies of power and values.

J. M. Coetzee argues, in his study *White Writing: On the Culture of Letters in South Africa* (1988), that Schreiner was South Africa's "great anti-pastoral writer," that as the pastoral requires the presentation of labor to enforce the link between the land and those who work it, Schreiner's elision of the black workforce on the novel's Karoo farm, and her portrayal of the idleness of white landowners, "mimics the idleness, ignorance, and greed of colonial society" (p. 4). The farm is arbitrarily imposed on an ahistorical landscape, he suggests. It has frequently been noted that the land's previous owners, the San people (or Bushmen), have left their mark in the form of rock paintings. Sitting on the kopje one day, Waldo encourages Em and Lyndall to consider the paintings:

> "Now the Boers have shot them all, so that we never see a little yellow face peeping out among the stones." He paused, a dreamy look coming over his face. "And the wild bucks have gone, and those days, and we are here. But we will be gone soon, and only the stones will lie on here, looking at everything like they look now."
>
> (p. 16)

This presentation of the land's apparent resistance to all attempts to inscribe it with meaning is an implicit critique of colonial and imperialist logic. Anne McClintock suggests that Waldo's spiritual crisis is in fact more significantly representative of the crisis of the colonial subject, who finds his legitimacy challenged by an inexplicable landscape, one which appears to have no available cultural meaning to a colonizing consciousness. The reader is not entirely sure whether the stranger's allegory and advice has been sincerely meant, or was merely a jest with a barely literate, rural youngster. But the validation of specific, localized knowledge embodied in Schreiner's depiction of Waldo is nonetheless a powerful affirmation of a spiritual but nonreligious relationship cast in South

African terms. Schreiner ascribes meaning to the colonial setting of her novel, and implicitly of her own upbringing (the formative childhood landscape is identical in *Undine* and *From Man to Man*). The colonial margins, after *The Story of an African Farm*, could never again be merely the site of escapist romance.

THE WOMAN QUESTION

The tale narrated by Waldo's stranger of the hunter's quest for the white bird of truth became one of the most famous passages of *The Story of an African Farm*. It appeared to appeal to a particular late-Victorian sensibility, offering an allegory of the seemingly ceaseless search for certainties in the face of a worldview changed utterly by evolutionary science and new, historical appraisals of the Bible. It is said that Herbert Spencer—whose writing Schreiner much admired in her youth—requested that it be read to him on his deathbed. It was much reproduced and excerpted, including in Schreiner's 1890 *Dreams*, which by 1930 had been reprinted twenty-four times. Schreiner regarded the kind of short prose in this volume, styled "dreams" or "allegories," as providing access to a state of consciousness in which attitudes and social structures might be imagined which were apparently antithetical to the status quo. In many ways, the texts collected in *Dreams, Dream Life and Real Life,* and *Stories, Dreams and Allegories* (posthumous, 1923), mostly written between 1887 and 1892, provided their author with a different means of advancing her arguments for alternative constructions of class, gender, and colonial race relations. The dream allegory operates on its own terms, and not according to those logical, rational, expostulatory, expository forms in which so many of the attitudes against which she positioned herself seemed to be embodied and expressed.

Among these pieces are several which merit brief mention. "The Sunlight Lay across My Bed" was published in the *New Review* in 1890 and collected in *Dreams* that same year. In a dream, God guides the speaker through hell and through heaven, before she wakes up to face a day in London filled with the challenges of inspiring others to work for greater equality and cooperation. In hell, the dreamer is shown revelers at a feast, ignoring the suffering of those who produce their wine—out of their own blood. Some of those at the feast realize their complicity in the suffering on which their enjoyment is based, but to question is to be cast out. Schreiner described this short piece as a reflection on socialism; it draws attention to the suffering of others, which was a constant concern in Schreiner's work on feminism. In another short text in *Dreams*, "I Thought I Stood," a woman dreams she is pleading for women's rights before the throne of God. She claims that men have blood on their hands, but God points out that she has blood on her feet, and the woman is made to realize the extent of her complicity in the suffering of women in the lower classes. Schreiner was adamant that the woman question was not one which should be posed only by and for middle-class women, and that neither, for that matter, should working-class men be expected to pay for women's liberation with increased oppression.

"Three Dreams in a Desert," written for the August 1887 issue of the *Fortnightly Review*, also appeared in *Dreams*. A traveler falls asleep under a mimosa tree on an African plain, and has three related dreams. In the first, two vast figures are seen in a desert, bound to each other. One, identified as a representative woman, has "a great burden on its back" (1891, p. 68); she is tied down by the "Inevitable Necessity" of childbearing and domestic labor (p. 70). The dreamer is told that this figure is stirring: "The Age-of-muscular-force is dead. The Age-of-nervous-force has killed him with the knife he holds in his hand; and silently and invisibly he has crept up to the woman, and with that knife of Mechanical Invention he has cut the band that bound her burden to her back" (pp. 71–72). As Schreiner would write in *Woman and La-*

bour and *From Man to Man*, women would achieve greater freedom only when the welfare of their society no longer required their submission. In the second dream, this female figure has arisen, and is attempting to cross a deep river to the "Land of Freedom" beyond (p. 76). She must first cross banks of Labour and waters of Suffering, however, and is forced to choose between Passion and Reason, but is promised that Passion will be replaced with Love when she does reach the other side. The final dream is of heaven on earth, a promise that women's rights would be won.

Schreiner began in the late 1880s to work up notes for a book on gender and sex relationships, but much of it was apparently destroyed when her house in Johannesburg was looted by British soldiers during the Boer War (after she had left for the Cape), or was never written. She worked on an introduction to a centennial edition of Mary Wollstonecraft's *Vindication of the Rights of Woman*, but it was abandoned. Ten years later, in 1899, she published an article in the *Cosmopolitan* in New York, "The Woman Question." This, in turn, formed part of *Woman and Labour* (1911). Schreiner was emphatic that labor is synonymous with social value, but conceded, pragmatically, that no women would, or could, successfully challenge their conditions if the welfare of society depended on their continued submission. This explained the continued subjugation of women in some cultures and countries, she argued. There was a danger, however, that social and technological changes in Westernized nations had alienated middle-class women from productive social labor. The challenge was for these women to resist the relatively easy option now available to them, that they merely rely on the passive performance of reproductive functions. Any woman who did rely on these functions, or, increasingly, on the "'*mere potentiality*' of her maternal duty" (p. 103) was "parasitic" (1978, p. 49).

Woman and Labour has been described as a "bible" of the early feminist movement, but it really looked back to the arguments about gender and evolutionism of the 1880s rather than to suffragette activism in the 1910s. Karl Pearson had developed a kind of eugenics which argued that women bore the evolutionary responsibility of marrying wisely, to produce strong offspring. This responsibility could be borne, and women could choose their partners freely, only if they were free of economic and social constraints which so often deprived them of choice in the marriage market. *Woman and Labour* is everywhere haunted by a late-Victorian concern with degeneracy and decline; women would contribute to the "decay of a nation or a class" if they merely accepted their passive role (p. 98). But Schreiner also predicates such passivity on the subjugation of others in society: "Behind the phenomenon of female parasitism has always lain another and yet larger social phenomenon; it has invariably been preceded, as we have seen, by the subjugation of large bodies of other human creatures, either as slaves, subject races, or classes" (p. 98). The wealth generated by these groups contributed to a state of leisure for the wealthy, which is directly connected with passivity and parasitism among middle- and upper-class women. This was a powerful argument, implicitly, against colonialism. Given the twentieth century's later experience of the consequences of eugenicist discourse, it is perhaps unsurprising that these arguments now seem dated. Schreiner's work also foreshadowed arguments later made by Virginia Woolf, among others, that war was related to the male domination of society. She argued that "when the woman takes her place beside the man in the governance and arrangement of external affairs of her race will also be that day that heralds the death of war as a means of arranging human differences" (pp. 170–171).

ANTIEVOLUTIONISM AND ANTICOLONIALISM

The novel on which Schreiner worked the longest was begun around the same time as *The Story of an African Farm,* and taken to Britain with her in 1881. She submitted the manuscript (entitled "Saints and Sinners") to both Chapman and Hall and Macmillan in 1881. Both rejected it, and she set about revisions in March 1882, hoping to have it completed by late 1884. However, according to Liz Stanley, she would spend several significant periods at various stages throughout the rest of her life revising the manuscript: 1884 to 1886, mid-1888 to spring 1889, 1901 to 1902, and 1906 to 1907 (2002, p. 95). It was only published in 1926, as *From Man to Man; or, Perhaps Only . . .,* its text reconstructed by her husband after her death. As he destroyed both the typescript and the manuscript, it is not possible to ascertain quite how much he amended his wife's text. Cronwright-Schreiner claimed that she had sent him a typescript of much of it in 1911 and that he found further, concluding fragments among her papers. He discarded the final thousand words as not advancing the plot, and included his own introduction, extracts from his wife's letters mentioning the manuscript, and a note on what she had apparently told him about the projected conclusion. It may be incomplete, and there may be doubts about Cronwright-Schreiner's heavy-handed editorial interventions, but the novel remains a fascinating statement of Schreiner's ideas about marriage, her indictment of the double standards in operation in Victorian attitudes to sex, and particularly toward prostitution. It is also, very significantly, a working out of the implications of her humanist ideas for South African racial affairs, and a comprehensive rejection of the social Darwinian ideas about racial degeneration harnessed so successfully by imperialist rhetoric.

The characters of many nineteenth-century novels progressed through courtship to a happily concluded marriage, whereupon they faded from the page. The novels of the "New Woman" often focused instead on the consequences of marriage; as Kate Flint argues, they presented women's lives as process, rather than as a movement toward fulfillment, justification, and confirmation in marriage. *From Man to Man* is just such a novel, and, while belonging quite firmly to the 1880s and 1890s in these respects, was a powerful exploration of the suffocation of a woman's intellect by the constrictions and expectations of marriage. It begins with what many critics regard as one of the most powerful passages in Schreiner's oeuvre, "The Prelude—The Child's Day," a description of the day in the life of the five-year-old Rebekah, a child on a remote Eastern Cape farm, on which her twin sisters are born. One survives, and is known to her family as "Baby Bertie." Part 2, "The Book—The Woman's Day," finds the sisters fifteen years later. The twenty-year-old Rebekah is about to marry her cousin, Frank, and move to Cape Town. Four years later, she returns to the farm for a visit, with three sons in tow. She is accompanied by Frank's brother, John-Ferdinand, who falls in love with the domestic, beautiful Bertie. Rebekah counsels her cousin to treat Bertie carefully—she has never left the farm, and appears very naive. John-Ferdinand reassures her that he loves Bertie as "the one absolutely spotless, Christ-like thing I have known" (1926, p. 122).

What neither knows is that Bertie had been seduced by her English tutor when she was fifteen, and has borne a burden of guilt ever since. When she shares her secret with John-Ferdinand, he casts her off as a sinner, and no longer the embodiment of virginal femininity. They conceal her secret from her immediate family, however, and Bertie leaves the farm to travel to Cape Town with her sister. John-Ferdinand marries Veronica Grey, an English-woman who had lodged with Bertie's parents. He tells her of Bertie's confession, and when in Cape Town, Veronica initiates the whispering among the town's gossips which seals Bertie's fate: she is viewed as a fallen woman, and is no longer in demand for croquet parties and fashionable dances, and is to be kept away from their daughters by the fashionable matriarchs of the colonial capital. Bertie flees to relatives in a rural Northern Cape town. Here she meets a

rich Jewish financier, on his way back to London from the diamond fields, and flees with him to London when news reaches her relatives of her reputation, and they decide to send her back to her parents in the Eastern Cape. The financier (who is, uncomfortably, grotesquely caricatured) keeps her as his mistress until he suspects her of being unfaithful and casts her out. She is "saved" by the man's cousin, and, it is intimated, becomes a prostitute.

Schreiner seeks to draw a comparison between Bertie's fate and the late-Victorian hypocrisy about female sexual expression which it embodies, and marriage. Rebekah discovers that her husband, Frank, is having an affair with the couple's maidservant, who is pregnant with his child. It is not the first time he has been unfaithful, and she demands new terms for the operation of their marriage. A chapter intriguingly titled "You Cannot Capture the Ideal by a Coup d'État" describes this attempt to secure a measure of security and independence on her own terms. "I am not afraid of you. I am not a woman speaking to the man who owns her, before whom she trembles," she tells Frank; "we are two free souls looking at each other" (p. 288). Either he must divorce her, and she will take their children away with her; or she will continue to live in their house and attend to the children and to his material needs, but there will be no more physical relationship, or other demands upon each other. It is this scenario which is chosen by them both, indirectly. Frank's response gives his measure: "No, there would be no divorce. It was impure, it was unclean for her even to talk of such a thing. It was enough to kill all a man's faith in women!" (p. 309). Rebekah has been able, under provisions of Roman-Dutch law in operation in the colony, which allowed women to buy land in their own right (with their husband's consent), to provide for herself from the proceeds of a small vineyard and fruit farm for several years. She continues to do so, and provides for Frank's mixed-race daughter, Sartje. Five years pass and the reader sees Rebekah, living in a separate extension to the house, still attending social functions with her husband, but beginning to form an attachment to a worthier man, the husband of Mrs. Drummond, the neighbor with whom Frank had an affair years previously and who took a leading role in blackening Bertie's name in Cape Town.

Rebekah owns Charles Darwin's *Variation of Plants and Animals under Domestication,* and is clearly well read in the natural sciences. Schreiner is particular about portraying her as a keen amateur naturalist, both in childhood and as an adult. She and Mr. Drummond appear, in the final passage of the incomplete novel, to have established a potentially enduring and affirmative relationship based at least in part on a shared interest in paleontology and the natural world, and all that such an interest implies. The manner in which social Darwinism underscored imperialist attitudes toward apparently inferior races in southern Africa disturbs Rebekah greatly, however, as it did Schreiner, and Rebekah offers one of Schreiner's most sustained critiques of its implications. If "keen perceptions and the power of dominating are characteristics of the to-be-preserved races," as argued by social Darwinists, what, she asks,

> if to me the little Bushman woman, who cannot count up to five and who, sitting alone and hidden on a koppie, sees danger approaching and stands up, raising a wild cry to warn her fellows in the plain below that the enemy are coming, though she knows she will fall dead struck by poisonous arrows, shows a quality higher and of more importance to the race than those of any Bismarck?
>
> (p. 197)

She questions whether there is "any superiority at all implied in degrees of pigmentations," and suggests that it is only "in their egoistic distortion of imagination" that Europeans are "more desirable or highly developed" than other races (p. 202). Prompted by her sons' refusal to be seen in public with their mixed-race half sister, Sartje, whom Rebekah is raising as her own

daughter, she offers an allegory which reveals the hypocrisy and injustice of imperialism. A race of aliens arrives on earth; they are whiter than white Europeans, and regard them as savage in consequence. They "laughed at the things we believed, and called us ignorant and superstitious savages"; they "would not ride in the same airships as us nor breathe the same currents of air; they called us 'The Inferior Races'" (p. 421). In a perceptive analysis of the violent psychology of racism, her story concludes: "Because they despised *us,* we began to despise *ourselves!*" (p. 422). She tells her children that no idea of racial superiority is tenable once it has been accepted that racial differences are superficial. Rebekah's alternative to the idea of the survival of the fittest is a belief that "the slow perfecting of humanity can find no aid from the destruction of the weak by the stronger, but by the continual bending down of the stronger to the weaker to share with them their ideals and aid them in the struggle with their qualities" (p. 223). Schreiner affirms supposedly womanly instincts, in particular a maternal protectiveness which she seeks to identify and awaken in the white women in the Cape and in Britain, as an ameliorating force in the centers of colonial power. This is the case in *Trooper Peter Halket of Mashonaland* (1897) and in *From Man to Man,* in particular, and while it may seem to venture close to a paternalism, it was envisaged as a quite different kind of response, one which sought both to reevaluate supposedly feminine attributes as potentially and positively universal, and to effect a just world for all oppressed groups and classes in society.

Rebekah's antievolutionism informs not only her anticolonialism, but also a revised apprehension of spirituality, and her ideal of a more equal relationship between men and women in marriage. She echoes Waldo's view of unity in the natural world in suggesting that "the Universe has become one, a whole, and it lives in all its parts," that "advancing knowledge has shown us the internetting lines of action and reaction which bind together all that we see and are conscious of" (p. 180). And this "new intellectual conception of the nature of the Universe" must influence "our spiritual and moral outlook" (p. 182). In particular, double standards with respect to gender relations must change. Rebekah has the strength, from within marriage, to renegotiate her position and escape a situation which Schreiner described elsewhere as a kind of prostitution. Frank's misdemeanors, which include affairs with underage girls, go unpunished. Bertie is less fortunate, however. Her aunt tells her that while men are seldom harmed by rumors of sexual impropriety, "a woman's character is like gossamer, when you've once dropped it in the mud and pulled it about it can never be put out again" (p. 326). Bertie is upset by the plight of prostitutes in London, but, as Frank informs Mr. Drummond, ends up in a brothel in Soho. Cronwright-Schreiner noted at the end of his edition of his wife's text that she had told him of her intention to have Bertie return to the Cape, where Mr. Drummond finds her. She is ill, and although Rebekah nurses her, she dies. Rebekah and Mr. Drummond grow to love each other, but decide that they cannot marry, as it would destroy their affection. Rebekah leaves Frank to live at Matjesfontein, where she brings up her children and Sartje. Olive Schreiner intended to end the novel in the same open-ended manner she had employed in *The Story of an African Farm*, with Rebekah standing on an outcrop in the Karoo, outlined against the sunset.

THOUGHTS ON SOUTH AFRICA (1923)

The growing and potentially invidious power of capital in southern Africa worried Schreiner tremendously during the 1890s. She was concerned at the threats posed to the agrarian Dutch republics by a rapacious emerging class of entrepreneurs and mining magnates, and their alignment with imperialists. She believed that the virtues she saw in the Boer, particularly the independent-minded Boer women, would be destroyed, and that the rights of black Africans would be abrogated in the rush to secure control of gold production in the Transvaal. She published several essays on these subjects in the late 1890s, including "The Boer Woman and the Modern Woman's Question," published in *Cosmopolis* in April 1898. These essays were collected in *Thoughts on South Africa* in 1923. Schreiner became particularly hostile to Cecil Rhodes's imperial ambitions in the region. In 1889 his British South Africa Company was granted a royal charter, and troops crossed the Limpopo River to colonize Mashonaland and Matabeleland, territories which would become Rhodesia (now Zimbabwe). There was a rebellion of Shona and Matabele against the company in 1896, a year in which their cattle had been decimated by a plague of a deadly cattle disease, rinderpest. Schreiner's long parable, *Trooper Peter Halket of Mashonaland*, published in London in 1897, was written in response to the campaign to quell these rebellions. Schreiner's protagonist, Peter Simon Halket, has come to South Africa from England dreaming of making his fortune: "Other men had come to South Africa with nothing, and had made everything,—why should not he?" (1897, p. 14). He soon leaves work on the mines, tempted by the promise of "lots of loot to be got, and land to be given out, and that sort of thing," to join up for the British South Africa Company's campaign against the insurrection in Matabeleland (p. 27). His party burns crops, machineguns and torches native villages, blows up caves in which fleeing natives were hiding, shoots and hangs surviving men as spies, and rapes women. After being out scouting, Halket is unable to find his way back to the camp, and spends the night on top of a rocky outcrop. He is joined by a mysterious man, dressed in robes, with long curly hair and nail marks on his feet; he declares himself a Jew of Palestine, and is clearly meant to be a Christ figure. Schreiner's friend, W. T. Stead, editor of the London *Pall Mall Gazette*, had speculated in an article in 1894 what Christ would find if he arrived in contemporary Chicago; Schreiner had admired the piece, and offered this work as her speculation about Christ's response to imperialism in southern Africa.

The Christ figure listens to Halket's disturbingly blasé accounts of his sexual abuse of black women, his jingoistic and racist opinions, and his boasting descriptions of his disregard for black life. He answers quietly, trying to make Halket apprehend the injustices of which he has been part. He draws a comparison between the Armenians under the yoke of the Turks, much in the news at the time Schreiner was writing the narrative, to the suffering of the Matabele under the British South Africa Company. Halket protests: "But it's quite a different thing"; the Armenians are "almost" white, and are "Christians, like us!" (pp. 45–46). Schreiner's allegory draws attention to the double standards applied to different races, and exposes the hypocrisies of supposedly Christian Englishmen and their institutions; "But here, in this world, what is a Christian?" the stranger asks Halket (p. 47). He tells Halket of a preacher in Cape Town who alienates much of his congregation by comparing the Old Testament story of Ahab, who sought to deprive Naboth of his vineyard, to the desire of Rhodes and others to annex the Boer Republics and dispossess black tribes (p. 55). The stranger exhorts Halket to become an evangelist for a new humanism, to reveal the truth about imperial aggression to the mothers, the women, and the working classes in Britain. The stranger's arguments convince Halket of the illegitimacy of Rhodes's violent operations in Matabeleland and Mashonaland, and when the rest of his party reaches him the following day with a wounded black man they have captured and plan to hang as a spy, Halket pleads for the man's life. He argues with his captain, exclaiming that "they would fight against the French if they came and took England from us" (p. 106). As punishment for this impudence, and for his unacceptable pro-native opinions, he is made to guard the man in the blazing heat. During the night, Halket releases the man. The soldiers in the camp awake, thinking that they are under at-tack, and in the ensuing confusion, Halket is shot. Two of the troopers realize, however, that Halket had released the prisoner; they resolve not to speak of it, and they ride off to continue their campaign, wondering whether Halket is lucky to be out of it.

In the Christ figure's story of the Cape Town preacher, it is the Jameson Raid in particular which is compared with Ahab's injustice. It was this event, more than any other, which galvanized Schreiner into virulent opposition to Rhodes and the brand of imperialism for which he stood. The discovery of gold in the Transvaal in 1886 had led to a huge influx of prospectors, financiers, and allied foreign workers, many of them English. A new city, Johannesburg, grew up almost overnight. Paul Kruger, president of the Transvaal (known as the Zuid-Afrikaansche Republiek, or South African Republic), resisted the demands of these foreign nationals, termed "Uitlanders" (literally, those from "out of the country"), for political representation, on the grounds that their vote would outweigh that of the Boer citizens of the Republic. At the end of 1895, Leander Starr Jameson, one of Rhodes's leading supporters (and later prime minister of the Cape), crossed into the Transvaal from the British Bechuanaland Protectorate (Botswana) with a force drawn from the British South African Police, effectively Rhodes's private army. His incursion was to have sparked an organized revolt by Uitlanders in Johannesburg, but this failed to materialize, and the raiders and the leading Uitlander agitators were arrested and dealt with harshly. The affair was deeply embarrassing for Britain. In the Cape, Rhodes was forced to resign his premiership. He faced an inquiry in the Colony's parliament (the Colony was self-governing) in Cape Town, and was summoned to London to explain himself to a parliamentary committee looking into the matter. In 1897 he traveled to Britain to these hearings on the same ship as Schreiner, on her way to find a publisher for *Trooper Peter Halket of Mashonaland*. They did not speak on board. Schreiner felt sure that Rhodes and the company

OLIVE SCHREINER

would proceed against her for libel, but they did not. The book attracted considerable press interest, but most papers ignored its politics. Those that did not (like *Blackwood's Magazine*), dismissed her indictment of Rhodes as exaggerated personal abuse.

The Jameson Raid and the British South Africa Company's operations in what would become Rhodesia strengthened Schreiner's support for the Boer, the proto-Afrikaner, in the two Dutch republics. She wrote to Jan Smuts in January 1899, in a letter in Richard Rive's edition of her letters: "I look upon the Free State and the Transvaal as the two last little sluice-gates we have left keeping out the flood of capitalism which would otherwise sweep in and overwhelm South Africa" (p. 344). Smuts was the state attorney in the Transvaal government, and would become one of the most successful generals in the Boer War, and ultimately prime minister of South Africa (1919 to 1924, and again between 1939 and 1948). Schreiner published several pieces of political commentary on the tensions in the area, including *The Political Situation* (1896) and *An English-South African's View of the Situation: Words in Season* (1899). War was inevitable, however, particularly after Sir Alfred Milner's appointment as the British High Commissioner in the Cape in 1897, and when it came in 1899, Schreiner and her husband left Johannesburg for the Cape. The Anglo-Boer War had changed by the end of 1900 from direct engagement to a guerrilla war waged by small groups of dedicated Boer commandos, which dragged on for another eighteen months. The British authorities responded with a scorched-earth policy, hoping to end the provisioning of the fighters and destroy their morale. Women and children refugees, largely created by this program, were interred; at least twenty thousand (and as many as twenty-eight thousand) died of disease in these concentration camps (as they were called). Martial law, and ill health, prevented Schreiner from active opposition to the Anglo-Boer War. She spent much of the war confined to Hanover, a small town under martial law, in the northern Karoo. She did address protest meetings, however, or sent messages of support, and attracted much media attention.

In the early years of the twentieth century, Schreiner and her brother Will were among the chief proponents of a federal model for the country which would emerge from the joining of the two British colonies (the Cape and Natal) and the two former Dutch republics (the Orange Free State and Transvaal), which had come under British control at the end of the war in 1902. She published her argument in *Closer Union: A Letter on the South African Union and the Principles of Government* (1909), but most politicians wanted a union, rather than a federation, and Schreiner felt increasingly marginalized in political debate during this period. She became increasingly alarmed, too, at the manner in which the rights and aspirations of black South Africans were disregarded by Britain, and by the white political establishment in the South African colonies. Reconciliation between English speakers and Afrikaners became the primary concern of political parties in the country, an expedient which proved shortsighted.

SCHREINER'S GHOST

In a cruel echo of the fate of Lyndall's child in *The Story of an African Farm*, Olive Schreiner gave birth to a baby daughter on 30 April 1895, but the child lived for only a few hours. Cronwright-Schreiner became a member of Parliament and Schreiner's health precluded her living with him in Cape Town, so she lived for many years in small provincial towns in the dry interior—the child's lead-lined coffin moving with her. She visited Britain in 1913, and was lionized by London's literati. Stranded in Britain by the outbreak of hostilities in 1914, she spent the duration of World War I alone in London, involved in pacifist and suffragette activities. She returned to South Africa in August 1920, and died in a boardinghouse in Cape Town on 10

December of that year. She was reburied on a rocky mountaintop in the Karoo near Cradock a year later.

Schreiner remained humble and self-deprecating about her writing, but in a letter to Karl Pearson in October 1886 (collected in Rive's edition of the letters), she does give an indication of the popularity and influence of her most famous novel:

> An untaught girl, working ten hours a day, having no time for thought or writing, but a few in the middle of the night, writes a little story like *An African Farm*; a book wanting in many respects, and altogether young and *crude,* and *full of faults*; a book that was written altogether for myself, when there seemed no possible chance that I should ever come to England or publish it. Yet, I have got scores, almost hundreds of letters about it from all classes of people, from an Earl's son to a dressmaker in Bond Street, and from a coalheaver to a poet.
>
> (p. 109)

If, she asked, a work of art so childish and "full of *faults*" has had such an influence, "what of a *great* work of art?" (p. 109). Whether or not *The Story of an African Farm* is a "great" work of art, its author's reputation and influence has indeed proved enduring; Schreiner is still frequently cited as the author of one of the first and most important novels in English in southern Africa.

Selected Bibliography

WORKS OF OLIVE SCHREINER

NOVELS

The Story of an African Farm. London: Chapman and Hall, 1883; New York: George Munro's Sons, 1887; London: Hutchinson, 1891; London: Chapman and Hall, 1892; London: Unwin, 1924 (with an introduction by S. C. Cronwright-Schreiner); Boston: Little, 1924; New York: Modern Library, 1927; London: Benn, 1929; London, and London and Glasgow: Collins, 1929; West Drayton, and Harmondsworth, U.K.: Penguin, 1939; New York: Fawcett, 1968; Johannesburg: Donker, 1975; New York: Garland, 1975; New York: Schocken, 1976; Chicago: Academy, 1977; New York: Penguin, 1986; London: Hutchinson, 1987; New York: Crown, 1987; London: Virago, 1989; Oxford: Oxford University Press, 1991; New York: Dove, 1998. (Until the early 1890s, the novel appeared under the pseudonym Ralph Iron) .

Trooper Peter Halket of Mashonaland. London: Unwin, 1897; Boston: Roberts, 1897; London: Benn, 1959; Johannesburg: Donker, 1974, 1992.

From Man to Man; or, Perhaps Only . . . London: Unwin, 1926; New York: Harper and Brothers, 1927; New York: Johnson Reprint Corp., 1927; repr. Chicago: Cassandra Editions, 1977.

Undine. New York and London: Harper, 1928; London: Benn, 1929.

SHORT FICTION AND ALLEGORIES

Dreams. London: Unwin, 1890; Boston: Little, Brown, 1916; London: Benn, 1930; London: Wildwood, 1982.

Dream Life and Real Life: A Little African Story. London: Unwin, 1893; Boston: Roberts, 1893; Chicago: Academy, 1977.

Stories, Dreams and Allegories. London: Unwin, 1923, 1924 (1924 edition includes parts of "The Dawn of Civilization"]; New York: Stokes, 1923; London: Benn, 1931.

SOCIAL AND POLITICAL WRITING

The Political Situation. London: Unwin, 1896.

An English-South African's View of the Situation: Words in Season. London: Hodder and Stoughton, 1899; repub. as *The South African Question.* Cape Town: South African Newspaper Company, 1899; Chicago: Segel, 1899.

A Letter on the Jew. Cape Town: Liberman, 1906.

Closer Union: A Letter on the South African Union and the Principles of Government. London: Fifield, 1909.

Woman and Labour. London: Unwin, 1911, repr. 1978; New York: Stokes, 1911; London: Virago, 1978.

Thoughts on South Africa. London: Unwin, 1923; New York: Stokes, 1923; Johannesburg: Donker, 1992.

"Introduction to the Life of Mary Wollstonecraft and The Rights of Woman." In *History Workshop Journal* 37 (1994).

LETTERS

The Letters of Olive Schreiner, 1876–1920, ed. by Samuel Cron Cronwright-Schreiner. London: Unwin, 1924.

Olive Schreiner Letters, Volume 1: 1871–1899, ed. by Richard Rive. Cape Town: David Philip, 1987; Oxford U.K.: Oxford University Press, 1988.

"My Other Self": The Letters of Olive Schreiner and Havelock Ellis, 1884–1920, ed. by Yaffa Claire Draznin. New York: Longman, 1992.

MANUSCRIPTS

Various archives hold letters and other primary material, chief amongst them are: the Albany Museum, Grahamstown, South Africa; the National English Literary Museum, Grahamstown; the Cory Library for Historical Research, Rhodes University, Grahamstown; Harry Ransom Humanities Research Center, University of Texas at Austin; Cullen Library, University of the Witwatersrand, Johannesburg; the National Library of South Africa, Cape Town Division.

STAGE ADAPTATIONS OF SCHREINER'S WORKS

Brown, James Ambrose. *Lyndall: An Adaptation in Two Acts of Olive Schreiner's The Story of an African Farm* (Johannesburg: Dramatic, Artistic and Literary Rights Organization, 1978.

Hodge, Merton. *Story of an African Farm: A Play in Three Acts.* London: William Heinemann, 1939.

COLLECTIONS

Barash, Carol, ed. *An Olive Schreiner Reader: Writings on Women and South Africa.* London and New York: Pandora, 1987.

Cherry, Clayton, ed. *Olive Schreiner.* Johannesburg and New York: McGraw-Hill, 1983 (Includes both primary material and reviews and essays on Schreiner, including a review by Nadine Gordimer of the Ruth First/Ann Scott biography.).

Krige, Uys, ed. *Olive Schreiner: A Selection.* Cape Town and New York: Oxford University Press, 1968.

Purcell Anna, ed., *Olive Schreiner's Thoughts about Women.* Cape Town: South African News, 1909.

Nuttall, Neville, ed., *The Silver Plume.* Johannesburg: APB, 1956.

Thurman, Howard, ed. *A Track to the Water's Edge: The Olive Schreiner Reader.* New York: Harper and Row, 1973.

BIBLIOGRAPHIES

Davis, Roslyn. *Olive Schreiner, 1920–1971: A Bibliography.* Johannesburg: University of the Witwatersrand, 1972.

Hinchliff, Shaen, and Margaret Houliston. *The Olive Schreiner Collection at Cradock Public Library.* Cape Town: Cape Provincial Library Service, 1983.

Verster, E. *Olive Emilie Albertine Schreiner.* Cape Town: University of Cape Town, 1946.

CRITICAL AND BIOGRAPHICAL STUDIES AND HISTORICAL BACKGROUND

Ardis, Ann L., *New Women, New Novels: Feminism and Early Modernism.* New Brunswick N.J.: Rutgers University Press, 1990.

Barash, Carol L. "Virile Womanhood: Olive Schreiner's Narratives of a Master Race." In *Speaking of Gender.* Edited by Elaine Showalter. New York: Routledge, 1989.

Beeton, Ridley. *Facets of Olive Schreiner: A Manuscript Source Book.* Johannesburg: Donker, 1987.

Berkman, Joyce Avrech. *The Healing Imagination of Olive Schreiner: Beyond South African Colonialism.* Amherst Mass.: University of Massachusetts Press, 1989 (An excellent critical account of Schreiner's theories of race, class, and gender, with an extensive bibliography).

Bristow, Joseph. Introduction to Olive Schreiner, *The Story of an African Farm,* ed. by Bristow. Oxford, U.K.: Oxford University Press, 1992.

Buchanan-Gould, Vera. *Not Without Honour: The Life and Writings of Olive Schreiner.* London and New York: Hutchinson, 1948.

Burdett, Carolyn. *Olive Schreiner and the Progress of Feminism: Evolution, Gender, Empire.* Houndmills, U.K., and New York, 2001. (An excellent account of Schreiner's engagement with evolutionary theory and its influence on her ideas about progress and the position of women, colonial subjects, and "native races.").

Chapman, Michael. *Southern African Literatures.* Londonand New York: Longman, 1996. (Provides a useful summary context within which to consider Schreiner's achievement.).

Chrisman, Laura. "Colonialism and Feminism in Olive Schreiner's 1890s Fiction." *English in Africa* 20.1: 25–38 (May 1993).

———. "Empire, 'Race' and Feminism at the *Fin de Siècle*: The Work of George Egerton and Olive Schreiner." In *Cultural Politics at the Fin de Siècle,* ed. by Sally Ledger and Scott McCracken. Cambridge U.K., and New York: Cambridge University Press, 1995.

———. *Rereading the Imperial Romance: British Imperialism and South African Resistance in Haggard, Schreiner, and Plaatje.* Oxford, U.K., and New York: Clarendon, 2000. (Considers *Trooper Peter Halket of Mashonaland* in particular, in the context of the romance tradition.).

Clayton, Cherry. *Olive Schreiner.* New York and London: Twayne, 1997.

Coetzee, J. M. *White Writing: On the Culture of Letters in South Africa.* New Haven Conn.: Yale University Press, 1988 (see especially chapter 3).

Cronwright-Schreiner, S. C. *The Life of Olive Schreiner.* London and Boston: Unwin, 1924.

Cunningham, Valentine. "Mad Pilgrims, Aimless Discontinuities, Painful Transitions, Faith and Doubt in Victorian Fiction." In *Victorian Studies* 22.3: 321-334 (September 1979).

Davenport, T. R. H., and Christopher Saunders. *South Africa: A Modern History,* 5th ed. Houndmills, U.K.: Macmillan; New York: St. Martin's, 2000.

First, Ruth, and Ann Scott, *Olive Schreiner.* London and New York: Deutsch, 1980; repr. London: Women's Press, 1989.

Flint, Kate. *The Woman Reader, 1837–1914.* Oxford U.K., and New York: Clarendon, 1993.

Gilbert, Sandra M., and Susan Gubar. *No Man's Land: The Place of the Woman Writer in the Twentieth Century,* vol. 2, *Sexchanges.* New Haven Conn.: Yale University Press, 1989.

Gregg, Lyndall Schreiner. *Memories of Olive Schreiner.* London: W. & R. Chambers, 1957.

Gorak, Irene E. "Colonial Allegory: *The Story of an African Farm.*" *Ariel* 23, no. 4: 53–72 (1992).

Hobman, Daisy Lucie. *Olive Schreiner: Her Friends and Times.* London: Watts, 1955.

Jacobson, Dan. Introduction to Olive Schreiner, *The Story of an African Farm.* Harmondsworth, U.K.: Penguin, 1971.

McClintock, Anne. *Imperial Leather: Race, Gender and Sexuality in the Colonial Conquest.* New York and London: Routledge, 1995. (see especially chapter 7, "Olive Schreiner: The Limits of Colonial Feminism").

McCracken, Scott. "Stages of Sand and Blood: The Performance of Gendered Subjectivity in Olive Schreiner's Colonial Allegories." In *Rereading Victorian Fiction.* Edited by Alice Jenkins and Juliet John. London: Palgrave, 2001.

Meintjes, Johannes. *Olive Schreiner: Portrait of a South African Woman.* Johannesburg: Keartland, 1965.

Monsman, Gerald. *Olive Schreiner's Fiction: Landscape and Power.* New Brunswick, N.J.: Rutgers University Press, 1991.

Packenham, Thomas. *The Boer War.* London: Longman, 1979.

Pechey, Graham. "*The Story of an African Farm*: Colonial History and the Discontinuous Text." *Critical Arts* 31: 65–78 (1989).

Raiskin, Judith L. *Snow on the Cane Fields: Women's Writing and Creole Subjectivity.* Minneapolis: University of Minnesota Press, 1996. (see especially chapter 1, "'An English South African': Olive Schreiner's South Africa, Land and Language.").

Roberts, Brian. *Cecil Rhodes: Flawed Colossus.* London: Hamish Hamilton, 1987.

Sanders, Mark. "Towards a Genealogy of Intellectual Life: Olive Schreiner's *The Story of an African Farm.*" *Novel* 34.1: 77–97 (fall 2000).

Schoeman, Karel. *Olive Schreiner: A Woman in South Africa, 1855–1881.* Translated by Henri Snijders. Johannesburg: Ball, 1991.

————. *Only an Anguish to Live Here: Olive Schreiner and the Anglo-Boer War, 1899–1902.* Cape Town: Human and Rousseau, 1992.

Stanley, Liz. "How Olive Schreiner Vanished, Leaving Behind Only Her Asthmatic Personality." In *Feminism and Friendship: Two Essays on Olive Schreiner.* Manchester U.K.: Department of Sociology, University of Manchester, 1986.

————. *Imperialism, Labour and the New Woman: Olive Schreiner's Social Theory.* Durham: Sociology Press, 2002.

Stanley, Liz. and Malvern van Wyk Smith. "Napoleon and the Giant: Discursive Conflicts in Olive Schreiner's 'Story of an African Farm.'" In *Ariel: A Review of International English Literature* 30.1: 151–163 (January 1999).

Steele, Murray. "A Humanist Bible: Gender Roles, Sexuality and Race in Olive Schreiner's *From Man to Man*" In *Gender Roles and Sexuality in Victorian Literature.* Edited by Christopher Parker. Aldershot, U.K., and Brookfield, Vt.: Scolar, 1995.

van der Vlies, Andrew. "The Editorial Empire: The Fiction of 'Greater Britain,' and the Early Readers of Olive Schreiner's *The Story of an African Farm.*" In *TEXT: An Interdisciplinary Annual of Textual Studies* 15: 237–260 (2002).

van Wyk Smith, Malvern and Don Maclennan, eds. *Olive Schreiner and After: Essays on Southern African Literature in Honour of Guy Butler.* Cape Town: David Philip, 1983.

Vivan, Itala, ed. *The Flawed Diamond: Essays on Olive Schreiner.* Sydney: Dangaroo, 1991.

Paul Scott
(1920–1978)

JOHN LENNARD

BETWEEN THE AGES of twenty-three and twenty-six, Paul Scott served in India and witnessed the passing of British rule. In 1942, the year before he arrived, the internment of Gandhi and sixty thousand Congress activists sparked weeks of rioting; in 1947, the year after he left, partition of the subcontinent into India and East and West Pakistan fueled sectarian massacres in which at least 430,000 Hindu, Muslim, and Sikh refugees were murdered. While Scott was there the political bankruptcy of the Raj and its Pax Britannica was underscored by the revelation of the Indian National Army (INA), raised by the Japanese from among Indian prisoners of war to fight alongside them against the British. Yet most Indian soldiers were fiercely loyal to the Allied cause, Indian labor was essential to the war effort, and despite the political tensions of the struggle for independence there was goodwill on both sides. The catastrophic descent into civil violence in 1946–1947 surprised and horrified most Indians as much as it did the British.

Scott never forgot his Indian experience, and he devoted his life as a novelist to understanding what he called the British "coming to the end of themselves as they were." In his first eight novels, published between 1952 and 1964, he trained himself in the novelist's craft and systematically explored the background and politics of the Far Eastern theater in Word War II. Little noticed by critics, these novels form an impressive body of fiction, richly inventive and structurally innovative, yet faithful to history and cast with increasing power as tragedy. On their own a major achievement, they have been eclipsed by the five novels that followed. *The Jewel in the Crown* (1966), *The Day of the Scorpion* (1968), *The Towers of Silence* (1971), and *A Division of the Spoils* (1975) form the *Raj Quartet,* with *Staying On* (1977) as a poignant, comedic coda. Televised to enormous acclaim in 1984 under the umbrella title *The Jewel in the Crown,* the *Quartet* is the most important British fiction of imperial India since Rudyard Kipling's. It is unique in its depth of political analysis and ferocious insistence on a British as well as Indian tragedy—so much so that some English readers recoil, damning Scott for betraying the glories of the imperial past. Many more are humbled and shamed by a portrait of racism, snobbery, suppressed sexuality, and hapless virtue they find all too believable, and the *Quartet* is recommended reading for imperial historians throughout the Commonwealth.

Scott did not live to enjoy his success. His death from cancer in 1978, only a year after *Staying On* brought his life's work to an astonishing conclusion, and is a measure of the effort he had expended. In life he won only three literary prizes—the Eyre and Spottiswoode Literary Award for *Johnnie Sahib* in 1952, the *Yorkshire Post* Fiction Award for *The Towers of Silence* in 1972, and the Booker Prize for *Staying On* in 1977. But since his death, his reputation has grown steadily throughout the English-speaking world, and the *Quartet* has begun to be translated into other languages. Shelley C. Reece has edited a volume of his essays and lectures, *On Writing and the Novel* (1987); there is a full-length biography, Hilary Spurling's *Paul Scott: A Life* (1990), and a body of criticism is steadily growing. His letters and personal library are held at the McFarlin Library, University of Tulsa, Oklahoma, and his literary manuscripts at the Harry Ransom Center, University of Texas, Austin. Critical interest is notably greater in the United States and Commonwealth countries, including India, than in the United Kingdom—a reflection, perhaps, of continuing hostility to the revisionism of Scott's history.

EARLY LIFE AND NOVELS

Paul Mark Scott was born on 25 March 1920 in Fox Lane, Palmer's Green, a "respectable" suburb of north London. His father, Tom Scott (1870–1958), was a freelance commercial artist born in Leeds and a proud Yorkshireman; his mother, Frances (née Mark, 1886–1969), had artistic talents and fierce social ambitions inherited from her own father, a laborer living in working-class South London. Tom and Frances married in 1916, and Paul's elder brother, Peter, was born in 1918.

From 1929 Paul attended Winchmore Hill Collegiate, a small private school where he shone and seemed likely to fulfill even the wildest of his mother's ambitions. His father's business, however, was crippled by the Great Depression: the family moved in with relatives in 1933, and in 1934 both Peter and Paul had to leave school to work, Peter as a car salesman and Paul as a

junior clerk in an accounting office. It was an emotional blow he never forgot or forgave, a loss both of present privilege and of the social ambitions he and his mother nurtured; similar losses befall many of his fictional characters, including (in severe form) Hari Kumar in the *Raj Quartet*. Of necessity Paul buckled down to earning money, but he did not abandon artistic hopes: influenced by reading Rupert Brooke, he wanted to be a poet, and by the later 1930s he had met bohemian friends who introduced him to modernist literature, especially T. S. Eliot. Evidence is uncertain, but it seems likely he also began at this time to explore his bisexuality.

In 1940 he completed a trilogy of religious poems (published in 1941 as *I, Gerontius*) but also received his call-up papers. At first military service was not unpleasant, as he began officer training in Torquay, but in the winter things changed. In November two of his aunts were killed in the Blitz on London, and in January 1941 there was an incident of some kind with a superior officer. Details are unknown, but it seems to have involved Paul's sexuality and led both to immediate demotion to private and a long delay in obtaining a commission. Whatever truly happened, Paul became more guarded and inward and appears from then on to have expressed his bisexuality only in fiction, a determined self-censorship publicly sealed after a whirlwind courtship by his marriage in October to Nancy Edith ("Penny") Avery, a nurse.

Finally, in 1943, Paul was sent to India and commissioned. Most of his time there was spent in Assam, serving in the air supply corps that supported General Slim's reconquest of Burma (1944) and advance on Malaya (1945), but initial training and post–VJ Day movement took him all over northern India and to Malaya, visiting cities and many smaller stations and cantonments. The acutely racist and class-conscious world of the Raj, its profound insecurities exposed in wartime, made an indelible impression, yet seemed closely related to the social ambitions nurtured by his mother: "In Palmer's

Green when I lived there we were as aware of social distinctions as they were in Mudpore," he explained long afterwards. "To that extent India was *never* a surprise to me" (Spurling, p. 4). This insight underpins the ways in which his novels are not simply historical but sharply relevant to contemporary Western readers.

Demobbed in 1946, Paul became bookkeeper, and later company secretary, at Falcon and Grey Walls Press. He and Penny had two daughters, Carol (b. 1947) and Sally (b. 1948), and Paul managed to have a play, *Pillars of Salt* (1948), published, but not performed. In 1950 he became a literary agent with Pearn, Pollinger, and Higham, and while continuing to write radio drama (*Lines of Communication,* 1951; *Sahibs and Memsahibs,* 1958) began to concentrate on novels: *Johnnie Sahib* (1952) was followed by *The Alien Sky* (1953; U.S. title *Six Days in Marapore*) and *A Male Child* (1956). All were respectfully reviewed but had limited sales.

In some ways journeyman work, all three novels nevertheless display Scott's central concerns and stylistic gifts. *Johnnie Sahib,* like many first novels, is closely autobiographical, the eponymous hero serving in Slim's Air Supply and finding himself socially ill at ease in a colonial world where his skin color and wartime rank give him an automatic superiority he would never have had in the U.K. But Scott was also concerned with the way others saw Johnnie, and his narrator remarks how

> it was easy, once an illusion had been swept away, to recreate a man in the imagination; recreate him out of his period when the impact of his personality was lost through his absence; to turn one's judgement of him upside down; trace back from the effect to find the cause; selecting the effects to find the cause one wanted to find; to find in the end a Johnnie who had been selfish, arrogant, childish and bitter; to find, like that, a Johnnie one could resent, exorcise like an undesirable spirit from which one could not escape, even in Pyongiu.
>
> (p. 166)

Memory and witness are already complicated by awareness of how memory can be self-serving and evidence tainted, a theme that develops throughout Scott's fiction.

In *The Alien Sky* the canvas is sharply expanded from a primarily white, male, and military world to the professional and familial worlds of civil India. Dorothy Gower is Eurasian (of mixed British/Indian blood) but passing as white English and has married a white English journalist and experimental farmer. She suffers the twin terrors of her deception—meeting a white person who knows the English town where she claims to have been born, and bearing a child whose skin would reveal its Indian ancestry—and Scott's sympathetic portrait marks a capacity to create and understand female characters that is distinct and unusual. The troubling figure of Johnnie Sahib is doubled: as Tom Gower, superficially liberal but revolted by miscegenation, and as John Steele, Gower's farm manager, who sleeps with Indian prostitutes but despises Indians and their aspiration to dignified independence, a *"man you depend on in a tight spot. But in reality, the man who brought the tight spot with him"* (p. 156). Indian and colonial politics are represented, notably in the presence of the *Rashtriya Swayamsevakh Sangh* (National Self-Help Army), a Fascist and Hindu-supremacist group founded in 1922 and still active, which is implicitly responsible for having Steele killed to revenge the death at Steele's hands of an Indian. The wartime and postwar U.S. presence in India is registered in Joe MacKendrick, visiting to investigate the wartime death of his brother.

India is present as background in *A Male Child,* but the novel concentrates on the other end of the colonial connection, the effects of colonial service on families, particularly siblings, in the U.K., principally represented by London as both imperial capital and the place of sprawling suburban ambitions. In the brooding house called Aylward, Mrs. Hurst, gin-drinking and emotionally violent, mourns her favorite son, Edward, killed in the war, and resents her surviving son, Alan; the narrator is an army friend of Alan's, Ian Canning. Alan represents an ethic of self-sacrifice and duty, suppressing his own feelings to humor his mother and sustain a wretched marriage, but also a muscular energy and no-nonsense approach; Ian, mysteriously ill, prone to depressive inertia, and struggling to become a writer, is also unhappily married, but later divorces and tries to articulate what Alan cannot. There are some memorable minor characters, notably the opportunistic widower Rex Coles, but the most haunting figure is Mrs. Hurst, who "had twisted the truth into a pattern of her own choosing, and . . . to unravel it face to face, heart to heart, would be more than she could bear" (p. 131). The worry that in *Johnnie Sahib* attended a false construction of others here becomes an understanding that such false constructions imprison those who create or believe in them—an understanding that would in the *Raj Quartet* be transformed into a scathing analysis of delusory national pride and sugarcoated imperial history.

MIDDLE NOVELS, 1958–1964

By the mid-1950s Paul was a partner in his firm and a sought-after literary agent whose clients included John Braine, "M. M. Kaye," Muriel Spark, Arthur C. Clarke, Morris West, Mervyn Peake, Ronald Searle, John Fowles, and Elizabeth David. Working closely on their manuscripts improved his own prose, but his own fourth novel, *The Mark of the Warrior* (1958), marks a different breakthrough. His attempt to represent the diverse complexity of British and Indian lives in the Raj needed a large cast of characters and an ever-ready *copia* (inventiveness) of plot that in *The Alien Sky* had threatened to run out of control. Now, perhaps inspired by Samuel Beckett's famous play *Waiting for Godot* (Paris, 1953; London, 1955), he developed a technique of creative iteration in which, instead of inventing something new at every turn, a different aspect of something already created was revealed.

The Mark of the Warrior begins with a prologue narrating the deaths of a young lieutenant, John Ramsay, and a group of men during the shambles of the British retreat from Burma in 1942; Ramsay's commanding officer, Major Craig, survives, and back in India is posted to an officer cadet training unit to teach others what he has learned about jungle warfare and from defeat. Among the cadets is Bob Ramsay, John's brother, who reveals outstanding qualities of command, potentially far greater than Craig's, and as the novel develops, deeply disturbing questions arise about what actually happened in the jungle and how John Ramsay died. The training course culminates in a realistic passing-out exercise, held in a nearby patch of jungled hill terrain, the Chota Bandar, during which the cadets are under Bob Ramsay's command. In a first glimmer of the INA (Indian National Army), Indian troops are cast as the Japanese enemy, and political tensions within the exercise multiply alarmingly as Ramsay develops his "fictional situations which might involve actual hardship" (p. 98). During the final attack one of the cadets gets into trouble crossing a swollen river: Ramsay manages to save him but is himself swept away and drowned.

One would think the accidental death of a cadet far too small a peg on which to hang an imperial tragedy, but in the bouncing echoes between the deaths of the Ramsay brothers under Craig's command, and the intense detail of an enclosed world, Scott's theme grows and resonates in a way that makes *The Mark of the Warrior* a much bigger novel than its two hundred pages suggest. The title also becomes intimately and persistently resonant within the plot: it is the Ramsay brothers who bear the mark and can take to the jungle as a place in which to kill, while Craig lacks the mark and can think of the jungle only as a place in which it is difficult to survive. But it is the Ramsays who die there, and Craig who survives—at least in part because he is capable, as the Ramsays seem not to be, of mutual love with a woman. Craig's wife, Esther, is the only substantial female character, but as such she brings a vivid depth to the male world in which she is isolated, and a powerful sense of judgment attends her love for Craig and instinctive dislike of both Ramsays. The novel achieves an austere and haunting tragedy and points directly toward the *Raj Quartet.*

The use of iteration to structure and discipline *copia* is also evident in *The Chinese Love Pavilion* (1960), a tale reminiscent of Conrad. The narrator is Tom Brent, a rather ordinary man wounded during the war, but the principal focus is Brian Saxby, a wealthy spiritual adventurer whom Brent first meets in the mid-1930s. Saxby helps Brent to get work on an experimental farm in the Punjab but himself disappears into the jungles of Malaya, where he lives with the Sakai, isolated tribes of the far interior. Immediately after the war Brent discovers that Saxby stayed in Malaya during the Japanese occupation, participating in guerrilla warfare, and is now suspected of masterminding a campaign of revenge in which Malays or Chinese who had collaborated are burned alive. The trail leads to the town of Bukit Kallang, and so to the extraordinary figure of Teena Chang, a prostitute and brothel madam who protected a group of women by coming to a civilized arrangement with the local Japanese officers and simultaneously providing women to the local guerrillas. Her brothel is the eponymous Love Pavilion, an ornate folly in the garden of a wealthy Malay merchant; the garden was also used for executions and is known locally as the "Garden of Madness" because so many people "lost their heads" there. The British occupying force, under Major Reid, has simply taken over the civilized arrangement, assigning Teena's girls to various officers; Brent falls in love with Teena; and Saxby, believing her to have been a collaborator, threatens her life.

Readers expect the denouement to involve Saxby, and Brent's evolving accounts of Saxby are central. In the end, though, Saxby turns out to be a creature as much of rumor as of reality, and amid the confusion a less heroic and more

wasteful tragedy blooms the death of Teena Chang, either by her own hand or at those of a young subaltern to whom Reid had awarded her in celebration of his first kill, his "blooding" as a man and officer. The uncertainty of what really happened and Brent's unwillingness to acknowledge either his betrayal of Teena or his larger responsibilities, provoke a need to reassess his reliability as a narrator—a distinct sharpening of the theme announced in *Johnnie Sahib* and developed in Mrs. Hurst, and (like Reid's desperate confusions of sexuality and violence) another clear pointer toward the *Raj Quartet.*

Malaya remains central to *The Birds of Paradise* (1962), but in the grim form of "Pig-Eye Camp," based on Changi, the most notorious of the Japanese civilian detention camps. The narrator, Bill Conway, is the son of an Anglo-Indian political resident whose job was to superintend the running of a small, nominally autonomous princely state (of which more than six hundred survived in British India until 1947). Conway's memories, scarred by his experiences in Pig-Eye, reach back to his childhood in that native state, Tradura—rich in friendships with a white girl (Dora), the prince's son (Krishanramarao), and such adventures as tiger hunting, but poor in the emotional coldness and severe discipline of his father. The use of these memories within Conway's narrative invokes a subtle and detailed image of the Raj both as polity and society, and the course of Conway's life from Tradura to Pig-Eye and back again weaves a still larger picture, showing both a general prewar image of the Raj and the impact on it of wartime events. The reappearance of Conway Senior in the *Raj Quartet* signals how close Scott was coming to the assemblage of materials and techniques he needed to bear full witness as a novelist to what he had experienced as a soldier.

The title of *The Birds of Paradise* draws on an old myth, fueled by native hunters who removed the feet postmortem, that such birds were footless and always on the wing, and an account of the novel's composition that Scott gave in 1961 suggests how richly his imagination was working:

> An Indian Prince. They still call them princes, but they have all been divested of their power since the British went. Their feet, you could say, have been cut off. You know something about the princes. . . . You have always been interested in their changed fortunes. While the British ruled, the princes were kept going in all their feudal magnificence. Their fine feathers were kept shiny. But when the British went and all their lands were merged with the lands of the new dominion they appeared, you might say, in their true light—they had been dead all the time, stuffed like the birds in the glass cages in the central hall of the Natural History Museum. . . .
>
> I remember . . . when the idea of the cage first came. A wet June Saturday afternoon, at about four o'clock, staring at a white wall. It had an onion-shaped dome and bars wrought like lattice-work; once painted gold, but flaked and faded now. It was a big cage, big enough to have housed several fully grown giraffes. And hanging from its tin roof in simulated flight were stuffed specimens of the birds of paradise; below them, as a setting, the trees and shrubs of their natural forest. It was a fine cage; but also curious. The beautiful, ridiculous folly of a man rich enough to indulge an expensive fancy. An Indian Prince. But of the old school. The grandfather, say, of the kind of modern prince who went to Harrow and played cricket for Bombay Province. And however symbolic the cage is to me it is equally symbolic to the old Indian Prince, because he had a joke about it. The birds were like the British: proud, convinced that they excited the admiration and wonder of all who saw them but, in truth, stuffed, dead from the neck up and the neck down.
>
> (*On Writing and the Novel*, pp. 31–32)

The birds begin as a condescending image of the princes as outmoded, feudal relics, gorgeously useless, but end as a joke all Indians might share about the vanity and self-delusions of the British as colonial rulers. That the image is made to cut both ways, equally reflecting and embodying mutually derogatory views, makes it larger and more telling than either of those views, and Scott's evenhandedness, a honed inclusivity of imagination, is one foundation of his greatness as a novelist of conflict.

The last two pre-*Quartet* novels completed his preparations. *The Bender: Pictures from an Exhibition of Middle Class Portraits* (1963) is, as title and subtitle suggest, a comedy of manners, centered on a demand by the apparently successful Tim Spruce that his down-at-heel and rather alcoholic brother George repay an old loan. Ludicrous family shenanigans ensue, and the novel is Scott's funniest, openly comic in a way he ruthlessly excluded from the epic tragedy of the *Quartet* (though tragicomic release fills *Staying On*); one function of *The Bender*, then, may have been to satiate a talent for comedy that would be rigidly disciplined in the great work to come.

The Corrida at San Felíu (1964), conversely, is both tragic and a shimmering exercise in narrative complexity, reminiscent of Nabokov. It is cast as four fragmentary stories and a novella, identified in an anonymous editorial introduction as pieces found among the effects of an expatriate writer, Edward Thornhill, recently killed in a car crash; reading between the lines and fragments, readers can follow various possible understandings of Thornhill's life and death. The Spanish material derives from Scott's family holidays on the Costa Brava in 1959 and 1962: though India is a setting for one fragment, the completion of a novel about a culture quite different from that of the Raj signaled the end of the training process to which Scott had subjected himself since 1946—but he did take from bullfighting lore one critical idea, that of the *querencia*. Literally a "lair" or "haunt," from the verb *querer* (to want or wish for), the *querencia* is a spot in the ring that a bull chooses as home, a spot it will defend and return to: "You can stop him going to the querencia, provoke him to leave it, distract him from finding a secondary querencia, but the mystery of the animal's choice remains unsolved. A shadow on the sand, a damp patch, a blood stain: any of these may mark the spot. But why?" (p. 81). A sense of its *querencia* is emotionally vital to the bull, but does it no good, serving only to guide the matador as he cites the bull to charge and enabling him to prolong the bull's suffering in a theatrical display simultaneously invoking and postponing sacrifice. The term *querencia* never surfaces in the *Raj Quartet,* where a language of bullfighting would be utterly out of place, but the idea of a place of false safety within the arena to which the goaded helplessly cleave becomes richly entwined with the ideas of edited memory and false constructions of history that Scott had latched onto in *Johnnie Sahib.*

RETURN TO INDIA, 1964

In 1960 Scott resigned from Pearn, Pollinger, and Higham to write full time. He was working productively, but financial worries and persistent stomach troubles were sapping confidence; his mother, widowed in 1958, was declining, he was beginning to drink heavily, and his marriage was strained to the point of domestic violence. Conscious of 1963 as "my shit-or-bust year" (quoted in Spurling, p. 263), he decided in December to revisit India, and, if that did not enable him to write as he wanted, to return to full-time employment.

He flew to Bombay in February 1964 and traveled for six weeks. Many people he met, notably Dorothy Ganapathy and the English-educated Neil Ghosh, inform characters in the *Quartet;* the generous hospitality and help of Indians refreshed Scott's love of the country. His critical encounter, however, was a visit to Narayan Dass in Timmapuram, a small village in Andhra Pradesh; Dass served under Scott during the war, and they had corresponded warmly, but Scott badly underestimated his ability to cope with rural India. Timmapuram had limited electricity, no plumbing, and deeply traditional Hindu attitudes that labeled him both "honored guest" and (as a non-Hindu) "unclean." Initially he was delighted by his welcome, but food saturated in ghee gave him terrible diarrhea, and repeated public treks to the fields induced paranoia and hatred. After ten days he fled:

> I arrived in Hyderabad next morning, still stunned and vicious. I knocked the hand of a beggar woman off my arm, gave the tongah wallah less than he asked for, ignored his protests and stalked into the Ritz Palace, called for beer and complained about the price. And then sat down in the blessed privacy of a civilized bedroom, with bathroom attached—blessed, blessed bathroom with all mod cons.
>
> My relief is indescribable. But already in that relief there was the shadow of something that appalled me—the growing shadow of my ingratitude, my ridiculous irrational fears, my utter dependence upon the amenities of my own kind of civilization. But the sense of relief was enough to keep the shadow at bay, for a while.
>
> (*On Writing and the Novel,* p. 136)

And only "for a while." Confronted by racism and anger in himself, Scott did not flinch but stared hard into the mirror, and his understanding of the prejudices that flourished in the Raj, among people far from home who ruled as an isolated minority, was exponentially deepened.

Back in the U.K., still with awful gastritis, he was sent by a friend to Dr. George Farréras in Paris, who diagnosed amebiasis, a parasitic illness causing recurrent diarrhea and linked to tiredness, depression, and mood swings, from which Scott had probably suffered since 1943. The cure was traumatic, but by late June he felt better than for years and wrote himself a bold instruction: "Risk all. The Indian novel I ought by now to be able to write" (quoted in Spurling, p. 310). Next day he began *The Jewel in the Crown,* and the *Quartet* grew steadily during the next decade.

RAJ QUARTET

Scott's sequence is complex, diverse, and nonlinear, the two central novels covering many of the same events from perspectives that may complement, supplement, or clash with one another. In reading, what is learned when and from whom is of absorbing interest and vital to the moral exposure of short-circuited judgments; in criticism an overview is needed.

All four novels have an anonymous narrator, the Stranger, sometimes explicitly present as an interviewer of characters, who has assembled documents and reconstructed the evidence of the dead. A publisher's reader, he found (c. 1964) in some military memoirs a passage about the gang rape of an English girl, Daphne Manners, in Mayapore, a small cantonment town, on 9 August 1942—the day riots sparked by Gandhi's arrest began. Rapes of Englishwomen, though a fear by which the Raj was hag-ridden after the Mutiny of 1857, were extremely rare, and the Stranger set out to investigate.

Mayapore means "City of Illusion" (from Hindi *maya,* "the illusion of the material world"), and is a fiction, but, with its surrounding towns, mechanisms of administration, railway lines, and neighboring Princely State of Mirat, conjointly forms an archetypal province within the historical Raj—something like Faulkner's Yoknapatawpha County, Mississippi. Scott makes no formal distinction between fiction and history, scrutinizing imaginations and events with equal sympathy and skepticism; on a paper napkin (now archived in Austin) he told himself to "Forget the fact that it never happened," and readers must do likewise. Historical events and places in the *Quartet,* and the relevant actions of historical people, are reported with stringent accuracy, and the fiction drives toward the largest possible truth, consistent with history books but including personal truths and reflections too small or awkward for official historians to notice. A systematic reader and reviewer of Indian materials since the 1940s, Scott was a fine amateur historian, particularly of subjects (like quotidian life and the INA) that professionals ignored or suppressed. A historical education is skillfully worked into the novels and in the TV adaptation is brilliantly

represented by archive newsreels. General Western ignorance of Indian history and imperial structures means many readers need that education.

The story the Stranger uncovered is haunting. Miss Manners is staying in Mayapore with a Rajput widow, Lady Chatterjee, and forms a close friendship with an Indian journalist, Hari Kumar, English educated and exquisitely spoken but impoverished. White Mayapore is suspicious, and the district superintendent of police, the socially mobile, impressive, and disturbing Ronald Merrick, warns Daphne to drop Kumar—advice she ignores because she is in love with Kumar, and Merrick himself is courting her. Unknown to Daphne, Merrick had once arrested Kumar, and his suspicions about Kumar's involvement with extremists, though almost certainly mistaken, are not wholly unreasonable.

Reason, however, is at a premium: between January and June 1942 the Japanese blitzkrieg was racing from the China Sea to the River Chindwin, pushing the British out of Malaya, Singapore (where 100,000 Allied troops surrendered), and Burma, and threatening northern India. Gandhi, appalled by Britain's apparent inability to defend India, called on the British to "Quit India!" and leave her "to God or to anarchy"—in practice, to the Japanese. Political tensions soared, groups like the RSS who despised Gandhian nonviolence became more active, and British attitudes to "treason" hardened. When Congress passed the Quit India! motion on 8 August the whole organization was banned and activists down to subdistrict level interned; then came the riots.

Miss Manners is not the only victim of 9 August. In the afternoon an elderly mission school superintendent, Miss Crane, driving back from an outlying school with an Indian teacher, Mr. Chaudhuri, is attacked by a mob; unwilling to speed through the rioters, she stops and is dragged from her car. She is beaten and Mr. Chaudhuri killed; the police find her holding his dead hand, saying "There's nothing I can do"

(*Jewel*, p. 69). That evening, with Mayapore apparently calm, Daphne and Hari meet in a deserted park, the Bibighar Gardens, and become lovers, but they are observed by unknown people, probably Indian rioters, who bind Hari and gang rape Daphne. Traumatized, and terrified that Hari will be accused, Daphne swears him to silence, suppressing his presence in her statement to police. He is arrested anyway, with five other young Indians found drinking hooch near the crime scene. Though obviously bruised (by the rapists), Hari refuses to answer questions: Merrick's suspicion that he is both rapist and political subversive is intense, the two being (for Merrick and many Anglo-Indians) in any case related. Merrick almost certainly tortures Hari, who comes close to confessing whatever Merrick wants. Without Daphne's evidence no rape case can be made, and in the end Hari and the other suspects are made political detenus, a decision taken at a level far above Merrick. Two months later Miss Crane becomes *sati* (suttee), burning herself to death in the manner of Hindu widows. (Death by fire is a recurring image in the *Quartet*.)

Scott's concern in *The Jewel in the Crown* with Daphne's rape and its aftermath serves several related purposes. "Bibighar" means "the house of women," and at the Bibighar in Cawnpore (Kanpur), during the 1857 mutiny (First War of Independence), some two hundred British women and children were imprisoned, ritually humiliated, and eventually murdered, their bodies stuffed into a well. The British troops who discovered the carnage, rapidly followed by journalists and public opinion, became convinced of mass rape and mutilation before the murders, and barbaric revenges were taken upon captured mutineers (see, for example, Christopher Hibbert, *The Great Mutiny*, 1980). In fact there had been no rapes or mutilations, and from the mid-1860s most historians admitted as much, but in the Anglo-Indian imagination threats of Indian rebellion remained threats of rape. In Mayapore one rape (by unknown men) certainly happens, but another (by Kumar) does not happen, although white Mayapore compulsively supposes it to have happened, and Merrick acts accordingly. Scott's novel, examining history through fiction, exposes historical mechanisms of distorted judgment and rewrites E. M. Forster's famous novel about an imaginary rape, *A Passage to India* (1924), as savagely as William Golding's *Lord of the Flies* (1954) rewrites R. M. Ballantyne's cozy fantasy of civilized shipwreck, *The Coral Island* (1854).

As the Quit India! riots subside, Daphne, pregnant either by Kumar or a rapist, decides to bear the child and is ostracized by the English, especially women. She goes to stay with her widowed aunt, Lady Manners, on a houseboat in Kashmir, and in May 1943 dies in childbirth. Her daughter survives and is adopted by Lady Manners as Parvati Manners—again horrifying the white community. The thrust of the sequence then turns to follow an army family on holiday, the Laytons, disturbed on the neighboring houseboat by Parvati's crying. Mildred Layton and her pretty, conformist younger daughter Susan cut Lady Manners and revile poor Daphne; Sarah Layton, the elder and tougher-minded daughter, secretly goes to see Parvati and apologizes to Lady Manners for her family's bigotry. A second set of connections is established through a retired mission schoolteacher, Miss Batchelor, an ex-colleague of Miss Crane's and a paying guest of Mildred's stepmother-in-law, Mabel Layton, in Pankot, the hill station where Mildred and her daughters live. Colonel John Layton, Mildred's husband and commanding officer, First Battalion, Pankot Rifles, is a POW in Germany, captured with most of his men in North Africa.

The histories of the Laytons and Barbie Batchelor between 1943 and 1947 form the bulk of the *Quartet*. Mildred Layton, drinking to the point of alcoholism, has a grass widow's affair with the desiccated regimental adjutant, Kevin Coley, and conducts a savage campaign against Barbie (evicted after Mabel's death on D Day, 1944), but insists on the rigid maintenance of her own privileges and of social protocols in general.

Sarah has to obey while discreetly paying her mother's bridge debts and trying to protect her sister, Barbie, and the memory of her absent father. In mid-1944 she loses her virginity to a cheerful cad, Jimmy Clark, and has an abortion—which her mother insists on but never emotionally acknowledges. Susan tries in October 1943 to escape more conventionally, marrying a young officer, Teddie Bingham, and getting pregnant legally. In April 1944 Teddie is killed at Imphal, and in June (after discovering Mabel's corpse) Susan gives birth prematurely. Her son is to be christened Edward after his dead father, but the day before Susan dresses him in a lace gown worked with butterflies, places him on the lawn, pours kerosene around him, sets fire to it, and becomes peacefully catatonic. Barbie, lingering in Pankot as a guest of the vicar, slowly loses her faith and suffers repeated humiliations. Horrified by her accidental witness of Mildred's adultery, obsessively reading Emerson's essays "On History" and "On Self-Reliance," haunted by what she believes was the misburial of Mabel, she finally becomes deranged after a tonga accident and dies in a mental asylum on the morning of Hiroshima.

Another strand of material is introduced by Susan and Teddie's 1943 wedding in Mirat, where Teddie is stationed. The wedding party is staying in a guesthouse loaned to the army by the Nawab of Mirat, a Kasim. His distant relation, Mohammed Ali Kasim (known as MAK), a senior congressman, is a political detenu, and the Nawab employs MAK's younger son, Ahmed, as his social secretary. The Laytons meet Ahmed, whom Sarah begins to love, and the Wazir (prime minister), an elderly White Russian named Dmitri Bronowsky, a skilled raconteur, machiavel, and spymaster. They also have an encounter with far-reaching consequences: Teddie's best man falls ill before the wedding, so Teddie asks his roommate to stand in—Ronald Merrick, turned captain in intelligence and INA expert, and pursued since leaving Mayapore by a sinister campaign of persecution revenging his

treatment of Kumar and the other Indians he arrested. A probable agent of that persecution, Pandit Baba, turns up in Mirat before the wedding, and on the day, as Teddie and Merrick are being driven to church, someone throws a stone. Teddie suffers a cut cheek, the ceremony has to be briefly postponed, and guards posted outside the reception refuse entry to the Nawab, the guest of honor. The wedding seems jinxed, and after Bronowsky reveals Merrick's former identity as a controversial policeman, Teddie and the Laytons blame him for agreeing to be best man. The unfairness of their judgment, founded on class bigotry disdaining the police as an inferior service and Merrick as a social climber, is underscored by knowledge that it was Merrick on whom Teddie had relied to organize the wedding. But the connection Merrick makes with an apologetic Bronowsky is advantageous, if complicated by Bronowsky's belief that Merrick is (like himself) homosexual.

When Teddie, a regular soldier, is briefed on the INA, he becomes terrified he will meet turncoat soldiers from his own proud regiment, the Muzzafirabad Guides. At Imphal, interrogating a captured INA man with Merrick, he does: the turncoat says that other ex-Muzzies are nearby, and when Merrick's back is turned Teddie goes forward in a jeep, relying on regimental loyalty to make the turncoats surrender, and is ambushed. Merrick manages to save the Indian driver, but the prisoner, the jeep, and Teddie are lost; Merrick himself, facially burned and minus his left arm, is recommended for a medal. The news disturbs the Laytons and Pankot: on one hand it seems like the stone in Mirat, Teddie's death tainted by Merrick's proximity as his wedding had been; on the other, Merrick's heroism seems to cancel out his low birth and make him what he perhaps yearns to be, "one of us." For readers there is a major complication, the reexamination and release of Kumar, and his allegations about Merrick's awful treatment of him. Kumar's interrogator this time is Nigel Rowan (who knew him at school and later became friendly with Sarah), and the authorities he represents want to offset Merrick's probably illegal cruelties in 1942 against his to-be-decorated gallantry in 1944, and take no other action. For the grief-stricken Susan, however, the Laytons are simply beholden to Merrick, and on her insistence Sarah visits Merrick in the hospital to ask him to be Edward's godfather.

Merrick refuses, but his connection with the Laytons is renewed. After an interval in which he recovers, Sarah has her abortion, and Susan (institutionalized after endangering Edward in her fire ritual) is partly restored to mental health by a Reichian psychiatrist, he begins to turn up in Pankot, meeting Barbie Batchelor on the day of her tonga accident and slowly becoming an intimate of the Laytons. In mid-1945 Colonel Layton returns from Germany with all his men but one—Havildar Muzzafir Khan, who has joined the *Frei Hind*, the equivalent of the INA in the European Theater. Repatriated to India and isolated (by general order) from former comrades and officers, including Colonel Layton, the Havildar commits suicide after repeated interrogation by Merrick. This awful news coincides with Susan accepting Merrick's proposal of marriage. Despite frantic opposition from Sarah, who dislikes Merrick and thinks Susan mentally unstable, the engagement is announced, and the wedding takes place early in 1946.

The last years of Merrick's war service as an INA expert are complicated by Lieutenant Sayed Kasim of the Ranpur Regiment, MAK's elder son, recaptured in mid-1944 as an INA major—which leads directly to MAK's release from detention and represents an impossible problem. Congress has to support the INA men, of whom there are thousands, but MAK, a devout Muslim and trained lawyer who thinks contract a sacred foundation of civil order, cannot condone Sayed's treason. Division is exacerbated by MAK's continuing loyalty to Congress's vision of a united, secular India,

while Sayed has become a devotee of Jinnah's Muslim League, advocating a separate Islamic state, Pakistan. As Sayed's case officer, Merrick superintends his meeting with MAK, a tour-de-force of writing in which the conflicts between religions and loyalties that would in 1947 rip India apart are superbly portrayed. Merrick's duties bring him renewed contact with Dmitri Bronowsky and in late 1946 a job overhauling the Mirati police to ensure impartial policing of sectarian conflict.

With peace and renewed domestic politics, independence becomes imminent, and the Muslim League demands Partition. Congress balks, negotiations stall, and violence escalates, but in Mirat, Merrick maintains the Pax Britannica. As Bronowsky explains, "He treated the whole thing as if it were just a silly quarrel between naughty children. And in a way he was right. He inspired confidence with his impartiality and his absolutely inflexible and unshakable sense of his own authority. It can be a very dangerous combination" (*Division*, p. 561). Yet Merrick is uneasy: like Kipling's Kim, and some real policemen, he has Indian informants and sometimes cross-dresses as a Pathan to gain knowledge not available to white Sahibs. He sends Susan and Edward back to Pankot, though Sarah (tutoring the Nawab's daughter) chooses to stay. When he is thrown from his horse, he claims another stone had been thrown, but no one else saw the thrower and Bronowsky dismisses the story. Partition had been announced, and ten million refugees were on the move, so everyone was frantically busy: Who had time now for a stone? Then Merrick is murdered, in his own bedroom, dressed in Indian clothes and brown face paint, strangled and hacked about, the word "Bibighar" scrawled on a mirror. Bronowsky thinks it a revenge made possible by Merrick's involvement in a homosexual underworld, and to preserve public order and decency facts are suppressed and a fulsome funeral arranged. A few days later Sarah accompanies a devastated Susan back to Pankot, and Ahmed Kasim joins them to be with his father for Independence Day. But just after departure the train is attacked by Hindu extremists, and all Muslims on board, including Ahmed, are massacred, raising the awful possibility that Merrick's murder was not revenge but preparation. Sarah is a paralyzed witness: at the next station, kneeling in mud at a water tap as the survivors try to help the dying, she can only echo Miss Crane's impotent lament over Mr. Chaudhuri's body (*Jewel*, p. 69, *Division*, p. 587). So the *Quartet* ends, just short of a necessary but mutilated and blood-spattered independence.

Much of the last novel is focused through Guy Perron, a young historian who has chosen to serve in the ranks for the professional insights he hoped it would afford him. He met and seduced Sarah in 1945 and briefly served under Merrick, whom he loathed, so his views are slanted, but as a professional he acknowledges duties to facts and fairness and has a more detached British rather than Anglo-Indian perspective. In some ways distinct—he alone, for example, understands Barbie Batchelor's late obsession with Emerson—Perron is tied into the web of the *Quartet* by his schooling at Chillingborough, the alma mater of Colonel Layton, Jimmy Clark, Rowan, and Kumar (after his release from political detention, scraping a living by tutoring schoolchildren). Perron, back in India for the transition to independence and to see Sarah, is another helpless witness of the train massacre. A few days afterward he tries to visit Kumar, but Hari is out, and Perron can only leave his card, wondering (as departing imperialists must) "what harm or good [he'd] done" (*Division*, p. 597).

TITULAR ARCHITECTURES

One way of analyzing how Scott shaped his extended plot is to consider the various titles he gave to the constituent parts of each volume. Throughout the *Quartet*, section titles emphasize and invite comparison of places and times—The MacGregor House, The Bibighar Gardens, The Tennis Court, The Moghul Room, The Dak Bungalow, and The Circuit House, 1945 and 1947, An Evening at the Club and another at the Maharanees. There are logical progressions, from arrest to release and wedding to christening, but also hollow, resonant clichés questioning loyalty and regimental honor, or invoking the mythic hopelessness of Pandora's Box. Above all arch the volume titles, each a diagnostic image. *The Jewel in the Crown*, a traditional tag for India's place in the British Empire, is also an allegorical print showing Queen Victoria (who never visited India) receiving tribute from Indian princes while plump angels soar above; both Miss Crane and Miss Batchelor have copies, used for teaching. Merrick sees Miss Crane's after her death and is given Barbie's because, "One should always share one's hopes" (*Towers*, p. 388). He passes it on to his stepson, Edward, but the pious, pompous hopes embodied in the print have long failed.

The Day of the Scorpion is Sarah's and Susan's childhood memory: a garden boy shows them a scorpion encircled by fire appearing to commit heroic suicide. Puzzling over Susan's fiery encirclement of her baby, a Pankot officer explains that in fact the scorpion simply contracts as it scorches to death. It is an image of doom and false glamourization, the Raj as "an insect entirely surrounded by the destructive element, so that twist, turn, attack, or defend yourself as you might you were doomed; not by the forces ranged against you but by the terrible inadequacy of your own armour . . . your conduct, ideas, principles, the code by which you lived" (*Towers*, p. 296). *The Towers of Silence* are where Parsis leave their dead exposed to be eaten by vultures, thereby returning to nature—an image of hill stations like Pankot, sentinels over the plain yet retreats where British vigilance lapsed; of the moribund "stiff upper lip" that precludes honest speech; and of Barbie's mortified faith, unheard voice, and final silence. Dividing ill-gotten gains is proverbial, but after three titles with definite articles the indefinite *A Division of the Spoils*—one that is casual, and could have been otherwise—horribly complements the queasy sense of spoils as both loot and something vandalized, as the subcontinent was by Empire and Partition. The arc from imperial hopes, through a fiery death supposed a brave suicide, to silent decay and a robbers' carve-up is Scott's epic tragedy, the fullest account of Britain's imperial abnegation and death, and the fissile creation of the Indo-Pakistani conflicts that continue to this day.

LITERARY STYLE AND VENTRILOQUY

Scott was an extraordinary prose stylist, and the remarkable sentences peppering the *Quartet* are among its great pleasures. His ventriloquy is the ability to write as one of his characters, creating distinct styles for each: to compare passages from Daphne's journal, the memoirs by Guy and Sarah, and the various inset letters is to see a master a work. Consider, for example, a brief excerpt from one subsection of "Civil and Military," an extract from *A Simple Life,* the memoir by Brigadier Reid that set the Stranger on his quest, describing Merrick in 1942:

> I told him I would appreciate it if he stuck his neck out occasionally. I had not mistaken my man. He was young enough still to respond to simple issues with the right mixture of probity and keenness. I could not help but admire him, too, for his outspokenness. He was a man who came from what he called "a very ordinary middle-class background." The Indian Police had been the one job he felt he could do. I knew what he meant, and liked him for his total lack of pretence.
>
> (*Jewel*, p. 293)

The clipped sentences and bluff tone superbly mimic the style of military memoirs and are more tendentious than they seem. Merrick, lacking pedigree and inherited wealth, could not have joined any imperial service but the police,

for none would have taken him, and both the army and civil service thought the police inferior for having officers who were not gentlemen. That is what Merrick meant, and might be what Reid understands—but is not what either actually says.

Compare this with a paragraph by Perron the professional historian about the Merrick he knew in 1945:

> I attributed to him the grossest motives and the darkest intentions without a scrap of real evidence. The interesting thing is that I was convinced that he knew this, that my instinct to hold him in such intense dislike and suspicion was clear to him from the beginning and was one of the reasons why he had chosen me. I believe he found it necessary to be close to someone whose antagonism he knew he could depend on and that without this antagonism he had nothing really satisfactory by which to measure the effect of his behaviour. My antagonism was like an acid, acting on a blank photographic plate which had been exposed to his powerful and inventive imagination. It made the picture emerge for him. This excited him, the more so because my antagonism could not be expressed openly without risk to myself of being guilty of insubordination. There were moments in our association when I felt my animosity inspired in him a gratitude and a contempt both so overwhelming that he felt for me the same tender compassion that is often said to overcome the inveterate slaughterer of game in the split second before he squeezes the trigger.
>
> (*Division*, pp. 230–231)

More honest and complex thoughts inhabit more complex sentences, and Perron's wider reading and greater modernity are reflected in his diction and imagery. Yet the repetitions of "antagonism" embody the distorting obsession Perron reports. The third sentence ("I believe . . . . his behaviour") and the last ("There were moments . . . the trigger"), consistent with Perron's style, also show Scott's ability to omit commas yet drive forward with clarity: in thirty-eight and fifty-one words respectively there are no marks, no pause from capital letter to full stop, and no ambiguities. Grammatically remarkable, this capacity for the seamless coexists with exposures of character, for Perron's final image, of Merrick as one of Hemingway's sentimental blood sportsmen, is profoundly false to Merrick's class background, mind-set, and tastes. Readers also have the interesting task of squaring Reid's and Perron's estimates of Merrick.

Scott's control of extended leitmotifs also deserves comment, and readers may track, among others, the images of birds and aeroplanes, monsoons and rainwear, Indian light, doorways and architecture, smell, and the passing of days held in trust. He was also a master of present (as well as absent) punctuation, and his colons and semicolons reward aesthetic as much as grammatical attention. There are also many moments when an apparently casual metaphor is extended far beyond its likely breaking point, yet in extension acquires ever-greater force and analytical cogency. A single example must suffice, Pankot's collective sense of the reclusive Mabel Layton:

> Her withdrawal was accepted with feelings that lay somewhere between respect and regret; which meant that they were fixed at a point of faint disapproval, therefore seldom expressed, but when they were, an idea would somehow be conveyed of Mrs Layton's isolation having a meaningful connexion with an earlier golden age which everyone knew had gone but over whose memory she stood guardian, stony-faced and uncompromising: a bleak point of reference, as it were a marker-buoy above a sunken ship full of treasure that could never be salvaged; a reminder and a warning to shipping still afloat in waters that got more treacherous every year.
>
> This sense of danger, of the sea-level rising, swamping the plains, threatening the hills, this sense of imminent inundation, was one to which people were not now unaccustomed and although the outbreak of war in Europe had momentarily suggested the erection of a rocky headland on which to stand fast, the headland was far away, in England, and India was very close and all about.

And as the war in Europe began to enter its disagreeable phases it looked as though the headland had been either a mirage or a last despairing lurch of all those things to which value had been attached and upon which the eye, looking west from Pankot, had been kept loyally fixed through all the years in which the encouraging sensation of being looked at loyally in return was steadily diminished until to the sense of living in expectation of inundation had been added the suspicion that this inundation would scarcely be remarked, or, if it were, not regretted when it happened.

(Towers, pp. 32–33)

LAST YEARS: *STAYING ON* AND AMERICA

By the time he finished the *Quartet* Scott was in poor health. Use of tobacco and alcohol to fuel his writing had compromised his body and his behavior. In 1975 Penny left him and in 1976 filed for divorce: though shocked and naturally devastated, Scott also knew he could have no complaints. He had admitted years before that India was his true mistress, and despite the destructive honesty of Penny's judgment and departure, his creative drive was still running strongly. He did set about preserving friendship with Penny and restoring his equally neglected relationships with his daughters, but he continued to write, and the problem of domestic loneliness was partly solved by a new venture into teaching. Scott had lectured before for the British Council, and in 1975 had undertaken a lecture tour in the United States. After completing his last novel, *Staying On,* in mid-1976, he took up an appointment he had secured at the University of Tulsa, teaching a creative writing course for the fall semester. Though nervous, and skeptical of grading creative work, Scott proved a great hit with both faculty and students. He returned in the summer of 1977, and it was there that he was diagnosed with colon cancer; after one operation in Tulsa he had to return to the U.K. for further treatment. The warmth of his relations with the university is commemorated in its extensive holdings of his letters and papers, in the Special Collections of the McFarlin Library.

Staying On is a coda to the *Quartet* but also a freestanding and very fine tragicomedy. It picks up the lives of two minor characters, Major "Tusker" Smalley and his wife, Lucy (née Little), who were in Pankot during the war. When independence came in 1947 they decided not to return to the U.K., where jobs and money, not to mention servants and sympathy for displaced colonials, were in short supply, but instead to stay on in India. After a brief and not very successful venture into commercial life, Tusker retired to Pankot, and by 1972 he and Lucy are the last English inhabitants, living cheaply on sufferance at Smith's Hotel. The novel covers a few days in spring, including the carnivalesque Hindu festival of *Holi* (at which Tusker makes a considerable fool of himself), and memorably features the hotel manager, Mr. Bhoolabhoy, who likes Tusker and Lucy but is browbeaten by the hotel owner, his grossly overweight wife. The servants with whom the Smalleys have grown old, Ibrahim and Minnie, are also a part of the comedy, as is an extended and absurd dispute with Mrs. Bhoolabhoy about whose responsibility it is to employ a gardener. And there is Tusker's dog, actually called "Blackshaw" but known to almost everyone in an Indian mispronunciation, "Bloxsaw," who inevitably gets where he shouldn't.

The rich minor key of the comedy is, however, darkened and made whole by the bass line, for *Staying On* is not the story of Tusker's life and marriage but of his last days and long-feared but still unexpected death, alone, unseen, and in exile. There is also the unsung fate of Lucy, whose sharper memory and greater energies produce an exchange of letters with Sarah Layton that gives some glimpses of other characters from the *Quartet:* she is now married to Guy Perron, Susan has remarried for the second time, finding happiness at last, and little

Edward has grown up to be a doctor; John and Mildred have died. But when Lucy is widowed, and left the only white person for a hundred miles, the consolations of correspondence are slight:

> All I'm asking, Tusker, is did you mean it when you said I'd been a good woman to you? And if so, why did you leave me? Why did you leave me here? I am frightened to be alone, Tusker, although I know it is wrong and weak to be frightened—
>
> —but now, until the end, I shall be alone, whatever I am doing, here as I feared, amid the alien corn, waking, sleeping, alone for ever and ever and I cannot bear it but mustn't cry and must must get over it but don't for the moment see how, so with my eyes shut, Tusker, I hold out my hand, and beg you, Tusker, beg, beg you to take it and take me with you. How can you not, Tusker? Oh, Tusker, Tusker, Tusker, how can you make me stay here by myself while you yourself go home?
>
> (*Staying On*, p. 255)

So Scott's last and most widely read novel ends, as the empire that shaped him had done, in desperate lament.

Staying On was greeted with acclaim. As a one-volume tragicomedy rather than a four-volume epic tragedy, a gentle work shaded with rueful laughter and distanced from the moral anger of the *Quartet* that produced it, it was more acceptable to critics and nostalgics, and in 1977 it won the Booker Prize, presented in absentia because Scott was too ill to attend. Filmed in 1979 by Granada TV as a pilot for their adaptation of the *Quartet,* the success of *Staying On* began an upsurge in Scott's reputation and sales that still continues. Scott did complete one final piece of writing, a version of Cinderella illustrated by his daughter Sally and published in a limited edition in 1979 as *After the Funeral.* But he was being eaten alive by cancer and remorse and, with his astonishing act of witness profoundly and unmistakably complete, needing no further attention or effort, died at the Middlesex Hospital in London on 1 March 1978. He was only fifty-seven.

Selected Bibliography

WORKS OF PAUL SCOTT

NOVELS

Johnnie Sahib. London: Eyre and Spottiswoode, 1952.

The Alien Sky. London: Eyre and Spottiswoode, 1953; as *Six Days in Marapore,* New York: Doubleday, 1953.

A Male Child. London: Eyre and Spottiswoode, 1956; New York: Dutton, 1957.

The Mark of the Warrior. London: Eyre and Spottiswoode; New York: Morrow, 1958.

The Chinese Love Pavilion. London: Eyre and Spottiswoode; New York: Morrow, 1960.

The Birds of Paradise. London: Eyre and Spottiswoode; New York: Dutton, 1962.

The Bender: Pictures from an Exhibition of Middle Class Portraits. London: Secker and Warburg; New York: Morrow, 1963.

The Corrida at San Felíu. London: Secker and Warburg; New York: Morrow, 1964.

The Jewel in the Crown. London: Heinemann; New York: Morrow, 1966. (The first volume of the *Raj Quartet.*)

The Day of the Scorpion. London: Heinemann; New York: Morrow, 1968. (The second volume of the *Raj Quartet.*)

The Towers of Silence. London: Heinemann, 1971; New York: Morrow, 1972. (The third volume of the *Raj Quartet.*)

A Division of the Spoils. London: Heinemann; New York: Morrow, 1975. (The fourth volume of the *Raj Quartet.* The *Quartet* has been issued in a variety of box sets and omnibus editions.)

Staying On. London: Heinemann; New York: Morrow, 1977. Edited by Roy Samson, London: Longman, 1991. (The Longman edition is annotated for U.K. school use.)

ESSAYS, ARTICLES, AND LECTURES

On Writing and the Novel: Essays. Edited by Shelley C. Reece. New York: Morrow, 1987. In the U.K., differently paginated, as *My Appointment with the Muse: Essays, 1961–75,* London: Heinemann, 1986.

"The Raj." In *John Kenneth Galbraith Introduces India.* Edited by Frank Moraes and Edward Howe. London: Andre Deutsch, 1974. Pp. 70–88.

"How Well Have They Worn?—1: *A Passage to India.*" *Times,* 6 January 1966, p. 15.

"India: A Post-Forsterian View." In *Essays by Divers Hands, Being the Transactions of the Royal Society of Literature.* New series, vol. 36. Edited by Mary Stocks. London: Oxford University Press, 1970. Pp. 113–132. (A later but shorter version of this lecture is printed in *On Writing and the Novel.*)

"Imperial Fathers." *Sunday Times,* 16 November 1975, p. 40.

(Scott is known to have written more than 800 reviews. Some were unsigned, and not all have been identified; those that have been, many in the *Times Literary Supplement* or *Country Life,* are held in the Scott Collection, McFarlin Library, University of Tulsa.)

OTHER WORKS

I, Gerontius: A Trilogy: The Creation—The Dream—The Cross. Resurgam Younger Poets 5. London: Favil Press, 1941.

Pillars of Salt. In *Four Jewish Plays.* Edited by H. R. Rubenstein. London: Camelot Press/Victor Gollancz, 1948.

After the Funeral. Andoversford, U.K.: Whittington Press/Heinemann, 1979. (A version of *Cinderella* with illustrations by Sally Scott; a posthumous edition limited to 500 copies.)

RADIO AND TELEVISION PLAYS

Lines of Communication: A New Play Written for Broadcasting. Broadcast on BBC Home Service 12 February 1951. (Microfiche in the BBC Document Archives, Reading, U.K.)

Sahibs and Memsahibs: A Play for Broadcasting. Broadcast on BBC Home Service 2 June 1958. (Microfiche in the BBC Document Archives, Reading, U.K.)

The Situation: A Play. Typescript with autograph corrections, in the Scott Collection, McFarlin Library, University of Tulsa.

Scott's Raj— Or India Returned, also entitled *A Division of the Spoils: Outline for a Possible TV Book Programme.* Dated May 1975. Scott Collection, McFarlin Library, University of Tulsa.

ARCHIVES

Scott's personal papers, letters, and books, plus the autograph manuscript, corrected typescript, and corrected proofs of *Staying On* are at the McFarlin Library, University of Tulsa, Tulsa, Oklahoma. His literary papers, including the autograph manuscripts, corrected typescripts, and corrected proofs of all his novels except *Staying On* are at the Harry Ransom Center for the Humanities, University of Texas, Austin, Texas. Online catalogs of these collections may be viewed at: http://www.hrc.utexas.edu/research/fa/scott.paul.html and http://www.lib.utulsa.edu/Speccoll/Scottp00.htm

TELEVISION ADAPTATIONS OF SCOTT'S WORK

Staying On. Directed by Silvio Narrazino. Granada TV, 1983. Video release. (Pilot for the $10 million TV adaptation of the *Raj Quartet.*)

The Jewel in the Crown. Directed by Christopher Morahan and Jim O'Brien. Screenplay by Ken Taylor. Granada TV. First broadcast in fourteen parts, 1984; released on video in various formats. (This series covers the whole of the *Raj Quartet.*) It was also broadcast in the United States on PBS's *Masterpiece Theater* and in India, and has been multiply rebroadcast and transmitted via cable and satellite worldwide. As well as prompting critical attention to Scott, it has been discussed in its own right by television historians. Web sites giving information about the series and an online course pack may be found at: http://www.museum.tv/archives/etv/J/tmlJ/jewelinthe/jewelinthe.htm and http://www.cocc.edu/cagatucci/classes/eng339/coursepack/makingJewel.htm.

BIOGRAPHICAL STUDIES AND INTERVIEWS

Gant, Roland. "Paul Scott." *Bookseller,* 11 March 1978, p. 1786.

Price, Alice Lindsay, ed. *After Paul: Paul Scott's Tulsa Years.* Tulsa, Okla.: HCE Publications/Riverrun Arts, 1988.

Ringold, Francine. "A Conversation with Paul Scott." *Nimrod* (University of Tulsa), 21:16–32 (Fall–Winter 1976).

Spurling, Hilary. *Paul Scott: A Life.* London: Hutchinson, 1990; New York: Norton, 1991 and Random House, 1996. (The major biography, excellent on facts but prone to rather simplistic readings of the novels as autobiographical.)

Zorn, G. Jean. "Talk with Paul Scott." *New York Times Book Review,* 21 August 1977, p. 31.

CRITICAL STUDIES

Ali, Tariq. "Fiction as History, History as Fiction." *Illustrated Weekly of India,* 8 July 1984. (Ali, a Pakistani Briton, is Scott's most senior champion of subcontinental origin; this essay particularly praises Scott's representation of Indian politics in the 1940s.)

Badiger, V. R. *Paul Scott: His Art and Vision.* New Delhi: Atlantic Publishers and Distributors, 1994.

Banerjee, Jacqueline. "A Living Legacy: An Indian View of Paul Scott's India." *London* magazine, April–May 1980, pp. 97–104.

——. *Paul Scott.* Plymouth, U.K.: Northcote House/British Council, 1999. (This "Writers and Their Work" booklet is a good basic introduction in a generally sound series.)

Beloff, Max. "The End of the Raj: Paul Scott's Novels as History." *Encounter,* 46.5:65–70 (May 1976). (Beloff was a professional historian; Scott saw and was delighted by this influential essay.)

Brandt, George W. "*The Jewel in the Crown* (Paul Scott—Ken Taylor): The Literary Serial; or the Art of Adaptation." In *British Television Drama in the 1980s.* Edited by George W. Brandt. Cambridge and New York: Cambridge University Press, 1993. Pp. 196–213.

Brann, Eva. "Paul Scott's Raj Quintet: Real Politics in Imagined Gardens." In *Poets, Princes & Private Citizens: Literary Alternatives to Postmodern Politics.* Edited by Joseph Knippenberg and Peter Lawler. Lanham, Md.: Rownan and Littlefield, 1996. Pp. 191–209.

Childs, Peter. *Paul Scott's* Raj Quartet: *History and Division.* Victoria, B.C.: English Literary Studies Monograph Series 77, 1998. (The only critical study so far to tackle Scott's use of Emerson.)

Degi, Bruce J. "Paul Scott's Indian National Army: *The Mark of the Warrior* and the *Raj Quartet.*" *CLIO: A Journal of Literature, History, and the Philosophy of History,* 18:41–54 (Fall 1988).

Farrell, J. G. "Indian Identities." *Times Literary Supplement,* 23 May 1975, p. 555. (Farrell also wrote fictions of Anglo-India.)

Gooneratne, Yasmine. "Paul Scott's *Staying On:* Finale in a Minor Key." *Journal of Indian Writing in English,* 9:1–12 (July 1981).

Gorra, Michael. *After Empire: Scott, Naipaul, Rushdie.* Chicago and London: University of Chicago Press, 1997.

Granada Television. *The Making of* The Jewel in the Crown. New York: St. Martin's Press, 1983.

Haswell, Janis Tedesco. *Paul Scott's Philosophy of Place(s): The Fiction of Relationality.* Oxford and New York: Peter Lang, 2002.

Hitchens, Christopher. "A Sense of Mission: *The Raj Quartet.*" *Grand Street,* 4:180–199 (Winter 1985).

Hubel, Teresa. *Whose India? The Independence Struggle in British and Indian Fiction and History.* London: Leicester University Press, 1996.

Moore, Robin. *Paul Scott's Raj.* London: Heinemann, 1990. (An extremely useful study of Scott's historical sources and accuracy by a professional historian.)

Parry, Benita. "Paul Scott's Raj." *South Asian Review,* 8.4:359–369 (July–October 1975).

Rao, K. Bhaskara. *Paul Scott.* Boston: Twayne, 1980.

Rushdie, Salman. "Outside the Whale." *Granta,* 11:125–138 (Spring 1984). Reprinted in Rushdie's *Imaginary Homelands: Essays and Criticism 1981–1991.* Harmondsworth, U.K.: Penguin/Granta, 1991. (This polemical essay savagely attacks Scott for Anglo-centricity and nostalgia; though often cited, particularly with regard to what Rushdie called a "Raj Revival" fueled by the Falklands War, Rushdie carelessly conflates the TV adaptation of the *Quartet* and its reception with Scott's novels, and is more interested throughout in insult than analysis.)

Scanlan, Margaret. "The Disappearance of History: Paul Scott's *Raj Quartet.*" *CLIO: A Journal of Literature, History, and the Philosophy of History,* 15.2:153–169 (Winter 1986).

Suleri, Sara. *The Rhetoric of English India.* Chicago and London: Chicago University Press, 1992.

Swinden, Patrick. *Paul Scott: Images of India.* London: Macmillan, 1980.

———. *Paul Scott.* Windsor, U.K.: Profile Books, 1982.

Tedesco, Janis, and Janet Popham. *An Introduction to the* Raj Quartet. Lanham, Md.: University Press of America, 1985. (A handy beginners' guide, but confusingly organized and sometimes misleading. See also under Haswell above.)

Verma, Anil Kumar. *Paul Scott: A Critical Study of His Novels.* New Delhi: Radha Publications, 1999.

Weinbaum, Francine S. *Paul Scott: A Critical Study.* Austin, Tex.: University of Texas Press, 1992. (Weinbaum knew Scott in his last years; her study is strongly psychoanalytical.)

REFERENCE AND HISTORICAL WORKS

Bhattacharya, Sachchidananda. *A Dictionary of Indian History* (1967). In 2 vols., New Delhi: Cosmo Publications, 1994.

Brown, Judith M. *Modern India: The Origins of an Asian Democracy.* Oxford and New York: Oxford University Press, 1985.

Ghosh, Amitav. "India's Untold War of Independence." *New Yorker: The Fiction Issue: India,* 23 and 30 June 23 1997, pp. 104–121.

Hibbert, Christopher. *The Great Mutiny: India 1857* (1978). Harmondsworth, U.K.: Penguin, 1980.

Lewis, Ivor. *Sahibs, Nabobs and Boxwallahs: A Dictionary of the Words of Anglo-India* (1991). Delhi: Oxford University Press, 1997.

Palmer, Alan. *Dictionary of the British Empire & Commonwealth.* London: John Murray, 1996.

Ward, Andrew. *Our Bones Are Scattered: The Cawnpore Massacres and the Indian Mutiny of 1857.* London: John Murray, 1996.

Yule, Colonel Henry, and A. C. Burnell. *Hobson-Jobson: A Glossary of Colloquial Anglo-Indian Words and Phrases, and of Kindred Terms, Etymological, Historical, Geographical and Discursive* (1886). (Often reprinted; known as *Hobson-Jobson.*)

Vikram Seth
(1952–)

AMITAVA KUMAR

SINCE THE 1980s, fiction by Indian writers in English has found a prominent place on the bookshelves of readers worldwide. The rise of the Indian novel and its unprecedented popularity was owed primarily to the publication, in 1981, of Salman Rushdie's *Midnight's Children* (1981). In the ensuing years, many Indian writers followed Rushdie's example, winning for themselves readers and countless awards. One writer who took a different path from Rushdie's—and who established himself as a unique and creative force on the world literary scene—is the novelist and poet Vikram Seth. If Seth's uniqueness lies, in some measure, in his avoidance of magic realism and other forms of postmodernist stylistic bravura so characteristic of Rushdie, it should be stressed that his body of work is also utterly unlike the literary output of contemporary Indian writers, including Rohinton Mistry, who have written well-received examples of realist or naturalist fiction. This is because each of Seth's books, and this is especially true of his prose, are unlike any other he has written. Unlike Mistry, who has written mostly about small Parsi families living in a single city, Seth has relentlessly explored new forms and new places. In 2003 his works included novels, including one in verse and one of more than thirteen hundred pages, a travel book, a libretto, several volumes of poetry, translations of Chinese poetry, and children's books, making Seth among the most versatile of contemporary writers.

Seth's inventiveness, however, has taken a less overtly political and, in that sense, less transgressive form than Rushdie's, and this perhaps explains why he has not received as much critical attention as he perhaps deserves. Seth's writings have not been seen as paradigmatic examples of Indian literature in English, and he has not been regarded as a guide to an essential Indianness in the way that some of his contemporaries have been. This is not surprising. Of his books, only *A Suitable Boy* (1993) is set in India—his other books take us to China, California, London, Venice, and Vienna. It can be argued that his protean creativity as well as his disregard for ethnic markers in his work convey a cosmopolitan ease and creativity that challenge our very notions of what it means for a writer to have a national identity. To read Seth is to encounter an imagination that, without making claims for one or another literary or political position, discovers the human condition in different places and times in the twentieth and twenty-first centuries.

LIFE

Vikram Seth was born into an upper-middle-class Hindu family in Calcutta, India, on 20 June

1952. His father, Premnath Seth, was a business consultant to a Czech shoe-manufacturing company. His mother, Leila Seth, studied law in England when Premnath Seth was based in London in 1954; she resumed her law practice in Delhi when the family returned to India in 1957. Leila Seth eventually became the first woman to serve as chief justice in the Delhi High Court.

Seth's early education was at well-known boarding schools in northern India, first at Welham and then at Doon School. He won a scholarship to Tonbridge School in Kent, and later attended Corpus Christi College, Oxford, also on scholarship. At Oxford he studied philosophy, politics, and economics, and began to write poetry, learn Chinese, and develop his passion for Western as well as Indian classical music. Homesick, he left school for a year and returned to India, studying cattle and economic-development patterns. He went back to Oxford for his final year and then, in 1975, he traveled to the United States, entering Stanford University for graduate studies in economics. There, Seth met the American poet Timothy Steele, who became his mentor; another influence at Stanford was the British poet and critic Donald Davie.

Seth was awarded a Wallace Stegner fellowship in creative writing at Stanford for the period 1977–1978, which enabled him to pursue his interest in poetry. He obtained his M.A. in economics from Stanford in 1979. Seth's first book of poems, *Mappings,* was self-published in 1981. When the book came out, Seth was in China, doing research for his dissertation (projected title: "Seven Chinese Villages: An Economic and Demographic Portrait") at Nanjing University. In the summer of 1981, while studying at Nanjing, Seth participated in an organized student trip to the northwest, but broke away from the tour to hitchhike through Tibet to his family's home in Delhi. He had kept a journal during his trip and this resulted in the travel book *From Heaven Lake: Travels through Sinkiang and Tibet* (1983), which was awarded the Thomas Cook Travel Book Award in 1983.

Back in California, Seth grew more and more disenchanted with academic work. One day he wandered into the Stanford bookstore and bought several books of poetry—one of which was Charles Johnston's translation from the Russian of Alexander Pushkin's *Eugene Onegin.* He decided to write a novel using the same stanza form, and completed *The Golden Gate* (1986), a verse novel set in California. Reviewers and readers generally responded well to its lighthearted tale of love and loss. Seth had also continued to write poetry during this time and in 1985 published *The Humble Administrator's Garden.* This book, which included poems that referred to Seth's life in China, India, and California, won the Commonwealth Poetry Prize, Asian Region, in the year of its publication. During 1985–1986, Seth was the recipient of the Ingram Merrill fellowship; he was also working, during that period, as a senior editor at Stanford University Press.

The following year, Seth received a Guggenheim fellowship and shipped his library to India, where he stayed with his parents and did research for the project that took the shape of his mammoth novel, *A Suitable Boy.* Originally, Seth had planned to write five short novels about India but, as he began writing, the book grew and when it was published eight years later, it was longer than Tolstoy's *War and Peace.* Among the prizes that the book garnered in 1994 were the W. H. Smith Award and the Commonwealth Writer's Prize, although the book was left off the shortlist for the Booker Prize—the prestigious British literary prize which has often been won by writers from the former colonies. The omission surprised many critics and angered Seth's publisher, but Seth's own response was to keep quiet. A private person, he has remained guarded about his personal life as well, although he did read a poem from his first collection, "Dubious," for a televised profile: "Some men like Jack / and some like Jill. / I'm glad I like / them both."

In the years following the publication of *A Suitable Boy*—despite its heft and subject matter, which was at times unfamiliar to Western readers, the book sold more than a million copies worldwide—Seth lived in London. During these years, he published a libretto and more poems. The novel *An Equal Music* was published in 1999. The story is about two classical musicians and their ill-fated love, which is set to the plot of Orpheus and Eurydice from Greek mythology. Like Seth's other works, it represents a departure in terms of style and subject matter from the books that precede it in his oeuvre. In an interview with Akash Kapur, Seth could as well have been speaking about himself when he observed that what was inspiring about Pushkin was that he "wrote in all sorts of different forms. He didn't succumb to the temptation to repeat himself simply to please a public or a publisher." Readers can expect that Seth will continue to follow a similar course in future works.

FROM HEAVEN LAKE: TRAVELS THROUGH SINKIANG AND TIBET

From Heaven Lake, a book of travel writing, narrates Seth's overland journey from Nanjing, China, to his home in Delhi, India, in the summer of 1981, while a student at Nanjing University. The narrative opens not in Nanjing, however, but in the desert near Turfan in northwest China; it ends with a trip, by air, from Kathmandu, in Nepal, to Delhi. The book's most gripping feature is Seth's unexpected entry into Tibet, considered restricted to foreigners, and then his trek into Nepal from where he catches the flight to India. But the book as a whole has a less dramatic but no less appealing quality of conveying a sense of curiosity that is informed by compassion and humor. Already, then, in this first book of prose by Seth, we are introduced to a quality that the reader will grow to recognize as a characteristic of this writer—an interest less in exotica than in the ordinary, and its appearance on the page as contributing to the charm of daily life.

As Seth writes in the book's introduction, "The land route—for this was a hitch-hiking journey—from the oases of northwest China to the Himalayas crosses four Chinese provinces: Xinjiang (Sinkiang) and Gansu in the northwestern desert; then the basin and plateau of Qinghai; and finally, Tibet." Seth also informs his readers that the book was based on the journal he had kept during the journey as well as the photographs that he took as he made his way through sharply different landscapes and met a variety of people. Although Seth does not mention this in his introduction, the reader also finds scattered in the book a handful of poems that are often unadorned, conversational pieces about the sights and sounds that he encountered on the road. The inclusion of the poems signals in this early work what will become another recognizable feature of Seth's writing—the mixing of prose and poetry, seemingly without any need for explanation or commentary.

From its opening page, *From Heaven Lake* draws the reader into the sensory experience of travel: the dry, breezeless heat in the desert, the buzzing of flies, the brilliance of the light. But what is also present in the description is the voice of the writer, a student of Chinese society who is quietly intent on providing information about the nature of the population and the role of the state.

In the beginning of the narrative, Seth writes of his frustration with the regulations imposed by the government guide who is leading the student trip. As the writer's own voice is so warm and reasonable, the reader is able to easily identify with the irritation that Seth feels as someone interested in getting an unhurried and more meaningful sense of the country that he is traveling through. We are also able to then share with Seth the exhilarating sense of freedom when he breaks away from the tour and sets out on his voyage of discovery by himself. The narrative, and the journey itself, negotiates a tension that is present in China. On the one hand, what Seth describes is a culture that carries the legacy of regarding the foreigner with suspicion. This is the attitude about which Seth writes, "There is nothing like the xenophobia of the Cultural Revolution, when Beethoven was banned and diplomats beaten by mobs" (p. 9). This is also why, on catching sight of Seth, children often yell, "*Waiguoren! Waiguronen!*" (outlander) or "*Waibin! Waibin!*" (foreign guest). At the same time, however, this attitude coexists with a remarkable generosity on the part of the Chinese toward the foreigner in their midst. Before he leaves China, Seth is able to record this realization: "Time and time again, with no thought other than kindness, people have helped me along in this journey. And this experience is merely a continuation of what I have felt throughout my travels in China: a remarkable warmth to the outsider from a people into whom a suspicion of foreigners has so long been instilled" (p. 139).

Much of the appeal of *From Heaven Lake* is generated by the manner in which human happenstance is shown to cut through the bureaucratic red tape of Communist China. One evening, Seth finds himself singing a song from a Hindi film—an old 1950s Indian film astonishingly popular in China—to a crowd in Turfan. Seth's singing is enthusiastically cheered by his audience. The next day, it is the story of his singing that wins favor with a police officer who stamps Seth's passport, giving him the magical endorsement needed to travel to Tibet. Also of interest in the book are the accounts of the different conversations that the writer holds in English, Hindi, Urdu, and German, and, of course, Chinese—Seth's Chinese name is Xie Binlang—with the people that he meets. These provide the backbone to the travel narrative that relies as much on the writer's observations as it does on what other people have to say to Seth. It should be noted, however, that such exchanges are not always mutually agreeable. In one humorous passage, Seth rails at length against the young Chinese men who stop him on the street and insist on speaking in English with him.

> No place is safe, no privacy respected by the worst of these "language rapists," who are only interested in you for your language. You may be sitting on the balcony of the Drum Tower, sipping tea, watching the sunset, red and smoky, over the roofs of the city; you may be buying onions in the crowded market and trying to prevent yourself and your purchases from being crushed by your fellow customers; you may be standing in a bus, or at a bus-stop or at a counter in the post office; nowhere are you safe from the machinations of the language-rapist. He will smile at you determinedly, and begin a conversation—"Hello. Do you speak English? So do I. What country are you from?" The first few times this is attractive, but it quickly palls. It becomes increasingly apparent that he is not interested in you. You are merely a punch-bag for language practice.
>
> (p. 116)

As Seth makes his way by train to Heaven Lake, and then, in an eastward loop, to Xian, he reflects on his restlessness. "I sometimes seem to myself to wander around the world," he writes, "merely accumulating material for future nostalgias" (p. 35). Thus, traveling in China, Seth dreams of the past, of drinking sherry in California or eating *dalmoth* in Delhi. When reading this, it is impossible for us not to see Seth's travels through China—and also therefore the book we are holding in our hands—as if all of it were already delicately painted in the colors of nostalgia. And it is this sense of nostalgia that works to imbue in the reader an affection for the different characters that Seth meets on his journey: the chain-smoking Sui who drives Seth to Tibet in his truck, the Nepalese counsel Mr. Shah who provides Seth with scotch and a route to Nepal, the toy photographer-bear that, when wound up, raises its camera and presses the flash.

THE GOLDEN GATE

In 1986 Seth published his novel-in-verse, *The Golden Gate*. It was this book, a sonnet sequence of 590 rhyming poems—more than 300 pages of more than 8,000 tetrameter-rhymed lines—that first brought literary fame to the writer. In the book, even the acknowledgments, the dedication, the contents page, and the author page are in the sonnet form. (Since the *e* in the writer's last name is pronounced like a long *a* as in "fate," it can even be said that we are presented with a rhyme on the title page: "The Golden Gate / A Novel in Verse by / Vikram Seth.") As mentioned, Seth, inspired by Charles Johnston's translation of Pushkin's *Eugene Onegin,* adopted the verse form used in that work, iambic tetrameter fourteen-line stanzas. This device allows the narrative in verse to combine complexity with a great deal of flexibility and verve. It serves as a convenient vehicle for Seth's tale, by turns arch and colloquial, as it sheds light on the lives of a group of yuppies, in the early 1980s, living in the Bay Area in California. The novel gets its name, of course, from the famous bridge in San Francisco. Its narrator is Seth himself, often engaged in a spirited defense of his current attempt at versification, but there also appears twice an alter ego, Kim Tarvesh, bearing an anagrammatic relationship to Seth and drowning the prospects of his economics Ph.D. in a glass of chilled Chablis.

The Golden Gate opens in the year 1980 with John Brown, a twenty-six-year-old Silicon Valley computer programmer with a Defense contract. John is good-looking, but like a latter-day Onegin, he is lonely. We get a profile of this life in lines like the following: "Thus files takes precedence over friends, / Labor is lauded, leisure riven. / John kneels bareheaded and unshod / Before the Chip, a jealous God" (p. 7). John has two friends, Phil Weiss and Janet Hayakawa. Phil, an environmental activist, is divorced and the father of a boy. Janet, or Jan, is John's former lover. She is a sculptor as well as a drummer in a rock band called Liquid Sheep. At the story's start, John telephones Phil but doesn't reach him; he then calls Jan and leaves a message on her answering machine. They meet for lunch, and once she has assessed the situation, Jan decides that what is lacking in John's life is love; without telling John, she places a personals ad in the *Bay Guardian.* Eight-two letters arrive in response, and then seven more. It is the last letter in the second bunch that draws John's attention. The writer is Liz Dorati, an at-

torney, and the owner of a jealous cat, Charlemagne. John and Liz meet at the Café Trieste and the story of their relationship, told in Seth's elegant rhyming verse, appears to the reader's ears as both felicitous and inevitable. In other words, it is in the language of the tale that the narrative succeeds. This is clear in the poet James Merrill's remark about *The Golden Gate* (quoted from the 1986 Random House edition dust jacket): "Mr. Seth's beautifully conventional characters would self-destruct on the page of any prose fiction. But his verse sets them glowing from within, and the result is as humanly poignant as it is technically reassuring—in short, a cause for rejoicing."

The love between John and Liz does not last—and the story of their falling out is again colored by Seth's technical proficiency with rhymed verse. There is other turmoil in the novel, and not all of it has to do with affairs of the heart. John's friend, Phil, is active in organizing a protest against the area's Lungless Labs, which manufactures nuclear bombs. One of Phil's comrades, Father O'Hare, makes a speech in favor of nuclear disarmament—and the speech gets nineteen poems in the book. Phil also has a brief gay affair with Liz's brother, Ed, a troubled Christian who has a pet iguana named Arnold Schwarzenegger. But Phil's more abiding romance is with Liz herself, after she becomes estranged from John; in fact, the couple gets married hastily, partly to please Liz's mother, who is dying of cancer. As Liz's family owns a vineyard in the wine-growing Sonoma County, Seth also produces memorable portraits of the California landscape and the effects of the changing seasons. The novel, in its closing pages, returns to John. He has become Jan's lover once again, but Jan dies soon after their newfound love, in an accident—and the novel, which has often touched on the sadness of love's loss, now strikes a genuinely tragic note. And yet, despite the sadness, the abiding effect of reading *The Golden Gate* is that of pleasure, because the universe that Seth has created is an uncomplicated one, and its movements, while often bizarre, are, in a manner of speaking, well-composed. The Indian writer and critic Amit Chaudhuri, in *The Picador Book of Modern Indian Literature,* describes the experience of reading the novel-in-verse in the following words: "As small and well-travelled as Puck, Seth, like Puck, has, in this novel, delighted in bringing together and separating his mortals, in fuelling their confusions and resolving them, and both chafing and transubstantiating them with his magic" (pp. 508–509).

In his book Seth includes verses that self-reflexively comment on the anxieties evoked by his eccentric choice of form. In one sonnet, he writes of an editor taking his arm and asking him, at a reception to honor Seth's *From Heaven Lake,* about his next book. When Seth informs the editor that it is a novel in verse, the man "turn[s] yellow." "'How marvelously quaint,' he said, / And subsequently cut me dead" (p. 100). Seth describes feeling out of place among the "Professor, publisher, and critic," and his doubting friends, who are shown as asking such questions as: "Driveling in rhyme's all very well; / The question is, does spittle sell?" (p. 101). But Seth need not have been so pessimistic. While it is true that the book was rejected by several important publishers, once it was accepted and published, it got several wonderful reviews. The Yale-based poet John Hollander, writing in the *New Republic,* was of the opinion that "this brilliantly fashioned tale of life among a number of Bay Area yuppies is never anything less than quaintly, and most unqualifiedly, marvelous. . . . The use of expertly controlled verse to give moral substance and extraordinary wit and plangency to a far from extraordinary tale is an astonishing achievement in its own right." In a review for the *Washington Post Book World,* Thomas Disch notes: "Seth writes poetry as if it has not been written for nearly a century—that's to say, with the intention that his work should give pleasure to that ideal Common Reader for whom good novelists have always aspired to write" (p. 105). Other writers commenting on *The Golden Gate* struck a more critical note. In

the pages of *Commentary,* Carol Iannone wrote that, apart from the feat of versification, Seth's novel was "slender" and its characterizations were "sketchy." *The Golden Gate,* she elaborated, "sports a slick emotional veneer such as one associates less with serious fiction than with a Hollywood film like *The Big Chill,* with a few Snoopy greeting-card sentiments about love and friendship thrown in for good measure." However, Iannone's criticism went further than what she called the novel's "superficiality." The real problem according to this critic was that "Seth does not so much create characters, round or flat, as grade them on a scale of prefabricated moral possibilities." According to Iannone, the characters in the book were rewarded in a politically correct universe which was the creation of Seth's imagination. Thus, the idealistic, bisexual Phil, an activist for peace, is "obviously the most advanced on the moral scale," and Jan, because she is Asian (Iannone's word is "Oriental"), is constructed as someone who is warm and loving, while John, as a WASP, is presented as the product of a loveless home. Iannone's comment on this flawed moral economy is founded on a racial reading of the writer himself, which is evident from some of her comments, for example: "The presumed emotional aloofness of the Anglo-Saxon appears, indeed, to be a cardinal sin of the West in the eyes of the Indian-born Seth."

In criticism pitched at a different level, Marjorie Perloff, in a commentary in the *American Poetry Review,* took issue with the many critics such as Hollander who had offered words of praise for *The Golden Gate.* Interrogating the return to popularity of rhyme in poetry, Perloff argued that while in classics like *Don Juan* and *Eugene Onegin,* rhyme words functioned as rhetorical and metrical markers, in Seth's case, they had little value in excess of what she calls "the merely cute" (p. 39). The lack of a linguistic and semantic edge to the verse is related, in Perloff's mind, also to the deficient structure of Seth's narrative—"the twists and turns of the ensuing plot are as predictable as if they had been programmed on one of the computers our hero himself had built" (p. 39). Instead of social satire, the critic charges, what *The Golden Gate* offers are social stereotypes and clichés. Contrasting Seth's book with the literary ancestor that it had invoked for itself, Perloff concludes that "as a social document, *The Golden Gate* is closer to Neil Simon than to Pushkin" (p. 41). This is not a judgment only on Seth, however. The subject of Perloff's attack is the historical era that had given rise to the book and provided the cause for its popularity—the conservatism of the presidential administration of Ronald Reagan and what Perloff saw as a cultural retreat into a myth of simplicity:

> Like the series of dramas on colonial subjects currently featured on *Masterpiece Theatre,* like the two-day network coverage of the Royal Wedding, *The Golden Gate* speaks to the nostalgia that characterizes the not-so-golden late 1980s. As the millennium approaches, as Apocalyptic images come to haunt our fictions, as political and military decisions become increasingly complex and problematic, there is inevitably a longing for the Old Poetry, poetry written before the fall into free rhythms and abstruse, often seemingly prosaic locutions.
>
> (p. 43)

A SUITABLE BOY

The most-discussed feature of Seth's best-known novel is its length. *A Suitable Boy,* which was published in 1993, was two feet high in typescript and 1,349 pages long in hardback. In 2003 it remained the longest novel written in the English language. (In the rhymed dedication at the beginning of the book, Seth has addressed the following words to the reader: "Buy me before good sense insists / You'll strain your purse and sprain your wrists." The author, who is five foot three, has also described the book in an interview with Jeremy Gavron as "a very large novel written by a very small Indian.") The book's length places *A Suitable Boy* in the tradition of the panoramic nineteenth-century novels

such as George Eliot's *Middlemarch* and Tolstoy's *War and Peace.* The book's ostensible subject, the search for a husband for a young woman, also puts it in line with other, shorter novels of that period like Jane Austen's *Pride and Prejudice.* But it can also be proposed that *A Suitable Boy* is an attempt on the part of an Indian to write a capacious novel as voluminous as the Indian nation itself—at a time when the coherence of the Indian nation-state was under the threat of separatist struggles and widespread social turmoil. This would explain the novel's setting in the early 1950s when India, under Jawaharlal Nehru, was a newly born country and articulating an idea of itself as an independent nation. There is nostalgia here in that return to the past, but the story emanates from the anxieties and desperation of the period in which it was written. It is as if the six million words in the novel and the multiple stories woven together by the novelist's hand were serving to provide a narrative for a nation whose postcolonial present was tenuous.

Seth's novel opens with Mrs. Rupa Mehra and her search for a suitable husband for her youngest daughter, Lata. The daughter is intelligent and well read and has a mind of her own. Her rebellious search for a partner of her own choice introduces into the plot other suitors and provides the tension for this domestic drama. The search for a suitable boy for Lata Mehra gives Seth an opportunity to string together the tales of at least four families—the Mehras, the Chatterjis, the Kapoors, and the Khans. In addition, we come in touch with the smaller families of Kabir Durrani, the Muslim youth with whom Lata first falls in love, and then Haresh Khanna, the humble shoe-company executive whom she eventually chooses as her husband. The nineteen-year-old Lata is a student of English literature at the university in the fictional town of Brahmpur in the province of Purva Pradesh (Brahmpur resembles Varanasi in the eastern state of Uttar Pradesh in India). It is at the university that she meets Kabir Durrani, who is her classmate, a cricket player as well as an actor.

But while Lata is Hindu, Kabir is a Muslim. He is an unsuitable boy. The person who next comes into the picture is the poet Amit Chatterji, who, although he is a witty and cosmopolitan suitor, does not win Lata's heart, because she fears that he is too self-centered and involved in his writing. At the novel's end, Lata chooses the man her mother had found, the unsophisticated, lower-middle-class suitor Haresh Khanna, who is enterprising and intelligent, with his open, direct manner suggesting both vulnerability and ambition. In this case, the writer Anita Desai's observation about Seth's novel seems valid: "If any philosophy is being expounded here it appears to be that of Aristotle's golden mean—the avoidance of excess, the advisability of moderation, the wisdom of restraint, temperance, and control. Whenever these rules are flouted, grief results" (pp. 24). While it is true that there might be little passion and even less excitement involved in Lata's choice, it is possible to see in the young woman's exercise of judgment a quality of prudent compromise and an orientation toward the hardworking and dynamic sector of newly independent India.

The broader history of the new nation and the tensions and changes of its divided society provide the backdrop for Lata's search for a suitable boy. It is this sociohistorical background that gives the novel its density and heft. For example, Lata's elder sister, Savita, marries into a family headed by a political leader, a radical socialist who is the executor of India's laws for the abolition of the feudal system of land ownership. Through the vicissitudes of the political leader's career the reader is able to witness the debates around the rights of the landless and the so-called untouchables. However, what is even more remarkable about Seth's engagement with history's complexities is that he focuses mostly on the quotidian aspects of national life; the years and the people he chooses to write about are not the most celebrated ones. As Desai has remarked, "For all the breadth and the scope of the author's intention, there is at the heart of his work a modesty that one would have thought belonged to the miniature, not the epic scale" (pp. 23). This modesty, which one can also view as reticence or reserve, especially in comparison to the ambitions of someone like Rushdie, can be viewed simply as a writer's predilection. But a different case can also be made. In *A Suitable Boy,* the relentless pursuit of the ordinary marks an attempt to find the soul of a nation in the vernacular space of the provincial, small towns and its familiar, conventional, inhabitants.

Pico Iyer has written that "the singular appeal of *A Suitable Boy* lies in its fondness, and in its evocation of an unhurried, gossipy, small-talking India as teasing and warm as every family reunion I have attended." For Iyer, Seth's retreat from the cities of noise and action is of a piece with his obvious distaste for unpleasantness: "Charm is his calling card, and sunniness his forte" (p. 140). It is true that *A Suitable Boy* ventures into violence, both of the public and the domestic variety, but it quickly passes on to other matters. Seth's fictional account of Hindu-Muslim violence is uncannily prescient of the riots that erupted all over India while the book was in production. A mob of religious zealots had demolished a sixteenth-century mosque in a small town not far from the towns of Benares and Lucknow invoked in the novel. But Seth's entry into the subject is not sustained; the reader is not given the opportunity to learn about the causes of the mayhem nor expected to have any real curiosity about the consequences of such acts on the lives of the people he is writing about. Similarly, Seth's foray into the less visible world of domestic violence, when he writes of one man who sexually abuses his daughter, is also marked by a certain reticence. The writing is sensitive, but it is also slight. Here is Anita Desai's commentary on this aspect of Seth's writing: "There is only one truly nasty character in the whole book—Uncle Sahgal, who plods quietly down the corridor to his daughter's bedroom at night and then tries to slip into Lata's—but he is seen as a figure in a nightmare: daylight drives him into oblivion and no more is made of his sinister vice" (p. 25). Sahgal is seen only once again, eight hundred pages later, at Lata's wedding; he approaches the wedding couple, congratulates the bridegroom, fixes his eyes on Lata, looks "at her face, at the lipstick on her lips, with a slight sneer" (p. 1470), and quickly departs from the stage on which the festivities are taking place.

The above criticism would find its echo in critical reviews that commented that while *A Suitable Boy,* in its length, scale, and ambition, seemed to emulate a book like *War and Peace,* it was also clear that Seth was unable to fathom Tolstoy's taste for the darker aspects of life. A slightly different point was made by Richard Jenkyns in the *New Republic,* whose point of reference was not Tolstoy but other postcolonial writers, like Patrick White and Rushdie, who had written out of a sense of disappointment or frustrated nationalism. In comparison to those writers, Jenkyns argued, "Seth . . . has no ax to grind about India, no thesis to argue: he simply lays the life of his characters expansively before us. That, in itself, is fine. The question is whether he has anything to say" (p. 42). This is a matter that can be argued over, and the answer will depend in many ways on the individual judgments one brings to bear on the issue, judgments about what constitutes the true subject of postcolonial literature and whether it can be restricted to one theme or another. What is less open to question, however, is the fact that like the other postcolonial writers that Jenkyns mentions, Seth is able to show that English is the language of the Indian small town. In doing this, he can be seen again as departing from a writer like Rushdie, who he is often paired with. While Rushdie shows great linguistic dexterity and inventiveness in fashioning a polyglot tongue, his mixed-up English remains that of a cosmopolitan traveler. Not Seth's. In *A Suitable Boy,* it is a variety of registers in which English comes into play; it is the language at once of the Constitutional Assembly, the provincial civil-servants, the language Seth uses to present the talk on the streets of Calcutta and also Brahmpur; it is even the language of discourse in the parlor of a sophisticated courtesan who only speaks in poetic Urdu. English is adequate to the tasks of describing Hindu and Muslim festivals; it is also the language used in the house of an upper-class family in Calcutta where all the family members seem to converse in rhyming verse; it is the language without which "you can't do anything," as an illiterate peasant says at one point in the novel, adding, "If you talk in English, you are a king. The more people you can mystify, the more people will respect you" (p. 543); of course, it is also the language used when one of Lata's suitors, wooing her, takes her to the graveyard in Calcutta where lies buried the British poet Walter Savage Landor's "Rose Aylmer," as well as "Thackeray's father, and one of Dickens' sons, and the original of Byron's Don Juan" (pp. 489–490). Seth's wit finds favor even with Jenkyns, the critic quoted above, who chooses as "the best scene in the book" one in which Lata attends a meeting of the Brahmpur Literary Society and discovers what might be called the charm of one kind of Indian English. On that occasion, one Dr. Makhijani reads his verses to the assembled members:

Let me recall history of heroes proud,
Mother-milk fed their breasts, who did not bow.
Fought they fiercely, carrying worlds of weight,
Establishing firm foundation of Indian state.

(p. 164)

AN EQUAL MUSIC

An Equal Music begins and ends with a man standing beside the river in London's Hyde Park, looking at the dark water of the Serpentine. The image comes from Seth's own life. In a 1999 interview, Seth told Jeremy Gavron about an experience he shared with his friend Philippe Honore, to whom, incidentally, the book is dedicated: "It was a winter's day two years ago. We saw a man standing at the edge of a pond in Hyde Park, looking into the water. I told Philippe that this image was stirring thoughts in me. 'He is a musician,' Philippe said.

'What instrument does he play?' I asked. 'A violin,' Philippe answered. I had no plan then to write about musicians, in fact I didn't want to write about musicians. But the idea was planted, and that scene is how the novel begins." (The novel's title is taken from John Donne's *XXVI Sermons* (1660), which also supplies the book's epigraph: "No noise, nor silence, but one equal music, no fears nor hopes, but one equal possession.")

Like much of his earlier work, *An Equal Music,* which appeared in 1999, is about love. But it is a darker, more anguished work. Inward and intense, the novel is about love's loss—and the recovery, if not exactly of love, then of that which endures as understanding. While *A Suitable Boy* had been hailed as a tour de force of what one might call unmagic mimeticism, fooling some critics into accepting it as a triumph of an authentic Indian realism, in *An Equal Music,* Seth turned such assumptions on their head, because here it is a different world that is conjured with representational exactitude, a universe that is wholly and utterly European. *An Equal Music* is a moving tribute to Western classical music and performance. The book's dust jacket shows Il Padovanino's painting *Orpheus Leading Eurydice out of the Underworld.* As it was with Orpheus, it is music that offers the characters that populate Seth's novel a chance to restore, amid shattering loss and yearning, a measure of worldliness and grace. The high romantic tradition provides the ideological backdrop to this novel, and it sets in relief Seth's characters, with their binding solitude, their alienated silences, and also their eloquence.

The protagonist of *An Equal Music* is a violinist, Michael Holme. He is wracked by the ten-year-old memory of his estranged love, a talented pianist named Julia McNicholl. This yearning remembrance is entangled in the very music he hears, plays, breathes: Bach, Haydn, Beethoven. Michael plays in an English quartet, the Maggiore, but when he thinks of what had brought to life the voice in his hands, he recalls his past in Vienna where Julia and he were students and lovers, before he had a breakdown and left, without a word, himself wordless. The novel is an account of his journey back to her. It is also a story of Julia's loss of hearing and her struggle with, and through, music to find her own self again. And yet, the book is not about the charms of therapy. It poignantly reveals what haunts loss and eludes recovery. As Julia tells us, after noting how much she has learned in her lipreading classes even as she is beginning to go deaf, "As one of my teachers once pointed out, you will never be able to learn from the lips alone if someone has lost her glove or her love" (p. 152).

The novel's essential drama of love lost and gained plays on a dream of wholeness. The dream of the whole is the drama behind many of the relations in *An Equal Music*: couples, musical quartets, even the relationship between the musicians and their instruments. While the Maggiore Quartet plays Bach, the narrator, Michael, sees in his mind's eye the musical notes and the rise and fall of the instruments' voices. The reader hears Michael saying to himself, "Our synchronous visions merge, and we are one: with each other, with the world, and with that long-dispersed being whose force we receive through the shape of his annotated vision and the single swift-flowing syllable of his name" (p. 90). While playing Haydn, and Mozart, and then a Beethoven piece composed a year before the composer's death and which had delighted and consoled Franz Schubert as he lay dying, Michael imagines a miraculous unity or completeness:

A strange composite being we are, not ourselves any more but the Maggiore, composed of so many disjunct parts: chairs, stands, music, bows, instruments, musicians—sitting, standing, shifting, sounding—all to produce these complex vibrations that jog the inner ear, and through them the grey mass that says: joy; love; sorrow; beauty. And above us here in the apse the strange figure of a naked man surrounded by thorns and aspiring towards a grail of light, in front of us 540 half-seen beings intent on 540 different webs of sensation and cerebration and emotion, and through us the spirit of someone scribbling away in 1772 with the sharpened feather of a bird.

(p. 86)

In other places in the novel, the question of the individual's relation to the whole takes a more recognizably political cast. Michael has his origins in a butcher's family in a northern England town. A visit to his working-class home in Rochdale provides an occasion to speak of economic decline and the threat to the poor—and to music—present in such circumstances:

Because the comprehensive I went to had been the old grammar school, it had a fine tradition of music. And the services of what were known as peripatetic music teachers were provided by the local education authorities. But all this has been cut back now, if it has not completely disappeared. There was a system for loaning instruments free or almost free of charge to those who could not afford them—all scrapped with the educational cuts as the budgetary hatchet struck again and again. The music centre where the young musicians of the area would gather to play in an orchestra on Saturdays is now derelict. Yesterday I drove past it: the windows were smashed; it has been dead for years. If I had been born in Rochdale five years later, I don't see how I—coming from the background I did, and there were so many who were much poorer—could have kept my love of the violin alive.

(p. 71)

It is with feeling and repressed fury that Seth mocks the venality of bankers and auctioneers. Art in such instances has its stakes in the public sphere: "My small radio, which plucked music from the public air, was everything to me; I would listen to it for hours in my room. As with the public library in Manchester, I don't see how I could have become a musician without it" (p. 124). The loss that persists as a shading around the private one is the public ruin. Talking of his hometown, Michael says that in a period when "everything civic or social was choked of funds . . . the town which had been the home

of the co-operative movement lost its sense of community" (p. 71). At those moments when we hear the laments about how in twenty years' time it might become impossible for a butcher's son or daughter to become a violinist, it is easy to see how Seth moves away from the romantic overvalorization of genius and the imagination—and *An Equal Music* becomes, as a whole, a sensitive and finely controlled exploration of the structure of feeling that words, music, and love produce.

"Music to me is dearer even than speech," Seth writes in his author's note to the book. The book he wrote is undeniably a tribute to the beauty of music, and perhaps art in general, but does it also pay homage to the idea of love? When Seth had published his monumental epic, *A Suitable Boy*, some critics had likened it to a "soap opera." That suggestion haunts *An Equal Music* also. In fact, at one point Michael tells Julia, "I don't know how I've lived without you all these years" and then, immediately afterwards, he thinks to himself, "How feeble and trite my words sound to me, as if they have been plucked out of some housewife fantasy" (p. 232). The critic Michael Arditti, writing in the *Independent*, seemed to echo the suspicion voiced by Seth's narrator. Arditti wrote: "It would take a far harder heart than mine not to respond to the doomed love of its principal characters, but it would take a far less critical mind not to decry the totally unchallenging nature of Seth's universe, in which there are no complex ideas or motives, and no malevolent forces." A rather different view was taken by Akash Kapur, who wrote that "*An Equal Music* is a sensitive, meticulous novel that has something of the delicacy of a haiku. Gone is the grand sweep of *A Suitable Boy*—Seth's new book is an intimate and internalized story of love and music. . . . Narrated in the present tense, in an insistent first person, this meditation is intensely personal; unlike anything Seth has previously written, the novel is distinguished by remarkable psychological portraiture."

It seems clear that what Seth had established with the publication of *An Equal Music,* when seen in the context of his other works, was a landscape similar to the one he had written about in *From Heaven Lake*—"In Western China the main topographical features are also latitudinal, and this enhances the variety of a longitudinal journey. Thus sandy deserts have given way to basins and basins to cold plateau, aridity to pasture, pasture to glaciers, snow-peaks and high passes; and now suddenly I am in a rapid southwards descent to the warm foothills of the Indian subcontinent" (p. 163). The topography of Seth's writing is one of variety, with the sunny charm of *The Golden Gate* giving way to the long, seemingly unchanging season of *A Suitable Boy,* Seth's poetry, blooming in unexpected places, slowly overtaken by the lyrical but cold and wintry air of *An Equal Music.*

POETRY AND BEYOND

In an interview with Akash Kapur following the publication of *An Equal Music,* Seth spoke of his fundamental commitment to poetry: "I'm forced to confess that in terms of the actual number of words I've written, I've probably written more prose than poetry. But in terms of the books, seven out of my ten books are entirely in verse." He went on to say that even in his books of prose, he has "infiltrated" a substantial amount of verse, and added, "Of course, I have to consider that I've written a lot of prose, but I do in my heart think of myself as being originally, and still primarily, a poet."

It was with the publication of his novel-in-verse, *The Golden Gate,* that, to quote him from his interview with Jeremy Gavron, he took in a "fizzy gulp of fame." More than the novel, it was the novelty of the form that drew most of the critical attention at the time of the book's publication. Yet there were many who admired the book for its poetry. Thomas M. Disch wrote that *The Golden Gate,* like Pushkin's *Eugene Onegin,* portrayed "ordinary life without falling into banality, and one finishes both books with a sense that poetry too rarely yields, a sense that life, however messy it may get from time to time, is really, pretty much, a bowl of cherries" (p. 108).

It was four years after Seth self-published his first book of poems, *Mappings,* that the British publisher Carcanet brought out his second book of poems, *The Humble Administrator's Garden* (1985). *Mappings* was published only in a single edition of a few hundred copies. (Some of the poems in the book had originally appeared in venues such as the *Threepenny Review, London Magazine,* and *Sequoia Press.*) The book is dedicated to Steele and Davie, the two main poetic influences on Seth when he was a student at Stanford. There are forty-four poems in the book, most of them rhymed verse, and they are set in India as well as California. The poems are lyrical but conversational in tone; they are mostly personal, often confessional, and even if they do not always display the Seth trademark of making light of deep sorrow through word and rhyme, they give the reader a taste of Seth as a translator. Within the covers of this single book, Seth presents translations of poems from Chinese (Du Fu), Urdu (Faiz Ahmed Faiz), and Hindi (Surya Kant Tripathi Nirala). It is especially in the translations that Seth practices a clean art, with precise wording and no frills—and this quality of fine phrasing offers an intimation of an art that will find expression in his next book of poems.

The Humble Administrator's Garden has three sets of poems gathered in separate sections titled "Wutong," "Neem," and "Live Oak." The poems are divided, under those titles, into those that deal with Seth's Chinese, Indian, and Californian experiences. The poems are simple without being plain. In his language and imagery, Seth echoes the Chinese lyric poets whom he has studied and translated. A poem in the "Neem" section called "The Comfortable Classes at Work and Play" offers a fine sketch of Seth's own family. The crispness of the writing that distinguishes many poems in the collection is most evident in Seth's use of the *Babur-Nama*, the memoir of the first Moghul emperor of India, Babur, to produce a poem that is a wonderful specimen of narrative, lyric poetry. Babur had kept a journal throughout his life; he composed poems easily, even in the midst of battle. Seth's poem captures the banality and the beauty of the emperor's life—the striking mix of the ordinary and the extraordinary—which is present in Babur's own words. The poem is an exceptional distillation of a four-hundred-and-fifty-page memoir.

What he did with Babur's words, setting another person's words to a poetic form, Seth repeated with many other voices in his next book of poems, *All You Who Sleep Tonight* (1990). This book has more than fifty short and long poems. Most of the short poems, and several of the longer ones, are rhymed. They are lyrical and moving, but do not have any greater effect on the reader. They do not incite further thought, or disturb the mind, or, for those who look for such qualities in poems, define or question an age. In that sense, Seth's poems, on account of their strengths as well as weaknesses, call to mind the lines that he wrote in his introduction to a collected edition of his poems, *The Poems, 1981–1994* (1995), to explain his fascination with rhymed verse. While discussing why rhyme and meter should "lead to memorability," Seth wrote that the emotional power of such poetry, although difficult to explain, perhaps derived "from musicality, perhaps from compression, perhaps from a necessary attentiveness." At the same time, Seth conceded, those attributes could also lead to a corresponding fault: "Too great an enchantment with artifice or with antiquated diction, a lack of breath and pulse, a confining intellectuality." It is their memorability as well as their mannered style that one notices in poem after poem in *All You Who Sleep Tonight*, as in this stanza from "Protocols":

I cannot walk by day as now I walk at dawn
　Past the still house where you lie sleeping.

May the sun burn away these footprints on the lawn
　And hold you in its warmth and keeping.

Nevertheless, in the poems that are "in other's voices" in the same book, one finds the use of verse "in form" toward a substantially different result. In poem after poem—the words of one Tang dynasty Chinese poet writing to another; a rabbi in Lithuania responding to a question from the husband of a woman who has been gang-raped; the commandant at Auschwitz talking of his demanding work and the needs of his children; the nineteenth-century Urdu poet Ghalib sharing his woes in a letter written after the Indian mutiny; a Japanese doctor's journal entry from the day the bomb fell in Hiroshima; a monologue of a patient dying of AIDS—Seth frees the reader from the prison of his or her own particular place and age. The reader is quietly invited to share another life, and the force of the poetic form is such that the reader's transport to another self appears wholly seamless. What also comes to the fore here is Seth's gift as a storyteller. As Rajeev Patke writes in *An Illustrated History of Indian Literature in English*, "To have restored the drive of narrative to verse is Seth's principal contribution to poetry" (273–274).

Two years after the publication of *All You Who Sleep Tonight*, Seth published two rather different books of poems. One of them was a children's book of stories written in verse, titled *Beastly Tales from Here and There* (1992). In the introduction to the book, Seth wrote: "Because it was very hot in my house one day and I could not concentrate on my work, I decided to write a summer story involving mangoes and a river." (The work that he could not concentrate on was the writing of *A Suitable Boy*.) The beastly tales, with titles like "The Crocodile and the Monkey" and "The Frog and the Nightingale," were folktales that had come from India, China, Greece, and Ukraine, and also, in the case of the last story, from the "Land of Gup," that is, from the land of gossip or the imagination. The somewhat different book of poems that Seth published the same year was a superb translation of three Tang dynasty poets who had lived in the eighth century A.D. Seth's book was called *Three Chinese Poets*; and the poets were Wang Wei, Li Bai, and Du Fu. The three poets had distinct personalities: one was a Buddhist recluse who wrote about loneliness, the second was exuberant and impulsive, while the third held dear to his heart the central concerns of Confucianism, the sad state of society, history, the state and the times in which he lived. The poems in *Three Chinese Poets* are compelling because they convey a sense of both sharpness and delicacy. The effect on the reader—even without being able to read the poems in their original Chinese—is of the translator simply holding in his hands a clean pane of transparent glass.

In 1994 there was a further twist to Seth's career. He was commissioned by the English National Opera to write a libretto based on the ancient Greek legend of Arion, a young musician whose life is saved by dolphins. The opera, with music by Alec Roth, was performed for the first time in June 1994 in Plymouth, England. The children's book *Arion and the Dolphin* was published the following year. The book has since been made into a twenty-five-minute animated special which has shown in Australia, Canada, Iceland, Malta, New Zealand, and throughout the United Kingdom.

In an interview with Jeremy Gavron, conducted before the release of *An Equal Music* in 1999, it was mentioned that a new project was beginning to take shape in Seth's mind, "another departure, a biography of his grand uncle, an Indian dentist who lost his arm at Monte Cassino during the second world war, and his German Jewish wife." Seth's experiments with new forms might be an important aspect of his legacy to Indian, and world, literature. Amit Chaudhuri, in *The Picador Book of Modern Indian Literature*, sees Seth's formal and stylistic variations in terms of a larger cultural context:

> His career has been of ceaseless reinvention; from economist to poet, to travel writer, to novelist-in-verse, to popular literary novelist, to librettist, to who knows what next. Skipping from genre to genre, it's as if he's not just a writer, but a microcosm of the cultural ethos—the ethos of the post-Independence, urban, English-speaking middle-class—to which he belongs, an ethos that too has felt the need indefatigably and restlessly to reinvent itself. Lacking a clearly defined tradition to fall back on, the Indian writer in English, working in isolation, has laid claim . . . to all of Western and European tradition, besides his own, in a way that perhaps no European can; and so has Seth, taking whatever, and whenever, he chooses. . . . For him, writing is partly a matter of creating genres, as if it's not enough to create an oeuvre, but a whole tradition in miniature, by which he, and his contemporaries, might be evaluated.
>
> (p. 508)

Selected Bibliography

WORKS OF VIKRAM SETH

POETRY

Mappings. Calcutta: Writers Workshop, 1981.

The Humble Administrator's Garden. Manchester, U.K.: Carcanet, 1985.

All You Who Sleep Tonight: Poems. New York: Knopf, 1990.

The Poems, 1981–1994. New Delhi and New York: Penguin. 1995.

NOVELS

The Golden Gate: A Novel in Verse. New York: Random House, 1986.

A Suitable Boy: A Novel. New Delhi: Viking Penguin, 1993; London and New York: HarperCollins, 1993.

An Equal Music. New York and London: Broadway Books, 1999.

OTHER WORKS

From Heaven Lake: Travels through Sinkiang and Tibet. London: Hogarth Press, 1983; New York: Vintage, 1987. Illustrated with Seth's own photographs. Quotes in text are from the Hogarth Press edition.

Arion and the Dolphin: A Libretto. New Delhi and New York: Penguin, 1994.

Arion and the Dolphin. New York: Dutton, 1995. Children's book with illustrations by Jane Ray.

Beastly Tales from Here and There New Delhi: Viking, 1992; New York: HarperCollins, 1994. Illustrated by Ravi Shankar. Children's book of stories written in verse.

TRANSLATION

Three Chinese Poets: Translations of Poems by Wang Wei, Li Bai, and Du Fu. New York: HarperPerennial, 1992).

INTERVIEWS

Currie, Jay, and Michèle Denis. "Hearing a Different Music." *January* (http://www.januarymagazine.com/profiles/vseth.html), June 1999.

Field, Michele. "Vikram Seth." *Publishers Weekly* 240 (10 May 1993):46–47.

Gavron, Jeremy. "A Suitable Joy." *Guardian Unlimited* (http://www.guardian.co.uk/Archive/ Article/0,4273,3845046,00.html), 27 March 1999.

Kanaganayakam, Chelva. "Vikram Seth." In his *Configurations of Exile: South Asian Writers and Their World.* Toronto: TSAR, 1995.

Kapur, Akash. "The Seth Variations," *Atlantic Unbound* (http://www.theatlantic.com/unbound/ interviews/ba990623.htm), 23 June 1999.

———. "An Equal Music." *salon.com* (http://archive.salon.com/books/review/1999/05/13/seth/), 27 June 2003.

Knorr, Katherine. "Vikram Seth Plays to His 'Truest Judges.'" *International Herald Tribune* (http://www.iht.com/IHT/KK/00/kk042399.html), 23 April 1999.

Rachlin, Jill. "Talking with . . . Vikram Seth: Creating an Indian 'Romeo and Juliet.'" In *People Weekly* 39 (24 May 1993): 65.

Roy, Amit. Interview with Seth. *Telegraph* (Calcutta), 29 August 1992.

Sen, Sudeep. "A Poet at Heart." In *Wasafiri: Journal of Caribbean, African, Asian and Associated Literatures and Film* 21 (spring 1995): 22–25.

Wachtel, Eleanor. "Eleanor Wachtel with Vikram Seth." In *Malahat Review* 107 (summer 1994): 85–102.

CRITICAL STUDIES

Agarwalla, Shyam S., *Vikram Seth's* A Suitable Boy: *Search for an Indian Identity.* New Delhi: Prestige Books, 1995.

Atkins, Angela. *Vikram Seth's* A Suitable Boy: *A Reader's Guide.* New York: Continuum, 2002.

Baneth-Nouailhetas, Emilienne. "Forms of Creation in *A Suitable Boy*." *Commonwealth Essays and Studies* 22 (spring 2000): 69–83.

Bemrose, John. "Full-Lotus Fiction." *Maclean's* 106, no. 22 (1993): 46–48.

Chaudhuri, Amit, ed., *The Picador Book of Modern Indian Literature*. London: Picador, 2001. Pp. 508–509.

Curlin, Jay. "'The World Goes On': Narrative Structure and the Sonnet in Vikram Seth's *The Golden Gate*." In *Publications of the Arkansas Philological Association* 22 (fall 1996): 13–26.

Disch, Thomas. "Sunlight, Coffee, and the Papers: A Poem for Our Times." In his *The Castle of Indolence*. New York: Picador, 1995.

Gupta, Santosh. "*The Golden Gate*: The First Indian Novel in Verse." *The New Indian Novel in English: A Study of the 1980s*. Edited by Viney Kirpal. New Delhi: Allied Publishers, 1990. Pp. 91–100.

Hollander, John. "Yuppie Time in Rhyme." In *New Republic* 194 (21 April 1986): 39–47.

Paranjape, Makarand R. "*The Golden Gate* and the Quest for Self-Realization." *ACLALS Bulletin* 8, no. 1 (1989):58–73.

Patke, Rajeev S. "Poetry Since Independence." *An Illustrated History of Indian Literature in English*. Edited by Arvind Krishna Mehrotra. Delhi: Permanent Black, 2003. Pp. 243–75.

Perloff, Marjorie. "'Homeward Ho!': Silicon Valley Pushkin." In *American Poetry Review* 15, no. 6 (November/December 1986): 37–46.

Perry, John Oliver. "*All You Who Sleep Tonight*." *World Literature Today* (summer 1991): 549–550.

Wole Soyinka

(1934–)

J. CHRIS WESTGATE

ANY STUDY OF Wole Soyinka must begin with an understanding of the inseparability of his writing and his political activism. Soyinka's more than four decades of contributions to Nigerian literature have established him among Africa's most accomplished and acclaimed writers of the twentieth century. His highly eclectic body of work includes novels, poetry, autobiography, and cultural biography, a translation of D. O. Fagunwa's *A Forest of a Thousand Daemons* (1968), revues, radio plays, and award-winning stage plays. His dramaturgy, which integrates Nigerian festival tradition with modern theatrical conventions, has recuperated an indigenous literary heritage from the legacy of British colonialism. His theatrical troupes and scholarly endeavors have revitalized Nigerian English-language theater. In 1986 Soyinka deservedly became the first African to win the Nobel Prize in literature. Interestingly, though, Soyinka used his Nobel address to advocate the obligation of all civilized nations—especially Western powers—to confront injustice in general and South African apartheid in particular.

That Soyinka would bring politics into a celebration of literary excellence is hardly surprising. His expository writing repeatedly characterizes literature as a potent agent of social change, and his fictional writing frequently satirizes Nigerian political corruption and universally condemns injustice. Writing about injustice, however, is not always enough, as Soyinka argued in his Nobel address when he described the outrage he felt when, as a student in London, he was compelled to participate in a revue satirical of the British treatment of Mau-Mau detainees in Kenya. What outraged Soyinka, then and today, is the ethicality of devoting words but not actions to ending human suffering. And Soyinka has consistently dedicated more than his writing to effecting change in Nigeria, tirelessly advocating justice, freedom, and democracy. He was imprisoned for more than two years as a political detainee, and he spent many more years in political exile from his homeland, where his plays, widely celebrated abroad, have often been banned and denounced by Nigerian regimes. Yet Soyinka still maintains that the artist must devote himself to social change. What is abundantly clear, then, is that Soyinka the dramatist cannot be separated from Soyinka the dissident.

AN AFRICAN CHILDHOOD

Soyinka was born Akinwande Oluwole Soyinka on 13 July 1934 in Abeokuta, Nigeria, and grew up in the Anglican Mission compound in Aké, in western Nigeria. As a child he possessed an adventurous temperament that undoubtedly bordered on a penchant for misadventure for the parents he worried half to death with the many escapades fondly retold in *Aké: The Years of Childhood* (1981). His father, Samuel Ayodele Soyinka, whom Soyinka nicknamed "Essay" because of the fastidiousness that characterized so much of his father's life, was the headmaster of St. Peter's Primary School in Aké and a well-respected community leader. Many nights, people from throughout the region would assemble within the Soyinka household in order to debate politics, religion, or whatever issue was most pressing—sometimes for days at a time. Soyinka enjoyed eavesdropping on these discussions almost as much as he relished the books that he surreptitiously borrowed from his father's bookshelf. Soyinka's mother, Grace Eniola Soyinka, was a shopkeeper and raconteur, peopling her stories either with biblical figures or forest spirits—so much so that Soyinka dubbed her "Wild Christian." She was also a leading activist for women's rights during his childhood, often recruiting the young Soyinka as a messenger or as a tutor for Nigerian women discovering literacy.

Clearly his parents shaped Soyinka's attitudes toward literature, community, and duty. But the most significant influence in his upbringing was his inheritance of two differing, but not contradictory, cultural traditions. The Christianity of his parents was balanced by the traditional Yoruba (Nigeria's third-largest ethnic group) beliefs of his grandfather, which included ritual scarification of Soyinka's ankles and wrists during a family visit to Isara, his father's ancestral home, as well as the *egungun* festivals (where ancestral spirits manifest themselves within masked participants) that captivated the young boy as he watched them pass by the parsonage wall in Aké. As a child, Soyinka was so intellectually curious that the family joke was that he would question anyone to death if given half a chance. But that curiosity allowed him to absorb both cultural traditions eagerly and openly, so that they formed a dialectic for him (even though later in life he would reject much of his parents' Christianity). This dialecticism would become an epistemology that would shape much of his writing.

Always captivated with learning, Soyinka followed his older sister to school when he was only three years old. When the teacher discovered the future playwright among his pupils, Soyinka insisted that he be afforded the same educational opportunity. He got that opportunity officially in 1944, when he began his secondary education at Abeokuta Grammar School. Then, in 1946, he attended Government College in Ibadan, where his classmates included Christopher Okigbo, Chinua Achebe, and J. P. Clark—all three of whom would become major names in Nigerian literature during the 1960s. The years at Government College, Soyinka observes in his memoir *Ibadan: The Penkelemes Years* (1994), were as influential as his childhood in Aké, even though the most important of his lessons generally occurred outside the classroom. It was there that Soyinka first encountered, during a conversation with a white instructor, the racism that would only grow more palpable when he studied in London years later. It was also at Government College that he was first introduced to Euripides, whose writing would exert a major influence on his dramaturgy. And it was Government College that gave him a forum to begin publishing his writing, which had been little more than a hobby until then. He contributed poetry to the *University Voice* and edited a campus newsletter called the *Eagle*.

After graduating in 1950 he considered a career in journalism, but when he couldn't find a position he worked in a medical store—although he admits that much of his time there was spent sitting atop bales of medical supplies, reading books borrowed from the public library in Yaba and the British Council library in Onikan. In 1951 his short story "Keffi's Birthday Treat" was broadcast on the Nigerian Broadcasting Service; soon after, it became Soyinka's first story published in a national magazine, thereby inaugurating a highly prolific career that would span more than five decades.

STUDY IN LONDON

In 1954 Soyinka renewed his educational endeavors when he matriculated to the University of Leeds in London. There he studied under such notables as the leading Marxist critic of the day, Arnold Kettle, and the renowned Shakespeare scholar G. Wilson Knight. Under Knight's tutelage Soyinka began theorizing the interplay between ritual and tragedy that informs much of his dramaturgy, a hypothesis he later delineated in *Myth, Literature, and the African World* (1976). Studying with Kettle afforded Soyinka his first serious exposure to the Marxist thought that would later influence his writing (which fully acknowledges the centrality of class struggle) but that would also be critiqued in his work (which refuses to read class as the default explanation of all human conflict). Although Soyinka's voracious intellect undoubtedly enjoyed the rigors of his academic life, he must sometimes have felt like the three-year-old child who followed his sister to school because of the racism with which he was frequently confronted during his years in England, as evidenced by such poems as "Telephone Conversation" and his memoir *Ibadan: The Penkelemes Years.*

One of the few places he felt comfortable was among other writers, actors, and directors. He quickly became enthralled with the English dramatic revival of the 1950s and the experimentation that nurtured such playwrights as John Osborne, Arnold Wesker, John Arden, and Harold Pinter. Much of Soyinka's time in England, consequently, was devoted to Sunday night theatrical programs sponsored by George Devine, the manager-director of the Royal Court Theatre in London. It was during one of Devine's productions that Soyinka's first play,

The Invention, was staged (although it was anything but successful by his own account). It was also during one of these productions that he made his debut as an actor when, in 1958, he was compelled to take part in *Eleven Men Dead at Hola,* a revue critical of British colonial policy in Kenya, where Mau-Mau detainees had been beaten to death by British soldiers; the "official" story was that the detainees died after accidentally drinking from a poisoned water supply. This revue stayed with Soyinka for years largely because it established, or confirmed, in him the sense of moral responsibility that demands more than simply writing about injustice. It was also in 1958 that Soyinka married Barbara Dickson, with whom he had a son, although the marriage was brief. After graduating in 1959 he worked as a script reader, actor, and director at the Royal Court Theatre.

In 1958 Soyinka brought *The Swamp-Dwellers* to the stage (in a student production as an entry for the University of London Drama Festival). *The Swamp-Dwellers,* despite being among his earliest plays, illustrates much, in terms of both form and content, of what will characterize the majority of his more mature plays. The play works primarily through juxtapositions—of village and city life, of traditional beliefs and colonizing religions, of faith and apostasy—without trying to resolve these juxtapositions.

The play opens with the playful bickering of Makuri and Alu (husband and wife), providing the play's exposition as they lament the loss of their sons—first Awuchike and then Igwezu (along with his wife)—to the city and simultaneously illustrating the dark humor that frequently characterizes Soyinka's plays, since the lightheartedness of this opening exchange is in direct contrast to the floods that have destroyed much of the village's harvest prior to the play's inception. The urban migration of the village's youth is conceptualized as death through Alu's insistence that her sons were swallowed up by the swamp. That death is figurative, not literal, as the play centers upon

Igwezu's disillusionment most immediately, but not exclusively, with the city from which he has already returned for the yearly harvest. When Igwezu returns from inspecting his ruined fields, he reveals just how desperately he needed the harvest. His brother Awuchike abandoned not only his obligation to the family by leaving the village (which Igwezu does as well, suggesting his hypocrisy) but also the communal values of the village (to which Igwezu still managed to cling) by exploiting Igwezu financially and then stealing his wife when Igwezu migrated to the city. Clearly the city functions as a metonym for capitalism and the bourgeois values—ostensibly at odds with traditional values—that it endorses. Yet if the village functions as a metonym for a traditional African lifestyle within this play, it does not escape Igwezu's condemnation. If anything, Igwezu is equally outraged and disillusioned with the beliefs of the village, not only with the flood that destroyed the harvest despite his attempts to propitiate the deity of the swamp through sacrifice before leaving for the city, but also because while the village is suffering because of the flood, Kadiye, the priest of the serpent, has grown fat on tithes. (Corpulence is associated with hypocrisy and exploitation throughout Soyinka's plays.) While shaving Kadiye, Igwezu, who was, like his father, the village barber before leaving for the city, is unable to hide his contempt for the priest who exploits the villagers, just as his brother exploited him, and Kadiye fears for his life. Yet the play refuses to offer a blanket condemnation of religion, as Igwezu's apostasy is balanced by a Muslim beggar, who continually praises God and the prophets despite the blindness he suffered in childhood and the drought suffered by his people in the present. Thus the play critiques both village and city, religion and disaffection, brother and brother (though certainly not equally in all cases), ending ambiguously as Igwezu flees his parents' home before Kadiye can return with his followers to exact revenge for his mistreatment. The play, like many of Bertolt Brecht's plays, offers no answers; it only posits questions that leave the audience with a greater sense of self-awareness.

While Soyinka was still working at the Royal Court Theatre in London in 1959, his second play, *The Lion and the Jewel*, debuted at the Arts Theatre in Ibadan—the first staging of his plays in Nigeria. The first of Soyinka's comic satires, *The Lion and the Jewel* juxtaposes the conflicting worldviews of traditional African beliefs and bourgeois colonial values without romanticizing the former at the expense of the latter. In fact, Soyinka avoids simple denunciation of colonial assumptions and bourgeois values by filtering them through the comic misunderstanding of Lakunle, the prototype for the playwright's comedic buffoons; later manifestations include Chume of *The Trials of Brother Jero* (1964) and Salubi of *The Road* (1965).

Lakunle has dabbled enough with European values to reject traditional village beliefs—such as paying a bride-price in his courting of Sidi—as being backward and foolish and something that must be educated out of Africans. But his understanding of the bourgeois values he champions is superficial at best. His concept of a "civilized" marriage, as opposed to the appalling practice of polygamy by Baroka, the village leader, is having "breakable plates." Lakunle is, in other words, a caricature not just of colonial attitudes, though those are obvious enough, but also of the uncritical acceptance of bourgeois values by Africans.

Against Lakunle's inept courting of Sidi, Soyinka pits Baroka, who is considerably older than Sidi and Lakunle and who is clearly associated with a more traditional African worldview. In fact many critics have described him as an archetypal African trickster, especially given that his eventual seduction of Sidi (who initially rejects his advances because of her vanity) is accomplished by passing disinformation to her through his eldest wife, Sadiku, about his impotence. When Sidi hears this news she accepts Baroka's invitation to dinner, only to discover her mistake in underestimating the Bale, a village leader, when she finds herself in his bed. While Sidi does eventually choose Baroka over Lakunle despite the deception, her choice does not entail any idealization of African village life. In fact Soyinka critiques Baroka (though not as harshly as he does Lakunle) by showing us how Baroka bribes the "Public Works" authorities to divert the railway originally intended to pass near the village, thereby obviating the almost inevitable loss of status and power that would accompany such modernization. This scene, like much of the background of the play, is depicted through dance and pantomime—elements of Yoruba festival traditions that Soyinka incorporates into his dramaturgy. In fact, the play ends with a dance that celebrates Sidi's engagement to Baroka, transforming the play into ritual.

NIGERIAN HOMECOMING

In 1960 Soyinka, funded by a Rockefeller research grant to study indigenous African theater, returned to Nigeria. After several years of living in England (without ever feeling he truly belonged), he looked forward to this homecoming despite apprehensions about what he would eventually describe as the "peculiar mess" that was Nigerian politics during these years. Most of his first year home was spent traveling across Nigeria, witnessing, documenting, and theorizing about traditional African rituals, ceremonies, and festivals. Soyinka's fascination with this rich heritage was due in part to the sheer spectacle of these rituals. But it was also due to his belief that any national identity—which Nigeria, only recently emerged from British colonialism, was struggling to establish—must not only derive from but also uphold a native literary tradition.

To nurture that tradition, Soyinka began increasingly to incorporate dance, mime, and other elements of indigenous festivals into his plays, which would range from comedy to tragedy, from political satire to theater of the absurd. Toward that same end, he founded the 1960 Masks, a theater troupe dedicated to revitalizing Nigerian English-language theater (in the tradition of Hubert Ogunde). Soyinka's writing attempts to synthesize European dramatic conventions with Yoruba festival traditions, but he refuses describe this synthesis as the "return" of contemporary drama to its "primitive" origins. In fact he questions the (largely Eurocentric) argument that drama (whether African or European) evolves in a direct line from primitive to complex forms. In *Art, Dialogue, and Outrage* (1988), he suggests that contemporary drama may actually be a "contraction," or diminishing, of sacred ceremonies and rituals that evoke cosmic forces through their performance. In any event, Soyinka refuses to conceptualize indigenous ritual and modern drama as opposing points on a spectrum. If anything, they shape each other, constantly interpenetrating as does everything from inanimate objects to human consciousness within Yoruba cosmology. Only by recognizing the fallacy of compartmentalizing "ritual" and "drama," Soyinka argues, might society overcome its modern sense of alienation.

Soyinka's 1960 homecoming wasn't just about rediscovering the past, however. It was equally about inaugurating Nigeria's future. Soyinka was commissioned to write a play for Nigeria's Independence Day celebration that year, and considering that *The Lion and the Jewel* was frequently misunderstood as a blanket condemnation of colonialism, government officials undoubtedly expected a lighthearted play that would ridicule colonialism and celebrate all things African. What they got was *A Dance of the Forests* (1964). The play examines the means by which any society forges a national identity and eventually posits that any such identity cannot, however much it might desire to do so, deny its own past.

The play opens with a startling image of that past intruding upon the present, as Dead Man and Dead Woman, ancestors summoned by the villagers as part of the "gathering of the tribes" to celebrate their future, emerge from the earth. Unfortunately these ancestors are anything but the idealized heroes of myth and legend that the villagers had intended to summon. Consequently the villagers immediately set about driving the ancestors away, back into the heart of the forest, with the petrol fumes of a lorry (which offers an interesting commentary on the relationship between technology and traditional beliefs). Beyond the hubris of rejecting these denizens of the spirit world (which is folly enough considering the value placed upon one's ancestors in African beliefs), these villagers are guilty of denying their own cultural past—a past marred by multitudes of sins and crimes that have apparently been elided from history or displaced onto others, such as colonizing powers.

The villagers are compelled to confront the reality of their cultural history after the Forest Father (the most powerful deity of the forest) draws several of them into the depths of the forest and enacts the ritual of the court of Mata Kharibu, an ancient ruling house in the village's history. The villagers, possessed by the spirits of the dead, act out the transgressions of this ancient kingdom, including Madam Tortoise's seduction and destruction of men to satisfy her narcissism and the king who imprisons and then castrates Warrior, who refuses to fight in the king's war of conquest because such a war is an abuse of the king's power. The Forest Father's ritual (and Soyinka's play) erases the distinction between past and present, between spirits and humans, and compels the villagers (and the audience) to recognize the transhistorical nature of crime, corruption, and evil. Demoke's killing his apprentice by pulling him off the totem, an act of jealousy for carving the head, which Demoke should have done, derives not from the corruption of the traditional world by the modern world; it reenacts and reifies ancient crimes. What the play conveys, then, is the reality that all societies must earnestly confront their past before they can embrace any future.

This was far from the message the Nigerian officials who commissioned the play wanted to convey, however. Soyinka's play, consequently, was deemed too subversive and too cynical for the Independence Day celebration and was rejected. Fully aware of the irony of its rejection by the new government, Soyinka eventually staged the play with his 1960 Masks at the University of Ibadan, where he played Forest Father.

POLITICAL ACTIVISM

In 1963 Soyinka married Olayide Idowu, with whom he would have four children. But the years 1960–1965 are best characterized by his increasing political activism and concomitant artistic output (the two correlate throughout his career). These years saw Soyinka actively campaigning against censorship, corruption, and oppression as they manifested themselves under the First Nigerian Republic. His Orisun Theatre Company, founded in 1964 with several original members of his 1960 Masks, satirized a number of political targets with his revues *The Republican* (1964) and *Before the Blackout* (1965).

His plays during this period, not surprisingly, evince both his growing discontent with Nigerian politics and his unwavering belief that the artist is obligated to oppose injustice. His *The Strong Breed* (1963) thematizes this obligation.

The play depicts a small village upon the eve of its yearly ritual of cleansing and renewal, which requires a "carrier"—not unlike the "scapegoat" of Jewish tradition—that would absorb and thereby purge the sins of the society. Since no one in the village is willing to accept the physical or psychological burden of being the "carrier," the village elders routinely conscript outsiders, like the village idiot Ifada, to carry out this ritual. The ritual scapegoating is not condemned by the play; in fact, it argues for the duty of an individual to endure suffering for the benefit of the society (a frequent theme in Soyinka's writing). Through Eman, the play's protagonist and newcomer to the village, the play does condemn the village elders' practice of conscripting outsiders. When Eman learns of what awaits Ifada (who cannot understand what is happening to him) he takes the boy's place in the ritual, and in doing so, he fulfills the ancestral duty that he once fled. As a member of the "strong breed," he was destined from birth to endure the suffering of his society, just like his father before him. But he rejected this sacred duty in his youth, exiling himself from his community and eventually taking up new residence in this new village which observes the same ritual. He rejected this duty in part because of his love for Omae (no woman survives the birth of one of the strong breed) and in part because of the enormity of the duty. Like the tragic figures of Greek drama, Eman flees his destiny only to eventually confront it through his flight. When he takes Ifada's place in the ritual, he eventually sacrifices his life for a village that is not his own. This embracing of duty (to society, to a father) is among the most common themes in Soyinka's plays. But it is clearly more than that. Most scholars acknowledge that Eman and others like him in Soyinka's oeuvre allegorize the writer for Soyinka, who believes that personal sacrifice is often necessary for the benefit of the society.

In 1965 Soyinka was arrested (and later acquitted) for allegedly seizing a Western Region radio station to denounce fraudulent election results broadcast by the Nigerian Broadcasting Corporation. Unfortunately this electoral fraud was far from an isolated incident during the "peculiar mess" of Nigerian politics during the late 1960s. As Soyinka laments in his memoir *Ibadan: The Penkelemes Years,* the country was beset by government-sanctioned campaigns of intimidation and disinformation.

Considering this almost rampant corruption, it seemed inevitable that his writing would turn to political satire, as it did in *Kongi's Harvest* (1967). In the play, Kongi, the prototype for the tyrants that populate so many of Soyinka's later plays, has already displaced the Oba (the traditional leader) with his secular, militaristic regime. However, Kongi, who understands the relationship between statecraft and stagecraft, endeavors to arrogate legitimacy for his regime by having the Oba (who has been imprisoned for several months, though in some luxury) offer him the ceremonial New Yam during the Harvest Festival. Kongi is something of a buffoon, as evidenced by his commanding his "Reformed Aweri Fraternity" to "dispute" social and political problems—that is, not to reach any conclusion but simply to conduct "official" sounding disputations. But he instinctively appreciates the value of tradition to the populace and fully intends to exploit it. Kongi orders the Fraternity to fast during their disputations because such fasts are traditional, but the constant complaints of hunger from the Fraternity (which are funny) parody Kongi's hunger for power and legitimacy (which are frightening). His strategy for ensuring both is highly Orwellian. He works through euphemism and doublespeak, proclaiming the theme of the new government to be "Harmony" when it is really "control." His "Carpenter's Brigade" is really just a group of thugs whose only function is to intimidate the populace against potential uprisings.

Kongi's apprehension about rebellion, of course, is not paranoia. Opposed to his regime stands a group of dissidents led by Daodu and Segi. Daodu convinces the Oba to go along with Kongi's ritual not only because Segi's father is Kongi's prisoner but also because the dissidents are planning a coup. But when that coup fails and Segi's father is killed, she replaces the ceremonial yam with her father's decapitated head, so that it is delivered to Kongi during the ritual—a poignant image of the reality of tyranny. The play ends the rebellion apparently thwarted and many of the characters, including some of Kongi's followers, fleeing across the border. This ambiguity again echoes the political plays of Brecht, plays intended to effect genuine social and political change outside the auditorium.

Not all of Soyinka's plays during this period directly satirize Nigerian politics, of course. The sort of political corruption that dominates *Kongi's Harvest* is only a backdrop in *The Road* (1965), whose main subject is an exploration of the juncture of the material and spiritual worlds. That exploration is spearheaded by the Professor, who was expelled from the local church after an ambiguous scandal and who now dedicates himself to discovering the shadowy but sacred "Word" that derives from and in many ways embodies the realm of spirits. The Professor undoubtedly sees his quest as a search for religious and perhaps existential meaning (he is serious and even severe throughout the play), but the fact that he believes that the mysterious "Word" manifests itself in the material world as road signs, which he duly appropriates, suggests that his quest may owe as much to pathology as theology. That the Professor is preoccupied with road signs may not be as absurd as it sounds, however, considering the symbolism associated with roads in Yoruba metaphysics. The road is a point of ontological duality, the place where the living and the dead intersect, where travelers coexist with ancestors. It is also where Ogun, a major Yoruba deity, ambushes unsuspecting travelers, intending to consume them (it is common practice to sacrifice a dog to Ogun to appease the god's hunger).

The Professor likes to keep near him a villager named Murano, who was once struck by a lorry on the road while wearing the mask of Ogun during an egungun ceremony (during which he was possessed by the god as his body became an intersection of the human and the divine; Soyinka's *Myth, Literature, and the African World* offers a good definition of this ritual). That is why the Professor keeps Murano in his auto parts shop; Murano exists in what Soyinka describes as an "agemo" phase—that is, between worlds. Since the accident, he has existed in a trancelike state, having one foot in

the world of spirits and the other in the world of the living (which is why he limps, according to the Professor). But what does call into question the Professor's true agenda in stealing the road signs—thefts that may cause accidents—is that he owns a repair shop that sells automobile parts routinely scavenged from wrecks on the African roadways. Thus the Professor is as much false prophet as he is prophet. (The false prophet is manifested in different guises—often comic—in Soyinka's plays, manipulating others to achieve his own ends, whether economic, metaphysical, or some combination of the two.) Toward the end of the play, when Murano slips back into his ritual trance (and is possessed once more by Ogun), the Professor believes that "the Word" will be revealed at last. But, during a scuffle, another villager accidentally stabs the Professor, a wound that results in his death. The play itself is highly episodic, defying straightforward plot summary, and is composed of a wide range of characters (perhaps too many). It also defies simple genre categorization, as it would seem to be simultaneously the Professor's tragedy and political satire, theater of the absurd and mythopoesis.

IMPRISONMENT

Soyinka's political activism continued to intensify in the 1960s, and when Odemugwu Ojukwu led the secession of the Eastern Republic of Nigeria in 1967 to establish the short-lived Republic of Biafra, Soyinka actively intervened in an unsuccessful attempt to avert the Nigerian Civil War. Along with Victor Banjo and other Nigerian intellectuals, Soyinka formed a bipartisan Third Force to dissuade European powers from selling munitions to either side. He then traveled to the secessionist region during the early days of the hostilities to advocate a political alternative to open warfare. Upon his return in August of 1967, Soyinka (who, ironically had written and acted in a radio play called *The Detainee* just two years before) was arrested by the Yakubu Gowon regime and was subsequently imprisoned without even the pretense of a trial. He was a political detainee for more than two years—one year and ten months of which was spent in solitary confinement.

The ordeal of this imprisonment is recounted in *The Man Died* (1972), the title of which derives not only from an anonymous prisoner who died during the night while Soyinka was imprisoned but also from a telegram he received while writing the memoir after his release about Segun Sowemimo, a journalist who died under the Yakubu Gowon regime. Soyinka believes his imprisonment was designed to break his mind through rather predictable but nevertheless effective psychological torments, such as being granted privileges—books, paper, a radio—only to have them revoked the next day, or being assured of his imminent release only to have such assurances forgotten. He maintains, both in the memoir and in interviews, that the worst aspect of being imprisoned was being denied the opportunity to exchange thoughts with another person, whether through reading or speaking.

Against these torments Soyinka did whatever he could to hold onto his sanity. He experimented with geometric and algebraic formulas; he created mobiles (what he describes as "poetry sculptures"); he compiled notes for works he would write after his release. One of the most powerful ways of resisting his jailors was by fasting; it was a way of reclaiming his autonomy by controlling his body and ultimately his fate. But that did not stop the disinformation campaign that was used against him during his imprisonment. Stories of attempted escapes that never occurred were circulated by the government; stories of his death were allowed to linger for months in the press before being officially denied. To survive, Soyinka not only had to anticipate these maneuverings but also had to understand the self-justifications (no matter how flimsy) of his captors—something that undoubtedly contributed to his startlingly accurate depictions of tyranny in his later plays. The one positive thing that Soyinka took from his imprisonment, as he acknowledges in

interviews, was an understanding of just how much one's survival depends upon one's will.

Two more works published shortly after his release in 1969 derived either from notes compiled while he was imprisoned or from the imprisonment itself. The first of these was *Madmen and Specialists* (1971), an early version of which Soyinka directed at the Eugene O'Neill Theater Center in Waterford, Connecticut, and then in Harlem in New York City. The play opens upon the Mendicants—a group of beggars who suffer from various physical disablements—wagering their own body parts in games of chance. Through this dark humor, Soyinka immediately establishes the reality of living under oppressive regimes—not only the physical suffering that is registered by the Mendicants' bodies but also the psychological conditioning that makes such suffering seem natural—or at least not appalling—to the Mendicants. Interestingly the Mendicants function almost like a Brechtian chorus, performing songs and pantomiming political trials, military executions, and the decorating of soldiers guilty of committing atrocities that linger in the background of the play (but which are central events in Soyinka's other plays).

The Mendicants are anything but mere dramatic devices, however: they are characters with some complexity, as evidenced by their divided loyalties. They are spies for Bero, who was the village doctor before the anonymous war (which clearly echoes the Nigerian Civil War) that left the Mendicants' bodies scarred. Now Bero is a "Specialist," an Orwellian designation that nicely obscures his true function in the new government but which also highlights the euphemism and doublespeak that so often characterize Soyinka's tyrannical regimes. Further, it emerges that the Mendicants are disciples of the Old Man (Bero's estranged father) and his philosophy of "As." The exact nature of this philosophy, not unlike "the Word" in *The Road*, remains ambiguous throughout *Madmen and Specialists,* but it clearly evokes a cyclical view of history and the material world, as the Old Man advocates (and has apparently enacted) cannibalism: flesh returning to flesh. The ambiguity that surrounds "As" may actually be what makes the philosophy so threatening to Bero's government, so much so that the Old Man is condemned for corrupting the minds of the populace (like Socrates), and Bero is ordered to discover the secret of "As." Yet Bero's many attempts to extract the knowledge are futile. Ultimately Bero, the Old Man, and the Mendicants are presumably killed when the Old Women—earth mother figures of the village—set Bero's surgery on fire, with everyone inside, by throwing hot embers on it. The play's conclusion, almost as ambiguous as the Old Man's philosophy, suggests the necessity of destroying that which could be exploited by oppressive regimes as well as the importance of returning to primal states: ashes returning to ashes.

In 1972 Soyinka published *A Shuttle in the Crypt,* his second book of poetry. His first, *Idanre and Other Poems* (1967), was published the year he was imprisoned, although the poems were obviously written well before that. Juxtaposing these collections, then, affords some insight into how Soyinka's experiences shaped his aesthetic. His lyric and narrative poems in *Idanre and Other Poems* dramatize and generally celebrate a natural world alive with deities (most notably Ogun), thereby suggesting the animism of Yoruba metaphysics. These nature poems are balanced by humorous poems like "To My First White Hairs" and philosophical poems such as "By Little Loving." And not surprisingly, the collection includes several political poems, like "Harvest of Hate," wherein skulls are figured as walnuts indiscriminately crushed under boot heels. The centerpiece of the collection, "Idanre," is a lengthy narrative poem (almost a brief epic) in which the poet witnesses the mythical reenactment of Ogun's slaughtering of his own men during a drunken episode (the myth is recounted in *Myth, Literature, and the African World*). While the narrator walks with the gods, he simultaneously warns his audi-

ence to beware the consequences, as Ogun's men discovered, of evoking the divine. The poem ends with imagery of fecundity and renewal, as fruits are born from Ogun's body, transfiguring suffering into hope.

By contrast, the poems from *A Shuttle in the Crypt,* the majority of which were conceived, if not composed, during Soyinka's imprisonment, evince little optimism for the future. The dominant theme of these poems is the loss of human contact and the suffering inherent in isolation. Much of the collection documents his strategies for staving off the madness that continually threatened him during his time in solitary confinement. He wrote elegies like "To the Madmen" to his fellow prisoners, some of whom he saw led to their execution. Other poems were written to the walls, to a cockroach that entered his cell, anything that he could use as a point of reference to maintain his sanity. Toward the end of the collection Soyinka includes two types of poems: what he describes as "cursifying" poems (those that express his rage) and "Animystic spells" (those he used to hypnotize himself through constant and controlled repetition while fasting). Writing these poems, even if only in his mind, was more than just an artistic endeavor; they were life-saving acts of imagination that stood against the torments he endured.

WRITINGS IN EXILE

When the Biafrans surrendered to Yakubu Gowon's federalist forces in early 1970, ending the Nigerian Civil War, Soyinka was finally released from prison. While he undoubtedly celebrated his freedom, he was deeply troubled by the mind-set of the Nigerian populace that, in its relief to be one nation again, stubbornly refused to appreciate that the war had been only a symptom of Nigeria's dilemma and that the true disease was the military dictatorship under Gowon that was still in power. His dismay at this willful ignorance became so overwhelming that he went into voluntary exile and spent much of the next six years in Ghana, England, and America. In 1973, he was a visiting professor of English at the University of Sheffield and an overseas fellow at Churchill College, Cambridge. From 1974 to 1976 he edited the African journal *Transition* in Accra, Ghana.

During this period Soyinka published his second novel, *Season of Anomy* (1973). Unlike his first novel, *The Interpreters* (1965), which realistically depicts the disaffection and disillusionment of a group of African intellectuals, *Season of Anomy* offers an appalling dystopia that is easily the most Orwellian of Soyinka's dramatic worlds. The novel follows Ofeyi's (the head of the propaganda division for the Cartel) endeavors, as naïve as they are noble, to undermine the hegemony of the Cartel, which, like Orwell's Oceania, controls not only people's lives but also their thoughts through intimidation, propaganda, and economic monopolies. Ofeyi understands just how the Cartel works because he was once part of its propaganda machine, but after visiting the utopian community of Aiyèrò, he regrets and rejects his former life. His strategy for overthrowing the Cartel is to educate the populace by using the young people of Aiyèrò, who are already dispersed throughout the country but who have not succumbed to the Cartel's rhetoric, thereby undermining the Cartel's credibility. His nonviolence, though, is contrasted with the Dentist's campaign of political assassination and sabotage. Like Ofeyi, the Dentist is associated with Aiyèrò, but unlike Ofeyi, he argues for swift and immediate action: pulling the tooth before the decay can spread (hence his nickname). The theme of decay—of bodies left in the wake of the Cartel's thugs, of the legitimacy of the police and the military, of minds beset by madness or disillusionment—is constant throughout the novel. When Iriyise, Ofeyi's lover, is kidnapped by the Cartel, the novel shifts from political satire to something close to a quest narrative, as Ofeyi attempts to rescue her. The search for Iriyise takes him through an almost Conrad-like mythic landscape, where Ofeyi must cross rivers of dead bodies, witness the horrors of the Cartel's thugs as they murder and loot, and finally penetrate different levels of Temoko prison before eventually finding Iriyise. The novel ends, like so many of his plays, without resolution. Iriyise, though found, is in a coma; the rebellion against the Cartel, though begun, is anything but complete; and Ofeyi's future, though hopeful, remains uncertain.

In 1973 Soyinka not only returned to comic satire with *Jero's Metamorphosis* but also revived the original manifestation of the false prophet in his plays. Through the charlatan Jero, who debuted in *The Trials of Brother Jero* (1964), Soyinka initially satirized the economic exploitation that characterized Nigerian evangelism; the pun on "prophet" and "profit" is inevitable, as Brother Jero uses theology, psychology, or any number of improvised stratagems to keep his followers "dissatisfied"— that is, in need of the divine reassurance that Jero happily provides as long as those followers continue paying. This original play unfolds through a series of comic reversals that eventually turn Chume, Jero's most ardent disciple, against the prophet—to the point that Chume, armed with indignation and a cutlass, attempts to kill Jero at the closing of the play.

Jero's Metamorphosis opens several months after the first play ends, as the prophets of Bar Beach (where the various "religions" compete for disciples) are confronted by bigger problems than simply augmenting their congregations (as well as their wallets). Through Rebecca, a former secretary for the government and recent convert to his flock, Jero learns of the City Council's plans for purging Bar Beach of the prophets so that it can build a National Public Amphitheatre for executions—with the ultimate goal of increasing tourism! Instead of panicking, Jero, the consummate opportunist, calls a meeting of all the prophets and, after getting them drunk, unveils his plan: The prophets, along with their "churches," will establish a corporation so that they can negotiate with the government on its own terms. Only the puritanical Shadrach refuses to participate (much to his chagrin when Jero's strategy eventually works), and the prophets establish a religious syndicate titled the Church of the Apostolic Salvation Army (CASA) of the Lord. To "legitimate" their organization, the members take official military ranks (allowing Soyinka to parody the dictatorial vogue for bestowing titles upon oneself), culminating with General Jero. Then, when the Executive arrives, Jero blackmails him with the secret file that outlines the City Council's plans, forcing the Executive to sign a contract with CASA that grants it (or Jero, the corporation's leader) not only spiritual monopoly over the souls of those who will gather to watch the executions but also title to the seaside property necessary for such salvation. The play is devastatingly funny, a satire of political corruption and governmental buffoonery.

That same year saw the staging of *The Bacchae of Euripides* (1973) Soyinka's adaptation of the Greek classic, at the National Theatre at the Old Vic in London. That Soyinka would recognize an analogue for Nigeria, a nation repeatedly exploited by military dictators, in Euripides's Thebes, where Pentheus's secular regime has displaced his grandfather's traditional reign, is hardly surprising considering that Soyinka has written frequently of the affinities between Ancient Greece and Africa.

Interestingly, though, Soyinka's adaptation highlights neither Pentheus's hubris nor his hamartia (tragic flaw). Instead it focuses on Dionysos (the god of wine, fertility, and excess), who returns to Thebes to revitalize the rituals and ceremonies of his religion, which have been suppressed under Pentheus's government, as an archetypal force for societal redemption. In other words, it is not the story of a ruler's fall; rather, it is the story of individual sacrifice for the benefit of the society. That theme, dominant throughout Soyinka's writing, becomes clear at the beginning of the play. Just after Dionysos appears at his mother's tomb, Tiresias (the blind

seer of antiquity) enters, playing the part of the "carrier" of Thebes, allowing himself to be ritually flogged to purge the "rot" of the previous year. Normally this duty falls to one of Thebes's slaves, but Tiresias volunteers to take part in the ritual because he recognizes that the slaves, who have been abused by Pentheus, are on the verge of revolt. He is, in other words, sacrificing his body for the good of Thebes.

But it is Pentheus, not Tiresias, who will truly sacrifice his body for his society. When the impetuous ruler learns that the cult of Dionysos—a highly egalitarian group that welcomes slaves, women, and the elderly (including Kadmos and Agave, Pentheus's grandfather and mother)—has been revived in Thebes, he immediately orders the rituals stopped and Dionysos, whom he mistakes as a prophet of the god, arrested. Such an offense, of course, must be punished whether it takes place in Ancient Greece or Africa. After escaping from prison, Dionysos dulls Pentheus's faculties with his sacred wine, dresses him as a woman, and leads him into the hills to witness the gathering of the Maenads, the god's most devoted followers. There, Dionysos drives the Maenads into a frenzy, which results in the death and dismemberment of Pentheus. It is Agave, his mother, who proudly bears the decapitated head of her son on a staff, believing it to be the head of a panther, when the group returns to Thebes. Only within the city does she recognize what she has done. But the guilt and grief of a mother destroying her child are offset (though not overcome) by the imagery of rebirth and renewal as wine erupts from all the orifices of Pentheus's head. It is a difficult ending, one that reminds Soyinka's audience of the terrible price of associating with the gods but also one that reaffirms the consequences of denying long-standing and life-sustaining beliefs.

ANOTHER HOMECOMING

When Yakubu Gowon was deposed in 1975, Soyinka returned to Nigeria and renewed his commitment to revitalizing the country's literary tradition. He served as the secretary-general of the Union of Writers of African Peoples; he assumed leadership of the Department of Dramatic Arts at the University of Ife (a position he would hold until 1985); and he produced the play *Death and the King's Horseman* the following year in 1976. Based on historical events that took place in Oyo, ancient Yoruba city of Nigeria in 1946, the play is fundamentally concerned with duty, ritual, and sacrifice. By tradition, Elesin, the king's horseman, must die through ritual suicide one month after the king's death, and the play opens on the last day of that month. This ritual does more than simply demonstrate Elesin's allegiance to the king; it maintains order within the Yoruba cosmology where all thoughts, actions, and forces interpenetrate. Consequently the villagers devote themselves to satisfying Elesin's every appetite—for food, drink, sex—during that month, including Elesin's demand that Iyaloya's (a woman of the village who eventually conveys the villagers outrage for Elesin's failure to fulfill his duty) would-be daughter-in-law share his bed on the day of the ritual.

Elesin's duty is sacred, both for himself and for the villagers. But the Pilkings, the British officials in charge of this region, cannot appreciate the ritual, largely because they view African beliefs as childish, as something to be educated out of the indigenous population. They have already sent Elesin's son Olunde to medical school in England (against his father's wishes), and now they desecrate traditional beliefs by wearing *egungun* masks and robes, which are nothing more than exotic clothing to them, to a party for the visiting British prince. When they learn of the ritual suicide, they order it stopped and have Elesin arrested, in part because they find the idea abhorrent and in part because such an incident would create embarrassment for the visiting prince. While the Pilkings are little more than caricatures of colonial attitudes and assumptions, Soyinka's play refuses to exploit them as scapegoats for the ritual's failure. After

Elesin's arrest it becomes evident that the horseman had ample opportunity to complete the ritual before the soldiers arrived, but he wavered in his duty because he was tempted by the many pleasures he enjoyed during the preceding month. This is not only a violation of his duty but also a disruption of the Yoruba world, one that Olunde, who returns from England intending to bury his father, must resolve. Despite his English education, which the Pilkings believed would undo the cultural backwardness of Africa, Olunde willingly takes his father's place in the ritual, dying for his people and fulfilling what would have been his duty after his father's death. When Elesin sees his son's body, he recognizes the consequence of avoiding his fate (like so many Greek tragic figures before him) as well as shirking his duty, and he hangs himself in his cell. Like so many of Soyinka's plays, *Death and the King's Horseman* emphasizes the absolute necessity of ritual, duty, and personal sacrifice for the health of any community.

In 1977, while serving as administrator of the International Festival of Negro Arts and Culture, Soyinka produced *Opera Wonyosi* (1989) at Ife. The play, influenced by both John Gay's *The Beggar's Opera* (1728) and Bertolt Brecht's *The Threepenny Opera* (1928), examines the means by which criminality becomes sanctioned state ideology and practice.

Within the play, three different factions compete for the city's resources, with only the slightest pretense of legality. The first upon the stage is Anikura's (a con man who has disguised himself as a businessman to exploit the government) euphemistically titled "Home from Home for the Homeless," a corporate monopoly on begging which permitted the government to officially license beggers (for 50 percent of their daily earnings), assigns them to clearly demarcated districts, and issues them costumes and stories (including "the Cheerful Cripple," "War Casualty," and "Victim of Modern Industry")—all carefully calculated to maximize corporate profits. While many of Anikura's beggars are actual war refugees or political exiles, seemingly just as many belong to the bourgeoisie and have apprenticed themselves to him to perfect their talents for sycophancy (an invaluable skill for career advancement, as well as staying alive, when living under any totalitarian regime). The second faction, generally at odds with the beggar's association, is Macheath's gang of thieves. Macheath is a thief, con man, and something of a Don Juan. His gang of thieves are quintessential African thugs, operating through intimidation and blackmail until Macheath marries Polly, Anikura's daughter, and installs her as the leader of the gang. Almost immediately she transforms the motley group of thugs into a well-organized, almost respectable corporation (of criminality) that makes even more money than before by winning contracts and monopolies from the government. In effect, she does the same thing for Macheath's gang as her father does for the city's beggars. The last group is composed of Emperor Boky's soldiers, though most of them are merely extensions of the emperor's petulant will. A literary descendant of the dictator from *Kongi's Harvest,* Boky is a caricature of the African tyrant that Soyinka lamentably knows so well. Boky surrounds himself with sycophants, commands outlandish punishments for anyone who disobeys him, and revels in his narcissism, as evidenced by the titles (which provide their own punch line) that he bestows upon himself: "Emperor Charlemagne, Desire Boky the First, Lion of Bangui, Tiger of the Tropics, Elect of God, First among Kings and Emperors, the Pulsing Nugget of Life, and Radiating Sun of Africa."

Much of the play depicts the various clashes among these factions, most notably Anikura's attempts to have Macheath executed for marrying his daughter. But what becomes evident is that it is only through the connivance among the groups that tyranny sustains itself, largely by erasing the distinction between crime and politics. The results of this erasure are all too familiar for those living in Nigeria: Laws manipulated, trials parodied, and punishments staged. It all becomes endless theater, as Soyinka emphasizes through the narrator Dee-Jay, intended to pacify the masses.

Toward the end of the decade Soyinka grew increasingly disaffected with Nigerian politics. His Unife Guerrilla Theatre, which followed in the tradition of Hubert Ogunde's folk theater and the Alarinzo traveling troupes, was established in 1978 largely to satirize the Second Nigerian Republic under Alhazi Shagari. His first political satire of the next decade, *A Play of Giants* (1984), moreover, offers his most virulent, and perhaps most incisive, critique of tyranny up to 1984. Dedicated to Byron Kadadwa, who led his theater troupe to the Festival of Black and African Arts in Nigeria in 1977 and was arrested and found murdered after returning to Kampala, the play renders the amusing and appalling psychology of Third World dictators while simultaneously scrutinizing the economic and political complicity of world powers in such tyranny.

The centerpiece of the play is the petulance of Kamini of Bugara, one of the four African tyrants gathered in New York to pose for a sculpture intended to adorn the Delegates Passage of the United Nations. (These tyrants were modeled on real-life African leaders: Macias Nguema of Equatorial Guinea, Emperor Jean-Baptiste Bokassa of the Central African Republic, Mobutu Sese Koko of Zaire, and Idi Amin of Uganda.) That petulance is most evident when Kamini's expectations are thwarted. When the Chairman of Bugara informs Kamini not only that the World Bank refused to authorize the loan that the dictator anticipated but also that Bugara cannot simply continue printing money, as the dictator suggests, because it would further devalue Bugara's currency, Kamini orders the Chairman's head flushed in a toilet—for the duration of the play. When the sculptor carelessly insults Kamini, the dictator has him beaten (though his hands are not damaged, as they are necessary to complete the sculpture). And when news comes of a coup in Bugara, Kamini orders an attack on the UN.

Like most dictators throughout the world, Kamini's outlandish behavior would be laughable were it not for the huge arsenal and loyal soldiers at his disposal. Just as significantly, the play emphasizes the ridiculousness of the strategies used by tyrants to legitimate their regimes: proclaiming a lineage derived from a historical figure such as Chaka Zulu or Napoleon, rewriting history to elide anything incongruous, and bestowing titles upon oneself (like Boky in *Opera Wonyosi*). Nothing is safe from Soyinka's satire within this play, not even the misinterpreted (or exploited) Marxism that attempts to excuse tyranny as the consequence of such cultural conditions as colonialism (as does Professor Batey, one of Kamini's sycophants). The final image of the play is permeated with the irony of Percy Bysshe Shelley's "Ozymandias." As Kamini orders the attack on the UN, the sculptor works busily, capturing the essence of the tyrant for posterity.

CRITICAL AND THEORETICAL WRITING

Throughout his career Soyinka has been extremely concerned with, and dismayed by, the abundant misinterpretations of African literature when read through Eurocentric matrices. His expository writing consistently questions the (racial) assumptions and (political) agendas of those critics commenting on African writing without understanding African history, culture, or cosmology. His theoretical writing, therefore, is dedicated to establishing a cultural context within which to interpret, and even create, African literature.

Myth, Literature, and the African World, the first of Soyinka's theoretical offerings, begins with an overview of Yoruba cosmology, including a discussion of three central deities—Sango, Obatala, and Ogun—who embody archetypal forces that inhabit a "chthonic realm"; within this realm are the creative and destructive essences upon which the writer must draw in order

to create. Just as significant in this book is Soyinka's critique of the Negritude movement, which in his view ironically panders to the worst racist logic used by Europeans to denigrate Africans in its efforts to celebrate Africans. The book ends with his seminal essay titled "The Fourth Stage," a term he defines as the embodiment of the interfusion of opposites, the realm in which Ogun, who symbolizes the creative-destructive essence, undergoes what Soyinka describes as the dissolution and reassembly of self—the paradigm for the African artist.

Soyinka followed this first book with *Art, Dialogue, and Outrage* (1988), which addresses a number of literary and cultural subjects but which devotes itself primarily to establishing the cultural matrix through which African literature must be read. In such essays as "Towards a True Theater" and "From a Common Back Cloth," he condemns the vogue for an excessive imitation of European writing that blinds African writers to the artistic potential in the complexity of African life. In "Cross Currents" and "Aesthetic Illusions" he extends his criticism of Negritude to include neo-Tarzanism, which assumes the essentialist dichotomy between the European (intellect) and the African (emotion). Any art that derives from racist assumptions of African "simplicity," argues Soyinka, is banal at best and legitimates cultural stereotypes at worst. The essays that comprise these two works are often difficult reads, but they provide an invaluable cultural context for assessing and appreciating Soyinka's writing.

LATER LIFE AND WRITINGS

After retiring from the University of Ife in 1985, Soyinka served as president of the International Theater Institute in Paris in 1986 and as professor of African studies and theater at Cornell University in 1988. Then, in the 1990s, he published two new plays, beginning with *From Zia, with Love* (1992), an abbreviated version of which was originally performed as a radio play titled *A Scourge of Hyacinths* (1991). In *From Zia, with Love,* the playwright experiments with genres by juxtaposing two groups of political prisoners. The first group, led by the Commandant, impudently parodies the bureaucracy that masquerades as government under military dictatorships. They ridicule the authority that keeps them imprisoned by offering official "reports" on the suffering of the populace, debating their fate like the Reformed Aweri Fraternity in *Kongi's Harvest,* without any effort to alleviate that suffering. Against this comical metadrama, he depicts the distressing fate of Domingo and two others, who briefly share a cell with the Commandant's theatrical troupe. Through flashbacks Soyinka satirizes the Orwellian thought control—complete with a disembodied voice urging citizens to inform on each other—that dominates Domingo's world. What is most appalling within this play, though, is its ending. Even as the Superintendent of the prison reassures Domingo that his execution will be called off, Domingo and the others are led out of his cell, offstage, where anonymous gunshots ring out, while trustees rifle through the prisoners' possessions.

Instead of parodying political corruption, Soyinka's next play, *The Beatification of Area Boy* (1995), dramatizes determined, coordinated resistance against such corruption. It does this through Sanda, who was a college radical years before (along with his girlfriend, Miseyi) but now, perhaps because of his disillusionment, uses his job as a security guard to conceal his criminal endeavors as the leader of the Area Boys, a group of thugs that exploits tourists and torments the military. Sanda is reunited with Miseyi after she chooses him over her betrothed during her marriage ceremony, and he then decides to confront the pervasive government oppression. This oppression is made concrete within the play by war refugees—both Mama Potts, the shopkeeper who still has the bayonet that killed her brother, and the refugees of Marokos, a city razed by the military to make way for the government's urbanization program. The

play ends with rebellion begun and renewal promised, though not yet achieved.

In the latter half of the decade Soyinka increasingly dedicated himself to writing nonfiction intended not only to expose the political oppression that continues unabated in Nigeria and throughout much of the African world but also to elicit the aid of world powers in combating such oppression. *The Open Sore of a Continent* (1996) documents the 1993 Nigerian election of Moshood Abiola, which was annulled by the military leader at the time, General Ibrahim Badamasi Babangida, even though an international monitoring committee certified the election as fully democratic. Disgusted by this blatant disregard for the will of the Nigerian people, Soyinka, who advocates democracy as an invaluable first step toward insuring the justice that he so desires, condemned this abuse of Nigeria by the military. Just as significant is the frustration he expresses in the book over the apparent indifference—if not implicit approval—of the world toward General Sani Abacha, the dictator exploiting Nigeria at that time for his own benefit and making a mockery of justice by manipulating the courts to execute political dissidents such as Ken Saro-Wiwa. In effect, *The Open Sore of a Continent* renews the call to action that Soyinka originally made in his 1986 Nobel address. Then, he spoke against South African apartheid and did nothing to conceal his considerable indignation toward any country that would ignore that great injustice to humanity. Now Soyinka demands that his fellow Nigerians and the world confront equally unconscionable acts of injustice. His publication of *The Burden of Memory, the Muse of Forgiveness* (1999) expands his concerns about Nigeria to the African world in general, as he questions the wisdom of clemency, without any sort of reparations, for the atrocities committed under tyranny. Some reparations, he argues, may be necessary for any society to move forward, as they would both acknowledge history and guarantee that such history would not reoccur. What these last two books advocate directly are the same things that Soyinka's plays have always addressed indirectly (and the same things to which he has dedicated so much of his life): the fundamental human rights to liberty and justice.

Selected Bibliography

WORKS OF WOLE SOYINKA

PLAYS AND REVUES

A Dance of the Forests. London: Oxford University Press, 1964.

The Lion and the Jewel. Oxford: Oxford University Press, 1963.

Three Plays. Ibadan, Nigeria: Mbari Publications, 1963. (Includes *The Swamp Dwellers, The Trials of Brother Jero,* and *The Strong Breed.*)

Five Plays. London: Oxford University Press, 1964. (Includes *A Dance of the Forests, The Lion and the Jewel, The Swamp Dwellers, The Trials of Brother Jero,* and *The Strong Breed.*)

The Trials of Brother Jero. Oxford: Oxford University Press, 1964.

Before the Blackout. Ibadan, Nigeria: Orison Acting Editions, 1965. (Revue.)

The Road. London: Oxford University Press, 1965.

Kongi's Harvest. London: Oxford University Press, 1967.

The Strong Breed. Ibadan, Nigeria: Orisun Acting Editions, 1970.

Madmen and Specialists. London: Methuen, 1971; New York: Hill and Wang, 1972.

The Bacchae of Euripides: A Communion Rite. London: Methuen, 1973; New York: Norton, 1974.

Camwood on the Leaves. London: Methuen, 1973.

Jero's Metamorphosis. London: Methuen, 1973.

Soyinka: Collected Plays 1. Oxford: Oxford University Press, 1973. (Includes *A Dance of the Forests, The Swamp Dwellers, The Strong Breed, The Road,* and *The Bacchae of Euripides.*)

Soyinka: Collected Plays 2. Oxford: Oxford University Press, 1974. (Includes *The Lion and the King, Kongi's Harvest, The Trials of Brother Jero, Jero's Metamorphosis,* and *Madmen and Specialists.*)

Opera Wonyosi. London: Rex Collings, 1981; Bloomington: Indiana University Press, 1981.

A Play of Giants. London and New York: Methuen, 1984.

Requiem for a Futurologist. London: Rex Collings, 1984.

Soyinka: Six Plays. London: Methuen, 1984. (Includes the Jero Plays, *Camwood on the Leaves, Death and the King's Horseman, Madmen and Specialists,* and *Opera Wonyosi.*)

Childe Internationale. Ibadan, Nigeria: Fountain Press, 1987.

From Zia, with Love and *A Scourge of Hyacinths.* London: Methuen, 1992.

The Beatification of Area Boy: A Lagosian Kaleidoscope. London: Methuen, 1995.

POETRY

Idanre and Other Poems. London: Methuen, 1967.

Poems from Prison. London: Rex Collings, 1969.

A Shuttle in the Crypt. London: Rex Collings, 1972; New York: Hill and Wang, 1972.

Ogun Abibiman. London: Rex Collings, 1976. (Long poem.)

Mandela's Earth and Other Poems. New York: Random House, 1988; London: Methuen, 1989.

NOVELS

The Interpreters. London: Andre Deutsch, 1965.

Season of Anomy. London: Rex Collings, 1973.

AUTOBIOGRAPHY AND MEMOIRS

The Forest of a Thousand Daemons. London: Nelson, 1968. (A translation of D. O. Fagunwa's novel *Ogboju Ode Ninu Igbo Irunmale.*)

The Man Died: Prison Notes. London: Rex Collings, 1972.

Aké: The Years of Childhood. London: Rex Collings, 1981; New York: Random House, 1981.

Isara: A Voyage around Essay. London: Methuen, 1989; New York: Random House, 1989.

Ibadan: The Penkelemes Years—A Memoir, 1946–1965. London: Methuen, 1994.

CRITICISM, ESSAYS, AND ADDRESSES

Myth, Literature, and the African World. Cambridge and New York: Cambridge University Press, 1976.

The Critic and Society: Barthes, Leftocracy and Other Mythologies. Ife, Nigeria: Ife University Press, 1981.

Art, Dialogue, and Outrage: Essays on Literature and Culture. Ibadan, Nigeria: New Horn Press, 1988.

The Credo of Being and Nothingness. Ibadan, Nigeria: Spectrum Books, 1991; Jersey, Channel Islands: Safari Books Export, 1991.

The Open Sore of a Continent: A Personal Narrative of the Nigerian Crisis. New York: Oxford University Press, 1996.

The Burden of Memory, the Muse of Forgiveness. New York: Oxford University Press, 1999.

CRITICAL AND BIOGRAPHICAL STUDIES

Adejare, Oluwole. *Language and Style in Soyinka: A Systematic Study of a Literary Idiolect.* Ibadan, Nigeria: Heinemann Educational Books, 1992.

Adelugba, Dapo, ed. *Before Our Very Eyes: Tribute to Wole Soyinka.* Ibadan, Nigeria: Spectrum Books, 1987.

David, Mary T. *Wole Soyinka: A Quest for Renewal.* Madras, India: B. I. Publications, 1995.

Gibbs, James. *Wole Soyinka.* London: Macmillan, 1986.

———. *Talking with Paper: Wole Soyinka at the University of Leeds, 1954–1958.* Powys, Wales: Nolisment, 1995.

Gibbs, James, ed. *Critical Perspectives on Wole Soyinka.* Washington D.C.: Three Continents Press, 1980.

Jeyifo, Biodun, ed. *Conversations with Wole Soyinka.* Jackson: University Press of Mississippi, 2001.

Jones, Eldred Durosimi. *The Writing of Wole Soyinka.* London: Heinemann, 1973.

———. *Wole Soyinka.* New York: Twayne, 1973.

Jones, Eldred Durosimi, Ketu H. Katrak, and Henry Louis Gates. *Wold Soyinka: A Bibliography of Primary and Secondary Sources.* Westport, Conn., Greenwood Press, 1986.

Katrak, Ketu H. *Wole Soyinka and Modern Tragedy: A Study of Dramatic Theory and Practice.* New York: Greenwood Press, 1986.

Maja-Pearce, Adewale, ed. *Wole Soyinka: An Appraisal.* Oxford: Heinemann Educational Publishers, 1994.

Moore, Gerald. *Wole Soyinka.* 2d ed. London: Evans, 1978.

Ogunba, Oyin. *The Movement of Transition: A Study of the Plays of Wole Soyinka.* Ibadan, Nigeria: Ibadan University Press, 1975.

Msiska, Mpalive-Hangson. *Wole Soyinka.* Plymouth, U.K.: Northcote House Publishers, 1998.

Wright, Derek. *Wole Soyinka Revisited.* New York: Twayne, 1993.

———. *Wole Soyinka: Life, Work, and Criticism.* Fredericton, N.B., Canada: York Press, 1996.

Christina Stead

(1902–1983)

RICHARD DAVENPORT-HINES

SAUL BELLOW, ROBERT Lowell, and Lillian Hellman all believed that Christina Stead deserved the Nobel Prize for Literature. Other critics have questioned whether she was a great writer or merely a good one. Her acceptance as among her century's finest novelists must depend on reading her novels, savoring the richness of their language, the energy of their action, their remorseless details, and their powerful characterization. Her books contain the acute observation and meticulous analysis of a high-grade research scientist, but their bold scale and linguistic exuberance recall Balzac and Joyce. As a canon they can seem fragmented, and somehow diffuse, unless one knows the variegated, cosmopolitan story of her life. Stead was an international adventuress: a woman who fled her homeland at her first chance and was lucky to escape the toils of the police on two continents for her involvement in financial chicanery and political subversion. In the first fifty years of her life she lived in Sydney, London, Paris, Spain, Antwerp, New York, Hollywood, Montreux, Bologna, Basle, Brussels, Lausanne, and The Hague, among other places. Her transatlantic and transpacific escapades, and the long, depressing anticlimax of her later life, provide the context for her novels. Understanding the woman's experiences and rel-

ish for her novels are integrally related. Both Stead and her books were awkward, unpredictable, intense, and demanding. The life and the work converge in their ferocious energy, intransigent vision, and inconsolable bleakness.

Stead had the outlook of the unnamed Musical Critic in her first published novel, *The Salzburg Tales* (1934). "I am a connoisseur of the things people say in the dark," the Critic explains. "I look at life altogether, as a spectator who looks at a vast stage-setting. If you have five minutes to observe a man, from a secret cranny, you will find out a great deal about him." Stead's Critic was inquisitive, voyeuristic, and guilt-free. "I am an inveterate and shameless eavesdropper, I listen at the doors of rooms, I pussy-foot along the corridors, I read private letters and stare at people in their emotion. My own life is too calm for my energy, I suppose that is the reason" (pp. 367–368).

Her career was a flop until the final decade of her life: during the preceding thirty years publishers canceled contracts, reviewers were uncomprehending, readers were scant. Although her books were rediscovered in the 1960s and promoted by the British feminist publisher Virago in the 1980s, her reputation remains mixed. The trouble is that many of her novels are huge and tiring. They have diverse tempers and modes, and she suffered the penalty of her originality: her books cannot be easily docketed and packaged any more than she could. Perhaps her characters and locations were too cosmopolitan for her chauvinist century; possibly her misanthropy seemed excessive too.

AUSTRALIAN UPBRINGING AND EARLY YEARS

Christina Ellen Stead was born on 17 July 1902 in a two-room cabin in the Sydney suburb of Rockdale. Her father, David George Stead (1877–1957), was the son of an Englishman who had emigrated to Australia in 1862. Her mother, Ellen Butters (1876–1904), had worked as a seamstress before her marriage in 1901. David Stead, who had little formal education, was an ardent naturalist, who escaped from his humdrum job shortly after Christina's birth to become scientific assistant to Australia's director of fisheries. When Christina was two-and-a-half years old, her mother died, and David Stead took over the mothering. At night, trying to talk her to sleep, he instead talked her awake with stories about nature, the Australian outback, the prehistoric world, and (she later recalled) "innumerable stories about imaginary people" (Rowley, p. 7).

David Stead was a zestful communicator who taught her botany, zoology, and geology; he kept a menagerie in their garden. He venerated the memory of Charles Darwin and had a naive, eager dedication to progressive causes. Unfortunately, he closely resembled Virginia Woolf's description of her father in "A Sketch of the Past" as exacting, histrionic, self-centered, self-pitying, and alternately lovable or hateful. He was a handsome man who insisted that good looks were an exterior sign of inner goodness; female beauty meant so much to him that he advocated breeding out ugliness from the human race by applying eugenic theories. Unfortunately he was disappointed by the physique of his eldest daughter, whose shape, weight, and features he routinely denounced. Christina was convinced of her plainness. Physical beauty became a lifelong preoccupation of hers.

In 1907 David Stead married Ada Gibbins (1879–1951), whose father had a thriving oyster and pearl business. The Steads moved into an imposing house on the shores of Sydney harbor with fine views of the Pacific Ocean, paddocks, and an orchard; but the pleasures of life there were spoiled for Christina by her stepmother, who treated her as a second-class child.

> Sometimes servants thought I was my father's illegitimate child, at other times, they fancied I was an orphan on my step-mother's side: friends who came to the house took me aside and told me what I owed to the kind people who had taken me in. I myself with dark, thunderous looks, frowns and portentous behaviour did nothing to discourage the idea I was something the gypsies had left behind.
>
> (Rowley, p. 15)

Her stepmother became exhausted by childbearing and increasingly excitable, querulous, manipulative, and unhappy. David Stead's charm and boisterousness contrasted with his wife's rasping discontent. The domestic atmosphere deteriorated when they were forced to move to a weatherboard house at 10 Pacific Street, Watson's Bay, in 1917. Watson's Bay was then a remote and windy fishermen's village popular with the inhabitants of Sydney for weekend picnics; only later in the twentieth century was it transformed into an elegant residential district. Ada Stead detested Watson's Bay's stink of fish and seaweed; she repined for the lost elegance of their previous house.

Christina grew into an ardent, romantic, and indignant young woman who was determined to become a novelist, although her father deplored fiction as frivolous. It was inevitable that he pervaded her life, for they had much in common: eloquence, formidable imagination, intensely focused ambition, passionate but systematic curiosity, and a compulsion to narrate stories. However, when Christina began to show independence of mind at the age of fifteen or sixteen, he started teasing her and making snide comparisons to other girls. Under this systematic belittling she became sullen. David Stead could not respect other people's emotional privacy or understand that their wishes, plans, and ideas were separate from his own. As a result of his invasiveness, his daughter was withdrawn and reticent throughout her life. Growing up on the shores of a great international port she daydreamed about sailors and explorers. Like her heroine in *For Love Alone* (1944) she yearned to "sail the seas, leave her invisible track on countries, learn in great universities, know what was said by foreign tongues, starve in cities, tramp, perhaps shoeless, along side roads, perhaps suffer every misery, but she would know life" (p. 265).

In 1917 Christina became a pupil at Sydney Girls' High School, where she became more self-confident and was sometimes happy. Although she had few close friends, because of her odd looks and clothes, other pupils respected her, especially after she became editor of the school magazine. Her standing with the staff was such that she was chosen to be a senior prefect despite professing to be a socialist, pacifist, and atheist. She read voraciously and was saturated with the ideas and atmosphere of the great nineteenth-century French novelists, supremely Balzac but also Guy de Maupassant, Victor Hugo, and Emile Zola.

In 1920, at age seventeen, she reluctantly enrolled at Sydney Teachers' College. Teaching was associated with spinsterhood, by which Stead was horrified, because Australian women were expected to resign from teaching when they married so as to provide job vacancies for single women who needed the income. She felt sexually frustrated and ashamed of her virginity; sexual deprivation she identified with madness. Throughout the 1920s she felt confused by profound feelings of worthlessness that could not be reconciled with her conviction that she had a great personal destiny.

After working briefly as a psychologist's research assistant investigating intelligence tests, she began teaching at Darlinghurst Girls' School, in an inner-city slum, in 1923. A minutely observed account of these Sydney schools is contained in chapters 7 and 9 of her novel *For Love Alone*. Her detestation of teaching, and her terror of becoming an old spinster teacher, manifested itself psychosomatically: this great novelist of human voices kept losing her voice in class. Consequently she was obliged to transfer to teaching backward and educationally subnormal children at a special school. Meanwhile Stead attended night school to learn stenography, as she had determined to travel after 1927, when her contractual obligation to teach expired, and she knew that she could find work overseas as a secretary.

She developed a romantic longing for a young man named Keith Duncan, an extramural lecturer who did not reciprocate her ardor. When he left Australia to study at the London School of Economics, she deprived herself of food and other pleasures so as to save the money to follow him to Europe. Her unrequited passion was humiliating, lonely, and destructive. She was both ashamed and inwardly exultant about her feelings; she thought herself both cowardly and heroic. Her craving to leave Australia, and her reputation for clumsy eccentricity, made her an isolated, unhappy, and self-harming young woman.

STEAD REACHES EUROPE

She finally sailed for London in March 1928. She traveled as companion to an alcoholic young heiress who had tried to throw herself overboard, and was charged with preventing the woman from bribing stewards to give her gin. This experience she later commemorated in her bleak story of wretched futility, "Night in the Indian Ocean" (in *Ocean of Story*, pp. 53–66). After reaching London in May 1928 she got a job as a secretary in a grain business run by a charismatic and voluble Romanian called Alf Hurst. Its temporary associate manager was a short, plump, pale but genial New Yorker called William Blech (1894–1968), who hired her because she seemed so shy, bookish, and solemn.

Blech (William Blake as he was later known) had been born in St. Louis, the son of German Jews. He had married young, under family pressure, to someone who was, like his mother, manipulative of his emotions and needy of his attention. A political activist from the age of fifteen, he protested against U.S. entry into World War I and went underground as a conscientious objector. After the Russian revolution of 1917, he became an optimistic admirer of the Soviet system despite working as a stock exchange runner and later an investment manager for private banking interests on Wall Street. In 1926 he had moved to Paris, where he worked for a private American outfit called the Travelers' Bank, which speculated in foreign currencies, commodities, and stocks, and had a colorful international clientele of gamblers, playboys, adventurers, and aristocrats. Blech was erudite, with encyclopedic knowledge of politics, economics, the arts, and music. He had a compelling personality—vital, zestful, dashing, and opinionated—and was a charming raconteur and mimic. He resembled a character in *The Salzburg Tales*, Stead's first published novel: "a prodigious polymath, an artesian well of rhetoric. . . . In discourse he seemed even truculent and brusque as he rose on the hawk feathers of logic . . . but in private conversation he was reasonable, sweet and patient, earthy as a sparrow, deft as a martin" (p. 182).

During the summer and autumn of 1928 Christina's self-loathing, and the sense of worthlessness that was reinforced by Keith Duncan's indifference to her, led to constant acts of self-privation, including starving herself. As her friendship with Blech developed, her spirits rose and she resumed eating. Fascinated by him, she studied Jewish culture and bought an English-Yiddish grammar.

In January 1929 he persuaded her to accompany him as his secretary to Paris, where he was returning to his job at the Travelers' Bank. In a French hotel, on 17 February 1929, she finally lost her virginity, which had been so obsessively loathsome to her from the age of fourteen. They began living together—bravely, defiantly, and with passionate commitment on her side—with the expectation that they would soon marry. However, Blech's wife proved unrelenting in her refusal of a divorce. He worried about Christina's eating, writing to her in 1930: "Are you, or you are not spending the last fortnight in an orgy of fattening? Remember a skinny girl means *divorce*, a fat girl *perpetual love*" (Rowley, p. 132). Overall, Blech was a splendid life partner, who supported her literary ambitions with shrewd, self-effacing generosity.

Although Blech and Stead moved primarily in shady banking circles, they amused themselves in cafés favored by those expatriate writers and American dilettantes who were attracted to Paris as the cultural capital of the world. With her love of French realist writers like Balzac (who was particularly admired by Marxists), Stead relished Parisian culture. "Whether the French discovered long ago, like the Jews, that conversation is the cheapest of entertainments, or whether their love for it springs from their natural witty and analytic minds, no one can say," she later wrote. "In the cultured French circles, the ability to spin words, to reverse, invert, pervert and controvert ideas and to divine character makes every foreigner sit back in surprised (and often ashamed) silence" (Rowley, p. 112). It was always language—the helter-skelter of words—that most excited and gratified her. In her books the multiplicity of voices emphasizes the aloneness of her characters and the disordered structure of human existence.

Stead learned to flirt with men in Paris and to dress attractively. Clothes were important to her. Significantly, in *The Salzburg Tales*, one of the most admirable women in any of her early novels is defined by, as well as extolled for, both her clothes sense and her conversational grace.

> She was dressed in a costume of black and white silk in small stripes like hairs laid close together, with a belt of red leather and silver. She wore high-heeled black slippers and the finest silk stockings ever seen; they were of pewter grey. She wore a blue fox fur and a pair of white gloves, and when she took off her gloves, which were always clean, she had on a silver chased ring for a wedding ring and a platinum ring with a diamond as large as a shoe-button . . .
>
> When she spoke, she spoke excellently, with a firm caressing voice; to everything she said she gave an aphoristic turn; her conversation disarmed the jealous, dismayed the dull and sharpened with salt the wit of the witty.
>
> (p. 15)

In 1931 a London publisher agreed to publish Stead's first written novel, *Seven Poor Men of Sydney,* on condition that she produced another novel to be published first so as to whet readers' appetites for the more unorthodox book. She had visited the music festival at Salzburg, Austria, in 1930 and conceived the ambitious project of a cycle of stories resembling Boccaccio's *Decameron,* Queen Margaret of Navarre's *Heptameron,* and Chaucer's *Canterbury Tales* told by characters attending the Salzburg Festival. She wrote at great speed, at her desk in the Paris bank during the day, or on her kitchen table during the evenings.

STEAD'S FLIGHT TO THE UNITED STATES

The Wall Street crash in October 1929 hit the Travelers' Bank hard, but it survived for another six years by dint of speculative maneuvers and illegal transactions in which both Blech and Stead were intimately involved. Alarmed by their implication in criminality, they both left Paris for London during 1934. When the Travelers' Bank collapsed with large debts in 1935, Blech and Stead hurriedly sailed for the United States. While other defaulting directors were pursued across the Atlantic and arrested, they were fortunate to escape charges. The ignominy of Stead's flight with Blech, her left-wing sympathies, the malice of her mother-in-law, her position as an unmarried woman living with a married man, all made her existence more awkward in the United States than in Europe.

In 1936 Stead went to Spain, where Blech was investigating business possibilities. There she wrote the bulk of her great banking novel, *House of All Nations* (1938). With the outbreak of the Spanish Civil War they shifted to Belgium before returning to London, where she developed a strong attraction toward Ralph Fox, a left-wing journalist and activist, who had lived in the Soviet Union during the 1920s. After he was killed in 1937, while a combatant in Spain, she transmogrified his memory with her own intense passion. Fox is the model for Harry Girton in Stead's autobiographical novel *For Love Alone* and for Paul Charteris, a famous leftist soldier-journalist, in arguably Stead's finest short story, "A Harmless Affair" (collected in *Ocean of Story,* 1985). Charteris impresses a married New York couple, Lydia and Tom, when they meet. "Tom talked, talked, Paul answered him, argued with him, opulently showered him with his own ideas" (p. 175). The moment when Lydia realizes her infatuation has a thrilling authenticity:

> a dark storm rushed on her, and for a few seconds, everything in the room whirled around in a glorious delirium: the dark wind rushed on, but left, where had only been a joyful excitement, the surge of adult passion. This was not like her earlier crushes with their blind rages and aches: she had been living happily with a man for a long time and she knew what happy passion was, and this that was left with her now was the night-darkened heavenly garden of love.
>
> (p. 183)

Paul, who is miserably married, returns in a fatalistic mood to China, where he is soon killed in action. Thereafter Lydia (like Stead, one feels, after Fox's death), "dressed very carefully, tried her hair various ways, wondered if tonight, or next week, she would meet the other Paul that the contemporary world probably held" (p. 195).

Stead returned with Blech to New York in 1937. He had been widely known as "Bill Blake" for years and formally changed his surname shortly afterwards, at about the time he briefly joined the Communist Party (1938–1939). The early 1940s, when she lived in Manhattan, was one of the happiest periods of Stead's life. Some of the friendships made at this time were enduring. Her efforts as a scriptwriter for Metro-Goldwyn-Mayer in Hollywood during 1943 were less successful than those teaching at New York University's Workshop in the Novel during 1943–1944.

THE COLD WAR AND AFTER

Stead left the United States for Europe in 1947 and lived a nomadic life shifting between hotels across western Europe for nearly seven years. Both she and Blake were the objects of FBI investigation by this time. The FBI file on her was closed in 1948; but Blake's dossier, opened in 1943, was 200 pages long by 1962. After leaving the United States, joy and vibrancy receded from her life. She became resentful of its course, disillusioned in her personal relations, colder in her outlook, and more easily bored. Publishers in the United States and Britain rejected her new books as insufficiently commercial or malleable for readers to be worth handling. In consequence, her writing (apart from *The People with the Dogs*, 1952) grew more satirical and angry.

Blake and Stead left Switzerland abruptly in 1951 after being questioned by Swiss security police at the instigation of the FBI. A week after Blake finally obtained a French divorce in 1952, he married Stead in London—then a dismal, dilapidated, and uncomfortable place still smashed by war damage—where they were liv-

ing on a pittance. Stead was unnerved by their Cold War blacklisting but kept Blake's faith in Soviet Russia: they even spent an admiring holiday in horrible Soviet bloc East Germany in 1959. Throughout the 1950s and 1960s they continued to mix with London's Jewish communist intelligentsia.

Stead had to wait fourteen years (1952–1966) before she could get another novel published. They lived mainly in shabby homes in dreary places on the southern outskirts of London. Their existence was threadbare, high-minded, isolated, and unhappy—they were too poor to visit cinemas or to entertain—but Blake remained courageous, decent, and hopeful until his health and eyesight began to fail. Stead drank heavily, in private, without embarrassment to herself or others. Her dignity was compromised, though, by her continuing need to flirt with younger men and her hopeless, inappropriate crushes on them. Her infatuation with an English physician many years her junior lasted for much of the 1960s. His public opposition to the Vietnam War only intensified her admiration. During the mid-1960s she began severing her relations with her women friends. Letters from her would unexpectedly upbraid them for undisclosed betrayals or shortcomings. Her anger seems unbalanced.

None of her books was published in Australia until 1965. In that year her critical reputation began to revive, but despite growing acclaim, the final fifteen years of her life were personally miserable. Her life felt sundered after the death of her husband in 1968. With unerring insight she had faced this crisis, and foreshadowed her final phase when, in *The Salzburg Tales*, composed in the early 1930s, a grieving widow recalls her husband, a Lithuanian Jew of high personal principles but few financial rules.

> He had a golden heart and he was very ambitious and so cultivated. . . . He had such a deep appreciation of the roots of things! . . . He was emotionally endowed; and . . . he appreciated me properly: he

knew me. . . . When I met him, it opened a new world for me: it gave me a new emotional orientation. . . .

I don't know how I shall go on: only that lonely part of me will go on living, that lonely part of the soul which even a husband cannot reach, the simple and childlike part which is the heritage of the child in us women. Yes, that is the tragedy of married life, that with the person to whom you are most attached, you still feel yourself, at times, a complete stranger.

(pp. 298–299)

When Stead revisited Australia in 1969 for the first time in forty-one years, she was treated as a celebrity but seemed self-conscious and even ungracious. In her later novels, such as *The Little Hotel*, there is a spirit of triumphant survival: despite human monstrosity, she will not admit defeat. The temper of her real life, alas, was sadder and angrier. In 1974 she moved back to Australia, where she lived a tiring, unsettled existence. Throughout her life Stead had felt anxious about being emotionally rejected, especially by men, yet she often seemed to court rejection by behaving unreasonably. In old age she was, more than ever, dogmatic, prickly, and demanding, and reverted to her early habit of self-starvation. Sustained by a diet of steak tartare, with two liters of Martini Rosso daily, she was helped by sympathetic Australian academics until her death on 31 March 1983. She had left instructions for her cremated ashes to be scattered in Botany Bay, but no one could be bothered to collect them.

When writing a novel Stead would reread, for inspiration, Shakespeare, Ibsen, and Chekhov (especially, as her compassionate and perceptive biographer, Hazel Rowley, has noted, to refresh her dialogue). Her prose, at its best, was vital and luscious; her artistic vision unique and unblinking. She was a cosmopolitan, who liked to immerse herself in different cultures. Language, more than alcohol, intoxicated her: it drove her creative impulses even more than her rage and resentment. Arguably the least autobiographical of her books was the first to be published, *The Salzburg Tales*. Thereafter her life and novels were interlaced.

Stead was as ambivalent about her characters as about her intimates. Her girlish love for her inspirational, exciting father had been tempered by resentment of his egotism and cruelty. The shortfall between his ideals and his conduct produced in her a lifetime of mistrust and disillusion. He was a supremely eloquent man, and she remained highly susceptible to great talkers. The other leading man in her life, Bill Blake, was another great conversationalist, with a yawning discrepancy between his ideals about the brotherhood of humankind, his unswerving fidelity to Marxism and the tyrannous Soviet Union, and his willingness to be the cat's-paw of crooks and speculators. Her behavior, like her books, could be monstrous.

THE SALZBURG TALES (1934)

It is fitting that Stead's first published book should be full of different voices and a festival spirit, for she was supremely the novelist of polyphony and carnival. The verbal expressionism of *The Salzburg Tales*—its variety of styles, moods, and subjects—makes it a rich and mysterious book. Salzburg, an old, princely city in the Tyrol mountains, is the location of an annual musical festival. In Stead's conception, music lovers attending the festival meet in the woods above the town and divert one another by telling stories. The result is a book of luxuriant vivacity teeming with character portraits, anecdotes, and jokes. The stories themselves are variously tragic, gothic, comic, ironic, supernatural, and the stuff of twentieth-century myth. Overall they present a view of European life between the world wars that combines realism and reportage with romance and absurdity.

Something of the range of *The Salzburg Tales* is conveyed by an abridged list of its narrators and their stories. A Viennese conductor talks of a skinny, seedy old Russian pedagogue who fathers a child in his old age. An Italian singer describes how a grieving Dutchman comes to throw himself into the crater of Vesuvius clutching the purloined heart of his dead American mistress. A Scottish woman doctor tells the strange story of a blind youth who is rejected by his wife because of the erotic power of his hands in bed. An Irish spinster schoolteacher repeats the dialogue between two women scaling a peak called Mount Solitary. An aristocratic philosopher tells a fairy tale about lemons. A superstitious international financier recalls a goldfish that could predict stock exchange price movements by changing the hue of its flesh. A swaggering Hungarian lawyer recalls his part in a *crime passionel* that sundered a Magyar family. A Finnish mathematician recounts the misery and death caused by a mirror with supernatural powers. A foreign correspondent from China describes a school bursar who commits suicide out of vanity. A Danish bookbinder explains the reasons for the death of her jilted brother. A Wall Street broker commemorates a sexy Spanish toreador, and an Austrian town councilor tells a story about puppeteers. There are other captivating stories in similar exotic strains.

Stead included a parabolic self-portrait in the character of a Public Stenographer, who types committee papers for the League of Nations in Geneva. She is like Stead before Blech started sleeping with her.

> At night, over a shaving of cheese, dry and old, with a bitter mouldy flavour caught in the restaurant's damp pantry . . . she would . . . amuse herself with anecdotes of the comic, pathetic, marvellous in her long dull life. . . . She speculated about love and its thick mystery; she recalled breaths of the supernatural which had blown on her cheek; and the great strokes of luck which had passed within a hand's breath of humble workers she had known.
>
> (pp. 46–49)

The Stenographer's haunting tale depicts her sexual frustration and her resentment of her father, an atheistic English schoolmaster who heckled the village clergyman's sermons with provocative remarks about Darwin. His illicit love affair, taunting, and exuberant insincerity repel his children. "The Public Stenographer's Tale" ends with her brother dancing around the room singing, "We ALL hate the Old Man, We ALL hate the Old Man" (p. 485).

A few stories in *The Salzburg Tales* are too long; but the book can be read in segments and is never wearisome. The eccentricities of its structure are deliberate and playful. Its language and stories are abundant but never excessive. This distinguishes *The Salzburg Tales* from most of Stead's subsequent novels, which despite more continuous plots, can seem too discursive or demanding (and therefore tedious) in places.

SEVEN POOR MEN OF SYDNEY (1934)

This novel is a peerless portrait of Sydney in the 1920s. It begins with a vivid account of Sydney Harbor waking for the day: "liners from Singapore, Shanghai, Nagasaki, Wellington, Hawaii, San Francisco, Naples, Brindisi, Dunkirk and London, in the face of all these stone houses, decayed weatherboard cottages, ruinous fences, boathouses and fishermen's shanties" (p. 2). There are luxuriant accounts of Watson's Bay (called Fisherman's Bay), with superb evocations of a local economy based on "dark wirrah, spotted kelpfish, rainbow parrot fish, eels and octopus" (p. 224). It is a book about twentieth-century cities to rival those other great novels of the 1920s about urban energy and failure, John Dos Passos' *Manhattan Transfer* (1925) and Alfred Döblin's *Berlin Alexanderplatz* (1929). The city's plenitude and variety are emphasized. In a characteristic scene, one poor man of Sydney gazes from his rooming house in Woolloomooloo. "Tiny living-rooms with Japanese screens, fans and bead curtains, and reeking of bugs and kerosene, with bric-a-brac, vases, wilting flowers and countless rags and papers, sent out their heat and animal odours and old dust at seven in the evening when the hot day had gone down into the violet twilight, a deceitful shady moment promising cool, but bringing in the torrid night" (p. 138).

The protagonists of the novel are poor, desperate, and isolated. Some, such as the wheedling printer Tom Withers, are emotionally cut off from other people by their struggle to escape poverty. Michael Baguenault, who has returned from soldiering in World War I with his nerves broken, is estranged by his morbid self-absorption. After long, desolate scenes, he jumps from a cliff into the ocean. Michael had been incestuously devoted to his sister Catherine, whose virginity is a source of desperate misery to her. One chapter concludes with Catherine weeping to herself: "In the lowest places I find my answers: I've fought all my life for male objectives in men's terms. I am neither man nor woman, rich nor poor, elegant nor worker, philistine nor artist. That's why I fight so hard and suffer so much and get nowhere" (p. 214). Like Stead, she will not eat and seems potentially self-harming; she retreats from her difficulties by committing herself, voluntarily, to a mental asylum.

The novel's most attractive and luxuriant character, Baruch Mendelssohn, who is based on Bill Blech, escapes to a job with an American financier. His long monologues are sometimes overwritten, but their futility is acknowledged. "A person like me who talks only, and even becomes warm and radiant in talking, dies with each word as if he spat out nothing but sparks," Mendelssohn says. "Conversation is the fire of social life, and see how it dies" (p. 141).

There is much Marxist talk in the book, descriptions of Communist newspapers and labor organizers, federal police spying on activists, and critiques of consumerism. The subjugation of Australian interests to British colonial power is a subsidiary theme. The activists are "energetic and disputatious," which is how Stead liked her men (p. 176). The linguistic exuberance of the novels reflects the impact of James Joyce on Stead's imagination. The middle of one long sentence, for example, reads, ". . . palsied palimpsests, clerks, sharks, narks, shades, suspicions, university janitor, spiral-horned rams, stock exchange rampers, rabbits, whorlie-whorlies, willy-willies, whories, houris, ghosts, gouttes, knouts, ghouls, walking-gourds, grimalkins, widdershins . . ." (pp. 269–270).

THE BEAUTIES AND THE FURIES (1936)

This third novel again shows the influence of Joyce. It is a jumbled mixture of semiautobiographical episodes with ideas taken from gossip about the fast lives of expatriates whom Stead met in Paris. The result is a coruscating, often funny portrayal of infidelity, betrayal, and poisoned innocence. Its central protagonist, Elvira Western, deserts her physician husband in London to live in Paris with a young lover, Oliver Fenton, a self-infatuated poseur who is writing a doctoral thesis on French socialism. Oliver is a loquacious and zestful cheapskate whose character blends Blech's with Duncan's. Elvira and Oliver's social set in Paris lacks scruples about either sex or money. Eventually they separate, and Elvira returns to her husband.

The book shows Stead's preoccupation with physical beauty and suggests that Elvira has wasted her abilities because she is alluring. The scandals and violence of French politics during 1934, which provide the background for the story, reflect the influence of Blech's political activism on Stead's outlook. Some fashionable psychoanalytic ideas of the 1930s are a further influence. Stead seems to have become pregnant more than once during the early 1930s but chose to have an abortion on each occasion. Later, when she desired a child, it was lost by miscarriage. In her fiction, too, Elvira is irresolute when she conceives a child by Oliver, but she finally has a termination. Perhaps this scandalous incident contributed to the book's mixed reception. One review is worth quoting because it foreshadows complaints directed against many of her later books. "What the book does offer is oceans of talk, all of it clever and dextrous in the extreme, some of it brilliant, a little of it wise as well as sophisticated. But every character talks in the same style, and the style is not that of a living person. . . . pages and pages of verbal fireworks lose significance in this professedly realistic story" (*Times Literary Supplement,* 2 May 1936, p. 375).

HOUSE OF ALL NATIONS (1938)

This is another polyphonic novel with lots of jittery, voluble fly-by-night financiers talking with mesmerizing speed. It is the supreme picaresque novel about capitalism ever written. On the score of its technical accuracy and ethical authenticity, it should be prescribed reading for students in business schools who need to learn about the murky, volatile, opportunistic world of private banking and speculation. Patrick White shrewdly likened the book to Balzac's *César Birotteau.* It is so long and unsparing that it has deterred readers, who do not anticipate how funny it often is. *House of All Nations* is also one of the great historical novels picturing Europe in the 1930s. Set in Paris in 1931–1932, its characters execute their financial shenanigans in the context of Hitler's rise to power in Germany, Nazi book burning, the central European banking crisis, the financial collapse of the Swedish Match Company (the Enron scandal of the 1930s), Japan's invasion of Manchuria, the disintegration of the Labour government in Britain, and Hoover's defeat by Roosevelt.

Stead's fictional Banque Mercure is closely based on the Travelers' Bank, where she and Blech worked. The book's title likens this type of outfit to a whorehouse. Jules Bertillon, the seductive scoundrel in charge of Banque Mercure, is based on the Travelers' boss, Peter Neidecker, in reality a crooked, generous, enthusiastic, amusing, and resourceful American. There are neither important women characters nor any admirable individuals in 800 pages. One of the chief protagonists, Michel Alphendéry, is discontent, morally contaminated, and despicably weak in some of his choices, but Stead's affection for him is brazen, for he is Bill Blech.

House of All Nations is a huge, engrossing book that defies detailed summary or apt quotation. Although it had a disappointing critical reception, its grandeur is undeniable, and it deserves recognition as arguably Stead's most ambitious and certainly one of her most important, opulent, enjoyable, and creative books.

THE MAN WHO LOVED CHILDREN (1940)

This remains among the finest books on family life ever written—indeed "one of the great novels of the world" according to Patrick White (in David Marr, ed., *Patrick White Letters,* 1994, p. 297). It is the ultimate book of domestic claustrophobia, female domestic entrapment, and childhood disempowerment. It depicts the discrepancy in family life between professed feelings and actual conduct, and the sinister ways in which extreme family abnormality somehow comes to seem normal. The book is sensual, vivid, agonizing and emphatic; some sections seem excessive, and there are structural frailties. Stead's fictive version of her childhood did not seem objectively true to her siblings, but as literature it is conclusive.

Its current status, and the revival of Stead's reputation, owes much to a long, passionate, and closely argued essay by the American poet Randall Jarrell first published in 1965. He championed *The Man Who Loved Children* as a masterpiece comparable to Tolstoy's *War and Peace,* Dosteovsky's *Crime and Punishment,* and Proust's *Rememberence of Things Past.* Stead transposed her novel from Sydney to the United States because the publisher claimed that no readers would be interested in Australia, but she could not master all American nuances and slang. The book is set chiefly in Baltimore, Maryland, and Washington, D.C., but also has scenes in other U.S. localities and in British Malaya.

The novel is dominated by the verbal dynamism of Sam Pollit, a government-employed fisheries expert whose marital history and histrionic mannerisms and conduct resemble (but distort) those of David Stead. A bigoted prohibitionist who hates novels as much as alcohol, he avers that men should be virgins when they marry. His egotism masquerades as caring for other people. After the death of his first wife, he has married Henny, the improvident daughter of a once rich but now decadent family, who is a fictionalized version of Ada Stead. "She looked formidable . . . in her intemperate silence, the bitter set of her discolored mouth with her uneven slender gambler's nose and scornful nostrils, lengthening her sharp oval face, pulling the dry skinfolds. Then when she opened her eyes, there would shoot out a look of hate, horror, passion, or contempt" (p. 6). Amidst her desperate unhappiness, she particularly dislikes her stepdaughter Louisa, who is a self-portrait by Christina Stead. "I am so miserable and poor and rotten and so vile and melodramatic, I don't know what to do," Louisa wails. "I can't bear the horror of everyday life." She hates her appearance too. "I'm so messy. My elbows are out and I have no shoes and I'm so big and fat and it'll always be the same. I can't help it" (p. 405).

Pollit likes cruel jokes, and he seems never to stop talking. He has many different voices: exasperating baby talk, puerile nicknames, facetious slang, sententious moralizing, and the violent rage of a man whose marriage is a disaster. He is always planning priggish utopias but thrives on tumult and encourages a state of domestic pandemonium. Louisa eventually writes him a message: "Shut up, shut up, shut up, shut up, shut up, I can't stand your gassing, oh, what a windbag, what will shut you up, shut up, shut up" (p. 363).

Apart from the devastating family rows, there are powerful passages in the book: the anguished scene when Louisa's sensitive, ambitious brother Ernie discovers that his mother has robbed his money box; a later scene when Henny beats Ernie; the evening when Henny plays solitaire while Sam and his children boil a marlin for its oil. Other sections—Henny taking her children to visit her parents one summer, Sam's sojourn in Malaya and his homecoming party—are too long.

Henny has an affair with a "red cheeked, lusty, riotous giant" (p. 88), who fathers her last child. He dumps her with humiliating decisiveness when she grows too needy, and she never recovers. Some readers will celebrate her death near the book's close, after drinking cyanide, as a merciful escape from misery; others as a punishment for her self-absorbed nastiness. It is hard to say whether Henny's death is suicide or murder by Louisa; but it is all too clear that the Pollit family seethes with homicidal resentment and a craving for murderous revenge.

FOR LOVE ALONE (1944)

This equally autobiographical sequel to *The Man Who Loved Children* focuses on sexual frustration. The heroine of *For Love Alone*, Teresa Hawkins, resembles Stead in teaching Sydney children with special educational needs during the 1920s, in starving herself, and in following an unrequited lover to London. Teresa feels rejected, desperate, and so feverish with desire as to verge on mental illness.

> Since school, she had ravaged libraries, disembowelled hundreds of books, ranged through literature since the earliest recorded frenzies of the world and had eaten into her few years with this boundless love of love, this insensate thirst for the truth about passion, alive in their home itself, in her brothers and sisters, but neglected, denied, and useless; obnoxious in school, workshop, street. . . . At each thing she read, she thought, yes, it's true, or no, it's false, and she persevered with satisfaction and joy, because her world existed and was recognized by men. But why not by women?
>
> (p. 76)

Teresa fantasizes about men and is frantic to marry. Both at home, and, when on a country walk, an old man masturbates in front of her, she is confronted by the twisted results of sexual abstinence and repression: "chastity, for that is the name they give the abomination, brings such suffering" (p. 319). Stead depicts her own terror of spinsterhood and condemns society's hypocrisy about women's sexual, emotional, and social needs. "Religion, morality, consist of the word No!" (p. 254).

Teresa begins to hero-worship a young man called Jonathan Crow, Stead's vengeful portrait of Keith Duncan. Teresa starves herself to save the money to follow him to London, but when she finally reaches England is met with cruel and selfish indifference. He has become unpleasant in looks and character: "a shrewd and unscrupulous-looking man . . . with a hammered-out distorted and evil face and a syncopated rolling walk which looked like the business stroll of the second-rate spottable spy" (p. 429). Sexual repression has twisted him into a lustful misogynist who complacently describes watching three of his friends rape a servant girl: "we just sat and grinned" (p. 339). He is obsessed with sex and, like a prototype of Alfred Kinsey, circulates a questionnaire about sexual behavior to the graduate students of his university. The novel is full of his lascivious monologues and contains a painful section in which he behaves with hateful vindictiveness to spoil his brother's happy wedding day. Crow has a disgusting antagonism to interracial marriage, and his doctoral dissertation is full of racial and sexual bigotry. "The white European male has a natural superiority," he writes (p. 414). Crow is described as a "dim-faced bobbing pedant of the sort that climbs slowly but successfully on his undangerous stupidity, behind the backs of other men to be head of his department" (p. 430). Keith Duncan, who became professor of history and political science at the University of Adelaide, never forgave Stead for publishing her unsparing version of their relationship.

Teresa is almost dying of sexual rejection by this arid, hectoring academic until, in chapter 30, she begins an office romance with her American boss, James Quick, based on Blech. They become lovers and begin a life together. It is a happy and successful match, but in an extraordinary end to the book, she falls for Quick's best friend, Harry Girton, a radical pamphleteer. "She dreamed of him, and presently day-dreamed of him, and, differently from any other man until then, it was of his body that she dreamed; its secret nakedness became robed in incomparable, ever-flowing, ever-born, shadowy loves and nameless pleasures" (p. 467). Eventually they hire a room together. "The whole night passed before they slept and for hours they were as close as creatures can be" (p. 488). After he leaves to fight in the Spanish Civil War shortly afterward, she returns contentedly to Quick; but her infidelity comes as a final shock in the book. It seems to mean that for Stead—certainly for her heroine Teresa living with James Quick—a stable, caring relationship is the prerequisite for a woman to gain freedom of choice. Life with a man is the only way that a woman can achieve any independence that matters.

LETTY FOX: HER LUCK (1946)

There is a huge cast of characters in this boisterous book, the action of which runs from the 1920s to the 1940s and largely occurs in New York. Its eponymous narrator is a bright, cynical American college graduate who quickly declares, "I have bounce, I am preposterous, I elbow people out of my way and am out for myself" (p. 13). She comes from a noisy, grotesque family based on some of Stead's own relations: Solander Fox is a version of her father, for example, while Jenny Fox is drawn from Rosa Blech, Bill's mother.

The competitive edginess of Letty Fox's life as a career woman in New York in the 1940s is realistic and unappealing. So too is the bevy of strong, scheming women who populate the novel. They exploit, trick, and exhaust their men, who are for the most part absent or passive figures in the narrative. The genteel surfaces that can cover women's use of sex to obtain money, status, and power are well evoked. There is much lechery and scandal. The novel might, perhaps, have been subtitled *Sex in the City*, although it is the emotional manipulation of sex rather than copulation that dominates. Its narrative is deliberately copious, filled with inconsequential incidents, because Stead knew that human experience is unstructured: Letty's narrative, though, is as fatiguing as life itself.

Letty Fox satirizes Americans as faddish, foolishly susceptible to Freud's theories, and provides an unforgiving analysis of the New York phenomenon that over thirty years later became known as radical chic. The book, which does, however, acknowledge the generosity and energy of Americans, incensed Communists, led the FBI to open a file on her, and offended American puritans by its portrayal of a young woman's sexual feelings. "A kind of picaresque of sex American style," as Patrick White reflected, "it's extraordinary to think of that quiet, sedate woman writing anything so hilarious" (Marr, ed., *Letters,* p. 451). Letty Fox's sexual independence seemed aggressive and even corrupting to some early readers. The Australian Literature Censorship Board banned the novel in 1947 after reporting that it was "indecent and vulgar and grossly over-emphasises matters of sex" and would therefore harm adolescent readers (Rowley, p. 346).

A LITTLE TEA, A LITTLE CHAT (1948)

Stead wrote this mordant novel when she was irritable with boredom while living in Antwerp and London during 1947. Its central figure, the lavish, credulous, and self-centered Robbie Grant, is her resentful picture of Alf Hurst, the Romanian grain merchant who had exploited and disrupted Bill Blake's life. The velocity, histrionics, and bad grammar of Grant's monologues dominates this story of confidence tricksters, war profiteers, Wall Street sharks, and sex workers set mainly in the period after Pearl Harbor (December 1941). Grant is a money-grubbing opportunist scared by premonitions of an early death. In terror of his own mortality, he frantically chases women, whom he cheats both sexually and financially. Though he has affairs with many women, he is too impatient as a lover and gives no pleasure to his partners.

Grant's discarded mistress, Barbara Kent, an up-market prostitute with a talent for extortion, comes to obsess him. She introduces him to an easy-money crowd, "people in the soft, sophisticated and depraved mid-Manhattan set" (p. 216). It is a typical Stead demimonde:

> Floaters, promoters, "representatives," "agents," people who had once been in Hollywood or would go next month. . . . Some were customers' men getting orders in those haunts of boredom and perversity and small talent that get the curious on their quarterly jaunt from the suburbs and New Jersey. Some were shady businessmen, in the black market, full of schemes for evading currency and tax laws. . . . These men did business in bars, houses of ill-fame, and on the sidewalk in the fashionable district. Some had as their office a desk, an automobile, or a hotel bedroom. . . . They traveled by plane and Pullman, at times had money. Among them were self-introduced majors and counts, an occasional General X and Lady Y: an international scum which declared itself well-born and excellently educated, rich, but just now out of luck.
>
> (p. 166)

Grant fools many people into believing that he is sincere, well-meaning but weak; in fact his amorality is hateful. He double-crosses his most loyal friends and preys on the vulnerable with deadly ruthlessness. His victims include a fashionable Polish playwright, whose tirades in a medley of foreign languages are one of the high points of the book: at first amusing, they became heartbreaking as his babble speeds up into madness under the annihilating humiliation of Grant's cheating. Sometimes Grant's lies are absurd and amusing; on other occasions revolting. When a vulnerable girlfriend commits suicide after he has cheated her over the purchase of a motorcar, he tries to turn her tragedy into a play with himself as sunny hero. "Nothing to reproach myself with," declares this sentimentalizing, self-mythologizing egomaniac. "We want to fix it up a bit, gay, light-hearted, no funeral urns, modern, no tears, no lilies, we extract the gloom and put in the honey" (p. 277).

The section in which Grant sets private detectives to investigate Kent's past and is infected by the wartime spy paranoia in Washington, D.C., is perhaps too protracted. However, some of his skirt-chasing escapades, and his exuberant, chaotic attempts to coax an acquaintance into writing a novel about him entitled *All I Want Is a Woman,* are hilarious. There is a long scene (covering chapters 44–46) in which Grant's wife, son, and two mistresses discover one another in his hotel suite. The farcical misunderstandings, witty deception, and absurd dialogue result in a long comic scene of uproarious gaiety.

A Little Tea is another disorderly, polyphonic dark comedy wired by the nervous, staccato street talk of its sleazy profiteers. It offended some U.S. reviewers, who wanted to hear about the idealism of the American Way and the proud marvels of capitalism rather than wartime corruption. Grant's long speech to his son in chapter 48 provides the credo of a market fixer and capitalist buccaneer, leaving the reader with no illusions about market economics. The bellicose rant about homeland security in chapter 11, delivered by a despicable Wall Street broker with isolationist and antilabor views, was equally offensive to patriotic Americans. The searing satire of *A Little Tea, a Little Chat* remains uncomfortably pertinent half a century later.

THE PEOPLE WITH THE DOGS (1952)

Stead and Blake lived during the early 1940s at 212 East Sixteenth Street in Manhattan, a house owned by Asa Zatz, a young man with a kern terrier. Zatz rented out rooms and maintained a communal kitchen in the basement. His aunt Aida, who had two bull terriers, was married to a concert pianist called Max Kotlarsky, with whom she owned a rambling old house in the Catskills where Stead often stayed during the summers of the 1940s. The kindness of the little informal communities in the Zatz and Kotlarsky households impressed her; she thought their extended family offered a model for human existence. "I feel such affection thinking back to New York," she wrote in 1953. "I don't grow much attached to anywhere, but I think the New York people were my closest" (Rowley, p. 274).

The People with the Dogs, celebrating this phase of her life, is her gentlest book. Zatz is Edward Massine in the novel; the Kotlarskys were models for Oneida and Lou Solway. The novel (set at the close of World War II) opens with a man stabbing his wife during a row caused by the housing shortage, but if Massine's communal household is cramped, there is still ease, amiability, and mutual respect. Joking and leisured conversations fill the novel. There is no sentimentality in Stead's story, but many pleasant sentiments and sturdy personal attachments. Good clothes, delicious brunches, and summer days are lingeringly described; canine breeds are praised and honored; happy, enthusiastic amateurs stage a play. The repose, human tenderness, and natural beauty of Whitehouse, the Massines' country estate, are celebrated: its congenial summer visitors form a community in which it is "hard to distinguish family and friends" (p. 155). A caustic optician called Philip Christy, who "admired people in the measure that they were failures in life and had lost all ambitions" (p. 261), dies trying to save a whippet from a trolley car. Oneida's toad-faced French bull terrier bitch dies of old age. But the stresses in the communal family are mild, sometimes amusing, and individually its members are endearing. Edward Massine is indecisive in his courting of a long-term girlfriend, and after their breakup, he abruptly makes a good decision and marries another character, Lydia, on Valentine's Day.

COTTERS' ENGLAND (DARK PLACES OF THE HEART) (1966)

In 1949 Stead stayed with a friend's family in Newcastle-upon-Tyne, a northern English industrial city. This experience contributed to her novel *Cotters' England* (published in the United States under a title she disliked, *Dark Places of the Heart*). It is an imperfect book that does not hold the interest of all readers, but it is by no means a failure or unworthy of Stead. Its most poignant scenes are set in economically depressed Bridgehead, where the disheartened and defeated members of the Cotter family live and die.

One of the Cotters, Nellie, has married a man called Cook and moved to a mean, run-down house in London. She is a slatternly, chain-smoking bronchitic who works for a left-wing newspaper. During her husband's frequent absences she becomes involved with other women, whose lives she bullies and manipulates in a self-deluding way. "A beaky, restless, gabby person" with a "turbulent selfish soul," Nellie's "shameless curiosity and crafty use of her knowledge . . . trapped people," one of her victims decides (p. 294).

Nellie is an emotional vampire who impels one friend to suicide but sincerely believes that she has a warm heart. In this, at least, she resembles Robbie Grant, the chief protagonist of *A Little Tea*, though the scenes of her destruction are more intimate and domestic. She feels emotionally martyred and has a streak of paranoia. The ambivalence of her impulses and conduct increases the difficulties of assessing the novel, which teems with her ruminations on leftist politics and personal destiny. Despite her tobacco-related illness, with its noisy respiratory crises, her gruesome vitality animates the book. It ends with this incorrigibly intrusive nosey parker becoming a spiritualist seeking information about the unknowable.

THE LITTLE HOTEL (1973)

This novel is set in the Swiss-Touring Hotel, a middle-range hostelry, during the late 1940s. Both guests and staff represent a variety of nationalities and backgrounds in Stead's characteristic manner. Most of the guests are emotionally or financially manipulative and fret over protecting their capital in a time of international political instability. The vulner-

ability of Britain's economy is a recurrent theme. The book opens and closes with sinister deaths in other towns involving former guests; another guest, a Belgian mayor, proves deranged, and there are intrigues and maneuvers among both guests and employees. An American woman starts an anti-Communist witch hunt and makes fatuous speeches against interracial marriage: "Darwin showed that God has arranged it so that blood will tell," she says. "Our culture will break down and the Russians come in" (p. 38). There are hectic scenes when several guests go on a spree in the town and behave with monstrous cruelty to one another. Most of the protagonists are defeated people: even, in the end, Princess Bili di Rovino, a rich American widow of an Italian nobleman, who is betrayed by her young lover. The princess is an archetypal Stead character "with her chatter of race-courses, stock-exchange board-rooms, promoters, automobile owners, millionaire owners of horseflesh, all fashionable society; and she knew not only the elegants, the cream, but the go-betweens, those one has to know to get money exchanged at the best rate, little private businesses done" (p. 110).

Although this is a small, intimately proportioned novel, it has Stead's characteristic mix of vivacious voices and human vitality. The hotel's manager, Madame Bonnard, is the chief narrator and most attractive character in the book. Her marriage has gone stale, and she is harassed by worries about the lift gates, guests who cannot pay their bills, stolen scissors, and other commonplaces. In person she is lonely, affectionate, sensible, and efficient. As a narrator she is eager, effusive, almost childishly direct, and seemingly inconsequential in her story, which darts about in a seemingly random way: this disrupted, uneven narrative has the precisely contrived effect of a busy hotel teeming with unpredictable inmates.

MISS HERBERT (THE SUBURBAN WIFE) (1976)

Stead started writing this novel in 1955 but it was not published for over twenty years.

Although it is not Stead's most successful nor important book, it surpasses thousands of other mediocre novels that were taken on by publishers in this period. Perhaps it was rejected because Stead satirized British publishers of the 1950s in later sections of the book, but it must be conceded that some aspects of its plot—notably its protagonist's bitter, interminable divorce negotiations and her tussles with the publishing bureaucracy—are too lengthy. The novel is about a woman whose life becomes aimless in middle age. The humdrum futility of her existence, together with the frugality and small-mindedness of mid-twentieth century England, hangs heavily over the book.

Eleanor Herbert is a beautiful young woman in the 1920s with ambitions to be a writer. She travels and has a series of quick, random affairs with a variety of men. "She had made up her mind it was necessary for her to see 'the underdog's life' so that she can write from first hand. Because she was strong, she could work fairly hard, but she would also throw herself on one of the beds, made or unmade, and laugh to herself, thinking of her picaresque life. She was the real thing; she had guts" (p. 16). After her hopes peter out, partly because she is too much of a professional beauty, she compromises by marrying a Swiss man, with whom she has two children. He is full of pompous ambitions and proves snobbish, racist, and obnoxious. They run a lodging house for foreign students in North London until the marriage breaks up. In middle age she tries to scratch a living as a hack writer. Minor characters include the Blackstones, a Communist couple based on Stead and Blake, "living in a foul bed-sitting room in a side street," who eke out a meager living by reading books in foreign languages for publishers (p. 249).

I'M DYING LAUGHING: THE HUMOURIST (1986)

This posthumously published novel has all of Stead's grandeur, irony, and ruthless atomization of human weakness. She began writing this savage account of Communist idealism, political morality, hypocrisy, and betrayal while living in the United States during the 1940s. It was recognizably based on a married couple whom she knew, and even after the man had gassed himself in his garage, could not be published for fear of a libel action.

The chief male protagonist, Stephen Howard, is the scion of a rich American family who starts writing "clever, spiteful essays in economics and about the monied" while at Princeton. He marries Emily Wilkes, "an eccentric from Arkansas, whose grandfather had been a Pennsylvania coal-miner; whose mother a house-cleaner." As a result of witnessing the U.S. Depression in the 1930s, they become "parlour Reds." She earns a lucrative income writing for Hollywood until in the late 1940s they quarrel with the Communist Party there and decamp to Paris, where they profess to be radical activists while scheming for handouts from Stephen's millionaire mother (pp. 172, 386).

Emily is excessive: obese, greedy, exuberant, egotistical, and immoderate in her energy, emotions, and conduct. Black coffee and barbiturates help her through her violent, determined days. She writes journalism, labor propaganda, screenplays, corny tales of small-town Middle America, letters, domestic memoranda—anything to appease her forcefulness and need to communicate. She batters people with her tirades. Her hypocrisy is brutally exposed in a long scene in which she tries to bully her stepson's French schoolmaster into raising his grades. Emily's family pride—her ambitions for her children and stepchildren—are an expression of her frantic egotism.

Though Stephen Howard has literary pretensions, he is too self-indulgent to work for money and lives off Emily's energy and literary earnings. As in other Stead novels, there is a large, discordant supporting cast, including vexatious relations and quarrelsome friends. Written at a time when Stead was both poor and eating badly, money and food provide recurrent themes of

I'm Dying Laughing. The Howards typify twentieth-century Americans at their most sanctimonious and self-deceiving. They are desperate to be thought good people, prone to outpourings of verbal goodwill toward others; but they are equally desperate to preserve their personal comforts and oblivious of the ethical dilemma they epitomize. It is not that they are shameless in their callous exploitation of disadvantaged people. Rather, they are too self-absorbed, complacent, and highly strung to notice what they are doing.

The prolix and showy compassion of their early years is replaced by a cataclysmic selfishness that ensures misery and self-destruction. Emily's overworking ends in writer's block; as she befuddles herself with alcohol, Stephen decides to leave her and buys a little car with which to drive away to Switzerland. After participating in a May Day march, he drenches the car in gasoline and incinerates himself inside. Emily becomes a mad streetwoman in Rome.

When Stead prepared *I'm Dying Laughing* for publication in 1966, she was advised to rewrite passages so that the complexities of the McCarthyite Cold War era were less obscure to younger readers. Later she regretted her tamper-ing, and certainly the book's flaws are partly attributable to its unnaturally prolonged gestation. It remains, though, a mordant and psychologically unflinching satire.

NOVELLAS AND SHORT STORIES

The restoration of Stead's reputation initiated by Randall Jarrell resulted in the publication of *The Puzzleheaded Girl*, a collection of four novellas, in 1967. Her literary executor was responsible for the posthumous publication of her remaining uncollected short stories *Ocean of Story* (1985). Unsurprisingly the collection is of mixed quality, but it includes stories with all her power and passion. In several the leading woman character is a reinvented Christina Stead. A stray sentence in one of them could serve as Stead's epitaph. "Lydia hated this sort of party—to be with people who were famous made her feel that life had stopped and there was nothing more to live for, whereas she wanted to keep on living, and for that reason preferred people who had not arrived, at the top, or anywhere else, but who still nourished impossible ambitions and desires" (p. 170).

Selected Bibliography

WORKS OF CHRISTINA STEAD

NOVELS

The Salzburg Tales. London: P. Davies; New York: D. Appleton, 1934; Sydney: Angus and Robertson, 1974.

Seven Poor Men of Sydney. London: P. Davies; New York: Appleton-Century, 1934; Sydney: Angus and Robertson, 1965.

The Beauties and the Furies. London: P. Davies; New York: Appleton-Century, 1936.

House of All Nations. London, P. Davies; New York: Simon and Schuster, 1938; Sydney, Angus and Robertson, 1974.

The Man Who Loved Children. New York: Simon and Schuster, 1940; London: P. Davies, 1941.

For Love Alone. New York: Harcourt, Brace, 1944; London: P. Davies, 1945; Sydney, Angus and Robertson, 1966.

Letty Fox: Her Luck. New York: Harcourt, Brace, 1946; London: P. Davies, 1947; Sydney: Angus and Robertson, 1974.

A Little Tea, a Little Chat. New York: Harcourt, Brace, 1948; London, Virago, 1981.

The People with the Dogs. Boston: Little, Brown, 1952; London: Virago, 1981.

Dark Places of the Heart. New York: Holt, Rinehart and Winston, 1966; as *Cotters' England,* London: Secker and Warburg, 1967; Sydney: Angus and Robertson, 1974.

The Puzzleheaded Girl. New York: Holt, Rinehart and Winston, 1967; London: Secker and Warburg, 1968.

The Little Hotel. London: Angus and Robertson; Sydney: Angus and Robertson, 1973; New York: Holt, Rinehart and Winston, 1975.

Miss Herbert (The Suburban Wife). New York: Random House, 1976; London: Virago, 1979.

I'm Dying Laughing: The Humorist. London: Virago, 1986; New York: Holt, 1987.

SHORT STORIES

Ocean of Story: The Uncollected Stories of Christina Stead. London, New York, and Ringwood, Australia: Viking, 1985.

ANTHOLOGIES EDITED BY STEAD

Modern Women in Love: Sixty Twentieth-Century Masterpieces of Fiction. Edited jointly with William Blake. New York: Dryden, 1945.

Great Stories of the South Sea Islands. London: F. Muller, 1955.

TRANSLATIONS BY STEAD

Gignon, Fernand. *Colour of Asia.* London: F. Muller, 1955.

Giltène, Jean. *The Candid Killer.* London: F. Muller, 1956.

Piccard, Auguste. *In Balloon and Bathyscaphe.* London: Cassell, 1956.

SELECTED ARTICLES BY STEAD

"The Writers Take Sides." *Left Review,* 1.2: 435–463, 469–475 (July 1935).

"About Women's Insight: There Is a Sort of Folklore We Inherit." *Vogue,* September 1971, pp. 61, 130.

"On the Women's Movement." *Partisan Review* 1.2: 271–274 (1979).

"Some Deep Spell—A View of Stanley Burnshaw." *Agenda* (London) 21.1: 125–139 (1984).

INTERVIEWS

Beston, John. "An Interview with Christina Stead." *World Literature Written in English,* 15.1: 87–95 (April 1976).

Giuffre, Giulia. *A Writing Life.* Sydney: Allen and Unwin, 1990.

Kinross-Smith, Graeme. "Christina Stead—A Profile." *Westerly,* 1: 67–75 (1976).

Raskin, Jonah. "Christina Stead in Washington Square." *London* magazine, February 1970, pp. 70–77.

Wetherall, Rodney. "Christina Stead: An Interview." *Australian Literary Studies,* 9.4: 431–448 (October 1980).

CHRISTINA STEAD

Whitehead, Ann. "Christina Stead: An Interview." *Australian Literary Studies,* 6.3: 230–248 (May 1974).

CRITICAL AND BIOGRAPHICAL STUDIES

Brydon, Diana. *Christina Stead.* London: Macmillan; Totowa, N.J.: Barnes and Nobel, 1987.

Carter, Angela. "Unhappy Families." *London Review of Books,* 16 September 1982, pp. 11–13.

Fagan, Robert. "Christina Stead." *Partisan Review* 46: 262–270 (1979).

Geering, Ronald, ed. *A Web of Friendship: Selected Letters (1928–1973).* Pymble, NSW, Australia, 1992.

———, ed. *Talking into the Typewriter: Selected Letters (1973–1983).* Pymble, NSW, Australia, 1992.

Hardwick, Elizabeth. *A View of My Own.* New York: Farrar, Straus and Cudahy, 1962. Pp. 41–48.

Lidoff, Joan. *Christina Stead.* New York: F. Unger, 1982.

Pender, Anne. *Christina Stead: Satirist.* Altona, Victoria, Australia: Altona, Vic.: Common Ground Pub. in association with the Association for the Study of Australian Literature, 2002.

Rowley, Hazel. *Christina Stead: A Biography.* Port Melbourne: W. Heinemann, 1993; New York: H. Holt, 1994.

Sheridan, Susan. *Christina Stead.* London: Harvester Wheatsheaf; Bloomington, Ind.: Indiana University Press, 1988.

Williams, Chris. *Christina Stead: A Life of Letters* Melbourne: McPhee Gribble, 1989.

Yglesias, José. "Marx as Muse." *Nation,* 5 April 1965, pp. 363–370.

Derek Walcott
(1930–)

JOHN LENNARD

IN "TRADITION AND the Individual Talent" (1920), perhaps the most influential literary essay of the last century, the poet-playwright and critic T. S. Eliot (1888–1965) made a classic statement:

No poet, no artist of any art, has his complete meaning alone. His significance, his appreciation is the appreciation of his relation to the dead poets and artists. You cannot value him alone; you must set him, for contrast and comparison, among the dead. I mean this as a principle of æsthetic, not merely historical, criticism. The necessity that he shall conform, that he shall cohere, is not one-sided; what happens when a new work of art is created is something that happens simultaneously to all the works of art which preceded it. The existing monuments form an ideal order among themselves, which is modified by the introduction of the new (the really new) work of art among them. The existing order is complete before the new work arrives; for order to persist after the supervention of novelty, the *whole* existing order must be, if ever so slightly, altered; and so the relations, proportions, values of each work of art toward the whole are readjusted; and this is conformity between the old and the new. Whoever has approved this idea of order, of the form of European, of English literature, will not find it preposterous that the past should be altered by the present as much as the present is directed by the past. And the poet who is aware of this will be aware of great difficulties and responsibilities.

(Eliot, *The Sacred Wood*, pp. 49–50)

Eliot was probably thinking of modernist art (including his own): his phrases negotiate the gulf opened by the modernists' rejection of inherited, usually Renaissance paradigms of creative order (tonality, perspective, grammar, neoclassical prosody) and counter-formulation of new paradigms (atonality, cubism, stream-of-consciousness, free verse). At home in European literature, from Chaucer and Dante in the fourteenth century to Kipling and Rimbaud at the turn of the twentieth, Eliot could not abandon tradition, however strongly he responded to modernity, and his work profoundly fuses allusion and creation. What he was almost certainly not imagining was the advent of postcolonial literatures in English, the enormous problems, aesthetic and political, confronting writers for whom national feeling and independence must mean an independent national literature, but whose inherited literary traditions are those of an alien, cast-off master. Yet those writers have most persistently tested Eliot's claim, none more so than the St. Lucian poet-playwright, critic, and painter Derek Walcott.

Walcott was born a British colonial subject, and is now an independent West Indian endlessly on the move. His journey from a Caribbean island to Nobel Laureateship and international acclaim has been as much an investigation of the canonical and classical past as a passage into the future. From his earliest work, canonical luminaries have been formally and fluidly summoned, invoked in titles or turns of phrase and set to astonishing music amid the un-English landscapes of the New World. In turn and together, Langland, Donne, Marvell, Wordsworth, and Eliot find themselves parading in a carnival led by Walcott himself, omnipresent as narrator and commonly his own subject; or brought to tropical book by the juxtaposition of their temperate certainties with his vision, enforced by a life no longer English, nor certain, but shaped by English legacies and crimes. To have so commanded the canon is an amazing achievement, close to the heart of greatness, but it is on his own terms that Walcott must be confronted: as a founding father of West Indian literature, not as an appendage to the English, French, Classical, and American literatures that he has loved and plundered in pursuing his own course.

THE ST. LUCIAN, 1930–1950: "I HAD A SOUND COLONIAL EDUCATION"

Derek Alton Walcott was born on 23 January 1930 in Castries, St. Lucia, moments before his twin-brother, Roderick. His father, Warwick Walcott (1897–1931), a civil servant, was the son of a white Barbadian, Charles Walcott, who moved to St. Lucia, and a mulatto St. Lucian, Christiana Wardrope. His mother, Alix (1894–1990), a teacher, was the daughter of two St. Maartenians, white Johannes van Romondt and mulatto Caroline Maarlin, but lived on St. Lucia from an early age. Warwick and Alix had one older child, Pamela (b. 1928). In 1931 Warwick died after an operation for mastoiditis, and Alix was left to raise her children alone; she never remarried.

St. Lucia, gold-green and mountainous, is a Windward Island in the Lesser Antilles, ringed with fine beaches and enticing surf. From the white distances of Britain and America it is easy to fantasize a clichéd tropical paradise, and Walcott's poetry, drama, and painting have always celebrated the beauty of his home—the fall of sunlight, the colors of fruits and of the sea, the rhythms of waterside life. But the realities are complex products of a history and sociology little known outside the West Indies, and cannot be comprehended in picture-postcard views, or through the crude polarities of "white/black" and "first/third world." Walcott has successively rejected the claims of Leopold Senghor's Negritude, of 1970s "Black Power," and of Afro-American "Black Studies," and to understand the nature of his work one must understand the quilt of tensions he inherited.

Caribbean culture is neither uniform nor a happy melting-pot. Two broad types may be distinguished: the Anglophone "Afro-Saxon" culture of Jamaica, Barbados, and many Leeward Islands, predominantly Protestant; and the Franco- or Hispanophone cultures of the two great northern islands, Cuba and Hispaniola, and many Windward Islands, closer to the Venezuelan coast of South America than to Jamaica, and predominantly Catholic. In many islands one type wholly dominates, and in some they mix—nowhere more so than St. Lucia, which (with its superb natural harbor at Castries) changed hands between the French and British a dozen times in the seventeenth and eighteenth centuries, becoming predominantly French before being permanently ceded to Britain in 1814, in the post-Napoleonic settlement. In consequence, while the island's later ruling and social élites have been largely Anglophone, Anglican, and mulatto, with a limited white presence, the vast majority of the population, especially in rural areas inland, is blacker-skinned and Catholic (with predominantly white French priests), and speaks a French Creole. Between the two groups many tensions and differences tend to entrench themselves, particularly affecting religiously shaped attitudes to illegitimacy, education, and freedom of speech, but shared St. Lucian identity makes each more like the other than like their respective ancestors. Anglophone St. Lucians are unlike Jamaicans or Barbadians, who find them provincial, while the Creole of Francophone St. Lucians (spoken in parallel by most Anglophones, including Walcott) is mocked and censured by French citizens in Martinique, twenty miles to the north.

Systemic and personal consequences of this history and sociology are constant in Walcott's work in all media. He has remarked, for example, his adult shock at the overwhelmingly white armed gendarmes of Martinique, contrasting them and the colonial identity they represent with stereotypical Latin American cops, all gun and sunglasses, and the unarmed mulatto St. Lucian policemen of whom he remembers as a child being unafraid. Or again, from schoolboy poems to Nobel days, he has had to endure theological attacks on his poetry and spirituality by Catholic "authorities" in St. Lucia and elsewhere, and has sometimes bitterly criticized the economic and cultural poverty imposed by Catholic authoritarian conservatism. Even his sense of his artistic language is deeply affected by the differing attitudes of the French and British to creolizations of the mother-tongue, the British generally tolerating and patronizing patois, the French generally censuring and shaming deviations from the pure diction and grammar authorized by the Paris *Academie*. To be blunt, Walcott's achievements as poet-playwright would not have been possible had he grown up in nearby Martinique, or in the purely Anglophone island of Barbados, forty miles to the south-east.

To this intricate tessellation of color, faith, and speech, Warwick and Alix Walcott brought other complications. To have two white grandfathers and two mulatto grandmothers is common enough in the Caribbean and United States, and Walcott's Dutch-English-African mix

is not so unusual in the Windward Islands, but the strong Methodism of Alix's family was part of a mission to St. Lucia, and a distinct source of tension. She was from 1918 to 1958 head of the hugely popular Methodist Infant School, and often de facto Principal of the Primary School; Derek and Roderick attended both en route to the only major secondary school, Catholic St. Mary's College, and priestly attacks on the plays of both brothers, and on Derek's poetry, express tensions central to their mother's working life. Warwick Walcott, for his part, was a devoted reader and amateur water-colorist whose premature death was seen as a cruel cutting-off. Orphaned at fifteen months, Walcott has no direct memory of Warwick, but grew up surrounded by his books and paintings, being taught by his grieving mother that he had the genetic and cultural inheritance to fulfill his father's promise, and must constantly practice, with pen as with brush, to fit himself for that task.

This meant a childhood in which exploration and play were combined with more disciplined fun, copying paintings and imitating anthologized poems. One source was Thomas Craven's *A Treasury of Arts Masterpieces: From the Renaissance to the Present Day* (1939), reproductions from Giotto (c. 1266–1337) to Grant Wood (1892–1942): formal imitation is still prescribed in art-school, and the model for Walcott's early practice of poetic copying, for example following rhyme and line-movement but substituting personal or local content, or seeking to reply in a poem's own form and style. Adumbrating his mature poetic practice, this also marks an early equivalence in Walcott's understanding of poetry and painting, anticipating theater-work using tableaux and strong visuals (including sets, costumes, and images of his own design), and the centrality of painting to his later poetry, especially *Tiepolo's Hound* (2000).

As if cultural whiteness, mulatto skin, bilingualism in English and French Creole, Methodist discipline, a family mission, and synesthetic grasp of words and color were not enough, a major complication is embodied in St. Mary's College, which Walcott attended on a government scholarship from 1941 to 1947. Founded by a French priest, St. Mary's was modeled on English public schools, formally Anglophone, and devoted to providing "a sound colonial education" ("The Schooner *Flight,*" 1.41) in French, Latin, English literature and language, history, geography, religion, arithmetic, geometry, and algebra. Despite attacks on his teenage poetry by priests who detected dangerous "deism" in his Wordsworthian love of nature, Walcott's time there seems generally to have been happy, and was certainly profitable. The classics have never left him, becoming central to his acknowledged masterwork, *Omeros* (1990). The history and literature he learned, if Anglocentric and remembered critically in *Another Life* (1973), were in their own terms thorough, methodological, and rich. And he made lifelong friends, notably the painter and muralist Dunstan St. Omer (b. 1927), a major artist himself, and their art-teacher, Harold Simmons (1914–1966), a friend of Warwick Walcott.

To move on required a scholarship, and leaving St. Lucia; awards were very limited, and subject to more pressures than meritocratic examination. Walcott's prodigious talent, already evident in poems and short plays (some surviving but none collected), could not be denied, but he had to wait, and spent two years at St. Mary's beginning a teaching career that culminated in his Boston University chair (shared with Seamus Heaney and once held by Robert Lowell). Walcott took teaching seriously, but had energies to spare: his mother was active in arts as well as education, and it seems to have been a natural development for the Walcotts, St. Omer, and other friends to found an Arts Guild and begin mounting plays, and equally natural for Walcott to write verse-drama for their performances. In so doing he began, formally and institutionally, his long quest for a West Indian dramatic mode and theatrical style, necessarily a "Theater of Poverty" with infinitely inventive enthusiasm but few dedicated resources, adaptable to cramped, unequipped, and temporarily converted spaces, hugely ambitious in proclaiming pride and identity, and intensely aware of both the greatness and frequent irrelevance of canonical European dramatic conventions and practices.

Through Simmons and St. Omer, Arts Guild members encountered European modernism, including Eliot and Yeats, and Walcott had their dramatic vitality, alert to symbolist and expressionist theater, as well as the great Jacobeans to draw on—but neither knowledge nor experience of modernist (or any professional) stage-movement or dance techniques, later to be central to his theater-making. He also had access via the silver screen to the American musical in its golden age, and was sharply aware of the dramatic value of song, but lacked sufficient resources to use it himself. Not surprisingly, the Guild production of Walcott's first major play, *Henri Christophe* (1950), dramatizing the fall of Haiti's black king, was uneven, but contained scenes of great power, came close to achieving tragedy, and is now reckoned, with the Whitehall Players from 1948 in Trinidad, to mark the beginning of modern West Indian drama.

Modern West Indian letters were further on, led by the generation including the great historian-essayist and novelist C. L. R. James (1901–1989) that emerged in the 1930s, but Walcott also made his mark there, with two privately printed and distributed collections, *25 Poems* (1948) and *Epitaph for the Young: XII Cantos* (1949). Walcott has not preserved much juvenilia, but four lyrics survive in *Collected Poems 1948–1984* (1986), one a long-lined sonnet commemorating the destruction of old Castries by fire in 1948:

After that hot gospeller had levelled all but the
   churched sky,

      ...

By the smoking sea, where Christ walked, I
   asked, why

Should a man wax tears, when his wooden world
    fails?

        ("A City's Death by Fire," line 1, 9–10)

Besides the striking tone and content, there is enough in these three lines to make any critic with ears start listening very carefully, and to suggest to readers a poet they had better read aloud as often as silently. To the eye metrically loose, they have to the ear rhythmical integrity, and beneath them (especially the last) lurks the tremendous English history and discipline of the iambic pentameter, or "heroic line" ("ti-TUM | [t]i- TUM | [t]i-TUM | [t]i-TUM | [t]i-TUM")— the line of Shakespeare's blank verse and many rhymed forms, including most sonnets. In another early poem, "Prelude," Walcott says directly that his life "must not be made public / Until I have learned to suffer / In accurate iambics" (ll. 15–17), and in a third the heroic line sounds twice: "So I, since feelings drown, should no more ask"; "Braving new water in an antique hoax" ("The Harbour" lines 3, 12). The greatest aural shock, however, comes in the fourth poem, "As John to Patmos," which ends:

As John to Patmos, in each love-leaping air,
O slave, soldier, worker under red trees sleeping,
    hear
What I swear now, as John did:
To praise lovelong, the living and the brown dead.

        ("As John to Patmos," lines 14–17)

The first line could easily be a regular pentameter—"As JOHN | [t]o PAT- | [m]os IN | [e]ach LEAP- | [i]ng AIR"—but the compound "love-leaping" is unavoidably hypermetric, and the line attempts a prosodic imitation of its own meaning, its "leaping" prosody grounded by "love-." The second and third lines move away from the pentameter, going long and short (as the couplet-rhymes "air/hear" and "did/dead" avoid perfection), but the fourth repeats the hypermetric trick to devastating effect. "To PRAISE | [L]OVELONG |[t]he LIV- |[i]ng AND | [t]he DEAD" would be metrically easy,

lulled by the pleasant pun on "livelong" and the easy, naturally iambic swing of the clichéd phrase "the living and the dead": but thumpingly into its last foot comes "brown" ("the LIV- | [i]ng AND | [t]he BROWN DEAD"). The effect is to set against the music of the heroic line and the conventional sentiments (praising life, rhetoricizing grief) a trenchant declaration of what heroic sentiments traditionally ignore: the life and exploitation unto death of brown people, on which so much English and first-world wealth was founded and still depends. From an adult poet it would be striking; from one in his teens it is testimony of greatness, aurally as in its meaning a promise Walcott has amply honored.

St. Lucia could not provide the stage or the press Walcott needed, and his audience already extended beyond his island. In 1950 his scholarship became available, and he set off for the University College in Jamaica, itself a place of promise, but knew in his bones he could not abandon St. Lucia, whose contradictions he embodied and had already built into the foundations of his arts. He was also going to Jamaica not as a fresh eighteen-year-old, ready to mingle freely with new peers, but as a highly self-conscious and strong-willed twenty-year-old with two years' teaching, two published volumes, and a full-length play behind him; one who had survived five years of public theological denunciation, seen his capital city burn, and made the foremost public commemoration of that event. He was, in short, a leader, not only as he had been since preceding his twin from the womb and bearing as an orphan his dead father's hopes, but in the public arenas of the arts. His honed and driven capacity for such leadership and artistic example informs his whole career, but has been for him personally a source of great difficulty, troubling friendships, theatrical partnerships, and marriages. Better understanding must await a good biography, but it is clear that for several decades after he left St. Lucia, living on this island or that, Walcott was an artist bearing the artist's wound; there could, should, be greatness, art to justify all, but meanwhile there would certainly be tears to go with the sweat, and the promise.

THE WEST INDIAN, 1950–1977: "WHERE SHALL I TURN, DIVIDED TO THE VEIN?"

From 1950–1954 Walcott studied at the University College of the West Indies in Mona, Jamaica, taking a B.A. in English Literature, French, and Latin in 1953, and following up with a year's work towards a B.Ed. UCWI was founded in 1948 to provide higher education within the Caribbean, borrowing degrees, syllabi, and staff from the University of London, and served a subtle purpose: attracting and binding together the high achievers of many islands to create a regional network of professionalized alumni—the personnel of a putative "West Indian Federation." With independence for India, Pakistan, Ceylon (Sri Lanka), and Burma in 1947–1948, the British Empire had begun its spectacular implosion: nationalism stirred in the Caribbean, as elsewhere, but most British West Indian islands were thought too small to succeed as nations, and a federated archipelago seemed the best bet. To keep things fair, and encourage a regional as well as insular identities, institutions must be distributed—chief among them a collegiate university with campuses on several larger islands. UCWI Mona was the first, and Walcott joined the first Arts intake.

Unsurprisingly, as a star in the undergraduate firmament, Walcott's academic record was patchy, stirring with resentments and impatience, but his extracurricular record was phenomenal. He seems at will to have dominated student writing-clubs, then the Dramatic Society and University Players, forging from 1951 a partnership with Abdur-Rahman Slade Hopkinson (1934–1993), already an outstanding actor; their *King Lear* is still remembered. He masterminded two short-lived magazines, the satirical *Barb* and more generous *Pelican,*

providing prose-copy and artwork as well as the drive that made them happen. Nor did university terms slow creative production. In 1951 alone he published a third volume, *Poems* (none collected); had three new plays staged by the St. Lucian Arts Guild—*Paolo and Francesca, Three Assassins,* and *The Price of Mercy* (all lost); and heard *Henri Christophe* broadcast on BBC radio. Walcott also revised a radio-play begun at sixteen, *Harry Dernier,* about the last man in the world, and in 1952 had it published in Barbados, performed in Jamaica, and broadcast in London. A group of expatriate West Indian students, led by Trinidadian playwright-actor-director and scholar Errol Hill (b. 1921) and including a future prime minister of Trinidad and novelists George Lamming (b. 1927) and V. S. Naipaul (b. 1932), performed *Henri Christophe* and staged readings of other Walcott plays in the British Council's Colonial Students Residence in London. Word was spreading, and Walcott's work was published regionally and broadcast from London throughout the 1950s.

According to Walcott's biographer, his student-poems were strongly influenced by W. H. Auden (1907–1973), whom he still thinks a greater poet-playwright than Eliot; it was a necessary phase of imitative development that Walcott (without disavowing) has no wish to preserve. His plays were more experimental, but in both media the political was a given, not (as sometimes in Auden) an indulgence or option. To mention in any formal English poem the bloom of black skin, or breadfruit, was as unavoidably political as to live "in the castle of [that] skin" (*Epitaph for the Young*), or to see every day the beauty of breadfruit and yet write poems about English oaks and roses somewhere far to the north, beauties for ever out of reach and always blonde. To write parts rooted in black history for black actors was to make that history speak as it had never spoken. But politics was matched, especially in poetry, by raw angers of race, and the confusions (fueled by charismatic leadership) of a morally alert mind in a young male body. Walcott already smoked heavily, and had begun to drink regularly; he also became very active sexually. In a familiar Christian male artistic pattern, vices fuelled work but coarsened behavior and relationships, and made him feel guilty, which could make him cruel; some aspects of the pattern have persisted throughout his life, their representation and analysis part of his practical self-interrogation as a poet.

Without condoning excess, it may be said that Walcott was in a deeply invidious bind for which he bore no personal responsibility. The insular cultures and limited markets of the Caribbean archipelago could not support literary careers, or enable artists to develop; history dozed and was washed away in the sleepy heat; the only way up was the way out, flight to a distant imperial metropolis. The exile's stairway to heaven led also to cultured alienation, the loss of island home, and the heartbreaking politics of assimilation—a career exemplified most brilliantly, and sadly, in the life and work of V. S. Naipaul, the West Indian artist closest to Walcott in stature and most opposite in temperament. A Trinidadian Indian, Naipaul (whom Walcott watches like a hawk, and mocks as "V. S. Nightfall") left for London, flattered the center of the dying empire with assurances that it was still where history and culture happened, and amused the metropolitans with his watered, ironic analyses of Caribbean somnolence, cheerful fatalism, and complacent unimportance. The human heart might beat there, and love take almost living shapes, but for Naipaul it was an emotional and social necessity that the West Indies be known as a place worth leaving. For Walcott, a similar British literary career would have fulfilled his mother's aspirations by completing his father's life, and few mulattos of his own generation would have been anything but ruefully happy for his talent and fortune; thousands of West Indians had made the trans-Atlantic crossing every year since 1948. But Walcott knew, as poet and dramatist, that to write what was in him he must stay within his archipelago, not on the late imperial model UCWI was supposed to serve,

but in a way for which no infrastructure or precedent existed. Small wonder he was sometimes wild, and his middling degree and incomplete B.Ed., blocking academic routes to Britain, may have been in part a way of burning his bridges and forcing himself to face adult West Indian practicalities.

He also sank roots by marrying Faye Moyston, the light-skinned, privately educated daughter of a well-off Jamaican family, whom he had known since his first year in Jamaica (as the vice-principal's secretary) and courted with charismatic charm. The wedding, in August 1954 in Vide Bouteille, St. Lucia, was in a chapel decorated by Dunstan St. Omer, and with dry hindsight Walcott's real commitment that day was to the practice of art within the cultures of the West Indies. The need for income led successively to exhausting journalism in Jamaica, and teaching posts there as well as in Grenada and St. Lucia; logistics were increasingly difficult, and emotions soon rubbed raw. After the birth in 1955 of a son, Peter, the marriage failed, exacerbating Walcott's moody aggressions and beginning (not for the last time) a chapter of sorrows in his life. After extended separations he and Faye were divorced in 1959.

But the work of artistic creation did not, could not be allowed to, stop. Teaching, traveling, fathering, divorcing, or blessedly at rest, Walcott practices a fierce, religiously inflected discipline of writing, and work flowed. Two of his plays, *The Sea at Dauphin* (1954), angrily tragic, and *Ti-Jean and His Brothers* (1957), a St. Lucian French Creole folk-parable Walcott dramatized for the Arts Guild, are preserved in *Dream on Monkey Mountain and Other Plays* (1970)—effectively a "selected plays"—a dramaturgical history of progress-to-date, and a manifesto. *Ti-Jean*, now a Caribbean classic and Walcott's most performed play, was written at whirlwind speed after his first brief visit to New York, and reveals a characteristic paradox. Broadway had long been a dream, and Walcott's first experience of New York must have strengthened that (as well as giving a lesson in realities)—but his explosive reaction was a play plunging into French-African village life of the St. Lucian interior, and bringing to it a wit as sophisticated as folktales are wise:

> Evening. Rain. The heights of a forest. A CRICKET, a FROG, a FIREFLY, a BIRD. Left, a hut with bare table, an empty bowl, stools. The MOTHER waiting.
> FROG: Greek-croak, Greek-croak.
> CRICKET: Greek-croak, Greek-croak.
> [*The others join*]
> FROG: [*Sneezing*] Aeschylus me!
> All that rain and no moon tonight.
> CRICKET: The moon always there even fighting the rain
> Creek-crak, it is cold, but the moon always there
> And Ti-Jean in the moon just like the story.
>
> (*Ti-Jean and His Brothers*, Prologue)

The animal prologue, framing the story of brothers Gros-Jean, Mi-Jean, and Ti-Jean and their bet with the devil Papa Bois about not losing their tempers, suggests a style closer to Brechtian epic than 1950s Broadway naturalism. Extravagant scenery is superfluous, the construction dynamic, and acting rapport, the storyteller's hook in his audience, vital; the cackling song marking the diabolical consumption of Gros-Jean and Mi-Jean sounds best in its original Creole ("*Bai Diable-là manger un 'ti mamaille, / Un, deux, trois 'ti mamaille!*"); and the play's closest canonical model is George Peele's *The Old Wives' Tale* (1595)—none of which were likely to interest Broadway or London's West End in the least, and didn't. Everything that makes it so popular in the Caribbean, including eclectic demands on the audience, refusal to patronize them, and dedication to human rather than material resource, makes it unfit for the metropolis, confirming the rightness of Walcott's decision to be a resident West Indian, and the price he pays for it.

There were also breakthroughs in poetry, the two earliest poems for which he is now well-known. His postgraduate tutor, the poet-educator John Figueroa (1920–1999), took him in 1954 to a ruined plantation-mansion at Guava Ridge; the experience took shape in "Ruins of a Great House":

> Ablaze with rage I thought,
> Some slave is rotting in this manorial lake,
> But still the coal of my compassion fought
> That Albion too was once
> A colony like ours, "part of the continent, piece of the main,"
> Nook-shotten, rook o'erblown, deranged
> By foaming channels and the vain expense
> Of bitter faction.
>   All in compassion ends
> So differently from what the heart arranged:
> "as well as if a manor of thy friend's . . ."
>
> ("Ruins of a Great House," lines 39–48)

From its epigraph by Thomas Browne to its medley of Shakespearean words and quotations from Donne's "No man is an island," the poem is alive with older literary voices, yet utterly in a present filled with ruin, not glory. Walcott's deftness of prosody and rhyme, bossing allusions into order, generates tremendous power, but higher levels of art are also engaged. Though never explicitly named, the ruins he and Figueroa saw at Guava Ridge were not of any plantation-house, but those of a greater power, a mansion once used by Admiral Nelson, of honored memory, and later by Edward Eyre, the brutally repressive governor at the time of the Morant Bay Rebellion in 1865. Alive to that history, "Ruins" is generically a "country-house poem," with origins in praise-song, a poet's thanks to his noble patron. Between two masterpieces, Ben Jonson's "To Penshurst," collected in *The Forrest* (1616), and Andrew Marvell's "Upon Appleton House," written amid renewed threats of civil war in 1651, country-house poetry was a major form, but thereafter rapidly died out. Astonishingly revived by Yeats in the 1920s in "Meditations in Time of Civil War" (collected in *The Tower*, 1928), it was picked up by Eliot in two of his war-bound *Four Quartets*, "Burnt Norton"

(1935) and "Little Gidding" (1941–1942). By seizing on it, complete with seventeenth- and twentieth-century freight, as a frame for contemplating a ruinous slave-mansion and the bodies of a different, much longer war, Walcott confronts Jonson and Marvell with the aristocratic monies they took, Yeats and Eliot with their desire for pastorals. Invoking the whole business of poetry in relation to history, he enables himself to negotiate with all on equal terms, validating his own rage and compassion by validating theirs.

If "Ruins" finds compassion, it is also a wrenching lament. "A Far Cry from Africa," brooding on news reports of atrocities committed against white families in Kenya by Mau-Mau rebels, is wholly lament, famously spelling out Walcott's dilemma:

> The gorilla wrestles with the superman.
> I who am poisoned with the blood of both,
> Where shall I turn, divided to the vein?
> I who have cursed
> The drunken officer of British rule, how choose
> Between this Africa and the English tongue I
>   love?
> Betray them both, or give back what they give?
>   ("A Far Cry from Africa," lines 25–31)

One might expect "divided to the bone": Walcott's problem is not a death-wound, but how to live with all inheritances, balancing them within a living circulation that returns them to the heart. In the mid-1950s, as Britain's graceless and feckless "Scramble from Africa" began, Walcott had no answers, but stated the problem in clear and memorable poetry, and so came close to the territory of his mature art.

The final steps came in 1962 with his first major collection, *In a Green Night: Poems 1948–1960*, published in London by Jonathan Cape. The dates are mildly misleading, for most of the poems Walcott included were written after 1957, and substantive revision continued in 1961–1962: he has always shaped collected work in this way, to good purpose. Here the title

quotes from Marvell's imagination of the Bermudas as God's second Eden—"He hangs in shades the Orange bright, / Like golden Lamps in a green Night," an amazing choice for a poet committed to cultural independence—and the title-poem is fiercely Marvellian ("The mind enspheres all circumstance"), yet does not defer to Marvell, answering him in his own form and tongue. "In a Green Night" recalls the imitation Walcott practiced as a child, but mastery of manner is complete, parries and ripostes assured; other poems raise the stakes even higher. "Pocomania" takes on Eliot, answering his quatrain-poems in mocking patois ("De bredren rattle withered gourds / Whose seeds are the forbidden fruits"), while "Orient and Immortal Wheat" looks steadfastly at the mysticism of Traherne; but quite different notes sound in poems that speak directly of island, especially St. Lucian, life. "Brise Marine" ends with "The darkness closing round a fisherman's oar. / The sound of water gnawing at bright stone." "A Sea-Chantey" begins a poetry of names:

> Anguilla, Adina,
> Antigua, Cannelles,
> Andreuille, all the *l*'s,
> Voyelles, of the liquid Antilles,
> The names tremble like needles
> Of anchored frigates,
> Yachts tranquil as lilies,
> In ports of calm coral,
> The lithe ebony hulls
> Of strait-stitching schooners,
> The needles of their masts
> That thread archipelagos . . .
>   ("A Sea-Chantey," lines 1–12)

The metaphors weaving together compass-needles, masts, and threaded archipelagos exemplify a mature technique of fullness and vividness, a painterly, gestural comprehension that analysis reveals as powerfully coherent and wide-ranging, but that is in itself synesthetic, not analytical. Between musing apprehensions of the West Indies Walcott saw every day but Marvell never saw, and cultured responses to

Marvell's generous, dangerous imaginings of New World opportunity, gulfs remained: but the two kinds of work had each achieved maturity and been bound together, if only in a book.

Walcott's theater-practice was also coming together, and he began the central, most clearly marked phase of his life. Through contacts from broadcasts and productions, he secured in 1957 a major commission, a pageant to celebrate the inauguration of the West Indian Federation in Port of Spain (the Trinidadian and future Federation capital). *Drums and Colours,* by all accounts two parts chaos to five parts magnificence and in its nature unrepeatable, was performed in 1958, and hard on its heels Walcott was given a Rockefeller Foundation grant to study in New York for a year. He hoped to learn technical and organizational theater-making, but soon found most classes irrelevant to his needs in assuming large, well-equipped theaters as a given. Homesickness grew, and while in New York he wrote a strongly Caribbean play, *Jourmard,* about St. Lucian eccentrics. He did, however, study carefully with director José Quintero (1924–1999), famed for premièring plays by Eugene O'Neill and as co-founder of the Circle-in-the-Square, a theater-in-the-round then in Sheridan Square.

Above all Walcott saw things he could not have seen at home—*The Beaux Stratagem, The Family Reunion, The Balcony, Our Town, The Quare Fellow, Summer and Smoke*—and was able to read and discuss the great contemporary theater-makers, especially Brecht. Classes or no, he soon stocked his professional toolkit more richly than ever before; his second New York play, *Malcochon; or, The Six in the Rain,* combines St. Lucian creoles with Brechtian epic effects and scenes from Japanese cinema. Returning to Port of Spain in 1959, he founded the Little Carib (later Trinidad) Theatre Workshop, and for seventeen years tried to build Caribbean theater from the basement up.

The first Workshop production, an evening of scenes by Trinidadian actor-playwright Errol John (1923–1988), Tennessee Williams, G. B. Shaw, and Arthur Miller, went up in December 1959, and thereafter something was always going on. In July 1960 Walcott married again: Margaret Maillard was Trinidadian French Creole, a dancer with Beryl McBurnie's Little Carib troupe (which Walcott was drawing into the Workshop) who had studied in England, was one of the young Port of Spain élite, and gave up Catholicism to marry. They had two daughters, Elizabeth (b. 1964) and Anna (b. 1968), and raised Peter, Walcott's son by Faye Moyston; the marriage seems to have been strong in love and work, with Margaret constantly involved in the Workshop as performer and administrator. Never properly funded or equipped, the Workshop made tremendous efforts, especially in touring productions around the archipelago, but required ever-increasing energy and devotion to keep going.

From financial necessity Walcott's own writing energies were given to regular journalism for quality dailies and weeklies. For much of the 1960s he averaged several substantial articles each week, building a body of work that deserves collection—but his own dramatic output inevitably slackened. The only major play of this period was *Dream on Monkey Mountain,* begun in New York and work-shopped for years; drawing on the dream-plays of early modernism to treat racial (in)dependence in symbolic and visionary scenes and episodes, it was performed from 1965 but continued to evolve. In 1970 it became Walcott's breakthrough in the United States, playing in Los Angeles and on Broadway, and winning the 1971 Obie for Distinguished Foreign Play. Published in 1970, with *The Sea at Dauphin, Ti-Jean and His Brothers, Malcochon,* and a superb essay-introduction, "What the Twilight Says," *Dream* could not be what it is if the Workshop (and St. Lucia Arts Guild) had not repeatedly produced plays, allowing Walcott to experiment and develop; all continue to be performed at festivals and makeshift venues throughout the Caribbean.

With a proper publishing contract, Walcott's poetry developed rapidly. *In a Green Night* was followed by *The Castaway and Other Poems* (1965), creating in "Crusoe's Journal" and "Crusoe's Island" a shipwrecked, observant persona to survey West Indian realities and emotions:

> Now Friday's progeny,
> The brood of Crusoe's slave,
> Black little girls in pink
> Organdy, crinolines,
> Walk in their air of glory
> Beside a breaking wave. . . .
>
> ("Crusoe's Island," III.10–15)

In other poems, especially "Laventille," named for a shantytown in Port of Spain, the less picturesque Caribbean is considered, and some poems travel elsewhere, to New York and New England, poetically activated for Walcott by his friendship from 1962 with the great Boston poet Robert Lowell (1917–1977). *The Gulf and Other Poems* (1969) shows a similar mix, but begins a more systematic survey of Caribbean places ("Homecoming: Anse La Raye," "Landfall: Grenada," "To the Hotel Saint Antoine," the six-part "Guyana"), and a tendency to longer, potentially narrative sequences ("Guyana," "Metamorphoses," "The Gulf").

As the volume titles suggest, problems of alienation and division, the clash between formal discipline and politically responsive creation, were still unsolved. At least one poem in *The Gulf,* however, the magnificent "Nearing Forty," points towards a solution: fears of aging and finding oneself less able than one hoped are more universal than regional, yet the light, softly persistent rain, louvred windows, and humidity of the poem are specifically Caribbean, and the final balance (*inter alia*) renews Walcott's commitment to his region. At deeper levels intertextuality powerfully triangulates Walcott, John

Figueroa (the dedicatee), Dr. Johnson (epigraphist), and Conrad's Lord Jim: a full reading is available in *The Poetry Handbook* (Lennard, 1996), and, measuring "Nearing Forty" against "Ruins of a Great House," a gathering resolution, backed by technical mastery of exceptional power and subtlety, begins to become apparent.

The Gulf, with Lowell's help, became Walcott's first New York publication, issued, like *Dream on Monkey Mountain,* by Farrar, Straus and Giroux, whose literary list was the most distinguished in the world; they have since become Walcott's primary house, with their nearest U.K. equivalent, Faber, issuing British editions. As important as prestige, their legal and administrative help saw Walcott become, as the 1970s and 1980s progressed, a regular contributor to *The New Yorker* and *New York Review of Books,* and a popular reader commanding a rising fee. He also came to know the New York artistic circles in which heavyweights moved, and was recognized by them as a peer and friend.

With better finances, more time, renewed self-confidence, and a growing need, traveling outside the Caribbean, to explain himself, Walcott was able to complete a project he had been working on since 1965 in prose, and from about 1968 in verse. *Another Life* (1973) is the best (and longest) verse-autobiography in English since Wordsworth's *Prelude* (1805), a rich, digressive account of the formation of the poet's mind. In four books—"The Divided Child," "Homage to Gregorias," "A Simple Flame," and "The Estranging Sea"—Walcott charts and illuminates the reefs and sail-roads of his artistic life. Among the most anthologized passages are a direct rewriting of Wordsworth in chapter 7 ("About the August of my fourteenth year"), a fusion of poetry and carpentry opening chapter 12 ("I watched the vowels curl from the tongue of the carpenter's plane, / resinous, fragrant / labials of our forests"), and a history-lesson in chapter 11:

I saw history through the sea-washed eyes
of our choleric, ginger-haired headmaster

. . .

Nostalgia! Hymns of battles not our own,
on which our fathers looked with the black, iron
    mouths
of cannon, sea-agape,
to the bugle-coloured light crying from the West,
those dates we piped of redoubt and repulse,
while in our wrists the kettle drums pulsed on
to Khartoum, Lucknow, Cawnpore, Balaclava.

. . .

The leaping Caribs whiten,
in one flash, the instant
the race leapt at Sauteurs,
a cataract! One scream of bounding lace.

       (*Another Life*, 11.III.1–2, 8–14, 32–35)

As a parable, the mulatto's memory of being taught battles in which the hero-soldiers were white, the soon-to-die enemy black, powerfully illustrates why independence was a moral necessity and human right. The final quatrain typically recalls those whom white, black, and mulatto jointly displaced, the Carib Indians of the islands, one large group of whom chose race-suicide, leaping en masse from cliffs now named for them: Sauteurs. Even slavery was not such an end, and colonies' inheritance of expropriated lands gives all modern Caribbeans a stake in redeeming the past, or agreeing on a tabula rasa.

Another Life greatly extended Walcott's naming into poetry of the St. Lucian landscape and vegetation. Names sound constantly—Gros and Petit Morne, Castries, Anse La Raye—bringing the sounds of French Creole and Anglophone Caribbean lilts; the process deepens in *Sea Grapes* (1976), short, varied lyrics assembled round a tremendous five-part centerpiece, "Sainte Lucie." In the first part, "The Villages," Walcott again embraces rural St. Lucia, and in the untitled second calls home the most local textures:

Pomme arac,
otaheite apple,

pomme cythère,
pomme granate,
moubain,
z'ananas
the pine apple's
Aztec helmet,
pomme,
I have forgotten
what pomme for
the Irish potato,
cerise,
the cherry,
z'aman
sea-almonds
by the crisp
sea-bursts,
au bord de la 'ouvière.
Come back to me,
my language.
Come back,
cacao,
grigri,
solitaire,
ciseau
the scissor-bird
no nightingales
except, once,
in the indigo mountains
of Jamaica, blue depth,
deep as coffee,
flicker of pimento,
the shaft light
on a yellow ackee
the bark alone bare

          ("Sainte Lucie," II.1–36)

The ease with which English prosody and creole diction are melded, like the ease of humor and address ("pomme, / I have forgotten / what pomme for / the Irish potato"), mark a breakthrough, and in celebration the final section considers Dunstan St. Omer's superb altarpiece in the Roseau Valley church, a St. Lucian fine art to match Walcott's mastery of words.

But for Walcott breakthroughs are also times of crisis, in which the political and personal fuse into Gordian knots from which he frees himself by cutting loose. His general problem was political: the West Indian Federation lasted only until 1962, when some islands (including Trinidad and Tobago) became independent, and others reverted to colony-status (including, until 1979, St. Lucia). With the regional cultural vision of the Federation removed, national arts policies failed, and the Trinidad Theatre Workshop was never able to find a proper home, or achieve proper funding. Governmental corruption meant that even the considerable oil- and gas-wealth that Trinidad began to earn in the 1960s fattened very few pockets; in 1970 there was an abortive revolution, and over several years an active and influential "Black Power" movement developed. In the crude, angry terms of the new demagogues, Walcott, a mulatto using European forms, was a nothing, and his life in Trinidad became increasingly tense. He answered his critics in a major play, *In a Fine Castle* (1972–1973; later *The Last Carnival*), and a full musical with score by Galt MacDermot, *O Babylon!* (1978), both Caribbean successes; in between, a Royal Shakespeare Company commission to translate Tirso de Molina's classic *El Burlador de Sevilla* eventually came to nothing in England, but in the Caribbean produced Walcott's splendid refashioning of Molina's play, *The Joker of Seville* (1978). Yet whatever he did, the Theatre Workshop seemed unable to make progress.

After a brush with alcoholism in the later 1960s, Walcott had moderated his drinking, and Margaret had long tolerated his other vices, but in the mid-1970s he met another dancer and actor, Norline Metivier, and put his marriage on the rocks. Political, professional, and personal frustrations clogged him in Trinidad as American horizons and opportunities widened; temptation warred with undiminished commitment to the Caribbean, felt in the growing St. Lucian intensities of *Another Life* and *Sea Grapes*. Something had to give, and in 1976, over matters trivial and rivalrous, Walcott

abruptly resigned from the Workshop, forbidding them to perform his plays, left Margaret and Port of Spain, and with Norline in tow turned his attention away from old British connections with the Caribbean, towards the quite different prospects he could see in the United States.

THE INTER-AMERICAN, 1977–1987: "MY COMMON LANGUAGE GO BE THE WIND"

Leaving Port of Spain could no more mean abandoning the West Indies than leaving St. Lucia, but Walcott's movement was now northward; teaching appointments in Tobago, St. Croix, and St. Thomas, with visits to New York, led in 1981 to Boston University, where he still teaches a day or two a week with constant returns to the Caribbean. The ambivalence of partial departure is embodied in "The Schooner *Flight*" (1977), collected in *The Star-Apple Kingdom* (1979)—eleven sections of confessional speech by Shabine ("the patois for / any red nigger"), driven by personal demons and involvement with smuggling to ship out suddenly on an inter-island schooner:

> As I worked, watching the rotting waves come
> past the bow that scissor the sea like silk,
> I swear to you all, by my mother's milk,
> by the stars that shall fly from tonight's furnace,
> that I loved them, my children, my wife, my
>   home;
> I loved them as poets love the poetry
> that kills them, as drowned sailors the sea.
>
> You ever look up from some lonely beach
> and see a far schooner? Well, when I write
> this poem, each phrase go be soaked in salt;
> I go draw and knot every line as tight
> as ropes in this rigging; in simple speech
> my common language go be the wind,
> my pages the sails of the schooner *Flight*.
>
> (I.63–76)

Though looking back to corrupt Trinidad and the woman he left sleeping, Shabine is sailing north, past Blanchisseuse and St. Vincent to Castries and the ocean beyond. He also travels in history, encountering a "Middle Passage" of ghostly slave- and warships, the greedy violence of imperial history, and survives a cleansing storm; in "the fresh light that follows," he ends with powerful achievement: "Shabine sang to you from the depths of the sea."

Fused with the journey structure, as Seamus Heaney (b. 1939) admiringly observed in "The Murmur of Malvern," is a tremendous command of the canon, beginning in the opening lines:

> In idle August, while the sea soft,
> and leaves of brown islands stick to the rim
> of this Caribbean, I blow out the light
> by the dreamless face of Maria Concepcion
> to ship as a seaman on the schooner *Flight*.
> ("The Schooner *Flight*," I.1–5)

> In a somer seson • whan soft was the sonne,
> I shope me in shroudes • as I a shepe were,
> In habite as an heremite • vnholy of workes,
> Went wyde in this world • wonders to here.
> (*Piers Ploughman*, B-text, Prologue, 1–4)

Walcott's is not the only great twentieth-century chamber-epic to name a month in opening allusion to a great mediaeval poem: Eliot's *The Waste Land* (1921) begins "April is the cruellest month," as Chaucer's "General Prologue" to the *Canterbury Tales* begins "Whan that Aprille with his shoures soote," and in summoning Langland, Walcott also summons Eliot summoning Chaucer. One line sets it all up—Walcott : Langland :: Eliot : Chaucer—and between the four greats the whole canon resonates. Nor is that all, for Walcott's lines insist on a West Indian accent: speak them in Received Pronunciation, or "BBC English," and it sounds as if you are reprimanding Walcott for creole grammar—"while the sea *is* soft, if you don't mind." Instead, Langland, Chaucer, and Eliot must allow their voices to lilt with Walcott's own.

The division between more English and more Caribbean work, the agony of "A Far Cry from Africa," is at last healed, and other poems in *The Star-Apple Kingdom* show the range of Walcott's new power. "In the Virgins," "Sabbaths, W.I.," "The Sea Is History," "The Saddhu at Couva," and "Koenig of the River" deploy a remarkable range of styles unified by themes and even mastery, while "The Star-Apple Kingdom," a long meditation on Jamaica, ends the volume in the northeastern archipelago, as Shabine began it by leaving southwestern Trinidad. Clear structure and inner resolution are central to the volume's brilliance; another source of power is recorded in "R.T.S.L.," an elegy for Lowell (d. 1977), and the dedication of "Forest of Europe" to the exiled Russian poet Joseph Brodsky (1940–1996). For the first time Walcott had been able over an extended period to talk, argue, and drink with poets he recognized as masters, and found in their admiration for him assurance that he had not wasted his talents or failed his father. The sad absence of Lowell after 1977 was shared with Brodsky, and balanced by new friendship with Heaney; for the next twenty years the three future Nobel Laureates shared platforms, conference halls, and adjacent barstools whenever they could. All slowly realized that a new world-stage was being conjured into existence by the jumbo jet and microchip, and they, strongly local, strongly international wordmasters, could bestride it.

Freed from the structures and demands of the Theatre Workshop, Walcott also entered a new phase of dramatic creativity. *The Joker of Seville* and *O Babylon!* were published together in 1978; the plays in his next volume, *Remembrance & Pantomime* (1980), were very different, turning away from the high-energy, carnivalesque style of Workshop plays to more traditionally structured, prose plays of middle-class life. *Remembrance* (St. Croix, 1977; New York, 1979), a compact seven-character play, revisits Trinidadian Black Power via the memories of a retired schoolteacher whom the revolutionaries despised as an educated mulatto, and whose son, a revolutionary leader, died. *Pantomime* (Port of Spain, 1978; BBC, 1979) is a wry two-character play, the routines of a middle-aged white "actor" who runs a hotel and his long-suffering black factotum.

Both plays were popular, and Walcott, at ease in his new manner, next wholly reconceived *In a Fine Castle* as *The Last Carnival* (1981–1982), premiering it with Frances McDormand in Port of Spain, and embedding it in a Trinidadian trilogy with *Beef, No Chicken* (1986) and *A Branch of the Blue Nile* (1986). Spanning four decades of Trinidadian history, the trilogy was issued as *Three Plays* (1986), his third volume of drama in eight years—and, as always with Walcott, the published plays were barely half the story. The same period saw another full musical with Galt MacDermot, *Marie Laveau* (1979), premiered in St. Thomas; an experimental play, *The Isle Is Full of Noises* (1981), premiered in Connecticut; a television-play, *The Rig* (1981), filmed in Trinidad; a big celebration of the sesquicentenary of Emancipation, *The Haytian Earth* (1984), premiered in St. Lucia; and a political piece, *To Die for Grenada* (1986), premiered in Cleveland.

There were also three new volumes of poetry and a major collection, showing the new shape of Walcott's life. *The Fortunate Traveller* (1981), dedicated to Brodsky and invoking Thomas Nashe's picaresque *The Unfortunate Traveller* (1594), has first and third sections called "North" bracketing the larger "South" (which includes the marvelous "The Spoiler's Return," spoken by an old calypsonian). *Midsummer* (1984), dedicated to his now-adult daughters, comprises fifty-four poems written over one Trinidadian summer equally dominated by painting, brief, long-lined considerations in Part 1 of Trinidad, and in Part 2 of Boston and places visited. *The Arkansas Testament* (1987), dedicated to Heaney, similarly has two sections, "Here," St. Lucia, and "Elsewhere," ranging from Martinique ("French Colonial. 'Vers de Société'") to "downtown Newark" ("God Rest Ye Merry Gentlemen Part II") and Fayetteville

("The Arkansas Testament"). Two classically-minded poems, "A Propertius Quartet" and "Menelaus," shadow a direction Walcott would shortly take, but the striking declaration of these volumes, and the magisterial *Collected Poems 1948–1984* (1986), is their Farrar, Straus and Giroux covers, which variously reproduce his paintings.

Walcott knew from teenage lessons shared with Dunstan St. Omer that he lacked in his wrist what he had in his pen, that Dunstan's was the great St. Lucian brush, but has painted all his life, in watercolor and oils, for pleasure and to his highest standards. For years the scenic demands of the Theatre Workshop had absorbed his visual energy, but painting was becoming more important again, its relation to poetry a principal theme of *Midsummer*. The Farrar, Straus and Giroux covers, a technological luxury (other editions are unillustrated), materially support the juxtaposition of arts Walcott was exploring, placing before readers a vivid palette of West Indian color. They are very attractive, and Farrar, Straus and Giroux's investment was shrewd, beauty without matching beauty within and boosting sales into a new league.

Prestigious magazine publications of individual poems, coordinated by Farrar, Straus and Giroux as a teaser-campaign, and the insane schedule of readings/signings Walcott undertook year after year, also drove sales. The academic rise of commonwealth, postcolonial, and black studies helped set Walcott's stage, but it was the power and enchantment of his voice, gravity of his presence, and emotional impact of his poetry in the ear that made him, with Heaney, a reader in endless demand and a superb advertisement of his wares. But his punishing schedule, zigzagging across North America (and the Atlantic), tore private life apart: he and Norline married in 1981, but disparity in age, a miscarriage, and his endless travels broke the relationship; she left him in 1986, and they divorced in 1993. His partner since has been Sigrid Nama, a German-Flemish American whom he met at a reading in Pittsburgh.

THE INTERNATIONALIST, 1987–2000: "WHEN HE SMILED AT ACHILLE'S CANOE, IN GOD WE TROUST, / ACHILLE SAID: 'LEAVE IT! IS GOD' SPELLING AND MINE.'"

Sometime in the mid-1980s a discussion of Homer became a tremendous catalyst:

> "O-meros," she laughed. "That's what we call
> him in Greek,"
> stroking the small bust with its boxer's broken
> nose,
> and I thought of Seven Seas sitting near the reek
>
> of drying fishnets, listening to the shallows' noise.
> I said: "Homer and Virg are New England
> farmers,
> and the winged horse guards their gas-station,
> you're right."
>
> I felt the foam head watching as I stroked an arm,
> as
> cold as its marble, then the shoulders in winter
> light
> in the studio attic. I said, "Omeros,"
> and O was the conch-shell's invocation, *mer* was
> both mother and sea in our Antillean patois,
> *os*, a grey bone, and the white surf as it crashes
>
> and spreads its sibilant collar on a lace shore.
> Omeros was the crunch of dry leaves, and the
> washes
> that echoed from a cave-mouth when the tide has
> ebbed.
>
> The name stayed in my mouth.
>
> (*Omeros*, II.iii.1ndash;16)

Sixty-four three-part chapters in seven books, *Omeros* (1990) took three years to write and is the most popular long poem in English since Tennyson's cumulative *Idylls of the King* (1833–1891). Analysis of what it does, and how, has been contentious, but at its core is a juxtaposition of Homer's Aegean and Walcott's Caribbean archipelagos: not because Castries is a modern Troy, nor simply because West Indians are as capable of epic as the heroes of Greece, but because the Caribbean is the place through which Homer's life can now be most richly imagined. Classicists rather surprisingly agree, and *Omeros* has received their serious attention, but Walcott's epic cast members are not Greeks, only St. Lucians whose names have French forms, "Achille" (ash-eel), not "Achilles," "Philoctete" (feel-ok-tet), not "Philoctetes"— unforced bearers of latent, poetically apprehended classical identities, fishermen who innocently inherit cognomens given by French slave-owners, half-admiringly, half-ironically, to their abducted African forebears; as black Shakespeares and Miltons are found in Jamaica and Barbados. For their story the Trojan myths are a canvas, not a template; the tercet form only approaches terza rima, in which Dante told of his meetings beyond the dark wood with the heroes of myth; even Achille's erratically named canoe, *In God We Troust*, whose life from forest tree to working boat the poem charts, declares its emblematic misspelling with its nautical faith.

The melded classical richness of *Omeros* bears comparison with the works of another Nobel Laureate, Yoruban Wole Soyinka (b. 1934), and a Nobel contender, Yorkshireman Tony Harrison (b. 1937). All are poet-playwrights and teachers, formidable classicists in deep-seated argument with postimperial centers, who have never thought art anything but political and use languages overtly proclaiming regional difference and identity while commanding traditional forms. An interesting analogy with their common strategy is offered by the twinned European Union policies of *federalization,* taking some national powers to continental level, and *subsidiarity,* dealing with all matters of governance at the lowest appropriate level, to empower regions and localities: both strip powers from member-nations who for five centuries tore Europe apart with internecine wars. Fighting that same postimperial (and increasingly postnational) fight, the classical learning that Walcott, Soyinka, and Harrison display in regional voices similarly seizes power from old centers, revalorizing from below creolized or dialectal languages, regional accents, and local sensibilities that empires overrule, and reaching over London to its most honored models, Rome and its mother city, Troy. In claiming living guardianship of Homeric and Athenian legacies in demotic, regional English, all three men foreclose as bards on imperial mythologies, and each gives voice to a people.

The narratives of *Omeros* involve real and visionary journeys to confront English, Aegean, and African roots; all Walcott's themes are there: languages, exile, island beauty and vegetation, and the infinite, timely relations of history and the sea. Both in an earlier poem and in a later essay Walcott insists that "the sea is history," and *Omeros* marks him as the finest poet-playwright of the sea since Shakespeare (there have been two great marine novelists, Melville and Conrad, but *Omeros* is closer to *Pericles*). The facts are simple and terrible: the slave trade was intrinsically maritime, and the ocean tracelessly swallowed many thousands of fettered Africans, in shipwreck or by policy; all islanders must love and fear the waters that make them what they are, sustain and drown them; the sea has many voices, but is enduringly dumb. Consider for a moment the Athenian choric mask, on stage a phalanx of closely similar masks, wide-eyed, open-mouthed: that must see even the unseeable, speak even the unspeakable; witness horror, comedy, nobility withering in tears, and be made to speak of these things, many- and one-voiced, by the dramatizing poet. Within his epic of archipelago and distant, venial empires, comedies of survival and tragedies of dissolution entwine, but to all the actors, and

Walcott behind them, the Antillean seas and colder Atlantic play a ceaseless sibilant chorus. As Shabine in his chamber-epic heard the sea-voice, and saw the ocean's palimpsest flicker with ghosts, lighting the Middle Passage with spectral loss, so in *Omeros* Achille and the wounded Philoctete sense them in fully epic form. *Another Life* explained Walcott; *Omeros* explains his people, and has commanded deep respect and affection from a diverse readership.

Sales rose rapidly, driven by word-of-mouth and Farrar, Straus and Giroux's publicity. One immediate consequence was a Royal Shakespeare Company commission to dramatize *The Odyssey* (1993) working with director Greg Doran; where *Omeros* brought the Aegean to the West Indies, the play (premiered in Stratford in July 1992) projected the West Indies to the Aegean, bringing Homer home with Caribbean vitality to modern audiences. Walcott was simultaneously involved in a Stockholm production of *The Last Carnival*, again reshaped in translation, which proved prophetic: in October he was announced as Nobel Laureate in Literature, four days before the 500th anniversary of Columbus's landfall in the West Indies, and in December returned to Stockholm in triumph to deliver his stunning Nobel lecture, *The Antilles: Fragments of Epic Memory* (1993).

Walcott was not the first West Indian Laureate—the Francophone poet-diplomat Saint-John Perse (Alexis Saint-Léger Léger, 1887–1975), raised in Guadeloupe, won in 1960—nor even the first St. Lucian born on 23 January to win—Arthur Lewis (1915–1991), another alumnus of St. Mary's and fifteen years to the day his senior, was Economics Laureate in 1979. But of all late-century Nobels, only Heaney's (in 1995) was greeted with anything like as extended a party: a kind of blessed Walcott-mania erupted in creative circles throughout the Caribbean, and in Castries continued well into 1993, when Columbus Square became Walcott Square.

One consequence was a rapprochement with the Trinidad Theatre Workshop, but renewed collaboration had to wait. *O Babylon!* had been staged in London in 1988 (when Walcott won the Queen's Gold Medal for Poetry), and in 1989 perhaps his most important American play, *The Ghost Dance,* confronting the Amerindian genocide and the shame of the New World, premiered in Oneonta, New York. In 1991 a fourth musical scored by Galt MacDermot, *Steel,* about Caribbean steel-bands, premiered in Boston. After the excitements of Stratford and Stockholm, Walcott found his Nobel had generated French, German, Danish, Russian, and other translations and productions of his work, with which he became variously involved. Interest in his painting also soared, leading in 1998 to a full exhibition in Albany, New York. In the same year (along with publication of his first prose collection, *What the Twilight Says: Essays,* 1988), a long-brewing musical collaboration with Paul Simon, *The Capeman,* opened on Broadway and closed after sixty-nine performances, having taken a terrible critical drubbing: there were fundamental problems in theatrically matching Walcott's words with Simon's music, but the debacle involved New York minority politics (its protagonist, Salvador Agron, was a Puerto Rican murderer-cum-jail-celebrity) and vicious journalism. Walcott's dramatic work afterward increasingly aimed to develop a studio around his drama-teaching in Boston, with teaching visits by Workshop members linked to fund-raising for themselves, the studio, and an arts foundation Walcott created in St. Lucia.

The completion of *Omeros* coincided with the death at ninety-six of Alix Walcott, and *The Bounty* (1997) begins with an oddly eponymous seven-part elegy. "The Bounty" cannot escape being Bligh's mutinous ship, but Walcott's primary sense is of beneficence, goodness in fecundity, and in his mother's absence he thinks of the great Northamptonshire nature-poet John Clare (1793–1864). The form is loose, long-lined tercets; the prosody, especially in part 5, draws

astonishingly close to comedic triple and quadruple meters despite its burden of loss. Other poems in the volume are like those in *Midsummer,* twenty-plus long lines nestled within a page; fluid numbering and titling implies a single work, like a sonnet-sequence, verse-diary, or graphic novel in successive frames.

The subject of *Tiepolo's Hound* (2000), openly a verse-novel, is painting, a quest for

> a slash of pink on the inner thigh
> of a white hound entering the cave of a table,
>
> so exact in its lucency at *The Feast of Levi,*
> I felt my heart halt.
>
> (I.3.9-12).

In the Farrar, Straus and Giroux edition, amid 164 pages of loosely heroic cross-rhymed couplets arranged as twenty-six four-part chapters in four books, are twenty-six full-color plates, conjoining Walcott's brush with his pen more intimately than ever, but his painted canine quarry proves the opposite of Francis Thompson's "Hound of Heaven," not remorselessly pursuing but infinitely receding. In parallel runs a verse-biography of the impressionist painter Camille Pissarro (1830–1903), born in St. Thomas but abandoning the Caribbean for Paris, England, and Pontoise. Thinking of Pissarro standing with Monet in London before Turner's *The Fighting Téméraire,* which shows that warship being drawn by a steam-tug:

> Triangulation: in his drawing room
> my father copies *The Fighting Téméraire.*
>
> He and Monet admire the radiant doom
> of the original; all three men revere
>
> the crusted barge, its funnel bannering fire,
> its torch guiding the great three-master on

to sink in the infernal asphalt of an empire
turning more spectral, like the mastodon.

(XII.1.37–44)

Transatlantic triangulation (reversing the slave-triangle) brings together the shades of Warwick Walcott, Pissarro, and Monet to admire Turner; the tug's ember-flecked smokestream as martial banner leads to an image of its light as the "torch of life" passed down the imperial generations in "Vitaï Lampada," a notorious poem of school and empire by Henry Newbolt (1862–1938), who also wrote a popular piece on "The Fighting Téméraire." A spectral mastodon sinking in "infernal asphalt" seems a bizarre addition to Walcott's visions of ghost-fuming seas: the simpler, tackily memorable explanation is the doomed plastic mastodon installed in the La Brea Tar Pits in Los Angeles, where Walcott is often produced at the Mark Taper Forum, and the sentence quietly completes its underlying movement from the journey Warwick could make only in Derek's imagination, to the journeys Derek has made himself.

The technical mastery seems effortless, and is complete. Fifty years after "As John to Patmos," Walcott's pentameters remember the old trick with an additional beat: the hypermetric "three" in "of THE |[o]RIG- | [i]nAL; |[a]ll THREE MEN |[r]evere" insists metrically on his father's equivalence with two of the greats, and shows Walcott still at seventy making the loved "brown dead" live again. Simultaneously, the generous bilingual half-rhyme, "*Téméraire*/revere," slides into a prophetic English one, "fire/empire," and caps it with mosaic-rhyme, "-master on/mastodon," diagnosing imperial obsolescence while subtly enquiring how short the "a" in "master" or "mastodon" should be, in what creolized or metropolitan accents you hear and say them. The diction comprehends geometry and painting, archaism and neologism, history and Hell; the syntax is simple and straightforward.

Walcott's life is more an expanding area than a line. St. Lucia was never abandoned, in word

or deed, but again and again proclaimed into regional, American, and international consciousness: the heartwood around which Walcott builds ringing growth; the sea-home at the epicenter of his travels. In later essays—"A Letter to Chamoiseau" (1997), "A Frowsty Fragrance" (2000)—Walcott explicitly addressed the maturing creole literature of the Caribbean that he helped to father, not as a bastard child fathered by the enslaved on English and French literatures, but as a legitimate heir come into its full inheritance to use wisely for itself. And in *Tiepolo's Hound*, as his St. Lucian father through him talks with two great dead French artists of an English third, think again of Eliot:

> No poet, no artist of any art, has his complete meaning alone. His significance, his appreciation is the appreciation of his relation to the dead poets and artists. . . . existing monuments form an ideal order. . . . Whoever has approved this idea of . . . the form of European, of English literature, will not find it preposterous that the past should be altered by the present as much as the present is directed by the past. And the poet who is aware of this will be aware of great difficulties and responsibilities.

CRITICS' CORNER

Although criticism has built up, attention was long restricted to emergent postcolonial studies, and, if offering some accurate lessons in West Indian history and culture, commonly shed more heat than light. Two disputes stand as examples, the feminist attack led by Elaine Fido's article "Macho Attitudes and Derek Walcott" (1986), and Walcott's much-hyped spat with Barbadian poet Kamau Brathwaite.

Fido's article offered a reasoned account of Walcott as gender-politically a typical, conservative black West Indian male of his generation, and with some less reasoned close readings argued that where misogyny runs strong, poetry is diminished. Fido was uninterested in the nuances of what she condemned, and did not consider Walcott's Christianity or sense of mission; though morally substantive, her criticism is narrow and, more seriously, unconcerned with the profound differences between poetic personae and roles written for performance. No one aware of Walcott's marital history can doubt male shortcomings and worse in his private life, but his knowledge of suffering and his poetic empowerments do not exclude women. If Fido's criticism is proper, her imitators have often been no more than a lynch-mob manqué, sometimes calumniously resurrecting an unproven, almost certainly unfounded, and perhaps malicious accusation of having once propositioned and academically victimized a Harvard student.

The record of Walcott's "enmity" with Brathwaite also curdles with others' malice. The two are certainly rivalrous; as Barbadian and St. Lucian Anglophone poets born in the same year, some inter-island competition and a politics of language are to be expected. Relations supposedly soured in 1969 with the polarities of *The Gulf* and Brathwaite's poetic trilogy *The Arrivants,* completed in that year with *Masks,* and issued as one volume in 1973, coinciding with *Another Life.* Both poets said things they have been happy to qualify; academic thesis-hunting reified genuine differences into a crude pseudo-polarity, supposing Walcott's adherence to formal disciplines and knowledge of European literatures to be the badges of a cultural Uncle Tom, and Brathwaite's incantatory lines and African content a validating sign of cutting-edge blackness. The crudity betrays the legacy of Black Power, and spawned a further grossly reductive opposition, of Walcott with a generation of supposedly more street- and market-wise rap artists, "blacker" MCs who will again slay the old poet, this time for being an unfashionable father. Generational development is not necessarily hostile, let alone Oedipal; Walcott has already deeply influenced two generations of West Indian artists, and will extend his

influence while world culture endures; Brathwaite too has an honorable and secure place. Their poetic arguments are lively and interesting; the notion of a diagnostic rift is intellectually laughable for anyone who has read Brathwaite with an ear for influence (he acknowledged his debt to Eliot in *History of the Voice,* 1984), and requires persistently crass readings of Walcott.

Constructive attention began with Edward Baugh's study *Derek Walcott: Memory as Vision* (1978), backed by Lloyd Brown's edited collection on *West Indian Poetry* (1978), and Goldstraw's *Annotated Bibliography* (1984). Stewart Brown's collection, *The Art of Derek Walcott* (1991) and Rei Terada's *Derek Walcott's Poetry: American Mimicry* (1992) interestingly predate the Nobel, after which scholarship quickened. The fattest works are Bruce King's *Derek Walcott and West Indian Drama* (1995) and *Derek Walcott: A Caribbean Life* (2000), invaluable for data and insistence on Walcott as poet-playwright, exasperating as reference tools, and disappointing as criticism; the biography will certainly be superseded, and should be supplemented by William Baer's *Conversations with Derek Walcott* (1996). Close reading was strengthened by the use of "Nearing Forty" as the exemplary poem in *The Poetry Handbook* (Lennard, 1996). John Thieme's *Derek Walcott* (1999) and Paul Breslin's *Nobody's Nation: Reading Derek Walcott* (2001) suggest the future shape of criticism; lesser work still tends to ignore drama and apply inadequate, ahistorical theory to no one's satisfaction but its own.

The best guide to Walcott is his work. Maps of St. Lucia and the Caribbean help, as does hearing him on tape; audio-clips are online, with paintings, essays, interviews, and Antillean images. French sounds French, English creoles lilt: allow that, reading aloud for the sense with passion, not to enunciate form, and Walcott comes vibrantly alive even if allusions still need research. His distilled speech has for fifty years been of the highest political and aesthetic orders, memorably seeking truth within Plato's Republic, as without; to hear it best you must again make it speech.

Selected Bibliography

Walcott's work is very extensive, and the volume of critical material enormous: for fuller bibliographies see Goldstraw, *Annotated Bibliography* (1984) and King, *Derek Walcott* (2000). Major collections of his papers are held at the libraries of the University Colleges of the West Indies at Mona, Jamaica, and Port of Spain, Trinidad, and of Boston University. There are sometimes minor differences, intentional or accidental, between the New York and London editions of Walcott's collections of poetry.

WORKS OF DEREK WALCOTT

COLLECTED POETRY

25 Poems. Port of Spain, Trinidad: Guardian, 1948; Bridgetown, Barbados: Advocate, 1949.

Epitaph for the Young: XII Cantos. Bridgetown, Barbados: Advocate, 1949.

Poems. Kingston, Jamaica: City Printery, 1951.

In a Green Night: Poems 1948–1960. London: Jonathan Cape, 1962.

The Castaway and Other Poems. London: Jonathan Cape, 1965.

The Gulf and Other Poems. London: Jonathan Cape, 1969; as *The Gulf: Poems,* New York: Farrar, Straus and Giroux, 1970.

Another Life. London: Jonathan Cape; New York: Farrar, Straus and Giroux, 1973.

Sea Grapes. London: Jonathan Cape; New York: Farrar, Straus and Giroux, 1976.

The Star-Apple Kingdom. New York: Farrar, Straus and Giroux, 1979; London: Jonathan Cape, 1980.

Selected Poetry. Oxford: Heinemann, 1981 (Caribbean Writers Series). (This selection from Walcott's first six major collections is still available and in wide use; there is an introduction and useful basic annotation by Wayne Brown.)

The Fortunate Traveller. New York: Farrar, Straus and Giroux, 1981; London: Faber and Faber, 1982.

Midsummer. New York: Farrar, Straus and Giroux; London: Faber and Faber, 1984.

Collected Poems 1948–1984. New York: Farrar, Straus and Giroux; London: Faber and Faber, 1986.

The Arkansas Testament. New York: Farrar, Straus and Giroux, 1987; London: Faber and Faber, 1988.

Omeros. New York: Farrar, Straus and Giroux; London: Faber and Faber, 1990.

Poems 1965–1980. London: Jonathan Cape, 1992. (Reprints the Cape editions of *The Castaway, The Gulf, Sea-Grapes,* and *The Star-Apple Kingdom.*)

The Bounty. New York: Farrar, Straus and Giroux; London: Faber and Faber, 1997.

Tiepolo's Hound. New York: Farrar, Straus and Giroux; London: Faber and Faber, 2000. (The Faber edition omits twenty-six full-color plates of watercolors by Walcott.)

Derek Walcott reads a selection of his work [from] Collected Poems 1948–1984 *and* Omeros. Argo/Polygram, 1994; catalog no. 522-222-4.

A partial list of uncollected poems 1944–1986 can be found in King, *Derek Walcott,* pp. 666–667.

PUBLISHED PLAYS

Henri Christophe: A Chronicle in Seven Scenes. Bridgetown, Barbados: Advocate, 1950.

"Robin and Andrea," in *Bim* 4.13 (December 1950), pp. 19–23.

Harry Dernier: A Play for Radio Production. Bridgetown, Barbados: Advocate, 1952.

The Sea at Dauphin. Port of Spain, Trinidad: University of the West Indies Extra-Mural Department, 1954.

The Wine of the Country. Port of Spain, Trinidad: University of the West Indies Extra-Mural Department, 1956 (Caribbean Plays series). (A duplicated typescript).

Ione: A Play with Music. Kingston, Jamaica: University College of the West Indies Extra-Mural Department, 1957 (Caribbean Plays No. 8).

Ti-Jean: A Play in One Act. Kingston, Jamaica: University College of the West Indies Extra-Mural Department, 1957.

Drums and Colours: An Epic Drama, in *Caribbean Quarterly,* 7.1-2 (March 1961), pp. 1–104.

Jourmard; or, A Comedy to the Last Minute. University of the West Indies Extra-Mural Department, 1960. (A duplicated typescript.)

Dream on Monkey Mountain and Other Plays. New York: Farrar, Straus and Giroux, 1970. Later New York re-issues are by Farrar, Straus and Giroux's Noonday Press. (Comprises an important introductory essay, "What the Twilight Says: An Overture," and four plays: *The Sea at Dauphin, Ti-Jean and His Brothers, Malcochon; or, The Six in the Rain,* and *Dream on Monkey Mountain.* Following its 1971 New York production, *Dream on Monkey Mountain* won the Obie Award for Distinguished Foreign Play.)

The Joker of Seville & O Babylon!: Two Plays. New York: Farrar, Straus and Giroux, 1978; London: Jonathan Cape, 1979.

Remembrance & Pantomime: Two Plays. New York: Farrar, Straus and Giroux, 1980.

Three Plays: The Last Carnival; Beef, No Chicken; A Branch of the Blue Nile. New York: Farrar, Straus and Giroux, 1986.

Sista karnevalen. Stockholm: Wahlström and Widstrand, 1992. (This Swedish version of *The Last Carnival* differs from the version published in the Farrar, Straus and Giroux *Three Plays.*)

The Odyssey: A Stage Version. New York: Farrar, Straus and Giroux; London: Faber and Faber, 1993.

Lists of Walcott's unpublished plays, surviving and lost, and of his screenplays, can be found in King, *Derek Walcott.* Pp. 668–669.

PROSE

"The Caribbean: Culture or Mimicry?" *Journal of Interamerican Studies and World Affairs,* 16.1 (February 1974): 3–13.

"On Choosing Port of Spain." In *David Frost Introduces Trinidad and Tobago.* Edited by Michael Anthony and Andrew Carr. London: André Deutsch, 1975. Pp. 14–23.

"A Rediscovery of Islands." *New York Times,* 13 November 1983, XX. P. 21.

"Papa's Flying Machines." *New York Times Book Review,* 13 November 1983. Pp. 37, 51.

"A Colonial's Eye-View of the Empire." *Triquarterly,* Winter 1986. Pp. 73–84.

"On the Beat in Trinidad." *New York Times Magazine,* 5 May 1986. Pp. 38–44.

Ronald Duncan Lecture No. 1: The Poet in the Theatre. London: Poetry Book Society/ South Bank Centre, 1990. The text of a lecture delivered 29 September 1990.

"Jackie Hinkson." *Galerie* (Trinidad), 1.2 (1992). Reprinted in *The Massachusetts Review,* Autumn-Winter 1994, pp. 413–417. (Excerpts from this essay were used in the catalogue to "Island Light," a 1998 exhibition of Walcott's paintings at the University Art Museum, Albany, NY, and are available on-line with images of many of the paintings at http://www.albany.edu/museum/wwwmuseum/island_still/island.html.

The Antilles: Fragments of Epic Memory: The Nobel Lecture. New York: Farrar, Straus and Giroux; London: Faber and Faber, 1993. (This superb text, reprinted in *What the Twilight Says,* is also available at http://www.nobel.se/literature/laureates/1992/ walcott-lecture.html.)

"A Tribute to C. L. R. James." In *C. L. R. James: His Intellectual Legacies.* Edited by Selwyn R. Cudjoe and William E. Cain. Amherst: University of Massachusetts Press, 1995. Pp. 34–48.

Homage to Robert Frost, with Joseph Brodsky and Seamus Heaney. New York: Farrar, Straus and Giroux, 1996.

"The Sea Is History." In *Frontiers of Caribbean Literature in English.* Edited by Frank Birbalsingh. New York: St. Martin's Press, 1996. Pp. 22–28.

"Afterword: Animals, Elemental Tales, and the Theatre." *Monsters, Tricksters, and Sacred Cows: Animal Tales and American Identities.* Edited by James Arnold. Charlottesville: University Press of Virginia, 1996. Pp. 269–277.

"Reflections on *Omeros.*" In *The Poetics of Derek Walcott.* Edited by Gregson Davis. *South Atlantic Quarterly* 96.2 (Spring 1997). Pp. 229–246.

What the Twilight Says: Essays. New York: Farrar, Straus and Giroux, 1988; London: Faber and Faber, 1998. (Comprises "What the Twilight Says" (1970), "The Muse of History" (1974), "The Antilles: Fragments of Epic Memory" (1993), "On Robert Lowell" (1984), "On Hemingway" (1990), "C. L. R. James" (1984), "The Garden Path: V. S. Naipaul" (1987), "Magic Industry: Joseph Brodsky" (1988), "The Master of the Ordinary: Philip Larkin" (1989), "Ted Hughes" (1989), "Crocodile Dandy: Les Murray" (1989), "The Road Taken: Robert Frost" (1996), "A Letter to Chamoiseau" (1997), and "Café Martinique: A Story" (1985).)

"A Frowsty Fragrance." *New York Review of Books* XLVII.10 (15 June 2000): 57–61. (A review of *Caribbeana: An Anthology of English Literature of the West Indies,* edited by T. W. Krise.)

"The Great Exile." *New York Review of Books* XLIX.5 (28 March 2002): 27–30. (A review of Guillermo Cabrera Infante's *Guilty of Dancing the Chachachá.*)

Walcott is a prolific essayist, reviewer, and lecturer; a fuller list of uncollected prose can be found in King, *Derek Walcott,* pp. 669–672.

INTERVIEWS

Baer, William, ed. *Conversations with Derek Walcott.* Jackson: University Press of Mississippi, 1996.

Fleming, Carrol. "Talking with Derek Walcott." http://www.thecaribbeanwriter.com/ volume7/v7p52.html.

CRITICAL STUDIES

Banham, Martin, Errol Hill, and George Woodyard, eds. *The Cambridge Guide to African & Caribbean Theatre.* Cambridge: Cambridge University Press, 1994. (A useful A–Z, with entries on all the Caribbean theater personnel and institutions mentioned here.)

Baugh, Edward. *Derek Walcott: Memory as Vision:* Another Life. London: Longman, 1978.

Breslin, Paul. *Nobody's Nation: Reading Derek Walcott.* Chicago and London: University of Chicago Press, 2001.

Brown, Lloyd. *West Indian Poetry.* Boston: Twayne, 1978.

Brown, Stewart, ed. *The Art of Derek Walcott.* Chester Springs, Pa.: Dufour, 1991; Bridgend, U.K.: Seren Books, 1992.

Burnett, Paula. *Derek Walcott: Politics and Poetics.* Gainesville: University Press of Florida, 2001.

Fido, Elaine Savory. "Macho Attitudes and Derek Walcott." *Journal of Commonwealth Literature,* xxi.1 (1986). Pp. 109–118. Partly reprinted in, e.g., Denis Walder, ed., *Literature in the Modern World: Critical Essays and Documents.* Oxford: Oxford University Press/Open University, 1990. Pp. 288–294.

Glissant, Edouard. "Natural Poetics, Forced Poetics." In *Caribbean Discourse: Selected Essays* (originally published as *Le Discours Antillais,* Paris: Editions du Seuil, 1981), trans. J. Michael Dash. Charlottesville: University Press of Virginia, 1989. Pp. 120–134.

Goldstraw, Irma E. *Derek Walcott: An Annotated Bibliography of His Works.* New York: Garland, 1984.

Hamner, Robert D. *Epic of the Dispossessed: Derek Walcott's 'Omeros.'* Columbia, Mo., and London: University of Missouri Press, 1997.

Heaney, Seamus. "The Murmur of Malvern." In *The Government of the Tongue: The 1986 T. S. Eliot Memorial Lectures and Other Critical Writings.* London: Faber and Faber, 1988. Pp. 23–29.

James, C. L. R. "Here's a Poet Who Sees the Real West Indies." *Sunday Guardian* (Port of Spain), 6 June 1962, p. 5.

King, Bruce, *Derek Walcott and West Indian Drama: 'Not Only a Playwright but a Company': The Trinidad Theatre Workshop 1959–1993.* Oxford: Clarendon Press, 1995. (This is the fullest available study of Walcott's drama, and includes a Theater Calendar as well as a substantial bibliography including reviews of individual productions.)

———. *Derek Walcott: A Caribbean Life.* Oxford and New York: Oxford University Press, 2000. (An essential resource for facts, and important for its insistence on Walcott as a dramatist, this first biography is unfortunately badly written, under-illustrated, and lacking in literary intelligence.)

Lennard, John. *The Poetry Handbook: A Guide to Reading Poetry in English for Pleasure and Practical Criticism.* Oxford and New York: Oxford University Press, 1996. (Each chapter, on a particular element of poetry, ends by looking at that element in Walcott's "Nearing Forty," from *The Gulf.*)

———. "Classical Learning in Regional Voices: The Work of Derek Walcott, Wole Soyinka, and Tony Harrison." In *Regions, nations, mondialisation: Aspects politiques, economiques, culturels.* Edited by J. P. Lehners, G. Schuller, and J. Goedert. Luxembourg: Centre Universitaire de Luxembourg, 1996. Pp. 139–149.

———. *Reading Contemporary Poetry: Walcott, Hill, Harrison, Heaney.* Bloomsbury Online, 2001.

Sinnewe, Dirk. *Divided to the Vein? Derek Walcott's Drama and the Formation of Cultural Identities.* Saarbrücken: Königshausen und Neumann, 2001. (Reihe Saarbrücker Beiträge 17).

Terada, Rei. *Derek Walcott's Poetry: American Mimicry.* Boston: Northeastern University Press, 1992.

Thieme, John. *Derek Walcott.* Manchester and New York: Manchester University Press, 1999.

Todd, Loreto. *York Notes on Derek Walcott, Selected Poems.* London: Longman/York Press, 1993. (Though tending to oversimplify in general, this undergraduate crib has some detailed annotation that those finding Walcott difficult will find helpful.)

OTHER WORKS CITED

Brathwaite, Edward (Kamau). *The Arrivants: A New World Trilogy: Rights of Passage, Islands, Masks.* Oxford: Oxford University Press, 1973. The individual volumes first appeared in 1967–1969.

———. *History of the Voice.* London: New Beacon Books, 1984.

Eliot, T. S. "Tradition and the Individual Talent." In his *The Sacred Wood: Essays on Poetry and Criticism.* London: Methuen, 1920. (Very widely anthologized and reprinted.)

———. *Complete Poems and Plays.* London: Faber and Faber, 1969.

Marvell, Andrew. *Miscellaneous Poems.* London: Robert Boulter, 1681. (Widely anthologized and reprinted.)

Newbolt, Henry. "The Fighting Téméraire" and "Vitaï Lampada," in his *Collected Poems 1897–1907.* London, Edinburgh, Dublin, & New York: Thomas Nelson & Sons, 1918. (Widely anthologized.)

Yeats, W. B., *Collected Poems* (1933). 2nd ed., London: Macmillan, 1950.

Patrick White
(1912–1990)

JOSEPH DEWEY

LIKE "TRAGEDY," LIKE "miracle," the word "visionary" has lost its grandeur, its daring. In a media-driven age where turnpike pileups and house fires are tragic and infomercial makeovers and long-shot athletic championships are miraculous, urban planners, political strategists, and savvy entrepreneurs have become a culture's visionaries. To say, then, that the fictions of the Australian Patrick White explore the compelling role of the visionary in the twentieth century is to necessarily understate the gravitas of a body of work, unapologetically metaphysical, that introduced into a stubbornly secular century the complex and gloriously medieval assumption that the complicated circuitry of the human animal—that mysterious matrix of hungers and drives—is infinitely more complicated by a soul, an essence unreachable through the senses, undetectable by the sciences, and (particularly problematic for a writer) indescribable via language. Despite the abundant contrary evidence of White's midcentury culture—the pain and waste of near-ceaseless warfare, the ugly complacency of materialism, the unrestricted indulgence of the carnal needs, the ignorance of bigotry (each of which came under White's unblinking eye)—his fictions dared to affirm a larger beauty, a sense of unity and organization to nothing less than the cosmos itself. In the midst of a century in which science relentlessly crafted a model universe in which the tiniest particles were codable, White refused to concede the material universe to dumb matter and offered rather an energizing confirmation of a vast "something" beyond the arrogant presumption of measurement. His, then, is a body of fiction defined not by its grasp but by its reach, not by what it realizes but rather by what it implies, not by the promise of articulation but rather by the premise of illumination, a body of work defined ultimately (and ironically given the sheer bulk of each of White's novels) by what it cannot say.

Although too much a product of the post–World War I wasteland culture to endorse any institutional church, Patrick White was nevertheless one of the twentieth century's most impassioned religious writers. White's defining narratives are uncompromising parables that conceive of a universe as a grim cycle of copulation, survival, and mortality played out by vulnerable isolates amid inscrutable contingency where, nevertheless, matter and spirit interpenetrate, a conviction sustained without the drag and pull of any faith but rather constructed from studying the arguments of mystical Judaism, Christian apocalypticism, Hindu spiritualism, and the nature religions of

Australian aborigines. Like wisdom literature generally, White's parables can seem on first reading dense, forbiddingly textured, even inaccessible, largely because he dispenses with the assumption of so much of his own century's fiction, namely that the writer share intimacy with the reader via fictions that are more like cloaked autobiography. Dismissing such fictions as documentary and solipsistic, White stays elusive, more like a dramatist (his earliest love) whose character inventions necessarily displace the author's self in order to test ideas. These novels are parables of suffering and redemption—not the particular sort of twentieth-century physical suffering rendered by naturalist/realist writers enthralled by the graphic depiction of brutality and offering as reward for such tribulations the faux redemption of identity, love, or family, but rather the grand spiritual suffering of prophets and saints who undergo trials to confirm that beneath and beyond the pressing chaos, irredeemable banality, and gross materialism of their cultural moment lurks a sustaining essence.

Thus a reader, accustomed to the modest scope of so much contemporary serious fiction, discovers in the defining works of Patrick White—a patterned cycle of nine novels published over a thirty-year period—the sheer breadth of the dimension those other narratives have forfeited by accepting as sufficient the narrowed horizon of realism, content to record the press and feel of the accessible immediate, peopling the privileged fictional space with characters like those encountered down the street or across town. Drawn by the compelling metaphor of the Australian continent itself (its thin fringes of civilization ribboned around its immense, untracked interior), White sees vastness as the business of the artist. Against the larger midcentury genre of drab realistic literature transfixed by the humdrum logic of self-definition and compelled by the slender urgency of an epiphany that merely clarifies the conditions of a single character's life, White returns the epiphany to its religious roots. His central characters tap into a deeper sense of real-

ity, an unsubtle illumination that, far from clarifying the condition of a single self, transforms all selves by confirming the viability of a larger dimension, of Being itself (for lack of a better term), that manifests itself as individual particles, a universe whose complex integrity would be violated by description.

As a twentieth-century writer, then, White moves in uncertain company—where to place him? Within his own era, he clearly lacked patience with the diminished scope of the social realist writers (Kingsley Amis, Angus Wilson, Anthony Powell, and C. P. Snow in Britain; John Updike, William Styron, and Saul Bellow in America), and he could not endorse the playful skepticism and the exhilarating writerly experiments of emerging American postmodernists such as William Gaddis, William Burroughs, Jack Kerouac, or John Barth. His fictions clearly draw from disparate narrative traditions (most acknowledged by White): his sense of a multilayered central consciousness recalls the psychological realism of Henry James; his vivid sense of deftly created secondary characters recalls Dickens; his trenchant social commentary, Thackeray; his forbidding pessimism, Hardy; his dramatic sense of excess, Melville; his complex wrestling with spiritual realities, Dostoevsky; his fascination with nonlinear narratives (particularly the flashback) and the recursive narrative mechanism of stream of consciousness, Joyce; his inclination toward allegory, Hawthorne; and his conviction of the vitality of nature, Lawrence.

Ultimately, however, White recalls most completely not any novelist or narrative school but rather the urgent quasi-religious instincts of poets such as William Blake and Walt Whitman, more metaphysicians than artists. Indeed, White as craftsman has often been cited for architectural failings: episodic plots that dismiss action, mismanage suspense, hinge on coincidence, and struggle beneath an overwrought prose line burdened with gratuitous symbols and a suffocating seriousness and which is ultimately dependent on authorial invasion to render judgment on characters. But as with Blake and Whitman, White's considerable intellect was infused by the intuitive conviction that matter matters only if it partakes as well of the spiritual, that the finite discloses to those rare few the untranslatable confirmation of the infinite. As with Blake and Whitman, White cannot guide readers to similar spiritual confirmation—his fictions are neither facile invitations nor crude self-help books. Rather, like traditional religious literature, they can only testify to an unsuspected reality; resolution is mystery, not solution. The reward for the participatory reader sharing the parable-narratives of White's visionaries is the difficult gift of living on the edge of expectation, sustained by possibility, content with a compassionate love of living—despite the world's glaring ugliness, inexplicable perversions, and casual cruelties. Darkness thus coexists with illumination; sordidness with beauty; despair with affirmation; surface with depth; madness with clarity; death with redemption.

THEMES AND CHARACTERS

White's fictions begin with the misfit unplaceable within the constricting matrix of a materialistic world where humanity has dispensed with the spiritual dimension (or has reduced it to spiritless rituals involving drab symbolic transactions) and has consequently reduced itself to the animal, servicing the itches of the flesh and relishing the accessible comforts of the suburban middle class. Like characters in parables, these central characters are difficult to approach—they are physically unattractive, uncompromisingly honest, grandly flawed. They dismiss as insignificant the animal drives that compel the rest of us, and they reveal, by their undiminished hunger for even the slenderest confirmation of a spiritual dimension, the thinness of our complacency. Further straining reader sympathy, White's visionaries endure decidedly problematic fates. Tolerating inviolable isolation, emotional betrayals, and

physical hardships, they are rewarded with a compelling moment when the cosmos discloses its unifying spirit, an intuitive conviction that ignites both joy and confidence but that must nevertheless remain private, indeed beggars the capacity of language even to record it. White, not surprisingly, often relies on metaphors of music and painting to suggest the sensual/spiritual convictions of his illuminati. Thus, unable to share their redemptive moment of cleansing certainty, White's visionary elect cannot find significant use for such gained understanding. They cannot save others (White dismisses the Messiah complex as unforgivably hubristic); irreparably burned, they cannot abide the traditional comforts of love and family (for White, love inevitably turns on the predatory scratch of the flesh, and the family is riven by grudges, discontents, and hatreds); and they cannot settle for tending to the self. Blasted by insight, they understand now that the self is a vulnerable part of a mightier frame of reference—the visionary moment is a humbling moment of union, of ego-surrender. And without reference to a socially sanctioned established religion, the visionary is shunted to the margins, ostracized as odd, institutionalized as untreatably insane, or (as is most often the case in White's fiction) left fit only to embrace the experience of death itself. Insight thus becomes affliction. As with all wisdom literature, the visionary is both heroic and unenviable.

The nine novels that form the core of White's oeuvre together work out the implications of three aspects critical to the visionary experience: exploration, articulation, and communication. These aspects in turn can define chronological phases within White's own canon. Theodora Goodman (*The Aunt's Story*, 1948), Stan Parker (*The Tree of Man*, 1955), and Johann Ulrich Voss (*Voss*, 1957) each exemplify the initial visionary stage: exploration. Each yearns for illumination, restless within the complacent materialism of their culture, the press of its banality and depthlessness. Unable to tap into the prosaic satisfactions of involvement (betrayed or exploited within the bindings of family and marriage), each pushes alone outward into a spatial vastness in a dedicated gesture of exploration, a heroic quest that proves to be inward drive as the character seeks to define the self against the cosmos. Each in turn receives a slender gesture of illumination, a devastating moment of intensity that is left inaccessible to the reader.

Because these characters leave no legacy, indeed can find no convenient way even to express their certainty, White moved into a cycle of three novels specifically about articulation, *künstellromans* where the visionary figure is a misfit-artist who wrestles with expression. These include Alf Dubbo (*Riders in the Chariot*, 1961), Arthur Brown (*The Solid Mandala*, 1966), and Hurtle Duffield (*The Vivisector*, 1970). Compelled by the dynamic kinetics of the imagination, their eyes open to the complex weave of joy and suffering that makes up contemporary life, they respond by capturing that difficult certainty within forms that satisfy their own unerring sensibility for honesty and beauty, be it visual (brutal, primitive canvases), verbal (unpolished poems or unfinishable novels), or nonverbal (an impromptu dance).

Yet the dilemma is clear—these visionary-artists suffer in comfortless obscurity or forbidding isolation, their best work satisfying their own instincts for aesthetic expression but left unavailable to any larger community. Such resolution clearly does not satisfy White. It was perhaps inevitable that even as White himself emerged into international prominence and came to understand the reach of the contemporary artist, in the closing phase of three novels White introduced his visionary characters to the difficult responsibilities of communication. Elizabeth Hunter (*The Eye of the Storm*, 1973), Ellen Gluyas Roxburgh (*A Fringe of Leaves*, 1976), and Eddie Twyborn (*The Twyborn Affair*, 1979) struggle not merely to come to terms with the complicated certainties they have been gifted to experience but rather how to share with significant others if not the substance

of that vision then the compelling compassion generated by such a generous illumination. This struggle for placement within the social matrices—friendship, marriage, family—offers a difficult exuberance as each character engages the imperfect negotiations of the heart in honest gestures of need.

BIOGRAPHY: EXPLORATION TO ARTICULATION TO COMMUNICATION

White's own biography follows a track remarkably similar to this narrative patterning, beginning with an early period of restless exploration (and inevitable isolation). Then came an intense period of articulation, a commitment to furious productivity (and cantankerous reclusiveness). Finally there was a closing period of communication, an acceptance of the responsibilities of assuming abroad a place in the world community of letters as a Nobel laureate and at home becoming a voice in controversial causes that included resistance to the Australian involvement in the Vietnam War and support for gay rights, environmental politics, and nuclear disarmament.

Although born into a wealthy fourth-generation Australian farming family from New South Wales (with a land empire of more than 100,000 acres), White chanced to be born in London, 28 May 1912, while his parents were enjoying a two-year tour of Europe and the Middle East to celebrate their marriage. The family returned to Sydney when White was six months old. A delicate child plagued by asthma and raised more by servants than his parents, White retreated into the protective shelter of reading (his favorites included *The Secret Garden* and *The Swiss Family Robinson*). His precocious intelligence isolated him at boarding school. Fearing Australian schooling would prove insufficient for such a promising child, his parents sent White in 1925 to England's prestigious Cheltenham College, which White himself found comfortless and alienating. A pale and wheezy child, White made few friends among the children of the British aristocracy in part because of his Australian background. He did begin to write, producing by age fourteen his first "novel" as well as several blank-verse melodramas. During his five years in Cheltenham, he would come to terms with his homosexuality, which, although it did not alarm him (he believed it granted him a complex masculine/feminine sensibility), did compel him into a deeper isolation. In 1930, White, long enamored by the pageantry of acting and the way it rendered identity itself as irrelevant, told his parents he had decided to pursue acting. They suggested, however, that he first return to Australia and work as a jackeroo (a farmhand) on his uncle's sheep ranch in the remote Snowy Mountains of New South Wales.

Although outdoor labor improved his health, White was unable to adjust to feelings of estrangement from his Australian roots and could not entirely remove himself from his love of writing, at night scribbling drafts of novels by lantern. He returned to England in 1932 to pursue graduate studies in modern languages at King's College, Cambridge. For five years, with his parents' financial support, White embraced the life of a bohemian dandy, writing unstaged comedies and publishing (with his mother's backing) a collection of derivative poems that recalled the overdrawn angst of Edwardians such as A. E. Housman. In addition, he completed two apprentice novels: *Happy Valley* (1939) and *The Living and the Dead* (1941). Because White learned how to write novels by reading them, these early works reveal his fascination for the techniques and themes of modernism, specifically the nonlinear narratives and stream of consciousness technique of Virginia Woolf and James Joyce; the shifting, multiple narrative perspectives of William Faulkner; the forbidding sense of Western civilization as unredeemable wasteland from T. S. Eliot; and the belief in nature as the sole ignition site for passion, the disdain for dry intellectualism, and the romance of the working class from D. H. Lawrence. But

by the end of the 1930s modernism had lost its cultural cachet, and these early works, although they received sympathetic reviews, seem today borrowed and tentative. *Happy Valley,* an unsympathetic look at an isolated Australian mountain town, is a melodrama about an adulterous affair between a town doctor and a piano teacher in which the couple opts ultimately to forsake their passion and return to the banality and malignant sterility of their small town life. *The Living and the Dead,* rushed into print because of the onset of World War II, anatomizes the spiritual aridity of the contemporary London literary community by tracking the evolution into passion of a Prufrockian central character, an intellectual writer (the titular dead) who disdains complicated entanglements but who comes to learn the meaning of passionate engagement when his own free-spirited sister (the titular living) bravely follows her dead lover to Spain to take up the cause of the freedom fighters in that civil war.

Setting aside his writing ambitions to serve a four-year stint in the Royal Air Force Intelligence, much of it in the Middle East and the deserts of western Africa, White, amid the inevitable boredom, spent his time reading, discovering the spiritual angst of Dostoevsky and rediscovering the rich satires of Dickens. In 1946, emotionally soured by war, White returned to London but felt estranged from its cultural scene. He decided to return to Australia. Years later, he would explain how he responded to the deep pull of his continent's vastness, its sheer emptiness—both geographically and culturally. He settled in the relative seclusion of a six-acre farm outside Sydney with Manoly Lascaris, a Greek officer he had met in 1941 and with whom he had maintained a passionate epistolary relationship during the war. Lascaris would center White's emotional life for nearly fifty years. After several years spent adapting to the rigors of farming (including an epiphanic moment during a heavy rainstorm when, after falling into a massive puddle while trying to feed his menagerie of kenneled dogs, he embraced a belief in an unnamable divine influence), a reinvigorated White returned to writing.

Past forty, he began a remarkably productive twenty-year period. Never enjoying the writing task (comparing it to a difficult bowel movement), scribbling his massive manuscript drafts in longhand, White was prone to depression and tantrums. But by the mid-1960s his work had secured an international readership, although the critical reception in his native Australia was always qualified largely because White so caustically satirized its suburban culture and because his religious dimension so completely challenged the form that had long defined Australian serious fiction, the realistic novel, with its plainsong prose and stubbornly horizontal reach. Here were dense character studies of unapologetically vast scope, compelled by a suggestive weave of symbols (usually colors, birds, flowers, fire, or weather) and executed with a demanding, near-poetic prose line. Internationally his novels became anticipated publishing events, although the intensely private White never pursued his celebrity, forswearing interviews, regularly turning down speaking engagements, honorary degrees, and even prestigious awards. When, after years of being short-listed for the Nobel, he received the 1973 award, the first time it had been given to a postcolonial English language writer, White himself opted not to attend the Stockholm ceremony.

But clearly he felt the weight of this international recognition, and the last decade of White's life was defined by his decision to involve himself in the political and cultural life of his country, moderating his reputation for fearsome irascibility and forsaking his inclination for privacy to participate in political rallies, appear on television, and even give speeches in support of controversial issues including the banning of nuclear weapons, contested political races, aboriginal rights, and pressing environmental causes. In addition, he returned to the public arena of the theater. The novels of this time are themselves more reader friendly, their prose less studied, their plots better choreographed, and their endings unironically affirmative. Long believing in the essential absence of the writer from his work and long refraining from lengthy commentary about his own work, White published *The Twyborn Affair,* his first novel centered on a gay character, and in 1981 a quasi-autobiographical work, *Flaws in the Glass,* the title drawn from his strategy to concentrate on his character flaws, including his trenchant honesty, his abiding anger at his parents, and his own social awkwardness. In 1986 he published *Memoirs of Many in One,* a misguided attempt at the overdone writer-writing-a-biography-of-a-fictional-writer genre pioneered by midcentury postmodernists but a valedictory work that nevertheless provided insight into the private life of a writer who, at career's end, saw that his own identity had been fragmented into the characters he had created and that his own self had become a studied performance. By the mid-1980s, his health failing, White accepted being Patrick White, Institution, the international face of Australian culture, even participating publicly in what he sniffed was his country's garish 1988 Bicentennial celebration. Two years later, on 30 September 1990, White died of pulmonary failure. Typically, he instructed that the announcement of his death was to be made only after his ashes had been scattered in a Sydney park he loved.

NARRATIVES OF EXPLORATION

At midlife, after a grim adulthood of commonplace sacrifice tending to a tyrannical bedridden mother who has finally died, Theodora Goodman (*The Aunt's Story*), unmarried and childless, finds herself suddenly free. Since lightning had struck an oak near her when she was twelve, Theodora had yearned for a similarly galvanizing moment when the "opaque world [would] become transparent" (p. 56). She resisted the Christian God as too simple. Ever curious, gifted with a keen eye and a generous understanding, stirred enormously by the cutting depth of music and the outdoors, she grew up a misfit, boyish and homely particularly when set against her younger sister, upon whom her mother lavished affection. After the father's death, the family relocated to suburban Sydney. Because her sister had married, care of the invalid mother fell to Theodora for more than ten years. With her death, Theodora finds herself able to begin what will become the signature quest of White's visionaries: to defeat the self by achieving a moment of clarity that will turn it into a transcendental state "like air or water" (p. 122).

Theodora's journey begins with a densely woven first section, a stream-of-consciousness exercise as Theodora's sister and her family gather for the mother's funeral and Theodora recalls for her beloved niece the defining moments of her childhood. The section closes with Theodora's decision to travel; she is determined to discover the mystery of being after a lifetime of doing. Part 2 is an expressionist tour de force as Theodora (apparently) travels to a Riviera hotel and there (apparently) converses with longtime hotel residents that include decadent roués, selfish expatriates, and contentious wealthy socialites. But as the section unfolds, the conversations become disjointed and inexplicably hostile and the situations more bizarre (spinning into imagistic dream sequences), and Theodora herself begins to take on the role of a relative of these guests. The reader begins to suspect that the entire hotel may be a projection of Theodora's fragmented self after the liberation trauma of her mother's death. Given the section's movement toward destruction (a massive fire kills most of the guests), the section becomes a disturbing record of Theodora's careen toward borderline psychosis as she begins to lose her core self. Freedom and self-exploration here are done at great peril. Such complex interior fragility is suggested by the section's controlling image, a curled nautilus shell that belongs to one of the "guests" and that Theodora accidentally shatters.

In part 3, Theodora finds herself in a "New World," traveling by train across the American West. After disembarking at a remote New Mexico outpost, she makes her way on foot to an abandoned house in the mountains, along the way dropping her traveling documents and identity papers. Stripped of her self, she encounters the mysterious Holstius (most likely another projection—as indeed the entire western jaunt may be) who rebukes Theodora for simplifying reality and counsels her to live within the tension between joy and suffering (to accept the "grub at the heart of the rose"), to accept flux and dispense with the rage to understand in order to embrace the full range of existence ("there is sometimes little to choose between the reality of illusion and the illusion of reality," p. 272). Gifted by such a healing message, her essential self recovered, Theodora returns to civilization now radically unfit to participate in its stultifying charades. Unable to communicate the strange splendor of Holstius's message, she accepts as inevitable commitment to an asylum at the hands of well-meaning strangers.

Like Theodora Goodman, Stan Parker is compelled by the mystery of the natural vastness around him. The core narrative of *The Tree of Man* gets its epic feel from this simple pioneer Everyman and his heroic fifty-year struggle to wrest a farm from the forbidding bush country outside Sydney in the late nineteenth century. Even as he endures the roiling unpredictability of storms, floods, bush fires, and droughts and the grinding misfortunes common to outback farm life, he anticipates verification of cosmic design, despite the oppressive evidence of brutality and chaos. Although he lacks the formal education to articulate this longing, he cannot accept the passionless tidiness of Christianity. Unlike *The Aunt's Story*, here White maintains a scrupulous distance from his central character's interior and narrates rather with the omniscient feel of a nineteenth-century historic novel. We know that Stan is haunted by a glimpse of an old man, drowned during a raging flood, hanging upside down from a tree, a grotesque symbol of humanity's absurdity and evident pointlessness. He is haunted as well by the persistent discontent of his wife, who, greedy for romance, hungry for material comforts difficult to attain on the farm, and unable to handle the loneliness of prairie life, dreams of adventure and ultimately takes as lover a traveling salesman.

After a stint in World War I convinces him of a universe out of moral control and of the irrelevancy of the Christian God, Stan struggles to come to terms with his spiritual anxieties. He tries to be content with family (not only his wife but both his children prove disappointing—his daughter marries a lawyer and embraces materialism, his son turns to petty crime and dies violently); he struggles to write poems; he attends *Hamlet* during a visit to Sydney and responds to the angst of the title character; he even contemplates the hard logic of suicide. Only as he nears death (and his beloved natural world begins to feel the cold intrusion of developers) does he finally, unexpectedly, intuit (appropriately in his own garden) the abiding unity of the cosmos, the presence enough of what humanity calls, for lack of a better term, God: "One, and no other figure, is the answer to all sums" (p. 497). This summary—if cryptic—revelation recalls Holstius's dictum to Theodora to accept the unity of joy and suffering. Here, after a lifetime of being rocked by the unpredictable, an aged Stan dies savaged/salvaged by a stunning assurance of cosmic harmony that beggars language. (White as authorial voice-over actually relates the essence of the vision second-hand.) Hardly the sort of towering figure traditionally gifted with such visionary moments, Stan testifies to White's conviction that the extraordinary can touch the ordinary. (Stan is most often identified simply as "the man.") Of course, Stan's illumination dies with him, his "greatness" still a "secret" (p. 499). White offers

the slenderest hope in a two-page coda in which Stan's young grandson, in the same garden the day of Stan's funeral, vows someday to write an epic poem about "all life," about people who, upon waking up, "feel for their money and their teeth," a poem that would smell of "bread and kumquats," in short a work that would (like *The Tree of Man*) sort through the massive evidence of the prosaic to recover its poetry, the hope that "in the end, there was no end" (p. 499).

Against Stan Parker's unprepossessing Everyman, Johann Voss thunders into his narrative as a sort of Everygod, a Nietzschean *Übermensch*, a romantic nineteenth century–era explorer whose grand-opera ambition (the book was later the subject of operatic treatment) is to lead a small, hand-picked team of inexperienced volunteers across the vast empty heart of the unexplored Australian continent, a premise based on an actual ill-fated 1845 expedition. It is the very impossibility of the enterprise that creates about the striking figure of Voss a heroic futility. Rootless (he is a German immigrant, a lineage suggesting for White a passion for order and a Faustian rage for knowledge), Voss is proud, defiantly unconventional, unkempt, and supremely willful. He is a megalomaniac (White drew on his own wartime assessment of Hitler) who believes that the future is what the individual fashions, exhorting his anxious men as they move beyond the settled fringes of the coast that ambition cannot be diminished by faint heart, that the single willful man is God enough and death itself a petty fear of the timid.

Of course, White will not brook such unbound egoism. The journey into the Australian wastes becomes an allegorical trip inward as Voss must endure hardships—exhaustion, brutal heat, starvation, fever—even as he comes to terms with the limits of his presumed self-sufficiency. Helping in that difficult enterprise is Laura Trevelyan, the orphaned niece of the wealthy Sydney merchant who sponsors the Voss expedition. Unlike the coarse Voss, Laura is the epitome of High Victorian upbringing, well read and well mannered.

Nevertheless, they share kindred spirits: both are unconventional, proud, willful. Laura scandalously insists on helping a pregnant, unwed maid (indeed, she adopts the baby when the mother dies in childbirth); she cannot endorse her family's Christianity; and she rejects the inevitability of marriage. In the alternating chapters devoted to Laura, White fashions a droll Dickensian comedy of manners that lampoons the moral hypocrisies of Australia's nascent middle class.

Despite meeting only briefly before Voss departs, Voss and Laura exchange passionate letters that create an unconventional bond not defined (thus not limited) by fleshly expression. It is a compelling intensity achieved without touching, a telepathic intimacy measured by the paradoxical nearness of distance. We share the letters but they are merely words—the sustaining emotional register is left inaccessible to the reader. But it sustains Voss as he moves his grumbling team into the unexplored reaches of the deserts where, Ahab-like, he pushes them beyond their endurance (several are killed, one commits suicide) until his party begins to fragment into alliances, including several pragmatic followers who abandon the expedition after encountering aborigines. Voss himself moves toward a catastrophic encounter with the aborigines that will threaten not only his expedition but his life—even as his soul mate Laura in distant Sydney suddenly falls to brain fever. After Voss studies crude cave paintings and tracks the magnificent night-sweep of a comet, he begins to fathom the magnitude of the natural world. Shortly before his death—he is brutally decapitated and then cannibalized—Voss, "reduced to the bones of manhood" (p. 384), chances to see the Southern Cross in the night sky and experiences his epiphany: he concedes his vulnerability, accepts limits to his ego, and regrets the pain he has caused in this doomed exercise of his grotesque pride.

Yet such wisdom threatens to die with the visionary, much as it did with Stan Parker and Theodora Goodman. Across the continent, at the very moment of the decapitation, the life-threatening brain fever that had gripped Laura for days suddenly, inexplicably breaks. Even as the doctors fuss about her with leeches, Laura cryptically says, "When man is truly humbled, when he has learned that he is not God, then he is nearest to becoming so" (p. 381)—the very revelation Voss at death accepts, a sort of telepathic redemption. But Laura ultimately simplifies Voss's paradoxical legacy. Voss's fate is never determined, and Laura simply retreats: she never marries, rejecting the complications of entanglements; she teaches at a girls' school and raises her adopted daughter (allegorically named Mercy) within its protective sanctuary. Voss himself lingers as mystery. The head of an expedition that tries (unsuccessfully) to locate Voss's remains struggles to solicit some sense of him from Laura, who points out she had met Voss only briefly. When the town erects a statue in honor of Voss, Laura chances to meet at the ceremony one of the mates who had abandoned Voss and who now struggles awkwardly to recount the expedition's story. The dull-witted town of course canonizes in bronze only the simplest reading of Voss—the accessible myth of his vaunting ambition. The far more difficult reality of his visionary experience is left simplified by Laura ("If he was composed of evil along with the good, he struggled with that evil," p. 438) and grasped only imperfectly by White's reader. As with the other visionaries in this initial phase, Voss stays apart, his redemption a closed drama.

NARRATIVES OF ARTICULATION

In the epigraph to *Riders in the Chariot*, the prophet Isaiah (as rendered by William Blake) argues, "I saw no God, nor heard any, in a finite organical perception; but my senses discover'd the infinite in everything. . . . I cared not for consequences, but wrote." Such ambition summarizes the three landmark novels that comprise White's middle phase, each a complex narrative of articulation. The epigraph itself confronts the need to satisfy the stunning burn of the visionary experience by pressing it into form. In this middle phase, White explores the artist as seer: amid the complacency of contemporary suburbia the artist possesses the sensitivity tuned to spiritual illumination. With the half-caste painter Alf Dubbo, the mentally challenged poet Arthur Brown, and the internationally renowned painter Hurtle Duffield, White will anatomize the artist-visionary who accepts the challenge of capturing the lightning strike of the epiphany into a sustaining artifact of expression.

At different moments in their lives, the identical vision is shared by four misfits of contemporary Australia. One is an eccentric elderly spinster who lives in decadent isolation in her family's mansion-in-ruins (Mary Hare). Another is a former university professor and Jewish immigrant who escaped the Holocaust and who, as atonement after he fails to save his wife from the Nazis, works as a laborer in a factory, where he endures the bigotry of his coworkers (Mordecai Himmelfarb). The third is a good-hearted if impoverished mother of six, a British immigrant, who slaves as a laundress (Ruth Godbold). And last is a consumptive half-breed painter, an uncompromising artist who conjures wildly primitive religious canvases (Alf Dubbo). Their nearly identical vision is of the fiery chariot with four living creatures as recorded in the Old Testament prophetic book of Ezekiel, an iconic symbol of God's glorious protection of the visionaries who must nevertheless contend with life among the unenlightened. Stage managing the quartet so that their lives touch at unexpected moments, White gives each central character a defining trait. Mary Hare, given to strolling in her estate gardens and entangling herself (literally) in its unkempt underbrush, represents the untutored instinct, specifically a deep pantheism (her vision occurs during a magnificent sunset) and the sheer (if lonely) joy of sensation and touch. Mordecai Himmelfarb, who studies arcane Jewish mysticism and thrives in the university environment (his vision occurs while he peruses a description

of the chariot), represents the intellect. Ruth Godbold, the saintly washerwoman who serves her life within an unhappy marriage and with thankless children and who finds satisfaction for such quiet desperation within the conventional wisdom of her evangelical Christianity, represents the heart (her vision occurs during a hymn while at church).

Each response to the visionary experience, however, falls decidedly short. Too enamored by the wilds, Mrs. Hare has little use for people and, when tested, has no vocabulary for evil. In her self-enclosed naïveté, she hires as maid an unsavory woman who is suspected of murdering her husband and whose bastard son is the leader of the vicious thugs at the factory who lynch Himmelfarb as a gruesome prank. After witnessing that torture, Mary simply wanders away, lost and unreachable. Himmelfarb himself believes he can redeem lost souls by passive endurance of the excessive bigotry around him, including submitting to the mock-crucifixion. Given such an unyielding messianic self-conception, he ends up hurting others (his efforts to get the factory boss to acknowledge his Jewishness drives the man ultimately to suicide), and he loses even the opportunity to remedy the suffering of his wife and family, as he acknowledges as he lays dying after a house fire. Ruth Godbold's need to be needed leads only to difficult enslavement to a reprobate husband who cannot handle his wife's insatiable need to forgive and whose death leaves her responsible for a family she cannot support. Her unshakable and unexamined religious convictions (suggested by her name, heavy-handed to the point of ironic) lead her to interfere in others' lives, including trailing her husband to a brothel, making a misguided attempt to convert Himmelfarb, and ultimately burying him in Christian ground.

It is the artist Alf Dubbo who emerges, with the gift of the imagination, as valid heroic center. Art—not illumination—is here the reliable vehicle for redemption. Irredeemably alone, infected with syphilis, living in slum conditions, caught between cultural identities, Dubbo works as custodian at the factory. His spare time is devoted to creating whirling canvases of unleashed energy based on religious themes whose bold clashing colors suggest the tension between certainty and doubt. Can the infinite be expressed in pigment? In the factory washroom Dubbo reads Ezekiel to prepare for a canvas based on a vision he had had while studying a museum painting of the chariot. But his dedication to art costs him the easy touch of friendship. He cannot bring himself to intercede on behalf of Himmelfarb the afternoon of his crucifixion, although he will ultimately convert that angst into a powerful canvas with Himmelfarb as the crucified Christ. Dubbo's abuse as a child at the hands of an Anglican priest who was his caregiver compels him to equate love with the sterile frictions of lust. He is dedicated only to his art. In the end, driven by Himmelfarb's torture and his own sense of impending death, Dubbo completes his most compelling canvas, a re-creation of Ezekiel's chariot. This marks a first in the White canon: rendering the visionary experience within a form. And given that the novel actually closes with Ruth Godbold's more traditional illumination (after her husband's death, she is gifted—not surprisingly—in her church), the reader of White's larger canon recognizes that Ruth's is yet another vision doomed to kindle only the individual but lost to any larger communion. Vivified by her vision, Ruth tidily consigns her three lost friends to her Christian heaven—an unconvincing and blindly sectarian gesture given their eccentric lifestyles. It is Alf Dubbo's savage painting that suggests genuine generosity by endowing the tectonic moment of the visionary with imperfect realization. White acknowledges that the artist suffers to touch the infinite within (the dying Dubbo spits up blood that mixes with the paint), that the artist is compelled by inexplicable certainties and must perforce exist along the margins of society. Art here is an infinitely complicated if closed circuit; the vision recovered in form is the sole beauty in a repugnant material world.

What, then, makes a successful artist? When Waldo Brown (*The Solid Mandala*) is still a boy, he presumes to write a tragedy drawn from his ambitious reading regimen. It is a predictably derivative production about gods and kings, full of carefully fashioned lines but without heart, coldly executed for effect and compelled by the absurd ambition of this joyless, lonely boy to be taken seriously as a genius. When his half-wit twin brother, Arthur, in emulation, writes his own tragedy, his, set in a stumbling meter, is about a cow who adjusts to the loss of her calf by realizing that she can have others. It is a delightfully sensitive, deceptively simple affirmation of life, an intuitive, untutored endorsement of the difficult adjustments necessary in a world subject to the cutting intrusion of mortality, an inchoate vision open despite his tender age to the healing power of the natural world, a vision entirely opposite his precocious brother. White uses the device of these twins to explore the necessary halves of the artist: the soul, intuitive and emotional; and the mind, analytical and distant.

Each brother is given a section of the novel, each of which is rendered in the phrasing and cadences appropriate to that brother and each reviewing the same life events from different perspectives through the vehicle of flashbacks. Waldo has grown up to be a librarian who toils away on an unfinishable novel and who produces arid monographs about obscure writers, a gloomy self-loathing intellectual whose keen mind is uncomplicated by emotions and who thus maintains careful distance from any awkward entanglements. Arthur, on the other hand, has worked contentedly in a grocery store, a friend to his neighbors, a lover of music and sunsets, an inspiration to those who fall under his gentle spirit. He loves his aloof twin and struggles to find a way to connect. He collects beautiful marbles but gives away the most precious ones, his solid mandalas, as gifts. (Waldo, predictably, rejects his.) When he feels the deep intuitive glimpse of a compelling unity to the apparent chaos so typical of White's visionary (here White draws on the mandala figure, the square within the circle, to suggest the imposition of perfect order on chaos), Arthur, too mentally challenged to follow the discipline and structure of form and too hampered by a stammer that makes articulation difficult, gives over to a spontaneous dance "half clumsy, half electric" (p. 256). The dance is immodest in its extravagance, yet it weaves a story of his brother and their lives, carefully patterned to render a tight, visible form; it is a joy beyond words, a visual epiphany.

Within the narrative present, Waldo, now an old man, lives with his "dill" (slang for someone slow-witted) brother, seeing him as his lifelong sacrifice. Together they care for a houseful of dogs and lead what is on the surface a quiet life in suburban Sydney. But as White explores Waldo's haunted interior, the reader glimpses Waldo's frustrations. (Uncertain of his sexuality and rejected by the only woman who ever interested him, he finds odd comfort in wearing his dead mother's dresses.) At every turn he has found his mentally damaged brother more generously accepted, more finely in tune with the spiritual (when he happens upon an unkempt Arthur in the library reading Dostoevsky, he calmly asks him to please leave the library and adds "sir" to complete the insult) and more in sync even with the creative urge that Waldo believes is his special province as self-described genius. Despite reams of a pretentious novel-in-progress, Waldo finds in a simple poem his brother shows him an essential wisdom—how living is an excruciating choreography of joy and suffering—that has escaped his massive assaults of language. The poem reads in part, "all Marys in the end bleed / . . . they know they cannot have it any other way" (p. 284). Waldo reacts to this evidence of his brother's finer soul with violence. He burns his considerable pile of manuscripts and then, his long-simmering hate of his brother finally boiling, attacks the stunned Arthur. The physically imposing Arthur easily fends off the attack but ends up accidentally killing the fragile Waldo, which drives the sensitive brother into raging grief. He flees, abandoning his dead brother in their home. After several days, neighbors break in and discover the ravenous dogs have begun to feed off the corpse. When Arthur is later apprehended, his fullest self now lost with the death of his brother, he accepts as inevitable confinement within an asylum.

Ironically, given that White himself had been writing since the age of nine, the artist figure in his work thus far is not particularly attractive: one artist dead, the other confined among the lunatics. It would take White's landmark closing work of this second phase, *The Vivisector,* to affirm the detached artist with that fiery energy of the visionary imagination. At least initially, Hurtle Duffield promises little: he is gifted with the fine-tuned sensibility of the artist-visionary, alert even as a child to the aesthetic pleasure within the colors, forms, and textures of the visible environment. But his Australian working-class parents actually sell him to a rich British family that purchases the precocious child to compensate for having only a crippled, hunchbacked daughter. Naturally Duffield grows up suspicious of trust and prefers isolation and honest (to the point of heartless) observation. He comes to compare the artist to a vivisectionist after he sees in a London window display an example of that grim medical practice: a small stuffed dog writhing in agony as it is being studied "alive" under the dissecting knife of the vivisectionist. Brutalized by a lonely childhood, he comes to believe that art must cut unapologetically to the core of reality (for instance, in one defining series, he converts his deformed sister, naked, into a grotesque pythoness).

Not surprisingly, his violent paintings stun and shock the polite art community in Sydney, and he becomes a cause célèbre. The prostitute Nance Lightfoot, with whom he shares a stormy relationship in his struggling bohemian years, is for him more a study in the vitality of flesh (their lovemaking is coarse and violent), her mammoth body a complex of space, lines, and color that he ruthlessly exploits in his art despite her evident love for him. His studied indifference drives her to death among the rocks below a cliff near their tenement; Duffield is never sure if it is a suicide or an accident.

As his reputation grows and his paintings become more haunted (in one series, a generous moon defecates on lovers), Duffield, with evident disdain for his wealthy patrons, lives in stark simplicity, reveling in the smell of his own unwashed body. He loves only his art, the very feel of pressed paint itself. He will endure three relationships, each time resisting emotional involvement: the first with a childhood friend who is now a sexually frigid socialite and art collector; another with the wife of a wealthy Greek who, despite her transcendent beauty and spiritual nature (she conducts Duffield on a spiritual pilgrimage to a temple on a remote Greek island), reveals a lust for kinky physical love; and the third with a promising adolescent pianist who uses Duffield (both as lover and as mentor) and then casually abandons him to pursue her own burgeoning career. The only life he comes to recognize as "practical was the one lived inside his head" (p. 356).

Late in life, as he prepares for a grand retrospective, Duffield chances to be reunited with his estranged stepsister, who renounced her family fortune to live on the streets of Sydney and tend to half-starved alley cats. It is only now, ironically late in a successful career, that he undergoes the striking epiphany that finally ennobles his position as artist and leads him to a far deeper understanding of the artistic process, even as he is recovering from a stroke that has forced him, symbolically, to learn anew how to hold a paintbrush. He now knows that art must involve not only frank observation but compassion; the artist can never assume that truth is consistent and definable (suggested by Duffield's inability to speak following his stroke); at its core, reality discloses that beauty and ugliness are complementary elements of a harmonic whole (his deformed sister is the vehicle for this epiphany); and the ordinary can disclose the essence of beauty (he is moved inexplicably by the divinity of a simple hen he sees while in Greece).

Feverishly embracing now the possibility of God in all things (never articulated but rather suggested by his embrace of the color indigo), Duffield boldly commences a projected series of sumptuous indigo canvases. He is only beginning the series when a second stroke kills him, White's suggestion that this privileged insight of the artist must ultimately remain elusive. In the closing page of the novel, as the stroke completes its work language itself collapses into cryptic fragments, ambiguous bits straining without success after clarity. Fitting in this summary work of this second phase, the artist alone (like the visionaries in the first phase) realizes the urgent redemption of the visionary experience.

NARRATIVES OF COMMUNICATION

Elizabeth Hunter and her grown children (*The Eye of the Storm*) surely epitomize what an earlier White would have relished lampooning. She is an aged, wealthy invalid, a widow who, with rapier wit, brutalizes the nurses who tend her and dominates her children, who now have reluctantly flown home to Sydney for their mother's deathwatch. One, a rapacious daughter, is a frigid, nervous woman recently divorced after a loveless marriage to a sleazy French faux prince; the other, a pretentious son, is a knighted Shakespearean actor who has lost his stage touch and is now so distanced from his own identity that he is terrified by an offer to perform in an unscripted avant-garde production where each night he would simply have to be himself. Together the vindictive siblings scheme to commit their dying mother to a nursing home in order to tap into her estate, payback for what they both feel was a loveless childhood (*Lear* provides a subtext). As their mother lingers apparently just to spite them, brother and sister make a sentimental visit to their childhood country home and share a shocking incestuous night in their parents' old bed.

The Hunters promise little redemption—all of them thorough materialists who relish the ostentation of privilege, vulgar egoists, wrecked sensualists with bottomless cravings for more, irredeemable victims of the grasping horizontal mind-set, careless in their affections and destructive in their predatory sexual hunger. (Elizabeth, a striking beauty whose smoldering sexuality caused considerable friction with her much plainer daughter, recalls one of her many affairs, one with the family's lawyer, a man whose doltish wife Elizabeth delights in tormenting with innuendo, even as the wife lies dying.) Told through the vehicle of Elizabeth's recollections as triggered by chance remarks by those who attend her (thus her deathbed itself becomes something of the eye of a storm), the narrative is a harrowing look at the loveless emptiness of the contemporary world.

Except that Elizabeth has begun to understand the pressure mortality can exert—White is unsettlingly graphic in recording the physical indignities of her deathwatch. Unlike White's previous visionaries whose epiphanies came either moments before death or within a context that inevitably left them as outcasts, Elizabeth Hunter experienced her moment of stillness sixteen years earlier. During a ravaging cyclone, as the eye of the storm raked Brumby Island where she had been left (she had interfered with her daughter's flirtation with a handsome biologist), she tapped into that familiar vulnerability when White's characters pass beyond the reach of the immediate and the frets over the particle "I" and realize a universal webbing that magnifies the self even as that self is significantly diminished. But that vision never altered Elizabeth's life. Ironically now nearly blind, Elizabeth strives to re-vision that threshold moment, struggling to reclaim that humbling sense of the "I" at the very moment of its most profound vulnerability.

That such a determined drama of self-definition (Elizabeth's recollections evidence a formidable mind that remains alert) must be played against the shallow machinations of her duplicitous children (and against a disturbing subplot in which one of the nurses connives to have a child with Elizabeth's son as a way to avoid the inevitability of marriage to her dreary boyfriend) secures Elizabeth Hunter's position as the novel's viable, if imperfect, moral center. Confronting her discontent over a life spent attending to the carnal, Elizabeth closes her life in dramatic gifts of generosity. First she bestows expensive jewelry on her long-suffering nurses. Then, recognizing that her children want her dead, she pretties herself, dons makeup and wig, and simply wills herself to die as she attends to her morning bowel movement—a grand absurd gesture, at once humbling and transcendent, that vividly binds the crude flesh and the soaring spirit as she feels herself released into "endlessness" (p. 551). It is a sensibility lost on her children, who depart Sydney even before her funeral, never acknowledging any spiritual depth to their mother.

We are back within the familiar dilemma: gifted by insight, the visionary cannot find a way to share that certainty. But in this last phase White reveals an unexpected gesture of community, of outreach. White traces Elizabeth's unexpected influence over her compassionate night nurse, Mary de Santis. Mary, herself a plain middle-age spinster and grounded in her Greek Orthodox faith, selflessly assists the belligerent Elizabeth, certain that Elizabeth's is a soul in need of reclamation. Initially shattered by Elizabeth's death, as she is leaving the mansion days after the funeral to begin her work with a new patient (a paralyzed girl), she stops to feed pigeons at dawn in the mansion's courtyard and suddenly gains a striking validation, a vision amid the breaking light of day of the pain and beauty of the flesh/spirit, "herself possessed" (p. 608). Thus for the first time in White's fiction, visionary affirmation occurs within an accidental conspiracy (unlike Voss and Laura) sustained by authentic interaction, reassuring despite its evident fragility. Indeed, Mary's jewelry from the dying Elizabeth bears the image of a phoenix, suggesting perpetual renewal, and Mary promises to bring this sense of possibility to her new patient. It is the sort of love that amid the perversions, emotional terrorism, and casual betrayals White so mercilessly records promises an authentic sharing of grace, stranger to stranger.

In his two closing narratives, however, White moves his characters toward understanding without the visionary moment itself. They are novels in which the religious implosions that had defined his characters' reclamation adapt to a secular world. Ellen Roxburgh and Eddie Twyborn evolve toward reclamation through a process of education and hence provide telling closure to White's canon by introducing the possibility that redemption, long the province of the privileged few, might extend to the ordinary as characters discover that the heart itself can disclose what initially the soul and then the imagination had sought. Thus the novels are White's most celebratory, save that this fragile process of education occurs within a decaying cultural context that White still defines as irredeemably hostile to reclamation.

In *A Fringe of Leaves,* rendered in a pitch-perfect High Victorian diction that recalls the nineteenth-century novel of manners of Jane Austen and George Eliot, Ellen Roxburgh, a vibrant Cornish farmgirl with a natural love of the land (suggested by her vivid green shawl and her love of horses), is married off disastrously to a sallow-faced scholar nearly twice her age. The marriage is a polite arrangement, but Ellen has to make the transition from the moors and play lady of the mansion and dutiful wife. When the couple spends a year in the harsh wilds of Tasmania, she is seduced by and seduces her darkly mysterious brother-in-law, a miscreant who had immigrated to Tasmania just steps ahead of the law. That passionate affair begins what will prove to be Ellen's difficult education into the complex circuitry of the heart (she is pregnant when she leaves Tasmania). It is a movement toward a self she has never been permitted to explore although she has long kept a journal to testify to her hunger for explora-

tion, an education that will lead to a radical acceptance of the heart that is at once foul and aggressively carnal and yet profoundly spiritual and capable of transcendence.

As with all White's central characters, Ellen has lived in the expectation of touching some deeper reality than what her life has presented (as a child she was fascinated more by the devil than God). The title itself is a metaphor for the thin veil of civilization that masks the darker realities of humanity's unregenerate nature, the artifices of civilization here represented by the dry rituals of the church, the hypocritical justice system that creates the brutal Tasmanian prisons, the repressive institution of marriage driven largely by economic considerations, and the Enlightenment pretense to decode the heart into absolutes of good and evil. When the ship returning Ellen and her husband to England founders on a reef during a heavy fog, they begin a difficult four-day drift in open longboats before landing on a nameless island. Convinced their only hope is to return to the sea, they re-board the longboats and return to the open ocean (Ellen miscarries during this long drift). When they land again, Ellen is abducted by an aboriginal tribe after her husband takes a spear in the neck when he attempts to minister to a wounded comrade.

At the mercy of these primitives, Ellen comes to understand, even as she strips away the polite assumptions of her civilized nature and abandons her faith in a protective God, the raw power of the flesh; the simpatico possible if the heart communes with the telluric energies of the wilds; the inexplicable possibilities of magic; and the difficult absolute of death itself. She must overcome her initial repulsion over the primitive practices of her captors and her misdirected pity for their presumed backwardness. As she endures indignities—taunted, prodded, stripped, her hair crudely hacked off at the roots by a seashell, her skin blackened with mud and feces, forced to hunt small game and then eat their glutinous, half-roasted carcasses—Ellen gains insight ultimately into the shallowness of civilization and her own hypocrisies and gradually accepts a humbler reconstruction of her ego as she moves toward a sense of union with the sensual world represented by the tribal life itself. Her education closes in a shattering moment in which she engages in a cannibal ritual that she views as both ghastly ritual and "sacrament" (p. 272).

She is ultimately assisted in securing her freedom by the efforts of a renegade prisoner, a murderer who had killed his lover when he discovered her infidelity. He provides her with a direct experience of both unswerving compassion and gentlest passion. Ellen returns to civilization radically altered, renewed by learning the realities of a harshly paradoxical universe where good and evil are moral forces within the self. Strong enough now to stand on her own, she must witness the "humane" justice system flog recaptured runaways, a reminder of the fate awaiting her rescuer should he be captured. She feels a nauseating impotence until in a moment of culminating insight she realizes the imperfect construction of the heart, capable of kindness and cruelty, each guided by principle: "the truth is often many-sided, and difficult to see from every angle" (p. 378). Unlike the moments of visionary electricity that illuminated earlier White characters without explanation, Ellen's is a subtle but clear evolution toward clarity, an earned moment of stillness, a decidedly non-mystical gesture of understanding that White now extends as possibility directly to his reader, long alienated from the parables of his gifted visionaries. And when Ellen accepts the attentions of a London merchant, she moves into this relationship at one with the chiaroscuro reality of the human heart in a universe governed by accident, an affirmation that endows that potential union with a promising strength radically at odds with White's long-standing dismissal of such oppressive, suffocating matrices. Importantly when they meet they converse in Ellen's Cornish idiom, indicating that she has relaxed into her authentic self, which

promises a sharing uncomplicated by masquerade.

Masquerade, however, will serve as the central metaphor of White's last great work. For most of his adult life, Eddie Twyborn has experimented with rather than explored his identity. Victimized by a smothering mother (a tormented alcoholic lesbian) and an unemotional father (a staid judge), Eddie grew up uncertain of the implications of his own sexual identity and thus unable to define a coherent self. Eddie thus reconstructs himself and masquerades within the form of an intoxicating catamite, Eudoxia Vatatzes, the mistress of an elderly Greek tycoon in the south of France shortly before World War I. When his lover dies unexpectedly, Eddie returns to his native Australia, where his father arranges work for him as a jackeroo in the rugged Outback. Here he joylessly fathers a child with his boss's wife, a ravaged soul lost to promiscuity, and endures a brutal sodomizing by ranchhands. The child dead within months of its birth, Eddie himself goes off to what will prove to be distinguished service in the war.

Twenty years later, Eddie assumes a masquerade as Eadith Trist, the lonely, insomniac madam of a classy pre–World War II London brothel. Because Eddie exists within a world of surfaces, his self a thorough disguise, he is unable to experience the authentic connection assumed by intimacy, accepting as sufficient the casual collisions of sexual heat, here recorded by White as brutal and animalistic or as the mercenary fantasies of the patrons of Eadith's prostitutes. Unlike other White characters who search for their essential core, Eddie has no interest in finding such a reserve. He is all mask, convincingly depthless, a sharp costume.

After a chance reunion outside a London church with his estranged mother, who surprisingly offers acceptance ("I have always wanted a daughter," p. 423) and who begs him to return to Australia with her, Eddie dons an ill-fitting man's suit and, after a quick haircut, heads back to his mother's hotel to begin at last the generous work of self-exploration. In a fitting gesture of closure to a career that began with a narrative of the family as a constricting energy field of grudges, simmering hatreds, and dreary obligations, White here reclaims the family itself as a nurturing environment. But Eddie is suddenly killed amid the pandemonium of an air-raid bomb, a reminder of a universe clumsily engined by contingency and coolly indifferent to our finest exertions of love. Rather than the blinding light of insight that salvages earlier characters, here is the stabbing light of a meaningless bomb that renders Eddie's metaphoric fragmentation a grim reality. Thus White closes his long exploration of the religious dimension of human nature with a character who is overtired of a lifetime of exploiting the surfaces of the flesh, weary of a self defined by fragments, poised to begin that exploration (as Eddie returns to the hotel he recalls his remote childhood), and revived by the suggestion that an essential self, long denied, was ready now to reveal itself within that most fundamental matrix: the family. Unlike previous White characters who die in the throes of fulfillment, Eddie dies as we must live: ready to begin.

Thus White's considerable canon closes, appropriately, in expectation. The novel ends with Eddie's mother waiting in a nearby hotel shaken by the explosion that we know has killed her son. Despite efforts to coax the old woman to seek shelter, she waits for her son, watching the silvery planes in the night sky and dreaming of the return to Australia where, after a lifetime of estrangement, she and her daughter will "experience harmony at last" (p. 432). This dream of forgiving love is sufficient confirmation of what White has dared to assert since Theodora Goodman: that spirit finally animates matter.

GRACE IN A GRACELESS AGE

In "Morning Soliloquy," an early poem published in White's 1935 collection *"The Ploughman" and Other Poems,* a young White wished that he might unstop his soul, free it to "soar in equity among the stars / And there forget that we are hostages / Beating our futile wings against the bars." That wish, at once so tenderly expressed and so absolutely denied, prepares the reader of White's vast canon for its dilemma, how his narratives, like all religious literature, must celebrate the difficult tension implicit in the logic of hope. His illuminati butt their way through the tedium of the everyday and tolerate the absurd hunger of their animal nature sustained by the stubborn conviction that they participate nevertheless in an unsuspected cosmos. It is finally not so far from Theodora Goodman in the New Mexico wastes to Eddie Twyborn in bomb-ravaged London—they share the compelling conviction of all White's characters that the body cannot finally tolerate its own absurdity. Against an age defined by erupting materialism, a self-willed lurch toward computerized depersonalization, the curdling embrace of violence, and a manic licensing of the libido, White's narratives remind the lost souls of such a graceless age that grace itself is still a possibility.

Selected Bibliography

WORKS OF PATRICK WHITE

NOVELS

Happy Valley. London: Harrap, 1939; New York: Viking, 1940.
The Living and the Dead. New York: Viking, 1941. Reprint, New York: AMS, 1979.
The Aunt's Story. London: Routledge and Kegan Paul, 1948; New York: Viking, 1948.
The Tree of Man. New York: Viking, 1955; London: Eyre and Spottiswoode, 1956.
Voss. London: Eyre and; Spottiswoode, 1957; New York: Viking, 1957.

Riders in the Chariot. London: Eyre and Spottiswoode, 1961; New York: Viking, 1961.

The Solid Mandala. London: Eyre and Spottiswoode, 1966; New York: Viking, 1966.

The Vivisector. London: Cape, 1970; New York: Viking, 1970.

The Eye of the Storm. London: Cape, 1973; New York: Viking, 1974.

A Fringe of Leaves. London: Cape, 1976; New York: Viking, 1977.

The Twyborn Affair. London: Cape, 1979; New York: Viking, 1980.

Memoirs of Many in One by Alex Xenophon Demirjian Gray. London: Cape, 1986; New York: Viking, 1986.

SHORT STORIES

The Burnt Ones. London: Cape, 1974; New York: Viking, 1964.

The Cockatoos. London: Cape, 1974; New York: Viking, 1975.

The Night, the Prowler: Short Story and Screenplay. Ringwood, Victoria, Australia: Penguin, 1977; Harmondsworth, U.K.: Penguin, 1978.

Three Uneasy Pieces. London: Cape, 1988.

NONFICTION

Flaws in the Glass: A Self-Portrait. London: Cape, 1981. Reprint, Penguin, 1982.

Letters. Edited by David Marr. Sydney: Random House, 1996.

Patrick White Speaks. Edited by Paul Brennan and Christine Flynn. Sydney: Primavera 1989; London: Cape, 1990.

DRAMA

Big Toys. Sydney: Currency, 1978.

Four Plays. London: Eyre and Spottiswoode, 1965; New York: Viking, 1966.

Netherwood. Sydney: Currency, 1983.

Signal Driver: A Morality Play for the Times. Sydney: Currency, 1983.

POETRY

"The Ploughman" and Other Poems. Sydney: Beacon, 1935.

BIOGRAPHICAL STUDIES

Hansson, Karin. "Patrick White: Existential Explorer." Online resource. http://www.nobel.se/literature.

Marr, David. *Patrick White: A Life.* London: Cape, 1991; New York: Knopf, 1991.

"Why Bother with Patrick White?" Online resource. http://arts.abc.net.au/white.

CRITICAL STUDIES

Argyle, Barry. *Patrick White.* London: Oliver and Boyd, 1967.

Beatson, Peter. *The Eye in the Mandala: Patrick White: A Vision of Man and God.* Sydney: Reed, 1977.

Bliss, Carolyn Jane. *Patrick White's Fiction: The Paradox of Fortunate Failure.* New York: St. Martin's Press, 1986.

Colmer, John. *Patrick White.* New York: Methuen, 1984.

PATRICK WHITE

During, Simon. *Patrick White*. Melbourne and New York: Oxford University Press, 1996.

Edgecombe, Rodney Stenning. *Vision and Style in Patrick White*. Tuscaloosa: University of Alabama Press, 1989.

Hansson, Karin. *The Warped Universe: A Study of Imagery and Structure in Seven Novels by Patrick White*. Lund, Sweden: CWK Gleerup, 1984.

Kiernan, Brian. *Patrick White*. London: Macmillan, 1980.

Lock, Charles. "Patrick White: Writing towards Silence." *Kenyon Review* 23:72–84 (summer 2001).

McCulloch, A. M. *A Tragic Vision: The Novels of Patrick White*. St. Lucia, Australia: University of Queensland Press, 1983.

Morley, Patricia A. *The Mystery of Unity: Themes and Techniques in the Novels of Patrick White*. Montreal: McGill-Queen's University Press, 1972.

Tacey, David. J. *Patrick White: Fiction and the Unconscious*. Melbourne and New York: Oxford University Press, 1988.

Walsh, William. *Patrick White's Fiction*. Totowa, N.J.: Rowman and Littlefield, 1977.

Williams, Mark. *Patrick White*. New York: St. Martin's Press, 1993.

Wolfe, Peter. *Laden Choirs: The Fiction of Patrick White*. Lexington: University of Kentucky Press, 1983.

Wolfe, Peter, ed. *Critical Essays on Patrick White*. Boston: G. K. Hall, 1990.

765

List of Subjects by Nationality

AFRICAN

Chinua Achebe (Nigeria)

J. M. Coetzee (South Africa)

Jeni Couzyn (South Africa)

Bessie Head (South Africa)

Alex La Guma (South Africa)

Jack Mapanje (Malawi)

Lewis Nkosi (South Africa)

Ngũgĩ wa Thiong'o (Kenya)

Arthur Nortje (South Africa)

Ben Okri (Nigeria)

Alan Paton (South Africa)

Olive Schreiner (South Africa)

Wole Soyinka (Nigeria)

AUSTRALIAN

John Forbes

John Kinsella

Peter Porter

Christina Stead

Patrick White

CANADIAN

Margaret Atwood

Alice Munro

Michael Ondaatje

CARIBBEAN

Jamaica Kincaid

Caryl Phillips

Jean Rhys

Derek Walcott

CHINESE

Timothy Mo

INDIAN

Agha Shahid Ali

Amitav Ghosh

Hanif Kureishi

Bharati Mukherjee

V. S. Naipaul

R. K. Narayan

A. K. Ramanujan

Arundhati Roy

Salman Rushdie

Paul Scott

Vikram Seth

JAPANESE

Kazuo Ishiguro

NEW ZEALANDER

Fleur Adcock

Katherine Mansfield

Index

Arabic numbers in **boldface type** *refer to subjects of articles.*